P9-AON-748

Karl Marx

GARETH STEDMAN
JONES

Karl Marx

Greatness and Illusion

THE BELKNAP PRESS OF
HARVARD UNIVERSITY PRESS
Cambridge, Massachusetts
2016

Original edition first published by Penguin Books Ltd, London
Text copyright © Gareth Stedman Jones 2016
All rights reserved

First Harvard University Press edition, 2016
First printing

Set in 10.2/13.87 pt Sabon LT Std
Typeset by Jouve (UK), Milton Keynes

Library of Congress Cataloging-in-Publication Data

Names: Stedman Jones, Gareth, author.
Title: Karl Marx : greatness and illusion / Gareth Stedman Jones.
Description: First Harvard University Press edition. | Cambridge,
Massachusetts : The Belknap Press of Harvard University Press, 2016. |
"Original edition first published by Penguin Books Ltd, London."—Title page verso |
Includes bibliographical references and index.
Identifiers: LCCN 2016027565 | ISBN 9780674971615 (cloth : alk. paper)
Subjects: LCSH: Marx, Karl, 1818–1883. | Philosophy, Marxist. |
Communism and society. | Europe—Intellectual life—19th century. |
Europe—Politics and
government—History—19th century.
Classification: LCC HX39 .S74 2016 | DDC 335.4092 [B] —dc23
LC record available at https://lccn.loc.gov/2016027565

Contents

Illustrations

(1808–1868). (Berlin, Sammlung Archiv für Kunst und Geschichte/ AKG Images)

18. The title page of the *Deutsch-Französische Jahrbücher*, Paris, 1844. (Copyright © Mary Evans Picture Library 2015/INTERFOTO/ Sammlung Rauch)

19. The bodies of those killed during the February street fighting paraded through Paris. (Engraving by J Gaildrau in a history of France.)

20. Session of the *Commission des travailleurs*, Paris, 1948. (Copyright © Mary Evans Picture Library 2015)

21. Barricade fighting in Cologne, 1848. (Bildarchiv Preußischer Kulturbesitz. Copyright © Mary Evans Picture Library 2015/ INTERFOTO/Sammlung Rauch)

22. Berlin, 1848, illustration from Carl Schurz, *Reminiscences*, Vol. I (McClure Publishing Co., 1907). (The Bodleian Libraries, The University of Oxford. 23351 d.43 (V.1))

23. The Chartist Meeting on Kennington Common, 10 April 1848, from F. Dimond and R. Taylor, *Crown & Camera: The Royal Family and Photography 1842–1910* (Harmondsworth, 1987). (Royal Collection Trust/© Her Majesty Queen Elizabeth II 2016)

24. The First Edition of 'Neue Rheinische Zeitung' 1 June 1848. (Copyright © Mary Evans Picture Library 2015/Interfoto)

25. Thibault: The barricade of Saint-Maur-Popincourt 26 June 1848. ((PHO 2002 4 2). Paris, Musée d'Orsay, acquired by the National Museum with support from the Heritage Photographic, © RMN-Grand Palais (Musée d'Orsay))

26. Insurgents in custody. (Copyright © Mary Evans Picture Library 2015)

27. Opening ceremony of the International Exhibition. (Copyright © Mary Evans Picture Library 2008)

28. William Powell Frith, *Ramsgate Sands* (Life at the Seaside), 1851–54. (Royal Collection Trust/© Her Majesty Queen Elizabeth II 2016)

29. Aftermath of the Commune. (© BnF, Dist. RMN-Grand Palais/ image BnF)

30. Chinese poster from the Cultural Revolution celebrating the centenary of the Paris Commune. (Stefan R. Landsberger Collection, International Institute of Social History (Amsterdam))

Maps

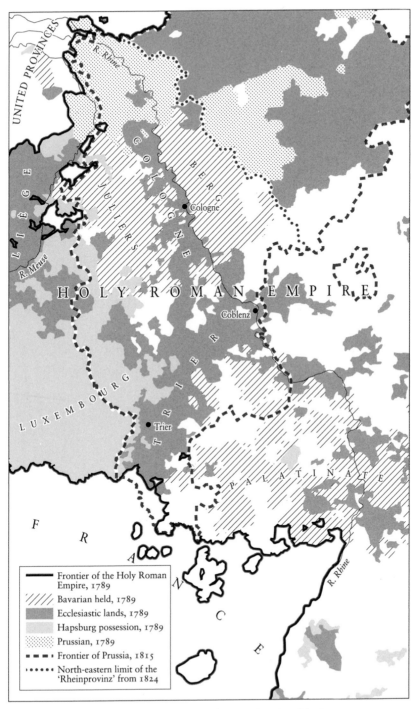

Map 1. The Rhineland before 1789 – 'The Monks' Corridor'

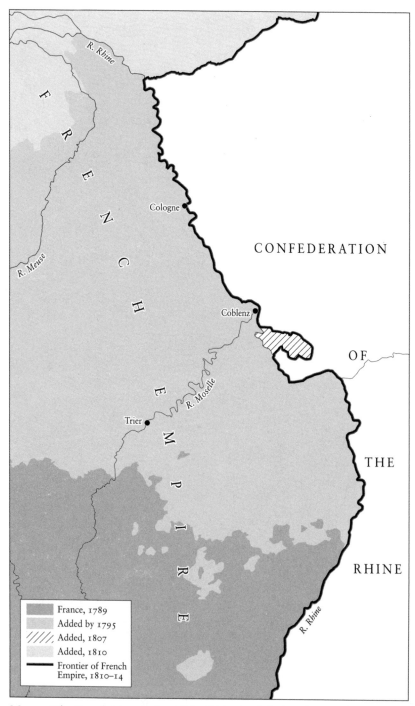

Map 2. The French Occupation of the Rhineland during the Revolution and the Napoleonic Era.

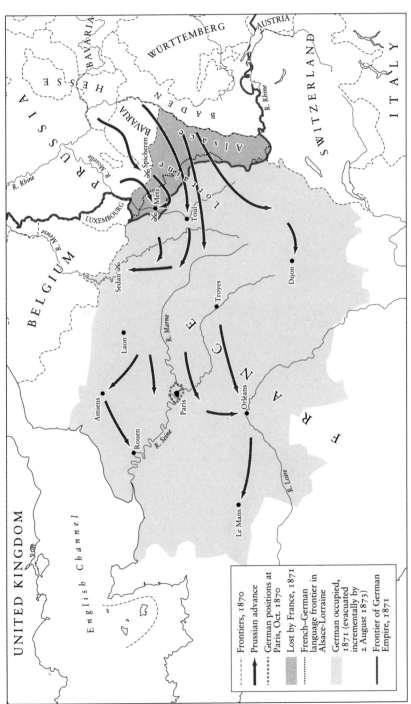

UNITED KINGDOM

English Channel

BELGIUM

LUXEMBOURG

PRUSSIA

HESSE

BAVARIA

WÜRTTEMBERG

AUSTRIA

BADEN

SWITZERLAND

ITALY

R. Rhine

R. Moselle

R. Meuse

R. Rhine

R. Rhine

Alsace

Lorraine

Spicheren

Metz

Toul

Dijon

Sedan

Troyes

Laon

R. Marne

Amiens

Paris

Rouen

R. Seine

Orléans

R. Loire

Le Mans

FRANCE

Frontiers, 1870
Prussian advance
German positions at
Paris, Oct. 1870
Lost by France, 1871
French–German
language frontier in
Alsace-Lorraine
German evacuated
1871 (evacuated
incrementally by
2 August 1873)
Frontier of German
Empire, 1871

Map 3. Paris and the Battles of the Franco-Prussian War

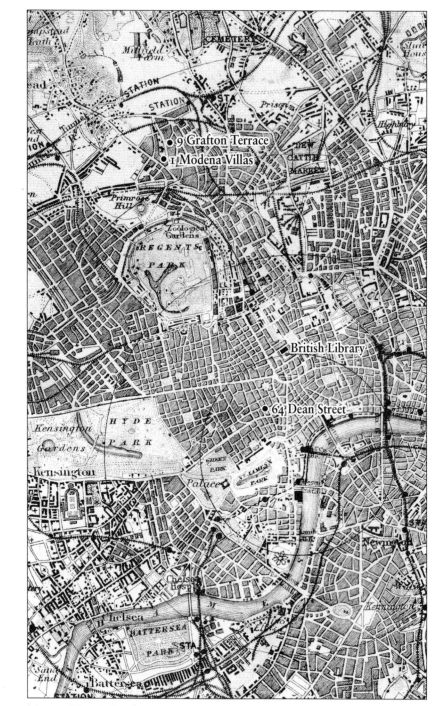

Map 4. Marx's London, 1848–1883

Acknowledgements

The study of Marx's life and works has inspired many distinguished writers, starting with the pioneering biography by the prominent German Social Democrat Franz Mehring, in 1918, and continuing almost without interruption through to the present. My book builds upon the innumerable insights contained in these works. But it is different in one important respect.

However interesting Marx's life was, his enduring importance derives from the impact of the ideas he developed in a remarkable series of texts, whose status and meaning have been the occasion of fierce political argument since their inception. Perhaps in order to steer clear of once violent and still simmering political passions surrounding these texts, scholarly biographers of Marx have tended to offer descriptive accounts of Marx's theoretical writings, and have preferred to concentrate on his life.

By contrast, I have decided to pay as much attention to Marx's thought as to his life. I treat his writings as the interventions of an author within particular political and philosophical contexts that the historian must carefully reconstruct. For all his originality, Marx was not a solitary explorer advancing along an untrodden path towards a novel and hitherto undiscovered social theory. Instead, whether as philosopher, political theorist or critic of political economy, his writings were intended as interventions in already existing fields of discourse. Furthermore, these interventions were addressed to his contemporaries, and not to his twentieth- or twenty-first-century descendants. My aim in this book is like that of a restorer, to remove the later retouching and alteration contained in a seemingly familiar painting, and restore it to its original state. This is why I have paid as much attention to the utterances and reactions of contemporaries as to Marx's own words. But this in turn can only be done if both Marx and his contemporaries are placed in a landscape larger than themselves. Hence the need, in part at least, to rethink the history of the nineteenth century, of which Marx and his contemporaries were a part.

The research for this book, and several colloquia related to it, have been made possible by the generous support over several years from the Edmond de Rothschild Foundation, led by Ariane de Rothschild and Firoz Ladak. I also owe a considerable debt to the forms of intellectual history practised for many years by my colleagues at the University of Cambridge, Queen Mary University of London, and the Institute of Historical Research: in particular, the late Chris Bayly, Duncan Bell, Eugenio Biagini, Richard Bourke, Christopher Clark, Tim Harper, Colin Jones, Shruti Kapila, Duncan Kelly, William O'Reilly, Jonathan Parry, Michael Sonenscher, Sylvana Tomaselli, Robert Tombs, Adam Tooze and Georgios Varouxakis. Marx's works require anchoring in specific lineages of political economy and natural law, and in these areas I learnt a great deal from members of the King's College Research Centre project on 'Political Economy and Society', including John Dunn, Bianca Fontana and Michael Ignatieff, and especially from the path-breaking work of the late Istvan Hont. Subsequently, I also benefited greatly from the research developed at the Cambridge Centre for History and Economics, led by Emma Rothschild and myself, and assisted by Inga Huld Markan and Amy Price. Emma's insights into the preceding history of political economy have greatly helped to shape the approach I adopt in this book.

My work was made possible by the still ongoing *Marx-Engels-Gesamtausgabe* (Marx-Engels Complete Works), a magnificent editorial project, both in its original conception in the 1920s and in the restoration of its scholarly integrity after its incorporation in the Berlin-Brandenburgische Akademie der Wissenschaften in 1991. I would particularly like to thank one of its current editors, Jürgen Herres, for his insights and assistance. The Karl-Marx-Haus in Trier, now part of the Friedrich-Ebert-Stiftung in Bonn and Berlin, and the International Institute of Social History in Amsterdam have offered me access to important archival material.

A number of friends and colleagues have played a vital role in helping me to think through the themes of this book. On German philosophy Douglas Moggach has been a source of constant support, just as Keith Tribe has been on political economy. Joachim Whaley has offered inspiring help and guidance on everything to do with nineteenth-century German language and literature. Over the years, I have also had the pleasure of supervising the doctoral research of a number of remarkable scholars in these fields, all now distinguished historians. I have enormously benefited from interactions with Carolina Armenteros, Callum Barrell, Duncan Campbell, Edward Castleton, Gregory Claeys, Simon Cook, David Craig, Isabel Divanna, David Feldman, Margot Finn, Tom Hopkins, Tristram Hunt, Thomas Jones, Christina Lattek, Jon Lawrence, Julia Nicholls, David Palfrey, Susan Pennybacker, Daniel Pick, Anna Plassart, Diana Siclovan, Nick Stargardt, Miles Taylor, William Whitham and Bee Wilson. I am warmly grateful to Sally Alexander for her helpful criticism and continuing engagement with the book. Numerous other friends and colleagues have also helped with comments and suggestions: Sylvie Aprile, Jonathan Beecher, Fabrice Bensimon, Jonathan Clark, Widukind de Ridder, Ludovic Frobert, Peter Ghosh, Samuel Hayat, Joanna Innes, David Leopold, Karma Nabulsi, Mark Philp, Iorwerth Prothero, Loïc Rignol, Amartya Sen, William Steinmetz, David Todd, Mark Traugott, Marcel van der Linden and Richard Whatmore.

It is a real pleasure to thank Mary-Rose Cheadle of the Centre for History and Economics; she is both a highly effective editor and a friend. With her linguistic and copy-editing skills and her eye for appropriate images she has expertly supervised the editing of the book from the early chapter drafts to the final manuscript. Maggie Hanbury has provided patient support over many years, and has ensured the best possible conditions for the book's publication. The team at Penguin has been formidable, particularly Chloe Campbell and Mark Handsley, who offered such intelligent editorial suggestions. Simon Winder at Penguin has offered thoughtful encouragement and support from the inception of the project.

I hope this book will be enjoyed by many readers outside academic circles. In thinking of such an audience, I always had in mind Abigail Thaw and Nigel Whitmey, intelligent and curious readers and observers of the world. I hope they like the book. Finally, and most of all, my warmest thanks to Daniel, Joseph and Miri – all three engaged in thinking and writing history – for their faith in the project, their love and their unfailing support.

Cambridge, 11 June 2016

Prologue: The Making of an Icon, 1883–1920

Karl Marx first became known to the wider world as the notorious revolutionary, who on behalf of the International Working Men's Association had defended the Paris *Commune* in 1871. As a result of this notoriety, growing attention was paid to his work as a theorist of socialism or communism. The publication of *Capital* in 1867, first in German and subsequently in Russian, French, Italian and English, made Marx the most prominent socialist theorist of his time, and created groups of followers across Europe and North America. Knowledge of his teachings was spread in particular by his closest friend and collaborator, Friedrich Engels, who claimed that thanks to Marx's work socialism was no longer a mere 'utopia'. It was a 'science'. *Capital* announced the approaching collapse of the current mode of production and its replacement by the socialist or communist society of the future.

The Russian Revolution of 1917 and a host of other attempted revolutions in Central Europe in the aftermath of the First World War were all attributed to Marx's teachings. These in turn were followed in the interwar period by the growth of Soviet-style communist parties, who after the Second World War, found themselves favourably placed to take control of states throughout much of Eastern Europe. In Asia, indigenous movements of national liberation, formed in resistance to imperialism and colonialism, carried out communist revolutions in China and Vietnam, also in the name of 'Marxism'. By the 1960s, movements inspired by communism or revolutionary socialism had also spread across Latin America and succeeded in Cuba. In South Africa, communism helped inspire the first sustained resistance to Apartheid, and movements to end white colonial rule throughout the rest of Africa.

In the aftermath of 1917 and the global spread of Soviet-style communism, Marx was celebrated as communism's epic founder and lawgiver in an increasingly monumental mythology. He was venerated as the founder of the science of history – 'historical materialism' – and together with his friend Engels as the architect of the scientific philosophy to accompany it – 'dialectical materialism'. In Communist countries, huge statues were erected in countless public squares, while the dissemination of popular editions of his works outstripped that of the Bible. This is the familiar story of twentieth-century communism and the development of the Cold War. Unsurprisingly, it has been identified with the emergence of 'totalitarian' states, in which the promulgation of an officially prescribed form of 'Marxism' was accompanied by purges, show trials, and a vigilant control of all means of communication.

More surprising is the fact that the mythology surrounding Marx had not been invented by the Soviet regime. It had already begun to be constructed at the time of Marx's death in 1883 and developed fully in the thirty years following. The invention of what came to be called 'Marxism' was initially in large part the creation of Engels in his books and pamphlets, beginning with *Anti-Dühring* in 1878. It was elaborated by the leaders of the Social Democratic Party in Germany, particularly, August Bebel, Karl Kautsky, Eduard Bernstein and Franz Mehring. The German Social Democratic Party in the years before 1914 was the largest socialist party in the world and exercised a preponderant influence upon the development of socialism elsewhere. Partly out of conviction, but mainly in order to buttress the authority of the Party, its leaders found it opportune to protect and to advance Marx's reputation as the revolutionary founder of a science of history. In Russia, 'Marxism' both as a philosophy and as a political movement was forcefully promoted in the 1880s and 1890s by Georgi Plekhanov and subsequently by Lenin. Elsewhere, in countries ranging from the Austro-Hungarian Empire to Spain and Italy, 'Marxism' offered a powerful alternative to nationalism, republicanism or anarchism. Even in countries, such as Britain and France, where the strength of an indigenous radicalism or socialism was much more deeply rooted, Marx's *Capital* drew support from small groupings and from prominent intellectuals.

The Social Democratic leaders in Germany were well aware of the vulnerability of their image of Marx and his theory. They were the appointed guardians of the Marx–Engels papers, and they discussed among themselves how to cope with the sometimes embarrassing gap between image and reality. They believed that an admission of Marx's failings, whether political or personal, might undermine the support of ordinary Party members, many of whom were sustained by the idea that the approaching demise of capitalism had been proved definitively in a book written by a great philosopher. It was also essential not to provide the imperial government of Wilhelmine Germany an opportunity to attack the credentials of the Social Democratic Party by discrediting the work of its founding thinker. Much of the standard picture of the personal character, political judgement and theoretical achievements of Marx was founded upon the need to protect this legacy.

The cost of this approach was an increasing inflation in Marx's reputation. Ever more expansive claims were made about the scale and significance of Marx's achievement, while areas in which his writings or activities had failed to meet these mythical requirements were glossed over or hidden. Marx was promoted as the philosopher who had accomplished as much in the human sciences as Darwin in the natural sciences. This invented parallel reinforced the claim that the Social Democratic Party embodied the *science* of socialism. Similarly, on the basis of the as yet unpublished Volume III of *Capital*, it was also maintained that Marx's theory propounded with certainty the coming downfall of capitalism. Between the 1890s and 1930s, the question of when exactly capitalism would collapse became a topic of prolonged debate. Known as '*Zusammenbruchstheorie*' (theory of collapse), the idea was that capitalism would come to an end, not so much as the result of workers' revolt, as because in the absence of new markets to exploit the system would reach a point of terminal breakdown.

As a result of the way in which expectations about the contents of Volume III had been raised, its actual publication in 1894 produced considerable disappointment. It encountered fundamental criticism from the Austrian economist Eugen von Böhm-Bawerk on account of its failure to produce a satisfactory theory of the relation between values and prices.[1] More immediately, it also provoked Eduard Bernstein's attack upon *Zusammenbruchstheorie*. The theory was based on the supposedly ever more acute polarization between classes and ever greater gulf between wealth and poverty. But empirical material did not support this claim. Bernstein's attack upon the theory was seen as particularly damaging, since he was one of the literary executors of the Marx–Engels papers. Engels completed the preface to Volume III on 4 October 1894. He died on 5 August 1895. Kautsky, the editor of *Die Neue Zeit*, the main theoretical journal of the Party, welcomed debate, and published Bernstein's eight critical articles. But Bebel, the leader of the Party, was alarmed and hoped Bernstein would resign from the Party. Bernstein's criticisms were debated at successive Party Congresses in 1898 and 1899, but were condemned as 'revisionism'. Henceforward Bernstein's view was classified as a heresy to be distinguished from 'orthodox Marxism'.[2]

From the beginning, what came to be called 'Marxism' had been built upon an unambiguously selective view of what was to count as theory, not only in relation to would-be heretics, but also in relation to Marx himself. The Marx celebrated from the 1890s and beyond was the theorist of the universality of capitalism and its inevitable global downfall.

Social Democratic leaders also had to decide what was to be said about Marx's personal character. In 1905 Franz Mehring, the first biographer of Marx, wrote to Karl Kautsky that it would be impossible to publish the correspondence between Marx and Engels in uncensored form. Mehring stated that if the correspondence were to appear in full, all the efforts made in the preceding twenty years to preserve Marx's literary reputation would have been in vain. The correspondence was full of insulting references to prominent Social Democrats. It also contained racist sneers against several figures, like the first Social Democratic leader, Ferdinand Lassalle. So, in 1913, the leader of the Party, August Bebel, together with Bernstein, finally went ahead with a four-volume collection of the letters, censored in the way that Mehring had requested. As Bebel wrote to Kautsky: 'by the way, I want to tell you – but please keep absolutely quiet about it – that some of the letters were not published, above all, because they were too strong for us. The two old ones had at that time a way of letter-writing, to which I can in no way reconcile myself.'[3] The letters were finally published in an uncensored edition by David Riazanov between 1929 and 1931.

What this account reveals is that, by the end of the nineteenth century, there were important differences between Marx himself – who he was, how he behaved, what he believed, what he thought about – and the ways in which he had come to be represented in political discourse.

4

The figure that had emerged was a forbidding bearded patriarch and lawgiver, a thinker of merciless consistency with a commanding vision of the future. This was Marx as the twentieth century was – quite wrongly – to see him. It was a picture brilliantly enunciated by Isaiah Berlin writing in 1939: Marx's faith in his own synoptic vision was 'of that boundless, absolute kind which puts an end to all questions and dissolves all difficulties'; 'his intellectual system was a closed one, everything that entered was made to conform to a pre-established pattern, but it was grounded in observation and experience'.[4]

The aim of this book is to put Marx back in his nineteenth-century surroundings, before all these posthumous elaborations of his character and achievements were constructed. Karl, as we shall henceforth call him, was born into a world just recovering from the French Revolution, the Napoleonic government of the Rhineland, the half-fulfilled but quickly retracted emancipation of the Jews, and the stifling atmosphere of Prussian absolutism. It was also a world in which there were escapes, even if for the most part only in the imagination. There were the beauty of the Greek *polis*, the inspiration of the poets and playwrights of Weimar, the power of German philosophy, and the wonders of romantic love. But Karl was not just the product of the culture into which he was born. From the beginning, he was determined to impress himself upon the world.

I

Fathers and Sons: The Ambiguities of Becoming a Prussian

Three years after the Battle of Waterloo, Karl Marx was born in the Rhineland, on 5 May 1818. Everywhere around him were the signs of the attempt to rebuild and restore Europe after thirty years of destruction and transformation brought about by the French Revolution and the Napoleonic Wars, and nowhere more so than in the Rhineland itself. Situated between France and the German Confederation, the population of the Rhineland was overwhelmingly Catholic – around 1.5 million out of 2 million souls. Before 1789, it had been dominated by three prince bishoprics – Cologne, Mainz and Trier – whose ancient privilege it had been, together with four secular princely electors, to elect the Holy Roman Emperor. But during the Revolution and Napoleonic Wars, not only had contending armies crossed and recrossed this *monks' corridor* as inhabitants called it, but the states commanding these armies had redefined the whole area; first, as part of revolutionary France in 1794, and after 1815 as part of the Protestant kingdom of Prussia. The Holy Roman Empire, in existence since the year AD 800, had been abolished by Napoléon in 1806, and the victorious allies meeting in Vienna in 1815 had made no attempt to restore it.

The scale of these wars needs to be recalled. An estimated five million Europeans perished in them, a number equal in proportion to those lost in the First World War. The scale of warfare itself was altogether new. In the eighteenth century, armies numbered tens of thousands; by contrast, the army which Napoléon led in his invasion of Russia in 1812 amounted to 650,000 troops. How warfare impinged upon society was also transformed. Eighteenth-century wars had largely been fought out between mercenaries, but in the wake of the

French Revolution 'national armies' were formed, first in France and then in Prussia. A new idea of 'national service' was devised, and with it came the practice of conscription. The Rhineland was relatively fortunate in avoiding the direct ravages of war, since major battles were fought elsewhere. But, as part of Napoléon's empire, it could not evade conscription. Between 1800 and 1814, the Rhineland contributed 80,000, or one in twenty of the population, to the two million troops mobilized by France. Half of this huge number never returned.[1]

Karl Marx was born in Trier, the centre of the wine-growing Moselle valley in the south-west of the Rhineland. As the centre of a purely agricultural region – with the exception of some iron manufacture in the Eifel – the fortunes of Trier were closely linked to grapes and timber. Vineyards and woodland occupied the slopes rising from the river, and beyond them were the forests of the poor Hunsrück region in the south, and the Eifel in the north. Founded as Augusta Treverorum in 16 BC, and claiming to be the oldest town in Germany, Trier became the capital of the Roman province of Gallia Belgica. At one time the chief centre in Gaul, the Roman city may have possessed a population of up to 80,000. After a decline in its administrative importance in the Early Middle Ages, during the twelfth century the archbishops of Trier became prince-electors of the Empire, and the town enjoyed another period of prosperity during later-medieval times. But by 1802, according to official returns, the population of Trèves (as its French occupiers renamed it) amounted to only 8,846, and fell further to 7,887 with the withdrawal of French soldiers and officials in 1814. Thereafter, its population rose again and by 1819 amounted to 11,432.[2]

Marx's father, Heinrich, had been born in 1777 in the contested frontier town of Saarlouis, the third son of Meier Halevi Marx, who was the rabbi of the town's Jewish community. In 1788, Meier Halevi moved to serve as rabbi at Trier, where he remained until his death in 1804. Heinrich's eldest brother, Samuel, succeeded his father, and continued in his office until his death in 1827, while Heinrich became a lawyer. He was successful in his profession, and in 1832 was awarded the status of *Justizrat* (the equivalent of QC). Widely recognized as a distinguished Rhineland jurist, Heinrich died on 10 May 1838. Karl's mother, Henriette, was born to a Jewish family in Nijmegen in Holland in 1788, where her father was variously described as a merchant, money-changer and collector of lottery funds. In 1814, she married

Heinrich, to whom she had probably been introduced by family acquaintances in Amsterdam. She bore Heinrich nine children and died on 30 November 1863.[3] Sometime around 1816–19, Heinrich was baptized into the Christian Evangelical church of Prussia. His children were also baptized around 1824, followed by Henriette in 1825.

I. REVOLUTION, EMPIRE AND THE JEWS OF THE RHINELAND

The historical drama which loomed behind these bare biographical facts was that of the French Revolution, which resulted in the French takeover of the Rhineland, the reforms of the Napoleonic Empire and in 1815 the acquisition of the Rhineland by Prussia, events which utterly transformed the fortunes of the Marx family. Heinrich could never have become a lawyer, but for the effects of the Revolution. He could never have acquired his legal qualification, but for the educational initiatives of Napoléon, and he could not have remained a lawyer, except by accommodating himself to the increasingly restrictive Prussian policy towards the Jews after 1815.

These momentous events also did much to shape the young Karl's conception of the world, his relationship with his parents, and his generally negative attitude towards his family's Jewish past. The long shadow cast by these events is explained by the enormous hopes awakened by the first years of the Revolution between 1789 and 1791: the promise of representative government, freedom of religion, freedom of speech and equality before the law, all couched in the universal language of the 'rights of man'. This dream had been a crucial turning point for Heinrich Marx's generation. But it is equally important to remember the later events, of 1792–4, which produced the dramatic replacement of France's discredited monarchy, and the establishment of a republic, a political form previously thought impossible in large, old and populous European states. The newly constituted republic had successfully defended itself against the rest of Europe with the help of a citizen army, a democratic constitution, and even a civil religion to underpin its vision of a new world. But it had also engendered the Terror, virtual bankruptcy and the downfall of radical Jacobinism. For radicals of Karl's generation, 1792 mattered more than 1789. The

Jacobin Republic served both as a source of inspiration and as the starting point of any attempt to explain why the Revolution finally foundered. This tension between liberal and republican conceptions of the Revolution would dominate the language of Rhineland opposition groupings through to the revolutions of 1848.

The changes brought about by the Revolution were momentous. The government of France before 1789 was organized on the basis of a hierarchically conceived estates system, built upon the supposed distinction between those who prayed, those who fought and those who worked. In the Revolution, a new nation was constructed. In its new constitution, those who worked – the 'Third Estate' – became the Nation itself. The privileges and separate existence of the other two estates, the aristocracy and clergy, were abolished. Furthermore, on the night of 4 August 1789, in town and country, feudal privileges and powers were abrogated. Serfdom was abolished and peasants were enabled to acquire possession of the land they had cultivated, either outright or else upon the payment of modest redemption fees. Finally, with the transformation of the Estates General into the National Assembly, the refounded Nation now rested upon a new and purely secular source of political legitimacy, the sovereignty of the people.

Yet it would be a mistake to assume that the events of the Revolution had been the result of a seemingly clear-cut revolutionary agenda. Only in retrospect could it be understood in this way. The process was considerably more ambiguous and confused.

At the beginning of the Revolution, 'the overwhelming majority of the deputies were convinced that all reforms must be accomplished under the auspices of the monarchy, in close cooperation with a king for whom they continued to show strong filial devotion'. The deputies persisted in a 'vision of a return to an idealized past, of a reform process in which historical precedent remained of considerable importance'. 'Yet somehow, in the space of six weeks of extraordinarily intense meetings' in the summer of 1789, these delegates reached 'a position that could only be described as revolutionary', a 'new concept of national sovereignty, fundamentally democratic in its implications'.[4]

At the beginning, it seemed most likely that the Assembly would adopt the historical monarchy, tempered by a balance of powers, which had been proposed by its Constitutional Committee and its respected chairman, Jean-Joseph Mounier. Instead, however, it adopted a radically new constitution based upon national sovereignty and a unitary legislative assembly, a proposal more in the spirit of Rousseau. The crown, now effectively defined as a subordinate executive authority, was given only a temporary power of suspensive veto, and this was further qualified by a resort to the people as the final court of appeal. This system, as the Girondin leader, Brissot, remarked, could only be made to operate with a 'revolutionary king'.[5]

Many of the representatives were unsure whether the National Assembly was attempting to reform an existing system, or to establish an entirely new one. The result, not surprisingly, was incoherent, a wholly unstable and virtually untenable combination of the Rousseau-based principle of the inalienable sovereignty of the general will and the categorically anti-Rousseau-based principle of a representative assembly.

Part of the reason for the confusion of aims was the weakness of a financially bankrupt executive powerless to prevent the adoption of a language of abstract universals, following the example of the Americans in 1776. Various members of the Assembly signalled the danger of adopting this language. The argument of Champion de Cicé, Bishop of Bordeaux, was characteristic: 'We must not be concerned with the natural rights fixed at the cradle of fledging peoples, but with the civil rights, the positive law of a great people that has been united for the past fifteen centuries ... let us abandon natural man to concern ourselves with the lot of civilized man.' Another moderate, Pierre-Victor Malouet, pointed out the obvious risks of adopting such an approach. Unlike in America, a society, he claimed, already 'prepared for democracy' and 'entirely composed of property holders', in France, 'announcing in an absolute manner to suffering men, deprived of knowledge and means, that they are equal in rights to the most powerful and most fortunate' could 'destroy necessary bonds' and incite 'universal disruption'.[6]

As the Revolution unfolded, this language of universal rights acquired a more and more coercive edge. In part, this can be ascribed to the radicalization of the Revolution in the face of escalating hostility from the Catholic church, the resistance and attempted flight of the king, the civil war in the Vendée, and the growing determination of European powers to combat what Burke called 'the armed doctrine' of revolution. In this state of emergency, in place of the *religion royale* of the *Ancien Régime*, a new form of the sacred was conceived, and it was located in the Nation. Old ecclesiastical structures were dismantled and the sacred bases of kingship were removed, even Christianity itself. The pressure to merge political and religious authority, now under republican auspices, became more intense. This was a process which culminated briefly in the summer of 1794 in Robespierre's foundation of 'The Cult of the Supreme Being', a republican civil religion along lines originally sketched out in Rousseau's *Social Contract*.

The differences between what would now be called 'liberalism' and 'republicanism' only emerged in the course of these escalating conflicts, but the disjunction between original intention and political result was there from the beginning. For, already in 1789, the National Assembly's resort to a language of natural rights and popular sovereignty generated outcomes that bore little relation to its original stated aspirations. What prevailed even then in those debates was a language of political will rather than of social reason, of absolute sovereignty, rather than government limited by the rights of man; a language which could also justify the Terror.[7]

This tension between liberal and republican visions of the Revolution was particularly clear in the case of Jewish emancipation. According to the Declaration of the Rights of Man of 1789, men were born and remained free and equal in rights. Furthermore no person was to be harassed on account of his or her opinions, even religious ones, provided that the manifestation of these opinions did not disturb 'public order established by the law'. On this basis, the Constituent Assembly accordingly granted French citizenship and all its attendant rights to the Jews on 27 September 1791.

Before 1789, those thinkers most well disposed towards the Jews had been Protestants, exiles in Holland like those around Pierre Bayle and Jacques Basnage, or in England free thinkers like John Toland, who claimed freedom of belief for all faiths. Montesquieu had also pressed for tolerance in the name of reason, but also as a measure of *raison d'état*, designed to ensure that Jewish mercantile activities were fully employed in the service of the state. Catholic attitudes voiced by Bossuet and Fleury were negative for theological reasons. It was true that Jews served as witness to the Glory of God, and formed part of traditional church history; therefore, they had to be protected. But they were also witness to God's anger; they must therefore either be kept in a humiliated state or be converted. Those most negative about the Jews, however, were not Christian believers, but one strand of opinion among the *Philosophes*, especially Voltaire, for whom the Jews combined 'the most sordid avarice' with 'the most detestable superstition'. These views were shared to a greater or lesser extent by other leading philosophers, Diderot, Jaucourt and D'Holbach.[8]

In 1789, the *Cahiers de Doléances* – the statements of grievance compiled by every locality and sent to Paris – revealed more mundane sources of anti-Jewish feeling, especially in Alsace and the eastern provinces bordering the Rhineland. Here, religious arguments were less frequent than economic complaints about the association of the Jews with usury. These resentments had a real basis in demographic and economic pressures upon agrarian workers, who suffered from the subdivision of holdings, scarcity of coinage and the lack of regular credit facilities; and they flared up in July 1789, around the time of the *Grande Peur*. The peasants rose up not only against the *seigneurs*, but also against the Jews, several hundred of whom were forced to flee from the Rhineland to Basle or Mulhouse. This partly explains why equality of rights was accorded by the National Assembly to Protestants and actors on 24 December 1789, and to the Jewish Sephardi community of Bordeaux ('the Portuguese') in January 1790, but was not extended to the Jews of the eastern provinces until September 1791, and then perhaps only because of the change in the political climate following the king's attempted flight to Varennes the previous June.

In 1792–3, French armies took over the southern Rhineland and established a Jacobin republic in Trier's fellow religious electorate of Mainz; in 1794, they took over the whole of the left bank of the Rhine (allegedly the true boundary of Roman Gaul, and a pre-existing goal of French expansion adopted by the revolutionary Danton) and remained there through to the downfall of Napoléon in 1815. The Rhineland had become part of the French Republic, and subsequently the First Empire. The doctrine of universal rights was, therefore, to be put to work there.

The situation of the population of 22,000 Jews in the overwhelmingly Catholic Rhineland varied significantly between territory and territory. In Cologne, for example, Jews had remained excluded from the city since their expulsion in 1424; in Bonn, Jews enjoyed toleration, while Protestants did not; in Aachen, even Protestants were forced to hold services outside the city gates; in Mainz, on the other hand, Jews and Christians were accorded the same rights – Jews could attend Christian schools and from 1786 both Protestants and Jews had been allowed to graduate from the local university. In Trier, Jews had experienced a particularly chequered history. Attacked around the time of the First Crusade in 1096, and again around the time of the Black Death, they had largely prospered in between. After they were expelled from the city for much of the fifteenth century and again at the end of the sixteenth century, the last major attack upon their property had occurred in 1675. In the eighteenth century, antagonisms seem to have diminished. Jews were treated with greater toleration and received more favourable treatment as one component of a movement of Catholic Enlightenment, which pressed for greater equality for religious minorities. In part, Catholic reformers, especially the 'Febronians' in Trier, were acting on principle. But they were also fearful of falling behind areas of Protestant Germany, where a combination of Enlightenment and the economics of *raison d'état* had brought about a steady increase of prosperity.[9]

Jews, however, were not treated as equal co-subjects of these various principalities, episcopies or city-states, but rather – in common with elsewhere – as members of a separate 'nation' exterior to the states concerned. They were thus restricted to certain quarters of cities, debarred from many occupations, and made subject to a discriminatory tax, justified as a form of protection money, levied on the local Jewish community as a whole and divided out between them.

Despite the ambivalence of attitudes towards the Jews, a bridge between universalism and Jewish emancipation was already established on the eve of the Revolution. However, the position developed amounted to less than a full and unconditional possession of equal rights. In France, whether formulated by reform-minded Catholics like the Abbé Grégoire, members of the 'Patriot Party' or Enlightenment sympathizers, the form taken by the argument remained either explicitly or implicitly conditional. The argument was that according equal rights would aid 'the regeneration' of Jews, meaning their accelerated assimilation into the 'national' community and effective disappearance within a few generations.

The terms of the debate had first emerged in Germany, where the partition of Poland with its 750,000 Jews between Russia, Austria and Prussia had raised unforeseen questions about how these new subjects were to be treated.[10] In Austria, it precipitated the 1781 Emancipation Decree of Joseph II. In Prussia, where the small Jewish population had doubled, and where rising anti-Jewish feeling in Alsace was causing increased anxiety, this new situation produced in the same year the first sustained non-Jewish argument for emancipation, by Christian Dohm, a professor of history and friend of the great exponent of Enlightened Judaism, Moses Mendelssohn. Dohm was an exponent of natural religion and rejected all 'positive' faiths. Much of the case he put forward in *On the Civic Improvement of the Jews* rested upon the Jews' capacity to become happier and more useful members of society, once there was an end to the oppression 'so unworthy of our age', which had corrupted them. The removal of legal discrimination, he assumed, would lead to the assimilation of Jews into Gentile society and the gradual disappearance of a specific Jewish identity. In place of their 'clannish religious opinions' they would be inspired by patriotism and love for the state. This would occur as part of a larger transformation of society as a whole from a hierarchy of estates into a social structure based upon merit.[11]

This book was rapidly translated and published in France, where it made an immediate impact. In 1787, it inspired a prize essay competition in Metz: 'Are there means of making Jews in France happier and more useful?' The most famous answer came from the Abbé Grégoire. Like Dohm, Grégoire argued for the removal of the disabilities of the Jews, both civil and political, not so much to increase their usefulness, but rather to accomplish their 'regeneration'. Grégoire was the first Catholic priest to write sympathetically about the plight of the Jews, but he also drew extravagantly upon an eclectic variety of sources to explain their 'corruption'. Not only had God punished them by dispersing them across the world, but Grégoire also concurred with Johann Kaspar Lavater, the Swiss clergyman and widely esteemed inventor of the 'science' of 'physiognomy', in believing that their moral degeneracy could be detected in their facial characteristics.[12]

After the outbreak of the Revolution, Grégoire became one of the champions of the new Constitutional church established by the National Assembly to rectify the abuses of the Catholic church during the *Ancien Régime*. With the advent of this new church and society, he believed, the Ashkenazi Jews would be dissolved into the nation. Furthermore, the argument for the 'regeneration' of the Jews was now expressed in universalistic terms. For all groups in the *Ancien Régime* had been corrupted to a greater or lesser extent before 1789. He was not in doubt that the new nation must possess a unified character, and therefore that all would now have to transform their customs and values. In particular, a new homogeneity would be achieved through intermarriage. Apart from the Jews, Grégoire paid special attention to the transformation of country people, free blacks and, his particular *bête noire*, the speakers of patois.

How far did the fortunes of the Marx family change in the ten years following the Emancipation Decree of 1791?[13] The evidence is only indirect and it suggests little significant improvement in the situation of Jews in the Rhineland. Greater freedom of residence was possible, and some broadening in the choices open to artisans. But there was now mounting Jacobin hostility towards all pre-existing forms of worship, culminating in the closure of all churches and synagogues between September 1793 and February 1795, or their transformation into Temples of Reason. The re-establishment of congregations in the traumatic aftermath of these events was often difficult, since many were now happier with their new secular status as equal citizens and refused to continue their former contribution to communal support. The billeting of French occupying troops and the requisitioning of provisions for the military were also problems. In neighbouring Alsace, the harsh years of the French Thermidorian regime (1795–9) brought a new surge of anger against usury. Despite the fact that Christian financiers had been equally involved, Jews were the chief targets of peasant animosity.[14]

Far more dramatic changes in the fortunes of the Rhineland's Jews occurred under the rule of Napoléon. In the 1790s, the Jacobins had generally adopted an exploitative attitude towards the local population. They had closed down all four of the Rhineland universities – Bonn, Cologne, Trier and Mainz – and had carted off local art treasures to Paris. Napoléon, on the other hand, was determined to court the collaboration of local elites. He abolished the revolutionary calendar and supported consensual local customs and holidays (not least St Napoléon's Day). While he was impatient with the humanities and traditional courses studied at universities, he was an enthusiastic promoter of vocational subjects. Apart from the applied sciences, he was particularly interested in promoting jurisprudence as a means of supporting his newly constructed and definitive legal code, the *Code Napoléon*. This was a project worthy of the founder of a second Roman Empire, and its new Justinian. On a state tour of the Rhineland in 1804, he stayed briefly in Trier, where he ordered that the magnificent Roman Porta Nigra be freed from the clutter of medieval buildings surrounding it, and ordained the foundation of a new Law School in Coblenz.[15]

In 1801, primarily in order to pacify the western French area of the Vendée, the heart of royalist and clerical resistance to the secular republic, Napoléon also made a Concordat with the Pope. Having removed Catholic objections to his rule, he followed this up with measures designed to extend administrative uniformity to other confessions, principally to Protestants and Jews. His justification was that 'the people must have a religion; this religion must be in the control of the government . . . My policy', he stated, 'is to govern men as the majority wish to be governed. That is the way, I believe, in which one recognizes the sovereignty of the people. If I ruled a people of Jews, I would rebuild the Temple of Solomon.'[16]

Napoléon seems to have possessed an instinctive dislike for the Jews, fuelled in part by his Catholic upbringing, in part by his reading of Voltaire. 'The Jews are a vile people,' he wrote in his *Memorial of Saint Helena*, 'cowardly yet cruel.'[17] But, at the same time, he was also determined to ease the tensions endemic to the new Empire's eastern provinces, in particular by accelerating the process of Jewish 'regeneration'. Despite his distaste, therefore, he did much to regularize the legal status of Jewish citizens and widen their occupational opportunities.

On 9 February 1807, along with seventy-one other rabbis and prominent Jewish laymen, Samuel Marx, the rabbi at Trier – brother of Heinrich and uncle to Karl – was summoned by Napoléon to 'The Great Sanhedrin' in Paris.[18] A previous gathering of Jewish notables had been asked a series of hostile questions designed to hasten their assimilation, by highlighting the areas in which Jewish law was thought to be incompatible with the laws of the nation. They were quizzed about their attitudes towards patriotism, intermarriage, state authority and usury. As a result of their Sanhedrin, two decrees reorganized the Judaic faith along state-approved lines. The members of the Rabbinate became state employees akin to Protestant pastors and Catholic *curés*, and the administration of the Jewish creed was entrusted to a General Consistory similar to that governing Protestant communities. Far more inflammatory was the third decree, the so-called 'infamous decree' (*décret infâme*). This measure continued the practice of discriminatory taxation, but purportedly was designed to stamp out obstacles to

Jewish 'regeneration', especially the practice of 'usury'. It not only urged diversification into other occupations, but also changed existing credit arrangements, obliged Jewish dealers to apply to the Prefect for the annual renewal of a licence to trade, forbade Jews – unlike other groups – to avoid conscription by payment for a substitute, and compelled them to register and, if necessary, modify their names to meet the new demands of civil registration.

Rhineland Jews were keen to demonstrate their patriotism by doing their best to comply with these decrees, particularly those directed against usury. On 16 August 1808, at a synagogue celebration of Napoléon's birthday in Trier, Marx's Uncle Samuel urged Jewish youth to apply itself to artisanal trades, agriculture or the sciences; his own son trained as a gardener. The newly established Consistory was also keen to act decisively against usury. A document from 1810 states that Samuel had 'left no opportunity unused to warn about the spirit of fanaticism so contrary to the principles of our religion'; and it went on to state that the Consistory would immediately report to the authorities any 'Israelite' who, as a result of usury, was found 'guilty of deception of a non-Israelite'.[19] It must also have been around the same time that Karl's father began his career as a lawyer. In line with the new demands of the civil administration, Heinrich – originally Herschel – now changed his name to Henri. He was recorded among those enrolled in the three-year licentiate law course at Coblenz, and in 1814 – the year in which he got married – he signed himself as a witness to the birth of his niece, 'H. Marx avoué'.[20]

But time was running out for Napoléon and his new empire. On the disastrous Russian campaign in 1812 Napoléon lost 570,000 men. The Russian army continued westwards, reinforced by the defection of the Prussian contingent of the *Grande Armée*. The Austrians rejoined the allied coalition, and in October 1813, at the Battle of Leipzig, Napoléon's army of 200,000 was defeated by a coalition of 365,000 Austrians, Prussians, Russians and Swedes. When the remnant of Napoléon's army entered Mainz in November, a further 18,000 were lost to typhus. By the end of January 1814, the whole of the left bank of the Rhine was in allied hands.

2. 1815: THE RHINELAND BECOMES PRUSSIAN

What would now happen to the Rhineland was a matter of contention among the victorious allied forces. Prussia hoped for a chunk of Saxony as its share in the spoils of victory. But after the collapse of the Austrian Netherlands in the 1790s, the British became determined that Prussia, for the most part an eastern power, should replace Austria as the western 'sentinel' against a fresh French military break-out. Prussia resisted this solution as long as possible. It would mean taking on the huge responsibility of defending the long western frontiers of Germany. The people of the Rhineland were equally unenthusiastic. The great majority were Catholic and would probably have preferred a Hapsburg ruler. They called the Prussians 'Lithuanians'; while the well-heeled lamented that 'we are marrying into a poor family'.[21]

The most immediate challenge for the Prussians was not Catholicism, but the threat posed by Rhenish law. If the Rhineland were to be incorporated into Prussia, Prussian law would surely replace the local legal system. But the Prussian legal code, the *Allgemeines Landrecht*, although enlightened in intention, largely predated 1789 and took virtually no account of the fundamental shift in legal and political assumptions which were to take place in the Rhineland as the result of the Revolution and twenty years of French rule. As in France, feudal lordship had been replaced by the sovereignty of private property, common rights had been privatized, guilds had been dissolved, administration had been streamlined and church land had been auctioned off.

The whole of this social and political transformation was presupposed in a new legal system, and it was strongly supported by the local population. These new judicial institutions were based upon the *Code Napoléon*, which presupposed equality before the law. Furthermore, a strange twist of events had pushed the system in a yet more liberal direction. Under Napoléon, juries had only been allowed in ordinary cases. Crimes of special interest to the state had been reserved for special tribunals consisting of judges and military officers, acting alone. During the allied invasion in 1814, however, the judges serving in these unpopular courts had fled and non-jury courts had closed down. As a result, the judicial system in the Rhineland now stood out as a model of liberal practice, and the principles embodied within it – trial by jury, public hearings, the separation of judiciary from executive and the outlawing of corporal punishment – survived to 1848, when it became the model of reformers all over Germany.

In 1815 the direction of Prussian policies for its new Rhineland province was as yet unclear. For the Revolution and the war had also forced Prussia to change. In 1806 in the Battles of Jena and Auerstedt, the Prussians had been utterly humiliated by Napoléon. It was the end of the political order of old Prussia – of 'the agrarian ruling class in uniform'.[22] In response to this fiasco, radicals within the Prussian administration had introduced a series of fundamental reforms. Conscription and promotion by merit were introduced in the army, a ministerial system was devised, servile tenure was abolished, guild restrictions were removed, and municipal self-government was established. These measures were accompanied by the introduction of universal primary education and the foundation of a new university in Berlin.

There was also a major shift in attitudes towards Jewish emancipation: promoted by the reforming Chancellor Karl von Hardenberg, the 1812 'Edict Concerning the Civil Condition of the Jews' swept away previous special jurisdictions, and turned Jews into 'citizens' of the Prussian state. The Edict did not go as far as the French legislation of 1791. There was still the expectation that changed status would be accompanied by changed behaviour. In addition, the question of whether Jews would be eligible for government employment was left undecided. Nevertheless, as a first step it was strongly welcomed by Jewish organizations.

Such a change played a significant part in the move away from the political assumptions which had governed feudal and absolutist Prussia of old. Change had been made necessary by the renewal of war against Napoléon in 1813. It had involved the mobilization of Prussia in the months leading up to the Battle of Leipzig, and for many at the time had meant the true birth of 'Germany'.[23] After the humiliation of 27 October 1806, when Napoléon and his victorious army had been cheered as they had ridden through the streets of Berlin, an extraordinary transformation had occurred. At that time, there had emerged the first sparks of *national* resistance to France. This had been confined to small circles of students and intellectuals, who defended a 'nation' in the sense of a linguistic and cultural community encompassing and transcending existing principalities and estates. Subsequently, this sentiment became conjoined with a growing reaction against the ruthlessness and exploitative behaviour of the *Grande Armée*, and as a result popular indifference turned into hatred of the occupying power. Reading groups, gymnastic associations and secret societies circulated propaganda among the educated classes, and found a wider reception, especially among the young in the towns, including students, artisans and day labourers.

In 1813, the conservative and absolutist Prussian monarchy had been forced to follow the example of the French revolutionary state and summon its own mass conscripted army. The whole eligible male population, irrespective of estate and including Jews, was called up, while a variety of voluntary groups, including women, provided backup across civil society. Momentarily, the cause of Prussia and the cause of an inchoate 'Germany' had come together. Thereafter, an endlessly embellished recollection of this moment of patriotic unity in 1813, when king and people allegedly stood together, nurtured a powerful reservoir of loyalist sentiment in the decades leading up to 1848.

The definitive victory over Napoléon at Waterloo by mostly British and Prussian troops on 18 June 1815 appeared as the culmination of the hopes engendered by Prussia's 'Reform Era' and by the patriotic mobilization of 1813. It had been preceded less than a month before by the Royal Edict of 22 May promising the calling of a representative assembly. There were also reasons to be optimistic about the future of the Rhineland. The province's government had been entrusted to prominent members of the reform camp, in particular Johann Sack, Justus von Gruner and Christoph von Sethe, who opposed the old aristocracy and favoured the Rhineland's liberal judicial system. For a moment, it seemed as if a new and more progressive Prussia might come to terms with its post-revolutionary province.

These hopes were soon dashed. The promise of a representative assembly was not kept. Metternich's establishment of the German Confederation, an old-world conglomerate of thirty-eight mainly princely entities, dampened visions of a new form of German unity. The disappointments and confusions of Romantic and nationalist activists, now enrolled in a new form of student association, the *Burschenschaft*, were passionately expressed in a new form of political gathering, commemorating the three-hundredth anniversary of Luther's Reformation, the

Wartburg Festival of 1817. There, among an assortment of hated objects, participants burnt the works of the playwright August von Kotzebue, who had derided Romantic nationalist ideals. A year later, dressed in an 'old German costume' designed by the Romantic gymnast Friedrich Jahn, a radical nationalist student from Jena, Karl Sand, assassinated Kotzebue in his home. This was quite enough to frighten the nervous Prussian king, Friedrich Wilhelm III, who had already been convinced by Metternich about the threat posed by 'demagogues' spreading Jacobinism and nationalism. Thus, in 1819, the German Confederation, prompted by Metternich, enacted the Carlsbad Decrees, which suppressed the student societies and imposed a crackdown on freedom of speech and of association.

In Berlin, conservatives had also already begun to gain the upper hand at the court of Friedrich Wilhelm III, and the marriage of his sister to the future Czar Nicholas I of Russia pushed him further in a reactionary direction. In contrast to the policies of the Prussian reformers, there was a new emphasis upon the centrality of religion. According to a memorandum of 1816, religion was the only bond powerful enough to transform a people into a 'unanimous whole', capable of unified and determined action 'in times of external threat'. This in turn meant a change in policy towards the Jews. Steps were taken to ensure that conversion was made easier, but, by the same token, as long as the Jew remained a Jew, he was strictly to be excluded from any position in the state.

Both as a lawyer and as a Jew, Heinrich Marx was caught up in the crossfire between these contending parties. On 13 June 1815, Heinrich wrote to the new Prussian provincial governor, Johann Sack, requesting that the new administration rescind the anti-Jewish Napoleonic decree of 17 March 1808. He referred to his fellow believers, *Glaubensgenossen*, arguing that while some were guilty of usurious practices, the remedy was not the current unequal legislation, but a clear law against usury. He went on to contest the claim that such discrimination was designed as a cure for Jewish degeneration. He gave 'eternal thanks to the Almighty for the fact that we still were, and are, human beings', and stated that any 'person who after such a long period of oppression has not been made wholly degenerate, must bear the unmistakeable stamp of a noble humanity; the ineradicable seeds of virtue reside in the breast; the spark of divinity inspires the spirit'. He also appealed to 'the gentle spirit of Christianity', often darkened by 'the spirit of fanaticism', to 'the pure morality of the Gospel tarnished by the ignorance of the priests' and to 'the will of the king as the wise lawgiver'.[24]

Heinrich was particularly concerned about his own ability to practise as an attorney. On 23 April 1816, reporting upon the numbers of Jews employed in the administration of justice, the President of the District Court, Christoph von Sethe, wrote to Berlin, arguing that while the 1812 Edict forbade Jews to practise as attorneys, three who were currently practising – including Heinrich – ought to be granted the exceptional right to continue to do so. They had chosen their profession in good faith, and had the monarch's assurance that no official should be ousted from his post as a result of the change of government. But Kircheisen, the conservative Minister of Justice in Berlin, did not think that exceptions should be made, nor did the Prussian Minister of the Interior, von Schuckmann.[25]

With reformers on the defensive or marginalized – Sack was moved to Pomerania soon after – the local administration could do little to help. Towards the end of 1816, Heinrich submitted to the 'Immediat-Justiz-Kommission' a report on the institution of commercial courts in the Rhineland. When the 'Kommission' invited him to publish his report, he agreed but only on condition that his name and place of residence be withheld. He was fearful of the possible consequences, if it became known that he lived in Trier. As he explained:

> unfortunately, my relations are of such a kind that as the father of a family I must be somewhat cautious. As is known, the confession to which nature has chained me enjoys no special esteem, and this province is certainly not the most tolerant. And if I have to endure many things, some quite bitter, and if I were to have to risk losing my small fortune almost completely, until such time as it could come to be accepted that a Jew might both possess some talent and be upright; I certainly cannot be blamed, if I have become somewhat shy.[26]

And so Heinrich was baptized as a member of the Prussian Evangelical church sometime between 1816 and 1819. No record of his baptism exists. But there is no cause to doubt the reason for it. It was because, as Karl's friend Wilhelm Liebknecht and his daughter, Eleanor, both stated long ago, the Prussian government left him with no other choice if he wished to continue as a lawyer.[27]

While there can be no doubt about the professional necessity for

Heinrich's baptism, it is not so certain that such a change was entirely contrary to his convictions. His references to the 'gentle spirit of Christianity' and 'the pure morality of the Gospel' suggest a strong respect for Christianity, while still a member of the Jewish community. What may have restrained him from making such a move earlier was consideration for the feelings of his parents. This may have been what he was referring to years later when in a reproving letter to the nineteen-year-old Karl, about the need to respect one's parents, he mentioned his own experience: 'how I have fought and suffered, in order not to distress them as long as possible'.[28] Karl's brother-in-law, Edgar von Westphalen, remembering forty years later, called Heinrich a Protestant in the manner of Lessing or according to Kant's model of faith and reason united in a higher morality.[29] This certainly agrees with the tone of another letter Heinrich wrote to his son Karl, in 1835: 'a great support for morality is pure faith in God. You know that I am anything but a fanatic. But this faith is a real [requirement] of man sooner or later, and there are moments in life when even the atheist is [involuntarily] drawn to worship the Almighty . . . for what Newton, Locke and Leibniz believed, everyone can . . . submit to.'[30]

In the 1820s, Heinrich seems to have prospered. Following his appointment to the Trier Appeal Court in 1818, he wrote another report on usury in 1821 and became a public advocate. He was evidently well regarded by his colleagues. The impressive house near the Porta Nigra bought in 1819 was purchased from a fellow jurist, and the godparents of his children were principally Trier advocates. Edgar von Westphalen claimed that he was one of the foremost advocates and most noble of men in the Rhineland. Nor did Heinrich lose all contact with the local Jewish community. The Marx family continued to share ownership of a vineyard at Mertesdorf with Dr Lion Bernkastel, a prominent member of the Consistory, and continued to seek his assistance in medical matters into the 1830s.[31] The family also remained on friendly terms with the widow of the rabbi, Samuel Marx.[32]

For Trier itself and its surrounding region, the 1820s was not a prosperous time. Under French rule, Moselle wine gained from easier access to the French market, but then suffered a prolonged and deepening crisis a few years after the region's incorporation into Prussia. Misled by the apparent monopoly position accorded to the industry by the Prussian tariff of 1818, wine growers vastly increased the acreage devoted to viticulture and at the same time diluted quality, lured by the promise of a Prussian mass market. By the mid-1820s, overproduction was leading to falling prices and this was turned into catastrophe by commercial treaties with Bavaria and Württemberg, which led to the displacement of Moselle wine by South German Pfalz and Rheingau wines. The crisis of the wine growers continued in the 1830s and 1840s to the point where their misery could only be compared with that of the internationally notorious contemporary case of the Silesian weavers.[33]

The other mainstay of the region was the forest, and during the first half of the nineteenth century there was a rising demand for wood, especially from the iron forges of the Eifel and coopers in the wine trade. Poor upland peasants benefited from this demand by selling the wood they collected from the forest floor. But the consolidation of private property rights during the period of Napoleonic rule and its confirmation by the Provincial Estates in the 1820s and 1830s threatened peasant livelihood by contesting the right to collect dead wood. Village resistance took the form of 'wood theft' mainly carried out by women and children. The rising numbers sentenced for wood theft by property-owning juries was one of the issues highlighted in an article by Karl Marx in the *Rheinische Zeitung* of 1842. But the issue was not so much, as he thought, a struggle between private property and subsistence agriculture, as rather a struggle by the poor to participate in the market for wood.[34]

If there was mistrust of Prussian rule in the 1820s, it was on the whole muted. There was no nostalgia for the Rhineland before the years of French rule. Berlin took little account of the economic interests of the Rhineland province; its free-trade policies were mainly designed to benefit the East Elbian corn exporters of the Prussian heartlands. But, like Napoléon, the Prussians tried to associate themselves with local culture. They returned looted treasure, restored Bonn University in 1818 (but not Trier) and patronized the growing Romantic cult of the medieval by supporting the project to complete Cologne Cathedral. Their main interest, however – and certainly in Trier – was military and strategic. Trier, a garrison town a few miles from the French frontier, was in the first line of defence against a potentially resurgent France.[35]

In the 1820s, the promise of the Prussian king to summon a representative assembly, originally prompted by Hardenberg and other ministerial reformers, was transformed by conservatives into the periodical holding of a provincial assembly organized along the lines of traditional estate society, and without budgetary powers.[36] Since, under Rhenish law, noble privilege remained illegal, the attempt to nominate a noble estate at the first meeting of the Rhineland Assembly in 1826 was generally treated with ridicule; Rhenish notables remained firmly bourgeois in their outlook and style of life. Nevertheless, despite their inappropriateness of form, local leaders managed to turn these assemblies into vehicles for the expression of discontent with the local Prussian bureaucracy.[37]

3. 1830 AND AFTER

In response to events in the 1830s, the demands of Rhenish liberalism acquired a much more clear-cut shape. The revolution of July 1830 in Paris toppled the regime of the Bourbon king, Charles X, brother of the executed Louis XVI and ended any ambition to restore the structures of the *Ancien Régime*. A month later, Belgium witnessed the beginning of a successful national revolt against the Dutch, and from November through to the following summer of 1831 the Poles made an attempt to throw off Russian rule. Among German liberals and radicals, there was general excitement. According to the poet Heinrich Heine, who was holidaying in remote Heligoland, when news arrived of the fall of Charles X, 'the fisherman, who yesterday took me over to the little island of sand where we bathe, smiled at me and said: "the poor people have gained the day"'.[38] In Brandenburg-Prussia, nothing much stirred. But in the Rhineland the fact that two of its most important neighbours, France and Belgium, had now become liberal parliamentary monarchies was greeted with enthusiasm. Politically, the intimidating presence of Prussian garrisons inhibited any overt challenge to the existing constitution beyond riots and disturbances in Aachen and Cologne.[39] But in the Bavarian Rhineland at Hambach in May 1832, an assembly of burghers, artisans and students reinforced by thousands of locally protesting peasants called for a German nation-state founded upon the sovereignty of the people. Predictably, the German Confederation reacted with another set of laws strengthening censorship and prohibiting all forms of freedom of association and freedom of assembly.

The reaction of Trier burghers was less visible, but not enough to escape official attention. The Prussian authorities had already noted with raised eyebrows the activities of the Casino Club, the main social club of the city's *Bürgertum*, which on several occasions had apparently omitted toasting the king's health. They had been even more concerned when tensions between members of the Club and the garrison led to a mass withdrawal of its officers from the Club. But the anxiety increased when, on 13 January 1834, the Club held a festive banquet for 160 guests to welcome back from the *Landtag* (Provincial Assembly) the four Deputies from Trier.

Heinrich Marx delivered the welcoming speech. 'One feeling unites us all at this ceremony,' he began, 'one feeling at this moment inspires the honourable citizens of this city; the feeling of gratitude towards their representatives, from whom they have the conviction, that they have struggled in word and deed, with courage and sacrifice for truth and justice.' He then proffered 'innermost thanks and warmest wishes to our benevolent king' for first instituting 'the representation of the people'. 'Of his own free will', the king had organized the calling of the estates 'in order that the truth should reach the steps of his throne'. And, he went on, 'where indeed should the truth lead us, if not there?' 'Where justice is enthroned,' he concluded, 'there also must truth make its appearance.'[40] As a loyal address, this was certainly somewhat arch. Heinrich Marx thanked the representatives of the city before the king; he spoke of the first establishment of 'the representation of the people', rather than the calling of estates, and he related the Provincial Assembly to the attainment of justice and truth.

The authorities treated the proceedings as an affront. The Justice Minister criticized a lunch society composed of private subscribers in the city of Trier 'presuming in an equally ignorant and unauthorized way to enlighten and criticize the proceedings of an assembly answerable to the majesty of the king'. And he was particularly alarmed that:

> the great majority of Deputies to the *Landtag* do not behave as Deputies to the *Landtag* from their respective German estates, but as representatives of the people; and, as in England, they will be encouraged along this path by the public, if in the taverns they give and receive speeches and are applauded by onlookers as tribunes of the people for their accomplishments in the *Landtag*, combating the perils and plans which threatened the *Landtag*, and which they staved off.[41]

For a government still anxious about the reaction of its Rhineland subjects in the aftermath of 1830, worse was yet to come. Less than a fortnight later, on 25 January 1834, there took place another celebratory supper to mark the anniversary of the foundation of the Casino Club. After most of the guests had left, a number of participants gathered at one of the tables, speeches were given and songs sung. While songs without political content were murmured, the 'Marseillaise' was taken up with more enthusiasm and that was followed by the 'Parisienne', and other revolutionary songs. One of the participants took out a silk tricolour napkin and stood on a stool and waved it around, then, stepping down and staggering backwards, caused others to kiss, embrace or even kneel before it. One of the lawyers present exclaimed, 'if we had not experienced the July Revolution in France, we would now be having to eat grass like cattle'. Again among those present was Heinrich Marx, though he left before the final rendition of the 'Marseillaise'.[42]

The Prussian administration was alarmed by the reports of the incident that it received from the military in Trier. The Mayor, on the other hand, attempted to smooth things over by arguing that the whole affair was simply the result of drinking too much wine, and should not be taken too seriously. Public opinion disapproved of the proceedings, but disliked even more the elaboration of the incident by the military. Nevertheless, the government went ahead with a charge of high treason against one of the participants, the lawyer Brixius. But the accused was acquitted in Trier, and yet again on appeal in Cologne, an eloquent testimony to the value and importance of the Rhineland's non-absolutist judicial system.

It was also some indication of the anxiety of Prussia's rulers that at the Trier *Gymnasium*, which Karl Marx attended between 1830 and 1835, alongside the headmaster, Johann Hugo Wyttenbach, a pronouncedly conservative co-director, Vitus Loers, was appointed and entrusted with political surveillance of the school. Wyttenbach was a history teacher as well as director. He was a cultured and progressive man, who had once saluted the storming of the Bastille as the dawn of freedom, and whose religious beliefs were informed by Kant. Heinrich reminded his son, when he reached the end of his times at the *Gymnasium*, to send some appreciative verses to Wyttenbach – 'I told him how devoted you are to him.' But he also reported that he had been invited to a luncheon held by Loers, who 'has taken it ill that you did not pay him a farewell visit'. Heinrich had told a white lie to excuse his son's disrespect.[43]

Despite the 1834 incident, the views of Heinrich were not those of a revolutionary, and, as he wrote to his son, he was 'anything but a fanatic'. In 1837 in an attempt to humour his son's youthful ambition to take up 'dramatic composition', he suggested a trial run and came up with a suggestion for a theme. The subject should come from Prussian history and relate to 'a crowded moment of time where however the future hung in the balance'. He pondered a theme, which would allot a role to 'the genius of the monarchy', perhaps via 'the mind of the very noble Queen Louise'. He lighted upon Waterloo. 'The danger was enormous, not only for Prussia, for its monarch, but for the whole of Germany'; and it was 'Prussia that decided the great issue here', a fitting topic for 'an ode in the heroic genre, or otherwise'. There has been some doubt whether this suggestion was entirely serious; Queen Louise had died in 1810. But there was no ambiguity in his condemnation of Napoléon a page further on. 'In truth, under his rule not a single person would have dared to think aloud what is being written daily and without interference throughout Germany, and especially in Prussia.' Anyone who had studied that history 'can rejoice greatly and with a clear conscience at his downfall and the victory of Prussia'.[44]

A Jew who had joined the Christian Evangelical church – the official confession of the Prussian monarchy – in a Catholic land clearly cannot be considered typical. Yet Heinrich Marx shared many of the values and attitudes of Rhineland liberals. Even in religious matters, at least until the conflict over mixed marriages flared up in the late 1830s, there was a much more consensual overlap in attitude among the Rhenish elite, whether Catholic, Protestant or Jewish, than the confessional divisions would suggest. In Heinrich's case, as has already been made clear, it was shaped by the legacy of the Enlightenment. According to his granddaughter, Eleanor, 'he was a real eighteenth-century "Frenchman". He knew Voltaire and Rousseau by heart.'[45] But similar enlightened movements of reform had made an impact among Rhineland Catholics too. In the late eighteenth century, Trier University had been much affected by the enlightened theology of Febronius and the teachings of Immanuel Kant, while in the University of Bonn students flocked to the radical theology lectures of Georg Hermes.[46]

The points of consensus were political. These included a determination not to destroy the benefits of twenty years of French rule, especially the Civil Code, the jury system and the abolition of the feudal aristocracy.

These changes had been accompanied by distaste for the fanaticism of the Jacobins and for the bureaucratic authoritarianism of Napoléon. There was also widespread dislike and suspicion of Prussian militarism, resentment about Prussian economic policy, which was thought to benefit the eastern provinces, and a desire for moderate parliamentary government, promised by the king back in 1815. For Heinrich's generation, the decisive years had been 1789–91 – the promise of a representative assembly, equality before the law, the abolition of the estates, the rights of man – and for Jews especially the year 1791 and the achievement of unconditional emancipation. These were the demands that inspired the new Rhineland leaders who came to prominence in the 1830s – Hansemann, Mevissen and Camphausen – and who would lead the liberal ministries in Berlin and Frankfurt in 1848.

For a younger and more radical generation, born and brought up entirely under Prussian rule in Metternich's Europe, reasoned arguments for constitutional monarchy and representative government were not enough. In 1830, when Karl was twelve, after fifteen years of severe repression, there was once again talk of revolution, as another generation witnessed anew the downfall of a Bourbon king in Paris. Parliamentary regimes were established in France and Belgium, and the suffrage was reformed in Britain. But throughout Europe there was radical pressure to push the reforms further and rifts began to appear between liberals and radicals, constitutional monarchists and republicans, Bonapartists, nationalists and democrats. In France and Britain differences became public and explicit almost immediately. But in Germany, where conditions remained repressive, disagreements within the 'Bewegungspartei' ('party of movement') remained muted and implicit. Ten years later, however, in the face of the Prussian monarchy's refusal to make any concession to the cause of reform, these divisions became as explicit and as polarized as elsewhere. It was at that point that the 24-year-old Karl Marx emerged as one of the most distinctive exponents of a new and peculiarly German form of radicalism, very different from the cautious hopes of his father. What has now to be explained is how family circumstance, the critical condition of German religion and philosophy, and, above all, Karl's own soaring intellectual ambitions combined to shape such a singular stance.

2

The Lawyer, the Poet and the Lover

1. HENRIETTE PRESSBURG AND HER CHILDREN

So far, nothing has been said about Karl's mother, Henriette, née Pressburg. Generally, she has received cursory and for the most part condescending treatment. In his classic study of 1918, Franz Mehring devoted less than half a paragraph to her, noting only that 'she was completely absorbed in her domestic affairs', and that she could only speak broken German.[1]

Why her German grammar and spelling remained so poor remains a mystery. It cannot simply be ascribed to her upbringing in the Netherlands, or her preference for Dutch, since her sister, Sophie, not only spoke and wrote good German, but also had mastered several other languages. Nor is there any evidence, as some have speculated, that the language spoken in Henriette's home was Yiddish. It is more likely to have been a Nijmegen dialect of Dutch. Similarly, there is no reason to think that she was in any way intellectually limited. Her daughter Sophie described her as 'small, delicate and very intelligent'; and what few fragments of evidence remain suggest that she was capable of critical judgement and wit.[2] At the time of her baptism, she is said to have responded to acquaintances who teased her about her new faith, 'I believe in God, not for God's sake, but for my sake.'[3] While in later life hardly having a good word to say about her, Karl Marx himself ruefully acknowledged in 1868: here he was with 'half a century on my shoulders, and still a pauper. How right my mother was: "if only Karell had made capital instead of etc."'[4]

How well Henriette fitted into Trier society is open to question. She came from Nijmegen and in later life considered returning, to her sister, who lived in Zaltbommel near Amsterdam. Holland remained important in her life and, for different reasons, in the life of her son. After Karl's trip to Holland at Christmas 1836, Henriette wrote to him with real pride, 'how do you like my native city – it is a really beautiful place and I hope it may have inspired you as to give you material for poetry'.[5] Much later, in 1851, when congratulating her niece, Henriette van Anrooij (born Philips), on the birth of her third child, she added, 'when one marries according to one's wish, one should not complain. But you have had much better fortune than I had. You have beside you your dear mother for every occasion. I was wholly alone in a foreign land.'[6] Like so many others in the middle of the nineteenth century, she linked her fears to those of the wandering Jew. In 1853, she wrote to her sister, Sophie, of the impending marriage of her daughter Louise and her intended move to South Africa: 'it seems that the fate of the people of I[srael] is once again being fulfilled in my case and that my children are to be scattered throughout all the world'.[7]

As for her absorption in domestic matters, more needs to be said about the reasons for this preoccupation. In her early letters, written soon after Karl had left home for Bonn University, while Heinrich advised or berated his son on his behaviour, values and career, Henriette focused on his physical well-being. Six weeks later, after Karl had begun at Bonn University, on 29 November 1836, she wrote, 'you must not regard it as a weakness of our sex, if I am curious to know how you arrange your little household'. After enquiring about what part 'economy' played in his life and how he prepared his coffee, she continued, 'you must never regard cleanliness and order as something secondary, for health and cheerfulness depend on them. Insist strictly that your rooms are scrubbed frequently and fix a definite time for it.'[8] After learning with 'disquiet' that Karl had been ill at the beginning of 1836, Heinrich declared that 'there is no more lamentable being than a sickly scholar', while Henriette offered practical advice:

I am sure that if you, dear Carl, behave sensibly you can reach a ripe old age. But for that you must avoid everything that could make things worse, you must not get over-heated, not drink a lot of wine or coffee, and not eat anything pungent, a lot of pepper or other spices. You must not smoke any tobacco, not stay up too long in the evening, and rise early. Be careful also not to catch cold and, dear Carl, do not dance until you are quite well again. It will seem ridiculous to you, dear Carl, that I act the doctor in this way, but you do not know how parents take it to heart when they see their children are not well, and how many anxious hours this has already caused us.[9]

In September 1837, when Karl was beginning his second year at the University of Berlin, she wrote of making for him 'for the autumn woollen jackets, which will protect you from catching cold'. Even in early 1838, when her husband was seriously ill, she was still anxious to learn 'what has been the matter with you and whether you are quite well again'.[10]

But it would be a mistake to present Henriette's anxieties as those of a small-minded Biedermeier housewife with nothing more important to occupy her mind. Once set against the family's health record, her concerns become easier to understand. Of the nine children born to Heinrich and Henriette, five died aged twenty-five or less. In the Marx household the great enemy was consumption; and a hereditary pulmonary weakness on the father's side of the family made Heinrich himself and the majority of his children – especially the males – particularly susceptible to it. Of those who survived into adulthood, only Karl and three sisters – Sophie (1816–86), Louise (1821–93) and Emilie (1822–88) – lived a normal lifespan. Karl's older brother, Mauritz, died at the age of four in 1819; Hermann aged twenty-three, in 1842;[11] Henriette aged twenty-five, in 1845; Caroline aged twenty-three, in 1847; Eduard aged eleven, in 1837. In two cases, the surviving letters provide glimpses of what this meant in human terms.

On 9 November 1836, Heinrich reported that Eduard was attending the *Gymnasium* and 'does want to show rather more zeal'. But on 12 August 1837, in the course of reproaching Karl for a failure to write, Heinrich claimed that letters from him – when he was free of 'that sickly sensitivity and fantastic, gloomy thoughts' – were 'a real need', and 'would have been particularly so this summer for your deeply feeling mother and myself . . . Eduard has been ailing for the last six months, and has grown quite thin, his recovery is very doubtful, and, what is so rare among children and so exhausting, he suffers from the deepest melancholy, really fear of dying. – And you know what your mother is like – she won't go from his side, she torments herself day and night, and I am for ever afraid that she will be overcome by these exertions.'[12] Eduard died on 14 December 1837.

Equally harrowing was the case of Henriette, the fifth child; Jenny Westphalen, Karl's future wife, wrote to him in Paris on 11 August 1844 that great preparations were already afoot in the Marx household for the wedding between 'Jettchen' Marx and Theodor Simons. But 'despite all the celebrations, Jettchen's condition becomes daily more wretched, as her cough and her raucousness grows worse. She can scarcely go anywhere any more. She moves forward like a ghost, but must be married. This is wholly dreadful and irresponsible . . . I don't know whether this can go well. If at least they were going to live in a town – but in a miserable village.' Jenny declared herself at a loss to understand the position of Marx's mother. Henriette believed that Jettchen had tuberculosis, but still let her marry. But it was not clear that there was much choice, since Jettchen so forcefully declared it was her wish.[13]

According to one of the daughters of the preacher Rocholl, the consumption took its course so rapidly that everyone foresaw her death:

> My father tried to postpone the wedding on the grounds that it was no longer possible. The groom also recognized this, but the bride hoped for a cure once she was married. And so it was carried out. She had stood up and was wearing a white dress; I did not recognize her any more, so pitiable did she look. After the wedding ceremony, the groom had to carry her onto a bed, from which she only stood up in order to be taken away in the carriage, so that she could die in her new home.[14]

The wedding took place on 20 August 1844 and she died on 3 January 1845.

While escaping the ravages of consumption, Karl himself was regularly prone to chest infections. Commentators have speculated fancifully on a school essay, written in 1835 – 'Reflections of a Young Man on the Choice of a Profession' – suggesting that it presaged his later 'materialist conception of history'.[15] But they have missed the more obvious point, the anxiety about his health. Karl wrote: 'Although we cannot work for long and seldom happily with a physical constitution which is not suited to our profession, the thought nevertheless continually arises of sacrificing our well-being to duty, of acting vigorously although we are weak.'[16] His father was alarmed by a description of his condition in Bonn at the beginning of 1836 and advised moderate exercise such as walking, and even riding.[17] Karl had no difficulty in acquiring an exemption from military service. Around June 1836, his father urged him to procure relevant certificates, adding that he could get one from their family physician, Herr Berncastel. 'You can do it with a good conscience. Your chest is weak, at least at present.'[18] Writing about the end of his first term at the University of Berlin in the winter of 1836–7, Karl wrote to his father that, after 'many a sleepless night' and having 'neglected nature, art and the world ... I was advised by a doctor to go to the country'. Having traversed Berlin to Stralow, he claimed, 'I had no inkling that I would mature there from an anaemic weakling into a man of robust bodily strength'.[19] Despite this transformation, however, his mother sent him the exemption certificate in February 1838, adding, like Heinrich, that 'he had every right to it'.[20] The military doctor who examined him in Berlin at that time declared him not fit for enlistment, 'on account of a weak chest and the periodic spitting of blood'.[21]

It is clear from the correspondence with his parents that Karl's health was a constant and worrying preoccupation. It also appears that his survival was regarded as an all but providential gift.[22] The only surviving account of Karl's childhood already emphasized his wilfulness. 'I have heard my aunts say', wrote Marx's daughter, Eleanor, that 'as a little boy he was a terrible tyrant to his sisters, whom he would "drive" down the Markusberg at Trier at full speed as his horses, and worse would insist on their eating the "cakes" he made with dirty dough and dirtier hands.'[23] As he grew up he was treated as a special person. Heinrich acknowledged his distinctive 'intellectual gifts'.[24] Above all, his parents seem to have considered him exceptionally favoured by fate. As Heinrich wrote on 9 November 1836, 'your mother says you are a favourite of fortune', or as he noted in a letter of 12 August 1837, 'you say yourself that good fortune has made you its pet child'.[25] What this seems to have nurtured in the young Karl was a high degree of self-absorption, a belief in his special destiny and a larger than normal sense of entitlement.

2. TRIER *GYMNASIUM* AND BONN UNIVERSITY

Between the ages of twelve and seventeen, from 1830 to 1835, the young Karl attended the *Gymnasium* at Trier. Of his classmates, only seven were members of the Protestant Evangelical church; the other twenty-five were Catholics (there were no Jewish pupils). Eight (nearly all Protestants) came from professional families, nine were the sons of artisans, six from peasant families, and five the children of merchants. In 1835, when they took their final examination, the *Abitur*, the ages of those who matriculated varied from sixteen to twenty-seven. Of the twenty-two who took the exam, almost half were theology candidates.[26] Recalling his school days in 1878, Marx wrote of 'the denseness' and 'advanced age' of 'the country bumpkins at our grammar school in Trier', 'who were preparing to enter the seminary' and 'most of them, drawing stipends'.[27] Theology was prominent because the sons of workers and peasants had little chance of prolonging their education, except through charity and grants from the church. The age range (seventeen pupils were twenty or older) was also explained by the numbers remaining at school to avoid military service.

The ethos of the *Gymnasium* in Trier, shaped by its long-term headmaster, Johann Hugo Wyttenbach, was that of the late eighteenth-century *Aufklärung*, the German Enlightenment. It consisted of a strong belief in a benign God, and a rational morality uncluttered by dogma. In his youth, Wyttenbach had been a committed Jacobin and during the period of French rule had argued that the future of the Republic depended upon the education of its youth; and so in 1799 he had composed *A Handbook for the Instruction in the Duties and Rights of Man and the Citizen*. Wyttenbach had originally been appointed head of the school in 1804, but had managed to retain the headship in 1815, when the incoming Prussians transformed the school into a state *Gymnasium*. He remained in the post until his retirement in 1846.

Despite the change of regime in 1815, the values preached by Wyttenbach changed very little. He believed that man's privilege over the beast consisted in the possession of reason and free will. Man's freedom, according to one of Wyttenbach's recommended history textbooks, consisted in the satisfaction of his bodily and spiritual needs; the former through the employment of mechanical skills and new inventions, the latter through the pursuit of truth, beauty, moral perfection and union with God – or what was described as 'culture' (*Bildung*). In two *Deutsche Lesebücher* (German reading primers), compiled by him, one for the lower, one for the upper school, there were selections of poetry and prose from Herder, Goethe, Schiller,

Klopstock, Wieland, Kleist, Schlegel, Albrecht von Haller. In 1834, Wyttenbach described the *Gymnasium* as an educational establishment in which young persons should be educated in the sacred belief in progress and moral ennoblement. 'Divine wisdom has established two stars, which have eternally shone forth ... the higher reason, which opens the holy shrine of truth and the longing of a pure heart, which exists only in the good and the noble.' Basing himself upon the 'pure' doctrine of God and the immortality of the soul, which he associated with Kant, Wyttenbach constantly reiterated the idea that the human being must always first and foremost work for others; by this means, the path to immortality would be opened up.[28]

Although Wyttenbach retained his post, the Prussian authorities were deeply suspicious of the ethos of the school, and anxious about the possible infiltration of subversive ideas. After the assassination of Kotzebue in 1819, by a member of the Halle student *Burschenschaft*, there was a wave of arrests and rounding up of suspects known as the 'persecution of demagogues' (*Demagogenverfolgen*). In addition, at the behest of the Austrian Chancellor, Metternich, the German Confederation issued the Carlsbad Decrees, which imposed tougher censorship and increased surveillance. In Trier, the *Gymnasium* vetoed applications to the University of Halle and dropped the teaching of French; French was only allowed back as an optional subject in 1822, and not restored to the curriculum until 1828. Similarly, instruction in gymnastics was suspended, because of its connection with the nationalist *Turnvereine* (gymnastic associations). Several of the teachers were also accused of travelling to Bonn to take part in 'demagogic activities'. In the early 1830s, one of Marx's teachers, J. G. Schneemann, was accused of being involved in the unfurling of the tricolour at the Casino Club, while a second, Schwendler, was clearly suspect as the Club's Secretary. Steininger, the teacher of maths and geology, was also denounced for having stated around 1818 that there was no proof of the immortality of the soul, and that the destruction of Sodom and Gomorrah had probably been the result of a volcanic eruption.

Among the pupils, as well, evidence of subversive opinions was a source of recurring alarm. In the late 1820s, there was widespread enthusiasm for the Greeks' struggle for independence, and for their freedom-loving hero, Botzaris. In the early 1830s, reports of the radical speeches at the Hambach Festival were said to have circulated around the school,[29] and it seems that there existed a branch of Young Germany.[30] In an attempt to exert more control over the direction of the school, therefore, the authorities in 1835 promoted the classics master, Vitus Loers, to become co-head of the school with Wyttenbach.[31]

In tune with the neoclassical and humanist culture of the German *Gymnasium*, and in addition to traditional religious teaching, considerable emphasis was placed upon the teaching of Greek, Latin, ancient history, German language and literature. These were subjects in which the young Karl performed well, according to his leaving 'Certificate of Maturity' issued after his passing of the *Abitur* in 1835. In these subjects he had shown 'a very satisfactory diligence'. His knowledge of 'the Christian faith and morals' was 'fairly clear and well grounded'. His mathematics was 'satisfactory'. On the other hand, his knowledge of physics was only 'moderate' and he showed 'only slight diligence' in French. Overall his performance was on a par with other Protestant professional pupils, good, but not outstanding. Out of the thirty-two in his year, he finished eighth equal.[32]

In his set-piece essay on the 'Choice of Profession' at the end of his years in school, Karl displayed an almost religious sense of vocation. The Deity left man 'to choose the position in society most suited to him'. A person's aim could be 'great' 'if the deepest conviction, the innermost voice of the heart declares it so . . . For the Deity never leaves mortal man wholly without a guide; he speaks softly but with certainty.' But this voice could easily be 'drowned' by delusion, self-deception or 'the demon of ambition'. Furthermore, even apart from ambition, enthusiasm might be aroused for a particular profession by the embellishments of the imagination or illusions about talent. A cursory reference was made to the counsel that might be given by parents, 'who have already travelled life's road and experienced the severity of fate'. But if after examining one's choice in cold blood, enthusiasm still remained, then 'we ought to adopt it . . . Worth is that which most of all uplifts a man, which imparts a higher nobility to his actions.' Therefore, providing a 'poor physical constitution' or lack of talent does not prevent a person from 'fulfilling their vocation', 'the chief guide which must direct us in the choice of a profession is the welfare of mankind and our own perfection . . . For man's nature is so constituted that he can attain his own perfection only by working for the perfection, for the good, of his fellow men.'[33]

It would be a mistake to make too much of the sentiments expressed in this essay. Concern about physical constitution and 'severity of fate' experienced by his parents may offer more intimate clues to Karl's state of mind. But apart from a more emphatic insistence upon work for the good of humanity as a prime goal, many of the formulations were a reiteration of Wyttenbach's teachings and were found similarly expressed in the essays of other pupils. The headmaster himself thought the essay 'rather good' and marked by a wealth of thought and a 'good systematised narration'. But he also considered it a characteristic 'mistake' that Karl 'constantly seeks for elaborate picturesque expressions' with the result that 'many passages' lacked 'the necessary clarity and definiteness'.[34]

On 27 September 1835, those who passed the *Abitur* left the school. Karl proceeded to the local university of Bonn to study Jurisprudence. As a riposte to the abolition of the Rhineland universities by the French, Bonn had been refounded by the Prussian monarchy in 1818. The aim of the new authorities was to demonstrate to Rhinelanders a broader cultural respect for higher education in contrast to the narrow vocational preoccupations of the French. It was also intended to encourage Protestantism in the province and to provide the requisite training for those wishing to enter state service.[35] But political surveillance of the new university was considerably increased in the panic accompanying the 'persecution of the demagogues' following the Kotzebue assassination in 1819. Bonn was seen as a prominent centre of student secret societies, encouraged, it was suspected, by prominent Catholic and nationalist polemicists like Joseph Görres and Ernst Moritz Arndt.[36] Thereafter, surveillance continued; and in his 'Certificate of Release' from Bonn University in August 1836, as a standard item on the form, the university authorities reported that Marx 'has not been suspected of participation in any forbidden association among the students'.

Bonn appeared dull to the more rebellious members of its faculty. According to Bruno Bauer, writing to Marx in 1840, Bonn meant 'mediocre insignificance', and he noted with exasperation how his colleagues ran away from every reference to the ongoing conflicts, which so galvanized the rest of Prussia.[37] But for the students Bonn offered associational life and conviviality. Karl's behaviour there was not that of a political subversive, but of an adolescent savouring his first release from parental scrutiny; and his excesses were for the most part those familiar in all student communities. The Certificate mentions a punishment for 'rowdiness and drunkenness at night'. But he also appears to have indulged in those vices more particularly associated with the aristocratic or pseudo-aristocratic rules of sociability found in many German universities. The Certificate of August 1836 records the accusation of 'having carried prohibited weapons in Cologne'. A letter from his father makes reference to a duel ('and is duelling then so closely interwoven with philosophy?'), which was apparently fought in Bonn.

The anxieties of his parents evidently found little place in Karl's new life; on 8 November 1835, three weeks after he left home, Heinrich wrote reproaching him for his 'boundless negligence' in not writing. 'You know your mother and how anxious she is.' It confirmed 'the opinion, which I hold in spite of your many good qualities, that in your heart egoism is predominant'. He should reply by return of post. Heinrich was also worried about his son's attitude towards money. In January 1836, he complained that his son's accounts were 'disconnected and inconclusive'. 'One expects *order* even from a scholar and especially from a practical lawyer.' In March, he agreed that the fact that 'you have somewhat overstepped the bounds' could be 'glossed over', while remaining convinced that it was possible 'to manage with less'.

Whatever else happened in Bonn, it seems that Karl remained a studious and conscientious student. In the first term, following his father's request for a prompt letter, he replied in 'a barely legible' letter that he was taking nine lecture courses. His father considered this 'rather a lot' and perhaps 'more than your body and mind can bear'. But he rejoiced that his son had found the beginning 'easy and pleasant' and that 'you are getting a liking for your professional studies'.[38]

This impression was borne out by the final report issued by Bonn University before Karl made a transfer to Berlin for the academic year 1836–7. In the winter term of 1835, he had taken six courses, three in law (Encyclopaedia of Jurisprudence, Institutions and History of Roman Law), and three in art and literature (Greek and Roman Mythology, Homer, Modern Art); and in each of these courses he was described as 'diligent' or 'very diligent' and 'attentive'. In the summer term of 1836, he took four courses, three in law (History of German Law, European International Law, Natural Right) and one in literature (the Elegiacs of Propertius) and was once again judged to be 'diligent' and 'attentive'.[39]

A hint of a more negative kind to the young Karl's state of mind is suggested by his attitude towards one obvious option, which an ambitious lawyer might have considered in the 1830s: 'Cameralistics' (*Staatswissenschaften*). This subject covered state policy and administration and drew upon the paternalistic traditions of small-state management. Originally conceived according to the model of the management of a household or an estate, described by Aristotle and elaborated by Luther and Melanchthon, it was considered particularly relevant in Protestant states, where government had taken over church land. Cameralistics had developed especially in eighteenth-century Prussia, where it was redesigned by Christian Wolff and others, according to the assumptions of natural law. But the huge debts accrued by Prussia during the Napoleonic Wars forced the state to sell off much of its land, and therefore to rely more and more upon taxation as the main source of its revenue. For this reason, political economy – the German word was *Nationalökonomie* – came to be included within the topics covered by *Staatswissenschaften*. During the years of the Prussian 'Reform Era', the prestige of the bureaucracy increased greatly, and in the period 1815–30 the number of law students increased by 89 per cent.[40] This was why Heinrich argued that it would be 'expedient' if his son were to follow 'a general introduction to Cameralistics', 'because it is always useful to have a general idea of what one will have to do some day'.[41] Karl did not dismiss the idea, but was unenthusiastic. After 1830, with the hopes of the 'Reform Era' at an end, the prestige of the bureaucracy had plainly declined, and the chances of state employment had in any case become extremely slim.[42] Later in Berlin, he wrote to his father that he had been advised to transfer to Cameralistics only after his third law exam, and that anyway 'I really prefer jurisprudence to all administrative science.'[43]

The true reason probably remained unavowed. Perhaps, as his father hoped, the law might still provide a livelihood. But Karl was destined for greater things. He was a poet.

3. A POET IN LOVE

According to his daughter, Eleanor, it was Ludwig von Westphalen, the father of his childhood companions, Edgar and Jenny, who first implanted in the young Karl a reverence for great literature. In later years, she wrote, Marx 'never tired of telling us of the old Baron von Westphalen and his surprising knowledge of Shakespeare and Homer. The baron could recite some of Homer's songs by heart from beginning to end and he knew most of Shakespeare's dramas by heart in both German and English.' It was said that Jenny Wishart, the baron's Scottish mother, had originally inspired this enthusiasm. It was also the baron, as Eleanor told Wilhelm Liebknecht, 'who inspired Marx with his first love for the romantic school'.[44]

Karl had already begun to write poetry while at school. Soon after he had left for Bonn, Heinrich wrote to him about Wyttenbach's distress at the appointment of Loers as the *Gymnasium*'s co-headmaster, and begged Karl to compose a few verses for him.[45] Early in 1836, his father was pleased to learn that Karl had become a member of a poets' circle in Bonn. Somewhat naively, he remarked, 'your little circle appeals to me, as you may well believe, much more than ale-house gatherings'. He was also relieved to be told that Karl's first work would be submitted to him for criticism 'before anybody else'. His reaction to an earlier poem sent by his son had been negative. 'I quite frankly confess, dear Karl, that I do not understand it, neither its true meaning, nor its tendency.'[46] As tactfully as he could, he tried to divert Karl's thoughts away from poetry as a vocation. 'It would grieve me to see you make your appearance as an ordinary poetaster; it should still be enough for you to give delight to those immediately around you in the family circle.'[47]

In the course of 1836, however, Karl fell in love with Jenny, the baron's daughter, and this fired his poetic ambitions even more strongly. As he explained to his father on 10 November 1837, when he had arrived in Berlin in the previous autumn, 'a new world had come into existence for me, that of love, which in fact at the beginning was a passionate yearning and hopeless love'. As a result, he continued, 'in accordance with my state of mind at the time, lyrical poetry was bound to be my first subject, at least the most pleasant and immediate one. But owing to my attitude and whole previous development, it was purely idealistic. My heaven, my art, became a world beyond, as remote as my love.'[48] He claimed to have burnt his poetry in the summer when he recovered from his illness. But it was only reluctantly, towards the end of 1837, that he began to abandon the belief in his destiny as a poet. In the meantime, he wrote for Jenny three volumes of poetry, two entitled

Book of Love, a third entitled *Book of Songs*. He also compiled *A Book of Verse*, dedicated to his father. This collection contained, in addition, some chapters from *Scorpion and Felix*, a 'humoristic novel', and scenes from *Oulanem*, a tragedy in verse.[49]

Literary scholars have traced the sources of Marx's poetic efforts in some detail.[50] In the earlier pieces, there is a strong debt in many of the compositions to the abstract poetry of the youthful Schiller and to the ballads of Goethe, while later compositions owe much to the satirical travel sketches of Heine. The main theme, the triumph and travails of love, is conveyed through a series of conventional Romantic images and narratives – the young man who remains true to his ideals and thus resists the song of the sirens, the knight who, returning to find his lover unfaithful and about to marry another, kills himself at her nuptials, the pair of harpists who weep as they sing outside a castle for him 'who soulful dwells within', stars indifferent to human fate, the beautiful lady eventually driven to delirium and death, the pale young maiden whose hopeless love of a knight leads her to drown herself.

These poems are oddly removed from current events, cultural or political.[51] Indeed one critic has called them 'curious anachronisms', going back to the earlier writings of Goethe and Schiller.[52] References dear to the more pious tropes of conservative Romanticism after 1810, the so-called period of *Hochromantik* (High Romanticism) – chapels, friars, Christian art, medieval or ancient Germany – are largely absent. But so are any references to Young Germany or the contemporary struggles of the Poles or the Greeks. The stress is upon a heroic action, to 'daringly advance in knowledge and seize song and art' within the world of culture:

> I can never pursue calmly
> What seizes the soul so powerfully,
> I can never remain comfortably at rest:
> Ceaselessly tempestuously, I rush on.[53]

Particularly distinctive is a sort of rhapsodic praise of action – will and activity, when conjoined with love, will triumph over the material world. In the 'Concluding Sonnet to Jenny', for instance:

> In ample glowing raiment bravely wrapped,
> With pride-lifted heart illumined,

Constraints and ties imperiously renounced
With firm step great spaces I traverse,
In thy presence I shatter pain,
Towards the tree of life my dreams radiate![54]

Or in 'Human Pride':

Jenny! Do I dare avow
That in love we have exchanged our souls
That as one they throb and glow
And that through their waves one current rolls?

Then the gauntlet do I fling
Scornful in the World's wide-open face.
Down the giant She-Dwarf, whimpering,
Plunges, cannot crush my happiness.

Like unto a God I dare
Through that ruined realm in triumph roam
Every word is Deed and Fire
And my bosom like the Maker's own.[55]

In the later poems, a battle against the world is invoked, but it is that of the poet or the artist against the philistine or bourgeois. The inspiration came mainly from the satirical sketches found in Heine's *Pictures of Travel*. A good example is the poem *Armide*. Listening to Gluck's opera *Armide*, the poet is trying to lose himself in 'the music's spell' but is interrupted by the silly chatter and annoying display of a foolish young lady sitting next to him.[56] A similar stance is adopted in an attempt to replicate the critical observations about the low standards of German criticism collected together by Goethe and Schiller in *Xenien* in 1797. In these epigrams, Marx employed sarcasm to defend the great artist against the judgement of the crowd. Thus Schiller 'played with Thunder and Lightning much, but totally lacked the common touch', while Goethe could be reproached, because 'he had beautiful thoughts, if sometimes odd, but omitted to mention – "made by God"'. Among these satirical verses was also an attack on Hegel:

Words I teach all mixed up into a devilish muddle,
Thus anyone may think just what he chooses to think.[57]

In the collection Karl sent to his father, two longer pieces were included: *Scorpion and Felix* and *Oulanem*. *Scorpion and Felix* was a laboured attempt to imitate *Tristram Shandy*, a form popularized not long before in the writings of Jean Paul, together with a play upon E. T. A. Hoffmann's notion of the *Doppelgänger*. In this fragment of a 'humoristic novel', whatever humour was intended was buried beneath a ponderous display of erudition. Karl himself in his letter to his father admitted its 'forced humour'. Perhaps its most interesting feature was its somewhat clumsy attempt to write of political matters in a literary form, an imitation of an approach associated with Sterne and Heine. Apart from the heavy-handed likening of primogeniture to 'the wash-closet of the aristocracy', there was the lament, again probably inspired by Heine, that 'in our day . . . no epic can be composed'. Great is followed by small. 'Every giant . . . presupposes a dwarf, every genius a hidebound philistine.' Thus 'Caesar the hero leaves behind him the play-acting Octavianus, Emperor Napoléon the bourgeois king Louis Philippe' and so on.[58] Without wit to hold it together, the whimsical thread of association appears clumsy and pointless.

The other fragment, 'Scenes from Oulanem, a Tragedy' in verse, concerns a mysterious German stranger, Oulanem, and his companion, Lucindo, who arrive in an Italian town to be greeted by Pertini, who unbeknown to them knows them both back to their very beginnings, and as an imitation Mephistopheles has sinister plans for them. Lucindo challenges Pertini's 'vile snake's bosom', but Pertini is nevertheless able to divert him by introducing him to what he suggests will be 'a succulent piece of woman'. This woman is called Beatrice. She and Lucindo find they are both German, and soon fall in love. But Beatrice has already been betrothed by her father to Wierin – 'no ape could ever look so sleek'.[59] Lucindo and Wierin prepare for a duel. Meanwhile, the mysterious Oulanem, an ageing Faust, sits at his desk, cursing the way of the world, and fearing the onset of a preordained doom:

> This pigmy universe collapses.
> Soon I shall clasp Eternity and howl
> Humanity's giant curse into its ear.
> Eternity! It is eternal pain,
> Death inconceivable, immeasurable!
> An evil artifice contrived to taunt us,

Who are but clockwork, blind machines wound up
To be the calendar-fools of Time.[60]

It is hinted that there are deeper connections between Lucindo, Beatrice and Oulanem than is first apparent. Not only do both Lucindo and Beatrice turn out to be German, but they may also turn out to be a long-lost brother and sister. Although only a fragment survives, it has been argued convincingly that the plot follows the conventions of what at the time was called 'the tragedy of fate', a type of gothic thriller popularized by Zacharias Werner and Adolf Müllner in the 1810s and 1820s.[61] Common motifs in this genre included the return of the apparently unknown but secretly recognized stranger, a destiny ruled by curses and the threat of incest between brother and sister.

Biographically, the main interest of this drama is that it gives the first indication that Karl was beginning to distance himself from German Romanticism. Lucindo has barely met Beatrice, when he bursts forth:

Oh, if my heart might speak, if it might only
Pour forth what you have quickened in its depths,
The words would all be flames of melody,
And every breath a whole eternity,
A heaven, and Empire infinitely vast,
In which all lives would sparkle bright with thoughts
Full of soft yearning, full of harmonies,
Locking the world so sweetly in its breast,
Streaming with radiance of pure loveliness,
Since every word would only bear your name!

Pertini at this point intervenes to explain:

You will not take it in bad part, young lady,
If I explain to you that he is German
And always raves of melody and soul.[62]

On 10 November 1837, Karl wrote to his father admitting that his dream of becoming a poet had come to an end. On that day he had received 'a highly unimpressive' note from Adalbert Chamisso, the editor of the *Deutscher Musenalmanach*, rejecting the poems he had submitted. 'I swallowed it [the note] with fury.'[63] A year before, his sister Sophie had told him that 'Jenny wept tears of delight and pain on receiving your poems'.[64] In the summer of 1837, when he 'again sought the dances of the Muses and the music of the Satyrs', he found that his attempts were becoming 'mere formal art, mostly without objects that inspire it and without any impassioned train of thought'. And yet, he continued, 'these last poems are the only ones in which suddenly as if by a magic touch – oh the touch was at first a shattering blow – I caught sight of the glittering realm of true poetry like a distant fairy palace, and all my creations crumbled into nothing'. Karl became ill, and when he recovered he burnt 'all his poems and outlines of stories'.[65] Around the end of August, he was toying with a plan for theatre criticism, but was reminded by his father that, even at its most brilliant, it would be received 'with more hostility than favour . . . The good learned Lessing pursued, as far as I know, no rose-strewn path, but lived and died a poor librarian.'[66] Once again, he attempted to steer his son back to a practical career, this time, an academic career, whether in law, philosophy or Cameralistics.

Karl's yearning to hold on to his literary destiny remained, and was evident in his November letter in the mannered style he chose to recount to his father how he had become a follower of Hegel. 'I had read fragments of Hegel's philosophy, the grotesque craggy melody of which did not appeal to me', wrote a twenty-four-page dialogue, 'Cleanthes', a 'philosophical-dialectical account of divinity, as it manifests itself as the idea-in-itself, as religion, as nature, and as history . . . My last proposition was the beginning of the Hegelian system . . . this work, my dearest child, reared by moonlight, like a false siren delivers me into the arms of the enemy . . . For some days my vexation made me quite incapable of thinking; I ran about madly in the garden by the dirty water of the Spree, "which washes souls and dilutes the tea".'[67]

Karl's infatuation with the idea of himself as a poet gradually subsided. It had definitely disappeared by 1839, when, instead of his own literary efforts, he put together for Jenny an international collection of folk-poems.[68]

4. THE WESTPHALENS

At the end of the summer term of 1836, Marx had secured permission to transfer from the University of Bonn to that of Berlin, and around the end of August he became engaged to Jenny von Westphalen. He had no difficulty in securing his own parents' consent, but the Westphalen parents were not informed until March 1837. Jenny was twenty-two years old, four years older than Karl. Karl had probably got to know Jenny through her younger brother, Edgar, in Karl's class in the *Gymnasium*. Jenny was also a school friend of Karl's elder sister, Sophie. It is said that Karl, Jenny and Edgar played together as children, that Edgar was a regular visitor to the Marx household, and that he had been attracted to Marx's sister Emilie. It is also clear that Heinrich and Ludwig von Westphalen, Jenny's father, would already have been professionally acquainted with each other. As a prominent local lawyer, Heinrich would have had to represent those in prison; and prisons were among Ludwig's official responsibilities as a Privy Councillor (*Geheim-Regierungsrat*), according to a list in 1824, alongside police, the fire service, hospitals, charities and the production of statistics.[69] Both were also members of the Casino Club.

Johann Ludwig von Westphalen was born in 1770, the fourth son of Christian Philipp Heinrich von Westphalen. His father had effectively acted as Chief of Staff to Prince Ferdinand of Brunswick-Lüneburg, the famous Commander of the Anglo-German forces against the French in Hanover and elsewhere during the Seven Years War (1757–63), and he had been ennobled for his services. Ludwig's mother, Jenny Wishart, the daughter of an Edinburgh preacher, was related to the Argylls. In addition to a good university education at Göttingen and elsewhere, Ludwig spoke English, and could read Latin, Greek, Italian, French and Spanish.

After university he entered government service in Brunswick. But, like so many in his generation, his career was disrupted by revolution and war. In 1807, when Brunswick was absorbed into the new Napoleonic state of Westphalia, he entered its civil service.[70] He was probably attracted by the reform programme of the new state.[71] From 1809 to 1813, he was Sub-Prefect of Salzwedel, where Jenny was born.

When French troops re-entered Salzwedel in 1813, Ludwig was imprisoned for having spoken out openly against Napoléon. Later in that year, after the French retreat, he became Prussian District President at Salzwedel, but had to relinquish the post when the local landed aristocracy reclaimed their traditional right to choose the president.

In 1816 he was probably disappointed to be transferred as First

Councillor to Trier on the extreme western border of the Prussian kingdom. Thereafter he stayed in this post and received no further promotion
beyond an honorific but automatic upgrade to *Geheim-Regierungsrat*
(Government Privy Councillor) on retirement.[72] Like many of the
liberal-minded Prussian officials with hopes of implementing progressive reforms in the immediate aftermath of the war, he found himself
stranded; and this lack of further prospects may have been especially
disappointing, since, whatever its aristocratic connections, his family
was not wealthy. A register of Prussian officials in the 1820s lists Ludwig as possessing 'no property', and it is known that he encountered
recurrent problems in settling debts and paying taxes. In 1832, officials
in Trier and Berlin discussed whether he should be pensioned off. It
was said in his defence that he was a tireless worker, but critics pointed
to verbosity, prolixity and an extremely shaky hand, which impaired
his performance. Ludwig felt deeply wounded on learning what had
been said. It was agreed to keep him on, but after another serious chest
infection he was retired in 1834.

Around 1830–31, it is clear that the political and social atmosphere
in Trier was extremely tense. There was a sharp increase in poverty,
among both the middle and the lower classes. One in four was dependent on some form of poor relief. Anger was directed at the level of
taxation and the inequalities of its incidence – particularly the 'meal'
and 'slaughter' taxes. Prussian officials feared the possibility of a popular revolt. From a letter Ludwig wrote to his nephew, Friedrich Perthes,
in 1831, it is clear that he too was deeply critical of the policy, which he
had to represent. Large inequalities of taxation led him to feel some
sympathy with the complaints of the people, and while hostile towards
the idea of a republic, he was critical of existing constitutional arrangements: there had to be progress towards 'true freedom' based upon
'order and reason'.[73]

Ludwig von Westphalen was married twice. His marriage in 1798 to
the aristocratic Elizabeth von Veltheim produced four children, Ferdinand (1799), Louise, known as Lisette (1800), Carl (1803) and Franziska
(1807). Elizabeth died in 1807. Ludwig's second marriage, in 1812, to
Caroline Heubel, the daughter of a Prussian official, produced three
children, Jenny, Karl's future wife (1814), Laura (1817, died 1821) and
Edgar (1819). The contrast between the children from the two marriages was striking. Indeed, the variety of convictions and directions

49

taken by the different members of this family read like an expression of the polarities of nineteenth-century Prussia played out in miniature within the confines of a single family.

Ferdinand, the eldest, trained as a lawyer, and although welcoming the advent of Louis Philippe in France in 1830, thereafter he became increasingly conservative. Between 1826 and 1830, and again between 1838 and 1843, he was stationed in Trier as an increasingly senior government official (*Ober-Regierungsrath und Dirigent der Abteilung des Inneren der Regierung*). In the aftermath of the 1848 Revolution, through the good offices of the conservative Leopold von Gerlach, he was introduced to the king, Friedrich Wilhelm IV. He was appointed Prussian Minister of the Interior and remained in the post between 1850 and 1858. Like the king's, Ferdinand's Christianity was conservative and Evangelical, and his main ambition as a minister was to re-establish a divine-right monarchy and a society based upon estates (*ständische Gesellschaft*).

Both his sisters, Lisette and Franziska, by all accounts, similar in outlook, became leading activists in the conservative religious revival, the *Erweckungsbewegung*, which had begun as a reaction to Prussia's military defeat at the Battle of Jena. According to one family account of Lisette, Jenny's eldest half-sister, despite a good husband, twelve children and a comfortable life on the Krosigk estate, she 'tortured herself and others with her preoccupation with sinfulness, and in her thoughts about sin, forgot laughter, joy and gratitude . . . Her actions, prompted not by the natural impulses of a swelling heart, but by duty, regulated her behaviour towards those nearest to her.' For that reason, mixed in with the love of her husband and children was always a trace of nervousness: 'one felt unworthy, when in the presence of the Holy one [*die Heilige*] and often longed for a heartfelt word, which might have diluted the incense-laden atmosphere emanating from within'.[74]

Jenny, her half-sister, was equally strong-minded, but diametrically opposed in her views. Lisette's granddaughter, drawing upon family correspondence, wrote that Jenny had, as a young woman, been hard to govern, with a strong sense of justice, and this could lead to passionate outbursts; she also had a thirst for knowledge, which already as a child had driven her to devour books. In the 1830s, she took her stand as a representative of Young Germany on the side of the radicals. It went so far that encounters between 'the proud woman' and her brother, Ferdinand, had to be avoided. True to her passionate convictions as a woman, as a young person and as an upholder of revolutionary politics, she castigated the backwoods views of the *bürgerlich* world. Her half-sister, Lisette, while wholly sharing her brother's opinions, nevertheless in human terms felt drawn to the readiness for self-sacrifice, purity of passion and ardent heart of her sister, 'who, for the sake of love and justice, grieved for those cheated by fate, the proletariat'.[75]

Jenny was by all accounts exceptionally beautiful. On a visit to Trier in 1863, Karl recalled, 'every day and on every side I am asked about the *quondam* "most beautiful girl in Trier" and the "queen of the ball". It's damned pleasant for a man when his wife lives on like this as an "enchanted princess" in the imagination of a whole town.'[76] Ferdinand himself had noted, in 1831, that Jenny was regularly 'swarmed around by *Curmachern*' (spa visitors), but proceeded unimpeded through a display of 'sang-froid', which in this case was put to good use.[77] In that year, at the age of seventeen, it seems she had been briefly engaged to an officer stationed in the garrison, but without any lasting emotional involvement.

The youngest of the Westphalen children, Edgar, as mentioned, was Karl's classmate in the *Gymnasium*. He was a very bright boy, of whom Jenny was especially fond, and by all accounts charming and easy-going. Edgar and Karl were also contemporaries in Berlin in 1837, both ostensibly following Jurisprudence, as was Edgar's best friend, Werner von Veltheim, the nephew of Ludwig's first wife. Both Edgar and Werner dreamt of going to America, and of living in a communist community. But Werner remained tied to the hereditary duties of a family estate. Edgar became a lawyer and held a succession of posts around Trier. But he remained restless, and in 1847 after a period with Karl and Jenny in Belgium, as a member of Karl's Brussels Communist Correspondence Committee, he realized his plan to go to the United States. Werner gave him assistance to establish himself in Texas, though noting, 'the idea of communism represented by Edgar is beautiful, but it depends for its realization upon men who are wholly ideal'. At the same time, Lisette reported, 'he is a good-hearted fellow, only he seems lacking in energy and resolve, still perhaps that will develop in him, once he has to rely solely upon himself'.[78]

But that was not to be. Only half a year later, Edgar was back, ill with yellow fever and afflicted by despair. In her journal, Lisette noted that 'experience has cured him of his communist ideas, but he is still constantly confused by socialist day-dreaming'.[79]

In 1851, he set off once more for Texas, on this occasion financially helped not only by his friend Werner, but also by his brother, Ferdinand. He finally returned again to Berlin, disappointed and without resources in 1865. Around that time, Jenny wrote to her friend Ernestine, Wilhelm Liebknecht's wife, 'he was the idol of my childhood and youth, my one and only dear companion. I clung to him with my whole soul . . . In recent times, I had so much to do with Karl's family, who were strange and distant to me, that I attached all the more of my inner self to the only member still remaining from my family.'[80] Around the same time, Karl wrote less indulgently to Engels that Edgar was 'vegetating', 'pondering the needs of his stomach from morn till night'. But as he was good-natured, and the children were fond of him, 'his egotism is that of a kind-natured cat or a friendly dog'. Edgar now wanted to be back in Texas again, but there would be no escaping 'the confrontation' with Ferdinand. Karl suspected that behind Edgar's 'present ideal' to 'set up a STORE – a cigar or wine STORE' lay the secret hope that 'this will be the surest way to apply oneself to the cigars and wine'.[81]

Back in Berlin, Edgar published a book of poetry and found employment with the judicial authorities. His political ideals remained those of an 1848 Frankfurt radical (a united Germany without Prussia, Austria or an aristocracy). He described himself as 'Auscultator ausser Diensten',[82] but he seems always to have been hopeless in the management of money and apparently died in 1890 without any resources in a charity hospital, the *Diakonissenhaus Bethanien*, for which twenty-five years previously his brother Ferdinand had endowed a free bed.

Conflict in the Westphalen household did not simply result from political difference. It appears that Ferdinand and particularly his wife, Louise von Florencourt, found it very hard to accept Ludwig's second wife, Caroline. The reason is not entirely clear, but is confirmed by the fact that in 1830 they had attempted to exclude Caroline and Jenny from a family trip they wanted to make with Ludwig. Some have suggested that at the root of the conflict was social snobbery – the disdain of the aristocratic Florencourts and Veltheims (the family of Ludwig's first wife) for the merely *bürgerlich* Caroline Heubel, the daughter of 'a small Prussian functionary' – in Karl's dismissive phrase. But it is equally likely that the antipathy was rooted in some more basic inability to accept the second marriage, and that the argument over the trip arose from the awkwardness of including Caroline and Jenny in a visit to the family home of Ludwig's first wife.

Far more serious was the deliberate snub committed by Ferdinand many years later, in 1859, when he published a book about his grandfather Christian Philipp Heinrich von Westphalen, the Chief of Staff to Ferdinand of Brunswick-Lüneburg, and his four sons. The section on Ludwig omitted any mention of Ludwig's second marriage to Caroline and the children born of the marriage. Jenny felt particularly incensed because he had not mentioned her mother, whose marriage to Ludwig had lasted thirty years and who had brought up the stepchildren as her own.[83] No wonder attitudes towards the older branch of the Westphalen family in the Marx household – even politics apart – were so scathing. According to Eleanor Marx in 1896, 'I really don't know about the Florencourts – except that some of them were very rich, very eccentric and very bigoted . . . My uncle Ferdinand v. Westphalen, was, as you know, a religious fanatic, and so *I believe* were the Florencourts . . . My uncle Ferdinand was the worst of all bigots – a Protestant one.'[84]

If the rift within the Westphalens had a larger significance, it was not so much a drama about class or kinship – Ferdinand's younger brother, Carl, remained relatively liberal, and Werner von Veltheim shared Edgar Westphalen's youthful communism. It was rather a clash between political generations. The generation of Ludwig von Westphalen and Heinrich Marx had believed that reason and progress were possible on the basis of a religion freed from superstitious dogma – 'man's release from self-incurred immaturity', as Kant had put it – a representative assembly and enlightened monarchical authority, be it Napoléon or the king of Prussia.

But for the next generation, this had been considered a cruel delusion. The well-ordered and rational state of Frederick the Great had collapsed in the face of Napoléon's army at Jena. Ferdinand and his two sisters grew up in the shadow of a revolution, merged with the Terror, and of the defeat of the old Prussian military aristocracy by the forces of republicanism and atheism. There were many diagnoses of the Prussian defeat, but the view most popular among the landed classes was that it was a judgement of God and a punishment for the shallow rationalism of the Enlightenment. In its reaction against secular reason, the *Erweckungsbewegung* was comparable to the Evangelical movement in Britain, but in the German-speaking world it was reinforced by the rediscovery of the German Middle Ages with its Christian art and folk culture. This was the formative experience of these children.

By contrast, the world of Jenny, Edgar, Werner and, of course, the young Karl – those whose coming of age came after 1830 – was of a world beyond Metternich and the penitential gloom of the Restoration. It was of a world made protean once more by a new wave of revolutions, and of hopes quickened by the appearance of new cultural and political movements – the Saint-Simonians, the Young Germans, the Young Hegelians and Mazzini's Young Europe.

Some of the conflicts, which would be provoked by the betrothal, could already be anticipated as Karl set off to Berlin in the autumn of 1836. On 28 December, Heinrich wrote to Karl that he had talked to Jenny, that 'she still does not know how her parents will take the relationship' and that 'the judgement of relatives and the world' would not be 'a trifling matter'. His impression had been that Ludwig knew already, but did not yet want to be told.

But if relations between the two wings of the Westphalen family were already polarized, matters could now only get worse, with the emergence of an assault even on the moderate liberalism of the generation of Heinrich and Ludwig. For, in Berlin, Karl had fallen in with a new group of friends, who were coming to believe that man's construction of God – and, in particular, the Christian God – and the mystification of social relationships that came with it had brought humanity to its present dismal condition. Once the reasons for this dismal condition were understood, humanity would embark upon a new and altogether unprecedented epoch of happiness.

3

Berlin and the Approaching Twilight of the Gods

I. THE NEW WORLD OF BERLIN AND THE DEATH OF HIS FATHER

Karl reached the rapidly growing metropolis of Berlin in October 1836. Between 1816 and 1846, Berlin's population had risen from 197,000 to 397,000. Two thirds of the estimated 10,000 new workers who poured into the city each year were effectively homeless and forced nightly to hire a sleeping space (*Schlafstelle*). Most of the city's burgeoning workforce of tailors and shoemakers remained beneath the tax threshold, and according to the socialist journalist Ernst Dronke,[1] one in seventeen of the city's female population – many of them country migrants and would-be domestic servants – turned to prostitution. Friedrich Sass writing in 1846 believed that no city except for St Petersburg did less for its poor. But even those whose standard of living was higher lived in unattractive conditions. Its 'broad plain streets with their prosaic houses' stood there 'like a regiment of soldiers'.[2] An English visitor, Henry Vizetelly, complained of 'clouds of sand, which in dry weather, at the slightest puff of wind, rise into the air and envelop everything they encounter in their progress'.[3] This was why Heine had famously described Berlin as 'the sandbox of the north'.

Berlin was the capital of Prussia, a state without parliament or independent judiciary. A constitution, promised by the king in 1815, had never materialized. There was no free press as heavy censorship was particularly applied to Berlin newspapers. As a result, there were only two newspapers in Berlin, and these, according to Edgar Bauer, were unable to grasp 'truly significant signs of the times. They can hardly digest the ideas the provinces send them.'[4] The middle classes did not offer opposition to the regime; nor did the new entrepreneurs developing their enterprises in the chemical and textile factories and workshops growing up around Berlin. Critics accused 'the bourgeois' of being loyal, politically inert and distinctive mainly for 'his sour and critical views of life, and his sickly piety'.[5]

Yet despite these drawbacks, for many Berlin was an exciting city. Its cultural vitality derived from its university, its theatres and its coffee houses, its pubs and beer halls. The university was founded by Wilhelm Humboldt in 1810 and was one of the most impressive achievements of the 'Reform Era', which followed Prussia's traumatic defeat by Napoléon at the Battle of Jena in October 1806.[6] It was designed according to liberal humanist ideals and its first director was the radical idealist philosopher Johann Gottlieb Fichte. It was remarkably inclusive in its intake and was considered by many to be the best in the world.[7] The university was situated in a city which was home to a flourishing tradition of performing arts, with a highly developed musical culture, an array of topical dramatists and over seventy theatres. According to a literary critic and Young Hegelian, Eduard Meyen, Berlin was 'the central point of German culture and German activity, like no other place in Germany'.[8] If not on the scale of Paris or London, Berlin nevertheless offered many of the attractions of a great nineteenth-century city, not only the pleasures and variety of city life, but also an escape from the philistine prejudice of the small town.

Karl came from Bonn to Berlin as a student initially committed to continue his studies in law. Our knowledge of his first year in Berlin derives from one ten-page letter to his father sent around 10 November 1837, and the only letter to have been preserved from this period.[9] It is a strange document: while it expresses Karl's passion for Jenny, his changing ideas about the philosophy of law, and the ups and downs of his poetic ambitions, it reads in large part like an exercise in *belles-lettres*, rather than a personal letter to an ailing parent. It opens portentously: 'There are moments in one's life, which are like frontier posts marking the completion of a period.' It then moves on, now in the first person plural: 'At such a moment of transition we feel compelled to view the past and the present with the eagle eye of thought in order to become conscious of our real position . . . world history itself likes to look back in this way.' It then reverts to the third person: 'At such moments . . . a person becomes lyrical, for every metamorphosis is partly a swan song, partly the overture to a great new poem.' Once more, Karl uses the first person plural: 'we should like to erect a memorial to what we have once lived through.' It is only at this point that the addressee looms into view, but even here this person must first be garlanded with wreaths of rhetorical finery: 'And where could a more sacred dwelling place be found for it than in the heart of a parent, the most merciful judge, the most intimate sympathiser, the sun of love whose warming fire is felt at the innermost centre of our endeavours!' Only once this courtly opening was concluded did Karl embark upon an account of his first year in Berlin, a declaration of his love for Jenny and then a discussion, for the most part, of his changing views about law and poetry.

Karl had come to Berlin in a state of total distraction. 'A new world had come into existence for me, that of love' – and at that point still 'a passionately yearning and hopeless love ... no work of art was as beautiful as Jenny'; and this meant that 'lyrical poetry was bound to be my first subject'. As previously mentioned, he had sent three volumes of poetry to Jenny in Trier, poetry which he described as 'purely idealistic ... nothing natural, everything built out of moonshine, complete opposition between what is and what ought to be'. He broke off 'all hitherto existing connections, made visits rarely and unwillingly', and tried to 'immerse' himself in 'science and art', and, to this end, began a lifelong habit of making extracts from books.[10]

Seven pages on law and poetry follow in this extraordinary letter and only in the last few paragraphs did Karl become more personal, though his tone is stilted and uneven. Genuine expressions of concern are crowded together with phrases that appear hurried and formulaic. 'Eduard's condition, dear Mama's illness, your own ill-health, although I hope it is not serious, all this makes me want to hurry to you, indeed it makes it almost a necessity.' He asks that the end of the letter be not shown 'to my angel of a mother. My sudden arrival could perhaps help this grand and wonderful woman to recover.' Finally, there are expressions of 'profound, heartfelt sympathy and immeasurable love' and a plea to take into account his 'much agitated state of mind' and to provide forgiveness where his 'heart seems to have erred', overwhelmed by his 'militant spirit'. This hasty ending was perhaps understandable since he was writing around four o'clock in the morning, 'when the candle has burnt itself out, and my eyes are dim'.

The letter was written barely a month before the death of his eleven-year-old brother, Eduard, and less than six months before that of his father. Since no other letters have survived, it is impossible to say how representative it may have been. But the solipsistic self-absorption, belletrist conceit, and apparent lack of real interest in the condition of his family – even in the face of the dark clouds that had been gathering around it in the preceding year – seem to have been a characteristic feature of Karl's letters home.

Such at least was the gist of the frequently reiterated complaints of his father and occasionally that of other members of his family during his time in Berlin. They all agreed that Karl's letters home were all too rare. On 28 December 1836, his father complained that they had not received a letter since early November. On 12 August 1837, writing from Bad Ems, where Henriette had sent him in a vain attempt to cure his persistent cough, Heinrich pleaded that a letter from Karl during the summer had been 'a real need'. He also wrote that twelve-year-old Eduard had been ailing for the last six months and had grown quite thin, that his recovery was 'quite doubtful' and that Henriette 'torments herself day and night'. On 16 September, Heinrich again urged Karl to 'write now and again a few lines for Eduard, but act as if he were quite well again', and his mother requested a few lines for his brother Hermann. By 17 November, Heinrich was pointing out that they had received no information about his address in Stralow, no letter for two months, and then 'a letter without form or content, a torn fragment saying nothing'. In the following letter of 9 December, although deeply fearful of sounding too harsh, he gave way to his exasperation with Karl:

> We never had the pleasure of a rational correspondence ... We never received a reply to our letters; never did your next letter have any connection to the previous one or with ours ... On several occasions we were without a letter for months, and the last time was when you knew Eduard was ill, mother suffering and I myself not well; and moreover, cholera was raging in Berlin; and as if that did not even call for an apology, your next letter contained not a single word about it, but merely some badly written lines and an extract from the diary entitled *The Visit* which I would quite frankly prefer to throw out rather than accept, a crazy botch-work, which merely testifies how you squander your talents and spend your nights giving birth to monsters.[11]

Heinrich Marx was equally concerned about Jenny's situation in Karl's absence, for although the Marx family knew about the engagement in the autumn of 1836, the Westphalens were not informed until March 1837. On 28 December 1836, Heinrich wrote to his son that Jenny was making a 'priceless sacrifice for you' and that she still did not know how her parents would take the relationship, and that 'the judgement of relatives and the world' (no doubt Ferdinand in particular) was not 'a trifling matter'. It was, therefore, particularly important to find out how soon he might hold an academic post. His sister Sophie, who had been acting as a go-between, added that if the difference in age worried Jenny (she was four years older), that was because of her parents, that she had 'wept tears of delight and pain on receiving your poems', and that once she had 'prepared' them, Karl should write. On 3 February 1837, Heinrich wrote again to his son to say that it weighed on Jenny's mind 'that her parents do not know or, as I believe, do not want to know'. He urged that a letter be sent, 'not dictated by the fanciful poet', but something informative, which would 'give a clear view of your relationship and elucidate and discuss the prospects'.[12]

On 2 March, Heinrich and Jenny were still deliberating how news of the engagement should be communicated to the Westphalens. This must have happened a few days later. But the whole process had generated in Heinrich an anxiety about Karl's character which he repeatedly sought to allay. On 28 December 1836, after reaffirming his 'high opinion of your kind heart', despite 'aberrations', he went on to state that 'high as I esteem your intellectual gifts, in the absence of a good heart, they would be of no interest to me at all'. In March, he returned to the theme:

> at times my heart delights in thinking of you and your future. And yet at times I cannot rid myself of ideas which arouse in me sad forebodings and fear when I am struck as if by lightning by the thought: is your heart in accord with your head, your talents? . . . And since that heart is obviously animated and governed by a demon not granted to all men, is that demon heavenly or Faustian? . . . Will you ever be capable of imparting happiness to those immediately around you?

These thoughts troubled him in relation to Jenny and the vulnerability of her situation: 'I note a striking phenomenon in Jenny. She, who is so wholly devoted to you with her childlike, pure disposition, betrays at times, involuntarily and against her will, a kind of fear, a fear laden with foreboding, which does not escape me.'[13]

A recurrent irritant was the aesthetic posturing of Karl as the would-be poet. In a letter in which he expressed his anxieties about Eduard's illness, Jenny's 'prolonged indisposition' and 'profound worry', and his ambiguous position in relation to the Westphalens, Heinrich reproached Karl for possessing 'a little more egoism than is necessary for self-preservation'. And he went on to accuse him of abandoning himself to grief 'at the slightest storm'. The 'first of all human virtues', Heinrich continued, 'is the strength and will to sacrifice oneself, to set aside one's ego, if duty, if love calls for it, and indeed, not those glorious, romantic or hero-like sacrifices, the act of a moment of fanciful reverie or heroic feeling. Even the greatest ego is capable of that, for it is precisely *the ego* which then has pride of place. No it is those daily and hourly recurring sacrifices which arise from the pure heart of a good person ... that give life its sole charm and make it beautiful despite all unpleasantness.' From the evidence of the surviving letters, during 1837 this self-absorption appears to have grown more intense, particularly once the issue of the engagement had been settled. At the end of the year, Heinrich complained, 'From your letters, one can hardly see that you have any brothers or sisters; as for the good Sophie, who has suffered so much for you and Jenny and is so lavish in her devotion to you, you do not think of her when you do not need her'.[14]

Heinrich was particularly repelled by Karl's apparent attraction to the Faustian and demonic paraphernalia with which Romanticism had associated the pursuit of knowledge. 'Disorderliness, musty excursions into all departments of knowledge, musty brooding under a gloomy oil-lamp; running wild in a scholar's dressing gown and with unkempt hair ... the love letters of a Jenny and the well-meant exhortations of a father, written perhaps with tears, are used for pipe-spills.'[15]

At a time when the ailing Heinrich worried that he would have to give up work, there were concerns about money too. He gently tried to steer Karl away from his ambition to found a journal of dramatic criticism. Would it yield significant financial profit? These worries about Karl's lack of realism and his thoughtless extravagance increased as the year wore on. The richest students, Heinrich claimed, spent less than

500 thalers, while Karl had got through 700 thalers 'contrary to all agreement'. Finally, in the last letter Karl's father had the strength to write, he once again reproached his son for his 'aristocratic silence' about money, and pointed out that he had already spent more money in the fourth month of the law year than Heinrich had earned during the winter.[16]

During the winter of 1837–8, Heinrich's condition steadily worsened. On 12 August 1837, he complained that for the last few months he had been 'afflicted by a painful cough'. The spa, Bad Ems, where Henriette had sent him in the summer, had brought no real relief – 'this fatal cough tortures me in every respect'; and by late August he was also suffering from 'the most painful boredom'. Back home, his condition continued to deteriorate, and on 10 February 1838 he wrote with great effort to his son that for the previous two months he had been confined to his room, and more recently to his bed. His mother added that 'good father is very weak', that she was really disappointed that Karl would not be coming home at Easter, but that Jenny 'takes an intimate part in everything' and 'often cheers us up by her loving childlike disposition, which still manages to find a bright side to everything'. His sister Sophie wrote that their father was 'very impatient' to be so 'behindhand with business matters . . . I sing to him every day and also read to him.' She urged Karl, 'write at once, it will be a pleasant distraction for us'. On 15 and 16 February 1838, Heinrich managed no more than a sentence of greeting to Karl. He died on 10 May.[17]

Karl's attachment to Jenny and his respect for his father remained strong. But as life at home had grown more disheartening, Karl appears to have become increasingly immersed in his life in Berlin. In Berlin, conversations flowed easily and news travelled fast. Even in the absence of a free press, theatres provided a vital outlet for the transmission of new ideas. These were in turn discussed in theatre reviews, in small intellectual journals like the *Athenäum* (the house magazine of the Doctors' Club), or out-of-town publications like the radical Hegelian *Hallische Jahrbücher*. Coffee houses, pubs and beer halls served as informal news agencies. In cafés like the Café Stehely, newspapers and journals from abroad and from other parts of Germany were made available on long tables, while correspondents gathered political news and gossip from foreign and provincial journals for dissemination through Central Europe and beyond.

2. THE BATTLE OVER THE MEANING
OF LAW

During the later years of the *Vormärz* – the years from 1815 to 1848 – Berlin's coffee houses, pubs and beer halls became famous as centres of free and open debate. The free discussion which flourished in these establishments probably represented for Karl the most stimulating aspect of life in Berlin, especially after the narrowly Catholic horizons he would have encountered in Trier and Bonn. According to Ernst Dronke, writing in 1846, Berlin 'wit' was political; it was a city in which 'a general preoccupation with politics' almost made up for 'the lack of a real political life'.[18] Each of the occupational and political groupings – higher civil servants, the military and businessmen, the theatre, the academy and literature – had its favoured meeting places. For radicals, intellectuals and theatrical people, the most famous *Konditorei* was Café Stehely, just across from the playhouse on the Gendarmenmarkt, and once allegedly patronized by Mozart and the influential Romantic author E. T. A. Hoffmann. In the decade after 1836 discussion centred increasingly upon philosophy, theology and politics.[19] There Marx first got to know members of the Doctors' Club and began to write his dissertation; there also a few years later, in 1842–3, meetings of the notorious group of free thinkers known as the 'Free' supposedly took place.

In his letter to his father, Karl provided a fairly detailed account of the progress of his legal studies. The so-called 'Historical School of Law' personified by its greatest representative, Karl von Savigny, dominated the Law Faculty. In 1836–7, Karl attended Savigny's lectures on the *Pandects*, the compendium of Roman Law compiled by order of the Emperor Justinian between AD 530 and 533. The only significant opposition to Savigny's approach came from a Hegelian, Eduard Gans. Karl attended Gans's lectures on Prussian Law (*Preußisches Landrecht*) in the summer of 1838.[20]

During his first few months in Berlin, Karl's primary preoccupation was still whether to accept the abandonment of his poetic vocation. By the end of his first term, he had spent 'many a sleepless night' and 'shut the door on my friends . . . Yet at the end, I emerged not much enriched.' He became ill and was advised by a doctor to seek a cure in the country. And so he journeyed to Stralow.[21] In Stralow he 'got to know Hegel from beginning to end'. Earlier 'the grotesque craggy melody' of Hegel had not appealed to him.[22] For in Hegel's conception of modernity, art and poetry occupied only a subordinate and derivative part. Why allude to the truth in symbols or stories or by means of pictorial representation, when philosophy had opened the way to 'absolute knowledge' and could therefore articulate the truth in plain unvarnished language? Karl described the change: 'my holy of holies was rent asunder and new gods had to be installed'. After one further attempt at emotional resistance, which would unite art and science, 'my dearest child, reared by moonlight, like a false siren' delivers me 'into the arms of the enemy'. His first reaction was 'vexation'. In a passage which rather belied his abandonment of literary pretension, he described how he 'ran about madly in the garden by the dirty water of the Spree', which, in Heine's words, 'washes souls and dilutes the tea'; how after he had joined his landlord in a hunting excursion, he 'rushed off to Berlin and wanted to embrace every street-corner loafer'.

In his letter to his father, Karl described his efforts to arrive at a satisfactory philosophical foundation for the law in the face of the formidable intellectual challenge represented by Savigny. His original political and ethical sympathies – both those of his father and of Wyttenbach at the *Gymnasium* – derived from a position 'nourished with the idealism of Kant and Fichte'.[23] But the defect of this approach was that discussion of philosophical norms or 'basic principles' was divorced from all 'actual law'. Furthermore, what he termed 'mathematical dogmatism' – mechanical approaches characteristic of the eighteenth century – had prevented 'the subject taking shape as something living and developing in a many-sided way'. More concretely, such an approach could not accommodate the history of 'positive law', or law as historical 'fact', and it was this insistence upon the law as 'fact' which constituted the starting point of Savigny.

Savigny's writings formed part of the first wave of Romantic nationalism that had developed between 1800 and 1810 in reaction to the conquests and domination of Prussia by Napoléon. In his *History of the Roman Law in the Middle Ages*, Savigny contested the belief that Roman Law had 'perished' with the fall of Rome and 'was revived by accident, after six hundred years of neglect'. His research documented the continuity of the development of laws, customs and institutions throughout the Middle Ages, based upon the creative confluence of Roman and German themes. It was a period, according to Savigny, 'abounding with examples of this awakened energy and restless enterprise'.[24]

Savigny's seminal work, *The Law of Possession (Das Recht des Besitzes)*, of 1804, argued that Roman Law treated 'possession' 'not merely as the consequence of right, but as the very foundation of right'.[25] From this starting point, he constructed a conception of law radically opposed to prevalent rationalist and idealist approaches. Law, and particularly the notion of private property, derived not from reason, but from the fact of possession embodied in the customs and languages of particular peoples in history. 'All laws depend more on the ever changing wants and opinions of those who obey them than on the mere fiat of any legislator.'[26] The law was not 'made', but 'found'. Following Herder, the law was aligned with language and culture; following Edmund Burke, emphasis was placed upon tradition and gradual change.[27] 'In the earliest times, law already attained a fixed character peculiar to the people, like their language, manners and constitution.'[28] Rights were not natural, but historical. Such an approach opened up 'a totally different view of the historical evidence'; for 'the law is part of a nation entwined with its existence and abrogated by its destruction'.[29]

In an attempt to clarify his own ideas, Karl wrote a 300-page manuscript on the philosophy of law. In the second part of this manuscript, in response to Savigny, he examined 'the development of ideas in positive Roman law', the area particularly investigated in Savigny's *On Possession*. Karl concluded, however, that there was no difference between 'positive law in its conceptual development' and 'the formation of the concept of law'. He wrote to his father to say that he now encountered in Savigny a mistake he himself had earlier made: that of imagining the matter and form of the law developing separately. It seemed then that neither the Kantians nor Savigny had provided a satisfactory connection between philosophical norm and historical fact. The problem became acute when Karl embarked upon the section on 'material private law', where central questions concerning persons and property would have to be addressed; and it was at this point that he abandoned the project. For it was plain that Roman concepts – the facts of possession, use and disposal – could not be forced into a rationalist system.

The resort to Hegel helped Karl at this point. In place of the separation between norm and fact, the development of law had to be studied as 'the concrete expression of a living world of ideas'. As he told his father, he had been led from 'the idealism of Kant and Fichte' to 'the point of seeking the idea in reality itself . . . If previously the gods had dwelt above the earth, now they became its centre.'

He had not reached this position unaided. Karl had not only read through Hegel, but also 'got to know most of his disciples', and 'through a number of meetings with friends in Stralow' had come across the Doctors' Club. This loose association of admirers of Hegel met and argued in favoured taverns, and included university lecturers, schoolteachers and journalists. Karl specifically mentioned Bruno Bauer, 'who plays a big role among them', and Dr Adolf Rutenberg, at that point 'my most intimate Berlin friend'. It also seems likely that, in Karl's first years in Berlin, Eduard Gans, one of the most prominent members of the Club, also helped him to redefine his ideas about law. Karl is recorded as having attended his lectures both in 1837 and in 1838.[30]

Gans was a professor in the Berlin Law Faculty, and a friend of the late Hegel. His early career had been blighted by the resurgence of anti-Semitism in the aftermath of 'the war of liberation'. Insulted by students in Berlin and Göttingen, he moved to Heidelberg, where he acquired a brilliant reputation as a law student under the rationalist and progressive jurist Anton Thibaut. In the early 1820s, he was a leading member of the Union for the Culture and Science of Jews, an attempt to bring together Jewish culture and Enlightenment values. At the same time and in accordance with the Jewish emancipation decree of 1812, he applied in 1822 for a professorship at the University of Berlin. The king personally intervened to declare that Jews were no longer eligible for academic appointments. In 1825, therefore, like his friend Heine, he converted to Christianity, and was appointed to the Berlin Chair in the following year. During this time he became a convinced Hegelian, and Hegel's closest ally and friend in the Berlin Faculty. It was not, therefore, surprising that in the 1830s he was chosen to prepare posthumous editions both of Hegel's *Philosophy of Right* (1833) and of his *Philosophy of History* (1837).

Gans was considerably more radical than Hegel in the post-1819 years. He was a dedicated member of the 'party of movement' and an active supporter of the 'Friends of Poland' following the suppression of the

Polish uprising of 1830.[31] He knew Paris and the activities of the Saint-Simonians[32] at first hand. He was also the first German writer seriously to study the 'social question'.[33] Particularly important in this context was his criticism of Savigny and of the Historical School of Law. In the absence of political parties or freedom of the press, open intervention in domestic politics was practically impossible. That was why, in the 1820s and 1830s, one of the most important battles over the future of Prussia was fought out in a controversy about the nature of Roman Law.[34]

Although Savigny avoided overt political partisanship, the political implications of his position had become clear at the end of the Napoleonic Wars. In 1814, the liberal jurist Anton Thibaut proposed that Germany should adopt a uniform legal code comparable to the *Code Napoléon*. In reply, Savigny launched in that year a fierce polemic, *Of the Vocation of Our Age for Legislation and Jurisprudence*. Napoléon, he argued, had used his *Code* as a bond to 'fetter' nations, 'which he had succeeded in subjecting to his rule'. In Germany the *Code* had 'eaten in further and further, like a cancer'. While in some areas it had been thrown off as 'a badge of political degradation', it was still in force in at least six states. Its continued spread would have ended in 'the annihilation of our nationality'. Codes, Savigny argued, dated from the middle of the eighteenth century, when the whole of Europe 'was actuated by a blind rage for improvement'; now 'a historical spirit has been everywhere awakened and leaves no room for the shallow self-sufficiency' of those times.[35]

There were several worrying implications in the position of Savigny, who was to become the Prussian Minister of Justice in the 1840s. Firstly, his advocacy of a return to Roman Law, as it had existed before the revolutionary epoch, perpetuated a situation in which laws of property and inheritance were subject to legal uncertainty and endless local variation. Secondly, his argument that the Roman Law of possession started from 'fact' rather than 'right' strengthened the claim of feudal lords to hold their demesnes by right of 'acquisitive prescription' or mere 'dominion over a thing'.[36] Finally, Savigny's position represented a particular threat to the Rhineland, where a modified form of the *Code Napoléon* was grounded upon the assumption of equality before the law, and where trial by jury was still in force.

Gans attacked the Historical School for its confusion of natural and legal fact. The fact of possession had no legal status. A 'right' could not be based on a 'wrong'. What the lawyers called tort presupposed the existence of a legal right that made wrongful violation subject to legal remedy.[37] More generally, Gans accused the Historical School of a refusal to acknowledge the creativity and forward movement of the World Spirit or World History. In place of rational progress, Savigny and his followers viewed history as a process to be uncovered by purely empirical means, a succession of events which became embedded in the form of traditions expressing the life and soul of the people. In this way, Gans argued, the present was subordinated to the past. Finally, Gans's vision of the significance of Roman Law was very different from that of Savigny's. Firstly, he stressed that much of its value derived from its promulgation as a *code* by Justinian. Secondly, in contrast to those who gloried in the immersion of Roman Law in native German custom during the Middle Ages, Gans praised the relative autonomy of Roman Law. Its long history suggested that legal rules could remain to some extent independent of political power, and this in turn suggested the existence in some form of natural law beneath it.[38]

Unlike the Kantians or the Historical School, Gans argued that a dialectical process of 'mediation' existed between philosophical norm and historical fact underpinning the historical and rational development of the concept of law. As he sought to demonstrate in his major study, *The History of the Law of Inheritance in Its Universal Development* (1826), there was a rational development of the concept of inheritance through the successive historical epochs of the progress of the Spirit. Karl attended Gans's 1836–7 lectures on the criminal law and those on Prussian civil law in the summer of 1838. In his letter to his father, he clearly echoed Gans's position in his assertion that 'the rational character of the object itself must develop as something imbued with contradictions in itself and find its unity in itself'.[39]

For all his interest in philosophy, Karl still appeared undecided about whether to continue a career in law. He wrote to his father of his preference for jurisprudence over administrative science, of the possibility of transferring as a 'justiciary' after the third law examination, of then becoming an 'assessor' and eventually attaining an extraordinary professorship. How far this reflected real indecision rather than a simple desire to humour his father is not clear. Back in September 1837, Heinrich had already stated, 'whether you make your career in one department of learning or in another [is] essentially all one to me'. His son should choose whatever was 'most in accord with [his] natural talents' whether in law or philosophy, but in either case not forget the need for patronage.[40] It also seems that his interest in jurisprudence persisted. Not only did he continue to attend Gans's lectures in the summer of 1838, but his contributions to the *Rheinische Zeitung* over three years later suggested a continued engagement with the concerns of rational jurisprudence.

3. THE EXCITEMENT OF PHILOSOPHY: IDEALISM FROM KANT TO HEGEL

By 1839, however, it was clear that Karl was fully committed to philosophy and ready to embark upon his doctorate. His father's death had removed any lingering inhibitions about changing course, while the death of Gans in the following year could only have reinforced his decision. Even more important was his sense of the cultural and political divisions that were opening up in *Vormärz* Prussia. Contemporaries noted the shift of interest at Café Stehely from literature and art to philosophy, theology and politics, and this matched the shift in Karl's own concerns. The appeal of Hegel – as he wrote to his father in 1837 – had been that of 'seeking the Idea in reality itself'. But the problem was that thought and being were not coming together in the way Hegel's position assumed. If anything, and particularly from the time of Hegel's death in 1831, thought and being had been driven further and further apart.

In the years following 1815, Hegel was the thinker who had most powerfully articulated the association between the Germanic world and the development of Universal Spirit. It was a discourse that made sense so long as it seemed credible that Prussia would continue the emancipatory programme of the 'Reform Era', begun in the aftermath of defeat by Napoléon in 1806. Hegel's appointment to the Chair of Philosophy in Berlin in 1818 can be regarded as part of this reform programme. The invitation had come from Karl von Altenstein, Minister of Education, Health and Religious Affairs, a protégé of Hardenberg, and a convinced rationalist.

In his lectures on *The Philosophy of History* delivered in the 1820s,

Hegel argued that two parallel paths could be traced in the modern history of freedom. One derived from the German Reformation, in which Luther freed religion from external authority and thus made possible the flowering of the German virtues of inward spirituality – *Innerlichkeit* – and reflective thought. This path of development culminated in the philosophy of Kant and the liberation of man from all received beliefs. The second path, that of politics, had led to the French Revolution, which despite its manifest imperfections had produced a situation in which man's internal and spiritual freedom could now be expressed in external political and institutional form. This combination of spiritual and political freedom, Hegel believed, was now being realized in Germany. In Prussia, a rational reform programme was accomplishing peacefully what the French Revolution had attempted to create by force.

Hegel's approach had come under fire from conservatives almost from the moment he was appointed. The Kotzebue assassination had rekindled fear of revolution in the king and his circle.[41] The Carlsbad Decrees of 1819 had led to the dismissal of 'demagogue' professors at the universities and severely curtailed freedom of publication, freedom of speech and freedom of assembly. It had also seemingly deterred Hegel from open avowal of the cause of political reform. In his newly written preface to *The Philosophy of Right*, published in 1821, he had disclaimed any intention to legislate for the future, and had apparently defended the rationality of the existing state of affairs.[42] The 1830 revolutions, which had sparked off violence and the demand for independence in Italy and Poland, had led to the separation of Belgium from Holland, and had delivered liberal constitutions in France and Belgium and Britain, further reinforcing the anxiety of political authorities. Alarmed by a mass democratic gathering at Hambach in the Palatinate in 1832, the German Confederation imposed further increases in censorship and political repression.

The increasingly defensive posture of the Prussian government was also a response to a larger cultural and political reaction against 'rationalism' and the Enlightenment, which had gathered strength in the decades following 1815. In Brandenburg-Prussia, there was a return to an Evangelical and fundamentalist form of Christianity, particularly among sections of the aristocracy and the professional classes. Followers of the new Evangelicalism believed that Enlightenment ideas had been responsible for the spread of rationalism and atheism, and that these in turn had led to the horrors of the French Revolution. This post-1815 world, dominated by the wish to turn its back on revolution and religious heterodoxy, was wholly different from that of the French Revolution and the crisis in orthodox belief occasioned by Kant's demolition of traditional theology and metaphysics. This was the world in which the philosophical approach of the young Hegel had first been formed, but was now seen as wholly at odds with the priorities of a renewed Christian fundamentalism and Romantic medievalism.

German radicalism, republicanism and socialism in the 1830s and 1840s – the aspirations of the 'party of movement' – were attempts to renew the forms of rationalism, which in different ways had supposedly guided the ambitions of Frederick the Great, defined the ideals of the Jacobins, shaped the philosophies of Kant and Fichte, and inspired the major innovations in the 'Reform Era'. Karl's thought was formed within this tradition and in important ways his approach remained a product of its expectations.

The rationalist heritage was particularly important in shaping the identity of what became known in the 1830s and 1840s as 'socialism', which in Germany as elsewhere arose from a battle about the status and character of religion. But in Germany this rationalism and the socialism which was constructed out of it assumed a different form from that found in the Anglo-French tradition.

In the Netherlands and the German world from the late seventeenth century, unbelief had taken on a 'pantheist' form, starting from Spinoza: God and Nature were the same thing, and this indivisible whole was governed by rational necessity. In Germany, the impact of Spinoza was lasting, leading Heine to declare in the 1830s that Spinozism was the secret religion of Germany. In Britain and France, there had been parallel conflicts over religion, but they had taken different forms. In contrast to Spinoza, the starting point had been predominantly deist (a 'clockmaker' God separated from his creation) rather than pantheist, and empiricist rather than rationalist. The starting point in both traditions, however, in contrast to the Christian emphasis upon original sin, had been the assumption that man was a natural being, whose ideas were formed through sensory perception, and whose activity was propelled by desire and the pursuit of happiness.

But in Germany, in the last third of the eighteenth century, there appeared a third major form of philosophy. It drew in important ways from Rousseau's conception of liberty as self-enacted law, but was formalized into what became known as *idealism* in the 'critical' philosophy of Kant. While equally sceptical of revealed religion, idealism stressed human freedom, the active role of the mind in shaping knowledge and activity, and the ability of reason to resist and overcome natural desires.

Idealism opened the door to a distinctive form of perfectionism or utopianism, built upon the displacement of man's limitations as a natural being by the advance of a realm of reason, in which man ultimately obeyed only those commands which had been formulated by himself. The formation of this distinctively idealist conception of human emancipation and its increasing separation from conventional religious belief can be clearly charted in Kant's later writings, in which the Christian conception of the afterlife is replaced by a quasi-secular picture of emancipation on earth.

In *The Critique of Pure Reason* of 1781, Kant had asserted that his purpose in eliminating all claims to knowledge about God's existence was to make room for faith.[43] This promise was fulfilled in 1788 in his *Critique of Practical Reason*, in which God together with immortality were restored as prerequisites or 'postulates'. But God's status was now far shakier. In traditional metaphysics it was God who provided the foundation for morality. In the new theory it was morality which (disputably) required the existence of God. The argument for the necessity of God now formed part of a larger requirement, as Kant understood it, to reconcile the moral law with the fact that human beings were embodied natural creatures, who pursued happiness.[44] In *The Critique of Practical Reason*, he argued that the connection between virtue and happiness was to be found in the notion of the 'highest good'. This was the condition in which happiness was distributed in proportion to virtue, and in which, therefore, each would receive the amount of happiness he or she deserved. Such an ideal, according to Kant, could never be achieved in this world, but since we believe it must be achieved, it was necessary to postulate a God who might distribute happiness to the virtuous in just proportion, and immortality of the soul as a means of allowing for however much time might be required to reach this ultimate result.

Kant tried in a number of ways to make these 'postulates' more compelling. In his *Critique of Judgement* of 1790, he wrote no longer about 'the highest good', but about 'the final end'. Putting the argument the other way round, he claimed that if God did not exist, the moral law would contradict itself, by demanding something which by its nature could not be fulfilled. The basic structure of the argument remained the same. In *Religion within the Boundaries of Mere Reason* of 1793, however, the distance from conventional belief was further increased. Christian supernaturalism encapsulated in the doctrine of the immortality of the soul was replaced by the vision of an 'ethical commonwealth', which would be the result of 'the victory of the good principle in the founding of a kingdom of God on earth'.[45] Here again an argument for the necessary relationship between the moral law, and God as the moral lawgiver, was developed. But the need for such a legislator was not fully established. The moral law was divine because it was binding, not binding because it was divine. Furthermore, Kant conceded that the idea of a 'final end' was introduced as something humans could 'love', and was a concession to 'an inescapable limitation of humanity'.[46] By the mid-1790s, therefore, it was clear that Kant had failed to re-establish God as a postulate of 'practical reason'.[47] The only way of preserving the moral argument for God was to identify the moral world itself as God.[48]

It was during the early and mid-1790s that Hegel's views together with those of his two brilliant fellow students, Hölderlin and Schelling, were shaped by his experience as a theology student in Tübingen.[49] The young Hegel was repelled by the rigidity of official Lutheranism, stirred by the events in France, and inspired by the challenge of Kant's philosophy. His response in his unpublished writings was to attempt to reformulate Christianity in the light of the post-Kantian prerequisites of autonomy and self-legislation. His ideas also drew upon Lessing's *Education of the Human Race* and Rousseau's conception of a civil religion, together with the vision of the spontaneous ethical harmony once supposedly enjoyed in Ancient Greece, according to the ideas of Goethe, Schiller and Herder during the time they worked together in the small court of Weimar between the 1770s and 1805.[50] In 1793, Kant himself had outlined the shape of a purely moral religion in *Religion within the Boundaries of Mere Reason*. But Hegel and his friends thought Kant placed too much emphasis on virtue as the fulfilment of duty. In 1796, they outlined their own conception of a 'religion of the people' (*Volksreligion*). Inspired by Schiller's *Aesthetic Education of*

Man, they stressed that Kantian ethical ideas must be coupled with the appeal of the beautiful: 'monotheism of Reason and heart, polytheism of the imagination and art, this is what we need'. The need was for 'a new mythology', 'a mythology of *Reason*'.[51]

Debates in the 1790s were not concerned with the historicity of the Christian narrative, but with the capacity of Christianity to form the basis of ethical life. In Hegel's view, the superiority of Christianity over other religions was incontestable because it alone was based upon the conviction that all were free. In his later writings, Hegel could therefore argue with justice that his conception of *Sittlichkeit* – the ethical norms and laws informing a modern culture and a rational state – was based upon Protestant Christianity. The absence of such a culture, in Hegel's view, was the main reason why the French Revolution had descended into terror and war. Religion in its untransformed state had been incapable of defending itself against the irreligious attacks of the Enlightenment. Hegel believed that his philosophy had broadened and enriched Christianity.

The doubts of conservatives about the compatibility of rationalism and Christianity were not allayed. Hegel's books and lectures placed Christianity as the last and highest in the development of successive forms of religious consciousness. While religion in earliest times had begun with mysterious gods surrounded by cults of nature and magic, from the time of the Reformation clarity had ultimately been attained in Christianity. Christianity had overcome the gulf between man and God. For in the Christian story of the Incarnation, the human had ceased to be alienated from the divine. Hegel placed at the heart of his Christianity the 'Holy Ghost', the third component of the Trinity. This was the Divine Spirit, which dwelt within each and every person and was celebrated in the act of Communion.

Christianity, however, claimed not only to be immanent, but also transcendent, and there was nothing in Hegel's writings to support the idea of a God separate from his creation or of life after death. Furthermore, it was clear from Hegel's presentation of the 'Absolute Idea' that in the light of the development of self-consciousness, religion, like art before it, was ultimately incapable of providing an adequate idea of the divine.[52] The rites and symbols of Christianity relied upon an ineffable form of symbolism; this vision of the Absolute was ultimately naive and its mode of communicating the truth unfree. The Christian religion was content to rest its claims upon Scriptural authority rather than upon the free determination of self-consciousness.

By the 1820s, such a position was increasingly isolated, confined to little more than Hegel's immediate followers. The brilliant generation of Romantic writers and philosophers, who had once espoused conceptions of the divine similar to Hegel during his years in Jena between 1800 and 1806, had all died or moved on. Novalis died young, Schleiermacher renounced his former pantheism, the Schlegel brothers became Catholics, and Schelling had retreated into mysticism. In the 1820s, there were repeated attacks upon Hegel from the followers of Schleiermacher, who emphasized the association of religion with feeling, while Pietists and Evangelicals, led by Ernst Hengstenberg, the editor of the newly founded *Evangelische Kirchenzeitung*, considered Hegel's rationalist translations of religious dogma presumptuous and heretical. Despite his protestations, Hegel was still accused of Spinozist pantheism, while others attacked him for 'panlogism', the subordination of freedom and reality to logical necessity.[53] In the face of these assaults, Hegel became increasingly defensive, and favoured his more conservative followers, who were intent upon demonstrating the compatibility of revealed religion and speculative philosophy.

4. THE BATTLES OF THE 1830S: STRAUSS AND THE EMERGENCE OF THE YOUNG HEGELIANS

The most intellectually challenging attack upon Hegel's position came in the 1830s, after his death, from his one-time friend at Tübingen, the now celebrated philosopher Schelling. Schelling had published nothing after his years at Jena and his position was only known by repute. But in 1827 he repudiated his youthful 'panlogism' and in 1834 launched a barely disguised philosophical attack upon Hegel's position. Like others who had turned their backs on their youthful philosophical radicalism, Schelling desired to recover a personal God free from the confines of logic or reason. As early as 1804, he had retreated from a vision of humanity overcoming all otherness within a totality and encompassing the identity of spirit and nature. He brought back the Christian language of the Fall, complemented a few years later by a conception of God as pure will beyond reason. God was now posited as the creator of the world, but eternally separate from it. What he revealed of himself to the world was attained, not through reason, but through revelation.[54]

The philosophical generation of the 1830s were generally unimpressed by Schelling's eccentric reconstitution of Christian apologetics, but they could not ignore the force of his criticism of Hegel. This took the form of a reassertion of the independence and prior reality of being, and an attack upon Hegel's attempted demonstration of the passage from logic to reality at the beginning of his *Science of Logic* (1816).[55] In contrast to philosophies that denied the autonomy of reality – 'negative philosophy' – Schelling posited a 'positive explanation of reality', 'positive philosophy'. The 'logical necessity' which 'negative philosophy' considered to order the world was in Schelling's view the result of God's will, which was unbound by any law. What speculative philosophy could not admit was the groundlessness of reality. Positive philosophy, on the other hand, presupposed the surrender of reason's autonomy to something external to it, to 'positive fact', which was only accessible through 'revelation'.

Schelling's 'positive philosophy' was amplified into a political philosophy by Friedrich Julius Stahl, an uncompromising anti-rationalist and friend of Savigny. In 1833, Stahl brought out his own *Philosophy of Right*, and in 1840 he was promoted to the Berlin Chair in Law in succession to Eduard Gans. According to Stahl, Hegel's philosophy suffered from the dangerous delusion that reason could know God. He accused Hegel of destroying divine – and by extension human – personality by depriving God of free will. Hegel's God ('Spirit') was encased within a universal principle of necessary development incorporating both nature and spirit and therefore unable to act as a freely self-revealing Supreme Being.

Stahl's objection to Hegel's conception of the monarch was similar; the monarch was immured in the substance of the state and beholden to the constitution. Just as God's will grounded being and reason, but was not limited by them, so the will of the monarchy should be similarly unbounded. For just as the all-encompassing being of God imparts unity to the whole of creation, so the personal sovereignty of the monarch should singly embody the authority of the state, and similarly not be bound by constitutional constraints. In practical terms, Stahl urged the restoration of 'the Christian state' with its *'cuius regio, eius religio'* principle established at the Peace of Augsburg in 1555.

By the mid-1830s, the conflict between the new conservatism and the 'party of movement' was becoming, in philosophical terms, more heated. It also began to take on a more explicit political form.

In the German Confederation, monarchs had successfully repudi-ated what small liberal gains had been made in Hesse–Kassel, Saxony and Hanover as a result of the 1830 revolutions. The writings of 'Young Germany', a literary tendency, which included Heine and Ludwig Börne, were banned throughout the Confederation. The political scru-tiny of academic appointments was tightened up. At the University of Erlangen in Bavaria, Ludwig Feuerbach was blocked from any prospect of gaining a Chair after writing a hostile review of Stahl.[56] Other prominent Hegelians, including David Strauss, Arnold Ruge and Bruno Bauer, were to suffer a similar fate.

The defining event in this struggle was the publication in 1835 of the Tübingen-based theologian David Strauss's *Life of Jesus, Critically Examined*.[57] Here at last a book had been published which spelled out plainly what might be meant by the Hegelian claim that the aims of reli-gion and philosophy might differ in form, but were identical in content. According to Strauss, the rational truth embodied in Christianity, the union of the human and the divine, could only become clear once the Gospels were freed from their archaic supernatural setting. In the New Testament, the 'Idea' had been encased in a narrative about the life and activity of a single individual. That narrative had been 'the product' of an unconscious mythologizing process shaped by the Old Testament picture of the Messiah. If Christianity were to be saved for modern science, the figure of Christ would have to be replaced by the idea of 'humanity' in the whole of its history. For only the infinite spirit of the human race could bring about the union of finite and infinite, as it was depicted in Hegel's portrayal of 'Absolute Spirit'.[58]

In the late 1830s, battles over the direction of the religious policy to be followed by the Prussian state became increasingly rancorous. Altenstein – still Minister for Education and Religious Affairs – allowed the publication and free dissemination of Strauss's *Life of Jesus* despite conservative outrage. But he was forced more and more onto the defen-sive, since conservative forces had gained increasing influence at court, particularly among the circle of the Crown Prince, which included

Stahl, Hengstenberg and supporters of the Romantic anti-rationalist view of church and state. In the aftermath of Strauss's book, more conservative Hegelians were also tempted to compromise with Stahl's aggressive promotion of the resurgent monarchical Christian German state. Altenstein was, therefore, unable to promote radicals to university chairs. He urged Göschel, Hegel's successor in Berlin, to reiterate the compatibility between Hegelianism and orthodox Christianity as a way of calming the passions about Strauss.

However unfavourable these portents were, the 'party of movement' still clung to the hope that events might lead the government to change course. The old king, Friedrich Wilhelm III, was famous for his high-handed amalgamation of the Lutheran and Calvinist churches back in 1817, a measure closer in spirit to the bureaucratic absolutism of Napoléon than it was to the post-1815 Evangelical revival. But now the government faced an unanticipated challenge from the right. The question concerned the relationship between the Prussian state and its Catholic subjects. In 1835, the new Catholic Archbishop of Cologne, Droste-Vischering, was a militant supporter of the 'ultramontane' tendency within the church. This meant an emphasis upon the authority of the Pope over the temporal affairs of civil governments and that a country's priests' first loyalty was to Rome rather than their secular leaders. He introduced a strictly enforced papal ban on mixed marriages. The church now required a written undertaking on the part of Protestant spouses of Catholics that their children would be brought up as Catholics. This meant not only the rejection of a long-standing Rhineland compromise on the issue, but a breach of Prussian law and a direct challenge to the authority of the king as 'supreme bishop' of the Prussian Union church. As a result, the archbishop was imprisoned in 1837.[59]

Not surprisingly, this confrontation between the Prussian state and the overwhelmingly Catholic Rhineland attracted unparalleled interest; the issue was debated in over 300 pamphlets.[60] It was also an issue upon which Hegelians could offer the state unqualified support.[61] *Athanasius*, the leading ultramontane pamphlet, was written by the well-known Rhinelander and former radical Joseph Görres. He claimed that Protestantism had led to the French Revolution. The Protestant counter-case was set out by the ex-Hegelian Heinrich Leo. But radical Hegelians thought the case was put too tamely. Their leading spokesman was Arnold Ruge, a lecturer at Halle and one time activist in the

Burschenschaft.[62] Together with Theodor Echtermeyer, he had founded the *Hallische Jahrbücher* (*The Annals of Halle*) at the beginning of 1838. This journal began life as a literary feuilleton drawing upon all shades of liberal and Hegelian opinion, but became increasingly identified with 'the independence of scientific enquiry' (meaning support for Strauss) and the supremacy of state over church. Ruge attacked both Görres and Leo in his pamphlet *Prussia and the Reaction*, for their hostility to rationalism, which Ruge claimed to be the essence of Prussia; he also accused Leo of being a 'semi-Catholic'. Ruge's attack in turn provoked an angry response from Leo, who dubbed Ruge, Feuerbach, Strauss and their allies 'the little Hegelians' (*die Hegelingen*). This was the origin of the term 'Young Hegelians'. Leo portrayed them as a group of atheists who relegated Christ's Resurrection and Ascension to the realm of mythology and were pressing for an entirely secular state.[63]

In response, Ruge reiterated the affinity between Protestantism and rationalism, and in the *Hallische Jahrbücher* embellished this theme with evidence gathered from Eduard Gans's just published posthumous edition of Hegel's *Lectures on the Philosophy of History*. Prussia as the land of the Reformation and the Enlightenment stood for religious toleration and freedom of thought. Strauss belonged to this rationally oriented Prussian Protestant tradition, which seemed now allegedly to be in danger of falling under the sway of Catholicism. In a further attack on Leo and Hengstenberg entitled *Pietism and the Jesuits*, Ruge argued that the seventeenth-century inner Protestant kernel of Pietism had disappeared, leaving only its irrational husk, Catholicism as a religion of externals.[64]

At the end of 1839, Ruge and Echtermeyer enlarged this polemical assault into a 'Manifesto' in a series of articles entitled *Protestantism and Romanticism*. Both Protestantism and Romanticism, they argued, were products of the Reformation, but whereas Protestantism constituted its rational 'kernel', Romanticism represented its irrational 'husk'. Romanticism was 'the subjective impulse of the free self', based upon the emotions and on nature rather than upon the universality of reason. It therefore embodied 'the unfree principle'. This representation of 'Romanticism' focused upon its 'irrational manifestations'. These included a taste for mysticism, proximity to Catholicism, affection for the Middle Ages and a preference for folk poetry. It was accompanied by an aversion to France, to the Enlightenment and to Frederick the Great.

5. EPICURUS: ATOMS AND FREEDOM

Other supporters took up this campaign, but no one was more enthusiastic than Karl Köppen in Berlin, a scholar of the novel nineteenth-century interest in Nordic mythology, member of the Doctors' Club and, according to many accounts, Karl's closest friend at the time.[65] Köppen had been writing for the *Hallische Jahrbücher* since May 1838. His approach to Nordic religion and mythology closely resembled that of Strauss: myth provided the inner account of the consciousness of a people before recorded history. As the controversy over Strauss and the character of the Young Hegelian campaign against ultramontanism unfolded, Köppen's writings became increasingly radical. He praised the medieval emperor Friedrich Barbarossa for his heroic opposition to slaves and priests, and emphasized the progression both of Hegel's thought and of Prussia itself towards constitutional rule. In 1840, he wrote an essay in praise of Frederick the Great on the centenary of his accession to the throne. The essay was turned into a book, *Frederick the Great and His Opponents*, and was employed to urge the new Prussian king, Friedrich Wilhelm IV, that he should follow the example of his great predecessor by making enlightenment and the battle against priestly fanaticism the guiding principles of his reign.

In the course of his study, Köppen drew attention to the fact that the Greek philosopher Epicurus was Friedrich's favourite thinker, and more generally that 'all the enlightened [the *Aufklärer*] of the last century were in many respects related to the Epicureans, just as conversely the Epicureans showed themselves to be the pre-eminent *Aufklärer* of antiquity'.[66] Epicurus was the philosopher most hated by Romantics, as the forefather of eighteenth-century French materialism and a mechanistic view of the world. His philosophy was, according to Friedrich Schlegel, 'the vilest of all ancient systems . . . which resolves everything into primary corporeal atoms'; Schlegel lamented that Epicureanism had grown to become the dominant philosophy of the latter half of the eighteenth century.[67]

All this helps to explain Karl's choice of Epicurus as the subject of his doctoral dissertation. Köppen dedicated his *Frederick the Great* to Karl, while Karl in the foreword to his dissertation praised Köppen for his treatment of Epicurean, Stoic and Sceptic philosophy, and his 'profound indication' of 'their connection with Greek life'.[68] Like Köppen, Karl was concerned to promote the recuperation of an affinity between the Prussian state and the ideals of the Enlightenment – what soon after in his journalistic articles he was to call 'the rational state'. But the dissertation also pursued other concerns. At a time when the Hegelian approach had been put on the defensive, the dissertation presented a general defence of idealism as a philosophy, directed firstly against 'the theologizing intellect' and secondly against the 'dogmatic' nature-based determinism of Democritus. Karl was concerned to refute the widely held anti-rationalist accusation that Epicurus was an advocate of materialism and determinism. For this reason he presented Epicurus as a precursor of the philosophy of self-consciousness.[69]

The dissertation concentrated upon the implications of Epicurus' theory of the 'atom'. It formed part of a larger project to study 'the philosophers of self-consciousness', the Epicureans, the Stoics and the Sceptics.[70] Examining the trajectories of these philosophies, which had arisen in the aftermath of Plato and Aristotle, offered a way of obliquely examining the contradictory developments in German philosophy following the death of Hegel and the break-up of his system. In 1837, Karl had written to his father as if the synthesis between thought and being announced by Hegel's philosophy were on the verge of completion. Now, like other followers of Hegel, he considered this reconciliation a goal to be attained in the future, an aim to be accomplished by a transition from theory to practice.

In the meantime, Karl had to examine the discrepant developments in post-Hegelian thought. For not only was it apparent that in Restoration Prussia the gap between reality and the idea had widened, but it also appeared that philosophy had become separated from the world. While subjective differences among Hegel's followers had increased, the state in alliance with 'Romanticism' had become ever more reactionary. Philosophy's objective universality was turned back into 'the subjective forms of individual consciousness in which it has life'. Or as he also put it, 'when the universal sun has gone down, the moth seeks the lamplight of the private individual'.[71] Once thought and being had fallen apart and philosophy was forced to adopt this subjective form, philosophical self-consciousness had taken on the appearance of 'a duality, each side utterly opposed to the other'. On the one side, there was 'the *liberal* party' that retained 'the concept'; on the other, was '*positive philosophy*', the '*non-concept*, the moment of reality'. This was Karl's description of the conflict between the Young Hegelians and the supporters of Schelling and Stahl. The former considered the problem to be 'the inadequacy of the world, which has to be made philosophical'; the latter considered that 'the inadequacy' was a problem for philosophy.[72]

The academic claim of Karl's dissertation was to have solved 'a heretofore unsolved problem in the history of Greek philosophy'. Commentators from Cicero and Plutarch to the church fathers had dismissed the work of Epicurus as a mere plagiarism of the pre-Socratic Greek philosopher Democritus. According to Democritus, atoms were strictly determined in their movement; the 'vortex' resulting from their repulsion and collision was 'the substance of necessity'. Epicurus, on the other hand, insisted that this motion could be un-determined; it could be subject to a 'swerve' or 'declination'. He thus introduced a way of resisting the 'blind necessity' and purely materialist physics of Democritus. Democritus, according to Karl, had seen 'in repulsion only the material side, the fragmentation, the change, and not the ideal side, according to which all relation to something else is negated and motion is established as self-determination'. The atom contained something in its breast which enabled it to fight back and resist determination by another being; and this, according to Karl, was the beginning of a theory of self-consciousness. 'Now, when matter has reconciled itself with form and been rendered self-sufficient, individual self-consciousness emerges from its pupation, proclaims itself the true principle.'[73]

One of the most distinctive features of Karl's dissertation was its attempt to represent the progress of the Epicurean atom as a foreshadowing of Hegel's portrayal of the emergence of self-consciousness. According to Karl, 'the absoluteness and freedom of self-consciousness', even if only in the form of individuality, was 'the principle of Epicurean philosophy'. 'Atomistics' with all its contradictions was 'the natural science of self-consciousness'. 'Atoms taken abstractly among themselves' were 'nothing but entities imagined in general ... only in confrontation with the concrete do they develop their identity ... The contradiction between existence and essence, between matter and form, is inherent in the individual atom endowed with qualities.' Thus the declination or 'repulsion' of many atoms was the realization of the law of atoms. 'It abstracts from its opposing being and withdraws from it', which could be done if 'the being to which it relates itself is none other than itself'. Repulsion was the first form of self-consciousness. All relation to something else was negated as motion was established as 'self-determination'. The indication of this was 'the heavenly bodies', where the atom is matter in the form of individuality. The heavenly bodies were therefore 'atoms become real'. In them matter acquired individuality. 'In this process, matter ceased to be abstract individuality and became concrete individuality.'[74] In this way, the 'repulsion' manifested by atoms in physical existence provided a paradigm for the existence of human freedom and self-consciousness.

The refusal of necessity led Epicurus to deny a central premise of Greek belief, 'the blessed and eternal role of heavenly bodies'. He did so by pointing to the activity of meteors, whose existence was impermanent and whose activity was disordered. The supposedly eternal nature of the heavenly bodies like everything else was subject to earthly transience. Nature was not independent. The highest principle was 'the absoluteness and freedom of self-consciousness'. The foreword declared, in words ascribed to Prometheus, that philosophy opposed 'all heavenly and earthly gods who do not acknowledge human self-consciousness as the highest divinity'. For this reason, Epicurus was 'the greatest representative of the Greek Enlightenment'.[75]

The shortcomings of Epicurus were also undeniable. The ancient philosophers of 'self-consciousness' had foundered because of their inability to move beyond a subjective notion of truth identified with 'the wise man'. In this respect, Marx followed Hegel's *Lectures on the History of Philosophy*: 'thought and the thinker' were 'immediately connected'; the guiding 'principle' of Epicurus was 'the impulse of self-consciousness towards self-satisfaction'.[76] According to Epicurus, 'all that matters is the tranquillity of the explaining subject'. The main concern of 'abstract individuality', which Epicurus designated as the principle of the atom, was the preservation of *ataraxy* (serenity). This meant that 'the purpose of action is to be found in abstracting, in swerving away from pain and confusion'. Thought remained separate from being, and thus the value of science was denied. Or, as Marx put it, the aim had been to achieve 'freedom from being, not freedom in being'.[77]

The danger of the Epicurean conception of self-consciousness as 'abstract universality' was that 'the door' was 'opened wide to superstitious and unfree mysticism'. This was what had made Epicurus vulnerable to the 'theologizing intellect' of Plutarch in ancient times, and had encouraged Gassendi to attempt to reconcile Epicurus and Catholicism in the seventeenth century. Much worse, however, was the threat represented by 'positive philosophy'. For once thought was severed from being, yet the assumption of the Absolute preserved, philosophy was free to restore transcendence and theology returned. This criticism was aimed particularly at those conservative Hegelians inclined to compromise with the reassertion of 'the Christian-German state' advocated by Stahl, and given philosophical backing by Schelling.[78]

Karl's dissertation and the notes accompanying it veered between confidence and uncertainty. 'Theory' had now to give way to 'practice', 'but the practice of philosophy is itself *theoretical*. It is the *critique* that measures the individual existence by the essence, the particular reality by the Idea.' It was, Karl thought, 'a psychological law that the theoretical mind, once liberated in itself, turns into practical energy . . . The inner self-contentment and completeness has been broken. What was inner light has become consuming flame turning outwards. The result is that as the world becomes philosophical, philosophy also becomes worldly.' In this sense, he was confident that 'only the liberal party achieves real progress, because it is the party of the concept, while positive philosophy is only able to produce demands and tendencies whose form contradicts their meaning'. But, as he conceded, 'the *immediate realisation* of philosophy is in its deepest essence afflicted with contradictions'. Ending his dissertation with a rhetorical flourish rather than a firm conclusion, Karl put his trust in the dialectic, 'the vehicle of vitality, the efflorescence in the gardens of the spirit, the foaming in the bubbling goblet of the tiny seeds out of which the flower of the single flame of the spirit bursts forth'.[79]

4

Rebuilding the *Polis*: Reason Takes On the Christian State

Cover your heaven, Zeus,
With foggy clouds
And try yourself, like a boy
Who beheads thistles,
On oak trees and mountain-tops.
You must still leave
my earth to me,
And my hut, which you did not build,
And my stove
Whose glow
You envy me.

I know no poorer creatures
Under the sun, than you, Gods!
You barely sustain your Majesty
From sacrificial offerings
And exhalated prayers
And would wither, were
Not children and beggars
Hopeful fools.

When I was a child,
And did not know where from or to,
I turned my wandering eyes towards
The sun, as if beyond there were
An ear to hear my lament,

A heart like mine
To take pity on the afflicted
From J. W. Goethe, 'Prometheus' (1772–4)

I. THE BREAK-UP OF THE FAMILY

In the five years following his father's death, Karl's relations with his family, particularly with his mother, grew steadily worse. When in Trier, Karl felt more at ease in the household of his future father-in-law, Ludwig von Westphalen, than in his own family home. But most of his time was spent outside Trier, in Berlin, Bonn or Cologne.

Heinrich's death on 10 May 1838 strained relations between the Marx and Westphalen families. Jenny had been attached to Heinrich, but had little rapport with Henriette. Six weeks after Heinrich's death, Jenny was still distraught when she wrote, 'the whole future is so dark, no friendly image smiles back at me'. Jenny recalled to Karl an afternoon she had spent with his father in the family's vineyard at Kürenz a year earlier. 'We talked for two or three hours over the most important matters in life, our noblest and holiest concerns, religion and love . . . He spoke to me with a love, with a warmth, a passion, of which only so rich a temperament as his own was capable. My heart reciprocated this love, this love which I have for him, which will last forever . . . He spoke much about the alarming condition of little Eduard' (Karl's younger brother, who had died on 14 December 1837) and of 'his own bodily weakness . . . His cough was very bad that day.' Later 'I picked for him a little bunch of strawberries . . . He became more cheerful, yes even witty and coquettish', mischievously fantasizing that Jenny was the wife of a high judicial official and to be addressed as 'Frau President'. Jenny included in her letter to Karl a lock of Heinrich's hair.[1]

There is little to indicate how Henriette bore the loss of her husband. Only one letter from her to Karl has survived. It was written over two years after her loss and is badly damaged. Yet what remains suggests the extent of her continuing distress compounded by a sense of being deserted. The letter began: 'You will be able to judge how many painful and bitter tears I have cried about your total renunciation of everything that was of value and dear to you, when you remember our earlier domestic circumstances – which contained extraordinary care and an unstinting motherly love.' She felt snubbed and discarded by the Westphalens. 'Six weeks after your beloved father was taken from us, from the Westphalen family, no friendship, no consolation came to us from that side. It was as if they had never seen us before . . . Jenny came once in four or five weeks and then instead of giving us consolation, she just complained and moaned.' There had evidently been a dispute, perhaps about the settlement of Heinrich's estate, though it is not really clear what was involved; and it appears that the Westphalens blamed her for mishandling it. 'All the pride and vanity of the Westphalens were offended . . . now I had to take the blame for not having presented affairs properly.' When she, the girls and Hermann (Karl's brother) went to offer condolences on the occasion of a Westphalen family bereavement, Hermann was not made welcome and 'Jenny behaved in a distant way.' Henriette felt threatened by what she believed to be their wish to dissolve the match. 'They only see in me a weak mother and doubt my feelings.' Only with great effort had she remained patient, so as not to break Karl's heart or say a harsh word to Jenny. If only Karl had done more to help. 'You will never make the moral sacrifice for your family which we all made for you.' She urged him once again to take into account 'what you consider you owe to your brothers and sisters, but that which we all tolerated and suffered, you can never repay'. As for the Westphalens, she urged Karl to remember that however much 'one recognises in a young woman whom one loves, the most beautiful and elevated virtues', every family 'has an essential character, which remains the same despite all circumstances'. In the case of the Westphalens, it meant one of the most exalted standards: 'no *juste milieu* for them – either one is transported into the heavenly sphere, or one must accept the abyss'.[2]

Family relations clearly survived the tensions created by this very long engagement. The chance survival of a letter from Karl's sister Sophie in March 1841 shows the family expecting a visit from Karl before he joined Bruno Bauer in Bonn in July, and their provision of 'whatever is necessary for your departure or other expenses'. But his relative detachment from the family remained, and is evident in Sophie's closing remark: 'if I had a truly loving brother, I would have very much liked to tell [him] about my own circumstances, but as it is, it is also good'.[3]

The family no doubt found Karl's career choices incomprehensible. Not only had he rejected the chance of a legal career or a position in government service, but as a doctoral student in philosophy he had chosen to work with one of the most notorious Young Hegelians in his department, a department hostile both to Bauer and to himself. Bauer, his new friend and mentor, understood the problem and suggested in March 1841, 'if only I could be in Trier to explain things to your family ... I believe that the small-town mentality is also contributing something to these complications.' But that summer he was too busy finishing off his own *Synoptics* to make a trip to Trier. Bauer also understood the importance of completing the doctorate without provoking unnecessary confrontation. 'You must also remember that you will also increase the financial woes for your Betrothed if you make your path to the lectern more difficult for yourself because of a popular *éclat*. You will have hardship enough afterwards in any case.' He urged Karl to leave Berlin within the next month. 'Shut yourself off, reassure your Betrothed, and make peace with your family.'[4]

Karl himself seems to have avoided the family home as much as was possible. In Trier, he was both cut off from the literary world and far away from the camaraderie of his Berlin companions. In January 1841, he got to know Eduard Meyen and the literary circle around the *Athenäum*, to which he contributed a poem. When he finally left the city, friends clearly missed his company. Köppen wrote in June 1841 that he was melancholy after a week's separation from Karl, and had now taken to walking with Meyen as his new *Schönheitsfreund* (beautiful friend). At least, he claimed, he was pleased that he could think for himself again, and no longer regard himself as a 'mutton-head'.[5] Bauer also bemoaned the fact that he would never again laugh as he had with Karl walking the streets of Berlin.[6]

The final breakdown in family relations occurred in the summer of 1842. From the beginning of that year, Karl had been staying with the Westphalens, while Ludwig von Westphalen – to whom he dedicated his dissertation – lay dying. His death on 3 March coincided with the dismissal of Bauer and the end of any chance of academic employment, and so the question of Karl's career came up again. But this time it was complicated by another death in the Westphalen family, that of Christiane Heubel, who had for many years lived with them.[7] It seems clear that Karl pressed his mother to grant him his share of the inheritance and that she refused. The only account written at the time comes in a letter from Karl to Arnold Ruge on 9 July. Ruge had been pressing him for articles he had been promising since the spring. Karl replied that 'from April to the present day I have been able to work for a total of perhaps only four weeks at most, and that not without interruption. I had to spend six weeks in Trier in connection with another death. The rest of the time was split up and poisoned by the most unpleasant family controversies. My family laid obstacles in my way, which, despite the prosperity of the family, put me for the moment in very serious straits.'[8] He repeated this point to Ruge at the beginning of 1843: 'as I wrote to you once before, I have fallen out with my family and, as long as my mother is alive, I have no right to my property'.[9] Karl's mother handed over the handling of her financial affairs first to her sons-in-law, Robert Schmalhausen, a solicitor in Maastricht married to Sophie, and Jacob Conradi, a hydraulic engineer married to Emilie, and later to her brother-in-law, Lion Philips, in Zaltbommel.[10]

Karl and his mother seem to have been equally strong-willed and unwilling to compromise. The few later comments by Karl about his mother were made between gritted teeth. He grudgingly admitted that she possessed an independent mind. After a trip to Trier in 1861, during which Henriette had paid off some of his old IOUs, he observed to Lassalle, 'incidentally the old woman also intrigued me by her exceedingly subtle esprit and unshakable equanimity'.[11] At his nastiest, he simply wished her dead.[12]

None of Karl's letters to Jenny have survived, but from what she wrote to him we can gain an insight into the texture of their relationship. There can be no doubt that during these years theirs was a sustained and passionate love affair. In 1839, she wrote:

> Oh my darling, how you looked at me the first time like that and then quickly looked away, and then looked at me again, and I did the same, until at last we looked at each other for quite a long time and very deeply, and could no longer look away ... Often things occur to me that you have said to me or asked me about, and then I am carried away by indescribably marvellous sensations. And Karl, when you kissed me, and pressed me to you and held me fast, and I could no longer breathe for fear and trembling ... If you only knew, dear Karl, what a peculiar feeling I have, I really cannot describe it to you.[13]

Sometimes these feelings were expressed in a language of self-abasement. In 1841, she declared, 'dearest Karl, please say, will I yet become wholly yours? ... Oh Karl I am so bad, and nothing is good about me any more except my love for you, that love, however, above all else is big and strong and eternal.'[14]

From these letters, Karl emerges as a would-be poet, dramatist or philosopher; he played the romantic lover to the hilt, furiously jealous about imagined rivals or any departure from feelings of exclusive devotion. In 1838, Jenny had to explain that her love for Edgar was that of a sister and a friend and that it did not impinge upon her feelings for Karl.[15] In 1839, Jenny tortured herself with the fear that 'for my sake you could become embroiled in a quarrel and then in a duel'. But perhaps to disarm him she fantasized a scenario along the lines of Jane Eyre's conquest of Mr Rochester, in which she was not entirely unhappy. 'I vividly imagined that you had lost your right hand, and Karl, I was in a state of rapture, of bliss because of that. You see, sweetheart, I thought that in that case I could really become quite indispensable to you; you would then always keep me with you and love me. I also thought that then I could write down all your dear, heavenly ideas and be really useful to you.'[16]

But such passion was always accompanied by an undertow of realism and an anxiety, which had already been noticed by Karl's father. Jenny was not altogether reassured by the 'beautiful, touching, passionate love, the indescribably beautiful things you say about it, the inspiring creations of your imagination'. She was concerned about the permanence of such love. 'That is why I am not so wholly thankful for, so wholly enchanted by your love, as it really deserves. That is why', she continued, 'I often remind you of external matters, of life and reality, instead of clinging wholly, as you can do so well, to the world of love, to absorption in it and to a higher, dearer, spiritual unity with you, and in it forgetting everything else, finding solace and happiness in that alone.'[17]

As the letters reveal, Jenny also had worries of her own. Not only was she fully engaged in nursing her sick father, Ludwig, but she also had to worry about the financial fecklessness of her brother, Edgar, and to shield her mother, Caroline, from the mess he was in. In 1841, she wrote that she had 'deliberately kept silent about the disordered state of Edgar's finances', but now could no longer do so, particularly since her own outgoings had increased so much. In addition, 'my mother has again begun to reproach me, since she warns me again about everything'. Caroline had insisted that Edgar collect her from Cologne 'simply to comply with outer and inner decorum, since I on the other hand could not otherwise visit you in Bonn'.[18]

Jenny felt increasingly bored and restless in the parental home and away from the excitements of Berlin or Cologne. In 1839, she wrote, 'if only I knew of a book which I could understand properly, and which could divert me a little'. She asked Karl to recommend a book, 'a bit learned so that I do not understand everything, but still manage to understand something as if through a fog, a bit such as not everyone likes to read; and also no fairy tales, and no poetry, I can't bear it. I think it would do me a lot of good if I exercised my mind a bit.'[19] In 1841, she was studying Greek, and longed to meet 'the synopticist' (Bruno Bauer).[20] The long years of engagement amid so much sickness, family tensions, financial anxiety and uncertainty about the future were taking their toll. Marriage could not come too soon. 'Tomorrow', she wrote, her father, who issued orders without pause, was going to be moved from the bed to a chair. 'If I were not lying here so miserably, I would soon be packing my bag. Everything is ready. Frocks and collars and bonnets are in beautiful order and only the wearer is not in the right condition.'[21]

2. BRUNO BAUER AND THE DESTRUCTION OF CHRISTIANITY

Between 1839 and 1841, while Karl was preparing his dissertation, Bruno Bauer was his closest friend and mentor. Bauer was becoming famous through his radical biblical criticism and his uncompromisingly secular reading of Hegel's philosophy (see below, pp. 93 ff.). At the time Karl became acquainted with him, he was a *Privatdozent*, an untenured lecturer, in the Theology Faculty of Berlin University. Karl had attended Bauer's lectures on the Book of Isaiah in 1836 and got to know him through his friend Adolf Rutenberg, Bauer's brother-in-law. In the summer semester of 1839, Bauer's lectures were the only ones Karl ever attended. While he remained in Berlin, Karl saw Bauer frequently in the Doctors' Club, where he was a leading light, and often also at the Bauer family home in Charlottenburg.

The first public sign of Bauer's move away from the position of *Accommodation* came in 1839, when he criticized 'the short-sighted theological apologetics' of his former ally, the leader of Christian Evangelical fundamentalism, Hengstenberg. Bauer's aim was to separate the spirit of Christianity from the dogmatic form it had assumed in the ethos of the Prussian Restoration state. Hengstenberg had gained increasing influence at court, and it is possible that Altenstein and Schulze as the last active and rationalist representatives in government of Prussia's 'Reform Era' had encouraged Bauer to make an attack. But such a move was also an acknowledgement of their increasing weakness. For, despite his move to Bonn, Bauer remained an unpaid and financially desperate *Privatdozent*, who, as Schulze admitted, had no prospects of promotion. In the winter semester of 1839, Altenstein, the Minister of Education, transferred Bauer to Bonn University to protect him from the controversy he had begun to provoke.

In 1841, after completing and submitting his dissertation in April, Karl spent two months back in Trier and then in early July followed Bauer to Bonn in the hope that Bauer might help him to acquire an academic position. In the first three months of 1842, he spent most of his time in Trier, where Jenny's father, Ludwig von Westphalen, was now terminally ill, but he also enlarged the dissertation, which he had originally submitted at Jena, with the aim of getting it printed and acquiring his *Habilitation* (his post-doctoral qualification) at Bonn. In March 1842, Bauer lost his post at Bonn and returned to Berlin soon after. Karl remained in Bonn somewhat longer, but eventually moved to Cologne, where he became involved in the newly founded newspaper the *Rheinische Zeitung*.

Behind these bare facts lay an increasingly dramatic sequence of events: the death both of Altenstein and of the old king, Friedrich Wilhelm III, followed by the spiralling confrontation between Bauer's ever more radical 'criticism' and the new and increasingly infuriated leaders of the Prussian 'Christian state'. This was a process in which Karl appears to have been an enthusiastic participant, but also one that annihilated his chances for academic employment.

Bauer's first letters to Karl after his arrival in Bonn in 1839 read like those of a supportive doctoral supervisor and friend. In December, he referred to Karl's 'logical investigations' and Köppen's worry that this might lead to sophistry. He went on to advise him on Hegel's unsatisfactory treatment of the transition from being to essence in *The Science of Logic*, while at the same time urging him first to get the dissertation finished. Through Karl, Bauer sent his greetings to Köppen and Rutenberg in Berlin and bemoaned the lack of anything in Bonn comparable to 'our club' with its constant flow of intelligent conversation. Colleagues in Bonn assembled at nine o'clock at the Casino or the 'Professors' Club at the Trier Hof, but only to exchange jokes and gossip; and at 11 p.m. everyone departed.' Despondently, Bauer noted that 'everything is wholly philistine'. In spring 1840, he urged Karl to get past his hesitations and 'the mere farce this examination is', only wishing that he could be there to discuss it.[22]

As the time for the submission of the doctoral dissertation approached, Bauer urged Karl in several letters not to provoke the examiner pointlessly. He should not, for example, include a provocative motto from Aeschylus on the frontispiece, nor include anything beyond philosophical discussion. 'Within that form you can indeed say all which lies within such mottos. Only not now! Once you are on the podium, and have developed a philosophical position, you can indeed say what you wish.'[23] With the help of Bruno Bauer's brother, Edgar, on 6 April, Karl dispatched his dissertation to the Philosophy Faculty of Jena, and on 15 April was sent his doctoral diploma.[24] Karl had requested the Dean of the Philosophy Faculty to act as quickly as possible in his case. But the remarkable speed with which the dissertation was examined was due to the help of an academic friend at Jena, Professor Oskar Wolff, who had provided precise instructions about the necessary documentation to accompany the dissertation.

The closeness of Karl's to Bauer's outlook during this period is attested by the foreword to his dissertation, in which Karl declared his hatred of 'all heavenly and earthly gods who do not acknowledge human self-consciousness as the highest divinity'.[25] 'Self-consciousness' was the central term in Bauer's reading of Hegel. It did not refer to immediate or particular awareness, but to what Bauer called 'singularity', or the process by which the particular elevated itself to the universal. In this way, the self became the bearer of reason or the dialectical unity of the universal and particular. The individual, possessed of singularity, had acquired those attributes which Hegel attributed to 'Absolute Spirit'. What Bauer called the progress of infinite self-consciousness now signified the progress of an external historical reality, which subjects recognized as their own accomplishment.

Bauer's notion of 'self-consciousness' formed part of his ambition to remove any residue of the existence of the transcendent from Hegel's philosophy. This was the loophole by which conservative Hegelians could persuade themselves that Hegel still reserved a place for a transcendent God. Orthodox Hegelians had maintained that religion and philosophy were identical; what one depicted in narratives and picture painting, the other articulated in concepts. Absolute Spirit in philosophy was therefore the equivalent of the Christian God. But in Bauer God was found exclusively in human consciousness; God was nothing more than self-consciousness actively knowing itself. By attacking any idea of *Spirit* as a power independent of rational spirits, Bauer had designated 'human self-consciousness as the highest divinity'.

Bruno Bauer, the son of a porcelain-painter at the royal court, had enrolled in Berlin University in 1828. He became Hegel's star pupil, and wrote a prize essay extending Hegel's arguments about aesthetics. As a result of this association, he had incurred the enmity of Schleiermacher, the theologian, and his supporters.[26] In 1834, he became a *Privatdozent* in the Berlin Theology Faculty and in 1836 editor of an orthodox Hegelian journal, *The Journal for Speculative Theology*. He was also chosen by Hegel's philosophical executors to edit Hegel's *Lectures on the Philosophy of Religion*, together with one of the most respected followers of Hegel, Philip Marheineke, a champion of the idea that a rational *Accommodation* could be found between philosophy and religion. At this early stage, Bauer's work was noteworthy because of the zeal with which he argued that every detail of the biblical letter could be established as historically true in a speculative sense according to Hegel's understanding of history. The goal of biblical exegesis, he argued, was to demonstrate 'the unity of the Idea in the separation of its moments as it is described in the Old Testament, and then its unmediated unity in the New Testament'. As Bauer himself recalled in 1840, 'like the immortal gods, the disciples lived with patriarchal calm in the kingdom of the Idea that their master had left behind as his inheritance'.[27] But the publication of Strauss's *Life of Jesus* in 1835, together with equivalent historical criticism of the Old Testament by Wilhelm

Vatke, had rudely shaken this speculative approach to religious truth. Hegel and Marheineke did not consider questions of historical criticism relevant to the question of the relationship between religion and philosophy. But now, in the aftermath of Strauss's book, this question became a burning issue.

Mainstream Hegelians looked to Bauer to provide a convincing answer to Strauss. This began with an unsuccessful attempt to demonstrate that the Gospels were not a collection of messianic myths, but rather multifaceted articulations of the 'Absolute Idea'. From there, Bauer constructed an alternative account of the historical status of religion in general, and of Christianity in particular, in relation to the development of self-consciousness. In 1838 in *The Religion of the Old Testament*, he presented the Old Testament account of the will of God as legal subordination to the will of another. This was to be superseded by the New Testament Gospel picture of universal immanence and the identity of human and divine. But by 1840 criticism, originally applied to the Old Testament, was extended to Christianity as a whole. Between 1841 and 1843, Bauer's attack was sharpened still further. Indeed, the polemical assault upon the credentials of Christianity in *The Trumpet of the Last Judgement against Hegel the Atheist and Anti-Christ* and *Christianity Exposed* was savage in a way not found in the works of Strauss or Feuerbach. Bauer wholly dismantled the edifice of religious belief. As he put it in 1841, 'Realized self-consciousness is that play in which the Ego is doubled as in a mirror, and which, after holding its image for thousands of years to be God, discovers the picture in the mirror to be itself . . . Religion takes that mirror image for God, philosophy casts off the illusion and shows man that no one stands behind the mirror.'[28]

Bauer had objected from the outset to Strauss's presentations of the Gospels as the product of the Jewish community and its tradition of messianic myths and prophesies. Bauer argued that Strauss's 'community' was just another name for the pantheist conception of 'substance' or 'being', which derived from Spinoza. Such an approach invoked a 'Universal' which was allegedly effective immediately without showing how it operated, how it was taken up or how it was internalized in the individual self-consciousness. Only individuals, Bauer argued, could give such a 'tradition' shape and form. Strauss's 'tradition' dissolved such individuals into an amorphous whole. As a matter of history as well, Bauer took issue with Strauss. Christianity was not grounded in the substance of mythology and tradition, of Jewish apocalyptic expectation or of the Old Testament God of Spinoza. Christianity was a response to the new universal conditions of the Roman Empire following the disappearance of the *polis*. It marked 'the death of nature' and beginning of self-consciousness.

The loss of any realistic prospect of academic employment helps to explain the increasing radicalism of Bauer's religious criticism after 1839.[29] This was signalled by the appearance of his *Critique of the Gospel of John* in May 1840, followed by three volumes of *The Critique of the Synoptic Gospels*, published in 1841 and 1842. *The Critique of the Gospel of John* highlighted the opposition between free self-consciousness and the religious principle. It argued that Christianity had been a necessity at one stage in the development of the human spirit, but also that that stage had now reached its term. The Gospel of John was taken as a demonstration of the 'positivity' of Christian dogma; it was a literary construction which invented dramatic incidents as pretexts for dogmatic pronouncements, and confused defence of the particular with the necessary manifestation of the universal. It was a Gospel in which Christ's pronouncements were confusingly mixed with expressions of the consciousness of later members of the religious community.

In the *Critique of the Gospel of John*, it was still implied that while John's was a literary invention, the first three 'Synoptic' Gospels might contain the original words of Christ. But in the *Critique of the Synoptic Gospels*, the attempt to undermine the pretensions of dogmatic Christianity went further. In the first two volumes, the claim that the Synoptic Gospels directly cited Christ's utterances was generally withdrawn as Bauer attempted to demonstrate that the incidents described were the products of religious consciousness rather than factual reports. He also stressed the extent to which reported events contradicted both nature and history. The Gospel of John, it was suggested, represented a further stage of reflection upon this religious consciousness, which converted the sayings found in the Synoptics into dogmatic form. Finally, in the third *Synoptic* volume, published in early 1842, Bauer argued not only that the Gospel of John was a literary artefact, but that so also were the Synoptic Gospels. Bauer finally disposed of the ambiguity still found in Strauss, where the mythic expectations of the Jewish people were aligned with the shadowy figure of a certain Jesus. In Volume 3, the supposed historical existence of Christ was presented as part of a fictional history of Jewish self-consciousness, and even the conception of the Messiah was depicted as a literary invention.[30]

Bauer's scholarly interventions launched the outbreak of open hostilities in a conflict that had been gathering momentum ever since the publication of Strauss's *Life of Jesus* and the battle between the state and the Catholics of Cologne. Under the old king, while Altenstein was still responsible for universities, tensions remained somewhat muffled. But in 1841, in the eyes of left Hegelians at least, and perhaps also of the circle around the new king, the open struggle between 'free self-consciousness' and the 'Christian state' began to acquire epic proportions. The 'Christian state' was no figment of left Hegelian imagination. The new king, Friedrich Wilhelm IV, was a Romantic conservative, a product of the religious awakening of the 1810s and 1820s, was firmly convinced of his divine right as a monarch and strongly believed in the necessity of rejuvenating a positive form of Christianity. Unlike his father's, his vision of Christianity was ecumenical, in line with the sentimental medievalism cultivated by the later Romantics. He allowed dissident Lutherans to break away from his father's United Evangelical church and was keen to patch up the quarrel with the Rhineland Catholics. He even married a Catholic and was an enthusiastic promoter of the gothic renovation of Cologne Cathedral.[31]

Some of Friedrich Wilhelm's first actions led some radicals to naively hope for the beginning of a new era. Bruno's brother, Edgar, wrote on 13 June 1840 that 'most people cherish the highest expectations of the government, the king will hold himself above the parties'.[32] The new king expressed approval of representative bodies and scepticism about bureaucracy; he released some long-standing political prisoners, supported aspects of cultural nationalism, and for a time in 1842 relaxed censorship. But none of these actions were straightforward. He quickly drew back from any commitment to political representation; he forbade the publication of Arnold Ruge's *Hallische Jahrbücher* in Prussia and put pressure on the Saxon government to ban it under its revised title, *Deutsche Jahrbücher*. He also forced the closure of the *Athenäum*, the tiny cultural journal of the Berlin Doctors' Club. The king's initial authorization of the appearance of the *Rheinische Zeitung* in 1842 was the result of a mistaken impression of its likely character. The vision behind these initiatives was not that of nineteenth-century liberalism built upon a free press and competing political parties, but of a king who listened to the voices of his subjects and acted for their welfare. Friedrich Wilhelm's belief was in a hierarchy of corporations and estates, and he even played with the idea of reconstituting the Jews as a separate estate until warned off the idea by horrified officials. Not surprisingly, rationalism and free thought – let alone the heresies of Hegel – had no place in his kingdom.

Meanwhile in Berlin, just as Stahl had succeeded Eduard Gans as Professor of Law, Friedrich Schelling was invited by the new king to take up the Chair in Philosophy once occupied by Hegel. In November 1841, Schelling delivered his first lecture, to a crowded auditorium which included the Russian anarchist Mikhail Bakunin, the young Engels and the Danish philosopher Søren Kierkegaard. Schelling's task was 'to remove the dragon's seed of Hegelianism' and to propagate his 'Philosophy of Revelation'. The new Minister of Education, Health and Religious Affairs was Johann Eichhorn, one of the architects of the *Zollverein* (the Prussian customs union) and once an ally of the Prussian liberal reformer Freiherr vom Stein. But it soon became clear that he regarded radical Hegelianism as a dangerous phenomenon and was happy to implement the king's conservative cultural policy.[33] In August 1841, Eichhorn sent out the first volume of the *Synoptic Gospels* to six theology faculties in a consultation over whether Bauer's *licentia docendi* – his 'licence to teach' – should be revoked for denying the divine inspiration of the Gospels. But before they decided, the government received reports of a banquet and a 'serenade' in Berlin organized without prior permission, and held at the Wallburgschen wine tavern by the Doctors' Club on 28 September 1841, in honour of the South German liberal editor of the *Staats-Lexikon*, Carl Welcker, a professor at Freiburg and a political activist in Baden. At this banquet, Bauer made a speech extolling his own radical reading of Hegel's vision of the state. Not only did it go far beyond the constitutionalist and reformist position of the South German liberals, but it also implied revolutionary opposition to the government. Welcker himself was 'very shocked', but the king was outraged, and demanded that participants at this event, especially Bauer and Rutenberg, should be denied access to Berlin and excluded from all official posts.[34]

3. *THE ARCHIVES OF ATHEISM* AND CHRISTIAN ART

Bauer's letters to Karl suggest that radical Hegelians were equally set upon what they confidently imagined to be a world-transforming confrontation. On 11 December 1839, he wrote, 'from my experience of Berlin, the university here and especially the Theological Faculty, Prussia is intent upon coming forward through another Battle of Jena'. In the spring of 1840, he advised Karl to make sure that he was 'alert to the moment'. The times were becoming 'more terrible' and 'more beautiful'. Political issues might be larger elsewhere, but those 'issues which concern the whole of life, are nowhere as richly and variously intertwined as in Prussia'. Everywhere, he saw 'the emergence of the starkest contradictions, and the futile Chinese police system, seeking to cover them up, which has only served to strengthen them'. Finally, he asserted, 'there is philosophy, which emancipates itself precisely in the context of this Chinese repression and will lead the struggle, while the state in its delusion lets control slip out of its hands'. A few weeks later in Bonn, after delivering a public lecture, in which he delighted in dashing local academic expectations that 'a Hegelian must always travel with a spear in hand', experience of 'this nice little bit of the world here' had convinced him of something, which he had not been able to admit to himself in Berlin: 'everything must be toppled . . . The catastrophe will be terrible . . . I might almost be inclined to say, it will become greater and more horrendous than the crisis which accompanied the entry of Christianity into the world.' In the spring of 1841, as Karl prepared to submit his dissertation, Bauer was keen 'to get the *Gospels* off my back in order to be able to start up other things'. He thought that 'the moment of decision inasmuch as it will express itself in an external rupture' was 'coming ever closer' and 'who can say how government will behave at that point'.[35]

For that reason, Bauer urged Karl not to abandon the cause of philosophy. The *Hallische Jahrbücher* had become tedious. It was clear that 'the terrorism of true theory must clear the field' and this meant that a new journal had to come into being. 'In the summer we must already get the material together', so that the journal could be published in Michaelmas.[36] 'It would be nonsense to devote yourself to a practical career. Theory is now the strongest form of practical activity, and we still cannot predict in how large a sense it will be practical.'[37] Talk about the new plan lasted between March and December 1841. The new journal would be entitled *The Archives of Atheism*.[38]

Unlike his brother, Edgar, Bauer had never expressed any confidence in the intentions of the new king; and even before the new reign he had expressed distrust of the Prussian government on account of its ambivalence on the question of Rhineland Catholics. As the letters to Karl revealed, even before the summer of 1841 Bauer was anticipating that an epic conflict between religion and free self-consciousness would be unleashed by his criticism, and that the lines of battle should be stated as clearly as possible. Thus, some months before the Welcker affair and the government reaction to the *Synoptic Gospels*, Bauer had begun to spell out the radicalism of his political and religious position in as clear a form as censorship would allow. He put his reading of Hegel as a radical into the mouth of a supposedly outraged Pietist preacher, who denounced Hegel as an atheist and a Jacobin; hence the mockingly misleading title, *The Trumpet of the Last Judgement against Hegel the Atheist and Antichrist*. Karl fully shared the position outlined in this pamphlet, and planned to contribute a 'treatise on Christian art' in the follow-up volume of *The Trumpet*.

The intended journal never came into existence, probably because of the difficulty of finding contributors and circumventing the new censorship regulations, issued on 24 December 1841. *The Trumpet*, however, was published in October 1841, and it was meant to be provocative. In the opinion of the pseudo-pastor, the ideas of the 'old' Hegelians, of the 'positive philosophers' or of the followers of Schleiermacher, all of whom in different ways attempted to reconcile religion and philosophy, must be exposed. The Christian message was safe only in the hands of evangelical fundamentalists like Hengstenberg, the author of *The Trumpet* thundered on: 'away with this rage of reconciliation, with this sentimental slop, with this slimy and lying secularism'.[39]

Even the opponents of Hegel had not realized 'the profound atheism at the ground of this system'. Hegel appears to present 'World Spirit' as 'an actual power guiding history to certain ends'. But 'World Spirit' was nothing but a form of words to describe the point at which self-consciousness entered the world, but was not as yet aware of its nature – the period between the inception of Christianity and the Enlightenment. But now 'a new epoch has arisen in the world . . . God is dead for philosophy, and only the self as self-consciousness lives, creates, acts and is everything.'[40] In Bauer's vision of history, the Hegelian identity of being and thought was retained, but no longer as a result which had already been attained, as it had been described in Hegel's *The Philosophy of Right* of 1821. This identity was now presented as an endless upward movement, whose momentum was located in the activity of rational subjects faced with irrational or 'positive' institutions.

In Bauer's reading, historical development was divided between three moments. First there was the time of the ancients – 'the moment of substantiality', in which thought was not distinguished from being and remained subordinate to it. Here, individuals were subordinate to community; their relationship to it was that of substance to accident. Individuals were not yet understood as possessing free subjectivity. The second moment, that of religious consciousness – pre-eminently Christianity – was one in which the 'universality' of the subject was recognized and distinguished from 'substance'. This subjectivity was not located in humanity, but in an alien and otherworldly domain. In the alienated world of religious consciousness, mankind perceived its own deeds as those of another. Man posited a transcendent God and abased himself before it. This was 'the moment of the Unhappy Consciousness'. In the third historical moment, that of the Enlightenment and the French Revolution, free self-consciousness was enabled to grasp its own universality, to remove the previous otherness of World Spirit, and to perceive its world as its own creation. Particular and universal were located within each citizen; nothing transcendent remained. 'The moment of Absolute Spirit' denoted a situation in which what had been perceived as transcendent being was now seen to consist of the individual rational subjects who composed it.[41]

Recent history was a period in which the development of the free self-consciousness that had emerged during the Enlightenment and the French Revolution was interrupted and halted by the Restoration governments, which had come into existence after 1815. The political task therefore was to provoke a resumption of the epoch of revolution. *The Trumpet* made frequent references to the Jacobins. They were saluted for their ruthless critique of all existing relations and for their refusal to compromise. Hegel became an apologist for Robespierre: 'his theory is praxis . . . it is the revolution itself'. Furthermore, Hegel's students – the

Young Hegelians – were not real Germans. They were not to be heard singing patriotic songs during the Rhine crisis of 1840. 'They revile everything German', they are 'French revolutionaries'.[42]

Bauer's subterfuge worked for only two months. In December, the *Trumpet*'s true authorship was exposed. The new law concerning censorship impinged directly upon projects such as *The Archives of Atheism*, and quickly halted the circulation of the *Trumpet*. These actions provoked Karl's first venture into political journalism, 'Comments on the Latest Prussian Censorship Instruction', an analysis of the intention behind the legislation.

Karl contrasted the new measure with the legislation of 1819. Unlike the old law that had sought to check 'all that is contrary to the general principles of religion', the new decree specifically mentioned Christianity. In 1819, according to Karl, a 'rationalism still prevailed, which understood by religion in general the so-called religion of reason'. In the old censorship law, one of the aims was also to 'oppose fanatical transference of religious articles of faith into politics and the *confusion of ideas* resulting therefrom'. But now 'the confusion of the political with the Christian-religious principle has indeed become *official doctrine*'.[43] Karl had originally sent the piece to Arnold Ruge for publication in his Dresden-based *Deutsche Jahrbücher*. But Ruge told him that the Prussian government would certainly censor the article and published it in the Swiss-based *Anekdota* instead.[44]

As for the fate of the second volume of the *Trumpet*, in January 1842 Bauer wrote to Karl informing him that he had completed his contribution to it. In the light of the ban, he changed the title to *Hegel's Teaching on Religion and Art from the Standpoint of a Believer*. Karl continued to work on his part of the text throughout the winter of 1841–2 and filled one of his notebooks with readings relevant to it. But on 5 March he wrote to Ruge stating that the revival of censorship in Saxony (and Prussia) would make it 'quite impossible to print my "Treatise on *Christian Art*" which should have appeared as the second part of the *Trumpet*'. He hoped that a version of it could be published in the *Anekdota*, to be published in Zurich, and therefore beyond the reach of German censors.[45] On 27 April, he wrote to Ruge that his essay was almost book length, but that because of 'all kinds of external muddles, it has been almost impossible for me to work'.[46]

The manuscript on Christian art has not survived, but its general argument can be inferred from Karl's previous aesthetic passions, from the argument in the *Trumpet*, and from the works consulted in his notebook.[47] It seems that Karl's identification with Weimar classicism remained undiminished. It had already been evident during his years at the Trier *Gymnasium*, where the headmaster, Wyttenbach, had propagated it. Even the reactionary Herr Loers must have been redeemed in Karl's eyes by his knowledge about and enthusiasm for Ovid. For some years later at Berlin, Karl continued to spend his spare time translating Ovid's *Tristia*.[48] During his time in Bonn in 1835–6, his continuing interest in classical culture and literature was testified by his attendance at Welcker's lectures on Greek and Latin mythology, Eduard d'Alton on art history, and Augustus Schlegel on Homer and Propertius. Much later, in 1857, he still marvelled at 'Greek art and epic poetry . . . Why should not the historical childhood of humanity, where it attained its most beautiful form, exert an eternal charm as a stage which will never recur?'[49]

Classical Greece had been an inspiration for the Jacobins, just as it had been for the builders of the Brandenburg Gate under Frederick the Great. In the *Trumpet*, Bauer claimed that Hegel was 'a great friend of the Greek religion and of the Greeks in general'. The reason for that was that Greek religion was 'basically no religion at all'. Greek religion was a religion of 'beauty, of art, of freedom, of humanity', in contrast to revealed religion, which was 'the celebration of servile egoism'. Greek religion was 'the religion of humanity'.[50] This was nearer to the poet and philosopher Friedrich Schiller's association between aesthetic and political freedom than to Hegel, who had accepted much of the neo-classical celebration of Greece and Greek art following on from Winckelmann[51], but thought that the Greek achievement was limited by its confinement to the physical world. For Hegel it had been the emergence of 'Spirit', embodied in the development of Christianity, which had liberated civilization from its bondage to nature.[52]

The claim that Greek religion was not a religion at all was an important one, as it allowed one to argue that *religion* was an imported, 'oriental' phenomenon.[53] The foundation of Greek life was unity with nature. According to one of the sources cited in Marx's notebook, C. F. von Rumohr, the Greek gods were 'pulsations of nature'.[54] By contrast, the gods of other pagan peoples were ugly and fierce, designed to instil fear. Nor was there any beauty in the God of the Old Testament;

it was a God of 'bare practicality, rapacity and crudity'. This God like other oriental gods possessed a predatory attitude towards nature and the propensity to combat it as a form of demonstrating its power: Karl was especially impressed by de Brosses's treatise of 1760, which identified religion with fetishism. In the religions of West Africa and Ancient Egypt, according to de Brosses, man-made objects were endowed with supernatural power. Their ugliness was intentional; de Brosses cited a grotesque representation of Hercules from Boeotia.[55]

The prospect of censorship was probably the main reason why Karl finally decided not to publish his treatise, which would have argued the fundamental continuity between Christianity and the repellent features of pagan religions. Christian art in the post-classical period reproduced the aesthetics of Asiatic barbarism. Citations from art historians and archaeologists, like Grund and Böttiger, originally inspired by Gibbon, focused on the continuity between the grotesque features of fetish gods and the distorted bodily forms found in Christian art.[56] According to Grund, gothic statues of saints were 'small in appearance, lean and angular in shape, awkward and unnatural in pose, they were below any real artistry, just as man their creator was below himself'. While in classical art form and artistry were essential, Christian architecture sought exaggeration and loftiness, and yet it was 'lost in barbaric pomp and countless details'. Man was made passive, while material things were endowed with the qualities of man himself.[57]

From Karl's analysis it could first have been inferred that the Christian release of 'Spirit' from the bonds of nature had not marked a major advance in human history, since it was based not upon science but upon the magical and the miraculous. Secondly, the intention of the 'Treatise' would have been to intervene in the battle over art, pursued by radicals ever since the politicization of the role of the artist by the Saint-Simonians in France. According to the Saint-Simonian mission at the beginning of the 1830s, artists were to become the 'avant-garde' prophets of the new 'religion of Saint-Simon', Evangelists of a new age of sensualism and 'the rehabilitation of the flesh'. Heinrich Heine in his exile in Paris and for a time an admirer of the Saint-Simonians had celebrated this coming age in his *History of Religion and Philosophy in Germany* of 1834. He challenged Hegel's identification of modernity with the spiritual by glorifying the sensualism of Eugène Delacroix's famous painting of *Liberty Leading the People* by describing her as 'a

Venus of the Streets'.[58] During his time as a would-be poet, Karl had been inspired by Heine's observation that 'the chaste monks have tied an apron around the Venus of antiquity'.[59] This point was of immediate political relevance since Friedrich Wilhelm IV was an enthusiastic patron and supporter of what became known as the 'Nazarene' school, a modern art which sought to revive the religious art of medieval Germany.

On 20 March 1842, Karl wrote to Ruge that the article 'On Christian Art', now retitled 'On Religion and Art, with Special Reference to Christian Art', would have to be 'entirely redone', since he was dropping the biblical tone of the *Trumpet* and now wished to add an epilogue on the Romantics.[60] That was virtually the last mention of the project. The joint campaign inaugurated by Bauer and Karl in the spring of 1841, intended to include an atheist journal and successive volumes of the *Trumpet*, was brought to a definitive end by the final dismissal from Bonn University of Bauer in March 1842. Bauer announced his intention to head back to Berlin and 'conduct proceedings against the Prussian Government'. Karl's future brother-in-law and 'aristocrat *comme il faut*', Ferdinand von Westphalen, told Karl that such a course of action would make people in Berlin 'particularly vexed'.[61] Before they parted company, Bauer and Karl 'rented a pair of asses' to ride through the city. 'Bonn society was astonished. We shouted with joy, the asses brayed.'[62]

4. THE *RHEINISCHE ZEITUNG*

With the definitive dismissal of Bruno Bauer, Karl lost all hope of academic employment. Like a growing number of educated but unemployed young men in *Vormärz* Germany, however, he had an alternative: he could turn to journalism. Despite censorship, this was an occupation in which opportunities for employment were increasing; and for Karl himself a particular opportunity had opened up in the Rhineland, the prospect of writing for a new liberal newspaper, the *Rheinische Zeitung*, which was to begin publication early in 1842.

The Prussian government desired the establishment of a moderate pro-Prussian newspaper in the Rhineland because of a concern about the loyalty of its Catholic population. In the neighbouring Low

Countries, a Catholic revolt against a Protestant state in 1830 had brought about the secession of Belgium from Holland. The growth of ultramontanism, which placed papal authority above that of secular monarchs, and the imprisonment of the Archbishop of Cologne by the Prussian authorities for denying the law over the question of mixed marriages had led to a pamphlet war, in which the undertow of anti-Prussian sentiment was clearly perceptible. According to a later account, 'the Catholics of the Rhine province, awakened from their slumber, rallied with unexpected ardour to the support of their chief pastor'.[63] The Catholic and ultramontane case was powerfully put in *Athanasius*, the work of the prominent former Rhineland radical Joseph Görres, ominously likened to O'Connell, the great agitator for the Catholic emancipation of Ireland.[64] The situation was made worse by the fact that opinion in the Rhineland was largely shaped by the Catholic *Kölnische Zeitung*, the leading newspaper of the Rhineland province with over 8,000 subscribers. Government officials were worried that during 'the Cologne troubles' – the conflict between the government and the Catholic archbishop – the stance of the *Kölnische Zeitung* had been unreliable.[65] In 1841, they had therefore attempted to establish a rival Protestant and pro-Prussian newspaper, the *Rheinische Allgemeine Zeitung*.

The failure of this short-lived project enabled a group of leading industrialists, lawyers and writers from Cologne to take over the project of establishing a newspaper in the second half of 1841. The group had originally come together earlier in the year to discuss the need for industrial development and economic reform. As a result of its Protestant and pro-Prussian position, the group won official approval and the appeal to take up shares in the new enterprise was a great success.

Prominent members of this group included Ludolf Camphausen (1803–90), a pioneer of railway development and briefly Prime Minister of Prussia in 1848, and Gustav Mevissen (1815–99), the founder of the Darmstädter Bank, a pioneer of German credit institutions, and a prominent member of the 1848 Frankfurt National Assembly. Their interest was both economic and political, for it was clear that further economic expansion depended upon reform of the state on the basis of representative institutions and equality before the law. Furthermore, although the chief shareholders were Cologne industrialists, the leading role in shaping the paper's policy on the Board of Management was taken by activist members of Cologne's educated and propertied intelligentsia. Particularly prominent within this group were Georg Jung and Dagobert Oppenheim. Both men were related to important banking houses in the city, but also attracted to the intellectual and political radicalism of the Young Hegelians. Lastly, there was Moses Hess, born in Bonn of a modest Jewish merchant family, a pioneer socialist writer and a leading participant in the formulation of editorial policy.

Karl first encountered this group while on his way from Trier to Bonn around July 1841 at the moment at which they had first conceived the project of establishing a daily newspaper in the Rhineland. He made a strong impression upon them, particularly upon Jung, Oppenheim and Hess. Jung described him as a 'quite desperate revolutionary' who possessed 'one of the acutest minds' he had come across, while Hess described him as his 'idol' and ranked him alongside major thinkers of the Enlightenment. As a result, he was invited to participate in the paper, when it was launched in January 1842.

With a great deal of current interest in the expansion of the *Zollverein*, the Prussian-dominated German customs union, and its impact upon the protection of the developing industries of the province, the group's first choice of editor was the celebrated advocate of a state-based and protectionist economic development Friedrich List.[66] But List was too ill to take up the position and recommended instead one of his followers, Dr Gustav Höfken, whose main preoccupations were not the protection of local industries, but German unity and the expansion of the *Zollverein*. This choice did not satisfy leading members of the Board, and on 18 January, after a short period of service, Höfken resigned. Under the influence of Moses Hess, a new editor was chosen from the Young Hegelians in Berlin, Karl's friend Adolf Rutenberg.

A provincial daily newspaper edited by Bruno Bauer's brother-in-law and organizer of the Welcker banquet, assisted by a group of Young Hegelians and socialists, was not what the government had had in mind. The king was furious and pressed for the paper to be banned, but other ministers were divided – including Bodelschwingh, the *Oberpräsident* of the province, and the Culture Minister, Eichhorn – and thought that the peremptory banning of the paper, so soon after its birth, would be seen as arbitrary and cause dissatisfaction among businessmen. According to Eichhorn, the destructive teachings of Ruge's *Deutsche Jahrbücher* had made little impact in the Rhineland; he therefore doubted whether 'the extravagances' of the Young Hegelians would have any effect. He was more concerned about the Catholic threat. Throughout the fifteen months of the paper's existence, argument went on between officials on whether it would be better to ban the paper or whether stricter censorship would suffice.[67]

Karl's first contribution to the paper appeared on 5 May 1842, following the confirmation of Bauer's dismissal. Not surprisingly, a strong continuity was evident between his preoccupations during his time with Bruno Bauer and the issues he intended to address on the paper. In a letter to Arnold Ruge on 27 April 1842, he promised to send four articles for the *Deutsche Jahrbücher*, on 'Religious Art', 'The Romantics', the 'Philosophical Manifesto of the Historical School of Law' and 'Positive Philosophy'.[68] In fact, only the essay on the Historical School of Law appeared. Yet his continuing engagement with these other and – as he thought – interconnected themes are evident in his writings for the *Rheinische Zeitung*.

Like other Young Hegelians – Ruge, Bauer, Köppen and Feuerbach – Karl progressed towards a more explicit commitment to a republican position during 1842. Referring to his intended essay on Hegel's political philosophy, Karl wrote to Ruge on 5 March, 'the central point is the struggle against *constitutional monarchy* as a hybrid which from beginning to end contradicts and abolishes itself'. But he also noted that the term *Res Publica* was quite untranslatable into German. In his contributions to the *Rheinische Zeitung*, therefore, he contrasted the 'Christian state' to the 'true state', 'rational state' or, sometimes, just 'the state'.[69]

An attack upon 'the Christian state' meant a critique of its theoretical underpinnings. These included the 'positive' philosophy of Schelling, the political theory of Stahl, the dismissal of reason as found in the 'Historical School', and the defence of religious censorship in the Catholic *Kölnische Zeitung*, the *Rheinische Zeitung*'s main local rival. To explain how these ideas found expression in political practice, Karl wrote lengthy critical articles on the proceedings of the Rhine Province Estates Assembly, dissecting what he perceived as its self-serving reasoning and its defence of private interests. He covered its debates on the freedom of the press, on the publication of its proceedings, and on new and harsher laws concerning thefts of dead wood.[70]

To describe these writings as journalism is somewhat misleading. Nearly all the articles were long, some exceedingly so – both accounts of the proceedings of the Estates were between forty and fifty pages long. They were not forms of investigative reporting aimed at uncovering the existence of concealed facts, and were almost exclusively concerned with the principle of press freedom, 'an embodiment of the idea', in contrast to censorship, 'the world outlook of semblance'.[71] Engels later claimed that Karl's awareness of the importance of economic facts first resulted from an investigation into the condition of the wine-growing peasants of the Moselle. But the *Rheinische Zeitung* article focused not upon the condition of the peasants, but upon the way in which censorship had undermined the claim of government officials to possess a superior insight into the plight of the governed. In short, Karl's articles can best be understood as exercises in applied philosophy. The conflict between the immanent and the transcendent, which from the mid-1830s had first pitted the Young Hegelians against the Prussian state in the sphere of religion and metaphysics, was now being played out in the realm of politics and history. Or, as Karl put it, philosophy had now come into 'contact and interaction with the real world of its day'. This would mean that 'philosophy has become worldly and the world has become philosophical'.[72]

Pre-1848 Prussia was a complex amalgam of feudal, absolutist, liberal and individualist features. Despite the continuity represented by its ruling house and the large manorial estates found in its eastern provinces, Prussia under Friedrich Wilhelm IV bore little relation to its essentially Eastern European and rationalist eighteenth-century forebear. It was a polity radically transformed by military defeat, restructured in the 'Reform Era', and then much enlarged in the non-Protestant west as a result of the post-revolutionary settlement of 1815. It combined feudal and absolutist features – lack of equality before the law and a hierarchical estate system – with vigorous economic expansion underpinned by the erosion of patrimonial relations in the countryside, the growth of a free market in land and migration to the towns; in the towns themselves, the partial opening up of occupations, the removal of guild privileges and the liberalization of the labour market.[73] For all its emphasis upon the restoration of traditional Christianity, the Prussian government of Friedrich Wilhelm IV in the 1840s made no attempt to reverse the process of economic change, introduced during the 'Reform Era'. The enlargement of the *Zollverein* and the extension of the free market remained central to its ambitions; the distress of the Moselle wine growers was one by-product of this government strategy.[74]

The anti-rationalist ethos of the regime was also far from traditional. Secular society in the arguments of feudal apologists, like von Haller, was akin to the state of nature.[75] In this way, authority and hierarchy could accommodate forms of activity that were aggressively competitive and individualist. In contrast to the views of rationalists and Hegelians, there was no bridge from logic to reality, since being or reality preceded thought. The creation of the universe was not an act governed by reason; it was solely a product of God's will. Stahl applied this reasoning to the monarch, who was no more bounded by the constitution than was God by his creation. By the same token, the rights of private proprietors were likened to the pre-social rights of individuals, and deemed as absolute as the monarch's over the state. The resulting state was an aggregation of transcendent authorities, while those beneath, the people, were merely a 'rabble of individuals'.[76]

In such a polity, claims made by the regime's supporters for the state or the nation as a political community were kept to the minimum. Man was an isolated and non-social being, and freedom was an individual property rather than a universal attribute. The inhabitants of this state were tied together by their commitment to the Christian faith. But there was no collective dimension to salvation; personal salvation was an individual matter. Confronted by the threat of revolution, which had once more re-emerged in 1830, and irreligion in its wake, the 'Christian state' required new ways to shape and control opinion. For this reason, as Karl argued, censorship had been redefined in such a way that the rationalism once embraced during the 'Reform Era' was now penalized as a threat to religion.[77]

In the *Rheinische Zeitung* articles, Karl retained the historical periodization which he and Bauer had employed in *The Trumpet*. In the golden age of Greece, 'art and rhetoric supplanted religion'. Similarly, in both Greece and Rome, the true religion of the ancients had been 'the cult of "their nationality", of their "state"'.[78] Conversely, in the centuries following the fall of the ancients, the people had been dominated by Christianity, feudalism and Romanticism. It was an epoch in which man was subordinated to an 'animal law'. Such a principle was paramount within the knightly estate, which was an embodiment of the 'modern feudal principle, in short the Romantic principle'. In their feudal conception of freedom as a special privilege belonging to certain groups and persons, it was believed that the privileges of the estates were 'in no way rights of the province'.[79] This was also true of the Assembly of Estates as a whole, which identified the law with the representation of particular interests.[80]

Karl continued to identify Christianity not only with feudalism, but also with fetishism. In the light of Bauer's dismissal and Ruge's conflict with von Rochow, the Prussian Minister of the Interior, Karl wrote to Ruge that although it was remarkable that 'the degradation of the people to the level of animals has become for the government an article of faith and principle', this did not contradict 'religiosity'. 'For the deification of animals is probably the most consistent form of religion, and perhaps it will soon be necessary to speak of religious zoology instead of religious anthropology.'[81]

The same thought was developed in Karl's account of the 'Debates on the Law on Thefts of Wood'. Having attacked 'the so-called customs of the privileged classes' as 'customs contrary to the law', he went on to argue that:

> their origin dates to the period in which human history was part of *natural history*, and in which according to Egyptian legend, all Gods concealed themselves in the shape of animals. Humans appeared to fall into definite species of animals, which were connected not by equality, but by inequality, an inequality fixed by laws ... whereas human law is the mode of existence of freedom, this animal law is the mode of existence of un-freedom. *Feudalism* in the broadest sense is the *spiritual animal kingdom*, the world of divided mankind.[82]

Equally guilty of fetishism were 'those writers of fantasy' who were responsible for enthroning 'the immoral, irrational and soulless abstraction of a particular material object and a particular consciousness which is slavishly subordinated to this object'. This *'abject materialism'* was the result of the belief that the legislator 'should think only of wood and forest and solve each material problem *in a non-political way*, i.e., without any connection with the whole of the reason and morality of the state'.[83]

This framework also enabled Karl to settle his differences with the Historical School of Law. The occasion was the fiftieth anniversary of the doctorate of its founder, Gustav Hugo.[84] Like the Young Hegelians, Hugo also claimed that his thought was inspired by Kant. But the Kant celebrated by Hugo was not the idealist, but the thinker who was sceptical about the limits of reason. 'He was a sceptic as regards the *necessary essence* of things.' All that mattered was 'the positive', the factual, and Hugo had taken pleasure in demonstrating that no rational necessity was inherent in positive institutions like property, the state constitution or marriage. By the same token, it was also possible to justify slavery. The slave might receive a better education and the lot of the slave might be preferable to that of the prisoner of war or the convict. If claims for reason could not be substantiated, then '*the sole juristic distinguishing feature* of *man* is his *animal* nature ... *Only what is animal* seems to *his reason* to be *indubitable*.'[85] Karl likened what he called Hugo's 'frivolity' to that of the 'courtiers' and 'roués' of the *Ancien Régime*. This conservative and empiricist emphasis on 'the positive' in history and law had thereafter been followed in the work of Haller, Stahl and Leo.[86]

5. REIMAGINING THE REPUBLIC

Karl's criticism in the *Rheinische Zeitung* was based upon the juxtaposition between 'the Christian state' and the 'rational' state. In contrast to the 'Christian state', which was 'not a free association of moral human beings, but an association of believers', philosophy demanded that 'the state should be a state of human nature', and this meant freedom, since 'freedom is so much the essence of man that even its opponents implement it while combating its reality'. 'The true "public" education carried out by the state' lay in 'the rational and public existence of the state; the state itself educates its members by making them its members, by converting the aims of the individual into general aims, crude instinct into moral inclination, natural independence into spiritual freedom, by the individual finding his good in the life of the whole, and the whole in the frame of mind of the individual.'[87] Freedom existed in the state as *law*, for laws were 'the positive, clear, universal norms in which freedom has acquired an impersonal, theoretical existence independent of the arbitrariness of the individual'. A 'statute law' was 'a people's Bible of freedom' and it was defended by 'the free press'.[88]

Although the *Rheinische Zeitung* advertised itself as a liberal news-paper, the 'rational state' invoked by Karl was quite distinct from that of constitutional liberalism. It was really an update of the Greek *polis*, which he and Bruno Bauer had lauded in the *Trumpet*. Atheism and republicanism went hand in hand. This was a republicanism which employed Hegel's notion of the forward movement and collective rationality of Spirit to restate the political vision embodied in Rous-seau's conception of the general will. Recent philosophy, according to Karl, proceeded from 'the idea of the whole'. It looked on the state 'as the great organism, in which legal, moral and political freedom must be realised, and in which the individual citizen in obeying the laws of the state only obeys the natural laws of his own reason, of human reason'.[89]

These articles made little or no reference to parliamentary represen-tation, the division of powers, or the rights of the individual. Clearly, representation was unacceptable in the local case of provincial estates, whose purpose was that of representing 'their *particular provincial in-terests* from the standpoint of their *particular estate interests*'.[90] But there was a larger objection to representation. 'In general, to be repre-sented is something passive; only what is material, spiritless, unable to rely on itself, imperilled, requires to be represented; but no element of the state should be material, spiritless, unable to rely on itself, imper-illed.' Representation could only be conceived as 'the people's *self-representation*'.[91] Such an idea did not recognize particular interests. It could only mean the representation of the whole by the whole. 'In a true state, there is no landed property, no industry, no material thing, which as a crude element of this kind could make a bargain with the state; in it there are only *spiritual forces*, and only in their state forms of resurrection in their political rebirth, are these natural forces en-titled to a voice in the state ... The state', he went on, 'pervades the whole of nature with spiritual nerves', and at every point, what was to be apparent was 'not matter, but form . . . not the *unfree object*' but the '*free human being*'.[92]

Young Hegelianism had grown out of the battle of ideas following the publication of David Strauss's *Life of Jesus* in 1835. By 1842, Karl's republicanism was one variant of a common position shared by the Bauer brothers, Ruge and Feuerbach. As the *Rheinische Zeitung* art-icles testify, it was a political position remote from the arguments of

Hegel himself. The main area of contention concerned the distinction, made in Hegel's *Philosophy of Right*, between the 'state' and 'civil society'. For the effect of this distinction was to exclude the possibility of the direct and democratic participation of the citizenry in the government of the modern state.

Hegel thought one of the most dangerous features of the French Revolution had been the untrammelled rule of a single assembly, such as that of the Convention in 1792–3, which had been based upon the assumption that all (males) were capable of discharging the duties both of man and of citizen. The disturbing association of popular sovereignty with terror proved a strong deterrent to further democratic experimentation in the aftermath of the revolutionary period. This had been evident in Hegel's conception of politics.

Hegel had first attempted to return to Aristotle's classical distinction between politics and household. In Aristotle's *Politics*, the state had been principally divided into two components, the *polis*, the public space for the political deliberation of citizens, and the *oikos*, the family or household, the habitat of women and slaves, the site of the material reproduction of life.[93] As Hegel had soon found, however, this classical distinction, at least as Aristotle formulated it, could not be sustained. The material reproduction of life was no longer confined to the household. Not only had slavery disappeared in medieval Europe, but, in addition to agriculture, much of the activity of the modern world was now dependent upon commerce. For this reason, Hegel had revised Aristotle's conception by introducing a third component, *civil society*, as a new space which had opened up between the family and the formal constitution of the state.[94]

Reacting against the democratic assumptions of 1792, Hegel had also attempted to formulate a modern version of Aristotle's assumption that the exercise of political virtue was dependent upon freedom from material necessity and need.[95]

In the *Philosophy of Right*, he attempted to preserve the connection between political virtue and material independence by embodying it in a 'universal' class of *Beamten*: tenured and economically independent civil servants. This was now to be contrasted with the sphere of 'civil society', or what he termed 'the state of necessity'. 'The creation of civil society', according to Hegel, belonged to 'the modern world'; it was what Adam Smith and others had described as 'commercial' society. 'In civil society, each individual is his own end and all else means nothing to him.' If the state was 'necessary' here, it was only because the individual 'cannot accomplish the full extent of his ends without reference to others; these others are therefore means to the end of the particular person'.

Civil society had come into being when antiquity had ended with the destruction of the Greek *polis* and of the Roman Republic. Thereafter, with the advent of the Roman Empire, the spread of Christianity, the development of Roman Law and the elaboration of a 'system of needs' (Hegel's term for the structure of commercial society) had each in different ways nurtured the growth of what Hegel called 'subjective particularity'. This encompassed the unmediated relationship of the individual to God, freedom of individual judgement, subjectivity, the self-interested pursuit of personal goals, individualism. This was a principle to which the ancient *polis* could assign no legitimate place.

According to Hegel, it was the ability of the modern state to incorporate subjective freedom within a political community that was also its great strength. But this achievement came at a certain cost. In contrast to the direct and immediate relationship between the citizen and the ancient *polis*, in the modern state members of civil society were only connected to the polity by a complicated system of 'mediations' (corporations, estates, etc.). Looked at in the aftermath of the 1830 revolutions, even sympathetic critics like Eduard Gans, Hegel's closest follower at the University of Berlin, characterized the state described in Hegel's *Philosophy of Right* as a form of tutelage. In the eyes of the Young Hegelians, the defect of Hegel's theory of the state was that the activity of the person was restricted to a role in civil society: to make contracts, to be part of a profession or trade, to enjoy freedom of religious and private life. What was missing was the ability to play a full and participant part as a citizen.

The end of the *polis* and the decline of the Roman Empire had also been accompanied by the growth of Christianity; and in the eyes of its republican critics from Machiavelli onwards the Christian religion was deeply implicated in, if not wholly responsible for, the genesis of civil society. Christianity detached the notion of a person from that of a citizen. The young Ludwig Feuerbach as a student under Hegel in 1828 argued that the Christian idea of the immortality of the soul originated as a replacement for the ancient idea of the citizen. But already in the eighteenth century Gibbon and Voltaire had highlighted Christianity's contribution to the decline of ancient political life and the fall of Rome. Rousseau pushed the argument further by blaming the combination of Christianity and commerce for the decline of patriotism, and by attacking Christianity in particular for its otherworldly preoccupations.[96]

The identification of the Prussian state with Christianity and civil society was common to Bruno Bauer, Arnold Ruge and Karl himself. In Karl's case, civil society was the Christian idea of the self, the feudal idea of freedom as privilege, and the rule of 'animal law', which embodied the competitive struggle associated with the law of nature. But the sharpest attribution of responsibility came from Feuerbach, who argued not only that Christianity fostered individualism, but that it actively prevented the emergence of a communal ethos. For it replaced the primordial species-unity of 'I and Thou' by the particular union of each individual with a personal external being: with Christ.

In the 1830s, the long-standing republican attack upon the relationship between Christianity and civic spirit was reinforced by a novel form of pantheistic criticism which came from France and was contained within the 'New Christianity' preached by the Saint-Simonians. Orthodox Christianity was criticized for its indifference or hostility towards 'matter', the body and productive work. Following the Saint-Simonians, therefore, the republicanism espoused by the Young Hegelians would be not only political, but also social. Production was what related the individual to society. All forms of activity, whether material or spiritual, would take place in the same communal context. In such a republic, civil society would be invigorated by public spirit. According to Ruge, material and spiritual pursuits would converge, and collective activity would replace the desire for private gain. The 'fellowship of prayer', as Feuerbach put it, would be replaced by the 'fellowship of work'. Or, as Karl argued, the activity of spirit was revealed equally in the construction of railways as in the political deliberations of the people.

In sum, the republican platform shared by the Young Hegelians of 1842 already possessed a distinctive social dimension provoked by the need to overcome the division between state and civil society delineated by Hegel. In Karl's case, therefore, the aim was not to discover a different way of combining civil society with the rational state, but to devise a state in which this distinction had disappeared.

6. THE END OF THE *RHEINISCHE ZEITUNG*

The battle between the king's ministers and officials carried on throughout the rest of 1842. In March, von Rochow, the Minister of the Interior,
had wanted the paper closed down, but Bodelschwingh thought more
strenuous censorship would be sufficient, while Eichhorn continued to
think the ultramontane threat was the greater. Von Rochow thought the
paper dangerous because it was spreading French liberal ideas, and the
king shared his view. When von Rochow was removed from his post,
the new Minister of the Interior, Arnim Boitzenberg, received no serious
complaints about the paper until the end of July. In November, the king
was enraged again by the publication in the *Rheinische Zeitung* of a leaked
draft of a new divorce law, and demanded to know its source. Arnim
Boitzenberg was unwilling to create a martyr or to give the impression
that this extreme draft was an accurate indication of forthcoming legislation. A compromise was therefore reached. The newspaper would
have to get rid of its ostensible editor, Rutenberg, and to put forward an
editorial position which could be compatible with the current law.

A reply was drafted by Karl in the name of the proprietor, Renard.
It was an adroit and cleverly framed document, making skilful use of
existing legislation together with royal and ministerial pronouncements.[97]
He argued that the *Rheinische Zeitung* supported Prussian leadership
in Germany, pushed for the expansion of the *Zollverein*, advocated
German rather than French liberalism, and promoted North German
'science' over French and South German 'frivolity'. The newspaper
would in future steer clear of religious issues, would moderate its tone
and would accept the dismissal of Rutenberg.

The position of the paper remained precarious, and worsened again
around the end of the year. Publications sympathetic to Young Hegelian positions were banned, including Ruge's *Deutsche Jahrbücher*,
Buhl's journal in Berlin and the Saxon *Leipziger Allgemeine Zeitung*.
Finally, on 23 January, the government announced that the paper must
cease publication on 1 April 1843.

The ban was not popular among provincial officials because it would
increase tension between the Prussian state and the local population.
Wilhelm von Saint-Paul, a civil servant from Berlin, was therefore

dispatched to oversee censorship during the remaining months. Earlier on, the paper had not made much impact upon the lower middle classes in the province – artisans, small merchants, shopkeepers and peasants. By October and November, there had been a significant increase in circulation from 885 to 1,880 copies. Furthermore, once the impending ban on the paper became known, the paper benefited from a wave of sympathy as a victim of arbitrary power, and by the end of January 1843 subscriptions had mounted to 3,400. At the same time, Jung and Oppenheim organized an effective petitioning campaign in major cities throughout the Rhineland to demand the lifting of the ban.

The increasing success of the paper was also due to the more coherent strategy of the new editor. Karl joined the editorial collective on 15 October, and quickly became known as the driving force behind its policy. It was he who had originally brought in his Berlin friend Rutenberg as editor. In July, he had admitted to Ruge that Rutenberg was 'a weight on my conscience', was 'absolutely incapable' and, sooner or later, would be 'shown the door'.[98]

As a result of Rutenberg's weakness and poor judgement, cronies from Berlin – Meyen, Köppen, Buhl and others – treated the paper as their 'docile organ' and spared no effort to interject anti-Christian polemic into the most inappropriate items. As Karl confessed to Ruge on 30 November, 'I have allowed myself to throw out as many articles as the censor' since 'Meyen and Co. sent us heaps of scribblings pregnant with revolutionising the world and empty of ideas, written in a slovenly style and seasoned with a little atheism and communism'.[99] Fortunately, the government had not realized that Rutenberg 'was not a danger to anyone but the *Rheinische Zeitung* and himself', and had demanded his removal.

As editor of the newspaper, Karl's best qualities and abilities came to the fore. His assumption was that 'the *Rheinische Zeitung* should not be guided by its contributors, but that, on the contrary, it should guide them'.[100] Secondly, as a Rhinelander, he had a clearer conception of the paper's likely constituency. He realized that in an overwhelmingly Catholic province, crude exercises in anti-Christian polemic would be counter-productive, and much feeling in the Rhineland, whether Catholic or Protestant, was not sectarian. On the other hand, defence of the liberties of the province against Prussian government interference was likely to receive widespread support. In his article on 'Thefts of Wood',

Karl concluded that 'the sense of right and legality is the *most important provincial characteristic* of the Rhinelander'.[101] Therefore any political position must be developed from the local and the concrete. Writing to Oppenheim about Edgar Bauer's attack upon 'half-hearted liberalism' or the *'juste milieu'* – a position with which Karl himself in principle agreed – he argued that 'quite general theoretical arguments about the state political system are more suitable for purely scientific organs than for newspapers', and that 'newspapers only begin to be the appropriate arena for such questions when these have become questions of the real state, practical questions'. The use of abstract and general arguments against the state was not only likely to result in the intensification of censorship, but also to 'arouse the resentment of many, indeed the majority, of the free-thinking practical people who have undertaken the laborious task of winning freedom step by step, within the constitutional framework'.[102]

Karl first expressed his irritation with the contributions from Berlin in July 1842. He wrote to Ruge, asking for details on the so-called 'Free', a new grouping of his Berlin friends. To declare for emancipation was honest, he argued, but to shout it out as propaganda would irritate the 'philistine' and only provoke more censorship. Dr Hermes, 'the mouthpiece of philistinism' and leader-writer in the Catholic *Kölnische Zeitung*, would 'probably saddle him with the "Free"'. He was relieved that Bauer was in Berlin and wouldn't 'allow any stupidities to be committed'.[103]

But Bruno Bauer doesn't seem to have exercised a restraining influence, and at the end of November matters came to a head. On a visit to Berlin, Georg Herwegh, the radical and formerly exiled poet, had been mocked by the 'Free' for his radical pretensions. He was attacked, in particular, for meeting with the king and for making an opportunistic marriage. Incensed by this reception, he wrote to the *Rheinische Zeitung*, complaining that 'the revolutionary Romanticism' of the 'Free' and 'this second-rate aping of French clubs' were compromising 'our cause and our party'.[104] Karl shared Herwegh's attitude and accused Eduard Meyen, one of the leaders of the Berlin group, of holding opinions which were 'licentious' and 'sansculotte-like'.[105] Ruge also visited Berlin to plead with Bruno Bauer to break with the 'Free' and adopt no other stance than that of an 'objective scholar'.[106] In turn, Bauer claimed that he could not abandon Meyen, Buhl, Köppen and Stirner. A few days later, he also wrote to Karl complaining about the misrepresentations and factual inaccuracies of Herwegh's claims, and attacked Karl for accepting Herwegh's position. But he ended on a more conciliatory note: 'I would rather write to you about things which are more pleasant and nearer to us.'[107]

1842 had been a disenchanting year for Bauer. In the previous year, his reputation among radical Young Hegelians had been at its peak. The two volumes of the *Synoptics* had pushed biblical criticism way beyond Strauss. Furthermore, his direct criticisms of Strauss's attempt to qualify the implications of *The Life of Jesus* had been strongly supported by Arnold Ruge in the *Deutsche Jahrbücher* even though this had led to Strauss's withdrawal, and the defection of moderate subscribers to the journal.[108] In his preface to the *Deutsche Jahrbücher* in July 1841, Ruge had also supported Bauer's claim that the movement of self-consciousness was identical with that of history itself. This was why Bauer sometimes imagined himself as the new Socrates come to break up the Christian world. Ruge had also endorsed as a transition from theory to practice Bauer's confidence in the power of 'criticism' to dissolve all merely 'positive' phenomena.

Bauer maintained this confidence up to his final dismissal. In March 1842 he had declared that a new epoch was beginning, while Karl added approvingly that 'philosophy speaks intelligibly with the state wisdom of these over-assured scoundrels'.[109] But once the summer passed, and Karl became more deeply involved in the *Rheinische Zeitung*, a distance developed between him and his former companions in Berlin. These had rallied round Bauer after his return to the city and used all journalistic means to publicize his arguments – especially, of course, in the *Rheinische Zeitung*, edited by Rutenberg, Bauer's brother-in-law.

There was no cosmic crisis of the kind anticipated by Bauer, or comically described among the Berlin Young Hegelians in a mock epic poem written by Friedrich Engels and Bruno Bauer's brother, Edgar.[110] Furthermore, while the general population of Brandenburg-Prussia remained unaffected by Young Hegelian religious criticism, that of the Catholic Rhineland was likely to be infuriated.

For the most part, the differences between Karl and Bruno Bauer in the course of 1842 were tactical and situational. How was philosophy to address the nation outside the enclaves of radical academia or Berlin bohemia? But as the fruitlessness of Bauer's atheist challenge became increasingly apparent in the course of the year, the position of Karl, Ruge and other Young Hegelians on the centrality of the religious question underwent a basic shift. In response to the complaints of Eduard Meyen in Berlin, at the end of November 1842, Karl wrote to Ruge, 'I asked that religion should be criticised in the framework of criticism of political conditions rather than that political conditions should be criticised in the framework of religion, since this was more in accord with the nature of a newspaper and the educational level of the reading public.' But this now also signalled a more fundamental change of position. 'For religion is without content; it owes its being not to heaven, but to earth; and with the abolition of distorted reality, of which it is the *theory*, it will collapse of itself.'[111]

In the last few months of its existence, the *Rheinische Zeitung* – with apparently nothing more to lose – became bolder. In response to anger provoked by the impending suppression of the newspaper, Arnim toyed with the idea of allowing some of the anti-Christian writing to be published uncensored as a way of alienating the Rhineland readership. The Prussian official Wilhelm von Saint-Paul, who reported to Berlin that Karl was the doctrinal middle point and theoretical inspiration of the paper, also speculated whether the newspaper might continue in a more moderate form if he departed. But the government remained adamant, not least because of pressure from Nicholas I, the Russian czar and brother-in-law of Friedrich Wilhelm IV, who had been outraged by a polemical article denouncing the alliance between the two countries.[112]

On 2 March 1843, Saint-Paul reported that in the present circumstances Karl had decided to give up his connection with the *Rheinische Zeitung* and to leave Prussia; and on 16 March Karl definitively resigned. The government came to think that it had over-estimated the dangers of the paper, given how little its abstract idealism influenced practical demands. Furthermore, given Karl's 'ultra-democratic' opinions, Saint-Paul wondered whether a moderate paper might take its place after his departure; others on the paper were instinctively radical, but were not so adept at connecting it up with the 'Ruge–Marx–Bauer' doctrine. But nothing came of it. As for the Catholic threat – the original reason for encouraging the establishment of the paper in the first place – Saint-Paul was able to establish good relations with Dr Hermes, the main leader-writer on the *Kölnische Zeitung*, and therefore to establish a friendlier treatment of the Berlin government in the future.[113]

Karl wrote to Ruge informing him about the banning of the *Rhein-ische Zeitung* and about his own resignation at the end of January 1843: 'It is a bad thing to have to perform menial duties even for the sake of freedom; to fight with pinpricks, instead of with clubs. I have become tired of hypocrisy, stupidity, gross arbitrariness, and of our bowing and scraping, dodging and hair-splitting over words. Consequently, the government has given me back my freedom.' He added, 'I can do nothing more in Germany.'[114]

5

The Alliance of Those Who Think and Those Who Suffer: Paris, 1844

I. PROLOGUE

One of the most enduring effects of the 1848 revolutions was to draw clearer lines between liberals, republicans and socialists. In Prussia, this divergence had taken place four years earlier, in the years 1843–4. Until that time, it had still been possible to think about a *'Bewegungspartei'* – a 'party of movement' ranging from the reform-minded liberal shareholders of the *Rheinische Zeitung* through to the socialism of Moses Hess or the republican nationalism of Arnold Ruge. Hopes still centred upon a reform of consciousness building upon radicalized versions of Kantian and Hegelian idealism and spearheaded by a free press. Aspirations were framed not in the language of happiness or well-being, but in that of self-determination and freedom. The aim was to realize a state in which 'the individual citizen in obeying the laws of the state only obeys the natural laws of his own reason, of human reason'.

As long as hope of change still prevailed, attention was paid to nuances of political position, to glimpses of struggles between contending parties behind closed doors, and to the possible re-emergence of a reform agenda within government and administration. The memory of the 'Reform Era' or of the national mobilization of 1813–14, and the presence until the beginning of the 1840s of influential veterans of those times, softened the lines of division within the forces of progress. But in the face of the intransigent stance of the new government, the removal of an oppositional press and the absence of effective resistance, positions soon hardened. Moderate reformers were reduced to silence, radicals were forced into exile.

This was a situation in which the broad alliance of the *Bewegungspartei* foundered and unity within the Young Hegelian movement broke down. By mid-1844, Karl was estranged from both Bruno Bauer and Arnold Ruge. He had become a 'communist', an advocate of 'social revolution'.[1] The fragility of the alliance between liberals and radicals had been apparent from the 1830s and was pinpointed by differences of attitude towards the parliamentary monarchy of Louis Philippe in France. This regime, which had attained power after the July Revolution of 1830, was the sort of government German liberals would have striven for. But it soon found itself, in 1831, embarked upon a programme of repression, both of republicans in Paris and of workers in Lyons and other provincial centres. Its *juste milieu* liberalism was attacked by Legitimist supporters of the deposed Bourbons, on the right, and by a broad array of radicals, republicans and socialists on the left.

Less readily understandable was the split between republicans and 'communists' within the Young Hegelian group. Why did Karl break with those who held a socially informed republican position? Three elements account for what otherwise might have looked like an arbitrary lurch on Karl's part towards 'communism' in the winter of 1843–4.

The first element was self-evident: the failure of the politics of self-consciousness to bring about any change in the policies of the state. The feebleness of the reaction to the suppression of the *Rheinische Zeitung* or Ruge's *Deutsche Jahrbücher* from any quarter of Prussian society also led to disenchantment with the strategy of 'criticism'. The second, and crucial, element was the emergence of an alternative philosophical path beyond Hegel, which had been outlined by Feuerbach. The politics of enlightenment and the development of self-consciousness were ideally suited to the process of religious and juridical criticism, but, unlike the position developed by Feuerbach, had no distinctive viewpoint in relation to the questions which were to dominate political life in the 1840s and to constitute the third element: the condition of the 'proletariat' and 'the social problem'. All three elements were closely interconnected. Seen from the perspective of 'criticism', it was difficult to accord special significance to the proletariat, a class whose distinguishing features were material misery and lack of education. But seen from the perspective of a 'human' or 'social' revolution, which Karl inferred from premises laid down by Feuerbach, such a class could be accorded a central role.

2. KREUZNACH

Karl finally withdrew from the *Rheinische Zeitung* on 16 March 1843. He had already decided to leave Germany, and from January had been looking for other work, first with Herwegh in Switzerland, then with Ruge in Saxony, Belgium or France.[2] He had also determined to get married. For, as he wrote to Ruge on 25 January, he would not leave without his fiancée. Once arrangements for the marriage were finally settled, he wrote again on 13 March, telling Ruge that he would travel to Kreuznach, marry and 'spend a month or more there at the home of my wife's mother, so that before starting work we should have at any rate a few articles ready'.

Marriage brought to an end long and bumpy years of engagement, which became particularly tense after the death of Heinrich, but even more so following the demise of Jenny's father, Ludwig. As Karl explained to Ruge:

> I have been engaged for more than seven years, and for my sake my fiancée has fought the most violent battles, which almost undermined her health, partly against her pietistic aristocratic relatives, for whom 'the Lord in heaven' and the 'lord in Berlin' are equally objects of religious cult, and partly against my own family, in which some priests and other enemies of mine have ensconced themselves. For years, therefore, my fiancée and I have been engaged in more unnecessary and exhausting conflicts than many who are three times our age and continually talk of their 'life experience' (the favourite phrase of our Juste-Milieu).

Despite all this, he told Ruge, 'I can assure you, without the slightest romanticism, that I am head over heels in love, and indeed in the most serious way.'[3]

The marriage took place on 19 June in Kreuznach in the Palatinate, eighty miles from Trier, and the centre of a wine-growing district famous for its Riesling and Silvaner grapes. Ludwig's death had been followed by that of an aunt, who also lived with them. Jenny then moved temporarily to Kreuznach with her mother, Caroline, probably

out of economic need; Karl had already visited her there. According to
Jenny's friend Betty Lucas, Bettina von Arnim, the famous Romantic
writer and social critic, visited Kreuznach in October 1842 and insisted
that Karl accompany her on a walk to the Rheingrafenstein, a famous
castle and local beauty spot, a good hour away from their home. Karl
had apparently followed Bettina 'with a melancholy glance at his
bride'.[4]

The marriage was celebrated in St Paul's church, Kreuznach, by a
preacher whose appointment dated back to Jacobin times; among the
witnesses were one of Karl's schoolboy contemporaries and a local inn-
keeper. Henriette did not attend the wedding, but sent her written
consent. After the wedding, according to Jenny's account, 'we went
from Kreuznach to Rhein-Pfalz via Ebernburg and returned via
Baden-Baden. Then we stayed at Kreuznach till the end of September.
My dear mother returned to Trier with my brother Edgar.'[5] Karl and
Jenny left for Paris at the end of October.

Karl had earlier hoped to co-edit *Deutscher Bote* (*German Messenger*)
with Herwegh in Zurich, and on 19 February Herwegh wrote about a
possible collaboration. But this plan ended when the authorities closed
down the *Bote* and expelled Herwegh. Arnold Ruge had also agreed to the
Bote plan, but his primary aim was to secure the 'essential rebirth' of the
Deutsche Jahrbücher. So next he offered Karl co-editorship and a fixed
income of 550–600 thalers with another 250 thalers for other writings.
The new journal would establish 'radical philosophy on the foundations of
the freedom of the press' and would 'articulate the question of the political
crisis or of general consciousness as it begins to form itself'. The immediate
aim would be 'to prepare ourselves, so that later we may jump in among
the philistines fully armed and knock them out with one blow'.[6]

Karl's politics had closely followed those of Ruge ever since the end
of the 1830s. In 1842 and 1843, their responses to immediate events,
not least the 'frivolous' diatribes of the 'Free', had remained very close.
An established author, and in possession of independent means, 'Papa
Ruge' – as Jenny called him – was clearly the senior partner in this collaboration. The banning of the *Deutsche Jahrbücher* in January 1843 as
the result of Prussian pressure, together with the suppression of the
Rheinische Zeitung, meant the effective silencing of Young Hegelianism within Germany. The aim of criticism, as it was employed among
Young Hegelians, was to highlight the gap between the demands of

reason and the behaviour of the government, but its failure to make any significant headway against the Prussia of Friedrich Wilhelm IV had also pushed them both towards an open criticism of Hegel's political philosophy.

During his summer in Kreuznach, Karl attempted to complete the critique of Hegel's *Philosophy of Right* which he had promised to the *Deutsche Jahrbücher* as far back as the spring of 1842. Initially conceived as a critique of constitutional monarchy, by the time he returned to the topic, his criticism of Hegel's philosophy had been fundamentally transformed by expansive application of Ludwig Feuerbach's philosophical approach. Feuerbach offered a different way of reading Hegel and this was spelled out in his essay entitled 'Preliminary Theses on the Reform of Philosophy', published in Ruge's *Anekdota* in Zurich in the spring of 1843, and developed further in his *Principles of the Philosophy of the Future*, published later that year.[7]

Feuerbach had become famous in 1840 as the author of *The Essence of Christianity*, which would be translated into English by George Eliot in 1854.[8] His argument was that religion was an alienated form of human emotion. Unlike animals, humans could turn their emotions into objects of thought. These emotions were re-embodied in an external being freed from the limitations of individual human existence, and in this way man had been led to project his own essence as a species upon a fictive being, God. As a result, the relationship between subject and object (or predicate) was reversed. Henceforth, it no longer appeared that man had created God, but that God had created man.

By contrast, Feuerbach began with 'man-in-nature'. 'Man' (the human being) was not simply a thinking being. Man embodied reason and freedom, but was first a 'sensuous being'. Man-in-nature was both active and passive. Just as thought had its genesis in 'real being', so 'suffering precedes thinking'. As a natural being 'man' stood in need of means of life that existed outside him, above all the elementary species-relationship, love. 'The first object of Man', wrote Feuerbach 'is Man.' As a creature of need, man depended on others. In this sense, he was a 'communal being'. The essence and starting point of man was not the 'self', but 'the unity of I and Thou'. Man came to consciousness of his humanity, of his 'species-being', through the agency of other men.

Feuerbach's construction of a 'species-being' out of the natural attributes of man led to a quite different vision of the significance of civil society from that found in Hegel. In the *Philosophy of Right*, Hegel had assigned a foundational role to need and human interdependence. What he called 'the system of needs' described the forms of exchange and interdependence that had been discovered by political economists, and which underpinned modern commercial society. But Hegel did not regard civil society as the true sphere of human freedom; nor did he see in it the capacity to become so. It was the sphere of necessity, the 'external state' governed by the selfish individual needs and desires of natural man. Man's true being as spirit could only be actualized in 'the state'. For Feuerbach, by contrast, man's only existence was that of a natural being, governed by need. On this basis, however, it was possible to conceive of the interdependence of civil society as the basis of the communal nature of man and to envisage the gradual flowering of a society which would be in accordance with the 'species-being'.

The development of Christianity had blocked the emergence of such a society. Christianity had transformed the communal character of the human species into the particular union of each individual with an external being. Religion was, therefore, responsible for the individualism of modern society. Between the individual and the universality of the species was now interposed an external mediator. In place of the primordial species-unity of 'I and Thou', the role of 'Thou' had been usurped by Christ. Protestantism, in particular, with its emphasis upon the individual conscience and the priesthood of all believers, had dismantled the spiritual community of medieval religion and inspired an egotistical withdrawal from communal life and a material world divested of sanctity.

In the 'Preliminary Theses on the Reform of Philosophy', Feuerbach extended his criticism to Hegel's philosophy. Hegel's incarnation of 'Absolute Spirit' in history presupposed an extra-human perspective that had no natural basis. It was an extension of Christian theology. Just as Christianity had originally alienated man from his emotions, so Hegel had alienated man from his thought, and common to both was the method of 'abstraction'. 'To abstract means to posit the *essence* of nature *outside nature*, the *essence* of Man *outside Man*, the *essence* of thought *outside the act of thinking*. The Hegelian philosophy has alienated Man *from himself* in so far as its whole system is based on these acts of abstraction.'[9]

These abstractions, as Feuerbach emphasized, possessed no independent existence. All could be resolved into empirical natural terms, and redescribed in the language of nature and history. Abstraction was an expression of man's own rational nature and capacities. The impression that such abstractions possessed an objective existence outside humanity was the result of man's alienation from nature, and in particular from his own social nature. This was particularly acute in the case of idealist philosophies like those of Fichte or Hegel, which began with the 'I' or 'self' in isolation. 'Two human beings are needed for the generation of man, of the intellectual as well as the physical one.' The defect of idealism was the desire to derive ideas from the 'I' without a given sensuous 'You'. The extreme case was that of Hegel's *Science of Logic*, where terms such as concept, judgement or syllogism 'are no longer our concepts', but presented as 'objective' absolute terms existing in and for themselves. In this way, Absolute philosophy externalized and alienated 'from man his own essence and activity'.[10]

Quite independently from Feuerbach, Ruge had developed his own critique of Hegel's conception of the state. Already in 1840 he had argued that Hegel's posthumously published *Philosophy of History* – which presented states as products of rational and historical development – was superior to *The Philosophy of Right*, which explained the state in categories employed in his *Science of Logic*. In the *Deutsche Jahrbücher* in August 1842, Ruge drew upon Feuerbach's insights to elaborate his political criticism.[11] Hegel's *Philosophy of Right*, he argued, had been a child of a time which 'totally lacked public discussion and public life'. Hegel had cherished the illusion that one could be 'theoretically free without being politically free'. He had veered away from 'the nasty "should" of praxis'.[12]

After Strauss, Ruge argued, this was impossible, for 'the times' were 'political'. The problem about starting from *The Science of Logic* was that it did not confront questions about existence. Only with the entry of history into the realm of science, did existence become relevant. For Young Hegelians, '*the historical process* is the relating of theory to the historical existences of Spirit; this relating is *critique*'. By contrast, *The Philosophy of Right* raised 'existences or historical determinations to logical determinations'. This lack of any explicit distinction between the historical and the metaphysical resulted in a 'foolish juggling act' in which hereditary monarchy and the bicameral system became logical necessities. Ruge abandoned his previous identification of Prussia with rational development and Protestantism. Like Feuerbach, he now presented the Reformation as the point of separation between religion and the community, and the beginning of Hegel's picture of the 'external state' or 'civil society', in which individuals were concerned only with their private affairs.[13]

3. ROUSSEAU REVISITED: TRUE DEMOCRACY VERSUS THE MODERN REPRESENTATIVE STATE

Ruge's critique of Hegel kept within the limits of a standard republican position; Karl's critique was much more drastic. After initially complaining to Ruge that Feuerbach devoted too much attention to nature and too little to politics, his own extension of Feuerbach's critical procedure was even more ambitious.[14] In 1842, Karl's target had been 'the Christian state'; now it was 'the modern state' or 'the political state'. Like Ruge, Karl applied Feuerbach's ideas about abstraction and inversion, but what excited him most about Feuerbach's approach was seeing religion as only one instance of a more universal process of abstraction.[15] All abstractions could be resolved into aspects of human nature. Through the translation of abstractions back into the natural and historical phenomena from which they derived, it was possible – so Feuerbach had claimed – to arrive at 'the unconcealed, pure and untarnished truth'.[16]

In Karl's view this insight could be applied as much to politics as to religion. Hegel was attacked for forgetting that 'the essence of a "particular personality"' was 'its *social quality* and that state functions, etc., are nothing but modes of being and modes of action of the social qualities of men'.[17] 'Just as it is not religion which creates man, but man who creates religion, so it is not the constitution which creates the people, but the people which creates the constitution.' If this was not clear, this was because the 'political' state was not a totality, but 'a dualism', in which each individual 'must effect a fundamental division within himself between the citizen of the state and the citizen as member of civil society'.[18]

Like Ruge, Karl used Feuerbach's ideas to attack Hegel's attempt to present his theory of the state as an application of his *Science of Logic*. Hegel had made the state the creation of 'the Idea'; he had 'turned the subject of the idea into a product, a predicate, of the idea'. His procedure was to transform empirical fact into speculation, and speculation into empirical fact. In this way, 'the correct method is stood on its head'. The transition from family and civil society to the state was not derived from the nature of the family or of civil society, but seen like the purely categorical transition from the sphere of essence to that of concept in the *Science of Logic*.[19] All the terms Karl later employed to explain his difference from Hegel in his 'Postscript to *Capital*', the attempt to derive a concept of the state from a sequence of abstractions, were reiterations of the terms employed here.[20]

Was it Hegel's theory of the state, or was it the post-revolutionary state itself that was guilty of abstraction? According to Karl, Hegel was right in treating the state as an abstraction, and in taking for granted the separation of civil and political estates. 'Hegel is not to be blamed for depicting the nature of the modern state as it is, but for presenting that which is as the nature of the state.' What was peculiar to the modern state was that the constitution had been developed into 'a particular actuality alongside the actual life of the people', and, as a result of the division between the state and civil society, a situation where 'the state does not reside within, but outside society'. In this process, Karl argued, 'the *political constitution* has been *the religious sphere*, the *religion* of national life, the heaven of its generality over against the *earthly existence* of its actuality'.[21]

Such an 'abstraction of the state as such' characterized modern times, as did its cause, 'the abstraction of private life'. Karl's picture of medieval feudalism remained that which he had developed while studying Christian art in 1841. It was a period in human society in which man was turned into an animal 'identical with his function', but also one where 'every private sphere had a political character'. 'The life of the nation and the life of the state were identical.' 'Man' was the principle of the state, even if it was 'unfree man'. It was 'the democracy of unfreedom'. The political state of modern times only came into being once the 'private spheres' – trade and landed property – had gained an independent existence. This transformation of political estates into civil estates took place under the absolute monarchy, and the process was completed by the French Revolution. Henceforth, differences between estates became simply 'social differences of civil life'.[22]

Only in the 'rational state', what Karl now called 'democracy', did there exist 'a true unity of universal and particular'. 'Democracy was the solved riddle of all constitutions.' Only here was the constitution brought back 'to its actual basis, the actual human being, the actual people'. 'In democracy, the formal principle is at the same time the material principle.'[23] An imagined point of comparison was once again classical Greece. Unlike the modern state, which was a compromise between the political and unpolitical state, the ancient state was 'universal', the unity of the formal and the material. There the republic was 'the real private affair of the citizens, their real content, the true and only content of the life and will of the citizens'. In the states of antiquity, whether Greece or Rome, the political state made up the content of the state to the exclusion of all other spheres.[24]

The 'democracy' to which Karl referred was not the post-1789 *political* democracy based upon the representative principle. In the modern 'political' state, democracy could only be 'formal', since such a state presupposed the coexistence of the 'unpolitical' and the 'political', the 'man' and the 'citizen'. This was true, whether in a monarchy, in a republic, or even in a state based upon universal male suffrage. The modern state was a compromise between civil society and the state or between the 'unpolitical' and the 'political' state. Judged by these criteria, 'the entire content of the law and the state is the same in North America as in Prussia, with few modifications. The *republic* there is thus a mere state *form*, as is the monarchy here. The content of the state lies outside these constitutions.'[25]

The dominant reality in modernity was 'civil society', with its guiding principles of individualism, the 'war of all against all', and the rule of private interests. Hegel claimed that the modern state was 'the actuality of the ethical idea', but 'the identity which he has constructed between civil society and the state is the identity of two hostile armies'. Furthermore, from his presentation, it seemed that the ethical idea was simply 'the religion of private property'. The constitution was 'guaranteed' by primogeniture, while the different subdivisions of trade and industry were 'the private property of different corporations'. Similarly, the bureaucracy, according to Hegel the universal interest, only constituted one particular private aim over against others. Private property was not just 'the pillar of the constitution, but the constitution itself'.[26]

In a true democracy, there would be no place for representation as it had developed in the 'political state'. Representation was only an issue 'within the *abstraction of the political state*', when 'universality' was turned into 'external multiplicity'. What was missing was 'universality' as an 'abstract, spiritual, actual quality of the individual', such that 'all' would participate as 'all', and not as 'individuals'.[27]

In a true democracy, civil society becomes political society, 'the significance of the *legislative* power as a *representative* power' would completely disappear. Legislative power in a true democracy would only exist in the sense 'in which *every* function is representative'; for example, 'the shoemaker, insofar as he satisfies a social need, is my representative, in which every particular social activity as a species-activity merely represents the species, i.e., an attribute of my own nature, and in which every person is the representative of every other'. Furthermore, in this situation decision-making was not the result of the conflict of wills, 'rather the actual law has to be *discovered* and *formulated*'. In other words, in a 'democracy', decision-making would approximate to Rousseau's vision of the exercise of the 'General Will' in *The Social Contract*.[28]

After 130 pages, Karl abandoned this 'essay'. But the direction of the argument was reasonably clear. Change would occur when civil society declared itself to be the political state. For this completion of abstraction would at the same time be the 'transcendence of abstraction'. Signs of such a possibility were suggested by movements for political reform in France and England. For '*electoral reform* within the *abstract political state* is therefore the demand for its *dissolution*, and also for the dissolution of civil society'.[29]

One of Karl's main purposes in the manuscript was to clarify rejection of the notion of 'criticism', which he had shared with Bruno Bauer. Karl's divergence from Bauer had developed gradually. He had become familiar with Feuerbach's work at least as far back as 1839, and his impatience with the narrow focus of religious criticism was already apparent by November 1842, when he had written that religion was 'without content'. But in March 1843 his praise for Bauer's 'Self-Defence' remained wholehearted, and as late as June 1843 he apparently shared Ruge's hope that Bauer might join the journal they had in mind.[30]

But, as the year wore on, Karl's distance from the assumptions of 'criticism' became more evident. Bauer did not accept that the process of abstraction, which Feuerbach had applied in his critique of religion, could be extended to the modern state. Nor did he accept, therefore, that 'political emancipation' could be criticized in the name of 'human emancipation'. This was the basis upon which Karl attacked Bauer in the first part of the essay 'On the Jewish Question', which Karl was to publish in the *Deutsch-Französische Jahrbücher* in early 1844.

Bauer's error, Karl wrote, was only to criticize 'the Christian state', not the state as such and therefore to regard 'the political abolition of religion as the abolition of religion as such'. Bauer did not investigate the relation between 'political emancipation' and 'human emancipation'. Nor did he take account of the limitations of 'the political state' and its relationship with civil society. According to Karl, where 'the political state has attained its true development', man led a twofold life: 'life in the *political community* in which he considers himself a *communal being*, and life in *civil society* in which he acts as a *private individual*'. This was what had happened during the French Revolution, which by 'smashing all estates, corporations, guilds and privileges' associated with feudalism had 'abolished the political character of civil society'.

Political emancipation embodied in the Rights of Man did not, as Bauer thought, contradict 'privilege of faith'. Both the French Constitution of 1791 and the Constitution of Pennsylvania of 1776 treated 'the privilege of faith' as a universal right of man. The religiosity of the United States, where there had been a complete separation of church and state, was proof that the existence of religion was not in contradiction to 'the perfection of the state'. Political emancipation meant that religion was relegated to the private sphere, the sphere of civil society. In this sense, 'the perfect Christian state' was 'the atheist state, the democratic state, the state which relegates religion to a place among the other elements of civil society'.

But if the existence of religion were compatible with 'the perfection of the state', this could only mean that there was an inherent inadequacy in the notion of *political* emancipation. For the existence of religion was 'the existence of a defect', and since 'we no longer regard religion as the *cause*, but only as the *manifestation* of secular narrowness', the source of the defect had to be sought in the nature of the state itself. Political emancipation was, of course, 'a big step forward'.[31] But Bauer did not understand what Feuerbach had demonstrated: that the emancipation of the state from religion did not mean the emancipation of real men from religion.

Christianity was still in the dock, but no longer because of the mystifications of the biblical narrative, highlighted by Bauer, but rather because it had become 'the expression of man's separation from his community'. Religion had become 'the spirit of civil society', the spirit of 'the sphere of egoism, of *bellum omnium contra omnes*'. Religion was 'the recognition of man in a roundabout way, through an intermediary'. Just as the state was 'the intermediary between man and man's freedom', so 'Christ is the intermediary to whom man transfers the burden of all his divinity'. Religion addressed the individual separated from the community. That was why 'political democracy is Christian, since in it man, not merely one man but every man, ranks as sovereign, as the highest being, but it is man in his uncivilised, unsocial form, man in his fortuitous existence, man just as he is, man as he has been corrupted by the whole organisation of our society . . . in short, man who is not yet a real species being'.[32]

Like Moses Hess, Karl denounced the 1789 Declaration of the Rights of Man and the Citizen as a proclamation of the primacy of civil society over the modern political state. The right of man to liberty in the Declaration was based not on the association of man with man, but on the separation of man from man. 'It is the *right* of this separation', and 'the practical application of man's right to liberty is man's right to private property'. It was the right to enjoy and dispose of property 'without regard to other men', in other words, 'the right of self-interest'; 'none of the so-called rights of man' went beyond 'egoistic man, as a member of civil society'. There was no conception of species-being or species-life. 'The sole bond holding them together is natural necessity, need and private interest.' In sum, the citizen was 'the servant of the egoistic *homme*'. Even in the euphoria of revolution, political life declared itself to be 'a mere means, whose purpose is the life of civil society'. It was not man as citizen, but 'man as bourgeois', who was considered to be 'the essential and true man'.[33]

The ideal of political emancipation was deficient. It meant the reduction of man to the egoistic independent individual or else to the citizen, the 'juridical person'. 'Only when the real individual man reabsorbs in himself the abstract citizen, and as an individual human being has become a species-being in his everyday life . . . and consequently no longer separates social power from himself in the shape of political power, only then will human emancipation have been accomplished.'[34]

Karl's manuscript and its use in the *Deutsch-Französische Jahrbücher* to distinguish his new position from that of Bruno Bauer were important because much that was argued was to remain a feature of Karl's subsequent thought. But even in Karl's own eyes the arguments advanced could have been neither conclusive nor wholly convincing: a point suggested by the fact that Karl attempted to restate his disagreement with Bauer on at least two later occasions.

Whatever the validity of Karl's attempt to theorize not just Hegel's state, but the modern state as such, the result was a rigid and impoverished construct, in which the differences between the Prussian and the American state, for example, became secondary and inessential. Secondly, the putative alternative to the separation between civil society and the political state, between man and citizen, rested upon a wholly unexamined vision of the '*social* character' of human nature and the '*universal*' character of the individual; supported only by a fleeting reference to the Greek *polis*. For this reason Hegel was criticized for forgetting that the essence of a particular personality was 'its social quality': a criticism that effectively ignored his reasons for distinguishing between the ancient and the modern state. This inability – or refusal – to think of individuality except as an alienation from social being found enduring expression in his distaste for the idea of rights even before he began to dismiss them as a 'bourgeois' phenomenon. Lastly, the remoteness of Karl's conceptions from the realities of radical politics in nineteenth-century Britain and France was underlined by his dismissal of the idea of representation and his expectation that radical movements would press for the overcoming of the division between civil society and the political state.

4. THE SOCIAL QUESTION AND THE PROLETARIAT

The second element which helped to account for Karl's shift in position was the dramatic emergence from around 1840 of the 'proletariat' and 'the social question' as central to political debate. By 1842, labour movements had come into existence both in Britain and in France.

In France, 'communism' had become the object of public attention in 1840. The word had been brought into use by the radical republican Étienne Cabet, as a supposedly inoffensive substitute for the forbidden idea of an egalitarian republic. But 'communism' could not so easily shake off its association with the violent and insurrectionary activities associated with the egalitarian tradition: part of the reason why, as the *Communist Manifesto* claimed, Europe was so soon to become haunted by its 'spectre'.

Ultra-radical republicans had been distinguished by their emphasis on equality and by their identification with the extreme Jacobin phase of the French Revolution. There were among them followers of Robespierre, of Hébert and especially of 'Gracchus' Babeuf, who in 1796 in the name of equality had attempted to organize an uprising against the Directory (the French government following the fall of Robespierre) – hence the frequent identification between 'communism' and 'Babouvism'. Memory of this event had been revived by the veteran revolutionary conspirator and survivor of the plot Philippe Buonarroti, whose account, *Babeuf's Conspiracy for Equality*, had appeared in Brussels in 1828. The aim of the 'Equals' had been to overthrow the corrupt government of Thermidor and replace it by an emergency committee of 'wise' men (a new version of Robespierre's Committee of Public Safety). Its purpose would be to expropriate the rich, take over the land, and establish a community of goods; it would then hand back power to the people, thenceforth constituted as an egalitarian and democratic republic.

Babeuf's doctrine had reappeared within the radical republican societies formed in the aftermath of the July Revolution of 1830, like the *Société des droits de l'homme* (Society of the Rights of Man). These societies, mainly composed of Paris-based students and artisans, regarded the parliamentary monarchy, propertied franchise and laissez-faire economics of the new 'citizen-king', Louis Philippe, as a 'betrayal'. Their repeated efforts at insurrection had provoked an increasingly repressive government response, and in 1835 not only were the republican societies outlawed, but all advocacy of a republic was henceforth forbidden.[35] Faced with this crackdown, one part of the republican opposition went underground. Secret societies were formed, such as the *Société des saisons* (Society of the Seasons), which attempted a badly botched uprising in 1839 under the leadership of Armand Barbès and Auguste Blanqui.

This was the background to Cabet's advocacy of the peaceful establishment of communist communities, set out in 1840 in his *Voyage to*

Icaria, a laborious imitation of Sir Thomas More's *Utopia*. Cabet's plan was to replicate 'the villages of cooperation' proposed in Britain by Robert Owen.[36] In the same year, however, opponents of Cabet's gradualism, the *violents*, Pillot and Dézamy, outflanked both Cabet and the dynastic opposition's growing banqueting campaign for suffrage reform by staging 'the first communist banquet' in the proletarian suburb of Belleville, an event attended by 1,200 people. Many held this banquet responsible for a wave of strikes which occurred in Paris soon after. Finally, towards the end of the year, the notoriety of 'communism' was underlined when a worker named Darmès, a 'communist' and a member of a secret society, attempted to assassinate the king.

The novel interest in 'communism', which developed in France in 1840, expressed a real shift in social and political preoccupations. This was the result of a growing overlap between older radical republican obsessions with equality and newer and predominantly socialist concerns about 'association' as a solution to the 'labour' question. Before the late 1830s, there had not been much common ground between these two positions. Communism was political, a revival of the revolutionary republican tradition, an extension of the cause of equality from the destruction of privilege to a generalized assault on private property. By contrast, socialism in France – a cluster of doctrines inspired by Saint-Simon and Fourier and initially of interest to students from new institutions like the *École Polytechnique* – was opposed to revolution, indifferent to political forms, hostile towards equality and more interested in church than in state. The goal of socialism was not equality, but the advent of harmony, made possible by a new social science. In the interim it pushed for 'association' or 'cooperation' as an answer to the 'antagonism' generated by competition and 'egoism'.

Two books published in 1840 gave shape to this new political landscape: Louis Blanc's *Organization of Labour* and Pierre-Joseph Proudhon's *What is Property?* Blanc's book attempted to merge socialism and republicanism. It focused upon a solution to the 'labour question': the question raised by a supposedly exterminatory system of competition accompanied by falling wages, the dissolution of the family and moral decline. The plight of labour was the result of 'bourgeois' rule, British hegemony and the pervasiveness of egoism. The remedy was the establishment of workers' associations under the aegis of a republican state. By contrast, Proudhon's socialism started from a non-state form of 'association'. Yet in his major object of attack, he seemed closer to the communists. For despite his vehement opposition to the asceticism and authoritarianism of the 'Babouvists', he like them argued that 'if you want to enjoy political equality, abolish property'. In these ways socialism, communism and the discontents of labour were becoming increasingly intertwined in public discussion.

In Britain, too, concern about the social question had taken a dramatic turn. Just as in France, where militant republicanism and subsequently communism had started as an angry reaction to the Orléanist 'betrayal' of the July Revolution, so Chartism in England with its demand for universal male suffrage began as a radical reaction to the limited constitutional settlement contained in the 1832 Reform Bill. In both countries, the numbers enfranchised were extremely small and, in both, the 'middle classes' or 'bourgeoisie' were blamed for abandoning the people rather than supporting them.

In the summer of 1842, there had also been a large-scale, and in part politically inspired, strike movement among workers in the Lancashire and Yorkshire textile districts – the 'plug-plot riots'. Some thought that these strikes had been deliberately fomented by employers; others accused the Chartists of attempting to turn these strikes into 'a revolution by legal means'. But whatever the original intention behind this movement, there was general agreement that it represented the most threatening aspect of Chartism so far. It seemed to confirm what Thomas Carlyle had written about 'the condition of England question', where he considered that, whatever the 'distracted incoherent embodiment of Chartism', its 'living essence' was 'the bitter discontent grown fierce and mad, the wrong condition therefore or the wrong disposition of the Working Classes of England'.[37]

Just at this moment – November 1842 – the young Friedrich Engels arrived in England to work in his father's Manchester textile firm, Ermen and Engels, after a year of military service in Berlin, where he had got to know the Bauer brothers and consorted with the 'Free'. His first impressions appeared to confirm all that he had heard about an approaching social revolution. In December 1842, he had quickly filed a report to the *Rheinische Zeitung* stating that 'the dispossessed have gained something useful from these events: the realization that a revolution by peaceful means is impossible' and that only 'a forcible abolition of existing unnatural conditions' could 'improve the material position of the proletariat'.[38]

There had also been a growing interest in the social question in Germany in the 1830s; Heine, Börne and the writers of Young Germany were fascinated by the social and religious ideas of the Saint-Simonians, but considered their political ideas untenable. In 1842, a German revival of interest in France was specifically related to questions about socialism and communism, but knowledge of their connection with the preceding French republican tradition was generally absent. Instead, communism was resituated as 'a rage for equality' and part of 'the social question'. It was identified with a primordial and extra-political force: 'the proletariat', 'the anguished cry of an unhappy and fanaticized class'; or as Heine put it, writing from Paris, the communists possessed a simple and universal language, comprehensible to all, a language built upon 'hunger', 'envy' and 'death'.

Discussion of these questions was greatly facilitated by the publication of a detailed study by a German research student based in Paris, Lorenz von Stein. Stein's *Socialism and Communism in Contemporary France* (1842) reinforced the association between hunger, envy and violence. It was widely read, not least because it was informative. He not only summarized the works of Saint-Simon and Fourier, but also introduced German readers to a successor generation of socialists, including Proudhon, Pierre Leroux and Louis Blanc. Once more, discussion centred on the proletariat. Stein treated communism as the specific product of post-revolutionary conditions in France, and assumed that no immediate threat was posed to Germany.

This sense of reassurance was short-lived. Mounting anxiety about the growth of 'pauperism' both in the cities and in the countryside from the end of the 1830s was given a political focus in 1843 by the arrest and imprisonment in Zurich of Wilhelm Weitling, a travelling tailor from Magdeburg and communist author. Papers found in his possession suggested that communism was already spreading among the German proletariat by means of a network of secret societies. In his official report, the local magistrate, J. C. Bluntschli, reinforced Stein's association of communism with the angry, destructive desires of the proletariat. 'Communism' had been brought to Switzerland by Weitling and others, who had fled after the failed Parisian uprising of 1839.

Weitling had called for a revolution to bring about the community of goods, and although in his published work, *Guarantees of Harmony and Freedom*, he had appealed to reason, his private correspondence revealed that the attainment of communism also required 'wild' and 'gruesome' actions on the part of the misery-stricken poor of great cities.[39] Bluntschli's report added considerably to an unreasoning fear of the communist threat which prevailed in Germany through to 1848.

For this reason, although Stein classed communism and socialism together as responses to the creation of the proletariat by the French Revolution, he also made a strong distinction between them. Socialism became the scientific response to the labour question, the solution to the split between society and the state. 'Communism' was its instinctive and destructive counterpart, embodied in a proletariat that was propelled by both its ignorance and its lack of property into the unrealizable pursuit of a once-and-for-all redistribution.

Stein was an impecunious law student, who had been dependent upon a government scholarship for his studies in Paris, and who had also supplemented his income by spying on German exiles (although this was not known at the time). The intellectual tradition from which Stein's book emerged was that of reforming *Staatswissenschaft*, the form of political science studied in German universities by would-be state officials. It derived from the paternalist economic and social policies of eighteenth-century Prussia, backed by a body of economic and administrative lore known as 'cameralism'. This governmental tradition was elaborated in the philosophy of Christian Wolff, the most important German philosopher between Leibniz and Kant. Wolff elaborated what was in effect a welfare state in his many publications. The state was made responsible for the defence, welfare and happiness of its subjects. Stein's conception of the state was also shaped by Hegel. Hegel himself in his discussion of day-to-day social and economic policies in the *Philosophy of Right* shared much of this administrative outlook. Stein's book was not, therefore, a simple description of the social problem and the condition of the French proletariat, but that of a passionate advocate of a considered form of state intervention as the answer to the social problem, when and if it reached Prussia.[40]

Within this *Staatswissenschaft* tradition, as an answer to the emergence of the proletariat, socialism did not need to be treated as a subversive political philosophy or the ideology of a particular class. It could be considered as a state-supported policy that afforded protection to the worker and political security to the state as a whole. Bismarck's later introduction of old-age pensions and social insurance owed much to this tradition. Others from the official class were coming to similar conclusions, and this helps to explain the interest shown by administrative reformers like Karl Rodbertus or Robert von Möhl in Louis Blanc's 1839 proposal for a state-managed 'organization of labour'.

'State socialism', as it came to be called, enjoyed an enduring appeal in Central Europe throughout the rest of the century. In the 1860s and 1870s, its legacy helped to explain the conflict between Lassalle's state-friendly *Allgemeiner Deutscher Arbeiterverein* (General German Workers' Association) and the anti-Prussian 'Eisenach' party of Liebknecht and Bebel, during the formation of the German Social Democratic Party. Its appeal was to be detected both in the proposals for social reform from 'the Socialists of the Chair' in the 1870s and in Bismarck's welfare measures in the 1880s that covered sickness, old age and unemployment.

More immediately, it explained the hostile reaction among Young Hegelians to Stein's work when it first appeared. This was powerfully articulated in 1843 by Moses Hess.[41] Hess questioned the reality of Stein's distinction between socialism and communism. Above all, he attacked the unpalatable implication of Stein's book, that the state could solve the 'social problem' or even practise 'socialism' without having to transform itself.[42]

Among radical Hegelians, interest in France focused not only upon the growth of the proletariat and the problem of pauperism, but also upon the defects of the *juste milieu* monarchy of Louis Philippe. This one-time model of liberalism was now associated with repression, both of republicanism and of social unrest. In Cologne, in August 1842, these concerns were evident in the formation by the management of the *Rheinische Zeitung* of a study circle, led by Moses Hess, to investigate the social question. Hess had travelled to France and in 1837 had produced a radical millenarian work entitled *The Sacred History of Mankind by a Disciple of Spinoza*. He was often regarded as the first philosophical advocate of communism in Germany. That book made little impact, but his next book, in 1841, *The European Triarchy*, attempted to rephrase his approach in Hegelian terms.

Hess argued against Hegel that man was not yet in a position to become 'at one with himself', and that this reconciliation would not happen if it were solely confined to thought. Such reconciliation could only be realized within a socialist society and under the aegis of a humanist creed; and this required action. Movements towards spiritual and social harmony already existed. In *The European Triarchy*, progress towards this ultimate harmony was embodied in three movements of emancipation found in three European nations. Germany, the land of the Reformation, was to realize spiritual freedom; France, the land of revolution, would attain political freedom; England, now on the verge of social revolution resulting from the mounting contradiction between pauperism and the 'money aristocracy', would bring about social equality.[43] Among those convinced by Hess's vision was Friedrich Engels, who passed through Cologne to England in the autumn of 1842. Hess claimed that after a meeting with him in the *Rheinische Zeitung* office, Engels shifted his position from Jacobinism to a form of socialism. It was Hess's vision that had inspired Engels' expectation of England's coming social revolution.

Karl was a regular participant in Hess's *Rheinische Zeitung* study circle; the 'rational state' invoked in his articles already contained a strong social component. But, at that stage, his attitude towards explicitly communist and socialist writings had remained guarded. In October 1842, in response to accusations of communist sympathies made by the *Augsburg Allgemeine Zeitung*, he replied on behalf of the *Rheinische Zeitung* that he did not think that communist ideas 'in their present form possess even *theoretical reality*'. He stated that such writings as those of Leroux and Considérant, and, above all, 'the sharp-witted work by Proudhon', could not be dismissed without 'long and profound study'.[44]

In this article, Karl was only prepared to consider 'communism' as a form of criticism rather than as a social movement. 'The real *danger*', he wrote, 'lies not in *practical attempts*, but in the *theoretical elaboration* of communist ideas, for practical attempts, even *mass attempts*, can be answered by *cannon* as soon as they become dangerous, whereas *ideas*, which have conquered our intellect and taken possession of our minds' were 'chains from which one cannot free oneself without a broken heart'.[45] It was only when Karl was able to consider man as a sensuous as well as a rational being that the impact of Feuerbach's philosophy upon him first became noticeable. This shift occurred in the spring of 1843 at the moment when he had abandoned any further hope of progress in Prussia and was preparing to leave the country.

Evidence of this shift is clear from the title of the journal adopted by Marx and Ruge: the *German-French Annals (Deutsch-Französische Jahrbücher)*. In his 'Preliminary Theses on the Reform of Philosophy', Feuerbach had stated, 'the true philosopher who is identical with life and Man must be of Franco-German parentage . . . We must make the mother French and the father German. The *heart* – the feminine principle, the *sense* of the finite and the seat of materialism – is of *French disposition*, the *head* – the masculine principle and the seat of idealism – of German.'[46]

Radical Hegelians were deeply impressed by this oracular pronouncement. Feuerbach's conception of man as both a sensuous and a rational being made possible a different way of thinking about the relationship between thought and being, or spirit and nature. In more concrete terms, it suggested a synthesis between Germany and France, or between philosophy and the proletariat. As Karl wrote to Feuerbach in the autumn of 1843, 'you were one of the first writers who expressed the need for a Franco-German scientific alliance'.[47]

A similar position was to be found in an essay by Hess published in 1843 in Herwegh's *Deutscher Bote*. Hess reiterated the claim that emancipation could only be the result of an equal emphasis upon thought and action. At present, while the Germans were barely aware of 'the modern social movement', the French had remained at a standstill in 'religious matters'. Saint-Simonianism 'was simply an aping of hierarchy', while in Germany the Young Hegelians had continued to 'be enmeshed in theological consciousness'. But now a new radicalism had emerged. 'In both countries, the radical party has come out against the official powers that emerged from the spiritual and social movement. Protestantism and the July Monarchy were under attack. Pierre Leroux, the French Arnold Ruge, is polemicizing against the *juste-milieu* government, just as his German equivalent is polemicizing against Protestantism, because they are beginning to see that these represent only a half-victory.'[48] A creative synthesis between French 'materialism', or 'sensualism', and German 'idealism', within the philosophical framework provided by Feuerbach, was now required, and in the mid-1840s 'humanism' – as this idea came to be known – inspired a generation of German intellectuals, previously radicalized by the writings of the Young

Hegelians, or Young Germany. But the question to be resolved was whether 'humanism' would take a republican or a socialist form.

5. THE *DEUTSCH-FRANZÖSISCHE JAHRBÜCHER*: PLANNING AND REALITY

In March 1843, in response to Feuerbach's call for a Franco-German alliance, Karl suggested to Ruge that publication of the journal should be switched from Zurich to Strasbourg and that French as well as German contributors should be enlisted. Ruge responded with enthusiasm, but still toyed with the idea of publication in Saxony, his former location. Karl replied that a reissue of the *Deutsche Jahrbücher* could only be a 'poor copy'. By contrast, the publication of a *Deutsch-Französische Jahrbücher* would be 'An undertaking about which one can be enthusiastic.'[49] Ruge accepted Karl's 'Gallo-Germanic principle', but between March and August, perhaps due to Jenny's misgivings, Karl dropped the Strasbourg idea.[50] Ruge explored the possibility of Brussels, but found it contained few intellectuals and nothing to compare with the 85,000 Germans supposedly living in Paris.[51] Paris was therefore agreed as the place of publication.

Some idea of what Karl and Ruge initially expected of the new journal was set out in correspondence from the spring and summer of 1843, which was later reprinted in the journal. Karl optimistically compared the Prussian king with the Stuarts and Bourbons, and likened Germany to 'a ship of fools' destined to go down in an 'impending revolution'.[52] Ruge's reply was deeply pessimistic, the result of his experience as a German republican, a political prisoner and a persecuted editor. There was no people more fragmented than the Germans, and – echoing Hölderlin's *Hyperion* – he went on, 'you see artisans, but no men, lords and serfs, young and established people, but no human beings . . . Is this not a battlefield, where hands, arms and other limbs lie all strewn, mixed up together, where the life's blood that has been shed drains away into the sand? . . . Your letter', he wrote, 'is an illusion . . . We will experience a political revolution? *We*, the contemporaries of these Germans? My friend, you believe in what you wish for.'[53]

Ruge argued that Germany was undergoing a repeat of the repressive Carlsbad Decrees of 1819. Talk of the Stuarts and the Bourbons was just talk. The Germans had never achieved a revolution. They fought as gladiators for others. 'Is there a single individual so stupid as to fail to understand our philistines and their eternal sheep-like patience?' They had now even lost their last cherished possession, freedom of thought. Germans not only tolerated despotism, but tolerated it 'with patriotism'. As a result, the princes had re-established their personal ownership of their land and people and once more abolished the rights of man as an imposition of the French. The Germans were 'a squalid people'.[54]

Faced with Ruge's scepticism, Karl enlarged upon his argument. It was true, he argued, that the old world belonged to the philistines, but there was a new order emerging, that of 'thinking beings, free men, republicans'.[55] 'The self-confidence of the human being' had first to be rekindled in 'the hearts of these people'. 'Only this feeling, which vanished from the world with the Greeks, and under Christianity disappeared into the blue mist of the heavens, can again transform society into a community of human beings united for their highest aims, into a democratic state.'

The Prussian king's attempt at reform had failed. His ambition to re-create a past full of 'priests, knights and feudal serfs' had clashed with the aims of 'idealists', who wanted 'only the consequences of the French Revolution'. Both the czar and the king's ministers had warned him that it would create an ungovernable and 'vociferous people' and urged him to 'return to the old system of slaves and silence'. It was a 'desperate situation', and this filled Karl with hope. It had led to a previously unattainable understanding among 'the enemies of philistinism . . . all the people who think and who suffer . . . The system of industry and trade, of ownership and exploitation of the people' was leading even more rapidly than the increase in population 'to a rupture within present-day society'.[56]

By September, Ruge had apparently stopped dwelling on the past. Karl outlined their strategy. They would not 'dogmatically anticipate' a new world, but rather 'find the new world through criticism of the old one'. Thus, from 'the conflict of the political state with itself', it would be 'possible everywhere to develop the social truth'.

Continuing the point he had developed in his critique of Hegel, Karl argued that an exposure of the contradictions contained within 'the political state' would lead to a 'reform of consciousness'. 'In analysing the superiority of the representative system over the social-estate system, the critic *in a practical way wins the interest* of a large party.' But then, by 'raising the representative system from its political form to the universal form and by bringing out the true significance underlying this system, the critic at the same time compels this party to go beyond its own confines, for its victory is at the same time its defeat . . . We merely show the world what it is really fighting for, and consciousness is something that it *has to* acquire, even if it does not want to.' The strategy was conceived in terms devised by Feuerbach. 'Our whole object can only be . . . to give religious and philosophical questions the form corresponding to man who has become conscious of himself.' Once this was done, it would become clear that 'the world has long dreamed of possessing something of which it has only to be conscious in order to possess it in reality'.[57]

Karl and Jenny arrived in Paris for the first time at the end of October 1843. Paris was after London the second-largest city in Europe, with a population of over one million. It specialized in the fabrication of quality fashion goods and the supply of specialized services. Its working-class population was by far the largest in France, but factory work was almost unknown. Its workers were largely members of skilled trades, employed in small workshops. In 1848, 50 per cent worked alone or were assisted by a single employee; and only one in ten shops employed more than ten workers. In the first half of the century, the city's population doubled. Immigrants were drawn to the city by the prospect of higher wages, and came not only from provincial France, but also from neighbouring countries. In the mid-1840s, there were estimated to be 40,000–60,000 German inhabitants in Paris, predominantly artisans – printers, shoemakers and tailors, but also teachers, writers and artists. The migration of artisans had begun in the years after 1815, as a result of the increase of population, the relaxation of guild restrictions and the consequent overcrowding of German trades. Educated and professional foreigners, on the other hand, were in large part political refugees, particularly those who came from Poland in what was called 'the great emigration' following the uprising of 1830–31. Their presence in Paris had been the result of successive waves of political repression in their homelands.[58]

Karl looked forward to leaving Prussia; he was happy to be destined for 'the new capital of the new world' and to escape from an atmosphere 'which makes one a serf'.[59] Ruge was more effusive, amazed by the size of Paris, particularly the view from the heights of Montmartre of a sea of houses as far as the eye could see. As he wrote:

> Vienna and Rome are large, their situation is beautiful, perhaps more beautiful than that of Paris; but unfortunately, one can never forget, if one looks more closely, that they are inhabited by donkeys, and only sparsely colonized by men, whereas here, and only here, is the focal point of the European spirit, here the heart of world history lies before us ... Above all, since the time of Athens and Rome, the history of men became the history of their absurdities; the renewal of the humanized world movement is still very young. It begins with the Revolution. For the Revolution has been the first reminder that heroes, republicans and free men once existed in the world.[60]

In their search for French authors, neither Ruge nor Karl took prior account of local realities. Ruge, helped by Hess, had made a grandiose start. He had approached notables such as Lamartine, Sand, Ledru-Rollin, Lamennais and the anti-slavery activist Victor Schölcher, together with the socialists Étienne Cabet, Théodore Dezamy, Victor Considérant and Flora Tristan. There was reason to be optimistic; the French were curious to learn about German Romanticism and nationalism, and particularly about Schelling, Young Germany and the Young Hegelians. Louis Blanc endorsed the project in Pierre Leroux's *Revue indépendante*.

Yet no French writers were prepared to contribute to the proposed journal. Ruge had believed that Feuerbach's philosophical humanism could unite the Germans and the French. The assumption that 'the people' would read a bilingual journal was far-fetched enough, but to assume that they would also warm to their Feuerbachian critique was to take no account of French intellectual development in the previous thirty years. As might have been expected, French authors almost without exception were reluctant to be associated with 'German atheism'.

From the 1820s, the hostility towards Christianity associated with the *Philosophes* and the Revolution had largely ceased to define the French left. Conceptions of the significance of religion had shifted. The battles of the Revolution highlighted the importance of what contemporaries called *pouvoir spirituel*, the cultural hegemony once exercised by the Catholic church. Counter-revolutionary and theocratic critics, most notably Bonald, argued that the Revolution had failed, in large part because of the inability of the Jacobins to establish a new source of 'spiritual power', capable of winning the hearts and minds of the people.

The socialism that emerged in France from around the end of the 1820s drew, therefore, not only upon an Enlightenment vision of scientific and social progress, but also upon the theocratic critique of Jacobinism and the Revolution. Saint-Simon's proclamation of the 'New Christianity' and the subsequent foundation of the Saint-Simonian church were attempts to harness this 'spiritual power' and apply it towards peaceful industrial and scientific goals. This helps to explain why in the plethora of democratic-social writing which followed the 1830 Revolution Christianity was redescribed or appropriated rather than attacked or dissolved.

Pierre Leroux, the former editor of *Le Globe* and one of the most famous socialist writers during the July Monarchy claimed to have invented 'socialism' in its modern sense in 1833.[61] But he had first called his new conception 'religious democracy'. 'Religious democracy' was placed between two extremes: on the one hand, that of Père Enfantin, the 'Father' of the Saint-Simonian church – 'this new crushing and absorbing papacy'; on the other, the 'individualism of English political economy', which 'in the name of liberty' would 'turn the behaviour of men towards each other into that of rapacious wolves and reduce society to atoms'.[62] 'Religious democracy' was an apt description of the language of the social movement in France in the years leading up to 1848. After 1830, it became common to portray the French Revolution as a decisive chapter in the religious history of mankind, with Jesus as its prophet.[63] Such an identification was common among socialist and republican groups between 1830 and 1848. The Robespierrist Alphonse Laponneraye described Jesus, Rousseau and Robespierre as 'three names which exist in inseparable unity'. Cabet declared communism to be Christianity in practice. Philippe Buchez, the ex-Saint-Simonian Christian Socialist and patron of the main artisan journal, *L'Atelier*, declared that socialism was the realization of the Christian promise of equality. Victor Considérant, Fourier's successor as leader of the Phalansterians, similarly claimed Fourierism to be the Christianity of the nineteenth century. According to him, social science would make a reality of the Christian promise of fraternity. Disconcertingly for the Germans, Louis Blanc declared that the left were the true defenders of Christianity against the scorn of Louis Philippe and the Orléanists, the new 'Voltairean' ruling class.[64] Not surprisingly, therefore, replacing Christianity by a humanist creed held little appeal for the French.

Their failure to anticipate how difficult it might be to convert the French to humanism suggests that Marx and Ruge were simply unfamiliar both with popular politics and with the world outside Germany. The problem had certainly been signalled by Moses Hess.[65] Ruge thought that fear of German 'atheism' and the sectarian party attachments of the French were problems which could be overcome.[66] By contrast, Marx, whose starting point was that religion as 'the existence of a defect' was incompatible with 'human emancipation', made no effort to address French assumptions.[67] According to Ruge, 'because of his cynicism and crude arrogance', Marx was 'anathema to the French'. 'His opinion' was that 'the whole culture of present-day France must disappear'.[68] He affected to believe that 'irreligion', formerly associated with the propertied classes, was now located in the proletariat, a largely unfounded assumption. His idea was another indication of the distance between French and German versions of socialism and republicanism in the 1840s and 1850s. More perceptive was the observation made by Friedrich Engels, not yet acquainted with Karl and writing from Manchester. In October 1843, he remarked how strange it was that English socialists, 'generally opposed to Christianity', had to suffer 'all the religious prejudices of a really Christian people', while 'French Communists, being part of a nation celebrated for its infidelity, are themselves Christian.'[69]

The inability to secure the cooperation of the French was only the first misfortune to befall the ill-fated joint venture. At a personal level, things went badly from the start. Ruge, so it was claimed, had originally proposed that they should establish a Fourierist phalanstery – the Fourierist version of a socialist community – next to the office of the *Jahrbücher* in the Rue Vaneau. The three families – the Ruges, the Marxes and the Herweghs, were to live on separate floors, but the women were to take it in turn to look after the cooking, sewing and organizing of a communal household. According to Marcel Herwegh, his mother, Emma:

rejected the idea at once. How could a nice little Saxon woman like Frau Ruge possibly get on with the highly intelligent and even more ambitious Madame Marx, who knew so much more than she? And how could the so recently married Frau Herwegh, who was the youngest of them all, possibly feel attracted to this communal life? Surely enough, Herwegh and his wife declined Ruge's invitation. Ruge and Marx and their wives went to live together in the Rue Vaneau. A fortnight later they parted.[70]

The editing of the single issue of the journal, published as a double number at the end of February 1844, was largely left to Karl, since Ruge was mainly out of town and afterwards ill. There were no contributions from writers living in Germany. Feuerbach claimed that there was no point in writing anything further about Schelling. There was nothing new he could say about him, save for making a semi-serious comparison between Schelling and Cagliostro.[71] The journal still contained some exceptional contributions: a comic hymn of praise for king Ludwig of Bavaria by Heine, together with poetry by Herwegh, the essays from Karl himself, and from Engels an essay on Thomas Carlyle together with a path-breaking critique of political economy, the initial inspiration of Karl's own investigations in the area.

6. 'THE EMANCIPATION OF THE GERMANS INTO HUMAN BEINGS'

Karl included two contributions of his own in the journal. In an essay on 'the Jewish Question', he added to what he had originally written in Kreuznach a new section much closer to a socialist viewpoint. In his original disagreement with Bauer, he had argued that the emancipation of the state from religion was not the same as emancipation of human beings from religion. In the second section, probably written after he reached Paris, Judaism was equated with the possessive individualism of civil society.

Karl took issue with Bauer's Hegelian treatment of Judaism and Christianity as successive stages in the development of Spirit. As an alternative to Bauer's 'theological approach', Karl attempted to specify the distinction between Christianity and Judaism in non-theological terms, and to identify the *social* element which would have to be overcome, if Judaism were to be abolished. His approach made substantial use of an essay by the socialist Moses Hess, 'On the Essence of Money', which was intended for publication in a subsequent number of the journal.

Hess argued that Christianity provided the 'theory and logic' of the 'upside-down world, currently inhabited by humanity'. Just as the activity of the species was not ascribed to the individuals who composed it, but rather to God as a species-essence conceived to exist outside these individuals, so, in practical life, money was the equivalent of this inverted God, a materialized Christian God, who stripped man of his social ties. In this modern 'Christian shopkeeper world', money represented the setting of species-life outside the individual. Money had become the alienated wealth of man, the bartering away of man's life activity.[72]

Hess's distinction between the Christian theory of an upside-down world and money as the equivalent in practical life to the inverted God was transformed by Karl into a theory of 'Judaism'. Money was 'the worldly God' of the Jew, and 'huckstering' his 'worldly religion', since the secular basis of Judaism, according to Karl, was 'practical need' and 'self-interest'. Both Hess and Karl were attempting to make use of Feuerbach's conception of abstraction. According to Karl, Man in the grip of religion can objectify his essential nature and turn it into something alien. He places his activity under the domination of an alien being and bestows the significance of alien entity – money – on them.[73]

In the present, Judaism constituted 'a general *anti-social* element'. Judaism as huckstering had developed through history to its present heights, in which money had become a world power and the worship of mammon had become universal. The Jew's lack of political rights was belied by his financial power.[74] For politics had become 'the serf of financial power'. Money was 'the estranged essence of man's work' and he worshipped it.

Egoism was the core of the Jewish religion, but it was also the 'principle of civil society'. As financial power grew, the affinity between the values of Judaism and those of civil society had become ever closer. Contempt for theory, art and man as an end in himself together with a debased view of nature were all contained 'in abstract form' in the Jewish religion. But these also formed 'the real standpoint of the man of money', for whom 'the species-relation itself, the relation between man and woman becomes an object of trade'. Similarly, 'the chimerical nationality of the Jew' was equivalent to 'the nationality of the merchant, of the man of money in general'.[75]

As a religion of practical need, Judaism could not develop any further; it could only find its consummation in practice. While it had reached its highest point in civil society, the perfection of civil society itself could only occur in the Christian world. Judaism lacked the theory to create 'a new world'. Yet out of Judaism there had developed Christianity, which created the theory that Judaism lacked. For only Christianity was able to make '*all* national, natural, moral and theoretical conditions extrinsic to man'. 'Only under the dominance of Christianity . . . could civil society separate itself completely from the life of the state, sever all the species-ties of man, put egoism and selfish need in the place of these species-ties and dissolve the human world into a world of atomistic individuals who are inimically opposed to one another.'[76]

Christianity had sprung from Judaism, but was now merging back into it again. For Christianity had only *appeared* to overcome Judaism through its creation of a Christian heaven. Now, however, that Christianity had completed the estrangement of man from himself and from nature, and everything had been turned into vendible, alienable objects, Judaism could finally achieve 'universal dominance'. Now 'the Christian egoism of heavenly bliss' was again merging with 'the corporal egoism of the Jew'. The tenacity of the Jew derived from the 'human basis' of his religion – practical need, egoism. Political emancipation therefore could not emancipate the Jew. Only human emancipation – emancipation from huckstering and money – would make the Jew 'impossible'.[77]

Karl's other contribution to the journal, his introduction to his 'Contribution to the Critique of Hegel's Philosophy of Right', also crossed the line between republicanism and socialism by presenting a particular group – the proletariat – as the privileged embodiment of the universal rather than couching his analysis in the form of an appeal to all potential citizens. This short essay reiterated some of the major themes of the unfinished 'Critique': the inadequacy of 'political emancipation' and the failure of 'criticism'. His confidence in the uses to which the critique of abstraction could be put remained undiminished. 'The criticism of religion', he announced, 'was now complete.' But 'the criticism of religion' was 'the premise of all criticism' and it ended with 'the teaching that *man is the highest being for man*, hence with the *categorical imperative to overthrow all relations* in which man is a debased, enslaved, forsaken, despicable being . . . To abolish religion as the *illusory* happiness of the people is to demand their real happiness.' The task of philosophy, once the holy form of self-estrangement had been unmasked, was to unmask self-estrangement in its unholy forms. Every sphere of German society must be exposed, 'these petrified relations must be forced to dance by singing their own tune to them'. Like Hess, he stressed the necessity of action, and the need to resort to force. 'The weapon of criticism cannot replace the criticism of weapons.'[78]

The present German regime was 'an anachronism . . . The last phase of a world-historical form is its *comedy*.' The fate of other *anciens régimes* had been tragic, but 'the modern *ancien régime* is only the *comedian* of a world order whose *true heroes* are dead'. The leaders of German industry, 'our cotton barons and iron champions', were equally anachronistic. They were demanding the introduction of 'protective duties' at just the moment when more advanced nations like Britain and France were beginning to abandon them. More generally, 'even the *moral self-confidence of the German middle class* rests only on the consciousness that it is the general representative of the philistine mediocrity of all the other classes.'[79]

For in Germany there was no class capable of acting like the French 'Third Estate' in 1789. Every class was struggling against classes both above and beneath it. That meant that in Germany it was not 'radical revolution' or 'general human emancipation', but 'political emancipation', 'the partial, the merely political revolution', which was a 'utopian dream'. In Germany 'universal emancipation' was 'the sine qua non of partial emancipation'. What was now required was a 'human' transformation carried through by a class outside and beneath existing society, a class with only 'a human title', 'a class with radical chains', a 'sphere' that 'cannot emancipate itself without emancipating . . . all other spheres of society'. In Germany, such a class was already coming into being. This was the proletariat, a class arising from '*industrial* development' and from the '*drastic dissolution* of society'. It was 'the complete loss of Man' and 'the dissolution of the hitherto existing world order'. For radical revolution to occur in Germany it would not be enough for 'thought to strive for realisation . . . reality must itself strive towards thought'. This requirement was now being met, for 'by demanding the negation of private property ... the proletariat merely raises to the rank of a principle what society has made the principle of the proletariat'.[80]

The proletariat represented the '*passive* element, a *material* basis' in the process of revolutionary change. In Feuerbach's vision, it represented 'the *heart* – the feminine principle, the *sense* of the finite and the seat of materialism'. The spark must come from elsewhere, from philosophy, 'the *head* – the masculine principle and the seat of idealism'. Germany's revolutionary past was theoretical – the Reformation. Just as present-day Germany was trapped in the clutches of an outdated *ancien régime*, so 'official' Germany on the eve of the Reformation had been 'the most unconditional *slave* of Rome'. But 'as the revolution then began in the brain of the *monk*, so now it begins in the brain of the *philosopher*'. If the original constituency of the journal had been 'people who think' and 'people who suffer', by the beginning of 1844 the role of suffering had been assigned to the proletariat. According to Karl's conclusion, 'as philosophy finds its *material* weapons in the proletariat, so the proletariat finds its *spiritual* weapons in philosophy ... The *emancipation of the German* is *the emancipation of the human being*. The *head* of this emancipation is *philosophy*; its *heart* is the *proletariat* ... Once the lightning of thought has squarely struck this ingenuous soil of the people, the emancipation of the *Germans* into *human beings* will take place.'[81]

As was to be expected, the Prussian government was alarmed by the publication of the *Jahrbücher*. It was considered to be a treasonable journal, and instructions were given that Karl, Ruge, Heine and Bernays (a young lawyer from the Palatinate and former editor of the *Mannheimer Abend-Zeitung*, recently expelled from Bavaria) should be arrested if they set foot on Prussian soil. Of 1,000 copies printed, 100 copies were found by the police on a Rhine steamer, while being transported by Bernays; another 230 were impounded at the frontier between France and the Palatinate.

The Zurich publisher Julius Froebel was also dismayed by the radicalism of the first number, which was far greater than he had expected, by the absence of French contributors and by the harassment of the authorities. He announced that funding for the journal was exhausted, and that he could not carry on without more money. Ruge refused to put any more of his own money into the journal and tried to convince Moses Hess to return the money he had advanced for unpublished essays; Karl was paid in unsold copies of the *Jahrbücher*. And so after one large number of around 350 pages, the Gallo-Germanic publishing project came to an end.

The financial emergency which Karl might otherwise have experienced was offset by his receipt of 1,000 thalers collected in support of his continuing literary activity by former shareholders of the *Rheinische Zeitung* through the initiative of Georg Jung, but relations with Ruge were tense. Of the occasion of Karl's breakup with Ruge, only Ruge's account survives, and it concerned the morality of the poet Georg Herwegh. Gossip suggested that Herwegh, very recently married to the daughter of a rich banker from Berlin, might be having an affair with the Countess d'Agoult, former mistress of Franz Liszt and future chronicler of 1848 in Paris under the name Daniel Stern. Ruge later recalled:

> I was incensed by Herwegh's way of living and his laziness. Several times I referred to him warmly as a scoundrel and declared that when a man gets married, he ought to know what he is doing. Marx said nothing and took his departure in a perfectly friendly manner. Next morning he wrote to me that Herwegh was a genius with a great future. My calling him a scoundrel filled him with indignation and my ideas on marriage were philistine and inhuman. Since then we have not seen each other again.[82]

Karl's ambition had once been to become a poet, and in Paris he was delighted to have the opportunity to get to know Heinrich Heine, whose satirical wit and stylistic artistry he vainly tried to emulate. Lonely and in poor health, Heine became friendly with the *Jahrbücher* group. According to Eleanor Marx's memories of her parents, there was a time in Paris when Heine called in practically every day and tried out new verses on Karl and Jenny. He seems to have been charmed by Jenny in particular, and unlike either Karl or Jenny had a practical turn of mind. According to Eleanor's account: 'Little Jenny Marx, a baby a few months old, was attacked one day by strong cramps which threatened to kill the child. Marx, his wife and their faithful helper and friend Helene Demuth were standing around the child in a complete quandary. Then Heine arrived, had a look and said, "the child must have a bath". With his own hands he prepared the bath, put the child in and saved, so Marx said, Jenny's life.'[83]

Like the Saint-Simonians, Karl believed that artists were endowed with a privileged vision of the future and so formed the elect avant-garde of humanity: they should not be assessed by the measure of ordinary or even extraordinary men.[84] It is also clear that whatever the shift in his philosophical views, Karl's fixation on poetic genius – which he associated with the disorder of creation – continued to define his life style. Ruge described his work habits:

> He has a peculiar personality – perfect as a scholar and author but completely ruinous as a journalist. He reads a lot; he works with unusual intensity and has a critical talent that occasionally degenerates into a wanton dialectic. But he finishes nothing, breaks off everything and plunges himself ever afresh into an endless sea of books . . . He is irritable and hot-tempered, particularly when he has worked himself sick and not gone to bed for three, even four nights on end.[85]

As Ruge's account of his time in Paris makes clear, Karl's view of poetry or his work habits were not the real issues which brought about the breach between the two men. Ruge considered that the published number of the journal had contained some remarkable essays, even though some of Karl's epigrams were forced and some of the essays 'unpolished'. But the main reason for the failure of the project had been the journal's gravitation from the beginning towards a most emphatic form of communism. This had caused his publisher, Froebel to withdraw, had frightened the booksellers and had alienated 'important talents'. Ruge was still attempting to find another publisher when his co-editor, Karl, 'a disruptive personality given to sophistry, whose practical talents I had greatly overestimated, explained to me he could no longer work together with me since I was only political, while he was a communist'. This came as a surprise, for from September 1843 to March 1844, Ruge continued, Karl remained silent about his progression to 'crude socialism', which in his letters (published in the *Jahrbücher*) he had 'very reasonably held forth against'.[86]

Ruge went on to attack Karl's communism. He argued to Feuerbach that neither the aims of the Fourierists, nor the suppression of property that the communists advocated, could be articulated with any clarity. 'These two tendencies end up with a police state and slavery. To liberate the proletariat from the weight of physical and intellectual misery, one dreams of an organization that would generalize this very misery, that would cause all human beings to bear its weight.'[87]

As for Karl himself, having once been convinced momentarily that he had discovered the new Luther, he now expressed no regret that his collaboration with Ruge had come to an end.

On 11 August 1844, Karl wrote to Feuerbach about 'the great respect and – if I may use the word – love which I feel for you'. And, referring especially to Feuerbach's *Principles of the Philosophy of the Future*, he went on, 'In these writings you have provided – I don't know whether intentionally – a philosophical basis for socialism and the Communists have immediately understood them in this way.' Feuerbach was saluted in particular for his understanding of 'the unity of man with man which is based on the real differences between them' and 'the concept of the human species brought down from the heaven of abstraction to the real earth, what is this but the concept of *society*?'[88]

7. 'OLD GERMANY, WE ARE WEAVING YOUR SHROUD!' *VORWÄRTS!* AND SILESIA

In December 1843, French and German authorities were forewarned of the appearance in Paris of two new German papers, one of them 'communist in tendency'. Metternich, the Austrian Chancellor, and Bülow, the Prussian Foreign Minister, hoped that preventive measures could be taken in the Frankfurt Diet, reiterating the prohibition of uncensored German-language journals, outside as well as within the German Confederation. German artisans were after all officially forbidden to leave the German Confederation: a measure impossible to enforce, but a good pretext for searching workers whenever they crossed frontiers. At the same time, uncensored German publications imported into the Confederation were liable to confiscation – as Bernays was to discover. Even so, the Prussian ambassador in Paris, Count von Arnim, considered these measures ineffective and pressured the French premier, François Guizot, to intervene. Guizot refused, having no wish to provoke the press outcry which would follow the expulsion of political refugees at the behest of the Prussians.

At the end of March 1844, however, the ambassador was pleased to report to Berlin that the *Deutsch-Französische Jahrbücher* had gone bankrupt. The trouble seemed to be over. But just for good measure, since the authorities were convinced that trouble was brought into the otherwise peaceful and loyal kingdom of Prussia by outside agitators, on 16 April 1844 warrants were issued for the arrest of Karl, Ruge, Heine and Bernays, should they set foot in Prussia.

The second journal, *Vorwärts!*, was set up in January 1844 by the theatrical director and translator Heinrich Börnstein, with the help of the composer Giacomo Meyerbeer.[89] Initially, the journal had hoped to remain politically inoffensive, emphasizing charitable help for distressed artisans. The presence of Adalbert von Bornstedt, reputedly funded by Prussia, provided further reassurance, though even the vaguest of commitments to 'unity' and 'freedom' made it liable to Prussian suspicion.[90]

Börnstein was unable to build up a viable circulation, and over the next few months he found it necessary to rethink the character of the journal. If he wanted able writers, he would have to recruit from among Parisian émigrés; if he wanted to build up a readership he would have to appeal to artisans. The collapse of the *Jahrbücher* provided him with a perfect opportunity. But the political émigrés were unlikely to participate so long as *Vorwärts!* was associated with Bornstedt, whom Heine had accused of being a spy as far back as 1838. Demand could also be stimulated among the artisans associated with radical educational associations, and the secret societies connected with them; they needed a journal in which political positions could be debated. This was particularly the case within the largest of the German radical associations, the League of the Just (*Bund der Gerechten*), which dated back to 1836.

Divisions within these groups were both political and generational. The older generation of émigrés from the 1830–34 period were primarily defined by different forms of nationalism from Romantic *Burschenschaftler*, Jacobin cosmopolitan republicans, Mazzinian nationalists to Hambach liberals. In age and political formation, Ruge was closer to this first group. The second wave of émigrés from the late 1830s were more likely to be defined by various forms of socialism and communism, ranging from Cabetist Icarians, followers of Weitling or Lamennais, advocates of various forms of Swiss-based Christian communism and, more recently, those, like Karl Schapper, drawn to London-based Chartism. Finally, there were the 'humanists' and 'neo-Hegelians', who had clustered around the *Jahrbücher*.

In response to this radical constituency, Börnstein broke with

Bornstedt and drew in former collaborators from the *Jahrbücher* and prominent members of the League. Börnstein himself claimed to have been converted to 'humanism' and, as he boasted with some justification, 'there soon gathered around *Vorwärts* a group of writers such as no other paper anywhere could boast . . . there wrote for the paper Arnold Ruge, Karl Marx, Heinrich Heine, Georg Herwegh, Bakunin, Georg Weerth, G. Weber, Fr. Engels, Dr Ewerbeck and H. Bürgers.' Börnstein went on to remember 'with pleasure' the weekly editorial conferences:

> From twelve to fourteen men used to gather . . . Some would sit on the bed or on the trunks, others would stand or walk about. They would all smoke terrifically, and argue with great passion and excitement. It was impossible to open the windows, because a crowd would immediately have gathered in the street to find out the cause of the violent uproar, and very soon the room was concealed in such a thick cloud of tobacco-smoke that it was impossible for a newcomer to recognise anybody present. In the end we ourselves could not even recognise each other.[91]

As in the *Jahrbücher*, the main battle was between republicans and socialists. Börnstein wrote of violent nightly arguments between the two tendencies. Socialists were in the majority and Ruge was the main target. Back in March, Börnstein had originally considered the *Jahrbücher* as Ruge's journal: Ruge was famous; he was 'the master', Karl his clever but obscure assistant. Ruge was also well-funded, and so Börnstein had proposed that together they should refound the journal. Ruge refused, not least because of his dislike of the increasingly strong 'communist' faction around the journal. But this led to increasing attacks upon his politics. On 22 June, Börnstein published a provocative open letter to Ruge accusing him of 'negativity' and challenging him to be more specific about his views. Why, for instance, did he stop at the 'rights of man', why not go beyond them like Karl? Additional interventions by Bernays and Ewerbeck put further pressure upon the republican position. But at this point (6 July) Ruge was reluctant to publicize his conflict with Karl and stuck to generalities.[92]

Ruge could have given a perfectly cogent reply. Like Karl, he had been inspired by Feuerbach's critique of abstraction, but saw no reason why its effects should be confined to one particular form like labour, or to one social group like the proletariat. Republican humanism entailed a struggle against all forms of abstraction (the assumption that concepts possessed an objective existence outside humanity, see pp. 127–8). He approved of the activities of socialist and communist groups in England and France, but thought the idea of a social revolution an illusion. All could be, and had to be, encompassed within a democratic national revolution along the lines of 1789. The problem of Germany, as he had insisted to Karl in the *Jahrbücher* letters of 1843, was apathy. His position was, 'There are no German people and only a revolution can create one.'

During the months following the collapse of the *Jahrbücher* in March, Karl had withdrawn from journalism to get on with his own work. On 1 May, his first daughter, Jenny, was born, and in early June Jenny and the baby went back to Trier to stay with her mother. Little Jenny was quite ill from the journey. She suffered from 'constipation and downright overfeeding' – and the doctor insisted that she must have a wet-nurse, since with 'artificial feeding she would not easily recover'. The wet-nurse, whom her father, Ludwig, had known as a child, turned out also to be able to speak French, and so was able to accompany mother and child back to Paris in September. Jenny wrote back to Karl from Trier around 21 June that 'everyone still hopes that you will decide after all to obtain a permanent post'. In Trier, she was happy to catch up with her mother, but she was also worried about the profligacy of her brother, Edgar. While her mother scrimped and saved, Edgar frequented the opera in Cologne; Edgar 'makes use of all the great signs of the times, and all the sufferings of society, in order to cover up and whitewash his own worthlessness'.[93] With some trepidation, she 'set out on my difficult journey – you know where to'. But all turned out well, and when the door opened, Jenny was greeted by Jettchen, who 'embraced and kissed me' and led her into the drawing room, where Henriette and her sister Sophie 'both immediately embraced me' and 'your mother called me "thou"'. Sophie looked to have been 'terribly ravaged by illness', and Jettchen was already in what was to become a terminal state of consumption. 'Only your mother looks well and flourishing.' Next morning, Henriette came to see the baby; 'can you imagine such a change?' She thought it due to their success 'or in our case rather *the appearance* of success'.[94]

Karl's own first aim during this period was to develop the argument he had been considering ever since his critical encounter with Hegel in Kreuznach – to write a history of the Convention (1792–5) during the

French Revolution.[95] This would provide a historical elaboration of his argument about the limitations of the 'political state'. For empirical detail he used the forty volumes of Buchez and Roux to provide a résumé of the parliamentary debates during the revolutionary period.[96] He did not make a strong distinction between 1789 and 1793. His interest throughout was in the inability of the 'political state' to transcend its conditions of existence. He had already made this the central point in 'On the Jewish Question' in his analysis of the distinction between the rights of man and the rights of the citizen. An account of how the efforts of the Committee of Public Safety to override the market price of bread had reverted back to the laissez-faire practices of Thermidor would have reinforced the argument. More generally, his aim would have been to account for the birth of the modern democratic citizenry and its illusions.

Karl had also been powerfully impressed by Friedrich Engels' essay in the *Jahrbücher*, 'Outlines of a Critique of Political Economy'. It revealed yet another way in which the process of abstraction dominated and distorted the relations between 'I and Thou'. Thus, between March and August, Karl took notes on Smith, Ricardo, Say, Sismondi, Pecqueur, Buret, James Mill, Wilhelm Schulz and MacCulloch. Out of this material, he prepared a preliminary draft of what was to become his central preoccupation over the next quarter of a century, the 'Critique of Political Economy'.[97]

When Engels passed through Paris on his way to Wuppertal to write up his book on England, he broke his journey for ten days between 28 August and 6 September 1844 to spend the time in conversation with Karl. This was the beginning of a lifelong partnership; its immediate result was an agreement with Engels to participate in a polemical attack that Karl was preparing against Bruno Bauer, and his new journal, the *Allgemeine Literatur-Zeitung*.[98]

But, in the meantime, exciting events drew Karl back into political controversy. Faced with continued pressure from socialists and communists, Ruge and his supporters were gradually withdrawing from *Vorwärts!*; Ruge went on instead to form a more congenial alliance with Louis Blanc and Ledru-Rollin on *La Réforme*. Before that happened, the argument acquired an unexpected German dimension. On 4–6 June 1844, the Silesian weavers of Peterswaldau attacked a local firm said to be responsible for low wages and degrading working conditions. They smashed the house and works of the employers and on the morrow reassembled in the neighbouring village of Langenbielau, where troops in panic shot down eleven weavers before being driven away by an enraged crowd that proceeded to ransack another owner's house.[99]

Events in Silesia appeared to suggest that the German Confederation had also finally acquired a proletariat. There were disturbances involving workers in Bohemia and elsewhere in Germany. In response, Friedrich Wilhelm IV of Prussia launched a debate on pauperism and encouraged the formation of charitable and Christian societies for 'the well-being of the working classes'. When uncensored reports of what had happened in Silesia reached Paris, enthusiasm bordering on euphoria gripped an editorial collective whose expectations had been shaped by Ludwig Feuerbach on the advent of 'species-being', Karl on the coming 'human revolution' in Germany, Moses Hess on the essence of money and Friedrich Engels' critique of political economy. After the failure to persuade Ruge to invest in the journal, Carl Bernays was appointed editor from the beginning of July. He praised the exemplary behaviour of the weavers, in particular that, instead of looting, they destroyed the firm's accounts books. 'They were the sublime harbingers of a universal revolt, which also proved that as long as political economy perpetuated its old routines, a truly human society would not be possible.' In the following number, *Vorwärts!* published what was to become one of Heine's best-remembered poems, 'The Poor Weavers', with its triple curse on God, King and Country and its arresting climax – 'Old Germany, we are weaving your shroud!'[100]

Ruge responded to the Silesian events at the end of July. He was not impressed by the actions of the weavers. His main concern was about the feebleness of the government response to the events; and he remarked that in an apolitical country like Germany it was impossible for partial distress in the manufacturing districts to be treated as a general question. Rather, like a flood or a famine, it was treated as a natural disaster, whose alleviation was left to Christian charity. As for the disturbances themselves, Ruge argued that this was a hunger-riot, characteristic of Germans who nowhere 'see beyond their hearth and home'. His intervention was anonymous, but signed 'A Prussian'.[101] Why he signed it in this way is unclear; not only was he a Saxon rather than a Prussian, but the only Prussian in the group was in fact Karl. This must have provoked Karl to intervene.

Karl had also been gripped by the euphoria which had spread among the *Vorwärts!* collective in July, as had Jenny. In the aftermath of the unsuccessful attempt by Heinrich Tschech, the disaffected *Bürgermeister* of Storkow (a province of Brandenburg), to assassinate the king, she wrote from Trier about the guns firing, the bells ringing and the 'pious crowd flocking into the temples' to offer their thanks for the king's deliverance. The mood in Trier convinced her that 'a political revolution is impossible in Germany, whereas all the seeds of a social revolution are present'.[102] She recalled the poems of Heine, who predicted – and as Jenny firmly believed – that the old world was really coming to an end, and human emancipation, embodied in the emergence of the proletariat, was in sight. Moses Hess's letter at the beginning of July was equally encouraging. 'The *Jahrbücher* have been a great success. New socialists are popping up everywhere: in particular, the party of philosophy has been wholly won over [to socialism] . . . The Silesian disturbances are now also contributing their own part to it . . . In short, the whole of educated Germany will soon be socialist, and in fact radical socialist, I mean communist.'[103]

In the same couple of weeks, Karl wrote effusively to Feuerbach of his first contacts with proletarians. According to reports by spies, Dr Hermann Ewerbeck, a leading League member and translator of Cabet, had taken Karl on a number of occasions to the public gatherings of German artisans at the Barrière du Trône in the Rue de Vincennes. Karl emphasized to Feuerbach 'the theoretical merits of the German artisans in Switzerland, London and Paris' but regretted that 'the German artisan is still, however, too much of an artisan'. But he had no such reservations about 'the French proletariat'. 'You would have to attend one of the meetings of the French workers to appreciate the pure freshness, the nobility which burst forth from these toil-worn men.'[104]

All this helps to explain the extraordinary terms in which Karl extolled the virtues of the German proletarian when he answered Ruge's dismissive observations on the Silesian disturbances in August 1844. He began by reiterating the argument about the impotence of the 'political state' that he had developed over the previous year. The argument of 'the alleged Prussian' that the king should have legislated for the education of uncared-for children missed the fact that such legislation would have been tantamount to 'the abolition of the proletariat'. The French Revolutionary Convention, Napoléon and the English government had all failed in the attempt to abolish pauperism. For the 'slavery of civil society' was 'the natural foundation on which the modern state rests'. The 'principle of politics' was 'the will' and this had led Robespierre to imagine that poverty, the main 'obstacle to pure democracy', could be remedied by the practice of 'universal Spartan frugality'. But even the Convention, which represented 'the maximum of political energy, political power and political understanding', could not achieve its purpose. For administrative action and charities were the only means available to government, and the state 'cannot abolish the shortcomings of administration without abolishing itself'.

In extolling the action of the Silesian weavers, Karl went far beyond Bernays: 'not one of the French and English uprisings had 'such a *theoretical* and *conscious* character'. The Silesian uprising began 'where English and French risings end'. The weavers were praised for attacking ledgers rather than machines, and bankers rather than the owners of industrial enterprises. Not only did the Silesian uprising possess 'the stamp of superior character' in relation to the English and the French, but in Weitling's book *Guarantees of Harmony and Freedom*, of 1842, Karl celebrated the 'brilliant literary debut of the German workers'. Truly, the German was 'the theoretician of the European proletariat', as the English was its 'economist' and the French its 'politician'. The political impotence of Germany was 'the impotence of the German bourgeoisie'; the Germans were 'classically destined for social revolution . . . A philosophical people can find its corresponding practice only in socialism' and therefore only in the proletariat can it 'find the dynamic element of its emancipation'. Unlike 'the narrow-minded spirit' that governed a 'political uprising . . . however *partial* the uprising of the *industrial* workers may be, it contains within itself a *universal* soul'. For the 'community of workers' was that of 'human nature . . . the true community of man'.[105]

From August to the end of 1844, Karl played an active role in *Vorwärts!* by offering lectures to artisans and by shaping the editorial line of the paper. The journal was now closely aligned with the activities of the League. He wrote to Feuerbach that 'the German artisans in Paris, i.e. the Communists amongst them, several hundreds', had been attending twice-weekly lectures, on *The Essence of Christianity*, 'throughout this summer'. Karl and others around the paper, notably

Georg Weber, lectured on political economy, drawing upon Engels, Hess on money and Karl's manuscripts. The journal fully reported industrial disturbances around Germany and also published articles, formerly destined for the *Jahrbücher*, notably Engels on the English constitution and Bernays on Weitling.

The Prussian authorities became increasingly restive after the assassination attempt on the king. They were outraged by Bernays's editorial, which suggested that in the face of such an attack German absolutism lost its 'divine and infallible nature'. Eventually Bernays was arraigned and sentenced to two months' imprisonment for a failure to pay caution money and more generally the encouragement of regicide. In December 1844, Guizot was prevailed upon to issue expulsion orders against Ruge, Heine, Bernays and Karl. Ruge insisted upon his Saxon citizenship and was therefore not subject to Prussian jurisdiction. Heine could not be expelled, because he had been born in Düsseldorf at a time when the Rhineland was part of France. Bernays once released from prison was forgotten. Only Karl, on 3 February 1845, whether through arrogance or incompetence, found himself on a coach together with his friend, Heinrich Bürgers, on his way to Brussels.

8. POSTSCRIPT: A NOTE ON MARX AND JUDAISM

Commentators have understandably treated 'On the Jewish Question' with some awkwardness, not least because of its cavalier and uncritical use of anti-Semitic imagery. It is also strange because, despite its reference to 'the real Jew', the 'Jew' in this essay was purely abstract, little more than a metaphor for the values and practices of civil society. In Karl's picture, with the downfall of the *polis* and the loss of knowledge or memory of participation in a political community, the inhabitants of the post-classical world constructed a sort of religion based upon practices arising out of self-interest and pure need. 'Judaism', according to Karl, was the religion which legitimated these practices and assumptions. According to his account, Judaism despised nature, was uninterested in art or love except for the financial value they might contain, while its interest in law was primarily in its circumvention. But a religion that merely rationalized everyday practice lacked the capacity to encompass a reality larger than itself or to transform it. Hence the emergence of Christianity, which completed man's severance from all species-ties. In this sense, the essay is not just a denunciation of Judaism, but of the whole Judaeo-Christian development, which followed the fall of the ancient republic. Even judged in its own terms, however, the analogy between Judaism and the practices of civil society was forced, and so, thereafter, it was dropped. When Karl settled in Paris and became more familiar with the discourse of French republican socialism, he abandoned the terminology of the 'Jew' and shifted to the more capacious notion of the 'bourgeois'.

But none of this explains the studied indifference and lack of empathy apparent in Karl's deployment of this language, nor why he chose to use it. It is noticeable that in the original extension of the alienation idea to encompass the money system, Moses Hess wrote of 'the modern Christian shopkeeper world', or the modern 'Judaeo-Christian shopkeeper world'. Karl's unconcerned usage of anti-Semitic tropes contrasts strongly with other radical Jewish writers who during the *Vormärz* period attempted to incorporate the history of the Jews into the history of progress. Heine, in his 1834 *On the History of Religion and Philosophy in Germany*, considered the Jews the first truly modern people because of their reverence for the law. Gans, who had founded the Association for the Culture and Science of Jews between 1821 and 1823 for the purpose of reconciling Judaism and Enlightenment, had eventually persuaded Hegel to consider Judaism the first religion of freedom. Hess himself in his 1837 *Holy History of Mankind* had also attempted to construct an alternative and Judaeo-centric philosophy of history running from Abraham through Jesus to Spinoza in place of conventional histories, in which Jews barely merited a footnote.

Nothing of this was found in Karl's writing. He did not share the view of some French socialists, notably the Fourierists or Proudhon, that the extent of indebtedness and pauperism had been made worse by the emancipation of the Jews at the time of the French Revolution. Karl supported a Jewish petition for the removal of Jewish disabilities to the Provincial Assembly in the Rhineland, though he claimed to do so only to increase pressure on the Prussian administration. He wrote to Ruge, 'However much I dislike the Jewish faith, Bauer's view seems to me too abstract. The thing is to make as many breaches as possible in the Christian state and to smuggle in as much as we can of what is rational.'[106]

It may be that because Heinrich had abandoned Judaism before Karl was born or because Karl had been brought up a Christian, he felt remote from the Jews and their problems. But whatever the reason, his treatment of the question was not simply unsympathetic, but a direct continuation and extension of the republican discourse about 'regeneration', which had characterized the French Revolution. Despite the best efforts of his father and his uncle, Karl unhesitatingly adopted Napoléon's secular equation between Judaism and usury. Not only did he attack the supposed monotheism of the Jew in the most insulting terms derived from Voltaire as 'a polytheism of many needs', but also went on to attack the Talmud as 'the relation of the world of self-interest to the laws governing that world'.[107] The only real difference between Karl's approach and that of republicans at the time of the Revolution was that his version of 'regeneration' now incorporated the all-encompassing notion of *human* as opposed to merely *political* emancipation. *Human emancipation*, 'an organisation of society which would abolish the preconditions of huckstering, and therefore the possibility of huckstering, would make the Jew impossible. His religious consciousness would be dissipated like a thin haze in the real, vital air of society.'

Karl's unreflective resort to catty anti-Semitic jibes incongruously combined with a sensitivity on the question of his Jewishness continued in later life too. Instances of the former were especially salient in relation to Lassalle. On his visit to Berlin in 1861, he could not refrain from remarking upon the voice of Lassalle's partner, Countess von Hatzfeldt, which had 'a Jewish intonation that has been acquired from and instilled in her by him'. Similarly, at a dinner party given by Lassalle, when seated next to Fräulein Ludmilla Assing, the niece of Varnhagen von Ense and editor of Varnhagen's correspondence with Humboldt, he could not refrain from remarking that she 'who really swamped me with her benevolence, is the most ugly creature I ever saw in my life, a nastily Jewish physiognomy, a sharply protruding thin nose, eternally smiling and grinning'.[108] On the other hand, he reacted sharply to the suggestion of his son-in-law, Charles Longuet, in 1881, that there had been hostility in Trier to Karl's marriage to Jenny von Westphalen, based on 'race prejudice'. Karl told his daughter that this was 'a simple invention' and that there had been 'no prejudice to overcome . . . Longuet would greatly oblige me in never mentioning my name in *his* writings.'[109]

6

Exile in Brussels, 1845–8

I. RESETTLING THE FAMILY

Karl travelled by coach ahead of his family to Brussels on 3 February 1845. Brussels was the capital of the new kingdom of Belgium, formed as a result of a successful revolt against Dutch rule in 1830–31. The city was the administrative centre of the new kingdom and the home of the new royal court, but was also famed for its manufacture of lace and furniture. Before June 1846, the country had been governed by a series of Catholic–Liberal coalitions. As one of the most tolerant and liberal regimes in the pre-1848 period, it had already provided refuge to Polish democrats, French communists and German republicans. But as a new, small and insecure state fearful of harassment by its more powerful neighbours, it could not wholly ignore diplomatic pressure. In Karl's case, the Belgian authorities resisted Prussian demands for his expulsion, but insisted that he sign an undertaking not to publish any article with a bearing upon current Belgian politics. When Prussian pressure continued, in exasperation Karl renounced his nationality in December 1845. Henceforth, he was stateless.

Arriving in Brussels, Karl's first thoughts were not about accommodation for his family, a subject which worried Jenny according to Karl's notebook.[1] There was the more exciting prospect of claiming a poet for the cause of revolution. According to Heinrich Bürgers, who travelled with him and was another member of the *Vorwärts!* collective, Karl had declared that their first task in Brussels would be to pay a visit to the celebrated young German poet Ferdinand Freiligrath, who had recently relinquished his court pension and joined the 'party of movement'; and so, Karl said, 'I must make good that wrong the *Rheinische Zeitung* did him before he stood "on the party battlements".'[2]

Following Karl's abrupt expulsion from Paris, Jenny was forced to sell off the Marxes' furniture and linen in order to pay for the journey to Brussels – 'I got ridiculously little for it,' she commented in her later reminiscences. The day after his departure, she wrote to Karl that Herwegh was playing with little Jenny, while Bakunin had unburdened himself to her with 'rhetoric and drama'. The Herweghs put her up for a couple of days and then, 'ill and in bitter cold weather, I followed Karl to Brussels'. Karl was unable to find suitable lodgings, and so for a month the family lodged at the modest Bois Sauvage Guest House. Thereafter, they stayed briefly in lodgings vacated by Freiligrath following his departure for Switzerland, and finally moved into a small terraced house in the Rue de l'Alliance in the Flemish quarter of the city, where they were soon joined by Moses Hess and his wife, Friedrich Engels, Heinrich Bürgers and a radical Cologne doctor, Roland Daniels. Jenny described a 'small German colony' that 'lived pleasantly together' with one or two radical Belgians, notably Philippe Gigot, and 'several Poles' to be found in 'one of the attractive cafés that we went to in the evenings ... What a colony of paupers there is going to be in Brussels', Jenny wrote in one of her letters in August 1845.[3]

The most important family event of 1845 was the birth on 26 September of Karl and Jenny's second daughter, Laura. In April, Jenny's mother, Caroline, had sent them her 'trusty maid' Lenchen, who was to stay with Karl and Jenny for the rest of their lives. Jenny also planned how the house might be rearranged in preparation for the new arrival. Her brother, Edgar, in Brussels searching for employment, could be housed more cheaply at Bois Sauvage. Once Laura was born, Karl was to move upstairs. 'The children's noise downstairs would then be completely shut off, you would not be disturbed upstairs, and I could join you when things were quiet.'

While Karl and Engels went on a research trip to Manchester in July and August, Jenny, Lenchen and little Jenny – by now fourteen months old – returned to Trier to keep Caroline company: 'oh if only you knew what bliss it is for my mother'. Dithering as to when she should return home, Jenny reflected that although 'people are petty here, infinitely so' and 'life as a whole is a pocket edition', she felt compelled to say, 'even in the face of you arch-Anti-Germans', that 'I feel altogether too much at ease here in little Germany.' Mockingly, she went on, for a woman 'whose destiny it is to have children, to sew, to cook, and to mend, I commend miserable Germany'. There 'one has the comfort of knowing in one's heart of hearts that one has done one's duty'. But now, she conceded, 'old watchwords' like 'duty, honour and the like no longer mean anything', and, she confessed, 'we actually feel in ourselves an urge towards sentiments of positively Stirnerian egotism . . . We, therefore, no longer feel any inclination for the lowlier duties of life. We, too, want to enjoy ourselves, to do things and to experience THE HAPPINESS OF MANKIND in our own persons.'[4]

Despite the thawing of relations with Karl's relatives, accomplished by Jenny on her trip from Paris in 1844, the relationship between Karl and his family in Trier remained strained. A year after Jenny's 1845 visit, Karl's sister Sophie wrote to thank Karl for his kindness towards their youngest sister, Caroline, yet another victim of consumption. Karl had evidently invited her on a trip after a visit to his Dutch relatives – his Aunt Sophie and her husband, Lion Philips – at Zaltbommel. Caroline had been very excited, but 'the poor child felt so weak, that the doctor strongly counselled against it'. Sophie was writing to suggest that for the sake of Caroline's 'peace of mind', Karl should explain to her that he had been prevented from carrying out their original plan, and that it should be postponed to another occasion.[5]

Sophie also went on to berate him for his indifference towards the rest of the family. 'I am so very curious to see your dear children one day; the profoundly sensitive Jenny and the radiant and beautiful little Laura . . . Give a kiss to the lovely little beings from their aunt who is wholly unknown to them . . . For', she went on, 'however lovingly and well you have treated a sister, everything else appears to you alien, and it seems to me, dear Karl, that you have attempted to reason away the intimacy of family relationships (and those still closer).' Sophie noted that, in her letter to Caroline, Jenny had congratulated Henriette on her birthday. But 'you, her own son, for whom she did more than she needed to . . . the poor suffering mother . . . who sees there dying her best-loved child, the most wonderful angel, despite all cares and troubles, you have not only failed to congratulate her, but have totally ignored her . . . I would only wish that you did not deny your heart to such an extent and did not wholly ignore our good mother and your three other siblings.'[6]

2. THE 'CRITIQUE' OF POLITICAL ECONOMY

When Karl had arrived in Paris in November 1843 and attempted to contact possible authors as contributors to the *Deutsch-Französische Jahrbücher*, one of the few he met was the socialist writer Louis Blanc. Blanc promised him an article and allowed him to use his address for letters sent from Germany. Through Blanc, Karl quickly became acquainted with the French radical and socialist analyses of free trade, factory production and the modern economy. These themes in large part stemmed from arguments originally put forward by J.-C.-L. Simonde de Sismondi in his *New Principles of Political Economy* of 1819. Sismondi had first established his reputation in 1803 as a follower of Adam Smith. But in *New Principles* he argued that the advent of the machine destroyed Smith's benign picture of the relationship between competition, the division of labour and the extension of the market. Writing in the aftermath of the Napoleonic Wars, when European and even global markets were saturated by English goods, Sismondi in 1819 was to 'protest against the modern organisation of society' and especially against English economists of the Ricardian School, who were its main defenders.[7] He argued that once the extent of market activity crossed national boundaries, 'overproduction' became a permanent property of the economic system. Overproduction was the consequence of mechanization. 'Europe has reached the point of possessing in all its parts an industry and a manufacture superior to its needs.' Competition on the world market was intensified because in each country production now surpassed consumption.

Competition was linked to the emergence of what Sismondi was one of the first to call 'the proletariat'. According to Sismondi, the rise in population, noticeable all over Western Europe in the early nineteenth century, could not be fully explained by Malthus's ratio between population and the quantity of subsistence (his famous claim that population increased 'geometrically', while increase in subsistence was only 'arithmetical). Population increase was limited, not by the quantity of subsistence, but by the demand for labour. He argued that the increase in population was the result of a fall in the age of marriage, consequent upon the displacement of peasants and artisans by a swelling class of day labourers. In England, where this class had almost wholly replaced peasants and artisans, begging and mendicancy were reaching epidemic proportions. Without the prospect of inheriting a landholding or becoming a master-craftsman, members of this new property-less class saw no reason to defer marriage. They were just like what the Romans had called 'proletarians'. 'Those who had no property, as if more than all others, were called to have children: *ad prolem generandum*.'[8] This class was a danger to itself and to others, a 'miserable and suffering population' which would always be 'restless and a threat to public order'.

Blanc elaborated and dramatized this picture; he perceived French society to be in crisis. According to his *Organization of Labour* of 1841, the 'bourgeois' revolution of 1789 had ushered in a 'commercial society' based upon egoistic individualism. The ensuing free-market competition was a system of 'extermination', which led both to the impoverishment of the workers and to the ruin of large sections of the bourgeoisie. Population increased, the artisan was displaced by the journeyman, the workshop was displaced by the factory, large factories swallowed up small, and exploitation everywhere became more intensive. In England, economists like Malthus and Ricardo were believed to have endorsed a process in which this gulf between rich and poor had been pushed to extremes.

Blanc's picture of France was reinforced by Friedrich Engels' reports from England, and thanks to the essay by Moses Hess 'On the Essence of Money', the situation could now be described in Feuerbachian terms: the worker was related to the product of his labour as an 'alien object'.[9] Karl had already built upon some of Hess's ideas in his essay 'On the Jewish Question'. In the *1844 Manuscripts*, he broadened further Hess's shift from consciousness to activity. Hess had defined life as 'the exchange of productive life activity' involving 'the cooperative working together of different individuals'. By contrast, in 'the inverted world' of money and private property, this 'species-activity' was displaced by the 'egoistic' satisfaction of private needs; man's species-attributes became mere means towards individual self-preservation. Karl built upon this shift of perspective by adopting 'conscious life activity' as his starting point. For, as he argued, 'religious estrangement occurs only in the realm of *consciousness* . . . but economic estrangement is that of *real* life'.[10]

It was not simply the accounts of social development in England and France that impressed Karl towards the end of 1843. What particularly captured his imagination was the connection which Engels made between these developments and the claims of political economy in his 'Outlines of a Critique of Political Economy'.[11] Karl first received an imperfect copy of this manuscript (it had been mangled by the police) that autumn but later published the whole text in the *Jahrbücher*. Engels interpreted the emergence of political economy as an effect of the expansion of trade, which had developed in parallel with the development of religion and theology. For this reason, Adam Smith was called 'the economic Luther', since he had proclaimed the virtues of free trade. But this was to replace 'the Catholic candour' of mercantilism by 'Protestant hypocrisy', to replace admitted rivalry by pretended friendship. Just as it was necessary to overthrow Catholicism, 'so it was necessary to overthrow the mercantile system with its monopolies and hindrances to trade, so that the true consequences of private property would have to come to light' and 'the struggle of our time could become a universal human struggle'. Smith had claimed that a system of liberty would inaugurate global bonds of friendship. But the reality of free trade meant the extension of exploitation across the globe, the onset of ever-fiercer competition between nations and the expansion of the factory system, leading to dissolution of the family.[12]

What was novel and arresting about Engels' 'Outlines' was its attempt to develop a systematic criticism of the categories of political economy. Engels surveyed the debate about 'value' among political economists and deemed it a 'confusion'. While English economists related value to cost of production (the amount of labour embodied in a commodity), the French, especially Jean-Baptiste Say, derived it from 'utility', the usefulness of a commodity in the eyes of the consumer. Engels assumed he had solved the question by defining value as the relationship between cost of production and utility, and price as an effect of the reciprocal relationship between cost of production and competition. He then moved on to attack Malthus's law of population and Say's alleged claim ('Say's Law') that there could never be overproduction by pointing to the periodic occurrence of trade crises. He also argued that these continuous fluctuations within the system undermined any moral basis for exchange.[13]

While Engels' targets were more systematic than those of Blanc, the tone of his attack was similar. Competition was responsible for 'the deepest degradation of mankind'. Just as Blanc summarized the discussion of French socialists, Engels built upon the economic criticism of the Manchester Owenite socialists.[14] In particular, he drew upon the work of the itinerant socialist lecturer John Watts, whose *Facts and Fictions of Political Economists* of 1842 provided the basis of most of his own arguments.

The most striking feature of Engels' essay – and in this he diverged from the Owenites – was that it conjoined his analysis of political economy with Proudhon's attack on private property. Political economy, according to Engels, presupposed private property, while never questioning its existence. As 'the science of enrichment born of the merchants' mutual envy and greed', political economy was largely 'the elaboration of the laws of private property'. Unbeknown to itself, however, Engels argued, political economy was 'a link in the chain of the general progress of mankind'. For by 'dissolving all particular interests', political economy prepared the way for 'the great transformation' towards which the century was headed, 'the reconciliation of mankind with nature and with itself'.[15]

Undoubtedly, it was this equation between political economy and Proudhon's idea of private property which inspired Karl to embark upon his own 'critique of political economy' in the early months of 1844: political economy provided the *theory* of civil society, or, as he later termed it, its 'anatomy'. It was the theoretical expression of this estranged world. As Karl developed the argument in the *Manuscripts* and *The Holy Family*, political economy mistook a world in which 'man' had alienated his essential human attributes for the true world of man. It conflated 'the productive life' of man with Adam Smith's 'propensity to truck, barter and exchange', and was therefore unable to distinguish species-man from the estranged world in which he currently had to act. This was why Karl claimed a few months later in *The Holy Family* that *What is Property?* had the same significance for 'modern political economy' as the famous 1789 text of Abbé Sieyès, *What is the 'Third Estate'?*, had possessed for 'modern politics'.[16]

Nine notebooks written in the first half of 1844 contained Karl's first engagement with political economy.[17] He took notes on Jean-Baptiste Say's *Treatise on Political Economy* and his *Complete Course of Practical Political Economy*, standard texts in France, as well as Smith's

Wealth of Nations, Ricardo's *Principles of Political Economy and Taxation* and McCulloch's history of political economy, together with works by the economists and philosophers Skarbek, Destutt de Tracy and Boiguillebert. But he paid little attention to the details of economic reasoning contained in these texts. Say was cited to confirm the idea that 'private property' was 'a fact whose explanation does not concern political economy, but which forms its foundation', thus confirming Engels' argument that political economy was 'in essence . . . a science of enrichment'.[18] There were extensive notes on Smith, but no overall comments except the remark that Smith's discussion of the relation between exchange and division of labour was a circular one. As to Ricardo, he read the French translation of the first edition together with McCulloch's appended notice on Ricardo's life and writings. He was therefore unaware of Ricardo's second thoughts about the labour or cost of production theory of value which he had adopted initially; this, despite the fact that the edition of Ricardo's works he had read contained relevant critical notes by Say. Karl seems not to have noticed the criticisms levelled against Ricardo in the 1810s and 1820s, and Ricardo's revisions in response; in particular, that the inclusion of capital in the value of a commodity introduced instability into the relationship between value and price.[19] Although he was to make a more attentive rereading of Ricardo in 1850–51, in the 1840s he still wholly depended upon McCulloch's dogmatic reiteration of Ricardo's argument from the first edition of *The Principles* in 1817. Karl's criticism focused not upon the ambiguities of Ricardo's theory of value, but upon 'the inversion' he discerned in the economists' representation of society: 'political economy, in order to lend its laws a greater consistency and precision, has to describe reality as accidental and abstraction as real'.[20]

Similarly, there was no examination of James Mill's *Elements of Political Economy* in its own terms, only an attack on money as 'the estranged mediator' in human exchanges, and yet another denunciation of abstraction: 'one sees how political economy *fixates* the *estranged* form of social intercourse as *essential* and *original*, corresponding to human determination'.[21] The social relationship involved in exchange was 'mere appearance'; 'our reciprocal complementarity' was likewise 'mere *appearance*, which serves mutual plundering'. By contrast, in a 'human' world, you could 'exchange love only for love . . .

Every one of your relations to man and to nature must be a *specific expression*, corresponding to the object of your will, of your *real individual* life'.[22]

The notes which provided the basis of Karl's 'critique' of political economy in the *1844 Manuscripts* consisted of three notebooks. The first notebook was divided into three columns – wages, capital and rent. Under each column were to be found transcriptions or paraphrases of observations in Smith, Schulz, Ricardo and others.[23] This was followed by a passage about labour and estrangement written across the whole page. The second notebook, only seven pages, deals with labour and capital as antitheses, and attacked feudal-Romantic conceptions of the landlord. The third notebook contains discussions of private property, labour, communism and the Hegelian dialectic.

Karl's intellectual development during this period cannot be reconstructed entirely from these notebooks. Not mentioned, but discussed in the *1844 Manuscripts*, were important works like Proudhon's *What is Property?* This was notable, not only for its attack on private property, but also because of its criticism of the wage relation and the remuneration of workers. Proudhon maintained that the worker retained the right to his product, even after being paid his wage, since the wage represented only a small proportion of the added value appropriated by the capitalist. Karl also maintained that the capitalist was the sole beneficiary of added productivity made possible by the cooperation between labourers. He thus touched upon the central question underlying radical criticisms of political economy. How did the apparently free and equal exchange between capitalist and wage-earner result in a disproportionate gain for the former and thus provide the basis of capital accumulation? The exchange between capitalist and worker was neither equal nor voluntary. Through the wage relation, producers of value were robbed of the fruits of their labour.

In a French context these arguments were not particularly original. Proudhon was drawing upon assumptions which had become widespread in French debates and were by no means confined to socialists. In 1836–7, Pellegrino Rossi, Say's successor at the Collège de France, had criticized the treatment of labour in the writings of Ricardo and McCulloch as if the worker were a factor of production just like any other. Rossi's approach was in turn developed and elaborated by Eugène Buret in his response to a prize essay question, set by the Académie des sciences morales et politiques: 'to determine the nature and signs of poverty in several countries' and 'investigate the causes that produce it'. He won the prize in 1840 and used his prize money to visit England. He wrote up his findings in *De la misère des classes laborieuses en Angleterre et en France* (*The Misery of the Working Classes in England and France*), where he argued that labour was not a commodity, a fixed quantity, which could be freely disposed of by the worker.[24] The worker was not in the position of a free seller in relation to the employer; labour could neither be accumulated nor saved: 'Labour is life, and if life is not exchanged every day for food, it soon enough perishes. For the life of man to be a commodity one would have to restore slavery.' Capital, on the other hand, was 'in an entirely different position; if it is not employed, it ceases only to make a profit, it is not destroyed'.[25]

Buret's work was important not just because of its descriptions of the condition of workers in England and France, but also because of its emphasis upon the fact that the commodity the worker sold was not labour, and that the daily exchange of 'life' for food entailed in the wage contract was neither free nor equal. In substance, this approach was not dissimilar to that eventually adopted by Karl in his distinction between 'labour' and 'labour power' around 1857–8. But that was not Karl's preoccupation in 1844. In the summer of that year, he read and annotated the first volume of Buret's study, but showed no particular interest in the critical discussion of the wage contract developed by Rossi, Buret, Proudhon and others in the 1830s and early 1840s.[26] Around 1844, Karl's reading of the works of Ricardo, Buret, Proudhon and others was almost solely governed by his search for evidence of immiseration. Karl's argument purported to be based upon what he called a 'wholly empirical analysis'. But what this meant was indicated at the end of his notes on wages, capital and rent in the first notebook: 'From political economy itself, in its own words, we have shown that the worker descends into a commodity, and the poorest sort of commodity, and that the poverty of the worker is in inverse proportion to the power and extent of his production.'[27] In that context, even Proudhon's work was unsatisfactory. It was the best that could be done from 'the standpoint of political economy'. But the point was to 'rise above the level of political economy'.[28]

This was the intention of Karl's analysis of 'estranged labour'. The greater the development of private property and the division of labour, the more the labour of the producer fell 'into the category of *labour* to earn a living, until it only has this significance'.[29] In contrast to the cynicism of political economists, who paid no attention to the worker's estrangement, Karl proceeded from 'an *actual* economic fact: the worker becomes poorer the more wealth he produces'. This 'fact', Karl claimed, meant that 'the worker is related to the *product of his labour* as to an *alien* object', the economic criticism of the French was now blended with a Feuerbachian inversion.

Estrangement related not only to the product of labour, but also to the activity of labour itself. The activity of the worker was 'an alien activity not belonging to him', a 'self-estrangement'. In other words, as in Hess's work, Man's *'essential being'* became 'a mere means to his *existence'*. The *'life of the species'* became 'a means of individual life'. Labour was no longer the satisfaction of a need, but 'merely a *means* to satisfy needs external to it' – animal needs to maintain individual physical existence. Thus man only felt himself 'freely active in his animal functions'. What was animal became human and what was human became animal.

Finally, estranged labour meant not only the estrangement of man from his species-nature, but also the estrangement of man from man. 'The *alien* being, to whom labour and the product of labour belongs . . . can only be some *other man than the worker.'* Every self-estrangement of man appeared in his relation to other men. His labour belonged to another and was therefore unfree. It was the labour 'of a man alien to labour and standing outside it', or the relation to it of 'a capitalist'.[30]

Karl stated, in what might originally have been intended as a preface, that the purpose of the text was once more to highlight the defects of the 'critical theologian' – Bruno Bauer.[31] But in the course of 1844 the aim of the work may have shifted. When he resumed his project in Brussels, the stated purpose in the contract signed with the Darmstadt publisher Karl Leske, on 1 February 1845, was to produce a two-volume work entitled *A Critique of Politics and of Political Economy*.[32] This particular contract was to be cancelled, but the idea of such a critique was to remain his major preoccupation over the next twenty-five years. The subtitle of *Capital (Das Kapital)* in 1867 was again 'Critique of Political Economy'.

The original aim was to build a 'German positive criticism of political economy' which would be 'positive, humanistic and naturalistic'. It would be based upon 'the discoveries of Feuerbach'.[33] This meant establishing a close link between Karl's picture of the economy and Feuerbach's picture of religion. Karl now claimed the more wealth the worker produced, the poorer the worker became. 'It is the same in religion. The more man puts into God, the less he retains in himself. The worker puts his life into the object; but now his life no longer belongs to him but to the object.'[34] This connection between the economy and religion was a continuation of the argument Karl had put forward in his essay 'On the Jewish Question', where Christian religious doctrine was likened to Judaic economic practice. The argument about spiritual abasement combined with the notion of capital as accumulated labour seems to have been the origin of the later argument connecting industrialization with material immiseration put forward in *Capital* and thereafter vigorously debated among economic historians from the 1920s to the 1970s.

Karl claimed political economy mistook a world in which man had alienated his essential human attributes for the true world of man. In civil society, where every individual appeared as 'a totality of needs' and in which 'each becomes a means for the other', these human attributes only appeared in alien guise. The patterns of behaviour observed and turned into laws by political economists were patterns produced by estrangement. Karl made no objection to the accuracy of these observations; nor did he make a specific economic criticism. The defects of political economy were not occasional, but fundamental. From the beginning, political economy treated the relation of person to person as a relationship between property-owner and property-owner. It proceeded as if private property were a natural attribute of man or a simple consequence of 'the propensity to truck, barter and exchange' described by Adam Smith. As a result, political economy was unable to distinguish 'the productive life' of man from the 'whole estrangement connected with the money system'. The task of the critic was to uncover the essential reality of species-man buried beneath this inverted world and to translate the estranged discourse of political economy into a truly *human* language.[35]

Like Fourier in his critique of 'civilization', authentic human passions found expression in it, but in a distorted and anti-social form. Thus the meaning of private property outside estrangement was 'the *existence of essential objects* for man'. Exchange – or barter – was defined as 'the social act, the species-act . . . within *private ownership*' and therefore 'the *alienated* species-act', 'the opposite of the *social* relationship'. The division of labour became 'the economic expression of the social character of labour within ... estrangement'. Money was 'the alienated *ability of mankind*'. In a 'human' world, the general confounding and confusing of all natural and human qualities expressed by money and exchange value would be impossible.[36]

Just as Feuerbach had argued that it was estrangement that had produced religion and not religion that had produced estrangement, so Karl maintained that it was estrangement that had produced private property.[37] There was no evidence to support this assertion, but without it Karl could not have reached his apocalyptic conclusion: that private property was the product of alienated labour, a 'secret' only revealed once private property had completed its domination over man. It was only once private property became 'a world historical power', and most of mankind was reduced to 'abstract' labour, and everything had been reduced to 'quantitative being', that the antithesis between property and lack of property was transformed into that between capital and labour, bourgeois and proletarian.[38]

In this way private property would be driven towards self-destruction by its own economic movement. As Karl wrote in *The Holy Family*, 'the proletariat executes the sentence that private property pronounces on itself by producing the proletariat'.[39] For as private property advanced to 'world dominion', the condition of the proletariat became ever more 'inhuman'. This polarization meant that at one pole there was the ever-greater sophistication of imaginary appetite (the dietary and sexual excesses of the metropolitan rich), while at the other were the treadmill and rotten potatoes (a reference to workhouse punishment and the meagre diet of the Irish poor).

But this journey of man through the vale of estrangement was not wholly negative. Firstly, private property forced man to become more productive, to the point where with the aid of steam power and automatic machinery, he now stood on the threshold of abundance.[40]

Secondly, dehumanization – which Engels would capture most graphically in his 1844 account of Manchester slums – was generating proletarian revolt. Revolutionary crisis was therefore imminent.[41] This would in turn usher in socialism, for 'when the proletariat is victorious, it by no means becomes the absolute side of society, for it is victorious only by abolishing itself and its opposite'.[42]

3. BETWEEN OWEN AND FEUERBACH: THE COMMUNISM OF FRIEDRICH ENGELS

The issues raised by Feuerbach, which were to the fore in Karl's reading of political economy, were reinforced by his meeting with Friedrich Engels, and the development of their close political companionship.[43] There had been a brief and not particularly cordial encounter in the offices of the *Rheinische Zeitung* in Cologne in November 1842. Thereafter, respect for each other grew as they discovered a need for each other's work. The friendship between them developed in the ten days they had spent together in Paris between 28 August and 6 September 1844.

Friedrich Engels was born in 1820 in Barmen, Westphalia, the eldest son of a textile manufacturer. While Karl possessed the qualifications of a university-trained classicist, lawyer and philosopher, Engels was equipped with the skills deemed requisite for a merchant. Brought up in a strongly Calvinist household, Friedrich attended the *Gymnasium* in the neighbouring town of Elberfeld before being sent to Bremen to study relevant commercial and accounting skills. But from school onwards, Engels had developed radical literary ambitions. Unlike Karl, his first political attitudes had been strongly shaped by the liberal nationalist literary movement of the 1830s. His earliest heroes had been drawn from Teutonic mythology; in Bremen, for example, he extolled the legend of Siegfried as a symbol of the courageous qualities of Young German manhood in its struggle against the petty and servile Germany of the princes.[44] He was drawn to Young Germany, particularly to the writings of Ludwig Börne, a Jewish radical and Parisian exile, whose republican denunciations of German princes and aristocrats were combined with a polemic against the Francophobe tendencies of German nationalism.

Engels gravitated towards the Young Hegelians after reading David Strauss's *Life of Jesus* in Bremen towards the end of 1839. He therefore chose Berlin, near Bruno Bauer and his circle, as the place to perform his year's military service. Military service was an activity which his patriotic father would support wholeheartedly, and so – at least for a time – Engels escaped the family firm. It was his first chance to break out from his home town and to savour life in a large city free from the surveillance of his elders. But peace-time soldiering brought its own forms of tedium, so Engels spent his spare hours socializing in the cafés and taverns frequented by the Young Hegelians. Young Hegelianism not only offered a bohemian diversion, but also gave him a chance to engage with what he called 'the ideas of the century'. He duly attended the famous Berlin course of lectures delivered by Friedrich Schelling, the erstwhile companion and now conservative foe of Hegel, and within weeks of his arrival, writing under the pseudonym 'Frederick Oswald', he published pamphlets denouncing Schelling's 'Philosophy of Revelation'.

When Engels first got to know Karl, he was impulsive, intrepid and eclectic. He had no contact with the university and no philosophical training; and so the growing disagreements between Young Hegelians appear to have made little impression upon him. Until he joined forces with Karl in Paris in the summer of 1844, Engels' journalistic writings showed no awareness of the growing rift between the supporters of Bauer and those of Feuerbach. He saw in them a common assault upon Christianity which would lead to the replacement of theology by anthropology. In politics, too, Engels was barely touched by Hegel. Unlike most of the other Berlin Young Hegelians, he was a republican and a revolutionary democrat before he became a Hegelian. In Berlin, he still believed he could combine Hegel's philosophy of history with Börne's republican view of politics. In 1842, in a satirical poem about Bruno Bauer's dismissal from his university post co-written with Bruno's younger brother, Edgar, Engels referred to himself as the Jacobin 'Oswald the Montagnard': 'A radical is he, dyed in the wool and hard / Day in, day out, he Plays the guillotine/a single, solitary tune and that's a cavatina.' Enthusiasm for Jacobinism together with the vehement rejection of Louis Philippe's *juste milieu* liberal constitutionalism in France was one way of expressing his off-the-record delight in shocking the respectable. Another was joining in with the anti-Christian excesses of the 'Free'.[45]

Engels' acquaintance with the character of Young Hegelianism was largely confined to the debate over Christianity. His distinctive voice developed not within the Young Hegelian circles of Berlin, but in England, to which he was sent to represent the firm of Ermen and Engels in Manchester between November 1842 and August 1844. There he regularly attended Owenite debates, and became more conversant with the Owenite philosophical assumptions expressed in the Manchester Hall of Science than with the philosophical tradition of German idealism.

During the summer of 1842 at the height of Chartist agitation, Hess – the foreign editor of the *Rheinische Zeitung* – foretold the final onset of an 'approaching catastrophe'. In a meeting with Hess in Cologne on his way to England in November 1842, Engels had been converted to 'communism'. For Hess's prophecy seemed to be coming true, and within days of his arrival in England Engels was writing in similar catastrophist terms.[46] In an article written in 1843 Engels defined his shift as a consequence of discussions among the Young Hegelians. He stated that in 1842 the Young Hegelians were 'atheist and republican', but that by the autumn of that year 'some of the party contended for the insufficiency of political change, and declared their opinion to be, that a *Social* revolution based upon common property, was the only state of mankind agreeing with their abstract principles'. He described Hess as 'the first communist of the party'.[47]

During his stay in England, Engels continued his double life. He was a businessman in office hours, but wrote frequently for the English and German radical press and began collecting materials for his book *The Condition of the Working Class in England*, which appeared in 1845. Outside his life as a businessman, he developed a relationship with a radical Irish mill worker, Mary Burns, and got to know some of the leading Owenites and Chartists around Manchester. Much of the enduring interest of his book derived from these encounters and from the first hand observation which resulted from them.

Engels followed Hess in believing that in each of the three major European nations, events were leading to the conclusion that 'a thorough revolution of social arrangements based on community of property' was an 'urgent and unavoidable necessity'. The English had arrived at this conclusion 'practically', the French 'politically' and the Germans 'philosophically by reasoning on first principles'. Engels was particularly impressed by the practical perspectives of the Owenites. In the autumn of 1843, he wrote that 'in everything bearing on practice, upon the *facts* of the present state of society, we find that the English Socialists are a long way before us'.[48] Around the same time he wrote 'Outlines of a Critique of Political Economy' – much of it again taken from

Owenite sources. In it he claimed that private property was responsible for the contradictions of political economy, and that after the approaching triumph of free trade, it would propel England towards its final social crisis.[49]

In subsequent essays, published in the *Jahrbücher* and *Vorwärts!*, Engels went on to enlarge upon this crisis and its historical causes. His starting point resembled that of Thomas Carlyle's famous essay of 1843, *Past and Present*: individualism was dissolving all social ties. After the dissolution of feudalism, mankind was no longer to 'be held together by force, by *political* means, but by *self-interest*, that is, by *social* means'. 'The abolition of feudal servitude has made "cash payment the sole relation between human beings"'.[50] Mercantilists had acknowledged the antagonism which underlay buying cheap and selling dear. But Adam Smith had praised commerce as 'a bond of union and friendship'.

This 'hypocritical way of misusing morality for immoral purposes' was 'the pride of the free-trade system'. All small monopolies were abolished 'so that the *one* great basic monopoly, property, may function the more freely and unrestrictedly'. By 'dissolving nationalities', the liberal economic system had intensified 'to the utmost the enmity between individuals, the ignominious war of competition'; 'commerce absorbed industry into itself and thereby became omnipotent'. Through industrialization and the factory system, the last stage was reached, 'the dissolution of the family'. 'What else can result from the separation of interests, such as forms the basis of the free-trade system?' Money, 'the alienated empty abstraction of property', had become the master of the world. Man had ceased to be the slave of men and has become the slave of *things*. 'The disintegration of mankind into a mass of isolated mutually repelling atoms in itself means the destruction of all corporate, national and indeed of any particular interests and is the last necessary step towards the free and spontaneous association of men.'[51]

The overarching framework of Engels' analysis was that of a final crisis of Christianity: 'the Christian world order cannot be taken any further than this'. His portrayal of the roots of this crisis drew upon both Bauer and Feuerbach without much discrimination. Following Moses Hess, he argued that the crisis was happening in England because 'only England has a social history ... Only here have principles been turned into interests before they were able to influence history'. 'Democratic equality', Engels wrote in March 1844, was a 'chimera'. But the democracy towards which England was moving 'was not that of the French Revolution, whose antithesis was the monarchy and feudalism, but the democracy whose antithesis is the middle class and property . . . the struggle of democracy against the aristocracy in England is the struggle of the poor against the rich. The democracy towards which England is moving is a *social* democracy.'[52]

The origin of the present crisis was to be traced back to 'the Christian-Germanic view of the world' whose basic principle was 'abstract subjectivity'. After the disintegration of feudalism, this idea had culminated in 'the Christian state'. More generally, it had elevated 'interestedness' which was 'subjective and egotistical' to 'a general principle' and the consequence was 'universal fragmentation, the concentration of each individual upon himself', the hegemony of individual interest and the domination of property.[53]

The most important effect of the eighteenth century for England was the creation of the proletariat by 'the industrial revolution'. The social upheaval of the industrial revolution and the expansion of trade were portents of 'the assembling, the gathering of mankind from the fragmentation and isolation into which it had been driven by Christianity; it was the penultimate step towards the self-understanding and self-liberation of mankind'. Engels had been confident about the 'irresistible progress' of the human species through history, 'its ever certain victory over the unreason of the individual'. 'Man has only to understand himself', Engels wrote in 1844, and 'to organise the world in a truly human manner according to the demands of his own nature and he will have solved the riddle of our time'.[54]

After his conversations with Karl in Paris, Engels somewhat modified his position on England. In *The Condition of the Working Class in England*, which he wrote up in the months following, the focus was no longer simply upon private property, individualism and social dissolution. These themes were now joined by an emphasis upon the redemptive role of the proletariat, a theme he had probably derived from a reading of Karl's depiction of its role in his introduction to his critique of Hegel's *Philosophy of Right*, published in the *Jahrbücher*, as well as from his discussions with him in August 1844. The story told in the book derived from the categories of Feuerbach. Starting from an account of the bucolic innocence of English pre-industrial textile workers, Engels recounted how industrialization had dragged these workers into the mainstream of world history and progressively reduced them to the horrific animal conditions detailed in his description of Manchester. But pauperization and dehumanization formed the essential prelude to the recovery of humanity through proletarian revolt, beginning with crude acts of individual violence and culminating with Chartism, the organized labour movement and social revolution.

Engels still aligned himself with the Owenites, but his view was becoming markedly more critical of their political passivity. In the summer of 1844 he still believed like the Owenites that 'social evils cannot be cured by People's Charters'. By 1845 in *The Condition of the Working Class in England*, he criticized the Owenites for their disapproval of 'class hatred' and for not discerning 'the element of progress in this dissolution of the old social order'. He now considered naive their ambition 'to place the nation in a state of communism at once, overnight, not by the unavoidable march of its political development'. He argued that they should 'condescend to return for a moment to the Chartist standpoint'; this might enable them to conquer 'the brutal element' in what would otherwise be the 'bloodiest war of the poor against the rich' ever waged.[55]

Engels was the first to identify the revolutionary possibilities of modern industry, to highlight the place of the factory worker and to dramatize for German socialists the character of modern industrial class struggle. His study of England connected the stages of the formation of proletarian class-consciousness to phases of industrial development. His focus on the steam-powered factory rather than on the workshop also led him to emphasize the relationship between workers and the means of production, rather than the product alone, and to describe the relation between classes, rather than the competition between alienated individuals; and this account made a deep impression on Karl. Almost twenty years later, Karl wrote to Engels, 'so far as the main theses in your book are concerned . . . they have been corroborated down to the very last detail by developments subsequent to 1844'.[56]

The result of the ten-day meeting between Engels and Karl in Paris was an agreement to produce a joint attack on Bruno Bauer. Although the ensuing pamphlet, *The Holy Family, or, Critique of Critical Criticism against Bruno Bauer and Company* appeared in February 1845 under both their names, only a dozen or so of its more than

200 pages – a small section dealing with conditions in England – were written by Engels. *The Holy Family* took the form of a prolonged attack on the *Allgemeine Literatur-Zeitung*, a journal produced between the end of 1843 and October 1844 by the Bauer brothers and their small coterie of supporters in Berlin.

The Holy Family began with the grandiloquent claim that '*real humanism* has no more dangerous enemy in Germany than *spiritualism* or *speculative idealism*.'[57] Its length and detail were excessive. Georg Jung, one of Karl's most devoted Cologne admirers, congratulated him on the pamphlet's treatment of Proudhon and of the popular novelist Eugène Sue, but found 'the many enumerations of trivia terribly tiring at first . . . I have only one request to make,' he went on, 'don't be deflected again by other works.' He urged him to get on with his work on political economy and politics.[58] Engels writing from Barmen in March 1845 pointed out the main defect of the book. 'The supreme contempt' evinced towards the *Literatur-Zeitung* was in glaring contrast to the length devoted to it. Furthermore, the criticism of speculation and abstract being in general would be incomprehensible to a wider public.[59]

The book did not add substantially to Karl's previous critique of Bauer's position. More interesting was its application in the discussion of some of the themes found in the *Literatur-Zeitung*. These included the French Revolution, Proudhon's political economy, Eugène Sue's *Mysteries of Paris*, and a discussion of seventeenth- and eighteenth-century Anglo-French materialism. The political scenario was still that originally laid out by Hess and reiterated by Karl in his attack on Ruge in *The King of Prussia and Social Reform*. Each of the three main European states, France, England and Germany, would pursue its own path to emancipation. Thus, in the case of France, against Edgar Bauer's attempt to cast Proudhon as a moralist, Karl declared his work to be a 'scientific manifesto of the French proletariat'.[60]

Back in Barmen and writing up *The Condition*, Engels pursued a similar course. He firmly predicted that England was destined to experience an apocalyptic social revolution; but, in Germany, he still hoped for a peaceful change inaugurated by the philosophers. In March 1845 he was delighted (incorrectly) to inform the readers of the Owenite *New Moral World* of 'the most important fact' that 'Dr Feuerbach has declared himself a communist' and that 'communism was in fact only the *practice* of what he had proclaimed long before theoretically'.[61] In speeches which he made around the same time to 'the respectables' of Barmen and Elberfeld, together with Moses Hess, Engels also argued that the transition to communism in Germany ought to be a peaceful one. Middle-class audiences were urged to embrace communism on prudential grounds. Their position, he warned, was being undermined by the polarization between rich and poor, by the impact of competition and by the chaos resulting from periodic trade crises. As an alternative to revolution, he argued for the benefits of planning and for the gradual introduction of community of goods. In the interim, helpful measures could be introduced – free education, the reorganization of poor relief and a progressive income tax.[62]

4. ANSWERING STIRNER

In October 1844, Max Stirner published his attack on Feuerbachian humanism, *The Ego and Its Own*. Both Engels and Hess read an early specimen copy sent by the publisher, Otto Wigand. Stirner's basic objection to this form of humanism was its quasi-religious ethos. Feuerbach's criticism of religion had focused upon the separation of human attributes ('predicates') from human individuals ('subjects') – hence 'the inversion of subject and predicate' – and their reassembly as attributes of a fictive God. But, as Stirner pointed out, Feuerbach himself did not return these alienated attributes to human individuals, but rather to another equally fictive creation, 'man' or 'species-being'. 'Man' continued to be presented to individuals as their 'vocation' or ethical goal. 'Man' was in effect just another version of the Protestant God; and this was an attack made worse by Feuerbach's own admission that he had taken the term 'species' from Strauss, who had employed it as a dynamic substitute for the place of Christ in orthodox Christianity. In place of Feuerbach's humanism, Stirner advocated the primacy of the ego:

> To the Christian the world's history is the higher thing, because it is the history of Christ or 'man'; to the egoist only *his* history has value, because he wants to develop only *himself*, not the mankind-idea, not God's plan, not the purposes of Providence, not liberty, and the like. He does not look upon himself as a tool of the idea or a vessel of God, he recognizes no

calling, he does not fancy that he exists for the further development of mankind and that he must contribute his mite to it, but he lives himself out, careless of how well or ill humanity may fare thereby.[63]

Engels and Hess disagreed about the book. Engels' first reaction was favourable. Writing to Karl from Barmen in November 1844, he compared Stirner with Bentham: 'We must not simply cast it aside, but rather use it as the perfect expression of present-day folly and, *while inverting it*, continue to build on it.' This, because it was so one-sided, he argued, would immediately result in 'communism'. 'In its egoism, the human heart' is 'unselfish and self-sacrificing'; 'we are communists out of egoism'. 'It is out of egoism that we wish to be *human beings*, not mere individuals.'[64]

Hess strongly disagreed. He was shocked that readers, unaware of Young Hegelian developments, might assume that 'recent German Philosophers' – in particular Stirner – 'have published their writings at the instigation of reactionaries'. Hess focused especially upon Stirner's assertion that 'as the individual is the whole of nature, so he is the whole of the species too'. Stirner's erasure of the difference between the particular man and the human species ignored the fact that this man remained 'divided'; and this division could only be resolved through 'socialism'. Instead of believing 'that we will only be something through a social union with our neighbouring men', the implication of Stirner's position, like that of Bauer, was that our misery could be cast out, that the divisiveness of our social isolation could be pushed aside and that 'we could be divinised and humanised by mere theoretical knowledge alone'. Socialists proposed that 'we should become *real species-beings*', and thereby create a society in which 'everyone can cultivate, exercise and perfect their human qualities'. Stirner wanted to 'know nothing of *this* actual man'. His response was: 'I, the egoist, have not at heart the welfare of the "human society", I sacrifice nothing to it, I only utilise it; but to be able to utilise it completely I transform it rather into my property and my creature; that is, I annihilate it, and form in its place the *Union of Egoists*.'[65]

Karl certainly felt targeted in Stirner's attack upon the religiosity of Feuerbach's language of 'man', and therefore required to reply.[66] In Paris, in December 1844, he wrote to Börnstein, the editor, explaining that his 'review of Stirner' for *Vorwärts!* would not be ready for the next number, but promising it for the following week.[67] His reaction to Stirner's book was evidently closer to that of Hess. For Engels wrote to Karl again from Barmen around 20 January 1845, regretting the first impression the book had made upon him. He stated that he was now in entire agreement with Karl, and with Hess, who 'after several changes of mind came to the same conclusion as yourself'.[68]

As in his polemic against the Bauers in *The Holy Family*, Karl's 'review' of Stirner was of inordinate length and lacking in any sense of proportion. The unpublished manuscript totalled more than 300 pages. The urgings of Jenny, of Engels and of Jung and other friends were to get on with his *Critique of Politics and of Political Economy*. But, despite this, the polemic against Stirner appears to have preoccupied Karl during the first half of 1845. In the summer of that year, it even prompted plans made together with Engels and Joseph Weydemeyer to produce a polemical volume akin to the *Deutsch-Französische Jahrbücher* criticizing 'German philosophy'.[69] Like Hess, in his 'review' Karl evaded Stirner's main point: the moralistic, normative and still quasi-religious character of socialist rhetoric. But Stirner's criticism was tacitly conceded. Karl replaced the normative tone by recourse to the notion of class struggle, an idea which had been commonplace in French political writing since the Revolution.[70] 'Communism' was redescribed. It was no longer 'an *ideal* to which reality' would 'have to adjust itself'. It was now 'the *real* movement which abolishes the present state of things'.[71]

Karl's attack on Stirner, 'Saint Max', was an elephantine elaboration of Hess's argument. Stirner's emphasis upon the identity of the individual and the species, according to Karl, implied that Stirner was intent upon some covert form of self-divinization. Just about acceptable as a *jeu d'esprit*, Karl's satirical polemic became silly when it was pushed too far, and especially so when it was accompanied by a leaden humour about saints and church councils. In fact, as Stirner replied to his critics, he had no belief in the metaphysical reality of the divine. Nor was he damaged by Karl's criticism that the Stirnerian 'ego' was shaped by the social and cultural environment of which it was part. All that mattered from Stirner's point of view was that the individual ego lived according to its own will.[72]

5. A MATERIALIST CONCEPTION OF HISTORY?

Forty years later, in the decade following Karl's death, Engels recalled, in his essay 'On the History of the Communist League', of 1885, his first extended meeting with Karl in Paris at the end of August 1844. 'When I visited Marx in Paris in the summer of 1844, our complete agreement in all theoretical fields became evident and our joint work dates from that time. When, in the spring of 1845, we met again in Brussels,' Engels went on, 'Marx had already fully developed his materialist theory of history in its main features.'[73]

This was a truly misleading account. Karl and Engels converged on certain points of current interest: the espousal of Feuerbach, for instance, the adoption of a socialist rather than a republican agenda, and, above all, a belief in the central importance of political economy. Engels' tendency to defer to Karl's intellectual authority also smoothed out some areas of possible contention. But their intellectual trajectories had been different and the differences between them persisted. The disagreement between Hess, Engels and Karl in their reactions to Stirner provides one important clue to their deeper differences. Both Hess and Karl over the previous year had emphasized a conception of life as 'the exchange of productive life activity' or 'conscious life activity'. There was no such emphasis in Engels, whose viewpoint had remained much closer to that of the Owenites, and who, therefore, thought that by a change of circumstances Stirnerian self-love could assume a 'communist' form.

The textual support for Engels' second claim about the foundation of a 'materialist conception of history' may have derived from his rereading in much changed circumstances of the opening lines of *The Holy Family*. There he read that '*real humanism* has no more dangerous enemy in Germany than *spiritualism* or *speculative idealism*, which substitutes "*self-consciousness*" or "*spirit*" for the *real individual man*'.[74] Engels' understanding of idealism remained superficial.[75] He may not therefore have seen any reason to distinguish between Karl's obsessive and mildly patricidal desire to differentiate himself from Bruno Bauer – his former *Doktorvater* – and the idealist tradition as a whole. Engels' elaboration of his account in the essay 'Ludwig Feuerbach and the End of Classical German Philosophy' (1886) compounded this error. He explained the philosophical conflicts of the period as a battle between 'two great camps': 'those who asserted the primacy of the mind over nature and, therefore in the last instance, assumed world creation in some form or other . . . comprised the camp of idealism. The others, who regarded nature as primary, belong to the various schools of materialism.'[76] This imaginary battle between 'idealism' and 'materialism' was a product of Engels' conflation of the debates of the mid-1840s with his particular version of a much later post-Darwinian materialism premised upon the primacy of nature. It was remote from the substance of the Young Hegelian debates of the 1840s.

These errors and misunderstandings contained in Engels' account of the advent of 'the materialist conception of history' were amplified in the work of Georgi Plekhanov (1856–1918), the so-called 'father of Russian Marxism'.[77] He presented Karl's learned attempt to correct Bauer's account of Enlightenment philosophy in *The Holy Family* as an endorsement of the Anglo-French materialism of the seventeenth and eighteenth centuries.[78]

The last steps towards the invention of this new theoretical tradition were taken in the twentieth century. Karl's theory was now called 'historical materialism'. The process was completed in the 1920s and 1930s with the publication of what was presented as the second joint composition of Karl and Engels, *The German Ideology*. It began with the publication by David Riazanov of a single chapter, 'I. Feuerbach' in Russian in 1924.[79] A German edition of this 'chapter' followed in 1926, and then – assembled together with the essays on Stirner and Bauer and a putative second volume dealing with 'the prophets of true socialism' – these manuscripts were published as a complete book in 1932. What purported to be the first chapter, entitled 'Feuerbach', soon became famous and was republished innumerable times as a supposed résumé of 'Marxism' or 'historical materialism'. But it has recently been demonstrated that it was 'factitiously' put together by Riazanov and his associates in the 1920s. The purpose of its publication during the early years of the Soviet Union was to complete the exposition of 'Marxism' as a system by connecting what Karl in 1859 had called a process of 'self-clarification' with Engels' claim about Karl's development of 'the materialist conception of history' in 1885.[80]

According to Engels, Karl developed his new 'materialist conception of history' between his completion of *The Holy Family* in the autumn of 1844 and his reunion with Engels in Brussels in the spring of 1845. During these months, Karl did not publish anything. The only piece of relevant documentation, which Engels discovered when going through papers dating from that period, was a two-page entry in one of Karl's notebooks, entitled 'Ad Feuerbach'.[81]

This document referred to materialism at various points. But its main aim was to criticize the passivity of the materialist approach; passivity was 'the chief defect of all previous materialism (that of Feuerbach included)'.[82] Such a criticism could not be construed as a contribution towards what Engels meant by 'the materialist conception of history'. The supposed battle between 'idealism' and 'materialism' invoked by Engels was a late-nineteenth-century preoccupation. During his years in Paris and Brussels, Karl's ambition – like that of all German philosophers in the pre-1848 period – was not to develop a 'materialist conception', but rather to construct a philosophical system that reconciled materialism and idealism, and incorporated nature and mind without assigning primacy to one or the other.

Feuerbach was criticized, both in the 'Theses' and in Karl's other writings of the time, for the passivity inherent in his association of man with sensuousness, rather than with '*practical* human sensuous activity'. According to Karl, Feuerbach did not see that the sensuous world he invoked was 'the product of industry and the state of society' and that 'the social system' was modified 'in accordance with changed needs'.[83] As will be seen, this was a criticism which derived not so much from 'materialism' as mainly from the legacy of idealism.[84] It is also important to remember that Karl was reluctant to concede too much to 'idealism' because its most obvious standard-bearer was Bruno Bauer. The argument that idealism 'does not know sensuous activity as such' was inaccurate.[85] So far as the claim had any validity, it mainly applied to Feuerbach, whose conception of activity was very circumscribed.

The one area in which Karl identified himself with a materialist position was in his support for Feuerbach's denial that abstractions possessed any existence beyond their empirical content. This was the basis of Karl's belief that there was a parallel between religious alienation in the spiritual realm and social alienation in the domain of material production. But this was not the product of a newly developing 'materialist conception' in 1845. The attack on abstraction had already become a prominent feature of his thought in 1843. Furthermore, it was to remain an important and recurrent theme throughout his subsequent work. As his well-known section on 'the fetishism of commodities' in *Capital* was to testify, it remained a central element in his 'critique of political economy'.[86]

In the mid-1840s, this critique of abstraction not only guided his criticism of economists, but also his approach to all forms of thought. At the end of 1846 in his letter to Pavel Annenkov, for instance, he explained his criticism of Proudhon: 'He fails to see that *economic categories* are but *abstractions* of those real relations, that they are truths only insofar as those relations continue to exist. Thus he falls into the error of bourgeois economists, who regard those economic categories as eternal laws, and not as historical laws, which are laws only for a given historical development, a specific development of the productive forces.' He claimed that Proudhon failed to understand that 'those who produce social relations in conformity with their material productivity – also produce the *ideas, categories*, i.e. the ideal abstract expressions of those same social relations'.[87]

The thought was equally present almost twenty years later. In the economic manuscripts of 1863, he wrote, 'The rule of the capitalist over the worker is therefore the rule of the object over the human, of dead labour over living, of the product over the producer . . . This is exactly *the same* relation in the sphere of material production, in the real social life process . . . as is represented by *religion* in the ideological sphere: the inversion of the subject into the object and *vice versa*.'[88] Lastly, it is worth noting Karl's continuing enthusiasm for this procedure in a somewhat different area of inquiry, his excitement about the concrete empirical origins of the language of abstraction in Hegel's *Science of Logic*: 'But what would Old Hegel say, were he to learn in the hereafter that the *general* [*das Allgemeine*] in German and Nordic means only the communal land, and that the *particular*, the *special* [*das Sondere, Besondere*], means only private property divided off from the communal land? Here are the logical categories coming damn well out of "our intercourse" after all.'[89]

6. THE LEGACY OF IDEALISM: A NEW VISION OF LABOUR

In these years spent in Brussels, Karl first declared his intellectual independence, not only from Bauer and Ruge, but also from Feuerbach. It is, therefore, a good point at which to pick out what was most novel and distinctive about Karl's political and philosophical position, just as its main features were beginning to acquire a permanent shape.

Most striking during these years was the change in his vision of socialism and the proletariat in the light of a new conception of the historical significance of labour. What inspired this new conception was not his putative materialism, but a particular appropriation of the basic assumptions of German idealism. This becomes clear when Karl's approach is compared with the approaches of other radicals and socialists at the time. Their outlook was shaped by a naturalistic version of materialism. Their starting point, standard in England from the time of Locke through to Bentham, prevalent among the *Philosophes* and *Idéologues* in France and the followers of Spinoza in Germany, was a conception of man as a natural being. This meant that man's actions were motivated by the pursuit of happiness and the avoidance of pain. As a creature of nature, man was primarily defined by his needs and impulses. Throughout the eighteenth century and the early nineteenth, this position offered a welcome alternative to the orthodox Christian emphasis upon original sin.

Not surprisingly, this was also the founding assumption of the many varieties of socialism that emerged in the 1830s and 1840s; and it was explicitly espoused by the largest socialist groupings, the followers of Owen in England and of Cabet in France. In this approach, man was a product of his environment, a consumer governed by his appetites and needs. By improving this environment through better education and a more enlightened attitude towards reward and punishment, it would be possible to transform human nature and increase the extent of human happiness. This had also been Karl's starting point in 1843, when he and Ruge planned the *Deutsch-Französische Jahrbücher* as a journal which would address 'those who think and those who suffer'.

Karl's innovation in the course of 1844 was to apply the insights of idealism to the understanding of labour, to recuperate its emphasis upon activity and man's position as a producer. Most striking was the connection made in these writings between two areas of discourse hitherto unrelated to each other: on the one hand, discussion of the social question and the plight of the proletariat and, on the other, the world-transforming significance accorded to labour in Hegel's *Phenomenology of the Spirit*. By making this connection, Karl identified socialism with human self-activity as it had been invoked in the idealist tradition following the philosophical revolution accomplished by Kant.[90]

Kant and Fichte had already challenged the passivity of the view of man as a natural being. But in the *Phenomenology*, Hegel built upon this idealist inheritance and translated it into a vision of history. According to Karl, Hegel had grasped 'the self-creation of man as a process' and in so doing had grasped the essence of labour, and comprehended the creation of man as 'the outcome of man's *own labour*'.[91] Man, according to Karl, was not merely a 'natural being', but 'a human natural being', whose point of origin was not nature, but history. Unlike animals, man made his activity 'the object of his will'. He could form objects in accordance with the laws of beauty. Thus history could be seen as the humanization of nature through man's 'conscious life activity' and, at the same time, the humanization of man himself through 'the forming of the five senses'. History was the process of man becoming *Gattungswesen* ('species-being') and the basis of man's ability to treat himself as 'a universal, and therefore a free being', not determined by his particular needs.[92]

The idealist tradition was crucial in focusing upon the capacity of subjects to resist or override natural desires or needs and to submit these impulses to rational scrutiny. Already in 1786, Kant had reinterpreted the biblical story of the Fall as a parable about man's escape from a natural condition. Despite his yearning to escape 'the wretchedness of his condition . . . between him and that imagined place of bliss, restless reason would interpose itself, irresistibly impelling him to develop the faculties implanted within him . . . It would make him take up patiently the toil which he yet hates, and pursue the frippery which he despises . . . Man's departure from that paradise . . . was nothing but the transition from an uncultured, merely animal condition to the state of humanity, from bondage to instinct to rational control – in a word, from the tutelage of nature to the state of freedom.'[93]

This ability to resist natural desires or submit them to rational scrutiny was what was meant by the term *spontaneity* in the idealist tradition. Spontaneity meant inward self-determination and was present in German philosophy from the time of Leibniz and became the centrepiece of Kant's conception of practical reason. Its crucial political implication was that individuals might shape their actions not in pursuit of welfare and happiness, but in the establishment of morality and right.[94] One of Hegel's crucial achievements in the *Phenomenology* was to show how the concept of right might extend beyond the conscience of the individual, and become embodied in institutions and in interpersonal relations, and form the basis of what he called 'ethical life'.[95] Karl's invocation of the self-making of man by labour in the *1844 Manuscripts* contained his version of spontaneity and freedom as human attributes. Labour was a form of activity which entailed a continuous process of interaction with nature, not one simply driven by need, for as the *1844 Manuscripts* emphasized, it could also be associated with freedom, for man could shape things according to the law of beauty. Labour as the activity of self-directed individuals was purposive and teleological (driven by pursuit of an end). The resistance to be overcome in any labour process was either natural – the operation of causal mechanisms in the physical world – or historical – the conflict it might occasion with existing social relations. In this sense human history might be understood as the continual and cumulative process of interaction between teleology and causality.

In the light of this approach, the depiction of man as a passive being, as a consumer dependent upon nature to supply his needs, became Karl's principal criticism of contemporary socialism. That was why his so-called 'Theses on Feuerbach', written early in 1845, were as much a criticism of socialism as of Feuerbach himself. This was certainly true of the third thesis, which argued 'that the materialist doctrine concerning the changing of circumstances and upbringing forgets that circumstances are changed by men and that the educator must himself be educated'.[96] It also explains part of Karl's objection to Proudhon. In Karl's view, the labour question was not simply about consumption or wages. The ambition of organized workers was not simply to attain 'greater happiness' through the acquisition of more material goods, but to change productive relations.

According to Karl's account in 1844, 'socialism' as the transcendence of 'self-estrangement had followed the same path of development as self-estrangement itself'. Its first crude emanation had been the extension of the category of worker to all men. In its most brutish form it had substituted for marriage (a 'form of exclusive private property') the 'community of women' and general prostitution. This type of communism was 'the logical expression of private property'. It was 'the culmination of envy' and 'the abstract negation of the entire

world of culture and civilisation', 'the regression to the unnatural simplicity of the *poor* and crude man, who has few needs and who has
not only failed to go beyond private property, but has not even reached
it'. Developed communism would get beyond 'the vileness of private
property which wants to set itself up as the positive community system'. Communism had still to reach the 'return of man to himself'.
True communism was 'the positive transcendence of private property
as human self-estrangement, and therefore as the complete return of
man to himself as a social (i.e. human) being – a return accomplished
consciously and embracing the entire wealth of previous development . . .
This communism as fully developed naturalism equals humanism, and
as fully developed humanism equals naturalism.' It was 'the riddle of
history solved'.[97]

The idea that freedom meant self-activity, and that the capacity to
produce was man's 'most essential' characteristic, led Karl to conclude
in 1844 that 'estranged labour' formed the basis of all other forms of
estrangement and, therefore, that 'the whole of human servitude' was
'involved in the relation of the worker to production'. For 'estranged
labour' was the inversion of 'conscious life activity'. Man's *essential
being* became a mere means to his *existence*. Karl never published
his 1844 reflections on 'estranged labour'. But his basic assumption
remained. In Kantian terms, wage work was a form of heteronomy, an
inversion of freedom conceived as the self-activity of the producer.

Contrast this with 'the materialist conception of history', as Plekhanov later understood it. In his conception, the role not only of politics
but also of the relations of production was given only a derivative and
secondary importance. Rather than falling for a 'dualism' between
'economy' and 'psychology', Plekhanov argued, both should be seen as
the product of 'the state of productive forces', which he, following Darwin, equated with 'the struggle for existence'. 'The struggle for existence
creates their economy, and on the same basis arises their psychology as
well. Economy itself is something derivative, just like psychology.'[98]
Karl Kautsky (1854–1938), the editor of *Die Neue Zeit* and a major
Marxist theorist of the Second International, went even further. His
intellectual ambitions were always dominated by the attempt to discover
universal natural scientific laws of development, to which human, animal and vegetable were alike subject. In particular, he was concerned
to prove the universality of the 'social instincts in the plant, animal and

human world'. It was these organic instincts and drives which he thought to underlie what philosophers had defined as ethics. According to *Ethics and the Materialist Conception of History*, published in 1906, 'what appeared to Kant as the creation of a higher world of spirits, is a product of the animal world . . . an animal impulse and nothing else is the moral law . . . the moral law is of the same nature as the instinct for reproduction'.[99]

This form of nature-based determinism had little in common with the forms of belief and behaviour which Karl, following Feuerbach, had defined as 'abstraction' or 'alienation'. Abstraction was a product of culture rather than nature and arose in a situation in which *self-determination* took a perverse form. Man makes himself the victim of the abstractions which he has created and builds upon these misperceptions. Thus the teleological forward movement, together with the energy embodied within it, remained, but expressed itself, on the one hand, in the 'political state' and, on the other, in a market fuelled by private interests. It was because this dynamic was the result of self-determination rather than natural determination that man retained the capacity to free himself from the alienating institutional structure which came into being with patriarchy, private property and religion.

7. RETHINKING THE HISTORY OF CIVIL SOCIETY

During his time in Brussels in 1845 and 1846, Karl elaborated his new insights into the place of labour or 'production' in the self-making of man. This meant transforming his ideas about civil society from an aggregation of fragmented exchangers, each driven by self-interest, to a relationship between producers. Such a conception provided a new basis for the existence of classes. To aid his depiction of labour in 1844, Karl used Hegel's depiction of 'external teleology' in his *Science of Logic*.[100] This enabled him to distinguish three moments in the labour process – 'the subjective purpose', 'the means' and 'the realized purpose'. When set against the ideal of *autonomy* (purposeful activity freely decided upon by the self or free self-activity), Karl was able to highlight the forms of *heteronomy* embodied in the ownership of the means of production or the determination of its purpose by another.

In the following year, 1845, Karl developed a second model, in which the function of labour was placed within an overall social and historical process.[101] In this account, the process and purpose of labour were presented as independent of the will of the labourers. This made possible a dynamic vision of history underpinned by a teleology punctuated by a succession of historical stages. In place of a vaguely delineated rise of a post-classical civil society, from feudal society to the French Revolution, he articulated a more precise historical sequence of property forms. This historical sequence relied on the researches of the German Historical School of Law, with 'tribal', 'ancient/communal' and 'feudal' phases.[102] 'The form of intercourse determined by the existing productive forces at all previous historical stages, and in its turn determining these, is *civil society*.'[103] Such an approach opened up ways of presenting a systematic and cumulative history of labour, and of introducing the idea of modes of production. These constituted different types of relationship between labourers, means of production and the product. 'History', Karl argued, 'is nothing but the succession of the separate generations, each of which uses the materials, the capital funds, the productive forces handed down to it by all preceding generations, and thus, on the one hand, continues the traditional activity in completely changed circumstances and, on the other, modifies the old circumstances with a completely changed activity.'[104]

In the course of 1845 and 1846, Karl managed to express more succinctly his picture of the relationship between social relations and productive development. In late 1846, in a letter to the wealthy Russian traveller and intellectual Pavel Annenkov, he outlined the new approach:

> If you assume given stages of development in production, commerce or consumption, you will have a corresponding form of social constitution, a corresponding organization, whether of the family, of the estates or of the classes – in a word, a corresponding civil society. If you assume this or that civil society, you will have this or that political system, which is but the official expression of civil society . . .
>
> Needless to say, man is not free to choose *his productive forces* – upon which his whole history is based – for every productive force is an acquired force, the product of previous activity. Thus the productive forces are the result of man's practical energy, but that energy is in turn circumscribed

by the condition in which man is placed by the productive forces already acquired, by the form of society which exists before him, which he does not create, which is the product of the preceding generation . . .

[If he is not] to forfeit the fruits of civilisation, man is compelled to change all his traditional social forms as soon as the mode of commerce ceases to correspond to the productive forces acquired.[105]

One of the ways in which Karl's thinking shifted in the course of rethinking civil society was in the place he now accorded to the bourgeoisie. Hegel's modernity was characterized by the tension between particularity and universality, civil society and the state, as necessary constituents of objective spirit. In Karl's essays on the attainment of a rational state in the *Rheinische Zeitung* in 1842, the part played by individual economic interest and private property was purely negative. In the *1844 Manuscripts*, similarly the dynamics of civil society were ignored except as part of a pathology of immiseration, which had ultimately turned a distinction between property and non-property into the antagonism between bourgeoisie and proletariat.[106] But, in 1847, in *The Poverty of Philosophy*, there was an altogether more positive appreciation of the development of the forces of production and class struggle as the underpinnings of the forward movement of history: 'the very moment civilisation begins, production begins to be founded on the antagonism of orders, estates, classes, and finally on the antagonism of accumulated labour and immediate labour. No antagonism, no progress. This is the law that civilisation has followed up to our days. Till now the productive forces have been developed by virtue of this system of class antagonisms.'[107]

By the time Karl composed the *Communist Manifesto*, his thought had come full circle. From the base defender of private property, the 'bourgeoisie' had become an epic hero of the forward march of humanity: 'It has been the first to show what man's activity can bring about. It has accomplished wonders far surpassing Egyptian pyramids, Roman aqueducts and Gothic cathedrals . . . In place of the old wants, satisfied by the production of the country, we find new wants requiring for their satisfaction the products of different lands and climes.'[108] The bourgeoisie was entering the last phase of its rule. Not only had there been the first instances of proletarian revolt, but there were the first signs that the further advance of production was being 'fettered' by the bourgeois property form.[109] But, in the meantime, what more powerful instance could there be that 'the self-creation of man' was 'the outcome of man's *own labour*'.[110]

Karl had developed a post-Kantian vision of the role of labour in history and its capacity for self-emancipation: a vision based on reason, spontaneity and freedom. But his adoption of this vision was only partial. Karl was silent about the individual rights to freedom and self-determination, and his position remained the one he had adopted in his reading of the 1789 Declaration of the Rights of Man. The rights of man were the barely concealed expression of the primacy of private property and the bourgeois individual in relation to the modern state. Similarly, while he ascribed a capacity for self-emancipation to the proletariat as a collective entity, he did not extend that capacity for freedom and self-determination to the plurality of individuals of which it was composed.

In this sense, Karl's picture of the proletariat was an ill-digested conflation between material need and the cause of freedom. In *The Holy Family* he wrote that 'man has lost himself in the proletariat' and 'yet at the same time has not only gained theoretical consciousness of that loss ... but is driven directly to revolt against this inhumanity'.[111] How this 'theoretical consciousness' was acquired is not explained. In its lack of private property, and in its absence of religion – which he imagined to be the case in Paris – the proletariat represented the imminent embodiment of species-being, 'the return of man to himself'. But, as individuals, these proletarians were accorded neither spontaneity nor self-determination. Their common consciousness arose from a shared condition. Driven by necessity they were presented as unreflective 'moments' of the whole. Need would drive them to revolt irrespective of any rational conviction they may have acquired. For, as Karl wrote in *The Holy Family*, 'It is not a question what this or that proletarian, or even the whole proletariat, at the moment *regards* as its aim. It is a question of *what the proletariat is*, and what, in accordance with this *being*, it will historically be compelled to do.'[112] Vocations were ascribed to classes in the same way in which Feuerbach had defined species-being or 'man' as the vocation of human individuals. This unexplained shift from *ought* to *is* was another facet of Karl's inability to provide a convincing answer to Stirner's charge that the arguments of Feuerbach and his followers were moralistic and still relied upon a set of assumptions derived from religion.

Like all philosophers in a post-Kantian tradition, Karl had acknowledged that man was both a natural being, subject to natural needs and desires, and a rational subject, capable of subjecting these desires to rational scrutiny, and of exercising will in accordance with self-imposed rules. But Karl did not endow his proletarians with individuality. They were subsumed under the presumption of common interests and predetermined ends. Any aberrant manifestation of individual behaviour on the part of a particular proletarian was ascribed to the pathology of estrangement.[113]

Not surprisingly, Karl's attempt to equate the universal path to human emancipation with the desires and needs of a particular class was one of the main issues in contention between republicans and socialists among the Young Hegelians in the mid-1840s. Alienation, Ruge claimed, was not a condition which afflicted the proletariat alone. Karl's picture was open to the same sort of criticism which Bruno Bauer had directed against Strauss and Feuerbach. Their employment of a pantheistic notion of immanence derived from the metaphysics of Spinoza, rather than of self-consciousness, to explain the displacement of Christianity by humanism or species-being.[114] In Bauer's view, this meant invoking an immediately effective, universal species-being, without showing how it came to be adopted, how it operated or how it was internalized by the individual. Karl's notion of proletarian class-consciousness was susceptible to the same sort of objection. But, in his case, the source of his position seems not to have been any particular affinity to Spinoza. The obstacle to an acceptance of the Kantian conception of the individual for him appears to have been the result of his distaste for any form of individualism, which he associated with the destruction of the ancient politics and its replacement by the distinction between 'man' and 'citizen' introduced by civil society. There was no distinction between the individual and the citizen in Aristotle's polity. The fall of the *polis* and the coming of Christianity had produced the emergence of the individual as a being apart from the citizen in civil society. The 'social question' and the advent of the proletariat contained the promise to end this division.

Republicans, while often sympathetic to the plight of labour, were sceptical. Labour, Bruno Bauer objected, was 'sunken in matter'.[115] The consciousness of workers was rudimentary, and immediate; it would fight for its particular interests. Due to a lack of education and its narrow surroundings, it was in a poor position to embrace the idea of its self-determination. How could the proletariat embody the trajectory of humanity as a whole? In what sense could the repetitive character of proletarian work make possible the vision of emancipation ascribed to such a class?

7

The Approach of Revolution: The Problem about Germany

I. A GERMAN REVOLUTION?

German socialism was born in exile. Its access to material or institutional support was minimal. The group around Karl survived through to the revolutions of 1848 thanks to a new vision, a sense of possibility, which held it together. Never in the past had German radicals, particularly those forced into exile, been able to sustain their conviction, in the face of what seemed to be the obdurate religious, military and royal reality of Germany. But in the coming crisis, it could now be foreseen, Germany could follow England and France on the path to social emancipation.

England had experienced its revolutions in 1640, and in 1688; France in 1789 and again in 1830. But no such dramatic events had taken place in Germany since the Reformation and the Peasants' War of the sixteenth century. But Karl and other German radicals of the 1840s wondered whether drastic changes could now engulf the states of the German Confederation. German radicals hoped that they might during the whole period of what came to be called the *Vormärz* (1815–48).[1] With Germany's contribution of new ways of thinking for a modern world, surely this would now be matched by a comparable transformation of its political institutions. The great chance that came with the revolutions of 1830 passed Germany by. However lofty and sublime the contribution of German thought to modernity might have been, any hope of real political transformation faltered and stumbled whenever forced to confront the reality of loyal and God-fearing, phlegmatic and provincial people who were unwilling to act out dramas of revolution.

There had of course been popular mobilization – if not popular revolt – in 1813, but unhappily it was led by the king of Prussia himself against the French. For this reason, dreams about universal emancipation were repeatedly disturbed by the need to dwell upon the persistent reality of a parochial people. Radicals increasingly assumed that theirs was a nation of 'philistines'.[2]

In the era of Kant, during the French Revolution of 1789, there had been no pressing need to consider the question. Kant's endorsement of the French attempt to construct a constitution based upon Reason was widely shared by educated Germans, but few assumed that a comparable upheaval would be required in Germany.[3] Furthermore, as the Revolution degenerated into terror and war, the poet Schiller voiced the predominant reaction. For a moment, he wrote in 1795, there seemed to have been 'a physical possibility of setting law upon the throne, of honouring man at last as an end in himself, and making true freedom the basis of political association'. But it was a 'vain hope'; the outcome was either 'a return to the savage state' or 'to complete lethargy'.[4]

This distancing from the course of events in France was reinforced by the German experience of the French occupation of the Rhineland after 1792; opposed – if not actively resisted – by all but a minority of Jacobin enthusiasts in the short-lived republic of Mainz. Subsequent reactions to Napoleonic rule were more ambivalent. Although, in retrospect, the abolition of feudalism and the reform of law were highly valued, the authoritarian style of Bonapartist government offset support for such measures.[5] Some, like Karl's father and uncle, worked with the regime, others, like Hegel's brother, became officers in the *Grande Armée*, or, like Jenny's father, briefly served as state officials in the Napoleonic state of Westphalia. But many of the younger members of the intelligentsia abandoned the political dreams of the 1790s. In these circumstances, few dissented from Madame de Staël's 1807 portrayal of Germany as a land of poets and thinkers. She cited 'one of the most distinguished of their writers', Jean Paul Richter, 'L'empire de la mer c'était aux Anglais, celui de la terre aux Français, et celui de l'air aux Allemands' – 'The empire of the sea was for the English, that of the land for the French and the empire of the air for the Germans.'[6]

After 1815, the progressive belief in an association between the 'German' and the 'universal' was most powerfully articulated by Hegel. It was a discourse that made sense so long as Prussia agreed to follow the emancipatory programme started in the 'Reform Era'. But by the 1820s, Hegel's approach had already begun to come under strain. The reforms once thought to be imminent – like the promise to summon a representative assembly – had not been realized. Instead, the government had established a series of provincial Diets, summoned along the lines of the traditional estates and denied any power over taxation. Similarly, the Carlsbad Decrees of 1819 had severely curtailed freedom of the press, freedom of speech and freedom of assembly. Finally, the 1830 revolutions, which delivered liberal constitutions in France and Belgium and brought to an end the 'Protestant Constitution' in Britain, had only increased the defensiveness of political authorities in Prussia and other German states. Alarmed by a mass democratic gathering at Hambach in the Palatinate in 1832, the German Confederation, prompted by the Austrian chancellor, Metternich, imposed increased censorship and political repression.[7]

The difficulty of attempting to restate a politically progressive future for Germany in the light of these developments was apparent in the case of Heinrich Heine. Together with other radical writers, he was forced into exile in Paris in the aftermath of the 1830 revolutions. In his *History of Religion and Philosophy in Germany* of 1834 Heine persisted in the attempt to develop Hegel's 'remarkable parallelism' between German Philosophy and the French Revolution. Thus, Kant was aligned with Robespierre, Fichte with Napoléon, Schelling with Restoration France, and Hegel with the 1830 Revolution. But by this time Heine was working under the spell of the Saint-Simonians in Paris, and so he identified Germany's contribution to human emancipation not as spirituality – or *Innerlichkeit* – but as 'sensualism' or, in philosophical terms, pantheism. According to Heine's narrative, Luther was identified with the 'sensualism' of everyday life. Luther's legacy bore fruit in the pantheism of Spinoza, which in turn was restated in the philosophy of the young Schelling. Here, however, the narrative broke down. Pantheism, according to Heine's argument, had completed its revolution in philosophy and was now ready to spill out into politics and everyday life. For this reason, Germany was on the eve of its own 1789, but one in which 'demonic forces' would be unleashed, and 'a play' would be enacted 'which will make the French Revolution look like a harmless idyll'. Nevertheless, the uncomfortable truth had to be faced, that Germany had missed the 1830 revolutions, and that in both

Schelling and Goethe pantheism produced forms of conservatism. The tract thereupon dipped despondently with Heine's admission of 'a depressingly paralysing effect on my feelings' made by this 'pantheist apostasy'.[8]

As has already been seen, a comparable impasse threatened in the aftermath of the last major attempt to sketch out in Hegelian terms a radically progressive path for Germany in the *Vormärz* period: that outlined by Karl in the *Rheinische Zeitung* and by Arnold Ruge in the *Deutsche Jahrbücher* in 1842. The Young Hegelian project of bringing about reform by raising to consciousness the real desires of the people failed. In 1843, the Prussian government closed down the *Rheinische Zeitung* and the rest of the opposition press without significant resistance from the people.

How could there continue to be faith in the democratic or republican capacities of a people so timid and parochial? The situation in 1843 only reiterated what had been said about the timidity of the German people in the previous decade. At the time of the 1830 revolutions, Ludwig Börne – in Parisian exile – had mocked Hegel's celebration of the Reformation and German *Innerlichkeit*. Perhaps precisely that Protestant spirituality had produced 'a people that despite its spiritual power and spiritual freedom, does not know how to free itself from a censor that destroys this power and this freedom'.[9] Börne added that the passivity of Shakespeare's Hamlet could be attributed to the time he spent studying German philosophy at the University of Wittenberg. Later in the decade, others began to make analogous attacks upon 'the Protestant principle' for its association with individualism and the specifically German preoccupation with privacy, individual security and a parochial relationship with the outside world. This was a condition that radicals contemptuously called '*Spiessbürgerlichkeit*' (petit bourgeois sentimentality).

Yet hope reappeared in 1844, the year in which German socialism was born. After the suppression of the press in 1843, constitutionalism – faith in the possibility of reforming the state – sharply declined. Karl's essay 'On the Jewish Question' and his introduction to the 'Contribution to the Critique of Hegel's Philosophy of Right' in the *Deutsch-Französische Jahrbücher* were influential statements of scepticism about political reform. Others were of equal importance, notably Feuerbach's 'Preliminary Theses on the Reform of Philosophy', and Moses

Hess's essay on the 'Philosophy of the Act'. Feuerbach's essay shifted the focus of concern from the 'progress of spirit' to the condition of the 'human'. Hess's essay was particularly striking since it attacked not only the radical constitutionalism of Bruno Bauer, but also the conservative reformism of Lorenz von Stein, who argued that socialism could resolve the social problem within the existing state. Socialism, Hess argued, was not simply concerned with the material needs of the proletariat; it was about the transformation of society as a whole. Furthermore, in his essay 'on the Essence of Money', Hess pushed forward from Feuerbach's conception of abstraction or alienation as a problem afflicting individuals towards a notion of alienation as a social problem, as powerfully present in economic relations as in religious belief.

Radicals did not initially expect to witness the emergence of socialism in Germany in the immediate future. There was alarm among conservatives as a result of the report by the Zurich magistrate Johann Bluntschli detailing the 'communist' activities of Wilhelm Weitling and of radicalized German-speaking artisans in Switzerland. But Stein had argued that the advent of communism in Germany was still distant, while Karl's essay in the *Deutsch-Französische Jahrbücher* hailed the coming role of the proletariat and implied that change would come from without. His last sentence read, 'The French cock will crow at dawn.'

This is why the Silesian weavers' rising in June 1844 was greeted with such excitement. The advent of proletarian revolt in a poor and remote part of Prussia showed that Germany had become part of the political mainstream of Europe. Unlike literary socialism, the 'rising' of the weavers – not least thanks to its overblown reporting – was an event large enough to enter popular consciousness, and even national mythology, inspiring poems, songs and pictures.[10]

The events in Silesia also prompted the crown to take action. In the autumn of 1844, the government founded the Association for the Welfare of the Working Classes, an organization which allowed the formation of local workers' associations (*Arbeitervereine*). Although the government thought of these associations as charitable institutions, definitions remained vague, thus allowing liberals, radicals and social reformers to attempt to shape them. Some, for example, followed the practices of migrant artisan clubs in Switzerland and provided communal dining facilities, thus leading to their superficial identification with 'communism'.[11] But whatever the precise character of particular associations, concern about socialism and the social question now acquired a visible and institutional presence.

The reaction to the Silesian events also generated the publication of a whole range of radical and socialist journals, dealing with social conditions and the position of the proletariat. A cluster of journals – including the *Deutsches Bürgerbuch*, the *Rheinische Jahrbücher*, the *Westphälische Dampfboot* and the *Gesellschaftsspiegel* – all appeared around the end of 1844 and beginning of 1845. The most important of these journals, continuing a tradition of specifically Rhineland radicalism, was the *Trier'sche Zeitung*, which predated this upsurge of socialist literature. After the closure of the *Rheinische Zeitung* in 1843, it became the foremost opposition journal in Germany. It employed socialist authors and devoted increasing space to the discussion of social issues. In particular it had taken on Karl Grün, a gifted author and journalist, soon to be seen as Karl's main rival in the formulation of a socialism appropriate to *Vormärz* Germany.

Like Karl, Grün had been a student in Bonn and Berlin. Towards the end of the 1830s he had fled to France to avoid military service. His radicalism derived from an admiration for the writings of Young Germany rather than for the Young Hegelians. After returning to Germany, he worked for a newspaper in Baden, and then moved to the Rhineland, where he was converted to socialism by Moses Hess. In March 1844, he himself attributed his socialism to a reading of Hess's 'Philosophy of the Act' and two essays of Karl's, 'On the Jewish Question' and the introduction to his 'Contribution to the Critique of Hegel's Philosophy of Right'.[12]

Like Hess and Engels in 1845, Grün played an active part in the campaign to develop the workers' associations in a socialist direction. In contrast to government paternalism, Grün believed that these societies could serve as starting points for the transformation of society and, like others inspired by Feuerbach and Hess, championed an anti-state, anti-constitutionalist approach. Only if politics were 'dissolved into socialism' could man ever hope to live in harmony with his 'species-being'. To reach such a point, private property would have to be abolished, labour reorganized communally, education and culture transformed. At the end of 1844, Grün was heartened by the fact that 'the question of socialism is starting to infiltrate current affairs in Germany too'. Newspapers were 'suddenly voicing those loaded terms: abolition of the proletariat, organisation of labour, the establishment of true social relations [*Vergesellschaftung*]'.[13]

Grün planned to set up a monthly journal, which would make socialism more widely known among the workers, but its publication was prevented by the censorship authorities, and in the autumn of 1844, he was once more forced into exile in Paris. There he published *The Social Movement in France and Belgium*, another attack on Stein's constitutionalist approach to socialism. While the destiny of France was political revolution, in Germany in 1845 he shared Engels' belief that the shaping power of philosophy itself could transform the country without the need for revolution. Like the Owenites in Britain, Grün combined his socialism with an interest in education and a concern about the emancipation of women.

In 1845, there was little visible disagreement among leading German socialists. The definition of socialism, and certainly the road to socialism, remained relatively vague. Socialism as a doctrine was as much cultural as economic, a concern with humanity rather than the project of any particular class. In the first instance, it was hoped to attract the middle class, as Engels and Hess attempted in their speeches in Barmen and Elberfeld; thereafter, it was believed, the working classes would follow.

But disagreements soon became visible. The group around Karl focused increasingly upon his critique of political economy, and this unavoidably focused attention on the labour question. For this reason, in 1845 Moses Hess, who had originally drawn Grün towards socialism, began to criticize him in 1845 for his lack of interest in political economy or the proletariat. He attempted to interest him in Karl's work, but Grün by now was unreceptive. What did engage him, when he reached Paris, were his encounters with Proudhon, which began late in 1844.

For Karl, Grün's relation with Proudhon posed a serious threat to his overarching project ever since he had first arrived in Paris at the end of 1843 – the building of a Franco-German political and philosophical alliance. Proudhon was crucial to the plan for he was the French proletarian who had attacked private property. In *The Holy Family* Karl had considered it imperative to rescue Proudhon from the interpretation of the Bauer brothers, in which he was presented as a mystic and as a 'moralist' believing in justice. Karl in contrast had praised him as 'a man of the mass', 'a plebeian and a proletarian'.[14] Proudhon was to be congratulated for making 'the first resolute, ruthless, and at the same time scientific investigation of the basis of political economy, *private property*'. He was not beyond criticism. His advocacy of equal wages was little more than a proposal for the better payment of the slave. But unlike others Proudhon had taken seriously 'the human semblance of economic relations' and sharply opposed it to 'their inhuman reality'. He had done 'all that criticism of political economy from the standpoint of political economy can do'. He had produced 'the scientific manifesto of the French proletariat'.[15] For Proudhon's acquaintance with German philosophy now to be mediated by Karl Grün was a development which Karl found intolerable.

2. THE 'DEMOCRATIC DICTATOR'

In February 1846, Karl, Engels and a Belgian friend, Philippe Gigot, set up a Communist Correspondence Committee in Brussels. The aim was to organize contacts with German socialists and communists 'on scientific questions', to 'supervise' popular writing and socialist propaganda in Germany, and to keep German, French and English socialists in contact with each other. Equally important from the start, however, whether avowed or not, was the ambition to eliminate rival visions of socialism.

In the case of Grün, Karl's hostility was clear from the beginning of 1846. On 18 January, he wrote to Grün's newspaper, the *Trier'sche Zeitung*, stating, 'I have *never* written a *single* line for this paper, whose bourgeois philanthropic, by no means communist tendencies are entirely alien to me.'[16] Once the Correspondence Committee was established, Karl also wrote to Proudhon on the Committee's behalf to invite him to join. 'So far as France is concerned, we all of us believe that we could find no better correspondent than yourself.' But Karl could not refrain from adding, 'I must now denounce to you Mr Grün of Paris. The man is nothing more than a literary swindler, a species of charlatan, who seeks to traffic in modern ideas.' Not only was this man writing '*gibberish*', but he was '*dangerous*'. 'Beware of this parasite.'[17]

There was also the need to deal with the radical artisan communist Wilhelm Weitling, who passed through Brussels and met the Correspondence Committee on 30 March 1846. Weitling was the best-known representative of the type of communism that had developed within secret societies of migrant German artisans in Paris, London, Switzerland and elsewhere since the revolutions of 1830. He had been the most important figure in the early years of the League of the Just, founded in Paris in 1836. The League's foundation had coincided with the impact of *Words of a Believer* by the dissident Catholic priest Félicité de Lamennais. During the years that followed, Christian radicalism had been at its height. According to Lamennais, 1789 had heralded the end of poverty, the advent of freedom and equality, and the imminent advent of the earthly paradise promised by Christ. Lamennais's vision was one of moral renewal, but in the writings of his German followers this was transformed into an aggressive argument for physical force and for 'communism' as the return to a Christian community of goods. The newly founded League had discussed these questions in 1837 and commissioned Weitling to report upon its practicability. His report of 1839, *Mankind As It is and As It Ought to Be*, was adopted as the League's official programme; it envisioned a social order premised upon equality, the universal duty to work and a centralized economy. Weitling thus became the uncontested leader of the League until challenged in 1843 by dissidents from Switzerland, inspired by the radical nationalism of Mazzini.

From that point on, Weitling's career appears to have foundered. In answer to criticism, he first attempted to provide a Christian foundation for his views by arguing that 'communism' and 'communion' stemmed from the same etymological root. When this argument was refuted, he attempted to provide a purely secular theory of communism, published as *Guarantees of Harmony and Freedom* in 1842. Karl praised this work enthusiastically in 1844 as 'this *vehement* and brilliant literary debut of the German workers'.[18] But the League was less impressed, and in response Weitling reverted once more to his Christian argument in *The Gospel of a Poor Sinner* of 1843. His imprisonment in Switzerland interrupted the book's publication: at his release in September 1844 the League in London gave him a hero's welcome but the book itself never made much of an impact.

Weitling still retained followers in Switzerland, but in London and

Paris the interests of many of the League members had moved on. In Paris under the leadership of Dr Hermann Ewerbeck, the League inclined to Cabet, and then in 1844–5 to the writings of Grün. In London, led by Karl Schapper, Heinrich Bauer and Joseph Moll, debates were held, in which the communist settlements of Cabet were rejected. Weitling's revised theory was also debated on a number of occasions, but was finally rejected in January 1846. In London there had been growing support for the pacific and rationalist approach of the Owenites. Weitling's polity was criticized for being 'too military'. Similarly, on the question of religion, not only was Christian-based communism now rejected, but there was growing support for an Owenite atheism or for the communist humanism of Moses Hess, in which God was 'the human species or mankind united in love'.[19]

By early 1846, therefore, Weitling's views had been rejected for the most part, both in London and in Paris. It was clear also that among the *'Gelehrte'* (the Brussels groups, seen by many of the artisans as a presumptuous educated clique) indulgence of Weitling's proletarian manners had worn thin. On 24 March 1846, Jenny wrote to Karl, 'just as he, coming from the artisan class, is perforce incapable of anything more elevated than to herald drinking bouts in popular poetry, so too is he capable of nothing more elevated than ill-fated undertakings which are obviously foolhardy and fail'.[20]

There was real pathos in the encounter between Weitling and the Brussels Correspondence Committee in March 1846. Weitling did not look 'an embittered worker, oppressed by the burden of work'. He was 'a handsome, fair, young man in a somewhat foppishly cut coat, with a foppishly trimmed beard. He looked more like a commercial traveller.'[21] Although he had been invited to join the Correspondence Committee, his reception by Karl and the others was bad-tempered and unfriendly. The encounter was memorably described by the Russian traveller Pavel Annenkov, whom Karl had invited to attend.

Karl asked Weitling, 'with what fundamental principles do you justify your revolutionary and social activity?' Weitling

> began to explain that his aim was not to create new economic theories but to make use of those that were best able, as experience in France had shown, to open the workers' eyes to the horror of their situation and all the injustices that had, with regard to them, become the bywords of

governments and societies, to teach them not to put trust any longer in promises on the part of the latter and to rely only on themselves, organizing into democratic and communist communes . . . He had a far different audience now than the one that usually crowded around his work bench or read his newspapers and printed pamphlets on contemporary economic practices, and in consequence, he had lost the facility of both his thought and his tongue.

Karl 'angrily interrupted' that the 'stimulation of fantastic hopes' led only to the ultimate ruin, and not the salvation 'of the oppressed'. This might do for Annenkov's country, Russia, where 'associations of nonsensical prophets and nonsensical followers are the only things that can be put together', but not 'in a civilized country like Germany'. Despite these attacks, Weitling went on with 'the recollection of the hundreds of letters and expressions of gratitude he had received from every corner of the fatherland'. He claimed that

his modest, preparatory work was, perhaps, more important for the general cause than criticism and closet analyses of doctrines in seclusion from the suffering world and the miseries of the people. On hearing these last words, Marx, at the height of fury, slammed his fist down on the table so hard that the lamp on the table reverberated and tottered, and jumping up from his place, said at the same time: 'Ignorance has never yet helped anybody' . . . The meeting had ended. While Marx paced the room back and forth in extreme anger and irritation, I hastily bid him and his companions good-bye . . .[22]

Following this confrontation, Karl insisted that there ought to be a 'sifting' of the Party.[23] What this meant became clear a few weeks later, on 11 May 1846, when the Correspondence Committee issued a 'Circular' directed against one of Weitling's allies, Hermann Kriege. Kriege, who was in New York and working as editor of *Der Volks-Tribun*, was accused of preaching 'fantastic emotionalism' under the name of communism and was therefore 'compromising in the highest degree to the Communist Party, both in Europe and America'.[24]

It is hard, however, to believe that something else wasn't also going on in this otherwise grotesquely self-important missive. In 1845, Kriege had been one of the companions of Engels and Hess, when they were preaching communism in Barmen and Elberfeld. Subsequently, he had defended Weitling's use of religion: 'he does not want to let go of the word 'God' as the expression of an emotive effect, and the use of Christ as a prophet of communism. In other respects, he is an out and out revolutionary.' He also raised queries about the extent of radicalism among English and French workers: 'The only country, where I now see an important movement is North America.' His words were also those of a rejected lover:

> I can tell you, they were the concluding words of your essay on *The Phil-osophy of Right*, which took me captive in love towards you. Not the art of rhetoric, not the sharp dialectic, not the strong life blood, which flows through these paragraphs, which connected me with you, it entered my whole being, and for a long time I only bore your children ... I would have gone with you wherever you wished. I came to Brussels and I found you as I knew you, but didn't think that you didn't know me and my love for you, hence my stupidities, which later became so boring in some letters.[25]

By the spring of 1846, Weitling and his supporters could be margin-alized without much risk. In June 1845, Ewerbeck had reported Weitling's difficulties in carrying his argument in London, while in 1846 the Chartist leader, Julian Harney, wrote to Engels that although Weitling might have friends in the London Society, it was certainly not the majority. 'S. [Schapper] is the man who leads, and properly so.'[26] This was important, because insofar as Karl and his Brussels group were ever to gain leadership within the League, it was due to the sup-port extended to them by Karl Schapper and the London members.

The threat represented by Karl Grün was altogether more serious than that from Weitling. Proudhon responded to the letter from Karl and the Correspondence Committee with a polite but firm refusal to join. He also expressed a reasoned disagreement with their project: he opposed the group's becoming 'the apostles of a new religion, even if it were a religion of logic, or a religion of reason ... Don't create a new theology like your countryman, Luther.' In order to turn political econ-omy in the direction of 'community', the burning of property on a gentle flame was called for rather than endowing it with a new strength by resorting to a 'St Bartholomew's Eve of the property owners'. This seemed to Proudhon also to be 'the disposition of the working class in France'. Just as Karl had earlier failed to understand French attitudes to religion when he had first approached French socialists with Arnold Ruge, so now he failed to understand their distaste for another revolution and a Jacobin-style state. Revolutionary action was not the way to accomplish social reform. As for Karl's attack on Karl Grün, whom he accused of 'selling socialist ideas', Proudhon replied that Grün had every right to do so, since he was living in exile with a wife and two children to support. 'What else do you want him to make a profit from, other than modern ideas? . . . I owe my knowledge of your writings', he concluded, 'and of those of Engels and Feuerbach to Grün and Ewerbeck.'[27]

Others also hastened to register their disagreement with the intolerant and imperious tone of the missives of the Correspondence Committee. The Committee in London asked, 'aren't you being too harsh against Kriege? . . . Kriege is still young and can still learn'. Similarly, Karl's Westphalian friend Joseph Weydemeyer reported that there was 'widespread regret that you have again got involved in such polemics'.[28] Hermann Ewerbeck, one of the leaders of the League in Paris and for a time a close collaborator with Grün, who had hailed Karl as a 'nineteenth-century Aristotle', could not understand why he should wish to attack Grün. Grün had done good work among cabinetmakers in Paris and had taken workers twenty times on tours of the Louvre.[29] As well as acting as the foreign correspondent of the *Trier'sche Zeitung*, he gave weekly lectures on art to Parisian artisans.

Most upsetting for Karl was the fact that Proudhon was now engaged in writing his own critique of political economy with the active assistance of Grün. Proudhon had been fascinated by what Grün had said about Feuerbach and intended to integrate it into his economic criticism, while Grün in turn celebrated Proudhon as 'the French Feuerbach'. Grün had been entrusted with the translation of Proudhon's *System of Economic Contradictions, or The Philosophy of Poverty* and announced its forthcoming publication in Germany as early as January 1846.[30] According to Ewerbeck, 'Grün boasts that he and Dr Mendelssohn will transplant the doctrine of Proudhon into Germany.'[31] Proudhon's book appeared in France in October 1846, while Grün's German translation, together with a lengthy introduction, was due to appear in May 1847.

Proudhon's criticism of political economy was based upon the claim that it reinforced inequality. He attacked the entry of the machine into the workshop. 'The machine or the workshop, having degraded the worker by setting above him a master, completes the process of cheapening him by ensuring that he sink from the ranks of the artisan to that of the manual labourer.' After reflecting on the generality of this phenomenon, he also, like Karl, saw an analogy between religion and the economy: 'With the machine and the workshop, divine right, that's to say, the principle of authority, makes its entry into political economy.' 'Capital, mastery, privilege, monopoly, partnership, credit, property' were 'in economic language' what were otherwise called 'power, authority, sovereignty, written law, revelation, religion, finally God, the cause and principle of all our poverty and all our crimes, which the more we seek to define it, the more it escapes us'.[32]

Proudhon's treatise attacked political economy as a modern form of competition, which resulted in a new form of poverty. The means employed by labour to create wealth entailed an inherent antagonism which produced poverty. Political economy was 'the affirmation and organisation of poverty'. Political economy was 'the false organisation of labour', which created 'pauperism'.[33] Grün went on to claim that Proudhon's book had finally achieved the unification of French socialism and German philosophy, that it marked a step forward in Lessing's notion of *The Education of the Human Race*.[34] Socialism was not simply a limited solution to the material concerns of the proletariat. It played a crucial role in the emancipation of humanity.

Grün's alliance with Proudhon fundamentally threatened Karl's idea of French–German unity. The Brussels Committee was no more successful than the *Deutsch-Französische Jahrbücher* had been in attracting non-German, non-exile participation. Not only Proudhon, but the London Chartist leader, Julian Harney, was reluctant to become involved. Even among the German diasporas, the reception was mixed. The sole definite success, the result of a suggestion by Harney, was the contact established with the leading member of the London League of the Just, Karl Schapper. Common ground was discovered here in a mutual rejection of Weitling's programme. On this basis a London branch of the Correspondence Committee was established. In Paris, on the other hand, Grün's high reputation and his popularity among German workers constituted a major obstacle to the expansion of the Correspondence Committee there, a situation made worse by the development of Grün's alliance with Proudhon.

Proudhon's book and its German translation also presented a challenge of a more personal kind. Karl's reputation throughout the German exile community was built upon the promise of his coming critique of political economy. But, as time wore on, even his publisher, C. J. Leske, became increasingly nervous about the character of the promised book and the likelihood of its completion. The evidence from Karl's notebooks suggests that little had been added to what he had written in 1844. He had accumulated English material on a research trip to Manchester in the summer of 1845, but there was no trace of the 'revised version of the first volume', which Karl claimed would be ready at the end of November 1846.[35] Work on the project was only resumed in September 1846. For Leske, the final straw was the appearance of 'a strong competitor' – Proudhon's book. On 2 February 1847, therefore, Leske demanded that the contract be annulled and the advance returned.[36] This threat to Karl's position helps to explain why, in contrast to the previous tardiness of progress on his economic critique, Karl sat down to write a book refuting Proudhon as soon as he received it. He started work on *The Poverty of Philosophy* in December 1846 and completed it in June 1847.

Anxiety about Grün and Proudhon as advocates of an alternative road to socialism in France and Germany dominated the politics of the Brussels group through most of 1846 and 1847. Karl wrote a polemical essay attacking Grün's *Social Movement in France and Belgium*, which was eventually published in the *Westphälische Dampfboot*.[37] In August 1846, Engels was dispatched to Paris to meet with members of the Parisian League of the Just and to denounce Grün's ideas as 'anti-proletarian, philistine and artisan'. News about his efforts to win over members against Grün dominated his letters to Karl through to December. His campaign was helped by a quarrel between Grün and Ewerbeck, which had occurred in April. But victories were not clear-cut. The prevailing impression was of continuing confusion. All this suggests that the main reason for members of the Brussels group to join the League of the Just was to be better situated in the combat with the ideas of Grün and Proudhon in Paris.

The conventional story of the transformation of the League, its acceptance of Marxian doctrine and its renaming as the Communist League is largely based upon Engels' reconstruction of events at a later date. Insofar as it was accurate, it was made possible by the fact that the League's London branch, led by Karl Schapper, Heinrich Bauer and Joseph Moll, was worried about the possibility of a return to the tenets of Weitling and was therefore prepared to make an alliance with the Brussels group. It also became possible because Schapper, for his own reasons, came to doubt the belief he had shared with the Owenites that a peaceful transformation was indeed possible. By 1846, Schapper saw revolution as inevitable. After alluding to this point in answer to a letter from Marx, Schapper and the London Committee continued, 'our task is to enlighten the people and to make propaganda for community of goods; you want the same, therefore let us join hands and work with combined strength for a better future'.[38] This convergence of interests was reinforced by the creation of a shared platform in support of the revolt in Poland, and was given a more durable institutional shape through the formation of the Fraternal Democrats.

Schapper and the London League were also responsible for the introduction of a new theme that was otherwise virtually absent from the writings of Karl or Engels. The discussions of 1845–6 were notable for the concern that communism should above all enable the free self-development of individuals. Weitling's communism like that of Cabet would stultify mankind; equality should mean equal opportunity, not equal consumption or equal enjoyment. Communism and individual self-realization must go hand in hand. It was probably as a result of Schapper's preoccupation with this theme that the *Manifesto* spoke of 'an association, in which the free development of each is the condition for the free development of all'.[39]

But while a satisfactory convergence of positions seems to have been established between London and Brussels, nothing comparable had been achieved among the branches in Paris. Ewerbeck, the League's main spokesman in Paris, had inclined to Cabet and then to Grün. He then moved closer to the Brussels group, but he was an unreliable ally. Engels had been dispatched to Paris in an attempt to contest the high standing of Proudhon and the popularity of Grün. But he was considered to be arrogant and rude, while Weitling supporters claimed that he was a member of a nasty academic clique with no time for the views of ordinary working men.[40] Joining the League and pushing forward a newly constructed reform programme strengthened the position of Karl and the Brussels group. But the extent of division and the continuing strength of Grün supporters were strongly conveyed in the

'Circular' of the First Congress of the Communist League on 9 June 1847. 'In the Paris League itself, there was no sign of the slightest progress, not the slightest concern with the development of the principle or with the movement of the Proletariat, as it was proceeding in other localities of the League.'[41]

From Engels' letters to Karl, it appeared that opponents of Brussels were being scattered from the field, and that once 'the Straubingers' were defeated, the group around Karl would triumph. But other sources suggest that these triumphs may have been hollow or illusory and that some of Engels' victories were based on manipulation or deceit. At the Conference of June 1847, Engels had only managed to get himself nominated as a delegate as the result of a 'presidential trick' on the part of his one-time friend, Stephan Born, who instead of encouraging a discussion of nominations, asked for those opposed to Engels to raise their hands. When a majority failed to do so, Born declared Engels elected. Engels congratulated Born on his 'beautiful' manoeuvre, but Born himself later felt ashamed of his action.[42] A little later, Engels boasted how he had managed to sideline what had been a majority in support of Moses Hess's draft of what ultimately was to become the 'Communist Manifesto'. In a letter from 25–26 October 1847, he confided to Karl, '*Strictly between ourselves*, I've played an infernal trick on Mosi. He had actually put through a delightfully amended confession of faith. Last Friday at the district, I dealt with this, point by point, and was not yet half way through when the lads declared themselves *satisfaits*. *Completely unopposed*, I got them to entrust me with the task of drafting a new one which will be discussed next Friday by the district and will be sent to London *behind the backs of the communities*.'[43] Late in 1847, Engels therefore managed to get the drafting of the League's 'Credo', or 'Manifesto', as it was now to be called, into his and Karl's hands.[44]

The resulting document,[45] which became the *Communist Manifesto*, written by Karl in January 1848, was not designed for posterity or even for the wider world. In the first instance, it was intended for the members of the League alone, and its aim was to bind the various branches – particularly those in Paris – to a single agreed programme. But despite Engels' manoeuvres, at the beginning of 1848 the challenge represented by the supporters of Grün and Proudhon persisted. It was for this reason that although it had received no mention in the previous drafts by Hess and Engels, a four-page section on what Karl called 'German' or '"True" Socialism' now appeared, and was described by the *Manifesto* as 'foul and enervating literature'.[46]

With the advent of revolution in Germany in March 1848, this debate lost its immediate relevance. With constitutional questions once more to the fore, the anti-political position represented by Grün lost its rationale. Grün returned to Trier in February 1848 and became a leading member of the *Demokratische Verein zu Trier* (Democratic Association of Trier). After the printing of a rushed version in London in February 1848, the *Manifesto* was shelved. Instead, Karl and 'the Committee' of 'the Communist Party of Germany' – Schapper, Bauer, Moll, Engels and Wolff – issued on 24 March 'Demands of the Communist Party in Germany'. The issue now was whether the revolution should be carried through by means of a republican state akin to the French Republic of 1792. The first demand of the 'Communist Party' was that 'the whole of Germany shall be declared a single and indivisible republic'.[47] The programme went on to include a state bank, nationalization of transport, progressive taxation and the establishment of national workshops (akin to those proposed in Paris by Louis Blanc). Grün, on the other hand, writing in the *Trier'sche Zeitung*, criticized the emphasis on centralization and nationalization; its results, he stated, would not be the emancipation of labour, but the replacement of individual monopolies by a 'collective monopoly' of the state, and the undermining of individual self-determination.[48]

The gains achieved by joining up with the League were limited, and with the long-awaited arrival of the revolution in Germany the benefits of continuing to operate within a still disunited party had become questionable. This was probably why, later in the year, Karl formally disbanded the Communist League.

3. INSIDE THE 'PARTY'

There are few surviving accounts of the domestic life of the Marx family in Brussels between 1845 and 1848. But the little evidence there is suggests that Karl and Jenny's marriage during these years was a happy one. Joseph Weydemeyer in a letter to his fiancée provided a glimpse of the social life of the household in 1846:

Marx, Weitling, Marx's brother-in-law [Edgar von Westphalen] and I sat up the whole night playing [cards]. Weitling got tired first. Marx and I slept a few hours on a sofa and idled away the whole of the next day in the company of his wife and his brother-in-law in the most priceless manner. We went to a tavern early in the morning, then we went by train to Villeworde, which is a little place nearby, where we had lunch and then returned in the most cheerful mood by the last train.[49]

Stefan Born described visiting Marx's home in autumn 1847: 'an extremely modest, one might almost say poorly furnished, little house in a suburb of Brussels'. He was particularly impressed by Jenny,[50] commenting, 'throughout her life she took the most intense interest in everything that concerned and occupied her husband' and 'Marx loved his wife and she shared his passion.'[51] During these years, it appears that she was as fully involved in the Brussels German Workers' Educational Association as it was possible for a woman to be. On New Year's Eve 1847, the Association organized a 'Democratic and Fraternal Celebration' at the Swan on the Grand'Place. Ladies and young women socialized with old workers and apprentices at an event where 130 guests were present. According to the report in the *Deutsche-Brüsseler-Zeitung*, after the speeches an amateur orchestra performed, and various poems were recited. 'Madame Marx was not the last to give to those assembled the benefit of her dramatic talent and thus provided a remarkable and extremely moving example of a distinguished lady devoting herself to the education of the proletariat.'

In December 1846, Jenny bore a son, named Edgar after her brother, but generally nicknamed 'Mush'. According to Wilhelm Liebknecht, 'he was very gifted, but sickly from birth, a real child of sorrow. He had beautiful eyes and a promising head which seemed too heavy for his weak body.' Liebknecht thought that he might have lived 'if he had peace and constant care and had lived in the country or by the seaside'. But 'in emigration, hunted from place to place and amid the hardships of London life' even 'the tenderest parental affection and motherly care' could not save him. In 1853, Edgar developed 'an incurable disease' and died in 1855.[52]

As for their German companions, Jenny later claimed that in the time spent in Belgium from 1845 to 1848 'the small German colony lived pleasantly together'. But there were evident frictions, produced by a life of exile, first in Paris and then in Brussels, and they became more acute as the stay in Brussels lengthened. Not only were these Germans in her words, 'a colony of paupers', cut off from normal channels of local and family support, but they were also attempting to establish a distinct form of political identity.[53] What had started as an informal collective gathered around *Vorwärts!* in Paris, and in some cases dating back to the preparation of the *Deutsch-Französische Jahrbücher* at the beginning of 1844, now acquired the aspiration to turn itself into a 'party'. The aim of this 'party', a grouping of a dozen people at most, would be to establish its ascendancy over other socialist groupings and currents of thought, both in Germany and in France. It was a further instalment of the Franco-German alliance so cherished by German radicals in the years before 1848. This was why so much time was apparently spent on the criticism of current German philosophy, a project in which not only Karl and Engels, but also Hess and Joseph Weydemeyer were for a time actively engaged. It was also a major motivation behind Karl's intended critique of political economy. The ambitions of the Brussels group were clearly stated in a meeting with Louis Blanc in the autumn of 1847. 'You, I said,' Engels wrote to Karl, 'were the chief: *vous pouvez regarder M. Marx comme le chef de notre parti (c'est-à-dire de la fraction la plus avancée de la démocratie allemande, que je représentais vis-à-vis de lui) et son récent livre contre M. Proudhon comme notre programme'*.[54]

As in other socialist groupings during this period, supporters tended to gravitate around an admired or even revered leader, the 'social father' like Robert Owen, or the founder of *Icaria*, Étienne Cabet. The style of governance of such leaders was autocratic, and was based upon the enunciation of doctrine. In Owen's case, it was inspired by the vision of 'a new moral world'; in the case of Cabet, the detailing of the social arrangements of his nineteenth-century rewriting of Thomas More's *Utopia*. In Karl's case, his status as undisputed leader was conceived and articulated in a language made familiar by Young Hegelianism; it was based upon the promise of his 'critique of political economy'. This was also strongly reinforced by his physical presence, which was vividly conveyed by the Russian traveller Pavel Annenkov:

> Marx himself was a man of the type made up of energy, will power and invincible conviction – a type of man extremely remarkable also in outward appearance. With a thick mop of black hair on his head, his hairy

hands, dressed in a coat buttoned diagonally across his chest, he maintained the appearance of a man with the right and authority to command respect, whatever guise he took and whatever he did. All his motions were awkward but vigorous and self-confident, all his manners ran athwart conventional usages in social intercourse, but were proud and somehow guarded, and his shrill voice with its metallic ring marvellously suited the radical pronouncements over things and people which he uttered. Marx was now in the habit of speaking in no other way than in such categorical pronouncements over which still reigned, it should be added, a certain shrill note superimposed on everything he said. This note expressed his firm conviction that it was his mission to control minds, to legislate over them and to lead them in his train. Before me stood the figure of the democratic dictator incarnate, just as it might be pictured in one's imagination during times devoted to fantasy.[55]

Whatever the intention, the aspiration to form a 'party' was seriously qualified by the personal rivalries and animosities that divided the group. While Karl's leadership was never challenged, conflict developed between those closest to him, in this case Engels and Hess. Engels had been a protégé of Hess and the two remained friends at least until sometime after their arrival in Brussels around April 1845. Together with Hess and Hermann Kriege, Engels had participated in a campaign to bring communism to the middle class of Barmen and Elberfeld in the spring of 1845. Writing from Barmen on 17 March, he described to Karl 'the long faces' of his parents on learning that he had spent the previous evening with Hess in Elberfeld, where 'we held forth about communism until two in the morning'.[56]

Once in Brussels, Engels and Hess had both promoted Karl's status as head of a 'party'. But in the spring of 1846 personal relations deteriorated to the point that Jenny Marx spoke of a 'radical breach'. Its causes were not entirely clear. One of the issues was certainly Jenny's open dislike of Engels' companion, Mary Burns, while another was the friction produced by the brief and forced cohabitation of the Hesses and the Engelses. It was a situation watched with amused scorn by Karl's Cologne friends Heinrich Bürgers and Roland Daniels. Assuming that the intention of the Brussels group was to produce another volume of the *Deutsch-Französische Jahrbücher*, Daniels wrote, 'I do not understand how you will be able to start on this with the two persons mentioned.' He and Bürgers had both 'a good laugh' reading Karl's description of the unfortunate situation in which he and Jenny had been obliged to take on both Engels and Hess and their female companions as sub-tenants. According to Roland Daniels:

> The 'tall chap' Engels, the *ami des prolétaires* whose company the limping Hess appears to seek because he is a copycat, or rather on principle – then the untameable proletarian woman [Engels' Manchester companion, Mary Burns], and the boring 'Frau' H.[57] – we have laughed over this for a week. The *ami des prolétaires* par excellence even goes so far – I have known several like him – as to blame fine linen, good clothes and the like on 'the malaise of present day society'. 'If you don't become like these proletarians, then you will not enter heaven.'

On Hess, Daniels observed, 'you don't write much about H; but very appropriately you call him "a sponge"'. On Hess's pretensions, he wrote, 'you must have conveyed to him your plan for an "analysis" of the Philosophy of Communism in yet another attempt to re-launch the so-called *Deutsch-Französische Jahrbücher*. Immediately, he writes, "*We* shall very soon conduct an 'analysis' – in order to separate the sheep from the goats."' Not only was his letter 'rather patriarchal', but also it seemed from his letter 'as if you too wanted to make Brussels into the ruling centre of communism, and Hess be its high priest'.[58]

In a letter to Karl from late February 1846, Bürgers also remarked upon 'the absolute impossibility of a humane communal existence between such heterogeneous elements that had suddenly been thrown together'. He saw it as 'a second edition enlarged and improved' of Karl's brief Parisian experience of cohabitation with the Ruges and the Herweghs. What disgusted him was:

> the cowardly manner in which these people too make your wife responsible for the fact that their ill-bred behaviour is not applauded . . . In order not to break with you, whom they need to have on their side, but who will never confront them with the bitter truth, they employ well-known speculative methods to turn you into a weak-minded husband, who for the moment for the sake of peace at home, gives in to the dictates of aristocratic arrogance and is persuaded into an unjust condemnation of his plebeian friends.[59]

On Engels, Bürgers commented, 'if your wife did not exist, he would convince himself that you wouldn't hesitate to recognise the pastures of free sexual relations, and possibly the object of his love'. 'Incidentally,' he went on, 'you are seeing how a new life situation completely destabilises easily excitable, but superficial characters like E. beyond all bounds.' Bürgers' judgement of Hess was similarly withering, if for different reasons. Because of his 'Spinozism and his spiritualising habits of mind', he was 'far too indifferent to the misery of our society in *small things* in their daily and hourly manifestations to think it worth the trouble to react strongly against such everyday occurrences'. And, he continued, 'he only ever sees what his intellectual preoccupations allow him to see; he is blind, when the reality of his imaginings takes on a threatening aspect . . . if someone agrees with Hess in the general condemnation of society, that is enough for him, whether the fellow acts out of polite hypocrisy, or conviction or from insight'.[60]

Some of these observations were confirmed by a letter written around the same time by Jenny, who was tending to her sick mother in Trier. On 24 March 1846, she wrote to Karl, 'it seems that murder and mayhem has broken loose among you! I am glad that this radical breach should not have taken place until after my departure. Much of it would have been attributed to the machinations of that ambitious woman, Lady Macbeth [i.e. Jenny herself], and not without reason.' She admitted that for too long she had been 'exercising *la petite critique*' (petty criticism), but demurred at the suggestion that Mary was a rare example of a woman 'as she ought to be' (a sarcastic reference to Weitling's *Mankind As It is and As It Ought to Be*). On the contrary, 'there is an abundance of lovely, charming, capable women and they are to be found all over the world'. On Hess, she agreed with the friends in Cologne. For 'Rabbi Rabuni', as she called him, 'all cats are of the same colour . . . He sees rosy tints appear in far away Poland; he forgets that the colour of these blood-red roses is not genuine.' Men like Hess were in fact 'nothing but ideologists, who actually have no real flesh and blood, but only as it were, an abstraction of the same'.[61]

As a result of what had happened, Hess wrote to Karl on 29 May 1846 apologizing for the tone of his previous letter. But, he continued, 'you have a right to be irritated, *but not Engels*, my letter was not intended in any way for him'. And he concluded: 'with you personally, I would still very much like to be involved; but I wish to have nothing more to do with your party'.[62] After this, matters got even worse. Perhaps because he was 'an excessive reconciler', as he himself admitted, Hess soon attempted to patch up his quarrel with Engels, and by July was requesting Engels' help in smuggling the passport-less Sybille from Brussels into France. Engels obliged, but was soon complaining to Karl that Sybille did not care about Hess, and was on the lookout for a husband.[63]

From the time he had joined Karl in Brussels Engels' attitude towards Hess had become steadily more hostile. Perhaps he was jealous of Hess's intellectual influence over Karl, or perhaps he wished to take revenge for 'all the dirty tricks', he claimed, 'they had played on Mary' around the time of the 'breach'. Whatever the reason, in 1846–7 Engels missed no opportunity to belittle, deride and ultimately humiliate Hess. In July, he referred to his 'stupidities', and in September he mocked Hess's attempt to 're-establish relations'; in Paris, he appears to have taken up with Sybille. In October, Engels referred to Hess, who had returned to Cologne because of lack of funds, as the member of a 'muddled school'. When Hess finally arrived in Paris at the beginning of 1847, Engels boasted to Karl that when 'the worthy man came to see me . . . my treatment of him was so cold and scornful that he will have no desire to return'.[64]

Eventually, in early 1848, Hess found out that Engels had had an affair with Sybille. He accused Engels of rape and spoke of challenging him to a duel. Engels' attitude was once again callous. On 14 January, he wrote to Karl, 'I was enormously tickled by the Mosi business, although annoyed that it should have come to light . . . Moses brandishing his pistols, parading his horns before the whole of Brussels . . . must have been exquisite.' The report of Hess's accusation 'made me split my sides with laughter'. In July 1847, he continued, Sybille, 'this Balaam's she-ass', made to him a 'declaration of love' and 'Her rage with me is unrequited love, pure and simple.'[65]

As for Engels, his correspondence with Karl clearly bears out the picture of an incongruous combination of dutiful subservience to Karl as his political fixer and louche pursuit of sexual adventure with street- or factory-women. In 1845, he had been keen to leave Barmen, not least because a love affair had come to its end. While protective of Mary Burns, when she came to Brussels in the spring of 1846, he still pursued further amatory encounters when in Paris later in the year. As he wrote to Karl towards the end of 1846, the informers from the Prefecture, who had been following him, must have acquired 'a great many entrance tickets to the *bals* Montesquieu, Valentino, Prado, etc.', and that he was indebted to the Prefect 'for some delicious encounters with *grisettes* and for a great deal of pleasure', since he wished day and night to take advantage of what Paris had to offer. For the days he spent there, he claimed, might be his last.[66] In March 1847, however, still from Paris, he wrote to Karl, 'it's absolutely essential that you get out of *ennuyante* Brussels for once and come to Paris, and I for my part have a great desire to go carousing with you'. In his own case, 'if there were no French women, life wouldn't be worth living. *Mais tant qu'il y a grisettes*, well and good'.[67]

4. THE BRUSSELS CRITIQUE OF POLITICAL ECONOMY

What held the ill-assorted Brussels group together was their faith in the promise of Karl's critique of political economy. Already in August 1845, Jenny was 'anxiously awaiting' its publication, while Ewerbeck enquired urgently, 'when will your great book appear?'[68] Beyond a small group of radical intellectuals, Karl was unknown. But within this group faith in his imminent 'greatness' was unanimous. Georg Jung in Cologne, a strong supporter since Karl's time on the *Rheinische Zeitung*, awaited the 'book on political economy and politics with the greatest eagerness ... You must become for the whole of Germany, what you already are for your friends. With your brilliant prose style and the great clarity of your argumentation, you must and will assert yourself here and become a star of first rank.'[69] The entreaties to get on with the book and not be diverted into other projects continued into 1846. Joseph Weydemeyer urged the importance of finishing the book soon, since the accounts in the *Deutsch-Französische Jahrbücher* and *The Holy Family* were too brief and there was 'nothing to recommend to those who want to read something sensibly argued about communism'.[70] Moses Hess wrote that he had thrown himself exclusively into the reading of economics and was looking forward 'with great excitement to the book'.[71]

The admiration of the Brussels group and of his friends from Cologne was not surprising. Karl was the first German radical to display a real knowledge of political economy and develop a radical critique of it. During the years from 1845 through to 1849 his writings, lectures and speeches presented this critique in an ever clearer form. During this time, he abandoned the Feuerbachian approach which had so impressed him in 1844 – the translation of the 'economic' into the 'human' – and instead began to develop a radical reading of political economy in its own terms.[72] While in 1844 he had criticized Proudhon for not being able to get beyond a critique of political economy, in 1846, faced by the challenge of Proudhon's *System of Economic Contradictions*, Karl adopted a new approach. Instead of dwelling upon the supposed silences and contradictions of political economy as an ideology, his aim was now to demonstrate his superior acquaintance with its findings.

In 1845, Karl had not yet added to his manuscripts of the previous year. But his trip to Manchester with Engels in the summer of 1845 must have strengthened his knowledge of economic literature in England and placed him in a better position to suggest an alternative to Proudhon's approach. This enabled him in particular to distinguish between the historical course of economic development and its representation in works of political economy. As he now observed in relation to what he had once attacked as the 'cynicism' of Ricardo, 'the cynicism is in the facts and not in the words which express the facts'.[73]

On the basis of his reading of Ricardo, Karl attacked Proudhon's ideal of the determination of value by labour time. He pointed out that 'determination of value by labour time – the formula M. Proudhon gives us as the regenerating formula of the future – is ... merely the scientific expression of the economic relations of present-day society, as was clearly and precisely demonstrated by Ricardo long before M. Proudhon'.[74] He was also able to show that the idea of equal exchange as an egalitarian application of Proudhon's formula had already been explored in the 1820s and 1830s by English 'socialists', including Thomas Hodgskin, William Thompson and John Francis Bray.[75] Finally, a better acquaintance with developments in the industrial economy in Britain led him to devote special attention to the 'automatic system' of machine production, described in Andrew Ure's *Philosophy of Manufactures*.[76] Rather than considering the machine a simple negation of the division of labour, as Proudhon saw it, 'the automatic system' heralded a new factory stage in the development of the division of labour. In it, as he was later to argue in *Capital*, the division of labour took place not between persons, but between machines, while the operatives were reduced to the role of simple machine-minders.

In speeches and lectures following *The Poverty of Philosophy*, notably a series of lectures given to the Brussels German Workers' Educational Association on 'Wage Labour and Capital' in the autumn of 1847, and in a speech on 'The Question of Free Trade' delivered to the Brussels *Association Démocratique* in January 1848, Karl put forward a critical account of the growth of 'the productive powers of capital' – the development of an industrial economy and its relationship with world trade.

For radical critics of political economy, the fundamental question was why should an exchange between the wage-earner and the capitalist, which was ostensibly free and equal, so disproportionately benefit the capitalist at the expense of the wage-earner. Like other critics of the period, Karl's answer to this question stressed that labour was not a commodity like any other. He cited John Wade: 'the saleable commodity labour differs from other commodities in particular by its *evanescent nature*, by the impossibility of *accumulating* and by the fact that the *supply* cannot be increased or reduced with the same facility as with other products'.[77] The wage was not 'the worker's share in the commodity produced by him'. Wages were 'part of already existing commodities with which the capitalist buys for himself a definite amount of productive labour'. The price of labour was determined by competition and fluctuated around the cost of production of labour. This price had nothing to do with the contribution made by labour to the value of the product; it was solely determined by the cost of production of labour (that which in Ricardo's terms is necessary to enable the labourer to subsist and reproduce his kind).

Capital consisted of 'raw materials, instruments of labour and food of all kinds which are employed to create new raw materials, instruments of labour and food. All these are creations of labour, products of labour, *accumulated labour*.' Capital was not simply an aggregation of physical goods. It was also 'a social relation of production', 'a *bourgeois production relation*'. Means of subsistence, instruments of labour and raw materials were 'utilised for new production under given social conditions, in definite social relations'. It is 'this definite social character which turns the products serving for new production into *capital*';

and the most important of these conditions was the existence of a class possessing nothing but the capacity to work; 'Capital does not consist in accumulated labour serving living labour as a means for new production. It consists in living labour serving accumulated labour as a means of maintaining and multiplying the exchange value of the latter.'[78]

This in turn served to explain the process of capital accumulation. 'The worker receives means of subsistence in exchange for his labour, but the capitalist receives in exchange for his means of subsistence labour, the productive activity of the worker, the creative power whereby the worker not only replaces what he consumes but gives to the accumulated labour a greater value than it previously possessed.' The worker in the cotton factory did not merely produce cotton textiles but produced capital: 'The wage labour can only be exchanged for capital, by increasing capital, by strengthening the power whose slave it is. *Hence, increase of capital is increase of the proletariat, that is, of the working class.*'[79]

The exchange value of capital – profit – increased to the same extent that the exchange value of labour, the day wage, fell and vice versa. There was a conflict of interest between labour and capital because if capital expanded, wages might also rise, but not in the same proportion, because profit and wages were in an inverse proportion. 'The indispensable condition for a tolerable situation of the worker' was '*the fastest possible growth of productive capital*'.[80] But the growth of productive capital meant 'the growth of the power of accumulated labour over living labour . . . of the bourgeoisie over the working class'; and this could be specified in various ways. When enlarged to include the whole world market, the results were 'uninterrupted division of labour, the application of new and the perfecting of old machinery precipitately and on an ever more gigantic scale . . . The greater *division of labour* enables *one* worker to do the work of five, ten or twenty . . . labour is *simplified*. The *special skill* of the worker becomes worthless. *Therefore, as labour becomes more unsatisfying, more repulsive, competition increases and wages decrease.*'[81] In sum, 'in the course of the growth of the productive forces the part of productive capital which is transformed into machinery and raw material, i.e. capital as such, increases in disproportion to the part which is intended for wages; i.e. in other words, the workers

232

must share among themselves an ever smaller part of the productive capital in relation to its total mass'.[82]

Many of the issues raised by the world-wide development of commercial society and the industrial economy were pinpointed in the debate about free trade. What position should socialists and communists adopt towards it? For Karl, there could be no doubt that the situation of the worker would be worsened by the coming of free trade; and in 1847 he reiterated the point often evaded by free traders in England when taunted by Chartists. As he wrote in the *Northern Star* in September 1847, 'we accept everything that has been said of the advantages of Free Trade. The powers of production will increase, the tax imposed upon the country by protective duties will disappear, all commodities will be sold at a cheaper price', but also, according to Ricardo, 'labour being equally a commodity will equally sell at a cheaper price'. It had to be accepted that 'under the freedom of trade the whole severity of the laws of political economy will be applied to the working classes'. But that was no reason for accepting protectionism, because 'by Free Trade all economical laws, with their most astounding contradictions, will act upon a larger scale, upon a greater extent of territory, upon the territory of the whole earth; and because from the uniting of all these contradictions into a single group, where they stand face to face, will result the struggle which will itself eventuate in the emancipation of the proletarians'. Or as Karl stated a few months later, in January 1848, 'the Free Trade system hastens the Social Revolution. In this revolutionary sense alone, gentlemen, I am in favour of Free Trade.'[83]

Karl's interpretation of the logic of political economy during these years did not as yet amount to a new theory. It presented an exceptionally clear, if selective, summary of the critical writings of Simonde de Sismondi, Louis Blanc, Pellegrino Rossi, Eugène Buret and Pierre-Joseph Proudhon; in England, it incorporated the work of Bray, Thomas Hodgskin, MacCulloch and James Mill. The readings were partial and, in the case of mainstream political economists, often misleading or distorted. His 1844 presentation of Adam Smith as an apologist of immiseration remained uncorrected, while in the case of Ricardo he took no account of the crucial qualifications Ricardo had made to his theory of the determination of value by labour time, subsequent to the first edition of

The Principles of Political Economy and Taxation in 1817. But, despite all this, his depiction of the pressures upon the proletariat created by the development of an industrial economy and its relationship with the growth of world trade powerfully captured some real aspects of the trajectory of economic development in the 1830s and 1840s.

Far less successful was Karl's account in the *Communist Manifesto* of how these developments were related to politics and class struggle. However highly stylized, the set of characters in play in his writings up until 1845 – 'the Christian state', 'the Philosopher', 'the rational state', 'the censor', 'civil society', 'the peasantry', 'the Germans', 'the Philistines' and even 'the proletariat' – had still borne some relation to local realities. But once Karl moved to France and Belgium, in texts running from the so-called *German Ideology* to the *Communist Manifesto*, these were replaced by a new cast of characters and processes – most prominently 'the modern state', 'the class struggle', 'the bourgeoisie' and 'the proletariat'. Although purportedly universal, these figures were more abstract and possessed less explanatory power than those which they replaced, especially in relation to Germany.

In the *Communist Manifesto*, Karl combined a brilliant thumbnail sketch of the development of modern capitalism with a depiction of the contemporary conflict between classes as its necessary outcome. The word 'bourgeois' was taken from the political debates in France during the years of the July Monarchy, and more specifically from the vocabulary of opposition journalists, especially Louis Blanc. Blanc characterized 'the social history of the bourgeoisie' as 'the banking interest enthralling industry and commerce; individual credit profiting the strong, injuring the weak; in a word, the reign of competition tending inevitably to overthrow small fortunes, and to undermine those of middle standard and all this for the purpose of arriving at a real financial feudality – an oligarchy of bankers'. 'From 1815 to 1830', Blanc continued, 'the bourgeoisie busied itself only with completing its domination. To turn the elective system to its own advantage, to seize on the parliamentary power and render it supreme after having achieved its conquest, such was for fifteen years the work prosecuted by liberalism.'[84]

But this 'bourgeois' was no longer the overfed businessman, sketched by Daumier, the coupon-clipper living off his *rentes* or the hard-hearted landlord deaf to the entreaties of poor tenants he threw onto the frosty Parisian streets. Nor was he simply the epitome of self-centred greed and mediocrity evoked a little later by Tocqueville.[85] The 'middle classes', the 'bourgeoisie', the *'Mittelklasse'* were no longer simply local translations of 'the possessing class', as they had been for Engels in 1845.[86] They were now the personification of capital itself.

In the *Manifesto*, impersonal forces – the division of labour and the unseen hand – conceived to be at work in the expansion of exchange relations and in the progress of commercial society, were presented as stages in the formation of the collective physiognomy of a class, and by the same token the portly representatives of the once inconspicuous European middle orders were endowed with the demonic energy of capital itself. Similarly, the *proletarian*, mainly thanks to Friedrich Engels' portrayal in the *Condition of the Working Class in England*, blended the uncompromising sectarian zeal of the Parisian revolutionary Babouvist with the mass democratic activism of the Lancashire Chartist.[87]

These classes were no longer struggling over anything as specific as the 'Prussian Christian state', the 'Reformed Parliament' or the 'July Monarchy'. The arena now described was that of the 'modern state'. But this notion, except in contrast to feudalism or the *ancien régime*, proved to be an empty category, and as late as 1875, in his *Critique of the Gotha Programme*, Karl was still trying to provide it with corresponding content. He criticized the German Social Democrats for talking vaguely about the 'present state'; given their empirical diversity, the 'present state' was 'a fiction'. But his own presumption continued to be that despite 'their motley diversity of form', modern states do have things in common: 'they all stand on the ground of modern bourgeois society'. 'They thus also share certain essential characteristics.' What were these 'essential characteristics'? Karl did not specify, and, as one critic has noted, the whole passage could be called 'an impressive sounding tautology'.[88] Karl himself seemed well aware of his failure in this area. In a letter of 1862 to his admirer Dr Kugelmann, he claimed that he had arrived at the basic principles from which even others could reconstruct his system 'with the exception, perhaps, of the relationship between the various forms of state and the various economic structures of society'.[89]

Even at the time, doubts were raised about the social and political scenario envisaged by the *Manifesto*. Harney, Engels' Chartist friend and editor of the *Northern Star*, wrote to him in 1846: 'Your speculations as to the speedy coming of a revolution in England, I doubt . . . Your prediction that we will get the Charter in the course of the current year, and the abolition of private property within three years will certainly not be realised – indeed as regards the latter, although it may and I hope will come, it is my belief that neither you nor I will see it.'[90] From London in 1845, Hermann Kriege wrote to Karl: 'my dear Marx, where are all these English workers that Engels is so enthusiastic about? I have had the opportunity to meet with the leading socialists here; I tell you that they are the most cockeyed philistines that anyone could meet'.[91]

After the tumultuous conflicts of the years 1831–4, there was also some despondency about the situation in France. In 1846, Carl Bernays wrote:

> Every day my hopes for France dwindle further. It is incredible how rapidly the *juste milieu* has gained credence amongst the lowest classes. Respect for property among the lowest classes is still much too much, much greater than in Germany and even than in the Rhineland. You will have seen in all the workers' uprisings, that the improvement of the condition of the workers is only sought in an indirect way through wage rises, and never by direct means. This desire is not only utterly contrary to communist principles, but also to communist instincts. The worker appears therefore not as an enemy, but rather as someone who enjoys making agreements.

Bernays thought a peasant *jacquerie* more likely than a workers' uprising.[92] As to Germany, there was just as much doubt whether the German *Bürgertum* would behave like a bourgeoisie. According to Heinrich Bürgers writing from Cologne:

> Now I have returned to the bosom of the German petit bourgeois. I have taken the opportunity to become familiar with the state of their consciousness and of their practice in the various circles of German society. I have come to the conclusion that both are located at a colossal distance from *our* consciousness, which has as its presupposition knowledge of the practice of the entire civilised world, and on that basis makes its critique of existing conditions. Nowhere is there even the beginning of the understanding of the questions that lead us to turn them into topics of public debate. The German bourgeoisie has so far not at all learnt to be a bourgeoisie in our sense; it is still richly infected by that philanthropism which

does not yet envisage the conflict against a class subordinated beneath it. Out of the whole manufacturing and trading public of Cologne, for example, there are perhaps not ten people, whom one could call intelligent and determined bourgeois.[93]

5. THE ADVENT OF REVOLUTION

In the course of 1847 events took a more hopeful turn. Chartist agitation, which had died down after 1842, appeared once again as hopes were invested in another petition to be presented to Parliament in 1848. In Prussia, financial difficulties forced the summoning of the estates in a 'United *Landtag*'. Its members, drawn from all the different Prussian provinces and chosen along traditional estate lines, had nevertheless refused to sanction a new form of tax, unless the government agreed to constitutional reform, whereupon the *Landtag* was adjourned. In France, as well, there was a revival of political agitation in the mid-1840s. Opposition centred on the narrowness of the franchise and took the form of a banqueting campaign – a tactic designed to circumvent the ban on political meetings. The campaign had originally been confined to the propertied classes, but increasingly attracted the support of republicans, democrats and the working classes in the streets. In January 1848, Engels claimed that the previous year had certainly been 'the most stormy we have experienced for a very long time'. He listed not only 'a constitution and a United Diet in Prussia', but 'an unexpectedly rapid awakening in political life and a general arming against Austria in Italy' and 'a civil war in Switzerland', where radicals from Protestant cantons expelled the Jesuits and defeated the Catholics. He could also point to unexpectedly liberal moves towards reform on the part of the new Pope, Pius IX, a rebellion against Bourbon rule in Naples, and the victory of the Liberals in the Belgian elections.[94]

In Brussels, Karl had also become more active in day-to-day politics. The Brussels Correspondence Committee turned itself into the Brussels branch of the Communist League. It then followed the example of London and formed the Brussels German Workers' Educational Association (*Deutscher Arbeiterbildungsverein*), a legal organization designed to attract resident German artisans. Regular meetings were held twice a week. On Wednesdays there were lectures, including Karl's on 'Wage Labour and Capital', while on Sundays there were weekly updates on the news by Karl's friend Wilhelm Wolff, followed by poetic recitals, singing and dancing.

Karl presented himself in public as a representative of this German Workers' Educational Association, and in this capacity he started to write for the *Deutsche-Brüsseler-Zeitung* in April 1847. The *Deutsche-Brüsseler-Zeitung* was a journal edited by Adalbert von Bornstedt, who had formerly been active in the running of *Vorwärts!* in Paris in 1844.[95] Both Heine and Freiligrath still believed Bornstedt to be a spy, and as the Prussian archives later confirmed, around the end of the 1830s Bornstedt had supplied spy reports. But by 1846 the increasing political boldness of his paper and the annoyance expressed by the Prussian authorities suggested not only that Bornstedt had ceased spying, but that he was a genuine convert to the radical cause. The *Deutsche-Brüsseler-Zeitung* was important since it was read by German artisans working in Brussels. Karl was therefore happy to urge his own circle to contribute to it.

During the same period, Karl also became actively involved in the *Association Démocratique*, an organization originally proposed by Karl Schapper during a meeting to honour Weitling in London in September 1844. Its aim was to unite democrats from all countries. In September 1845, after a meeting of 1,000 democrats of different nationalities to celebrate the anniversary of the French Revolution, the idea was further advanced by the Chartist leader, Julian Harney. It acquired institutional form in 1846 with the formation of the Fraternal Democrats, and in 1847 a secretary was appointed to represent each nationality. Harney represented the English and Schapper the Germans; their motto was the same as the German Workers' Educational Association: 'All men are brothers'.

In Belgium, on 27 September 1847, Bornstedt founded the *Association Démocratique* as the local branch of the Fraternal Democrats. He hoped to take advantage of Karl's temporary absence from the country to assume control of the organization, but was outmanoeuvred by Engels, who secured the position of Vice-President. In November 1847, Karl returned and was elected as the German representative, while its Belgian representative was Lucien-Léopold Jottrand, a prominent liberal lawyer and editor of *Débat Social*.

1. A portrait of the young Karl as a student

2. A portrait of the young Jenny von Westphalen

3. Karl Marx as editor of the *Rheinische Zeitung* (1842–3)

4. Heine in Paris with Jenny and Karl, *c.* 1844

5. Eleanor 'Tussy' Marx in 1873 at the age of 18, in pre-Raphaelite pose

6. Jenny and Laura Marx, c. 1865

8. Helene Demuth, maid in the Marx
family and mother of Freddy, in old age

9. Friedrich Engels in 1870

10. Moses Hess in 1847

11. Mikhail Bakunin

12. Pierre Joseph Proudhon

13. Andreas Gottschalk – a portrait by Wilhelm Kleinenbroich, 1849

14. Ferdinand Lassalle, c. 1860

15. Dr Eduard Gumpert,
Karl's physician in
Manchester

16. Wilhelm Wolff, friend
and associate of Marx
and Engels

The Belgian *Association* grew rapidly, especially in the depressed textile districts of Flanders; in Ghent, at a meeting attended by Karl, a branch of 3,000 members, mainly workers, was formed. The Belgian democratic leaders, particularly Jottrand, were inspired by the example of Chartism and aspired to found a comparable organization capable of mounting democratic pressure from without. Karl devoted much of his time to the *Association* but, unbeknown to the Belgians, also continued to fulfil his responsibilities in the clandestine Communist League. Thus, on 27 November, he embarked on a ten-day trip to London, ostensibly to represent the *Association* at a meeting of the Fraternal Democrats, but also to participate in the conference to agree upon the statutes of the Communist League. Karl was almost without resources and was only able to return to Brussels thanks to a loan from his Russian friend Pavel Annenkov. Previously, he had left Belgium to visit his relatives and press his claim for part of his inheritance. In January, he was similarly engaged both in the political direction of the *Association* and in writing up a final draft of what was to become *The Communist Manifesto*. The text was completed during January 1848, under pressure from the League, which threatened to withdraw the commission if he failed to meet his deadline.

The internal arguments among German radicals, which led to the need to produce what became the *Manifesto*, especially the aim to marginalize Karl Grün and his supporters, have already been discussed, but not the actual stages in its preparation.[96] The *Manifesto* was originally entitled the 'communist credo' or 'communist confession of faith' and had been under discussion since June 1847. Friedrich Engels was a vital intermediary between London and Brussels in the process of devising the new 'credo'. As an emissary from the Brussels Committee he put forward the original 'Draft of a Communist Confession of Faith' at the First Congress of the newly named Communist League, in London in June 1847. In September, he almost certainly contributed to the first and only number of the League's newspaper, *Die Kommunistische Zeitschrift*; and it is likely that he suggested the League's new watchword, 'Workers of the World, Unite!' in place of 'All men are brothers'.

At a meeting of the Paris branch of the League on 22 October 1847, Engels proposed a second draft of 'the credo', the so-called 'Principles of Communism', which he managed to get accepted in preference to the alternative put forward by Moses Hess.[97] Both Karl and Engels attended the Second Congress of the League in London between 28 November and 8 December 1847. At this congress, Engels' draft appears to have been accepted as the basis of a final version. A week before this congress, Engels wrote to Karl, providing a brief summary of the 'Principles'. He suggested that since 'a certain amount of history has to be narrated in it', they should 'abandon the catechetical form and call the thing the Communist *Manifesto*'. As for the congress itself, he assured Karl, 'THIS TIME WE SHALL HAVE IT ALL OUR OWN WAY.'[98]

After the congress, Karl and Engels spent a few days in London and then a further ten days together in Brussels before Engels returned to Paris. Engels did not return to Brussels until 29 January, while the manuscript of the *Manifesto* was apparently delivered before 1 February. Only one page of preparatory notes survives of a plan of section two, probably dating from December 1847. It seems, therefore, that Karl wrote up the final version alone in January 1848.

The structure of the *Manifesto* closely followed Engels' 'Principles'. Its first two historical sections correspond to questions 1–23 of the 'Principles'. Section three on communist literature elaborates question 24 of the 'Principles'; section four on communists and opposition parties relates to question 25. In substance if not in form, the *Manifesto* was not an original piece of work. Apart from Engels' 'Principles of Communism', his *Condition of the Working Class in England* and some of his shorter pieces, Karl drew heavily upon his own writings, particularly the unpublished Paris manuscripts of 1844 and *The Poverty of Philosophy*. Much of the thumbnail history contained in the *Manifesto* – its arguments about the transition from 'feudal' to 'bourgeois' society, about the growth of free trade and the world market, about the industrial revolution and the end of 'patriarchal idyllic relations', and about the formation of the proletariat – had already been expressed in 1844 in Engels' writings about England. The historical case for 'communism' placed at its centre a barely concealed account of what amounted to specifically English social and economic development. He also drew upon manuscripts assembled collectively for the *German Ideology*, and on some articles by Moses Hess. From these writings, Karl either paraphrased relevant propositions or simply lifted appropriate sentences and phrases.

The *Manifesto* is still rightly celebrated as Karl's most memorable text. Its phrases have resonated in literature and the political imagination long after the disappearance of the circumstances which originally brought them into being. Intellectually, the compelling power of its argument – or at least that of its most famous, first section – was the result of the bringing together of Karl's two most original insights in the 1840s. These were, firstly, his development of the legacy of German idealism – man was not just a creature or product of nature, but a being who transformed nature, both his own and the natural world, by his productive activity. Secondly, this was put together with his elaboration of the economic criticism, which had been developed by English and French authors, of the emergence of industrial capitalism and its relationship with the world market.

Building upon these insights, Karl was the first to evoke the seemingly limitless powers of the modern economy and its truly global reach. He was the first to chart the staggering transformation produced in less than a century by the emergence of a world market and the unleashing of the unparalleled productive powers of modern industry. He also delineated the endlessly inchoate, incessantly restless and unfinished character of modern capitalism as a phenomenon. He emphasized its inherent tendency to invent new needs and the means to satisfy them, its subversion of all inherited cultural practices and beliefs, its disregard of all boundaries, whether sacred or secular, its destabilization of every hallowed hierarchy, whether of ruler and ruled, man and woman or parent and child, its turning of everything into an object for sale.

But whatever its lasting importance in defining modernity during the last century and a half, judged by the circumstances of 1847–9 the political position adopted by Karl and his circle was impossibly self-contradictory. Since the battle with Weitling, Karl and his group were committed to the condemnation of a 'primitive' insurrectionism, a pose which took no account of changing circumstances. But equally as an answer to Grün and his supporters, it was impossible to accept the withdrawal from politics associated with many forms of socialism. Another option was simply to represent the particular grievances of the workers at a local level. This was to be the choice of another member of the Communist League, a doctor, Andreas Gottschalk, who later became the leader of the workers in Cologne. This position was rejected by Karl and his friends on the grounds that it would divide worker from bourgeois in the assault upon Prussia's feudal regime. On the other hand, given Karl's public criticism of political economy, it was no longer possible simply to merge into the democratic republican flank of a liberal-constitutionalist movement like Ruge or Heinzen. For since 1843 Karl had been committed to the exposure of what he considered to be the illusory vision animating the politics of republican democrats. The resulting position deriving from these diverse criticisms was contradictory and politically unsustainable. It meant supporting the liberals while at the same time pointing out that the achievement of liberal-bourgeois success would place the proletariat in an even worse situation than before. The communism of the *Gelehrten* (learned) involved support of the bourgeois revolution, but only as a prelude to a proletarian revolution, in which the bourgeoisie would be overthrown. This meant playing a contradictory dual role, both supporting and subverting political alliances at the same time.

As a leading member and spokesman of the *Association Démocratique*, on New Year's Eve 1847, Karl publicly saluted the liberal mission of Belgium in opposition to absolutism. He 'forcefully' expressed his appreciation of 'the benefits of a liberal constitution, of a country where there is freedom of discussion, freedom of association, and where a humanitarian seed can flourish to the good of all Europe'.[99] Yet on 6 February 1848 Karl angrily denounced the position of Lucien Jottrand, the President of the Association, when he cited the United States, Switzerland and England as examples where the 'system of government was in tolerable transition towards a more perfect system'.[100] Belgian democrats, Jottrand argued, were not utopians, but wished to make use of the constitutional right of association in order to obtain for the people the right to vote, a reduction of taxation and a more equitable distribution of tax burdens.

Karl chose to interpret Jottrand's disavowal of utopianism as an attack on German communism. He replied belligerently, firstly, that German communism was not utopian, but based upon historical experience; secondly, although Germany was 'retarded in its political development', it was a country of more than 40 million inhabitants and when it prepared for revolution, it 'will not seek the model for its movement in the radicalism in small free countries'.[101] His advice on free trade was similarly barbed. 'We must admit that under this same Free Trade the whole severity of the economic laws will fall upon the workers.' The freedom supported by free traders was not 'the freedom of one individual in relation to another, but the freedom of Capital to crush the worker'. If he supported free trade, it was because 'the Free Trade System hastens the Social Revolution'.[102]

Political questions, he maintained, were already turning into social ones. Poland at the time of the Cracow rising of 1846 was to be congratulated for combining national demands with the abolition of feudalism. The solution to Poland's national question would only be brought about through the resolution of its social question. For 'it is not only the old Poland that is lost. The old Germany, the old France, the old England, the whole of the old society is lost.' But this was no loss 'for those who have nothing to lose in the old society, and this is the case of the great majority in all countries at the present time'. The answer was 'the establishment of a new society, one no longer based on class antagonisms'. Therefore, the crucial issue for Poland was 'the victory of the English proletarians over the English bourgeoisie . . . Poland must be liberated not in Poland but in England.'[103] This reduction of the political to the social was, he thought, happening everywhere. Something similar had occurred in England, where 'in all questions from the Reform Bill until the abolition of the Corn Laws', political parties fought about nothing except 'changes in property rights', while in Belgium the struggle of liberalism with Catholicism was 'a struggle of industrial capital with large landed property'.[104]

Engels expressed the point more crudely. He could not 'forbear an ironical smile' when he observed 'the terrible earnestness, the pathetic enthusiasm with which the bourgeois strive to achieve their aims'. 'They are so short-sighted as to fancy that through their triumph the world will assume its final configuration. Yet nothing is more clear than that they are everywhere preparing the way for *us*, for the democrats and Communists; than that they will at most win a few years of troubled enjoyment, only to be then immediately overthrown.' The great denouement which was approaching had been brought about by machinery and modern industry. 'In England, as a result of modern industry, of the introduction of machinery, all oppressed classes are being merged together into a single great class with common interests, the class of the proletariat . . . as a consequence, on the opposite side all classes of oppressors have likewise been united into a single class, the bourgeoisie. The struggle has thus been simplified and so it will be possible to decide it by one single heavy blow.'[105]

This stance on the part of Karl and his Brussels circle created confusion among his democratic allies, suspicion and alarm among his governmental adversaries. As he was soon to discover, it was not a sustainable form of politics. In Paris, on 23 February 1848, soldiers fired upon a peaceful demonstration. The morning after, the city was filled with barricades, and the demand was no longer just for electoral reform, but for a republic. On the same evening, the Palais Royal was captured by insurrectionists. The king fled and his throne was put on a bonfire. A republic was declared and a provisional government was formed.

6. EXIT FROM BRUSSELS

On 26 February, the Paris train brought news of the revolution to Brussels. On board the train was a royal adviser, Comte de Hompesch, come to warn Leopold, king of the Belgians, of the gravity of the situation in Paris. Hompesch's solicitor was Lucien Jottrand, so as President of the *Association Démocratique* Jottrand immediately summoned the Executive Committee, of which Karl was a member; and it was agreed that an open meeting should be held the next day at the Old Court, Rue de Soeurs Noires.

According to an account written by Jenny a decade later, Karl helped to arm the workers in preparation for a republican insurrection. This point was reiterated in 1934 in the official communist chronology, *Karl Marx: Chronik seines Lebens*, and has been repeated in many biographical accounts ever since. Why Jenny made this statement, whether it was the result of confusion or of an unconscious desire to present a more heroic account of their exit from Belgium, is unclear. But the Belgian archives tell a different story, which clearly shows that Karl was totally uninvolved in any insurrectionary preparations.[106]

At the meeting at the Old Court on 27 February, a crowded and enthusiastic assembly agreed to Jottrand's proposal that the *Association* reassemble every evening to put democratic pressure on the government. Two addresses were voted on: the first congratulated the new French Provisional Government, a second expressed solidarity with the Fraternal Democrats. Another resolution pressing the government to call up artisans and workers to supplement the predominantly bourgeois Civic Guard was signed only by Belgian members of the Committee. Karl was punctilious in emphasizing that his participation was only in support of the cosmopolitan aims of the *Association*, thus honouring his official commitment not to become involved in Belgian politics.

The government feared trouble and by 26 February had increased police patrols and mobilized the army. It was therefore well prepared when, at the end of the meeting, younger members of the gathering, carried away by enthusiasm, prowled the streets shouting slogans like 'Vive la République' and attempted to enter the Grand'Place. Several arrests were made, including of Karl's companions Wilhelm Wolff, Philippe Gigot and Victor Tedesco together with other members of the German Workers' Educational Association. This was not the attempted insurrection that subsequent accounts have implied. It was a minor street disorder, and by 10.30 p.m. calm had been restored. The repressive response of the government continued. The mayor was asked to forbid public meetings, and special attention was paid to the surveillance of foreigners, who were to be verified or else be expelled from the country. Further arrests were made, including of a shoemaker called Dassy, who had shouted 'Vive la République' and was said to possess a dagger belonging to Bornstedt, and another shoemaker, called Merkens, accused of arguing for the use of the guillotine.

The government's alarm was not the result of the activities of the Brussels *Association Démocratique*, but of those Belgian republicans and refugees in Paris. One of these republicans, Blervacq, was recruiting members of a 'Belgian Legion' and was enlisting not only Belgians but unemployed French and Germans too. Furthermore, the process was unofficially encouraged by Paris's republican Police Commissioner, Caussidière, who was happy to pay for the travel of volunteers to the frontier, and was assisted by *préfets* who had opened up arsenals in Lille and Valenciennes.

In these circumstances, the suspicions of Charles de Bavay at the Brussels Court of Appeal focused particularly upon Karl. As a leading member of the German Workers' Educational Association and as an active participant in the *Association Démocratique*, Karl was already notorious. On his return from London on behalf of the *Association* on 13 December 1847, the *Journal de Bruxelles* had mocked his activist cosmopolitanism by comparing it with that of a notorious Low

Countries Jacobin, Anacharsis Cloots. On hearing of Karl's presence at the *Association* meeting of 27 February and of the subsequent disorderly behaviour of German and Belgian workers on the streets, de Bavay became convinced that Karl was at the centre of a conspiracy to mount an insurrection.

What particularly attracted de Bavay's attention had been Karl's recent financial transactions: through the good offices of his brother-in-law, Wilhelm Schmalhausen, Karl had finally secured 6,000 francs, a portion of his inheritance from his mother. De Bavay believed that the inheritance was just a cover story to conceal Karl's financing of the Belgian republican movement in Paris. On this basis, Baron Hody, Chief of National Security, asked the Minister of Justice to decree Karl's expulsion on the grounds that he had breached the terms of his residence permit. The Council of Ministers approved the measure on 1 March and the king confirmed the order on the next day. On 3 March, Karl was informed that he must leave Belgium within twenty-four hours.

At de Bavay's instigation an enquiry into the behaviour of the proscribed German took place on that day at the *Palais de Justice*. There it was revealed that a few days after receiving his inheritance, Karl and his family had moved from their residence in the Rue d'Orléans back to the more comfortable quarters of the Bois Sauvage hotel. Evidence was collected from restaurateurs, shopkeepers and a coachman to make up a dossier. It emerged that Karl had been visited by a number of foreigners, while a local saddler suggested that foreign persons might have been trying to acquire holsters and sword-belts. A coachman from a local inn, the Vigilante, reported that Karl and two other members of the *Association Démocratique* visited a bank to change 2,100 francs into banknotes, thus reinforcing the belief of the authorities that Karl was either preparing an armed insurrection in Brussels or else assisting the mobilization of Belgian revolutionaries in Paris.

While the judicial process continued, Karl contacted three lawyers at the Court of Appeal, including Jottrand, who tried to negotiate with the ministers a delay in the expulsion. But on the same day, 3 March, Karl received from his friend Flocon, editor of *La Réforme* and now a minister in the French Provisional Government, a letter rescinding his previous expulsion from France and inviting him back to Paris.

According to the report of the First Division of Police on the evening of 3 March, after a meeting at the Court of Brussels, several

individuals, mainly foreigners, exchanged loud words of 'exalted republicanism', and then made their way to Bois Sauvage at around eleven in
the evening. A meeting was held, which went on until after midnight.
This was a meeting with members of the German Workers' Educational
Association, followed by the Committee of the Communist League.
After the meetings were dispersed, Police Inspector Daxbeck entered
the Bois Sauvage and asked Karl to hand over the papers he was working on. Karl attempted to resist and as a result he – and later Jenny – was
arrested.

This official version of events was challenged a few days later and a
request lodged to investigate the conduct of the police. A new enquiry
took place at the *Hôtel de Ville* on 11 March in the presence of the
mayor and seven councillors. There it emerged that the original report
contained 'grave errors'. The raid on Bois Sauvage by Daxbeck was
unauthorized and in any case nothing untoward was found. The papers
seized by Daxbeck revealed that 'the society' of which Karl was Vice-
President had been dissolved and moved to Paris. The authorities originally
assumed that this 'society' must refer to the *Association Démocratique*,
thus showing that they were unaware of Karl's parallel role in the Communist League.

After his arrest, Karl was taken to the Amigo, a detention centre
next to the *Hôtel de Ville*. Jenny went to consult Jottrand about Karl's
plight. In the meantime Daxbeck returned to the *Hôtel de Ville* and
ordered that Jenny be arrested on her return on the grounds that she
lacked papers. She too was taken to the Amigo, where a Belgian friend,
Gigot, who tried to intervene on her behalf, was also imprisoned. Most
embarrassing in the eyes of the new enquiry was that Jenny, 'the sister
of the governor of Pomerania' (Ferdinand von Westphalen), had briefly
been forced to share a cell with three prostitutes. Brussels liberals were
outraged at the treatment of the Marx family, and Baron Hody
requested the dismissal of Daxbeck, contending that Belgium was a
free country and that the police had no right to seize Karl's papers, even
when it had emerged that they referred to the Communist League. But,
despite all this, de Bavay persisted in his suspicion about the connection
between Karl's inheritance and the financing of insurrection. He traced
the passage of the bill of exchange through the banking house of Fould
and Oppenheim in Paris and back to the original deposit in Trier.
All these enquiries confirmed that the funds had been legitimately

transferred from Frau Marx in Trier and were intended for her son. Finally, de Bavay was convinced that Karl had not financed an uprising.

Karl reached Paris on 4 March, having armed no Belgian workers. He wrote to the editor of *La Réforme* protesting at his wife's treatment. 'My wife, under the charge of vagabondage, was taken to the prison at the Hôtel de Ville and locked up in a dark room with prostitutes.' Her 'only crime consists in the fact that, although belonging to the Prussian aristocracy, she shares the democratic opinions of her husband'.[107]

8

The Mid-Century Revolutions

I. PARIS AGAIN

A fortnight after the Revolution of 22–24 February, Karl together with his family arrived in Paris, on 4 March 1848. Evidence of the February insurrection lay all around.[1] According to the German novelist Fanny Lewald, 'the paving stones are laid loosely at the street corners and not pounded down. Wrecked bread wagons and overturned buses show where the most important barricades were. Most of the iron fencing (except for a few remaining feet giving witness that there had been a fence there) had been torn down around a church. In the Palais Royal – or the Palais National as it is now called according to the sign – all the window panes and their frames have been broken . . . On the boulevards, the trees are felled, the pipes and columns of the fountains torn down. At the Tuileries, tattered white curtains flutter from the paneless windows; over all the doors, on the walls of the palace, you can read this inscription written in chalk or charcoal: "Hôpital des Invalides Civiles" (City Hospital).'[2]

During this stay in Paris – which proved to be brief – Karl met again with those he had known in 1844, in particular those associated with *La Réforme*, the left-leaning republican newspaper, now represented in the Provisional Government. He was in contact with Ledru-Rollin, just become the Minister of the Interior in the Provisional Government, but was closest to Ferdinand Flocon, the editor of *La Réforme* and soon to be Minister of Agriculture. Flocon was a friend who had first invited Karl back from Brussels. He had also apparently offered Karl money to restart the *Neue Rheinische Zeitung*, but the offer was refused.[3]

In early March, the Fraternal Democrats also sent a delegation to

Paris. The delegation, which was there to congratulate the new Provisional Government, included the Chartists Harney and Jones, and representatives of the German Workers' Educational Association in London, Schapper and Moll. The opportune presence in Paris of these leading members of the Communist League both from London and from Brussels made possible the re-establishment of a central office. Karl was reappointed President and Karl Schapper was again Secretary.

In the immediate aftermath of the February days, the atmosphere in Paris remained one of euphoria. Its spirit was evoked by the revolutionary enthusiast, Dussardier, in Flaubert's novel *A Sentimental Education*. 'Everything's fine! The People are on top! The workers and middle classes are falling into each other's arms! Ah, if only you knew what I've seen! What a splendid lot! How wonderful it all is! . . . The Republic's been proclaimed and now everyone's going to be happy! Some journalists talking near me a moment ago were saying we're going to liberate Poland and Italy! Do you realize there'll be no more kings? The whole world will be free, absolutely free!'[4]

In this heady atmosphere, in which it was believed that revolution would sweep across Europe, it was not difficult to kindle enthusiasm among exiles for the assembling of expeditions which would take the republic back to their native lands. The Provisional Government was keen to see political exiles and foreign workers return to their homelands, and it assisted their passage to the frontier; while, in Belgium, Karl had already found himself falsely accused of promoting the dispatch of revolutionary Belgian workers from Paris to Brussels. When he arrived in France, he learned that a similar plan was afoot among the Germans in Paris. At a large meeting of artisans and exiles, Karl discovered that 'German democrats of Paris have formed a legion to march and proclaim the German republic'; German and Polish democrats would 'march together'. They might join the uprising in Posen, and even go on to Russia itself. Gifts were required in the form of arms, ammunition, money and clothing. The first volunteers had already started drilling on the Champ de Mars. The plan was to proceed via Odenwald, the place where the sixteenth-century Peasants' War had begun, and launch an insurrection there.

This plan, which had been devised by Herwegh and Bornstedt, was vehemently opposed by socialists and communists, who held public meetings to condemn any attempt to establish a republic by means of armed intervention from without. In one of these meetings Karl made a long speech, in which he condemned the Legion, not so much for its Romanticism or its naivety, as for misreading the character of the current revolution. According to Sebastian Seiler, a fellow member of the Communist League, Karl argued that 'the February revolution was only to be regarded as the superficial beginning of the European movement. In a short time open fighting would break out in Paris between the proletariat and the bourgeoisie . . . On its result', he declared, 'the victory or defeat of revolutionary Europe would depend. He therefore insisted that the German workers remain in Paris and prepare in advance to take part in the armed struggle.'[5] As President of the reconstituted League, Karl was now able to break with any organization supporting Herwegh's Legion, and to expel Bornstedt from the League. Karl and his allies withdrew from the democratic organizations, and set up their own German Workers' Union, which by April had attracted 400 members.

But plans changed when on 19 and 20 March news reached Paris of revolutions in Vienna and Berlin. In the light of these events, the reconstituted leadership of the Communist League decided to encourage individual members to make their own way back to their home towns and there to work towards the formation of a national network of branches centred upon Mainz. Members were to prepare themselves for a revolution akin to that of 1789. As Karl explained in a reply to Weitling in a speech to the Cologne Democratic Society later in the year, 'we Germans' have 'only now arrived at the point which the French had already reached in the year 1789'.[6] All members of the League were to take with them copies of the *Communist Manifesto* and the seventeen 'Demands of the Communist Party in Germany', a document thought likely to appeal to peasants and artisans. In contrast to liberal reform programmes across Europe, these 'demands' contained no mention of individual rights, or freedom of speech, of assembly or of the press, and no reference to trial by jury.

The French revolutionary government had given help to the German Legion that marched out of Paris on 1 April. Similar assistance was offered to members of the Communist League, who left Paris on the same day. Karl and his family, together with Engels and Ernst Dronke, left Paris at the beginning of April, first making their way to Mainz. On 10 April, Jenny and the children moved to Trier, where they stayed for three months with her mother, until Karl obtained his residence permit. Karl himself moved to Cologne.

2. THE COURSE OF THE REVOLUTIONS

The revolutions of 1848 represented a spectacular collapse of political authority in Western and Central Europe: in Paris in February, in Vienna and Berlin in March. Governments were taken by surprise as some were brought down and others forced into reform. For this reason, most of the gains made by opposition forces – constitutional reformers, liberals, republicans and socialists – were achieved within the first few weeks or even the first few days following the victories of the crowds. Thereafter, in a protracted and sometimes precarious process, conservative forces regained the initiative and recaptured power. The forces of order re-established the fractured polities, but along new and unfamiliar lines.

Karl was fully engaged in the mid-century revolutions, both as a participant and as a critical observer. Before being issued a deportation order on 16 May 1849, he spent thirteen months in Cologne, as the editor of the largest-selling radical newspaper in the Rhineland, the *Neue Rheinische Zeitung*, and as a leading member of the Cologne Democratic Society. Later he also became involved in the direction of the Workers' Association. From Cologne, he proceeded to Frankfurt on 19 May and arrived back in Paris around 3 June. Two months later, he was informed that he had to leave Paris, which he did on 24 August, for London. In England in the aftermath of revolution between January 1850 and March 1852, he wrote two major texts: *The Class Struggles in France* and *The Eighteenth Brumaire of Louis Bonaparte*. These works were attempts to interpret the revolutionary sequence of events in the light of his new historical conception of 'class struggle': 'Forms of class struggle', he wrote to Joseph Weydemeyer, while composing the *Eighteenth Brumaire* in March 1852, were related to 'historical phases in the development of production'.[7] This conviction governed his political activity as a participant, and his subsequent judgements as a philosopher and a historian. How well it corresponded to the observable sequence of events can only be assessed in the light of an account of what actually occurred.

The possibility of a crisis gathering in Europe had become apparent in 1847. Chartist agitation began in England and a campaign to extend the suffrage started in France. In Switzerland, a civil war resulted in the victory of the liberal cantons over the Catholic ones, while in Palermo the king of Naples was forced to grant a constitution. In Prussia, King Friedrich Wilhelm was obliged to summon a United *Landtag* in order to authorize a loan to enable the state to build strategically important railways. The government's continued use of incongruous distinction by estates had been noted at the time, and comparisons were made with the summoning of the Estates General in 1789. Led by Rhineland liberals, the *Landtag* attempted to make its authorization dependent upon regular meetings and the authority to approve taxes. But this attempt to move towards representative government was refused and the *Landtag* was adjourned.

The uneasy awareness that official languages of political or social hierarchy no longer matched patterns of belief or behaviour affected both ruling and subordinate classes. This was particularly true in cities, where cafés, taverns and newspapers provided daily updates on political life. On 27 January 1848, Tocqueville asked the French Chamber of Deputies, 'have you no intuitive instinct, incapable of being analysed, but certain, that tells you the ground is trembling once more in Europe? Do you not feel – how should I say it – a revolutionary wind in the air?'[8] Even so, no one expected the Revolution to come precisely when it did.

It arrived three weeks later and in Paris lasted for three days – between 22 and 24 February 1848. It was the unanticipated outcome of the suffrage campaign that had been gathering momentum during the previous year. The Guizot ministry won a substantial victory in 1846, but on the basis of a franchise so narrow that it revealed little about political sentiment in the nation at large. Legitimists no less than republicans, and even the moderate 'dynastic' opposition within the Assembly, felt frustrated by the July Monarchy (the constitutional compromise that had followed the Revolution of July 1830). So a suffrage campaign began in the National Assembly in 1847 with Duvergier de Hauranne's proposal to create 200,000 new voters.[9] Since political demonstrations had been forbidden from the mid-1830s, support was to be expressed by a series of reform banquets held all over France. The dining was a pastime largely confined to the middle classes, while large numbers of workers looked on. One banquet in Rouen was attended by 1,800 guests, and Flaubert recorded his distaste at it: 'Such cuisine! Such wine! And such talk! . . . After nine hours spent before cold turkey and sucking pig in the company of my locksmith, who continually slapped me on the back at all the best parts, I came home frozen to the marrow.'[10]

The banquet campaign generated mounting excitement. The moderate 'dynastic opposition' – so called because of its acceptance of the July Monarchy – was only prepared to sanction a modest reform programme. It took fright at the plan promoted by radicals in early 1848 to hold a democratic banquet in the 12th *arrondissement* of Paris, a democratic stronghold around the Panthéon. An alternative plan was put forward, for a banquet near the Champs-Élysées on 22 February. The Prime Minister, Guizot, declared it to be illegal, so on 21 February the leaders of the parliamentary opposition backed down. But the poet Lamartine, famous for his recently published *History of the Girondins*, and for his move away from the conservative and Catholic deputies in the Assembly, announced his intention to attend the banquet, alone if necessary. Workers and students also refused to capitulate. On the morning of 22 February, therefore, considerable numbers from the eastern suburbs and from the Latin Quarter proceeded to the Place de la Concorde.

No one expected the marches and demonstrations to turn into a revolution. With the National and Municipal Guards the government had at its disposal three times the armed forces which it had commanded in 1840. Nevertheless, within forty-eight hours, Louis Philippe and his ministers were defeated, and the July Monarchy was over. The crucial mistake had been to depend upon the National Guard – the shopkeepers, masters, teachers, journalists and local officials, the so-called 'petite bourgeoisie in uniform'. During the years 1831-4, the July regime had relied on it as an armed force, but now its loyalties had become uncertain. The editor of *Le Siècle* and leading member of the National Guard, Louis Parée, reported that there was considerable ill-feeling against Guizot and that his legion would shout, 'Down with the system! Long live reform!'

Most observers expected that the contestation between the crowds and the regime would end in some sort of compromise between the king and the liberals. What happened later in the day, however, made any such compromise impossible. A long and festive column of marchers, adults and children, proceeded from Saint-Antoine to Porte Saint-Denis, where it mixed with a squadron of *cuirassiers* in what was seen as a celebration of solidarity between bourgeois and proletarian. The column soon passed the offices of *Le National*, the journal of the republican opposition, where it was addressed by the editor, Armand Marrast. He called for dissolution of the Assembly, parliamentary reform, and the prosecution of corrupt ministers. The marchers then made their way along the Rue de la Paix to the Ministry of Foreign Affairs in the Boulevard des Capucines, where they found their way unexpectedly blocked by 200 men of the 14th Regiment of the Line. Confused by the thick smoke from the demonstrators' torches, the soldiers felt threatened and began to shoot, at first by accident and then so it seemed in earnest. Once the smoke cleared, it emerged that fifty demonstrators had been killed, and many more wounded.

On the night of 23 February news of the 'Massacre of the Boulevard des Capucines' spread rapidly, and caused 1,500 barricades to be erected throughout the city. The king appointed Marshal Bugeaud to restore order – a tasteless and provocative choice, since Bugeaud was hated for his brutal suppression of the Paris riots of April 1834. Bugeaud found the insurgents too well entrenched to be dislodged. Abandoning the military solution and moving to a political one, Louis Philippe dismissed Guizot and appointed Thiers, who insisted that the opposition leader, Odilon Barrot, be appointed to the ministry and that the troops be cleared from the capital. But this was now too late to placate the crowd. The king abdicated in favour of his nine-year-old grandson, and left for England.

Talk on the streets had already moved towards a republic. The Tuileries Palace was overrun and the royal throne set on fire, and the Assembly was invaded by demonstrators. Not surprisingly, in a chaotic chamber, the regency proposed by the Duchess of Orléans made no headway and the nomination of members of a provisional government was adjourned to the *Hôtel de Ville*. There, further radicalization took place. Pressure from a vast crowd assembled outside the building – fed on angry memories of how the 1830 Revolution had been ended prematurely with the installation of the July Monarchy – ensured that attempts to leave the future form of government open had to be abandoned. A republic was declared. At the same time, the Chamber of Peers was removed, freedom of assembly and of the press was proclaimed, slavery in the colonies was abolished, and imprisonment for debt and the death penalty for political offences were brought to an end. A solution to the problems of labour was proffered in the appointment of a commission charged with hearings at the Palais de Luxembourg. Above all, in sweeping and unanticipated measures of democratization, universal male suffrage was proclaimed and membership of the National Guard opened to all.

In the eyes of its more radical supporters, the newly established Republic was not simply the 'Democratic Republic', but the 'Democratic and Social Republic'. Pressure from the streets ensured that the government included seven members from the liberal republican journal *Le National* and five more from the more radical, social-democratic *La Réforme*. The government now also included the socialist Louis Blanc and the worker Albert.[11] Lastly, on 25 February, in response to a further demonstration outside the *Hôtel de Ville*, the Provisional Government committed itself to 'guarantee work to all citizens' and to recognize that 'workers must associate themselves to enjoy the fruits of their labour'. In apparent recognition of the 'right to work' and as a means of removing unemployed workers from the streets, the new government sanctioned on 26 February the creation of 'National Workshops'.

The events in Paris produced great excitement in Germany. Berliners poured onto the streets in search of news. Coming on top of the liberal victories in Switzerland and Naples and the dismissal of conservative ministries in Saxony, Bavaria, Baden, Württemberg, Hanover and Hesse, the tide of reform appeared to be unstoppable. There were demonstrations in Rhineland cities. In Cologne, while deputies discussed a liberal petition demanding civil liberties and constitutional reform on 3 March, radicals burst into the Town Hall, demanding manhood suffrage (the right to vote extended to all adult males) and the abolition of the standing army. In Berlin, on 9 March, crowds similarly burst into the Council Chamber and turned the Municipal Assembly into a protest rally. At the 'Tents' in the Tiergarten, there were daily assemblies reaching some 20,000 participants at which constitutional changes were discussed, and artisans and labourers made known their economic discontents, and demanded a new law to protect labour.[12]

Tension mounted when on 13 March troops were brought into the city, and several demonstrators were killed in the palace precinct. The authorities were divided on how to react: whether to make concessions, as proposed by General Pfuel, the governor of Berlin, or to attack the insurgents, as was urged by Prince Wilhelm, the king's brother.

News from Vienna decided the issue. On 13 March, a large demonstration of citizens, students and artisans took place outside Vienna's *Landhaus* (the meeting place of the lower Austrian estates), where demands were made for reform and for the resignation of Metternich, the Empire's veteran Chancellor. Throughout the day, the demonstration grew, and, as in Paris, frightened soldiers responded with excessive force. But the crowd did not retreat; it regrouped in various parts of the city, particularly the depressed working-class quarters surrounding the centre. Rioting continued during the night, employers and officials were attacked and fires started. In response to the demands of the Civil Guard, Metternich resigned and left for England. On 15 March, after two days of revolutionary upheaval, the emperor abolished censorship, acknowledged the Civil Guard and promised to summon a constitutional assembly.

Following these events, on the morning of 17 March in Berlin it was also announced that censorship was abolished, that the United *Landtag* would be recalled and that Prussia would become a constitutional state. The city celebrated and illuminations were ordered. But it was too late to drop the plan to hold a political demonstration in the Palace Square. The demonstration would be a celebration of the crown's concessions. The crowd duly assembled, but was disturbed by the presence of the military. There were shouts that the soldiers should leave and the beginnings of panic. The order was given for the soldiers to clear the square, but, as the dragoons advanced, two weapons were accidentally fired. Anger mounted on both sides; and the square and its surroundings became a battlefield. As in Paris, the crowd saw the killing of demonstrators as a deliberate tactic, and in response built barricades across the city.[13]

By the end of the following day, there were 300 protesters and 100 soldiers dead, but no one controlled the city. The military commander, Prittwitz, together with Crown Prince Wilhelm, proposed that the city be evacuated, surrounded and bombarded. But much to the consternation of hardliners in the military, King Friedrich Wilhelm resisted this proposal, and at noon on 19 March troops were pulled out of the city, leaving the king in the hands of the Revolution. That afternoon, he and his wife were obliged to witness a procession of the corpses of the demonstrators carried across the Palace Square. As a sign of respect, he was required to remove his hat – an unheard of humiliation for a Prussian monarch. On 19 March, Friedrich Wilhelm issued 'An Address to My People and to the German Nation'. In it he implied that Prussia would lead a movement of national unification. At the same time, Prussian liberals convened with others to plan a national German Parliament. The king meanwhile rode through the city, stopping frequently to explain his actions and proclaiming himself proud to be protected by his citizens.

On 21 March, from Cologne, where Karl had formerly edited the *Rheinische Zeitung*, his friend the physician Roland Daniels wrote that people still depended on rumour to know what had gone on in Berlin: 'Everything here is in a state of excitement and tension. The whole population would be inclined to do something, but the uncertainty holds it back . . . The local population is in such a condition that if the town council declared a republic, all would agree.'[14] A few days later, another of Karl's friends, Georg Weerth, wrote, 'I have been in Cologne for some days. Everyone is armed. The promises from Berlin are not trusted. People will only be satisfied by universal suffrage, unrestricted freedom of the press and the right of free assembly. In the eyes of the people, the old *Landtag* [the United *Landtag*] is dead . . . People will only be content with a new *Landtag* chosen on the basis of universal suffrage. The same is true of the Frankfurt National Assembly.'[15] Excitement was palpable when on 29 March Ludwig Camphausen from Cologne, the leading liberal member of the United *Landtag* in 1847, was appointed Prime Minister, and when on 1 April the United *Landtag* enacted a law providing for elections to a constituent Prussian National Assembly. Elections were to be indirect, but based upon universal manhood suffrage.

3. COLOGNE

Karl arrived in Cologne on 10 April. Together with Engels, he had first spent two days in Mainz meeting Karl Wallau and Adolph Cluss, members sent in March by the Communist League to establish a Workers' Association along similar lines to those set up in London and Brussels.

The hope had been to make Mainz the centre of a network of Associations across Germany led by Wallau, a native of Mainz and President of the German Workers' Association in Brussels. Both he and Cluss were energetic, and by the time Karl and Engels arrived, they had set up a Workers' Educational Association and published a handbill addressed 'To All Workers of Germany! Brothers and Workers', urging the formation of Workers' Associations in every town and village to choose candidates for the coming German Parliament. Other League members had made similar efforts elsewhere: Stephan Born in Berlin, Wilhelm Wolff in Silesia, Karl Schapper in towns along the River Main, and Ernst Dronke in Coblenz.

But the reports sent back to the Central Authority were discouraging. Where local associations had been formed, they were above all concerned with local issues. The Mainz appeal had been virtually ignored. The first of the seventeen 'Demands of the Communist Party in Germany' stated that 'the whole of Germany shall be declared a single and indivisible republic'. But even where this neo-Jacobin proclamation did not encounter active hostility, it found no resonance. Before the February Revolution, the attempt to establish uniformity of outlook between the London, Brussels and Paris branches of the League had proved a fantasy. But artisans in these cities were at least aware of the array of political positions debated within exile communities. This was not the case in Germany itself. Except for a few Rhineland centres where the French occupation of 1792 had made a lasting impression, there was no republican tradition and no historical memory of the republic. Not only were local concerns to the fore, but – at least among urban crafts – hopes were still focused upon the revival of guild regulation. By the end of April, it had become clear that the League's attempt to establish a national network of Workers' Associations was failing. There was no shortage of grievances among artisans and outworkers, and no evidence of unwillingness to associate. But the ideals and aspirations which inspired these workers to act bore little relation to the League's neo-Jacobin conception of democracy.

Karl had decided to base himself in Cologne. It was a city of around 90,000 with a considerable working population located predominantly in declining port and riverside industries with an unemployment rate of 25 per cent; in 1848, one third of the population were on poor relief. The initiative in establishing an association there had been taken by

Andreas Gottschalk, a member of the Communist League, who was a local doctor and extraordinarily popular with the city's workers for his work among the poor. On 6 April, he placed an advertisement in the *Kölnische Zeitung* announcing that with some friends he intended to organize a 'Democratic-Socialistic Club'. The inaugural meeting on 13 April was a success, with several hundred in attendance, yet the identity they wished to assert was not that of democrats or socialists, but of workers. This was clearly stated on 23 April, in the first issue of the Association's newspaper, the *Zeitung des Arbeiter-Vereines zu Köln. Freiheit, Brüderlichkeit, Arbeit* (*Newspaper of the Workers' Association in Cologne. Freedom, Brotherhood, Work*). A short report on the inaugural meeting stated that the 'Democratic-Socialist Club was not favoured; the designation, Peoples-Society, was likewise rejected; the name, Worker-Society, universally accepted.'[16]

In line with the League's policy of returning activists to their home towns, Gottschalk assumed that Karl would be destined for Trier, and Engels for Barmen. He was a close friend of Moses Hess and had written, urging him not to get involved in Herwegh's 'Legion', but to come to Cologne.[17] Together they hoped to revive the *Rheinische Zeitung*, Gottschalk thought. It could be restarted on the basis of the sale of shares. The intention of the paper envisaged by Gottschalk and Hess was to combine a democratic perspective with particular attention to 'the social question' and would focus upon practical rather than theoretical issues. On 7 April, together with a radical ex-army officer, Fritz Anneke, Hess put a notice in the *Kölnische Zeitung* calling for support for the plan. But Karl's friend Heinrich Bürgers was also promoting the idea and wrote to Karl inviting him once more to become editor. What exactly happened when Karl and Engels arrived in Cologne is not known, but it is clear that within two days of their arrival, Karl was established as the prospective editor, while Gottschalk and Hess had been sidelined.

The Workers' Association established by Gottschalk did not correspond to the structure envisaged by the League. While the League treated workers as an undifferentiated group, members of the Workers' Association were divided into sections along guild and craft lines. Organization by trade went together with encouragement of the expression of workers' grievances: the highlighting of low wages, industrial disputes, and the exposure of bad employers. In contrast to the League's commitment to 'a single and indivisible republic', Gottschalk supported a federal principle and considered constitutional monarchy a more realistic goal. He wrote to Hess on 26 March: 'The name "republic" is highly unpopular and the proletariat is at least in this place not yet strong enough to act independently. For the time being, we should be content with what has been achieved already – a monarchy on a Chartist basis – which is more than England has after all.'[18] The very name republic, he added, frightened the bourgeoisie, who placed it on a par with 'robbery, murder and an invasion by Russia'.[19] In accordance with this position, and against most democratic opinion, he prevailed upon the Workers' Association not to oppose the return from England of the reactionary Crown Prince Wilhelm. All these positions were in line with the secondary status accorded to political questions in most forms of socialism in the 1840s. Gottschalk also strongly disapproved of the principle of indirect franchise and for that reason advised his supporters not to vote in the elections for the Prussian National Assembly or the Frankfurt Parliament. But as conflict increased over the summer of 1848, Gottschalk, like others close to the so-called 'True Socialist' position, found himself thrown back into the political battle, and in June declared his support for a republic.

The priorities of the Workers' Association clashed with the League's conception of the revolution in Germany. The group around Karl was convinced that Germany in 1848 would follow the course of France in 1789. There would be an initial 'bourgeois' or 'liberal' phase, in which both propertied and popular forces concentrated upon the overthrow of 'feudal' social relations. This would then be followed by a 'second', radical revolution, led by 'the German proletariat, the petty bourgeoisie and the small peasants'. As in 1792–3, this radical phase of revolution would be brought about by war. That is why, be it on the status of Poles in the Duchy of Posen, or the claims of the German minority in Schleswig, Karl and his allies always placed themselves on the most belligerent wing of the war party.

This also explained why after their arrival in Cologne Karl and Engels joined the Democratic Society, formed early in April, by a committee containing two of Karl's old friends and political allies, Heinrich Bürgers and Karl D'Ester. From then to the spring of 1849, the Democratic Society provided Karl's chosen political home. The *Neue Rheinische Zeitung*, whose subtitle was 'Organ of Democracy', formed part of the same overall vision. The paper made no reference to communism or class struggle. What was meant by the 'Democratic Party' in Germany in 1848, Engels later explained, was a commitment to direct and manhood suffrage, a single legislative body and the recognition of 18 March (in Berlin) as the foundation of the new order.[20] But 'democracy' for Karl and his followers was more a device than an ultimate principle. The demands of 'the proletarian party' were supposed to remain hidden, but on occasion spectacularly escaped their confinement, as would become clear in the reaction of Karl and Engels to the Paris workers' insurrection in June 1848.

It was impossible to rival the devoted following Gottschalk had gathered around himself during his years as a doctor in Cologne since 1843. Across the cities and towns of Western Europe in the 1840s, leaving aside domestic service, contact between the propertied or educated classes and the working classes or the poor was extremely limited. For this reason, the prestige and popularity of those doctors who devoted themselves to the lives of the poor and were some of the few who had first-hand acquaintance with workers' lives were high indeed. But Gottschalk was also a powerful orator and an intelligent leader. He led the Workers' Association with a firm hand. As one follower put it, 'he spoke and silence reigned in the great space of the Gürzenich [the largest public meeting hall at the time] . . . he commanded and they obeyed'. The success of his Association was phenomenal. Membership climbed from 5,000 in May to 7,000 in June. By contrast, the membership of the Democratic Society was a more modest 700.[21]

Needless to say, the division between the two camps was counterproductive. Gottschalk's campaign for abstention from elections reduced the strength of radical representatives in Berlin and Frankfurt, while the result of Karl's rigid application of his notion of democratic revolution meant that the *Neue Rheinische Zeitung* virtually ignored workers' grievances and initiatives in Cologne throughout 1848.

Gottschalk's departure from the original strategy of the League and Karl's inability to challenge Gottschalk's position publicly were probably the main reasons for the decision to disband the Communist League. At a meeting of the Cologne branch of the League on 11 May, Karl challenged Gottschalk's departure from the League's agreed positions. In response, Gottschalk repeated the point that his resignation had already been submitted, 'since the transformation undergone by the present conditions required also a recasting of the Rules of the League, and under the existing Rules his personal freedom was in jeopardy'.[22] The impossibility of maintaining the leadership of the League, even when its 'Central Authority' was located in Cologne, led Karl to dissolve it in early June. His stated justification was that since there now was a free press, the structure and activities of a secret society were no longer necessary. Yet despite its abolition, in some places – especially London – the League's shadowy existence continued and it re-emerged with disastrous consequences in the closing stages of the Revolution.

4. THE *NEUE RHEINISCHE ZEITUNG*

The first issue of the *Neue Rheinische Zeitung* appeared on 1 June. Raising funds to finance the paper had proved more difficult than expected. Subscriptions were not sufficient, and so stocks had to be sold. But the campaign to raise the necessary funds was not successful. Despite a public meeting of stockholders, by the end of May only 13,000 thalers in shares out of a hoped-for 30,000 had been subscribed, and only 10 per cent of these shares had been paid for. Engels went to the Wuppertal to raise funds, but not surprisingly in this loyalist Protestant area he met with a suspicious or hostile response. He warned that all would be lost if one copy of the seventeen communist demands were to become public there. He also ridiculed Karl's suggestion that he should approach Engels' father, who would rather 'pepper us with a thousand balls of grape[shot]' than 'present us with 1,000 t[h]alers'.[23] It seemed therefore as if it would be impossible to start the journal before the beginning of July. But Karl was convinced of the imminent danger of the return of reaction, and therefore insisted that the newspaper appear at the beginning of June.[24] As a result, despite an energetic circulation campaign, and the possible deployment of part of his inheritance by Karl himself, the newspaper's finances still remained precarious.[25]

Apart from Heinrich Bürgers, the editorial team was composed entirely of League members who had returned with Karl to Germany – Ernst Dronke, Friedrich Engels, Georg Weerth, Ferdinand Wolff and Wilhelm Wolff. As in Brussels, Karl as editor-in-chief continued to play this role in a dictatorial fashion. Engels looked after most of the coverage of foreign affairs, while Georg Weerth edited the lighter literary feuilleton or supplement. Karl concentrated on domestic politics and constitutional issues. Although based in Cologne, the paper devoted little space to local issues. It aspired to act as a national newspaper, drawing upon far-flung contributing correspondents, and attracting subscriptions from all over the German Confederation. As Karl stated when he represented the paper at a trial in February 1849, 'I prefer to follow the great events of the world, to analyse the course of history, than to occupy myself with local bosses, with the police, and prosecuting magistrates'.[26] In addition to its leading article on Germany, the first issue contained reports from Vienna, Belgium, Italy, the French Republic and Great Britain. In the next few issues there were also items on Spain, Sweden and the United States, and regular supplements made substantial additions to the coverage. The paper never managed to compete with the 17,000 subscriptions of the main Rhineland paper, the *Kölnische Zeitung*, but with 5,000 subscribers became established as Germany's most important radical newspaper, and an informed source of political events abroad. Not surprisingly it was one of the papers commended by the First German Democratic Congress at Frankfurt.

The paper did not foreground the grievances of workers, and it was also written in a style inaccessible to all except a propertied and educated bourgeoisie. In the first issue, explaining why the paper was appearing a month early, an arcane and unexplained reference was made to the French 'September Press Laws' of 1835.[27] In issue 3, the lead article by Karl, a two-column report attacking the Camphausen ministry, contained references not only to *Tristram Shandy*, but also to Shakespeare's *Richard III* and Goethe's *Faust*. The purpose of the article, hardly a contentious point among radicals, was to attack the attempt by the Prime Minister, Camphausen, to establish a legal continuity between the old 'United *Landtag*' and his own ministry without mentioning the revolution that had taken place between the two. This is how Karl's report concluded: 'Thus, a goose is transformed into an egg and an egg into a goose. Thanks to the Capitol-saving cackling, the nation soon realises, however, that the golden eggs of Leda, which it laid in the revolution, have been stolen. Not even Deputy *Milde* seems to be the bright conspicuous Castor, son of Leda.'[28] This ponderous display was a further reason for the ill-feeling of the Workers'

Association towards Karl's paper. According to Gottschalk's *Zeitung des Arbeiter-Vereines zu Köln*, the paper was taking advantage of the depressed economic conditions to assemble a 'submissive' labour force at low cost. The *Zeitung* also attacked the subtitle of the paper – 'Organ of Democracy' – both because of the dishonest concealment of its aims, and because it was a 'formal act of suppression of the proletariat, a betrayal of the people'.

In April and May, radicals still sensed that the course of events favoured them. The Prussian Assembly that met on 22 May was predominantly liberal or left-liberal. It aimed to reduce the power of the monarch, subordinate the army to the constitution and eliminate many seigniorial rights in the countryside. Democratic societies and Workers' Associations were established in many areas, especially in Saxony, Berlin and parts of the Rhineland. Radicals were particularly successful in Vienna, where on 11 May armed students and workers had forced the government to establish a more democratic franchise. In the following weeks the emperor was moved to Innsbruck, while the revolutionary movement remained in the ascendant in the city.

In Cologne, there was an increasingly charged atmosphere, both the fear of a reactionary counter-strike – the stated reason why the *Neue Rheinische Zeitung* appeared one month early – and a tense climate of revolutionary expectation, which only grew during the First German Democratic Congress of the All-German Democratic Party held at Frankfurt from 14 to 17 June. In addition to Karl's allies, Schapper, Moll, Dronke, Cluss, Weydemeyer and Freiligrath, this congress was attended by Gottschalk, who on his return was carried in triumph through the streets. The atmosphere in Cologne was also heightened by what had happened in Berlin, where a crowd enraged by the rejection of a motion put forward by Julius Berend in the Prussian Assembly proposing recognition of the service of those who fought on 18 March demanded arms and stormed the Berlin armoury to get them. In Cologne, it was rumoured that delegates returning from Frankfurt would similarly demand arms from the local military. This did not occur, but on 17 June there was tumult in the Altenmarkt, where police were mocked and stones were thrown at them, while the Civil Guard in attendance proved weak and ineffective. Handbills warned 'brothers' to be alert since the hour of deliverance was near. News of the attempted uprising led by Friedrich Hecker in Baden further increased the tension. The heading of its manifesto was 'Speak out the Great Word: German Republic! German People's State!' The local military also suspected the imminence of a planned insurrection.

Gottschalk returned from Frankfurt intent upon uniting into one 'Republican Society' the three democratic organizations in Cologne – the Workers' Association, the Democratic Society and the Society for Workers and Employers. Given the overwhelming numerical superiority of the Workers' Association, however, this was resisted by the two smaller societies. Instead, on 24 June a committee of six – two from each society – was appointed as both a local coordinating body and as the Democratic District Committee for the Rhine Province. Karl was to act with Karl Schneider II (analogous to the American, Schneider Junior), the President of the Democratic Society, on this joint committee; he was therefore placed in a privileged position to direct the Rhineland democratic movement.

By the second half of June, the moment of popular ascendancy was almost over. Friedrich Wilhelm IV had not abdicated. He had not fled as Louis Philippe had done, but nor had he left the city with his troops in order to bombard it into submission, as had been advocated by his brother, Crown Prince Wilhelm. By staying in Berlin without army protection, he had both saved lives and gained popularity. This meant that he was in a far stronger position to defend the monarchical prerogatives that had been so endangered in March.

The king's response to the constitutional proposals, both of the Camphausen ministry and of the Assembly, was an absolute refusal to countenance any diminution of sovereignty. He was determined that the proposed constitution should continue to specify that the king remained the monarch 'by grace of God', and that the constitution itself be regarded not as a law imposed on the sovereign by popular will, but as the outcome of 'an agreement' between Friedrich Wilhelm and the people. In practical terms, the king would retain exclusive control both over the army and over the conduct of foreign policy.

The beginnings of a crackdown became evident at the end of June. On 25 June, at a large general meeting of the Workers' Association at the Gürzenich, 2,000 activists wearing red ribbons in their button-holes clamoured to hear from their President news about the progress of the Revolution. Calls were made for insurrection and the declaration of a republic. Pressed by his supporters, Gottschalk responded cautiously: it was necessary to wait and see what happened in Berlin and Frankfurt.

Nevertheless, this was enough to incur prosecution, and on 3 July Gottschalk, Anneke and one of the Association's leading militants, Esser, were arrested. Their prosecution was pursued with deliberate slowness by the judicial authorities through the autumn and ensured that their imprisonment was prolonged. They were finally brought to trial – and acquitted – on 20 December.

From its creation on 1 June, the *Neue Rheinische Zeitung* was intent upon pushing the political situation beyond the liberal constitutional phase of the Revolution as quickly as possible. This was done firstly by ridiculing the procedures of the Prussian Assembly and the Frankfurt Parliament, and secondly by highlighting almost daily the supposed threat of counter-revolution. The Frankfurt Assembly was attacked in the journal's first issue for not having declared the sovereignty of the German people. According to Engels, it should also have drafted a constitution 'and the elimination from the regime actually existing in Germany of everything that contradicted the principle of the sovereignty of the people'.[29] 'A Constituent National Assembly must above all be an *active*, revolutionarily active assembly. The Assembly at Frankfurt is engaged in parliamentary school exercises and leaves it to the governments to act . . . It is the first time in world history that the Constituent Assembly of a big nation holds its sessions in a small town . . . The Assembly bores the German people instead of inspiring it.'[30]

If the ultimate demand were for 'a *united indivisible German republic*', the constitution-making in Berlin would be beside the point. But simply to ignore the constitutional conflict in Prussia would have been self-defeating. Instead, the activities of Camphausen and the Prussian Constituent Assembly were covered in the *Neue Rheinische Zeitung*, but in a wholly negative way. The Assembly was denounced as 'the Agreement Assembly', on account of its supposed preparedness to act in accordance with the royal formulation, that the constitution would be the result of an 'agreement' (*Vereinbarung*) between king and people. The Assembly was attacked particularly for its unwillingness to commemorate the fighters of 18 March. This was contrasted with the attack on the armoury by the people of Berlin. The Assembly's denial of this first revolution, it was stated, would soon be confounded by the beginning of the second; foretold by the attack on the arsenal.[31] As for the newspaper's preoccupation with counter-revolution and conspiracy, its headline reaction to the fall of the Camphausen ministry on

21 June was a good example. The paper had been predicting 'either a new revolution or a definitely reactionary Government' and that 'The attempt at a new revolution has failed', and it continued in bold letters: 'a Russophile Government will pave the way for the Czar'.[32] During the same period – from 19 to 26 June – in an effort to stoke up radical passions, the *Neue Rheinische Zeitung* helpfully serialized an account of the trial of Louis Capet, formerly known as Louis XVI, by the French Revolutionary Convention in January 1793.

5. THE *NEUE RHEINISCHE ZEITUNG* AND THE JUNE INSURRECTION IN PARIS

At this point, the attention of Karl's newspaper became transfixed by developments in Paris, where an announcement of the imminent closure of the National Workshops had led to an insurrection of more than 40,000 concerned workers. Having learnt of their impending dismissal on 22 June, workers had assembled on the morrow en masse in the Place de la Bastille and then retired to their respective *quartiers* to build barricades. To deal with the emergency, on 25 June the 'Executive Commission' (the government) followed republican precedent derived from Ancient Rome. It entrusted temporary dictatorial power to General Eugène Cavaignac, the republican War Minister who had played a prominent role in the conquest of Algeria. On 25 June, Cavaignac launched a counter-offensive, and on 26 June the last barricade was recaptured. From England, the Clerk to the Privy Council, Charles Greville recorded in his diary:

> Although distress and famine were the prime causes of this great struggle, it is remarkable that there was no plundering or robbery; on the contrary, they were strictly forbidden and apparently never attempted. It is the only example, so far as I know, that history records of a pitched battle in the streets of a great capital between the regular army and the armed civil power on the one side, and the populace of the town militarily armed and organised also on the other, nobody knowing how the latter were organised or by whom directed.[33]

Since Karl had left Paris in early April, the political climate in France had changed markedly. Throughout March and the beginning of April, the supporters of the Revolution had remained in the ascendant. But as militants flocked to Paris, the left assumed more provocative forms, especially in many radical clubs. On 17 March, a demonstration of 100,000 led by the former secret-society leader Auguste Blanqui had ensured that elections for the Constituent Assembly would be postponed from 9 to 23 April together with the promise (not kept) that troops would be progressively withdrawn from the town.

In April, lines of division became more visible. In another large demonstration on 16 April, a plan suspected to be by Blanqui to force a shift in the balance between moderates and radicals within the Provisional Government was thwarted by other radical leaders. These included Barbès, Blanc and especially Ledru-Rollin, the radical Minister of the Interior, who called out the National and Mobile Guards to defend the *Hôtel de Ville* against the possibility of a radical coup. As expected, the election of the Constituent Assembly on 23 April benefited the moderates rather than the left. Manhood suffrage produced an Assembly which was for the most part unsympathetic to the ideals of February: out of 900 representatives, there were 350–500 nominal republicans. The events of February had taken rural France by surprise; political mobilization of radical support in the countryside had scarcely begun. Not surprisingly, aristocrats, notables and clergy were disproportionately returned. Radical republicans polled less than 10 per cent of the seats. Many more seats were won by monarchists, whether Orléanist or Legitimist. The Provisional Government was replaced by a more conservative five-member 'Executive Commission', from which the socialist, Blanc, and the worker, Albert, were dropped.

But even more decisive in shaping the sequence of events leading to the June Insurrection had been the shift in attitudes towards the left as a result of the demonstration of 15 May. The ostensible purpose of this demonstration had been to press for French intervention in aid of Polish democrats. Thirty thousand had initially gathered on the Champ de Mars, but as the ulterior aim of the leaders of the demonstration became clear, many slipped away and numbers were down to 2,000 by the time it reached the Constituent Assembly. There, however, with the connivance of the local National Guard commander, entry was forced into the Assembly chambers, and amid the tumult the demonstrators declared the dissolution of the Assembly and the formation of a new Provisional Government. By this time, loyal units of the National and

Mobile Guards had arrived, and the radical leaders had been arrested as they had attempted to make their way to the *Hôtel de Ville* to install the new government.

By any criterion, these were acts of stupidity, and there have been suspicions ever since that the radicals had been set up by agents provocateurs.[34] The result was that a large part of the left's potential following was now alienated, and its leadership, in Maurice Agulhon's word, 'decapitated'.[35] The policy of compromise followed by the Executive Commission had been discredited. Leadership of the Constituent Assembly now passed into the hands of an increasingly intransigent coalition of conservatives, who abolished the Luxembourg Commission and began to plan the disbanding of the National Workshops.

Moderates as well as radicals had welcomed the National Workshops as a way of keeping the unemployed off the streets. Under the direction of Émile Thomas, the Workshops themselves were kept away from the influence of radicals and the activities of their clubs. But attitudes changed once Thomas was removed, the right of assembly was limited and democratic clubs were shut down. At this point in early June, it was becoming increasingly clear that the Workshops themselves were also about to be closed. Delegates from the Workshops met up with members of the disbanded Luxembourg Commission and protested against the abandonment of the democratic-social proclamations of the February Republic. Finally, after a debate on 20 June, a directive of the Assembly ordained the immediate dissolution of the Workshops. Younger members were directed to enlist in the army, while older ones were to be sent to rural work projects in distant provinces. Demonstrations against the decree were unavailing, and on the evening of 22 June a crowd of 100,000 in front of the *Hôtel de Ville* resolved to resist by force of arms. The insurrection began on the following day.[36]

French republicans condemned this rebellion almost without exception. For Karl's friend Flocon, the issue was simply that of refusal to obey a democratically elected republican authority. It was akin to an attempted coup d'état. Cavaignac, the general who suppressed the rebels, was a committed republican, and so was the cabinet he chose to serve with him until the presidential elections in December 1848. Although many papers were sympathetic to the plight of the workers, the democratic and republican press across Europe was equally scathing about the revolt.

Only the *Neue Rheinische Zeitung* – despite its claim to be an 'Organ of Democracy' – was prepared to celebrate the insurrection as a triumph of the workers. In his essay 'The June Revolution' of 28 June, Karl claimed that 'the workers of Paris' had been *'overwhelmed'* by superior strength, 'but they were not *subdued'*. This 'triumph of brute force' had been 'purchased' with 'the destruction of all the delusions and illusions of the February revolution'. The 'fraternity' proclaimed in February had found 'its true, unadulterated and prosaic expression in *civil war*, civil was in its most terrible aspect, the war of labour against capital'. The February Revolution had been 'the *nice* revolution, the revolution of universal sympathies'. The June Revolution was 'the *ugly* revolution' because 'the phrases have given place to the real thing, because the republic has bared the head of the monster [capital] by knocking off the crown which shielded and concealed it'. This was the first 'revolution' since 1789 to have assailed 'class rule' and the *'bourgeois order'*.[37]

Ever since his time in Brussels, Karl's political writings had suffered from a certain incoherence as a result of his attempt simultaneously to ride two horses – the democratic and the proletarian-socialist, the actual revolution and the next revolution but one. The treatment of the June Insurrection was a spectacular example of this contradictory attitude. The article opened up the democratic position to all the objections which could be made by Karl Grün and other socialists. If the workers were crushed by a democratic republic based on manhood suffrage, if democracy did not provide a solution to the social question, then why fight for the attainment of a republic? Despite his bluster – 'only weak, cowardly minds can pose such a question' – Karl's attempt to answer this objection was not satisfactory. He argued that 'the best form of state is that in which these contradictions reach a stage of open struggle in the course of which they are resolved'.[38] But the case made by democrats and republicans was not that democratic politics provided an arena in which the class struggle could be fought through to the end, but rather that, in a democracy, conflicts of interest would be amenable to peaceful and rational solutions.

Not surprisingly, other Rhineland newspapers attacked the *Neue Rheinische Zeitung* and ironized about its support for 'democracy'. Karl appears to have realized that he would have to rectify his position if he wished to retain his leading role in the Democratic Society. An opportunity to do this arose when, despite Karl's opposition, Weitling was given an opportunity to address the Democratic Society on 22 July. Two weeks later, on 4 August, Karl gave a speech in reply. His response to Weitling's advocacy of a virtuous dictatorship was that such a rule in Germany would be both impractical and quite unfeasible 'since power cannot be attained by a single class'. On the contrary, 'the governing power, just as the Provisional Government in Paris, must consist of the most heterogeneous elements'. In a very different tone from that employed in the June article, he argued that 'the disregard of the position of the various strata of the population to one another, the refusal to make reciprocal concessions and wrong notions about class relations have led to the bloody outcome in Paris'.[39]

Besides its homage to the June insurrectionaries in Paris, the *Neue Rheinische Zeitung* also attacked the heightening of repression in Cologne at the beginning of July. The paper alleged that Gottschalk and Anneke were arrested in order to provoke an uprising, which the army could then crush. Mrs Anneke claimed that in the case of 'the brutal arrest' of her husband, a servant girl had been mistreated and that no official complaint could be made since the gendarmes were not accompanied by a suitable official. These claims were hotly contested by the judicial officials, Zweiffel and Hecker, who were responsible for the conduct of the case.

In the light of the shift towards reaction on the part of the Prussian state and the growing numbers of instances – both personal and political – which set Karl against the Prussian authorities, it was scarcely surprising that on 3 August 1848 Karl was informed that his application for the re-establishment of his Prussian citizenship had been refused.[40]

6. THE REVOLUTION IN RETREAT

The Revolution in Germany came to an end in the three months following the Schleswig-Holstein crisis in September 1848. The Prussian Assembly lost the battle to establish a constitutional monarchy. The Parliament in Frankfurt was humiliated and marginalized, while both in France and in the Hapsburg Empire a decisive shift to the right was underway.

In France at the beginning of July, the Workshops were dismantled. The Assembly considered that the June Insurrection had not just been the result of socialism, but also a consequence of February. The Revolution had created too much freedom. It therefore supported measures to regulate the clubs and curb the press. The restriction on working hours decreed in February was relaxed, and 'the right to work' was omitted from the new constitution drafted by the Assembly between September and November. In the elections for the new executive presidency, created by the constitution, Cavaignac hoped to triumph by aligning himself with the Orléanists headed by Thiers (the so-called 'Rue de Poitiers group'). But he was trumped by Louis-Napoléon, the nephew of the former emperor, who now unambiguously aligned himself with a 'party of order', appealing not only to the Orléanists and Thiers, but also to the church, to strong rule and to the memory of the First Empire.[41] Cavaignac was also challenged on the left by Ledru-Rollin, who built upon the social-democratic republicanism associated with *La Réforme*. In November 1848, he and his supporters, associating themselves with the republicanism of 1792 or *La Montagne*,[42] issued an election manifesto, *La Solidarité républicaine*.

The results of the presidential election of 10 December came as an unpleasant surprise to the political class. Cavaignac polled 1,400,000 votes while Louis-Napoléon Bonaparte, whom Ledru-Rollin and Lamartine had attempted to outlaw from the Assembly the previous summer, polled more than 5 million. For the moderate left, Ledru-Rollin polled 400,000, while only 37,000 voted for the intransigent secret-society veteran, Raspail. The republic now seemed to be in danger. For the new ministry, put together by Bonaparte and the Rue de Poitiers Orléanists, contained no republicans, and its leader was intent upon restoring the imperial throne. The ministry was headed by the Orléanist politician Odilon Barrot, and defined itself as the 'Party of Order'. It attempted an energetic campaign of repression against what it construed to be the growth of a 'red menace', whether Ledru-Rollin's 'Démoc-Socs', who had been growing in parts of the countryside, or the remnants of the Blanquists in Paris.

The news from France was depressing, but it was not clear that the Revolution there had finally come to an end. Paris may have been stunned by the brutal subjugation of the June Insurrection, but elsewhere in France support for the 'Démoc-Socs' was growing. In Austria and Central Europe, by contrast, initial hopes for democracy in Vienna and for independence in Italy and Hungary gave way to a nightmarish sequence of reversals, in which the seemingly moribund Hapsburg Empire experienced first military triumph and then political renewal.

Over the summer, the Hapsburg armies were the first to turn the balance of forces in favour of counter-revolution. In June, an army commanded by Prince Windischgrätz defeated the Czech rebels in Prague. In July, an army of Croats under General Jellačić began to push the Hungarians back, and on 25 July the Austrian army in Italy under Radetzky decisively defeated the Piedmontese at the Battle of Custozza.

Radicals found themselves increasingly on the defensive. As in Paris, the commitment of the radical Viennese authorities to support a public-works programme attracted large numbers of unemployed to Vienna. But the costs became politically unsustainable and, on 23 August, the Council was forced to reduce wages, leading to clashes between workers and a middle class, reminiscent of Paris in June.

On the question of the Empire, there were also some crippling divisions among radicals and nationalists. The crushing of rebellion in Prague was in part the result of the division between Germans and Czechs in Bohemia. While democrats in Vienna identified with Germany and sent representatives to the Frankfurt Parliament, Czech national leaders supported an Austro-Slav programme outside German borders, and in June convoked a Pan-Slav Congress, supported also on the left by Bakunin. This congress was disrupted by an anti-Hapsburg insurrection on the part of those supporting Frankfurt, and was made worse by the shooting of Windischgrätz's wife. Threatened with destruction by Windischgrätz's army, the insurrection collapsed. But, thereafter, the leaders of the Czech national movement and the democrats in Vienna were pitted against each other. Other subordinate nationalities in the Empire – Croats, Serbs, Romanians and Slovaks – also found themselves increasingly aligned with the Hapsburgs against the revolution in Vienna and Hungary.

The final act in the Viennese Revolution was sparked off by the news on 5 October that regiments were to be dispatched to join Jellačić's Croat army to fight the Hungarians. On 6 October, the departure of these troops led to the erecting of barricades and an uprising in Vienna. The court once more fled the city, and conservative deputies withdrew. A revolutionary Committee of Public Safety (named after the Jacobin society which presided over the Terror in 1793) took over the running of the city, but the citizenry were soon alienated by its excesses. Revolutionaries were also undecided about how to act in the face of approaching Hapsburg armies. Hope was pinned on the Hungarians, but their help was not forthcoming until too late. There was therefore increasing panic as Jellačić's army moved in from the south-east and that of Windischgrätz from the north. Finally, on 23 October, Windischgrätz surrounded the city with an army of 60,000 and by the end of the month it was taken. A new and more decisive imperial government was formed under Prince Felix zu Schwarzenberg. The feeble-minded emperor was forced to abdicate and a new constitution was issued.

In parallel with the defeat of the democratic-social republic in France and the destruction of revolution in Vienna, from September onwards the German Parliament in Frankfurt experienced a series of comparable defeats. On 21 March 1848, liberals had been delighted when the Prussian king invoked the memory of the struggle against Napoléon in 1813 and announced his support for the formation of an all-German Parliament. On 18 May, following the assembly of the Pre-Parliament, the German National Assembly began its proceedings in Frankfurt. But doubt about its powers and status in relation to existing German states was there from the beginning. While liberal nationalists planned a federal monarchy, presided over by either Prussia or Austria, and a tiny minority of ultra-radicals like Karl dreamt of a unitary republic, the Germany imagined by Friedrich Wilhelm was something like a revival of the medieval Holy Roman Empire. Incorporating both Berlin and Vienna, it did not entail significant ceding of power to the Frankfurt Assembly.

These ambiguities were made brutally clear when the Frankfurt Assembly was forced directly to confront the problem of and authority over the issue of Schleswig-Holstein. On 21 March, the Danish government annexed Schleswig, a border province with a substantial minority of German speakers. Outraged by the annexation, which had met with revolutionary resistance on the part of the Germans of south Schleswig on 23 April, the Prussian army – with the endorsement of the German Confederation – marched into Schleswig and pushed out the Danes. The liberal nationalists in Frankfurt were delighted. But the Russian czar was alarmed to see Prussia acting in apparent alliance with revolutionary nationalists and threatened to send in troops. This in turn aroused the British government, worried that Russia might use the Schleswig-Holstein affair as a pretext to turn Denmark into a Russian protectorate and secure control over access to the Baltic. Faced with intense diplomatic pressure, under the terms of the Treaty of Malmo on 26 August 1848, the Prussians withdrew their troops, leaving northern Schleswig in Danish hands.

In signing this treaty, the Prussians paid no attention to the views of the Frankfurt Parliament. Deputies were enraged and on 5 September voted to block the treaty. But without an army or any constitutional means by which its decisions might be enforced within the German Confederation, the Parliament was powerless, and in a humiliating climb-down it voted on 16 September to accept the terms of the Malmo armistice. Much of the prestige of the Frankfurt Parliament was thereby lost. The decision caused consternation, and provoked another uprising in Baden. In Frankfurt, a mass meeting insisted that radical deputies secede from the Parliament; two conservative deputies were killed and a crowd tried to storm the Assembly.

The crisis in Frankfurt over the Treaty of Malmo coincided with a parallel ministerial crisis in Prussia over the control of the army. An incident in Schweidnitz in Silesia, which had originated in the intervention of the army in a dispute between the Civil Guard and their local commander, resulted on 3 August in an exchange of shots between the army and the Guard in which fourteen civilians were killed. This provoked widespread indignation throughout Prussia and resulted in a motion proposed on 3 August by Julius Stein, the democratic representative from Breslau, and accepted by the National Assembly, instructing the army to cooperate with civil authorities. This was unacceptable to the king for it threatened the notion of 'agreement' upon which dealings between the monarch and the Assembly were supposed to proceed. The Chief Minister, Hansemann, attempted to delay the implementation of the motion, but the Assembly backed by crowd pressure outside the building forced the issue. On 10 September, Hansemann was compelled to resign; liberals felt uneasy about the presence of the crowd.

In Cologne, the tension between soldiers and civilians took a different form. On the day after the Hansemann resignation, soldiers of the 27th Regiment in one of the town squares insulted a local girl, who appealed to local bystanders for protection. The hostility of the locals towards the soldiers provoked a riot of drunken soldiers, their sabres drawn and beyond control by their officers. Eventually order was restored by the Civil Guard, but anger in the city remained intense. A meeting of the Council reinforced by a crowd of radical demonstrators insisted that the regiment be moved, and that the Civil Guard patrol the city.

The hostility between Rhinelanders and East Elbian soldiers – 'soldeska', seen as foreign as well as reactionary – was long-standing.

Nevertheless, most assumed that there was no larger political agenda behind this senseless drunken affray. Yet while tension in Berlin and Frankfurt was at its height, and the possibility of the radicalization of the revolution seemed imminent, the left scented a conspiracy and so over-reacted. Radical companies in the Civil Guard, and, following them, the Democratic Society and the Workers' Association, proposed the formation of a Committee of Public Safety and the next day mounted the public election of its members. Members of the *Neue Rheinische Zeitung*, including Karl, were prominent among those elected. But the square was only half filled, other detachments of the Civil Guard and other societies objected, and seven leading members of the Democratic Society resigned. In the following days, the Committee backed down, protesting the legality of its intentions.

The ministerial crisis in Berlin was temporarily resolved by the formation of General Pfuel's ministry on 20 September. But in the meantime, anger about the Treaty of Malmo and the determination to support the Frankfurt Assembly's initial refusal to endorse the treaty had prompted the Workers' Association to organize a large-scale protest at Worringen, on the Rhine, ten miles north of Cologne. The meeting attracted between 5,000 and 10,000 people, many of them peasants recruited from the surrounding villages by the Workers' Association. At the meeting there was a unanimous declaration in favour of 'the democratic-social, the *Red Republic*', and an endorsement of the newly formed 'Committee of Public Safety'. Engels was elected Secretary and he committed the meeting to support the Frankfurt Assembly's stand on Schleswig-Holstein – they had not yet heard that Frankfurt had gone back on its decision. As 'assembled imperial citizens', those present were to disregard the Prussian position and commit their 'fortune and blood' to the battle with Denmark. Engels' speech at this meeting was cited as the reason for a warrant for his arrest later in the month. Karl himself was not at the meeting and the rejection of his appeal for citizenship had been confirmed on 12 September, so his continued residence in Cologne was wholly at the discretion of the authorities.

Once it was learnt that the Frankfurt Parliament had in fact ratified the Malmo treaty, Cologne was in turmoil. On 20 September, a protest meeting was arranged by the Democratic Society, the Workers' Association and the Committee for Public Safety, while further action was expected at the Second National Democratic Congress, due to be held on 25 September. In an attempt to forestall further radical activity, on 23 September warrants were issued for the arrest of Engels, together with Schapper, Moll, Wilhelm Wolff, Bürgers and others. The meeting of the Democratic Congress was cancelled, but the atmosphere in Cologne around the end of September remained extremely tense. There was looting and disorder, and windows were broken on many streets; a new stage in the revolution was thought to be imminent. The police and army moved in to occupy strategic positions within the city. Radicals, including Karl, addressed several meetings of the Democratic Society and the Workers' Association advising workers not to be provoked into premature action, but to remain disciplined and await news of events in Berlin.

Despite this warning a workers' meeting did assemble in the Altenmarkt in the late afternoon of 23 September. On hearing that soldiers were about to arrive, the crowd hurriedly dispersed, but at the same time embarked upon the building of barricades and by nightfall more than thirty had been erected. When, on the following morning, the soldiers did eventually advance on the barricades, they found no one there. The defenders had tired of waiting through the night and retired. After this moment of bathos, some mockery was directed at the *Neue Rheinische Zeitung*, to which Karl was unable to reply, since on 26 September martial law was declared in Cologne and the newspaper was unable to appear again until 12 October.[43]

The crisis in September was for the moment eased by Pfuel, who attempted to cooperate with the Assembly and ordered the army to conform to the Assembly's demands. But this attitude angered the king and annoyed the army. The situation became increasingly tense once the debate on the constitution began. The Assembly refused to accept the king's insistence upon royal authority 'by the grace of God' and went on to abolish titles of nobility. Crowd pressure from the left in Berlin steadily increased and was reinforced towards the end of the month after a takeover of the meeting of the German National Democratic Congress by a radical minority. What was left of the congress declared for a 'red republic' and organized a mass demonstration designed to force upon the Assembly a commitment to assist besieged Vienna, the Waldeck motion. On the other side, the king was strengthened by the army's return from Denmark under the command of

General Wrangel, who since 13 September had been in charge of all military units around Berlin. Direct confrontation was unavoidable.

Karl thought that developments in France determined the course of events. But the happenings in Austria seem to have made a greater impression on Friedrich Wilhelm and his circle, for just as the triumph of the crowd in Vienna had prompted Friedrich Wilhelm's concessions in Berlin in March, so in November the victory of the Hapsburg counter-revolution encouraged the Prussian king to regain full military control in Berlin. On 2 November, the king dismissed the moderate Pfuel ministry and installed instead his own uncle, the conservative Count Friedrich Wilhelm von Brandenburg, as Chief Minister. The Assembly refused Brandenburg, but without any attention being paid to its declaration. On 9 November, Brandenburg announced to the Assembly that it was adjourned for three weeks and would reconvene in the town of Brandenburg. At the same time, General Wrangel and 13,000 troops re-entered Berlin, without significant resistance from the Civil Guard. Wrangel proceeded to the Gendarmenmarkt and informed the Assembly that it must disperse immediately. In response, the Assembly moved to a shooting gallery and called for passive resistance. On 14 November, martial law was declared in Berlin and the Civil Guard disbanded, political clubs were closed down and radical newspapers banned. Karl's reaction in the *Neue Rheinische Zeitung* on 12 November was to call for a tax strike. On 15 November the radical remnant of the Assembly – urged on by Karl's friend Karl D'Ester – decreed by a unanimous majority of 226 to 0 that the Brandenburg ministry did not have the authority to collect taxes, so long as the Assembly was denied the right to meet freely in Berlin.

This seemed like the moment for which radicals had been waiting. The king was forced, for the moment at least, to disregard the idea of 'the Agreement Assembly', and revert to the position of an absolute monarch, driving the Assembly to outraged resistance. In Cologne, on 11 November, a large meeting attended by workers, merchants and officials passed a resolution declaring that the crown had no right to suspend the Assembly, a declaration subsequently signed by a further 7,000. The City Council was persuaded to endorse it, and so did the liberal-constitutionalist Cologne Citizens' Society. A delegation from Cologne was sent to Berlin to convey the opinion of the city to the government. Karl and Schneider II issued a proclamation in the name of the Democratic District Committee calling all Rhineland democratic societies to support the tax refusal. At the same time, the *Neue Rheinische Zeitung* published any news or rumours it could find to magnify the extent of resistance to the government. Soldiers were said to be fraternizing with the people, martial law in Berlin was being mocked and the provinces of Silesia and Thuringia were said to be in revolt. The Assembly's decree was to begin on 17 November and on that day the *Neue Rheinische Zeitung* printed on its masthead the headline 'No More Taxes!!!' A further proclamation by Karl and Schneider II proposed resistance to tax collection, the formation of a militia and the demand that all officials declare loyalty to the commands of the Assembly.

At the beginning, there was a promising response to the campaign for tax refusal. Pressure was put on city councils to join the tax ban. In Bonn, Düsseldorf, Coblenz and elsewhere, toll booths were destroyed, while cattle and flour entered the cities toll-free. An effort was made to mobilize the Civil Guard and the *Landwehr* in defence of the campaign. But the attempt to assemble such a force in a square in Cologne was prevented by the army and the prospective commander, von Beust, was compelled to flee. By 23–24 November, resistance was fading. Unlike in Britain or the United States the association between taxation and representation lacked historical potency. In Cologne, the City Council was prepared to protest against the Brandenburg coup, but was unwilling to join in tax refusal. Furthermore, the Civil Guard was not in a position to prevent tax collection in the city. As a major garrison town, Cologne was full of soldiers, and in addition the Guard had been disarmed in September.

How did the *Neue Rheinische Zeitung* respond to this crucial phase of the 1848 Revolution? As we have seen, Karl and his friends not only hated Russian czardom but feared its capacity to intervene and crush progressive movements across Central and Eastern Europe – and even in Denmark. For Karl and Engels, however, hatred of Russia was also a means to an end. Whether the issue was the assistance to be given to the Polish rebels in Posen or the military support to be given to Schleswig Germans in Denmark, the objective was to provoke war with Russia: 'Only a *war against Russia* would be a war of *revolutionary Germany*, a war by which she could cleanse herself of her past sins, could . . . make herself free within her borders by bringing liberation to those outside.'[44]

Such thinking was inspired by an analogy with the first French Revolution; Germany in 1848 was a replay of France in 1789.[45] But what particularly fascinated Karl and his colleagues on the *Neue Rheinische Zeitung* was not 1789, but 1792–3 when European war radicalized the Revolution. Revolutionary war had brought about the declaration of the Republic, the assembly of the Convention, the execution of the king, the formation of the Committee of Public Safety and the practice of the Terror. At the height of the Malmo crisis on 13 September 1848, Karl wrote, 'If the government continues in the way it has been doing, we shall have a Convention before long – not merely for Prussia, but for Germany as a whole – a Convention which will have to use all means to cope with the civil war in our twenty Vendées and with the inevitable war with Russia.'[46]

The use of such an analogy was dangerously misleading. It presumed that it was possible to anticipate events solely on the basis of 'social development', regardless of political forces and institutions. It took no account of the fact that in 1789 the French state was bankrupt, that it was indissolubly tied to a discredited church, that it could not rely on the army to control popular forces, and that by 1792 the monarch had been disgraced and rendered powerless by his attempt to flee the country. None of this applied to the Prussian king, whose control of army and bureaucracy remained unchallenged throughout the 1848 crisis.

In 1815, Talleyrand was reported to have said of the Bourbons that they had learnt nothing and forgotten nothing. But on the evidence of 1848 it was the left rather than the leaders of reaction who remained trapped in an outdated fantasy about revolution rather than coming to terms with new realities. As Engels had written to Karl back on 8–9 March, 'if only Friedrich Wilhelm IV digs his heels in! Then all will be won and in a few months' time we'll have the German Revolution. If he only sticks to his feudal forms! . . . But', he had to add, 'the devil only knows what this capricious and crazy individual will do.'[47] Engels was wise to add a note of caution. For the reactions of the king and his circle were far from stupid, not only in March but throughout the rest of the year. On 12 September, at the height of the crisis following the Treaty of Malmo and the departure of Hansemann, Karl wrote, 'we are facing a decisive struggle'. It revolved around the king's choice of government. Karl wrote: 'There are only two solutions to this crisis. Either a Waldeck Government, recognition of the authority of the German National Assembly and recognition of popular sovereignty; Or a Radowitz-Vincke Government, dissolution of the Berlin Assembly, abolition of the revolutionary gains, a sham constitutionalism or even the United Diet.'[48] Here at last was the conflict the radicals had been waiting for, the conflict between the Berlin Assembly 'acting as a *Constituent* Assembly, and the *Crown*'. Karl was confident that the king, particularly after the Assembly had yielded to the government on the Malmo treaty, would press ahead with a government of reaction. On 22 September, he wrote, 'It has happened after all! The government of the Prince of Prussia is in being and the counter-revolution intends to risk the final decisive blow ... The Don Quixotes of Further Pomerania, these old warriors and debt-encumbered landed proprietors will finally have their opportunity to cleanse their rusty blades in the blood of the agitators.'[49] In fact, however, whether as a result of indecision or of good judgement, the king deferred the decision about the new ministry until nationalist passion had somewhat abated, and then chose the conciliatory General Pfuel to head the government.

The attempt of the *Neue Rheinische Zeitung* to treat political struggles as 'merely the manifestations of social collisions' produced a reading of events that was far too crude. It treated all the ministries created between that of Camphausen at the end of March and that of the royal coup d'état in November as the conscious or unconscious tools of reaction. Just as, after the departure of Hansemann, Karl had predicted the arrival of a backward 'feudal' government, so he predicted exactly the same after the fall of Camphausen on 22 June. 'Camphausen has the honour of having given the absolutist feudal party its natural boss and himself a successor.'[50]

His treatment of the Prussian Assembly suffered from a similarly dismissive handling of political difference. Karl argued on 14 September that 'from the very beginning we blamed Camphausen for not having acted in a dictatorial manner, for not having immediately smashed up and removed the remains of the old institutions'.[51] It was certainly true that because Camphausen's liberal ministry was fearful of the popular forces that had established it in office at the end of

March, it did not press for major constitutional reforms at the moment when monarchical forces were at their weakest. But it was naive of the *Neue Rheinische Zeitung* to imagine that a liberal ministry would not also have taken account of the danger from radicalism and the anger on the streets.

For liberals were haunted by the memory of the French Revolution as much as the left. For them, the threat represented by popular forces on the street was even more to be feared than the resistance of the crown. If unchecked, it could lead to uncontrolled violence and the rule of the untutored masses. That this belief was shared by the bulk of the Berlin middle classes was apparent in a memorial procession in honour of the 'March fallen'. The event 'attracted well over 100,000 people, but these were virtually all labourers, working men and journeymen, or to put it more pointedly, people from the same social stratum as the dead barricade fighters themselves. Middle-class burghers of the kind who predominated in the National Assembly were conspicuous by their rarity.'[52] The aim of Camphausen, Hansemann and the liberal leadership of the United *Landtag* had never been to establish a republic, but to achieve a constitutional monarchy. Their aim was to find an acceptable compromise between monarch and parliament supported by public opinion – the opinion of the propertied and the educated. The last thing they wanted was to be at the mercy of the anarchic passions of the crowds.

The contemptuous tone adopted by Karl and Engels whenever they referred to 'the Agreement Assembly' provided another example of the *Zeitung*'s lack of political discrimination. It failed to accept that the inter-class nature of a 'democratic' revolution raised the need to build alliances rather than to resort to derision and condemnation whenever the Assembly was mentioned. Such an approach obscured the extent to which a struggle still continued between the crown and the Assembly. This was most immediately about control of the army, but ultimately over the issue of sovereignty – whether the king was beholden to the people or acted 'by the grace of God'.

As this conflict reached an acute phase at the end of October, culminating on 2 November in the dismissal of the Pfuel ministry, the *Zeitung* moved again towards the need for a united front. On 14 November, Karl declared that it was 'the duty of the Rhine Province to hasten to the assistance of the Berlin National Assembly with men and weapons'.[53]

The article acknowledged the refusal of the Assembly to back down, its condemnation of Brandenburg for treason, and the continuation of its proceedings in a shooting gallery after Wrangel had expelled it from the theatre in which it had met. This was a gesture which Karl compared with the use of a tennis court by the French 'Third Estate' after its own expulsion in June 1789.[54] Two days earlier the *Zeitung* had not been able to refrain from sniping at the 'bourgeoisie': 'the bourgeoisie would have liked so much to unite with the feudal party and together with it enslave the people'.[55]

So what should be done now? According to the paper, before declaring that 'we should refuse to pay taxes', Karl berated the National Assembly for its failure to resist Wrangel and his soldiers: 'Why does it not pronounce the *mise hors de loi* [outlawing]? Why does it not outlaw the Wrangels? Why does not one of the deputies step into the midst of Wrangel's bayonets to outlaw him and address the soldiers? Let the Berlin National Assembly leaf through the *Moniteur*, the *Moniteur* for 1789–1795.' This again was more a reference to the histrionics of revolution than to its actuality. In Karl's own case in the Rhineland, whenever the question of physical resistance was raised, his appeals were to 'conduct yourselves calmly', and not to react to any provocation which the soldiery might commit.[56]

As for Brandenburg and Wrangel themselves, in a witty attack, Karl ridiculed them as 'nothing but mustachios', and as '*the two most stupid men* in the monarchy'.[57] But, once again, he underestimated the ability of the leaders of reaction. Karl was right to assume that the king was determined to defeat any notion of popular sovereignty, but wrong to imagine that this would come about through the staging of the great final confrontation of which Karl dreamt. In reality, the king and his advisers were able to produce a solution which divided the opposition and rallied support for the crown.

On 9 November, the Prussian National Assembly was informed by royal decree that it was to be transferred from Berlin to Brandenburg, where it would reconvene three weeks later. But many of the deputies who rejected the decree stayed in Berlin. This meant, however, that there were too few deputies present in Brandenburg on 27 November and that it was not sufficient to make up a quorum. On 5 December, Brandenburg was therefore enabled to declare the Assembly dissolved. Wisely, however, he made no effort to revert to the non-parliamentary

Prussian practices of the pre-1848 years. He issued a new constitution, and scheduled new elections for a two-house Assembly in late January. The new constitution was similar to the one it replaced as it incorporated some important liberal demands. But it was still based on royal sovereignty with crown control over army, bureaucracy and foreign policy. This new constitution was a clever initiative which successfully split the opposition and isolated the radical left. It won approval from all parts of Prussia, not least the Rhineland. The *Neue Rheinische Zeitung* was almost alone in its wholesale condemnation. For, whatever their misgivings, many liberals found it an acceptable compromise, while Catholics were delighted by its effort to accommodate the church.

Karl found it impossible to accept that this could be the result of the 1848 Revolution in Prussia. Throughout the months between March and December, he had been predicting a reactionary *Junker*-led coup, which in turn would provoke a radical social revolution. In November, after the fall of Vienna, attacking what he called 'the bourgeoisie' in the shape of the National Guard, he also claimed that 'everywhere' the 'bourgeoisie' had come to a secret agreement with the forces of reaction, and this idea propelled him once more back to the repertoire of the French Revolution. After referring to the June events in Paris, and the October events in Vienna, he continued, 'the very cannibalism of the counter-revolution will convince the nations that there is only *one means* by which the murderous death agonies of the old society and the bloody birth throes of the new society can be *shortened*, simplified and concentrated – and that is by *revolutionary terror*.'[58] In December, in the aftermath of the Brandenburg coup he reiterated the point in a more extended article, 'The Bourgeoisie and the Counter-Revolution'. He claimed that 1848 had shown 'that a purely *bourgeois revolution* and the establishment of *bourgeois rule* in the form of a *constitutional monarchy* is impossible in Germany, and that only a feudal absolutist counter-revolution or a *social republican revolution* is possible'.[59]

Once again, Karl's was a static and anachronistic picture. It was true that a pure form of 'bourgeois rule' had not been established. But what had come into being was a hybrid creation, a form of representative state, but one in which parliament still lacked control over crucial aspects of the executive, notably the army and foreign policy. Developments in France under Louis-Napoléon were tending in the same direction. The crisis in political authority had produced a renewed predilection for strong government, but no longer in its traditional shape. The alternatives envisaged by Karl missed altogether the emergence of these new political forms, which encompassed, however demagogically, some form of a representation and a broader suffrage.

In historic Prussia, Brandenburg's constitution effectively brought the Revolution to an end. The second half of November was the nearest that Prussia had come to insurrection, not only in the cities but also in the countryside, particularly the wine-producing district of the Moselle valley. At that point, democrats commanded broad support, and they remained the strongest grouping in the new Parliament elected on 22 January 1849. The slogan 'No more taxes!!!' remained on the masthead of the *Neue Rheinische Zeitung* until 17 December, but ceased to carry any weight after the last week of November. In the Rhineland, forms of opposition and outbreaks of rebellion among peasants and outworkers continued through to the spring. But this was not enough to shake the government. For without leadership from Berlin, Vienna or Frankfurt, rebellions remained localized and opposition fragmented.

7. 1849 – FINAL MONTHS

The final phase of the Revolution occurred in the spring and early summer of 1849. On 27 March, having laboured to complete the drafting of an imperial constitution, a narrow majority of the Frankfurt Parliament voted to approve a royal constitution and to offer the imperial throne to Friedrich Wilhelm, making him the ruler of all Germany. To have accepted an offer from the Parliament would have implied an endorsement of popular sovereignty. Only a proposal from the crowned heads of the German Confederation would have been acceptable. After some delay, the king declined the crown, and refused to ratify the Frankfurt constitution. Furthermore, on 26 April, he dissolved the new Prussian Assembly, which had accepted the constitution and offered military assistance to other states which supported its rejection.

In the Rhineland, the response was divided. Catholics were happy to support a decision that preserved the pre-existing German Confederation, and Austria's pre-eminent place within it. Conversely, in Protestant districts, traditionally loyal to the Prussian crown, the king's response was met with disbelief. Elberfeld, near Engels' childhood home, and

Krefeld, a centre of outworking metal trades, became hubs of resistance. Along the Rhine, meetings of democrats and militiamen were held, and it is estimated that 10,000–15,000 participated in some form of resistance.[60] But the groups were short of weapons, and by mid-May the insurrection had run out of steam. In the south and the west, a military campaign to ensure the ratification of the Frankfurt constitution continued. But it stood no chance against Prussian forces and finally came to an end in July.

For the radical left crisis was welcome. But this was not the crisis for which they had yearned. How could republicans get involved in a campaign to induce Friedrich Wilhelm to accept the imperial crown? At least liberals in the liberal-constitutionalist citizen societies had felt sufficiently incensed to contest the actions of royal government. The Cologne City Council protested that the king had acted contrary to the will of the people, while that of Elberfeld appointed a Committee of Public Safety and sent a message of support to Frankfurt. Karl and other radicals had expected that some form of compromise would be reached between Frankfurt and Berlin. Since Malmo, Frankfurt was held in little respect by either the right or the left. The powerlessness of the Assembly had been underlined on 9 November by the shooting on the order of Prince Windischgrätz of Robert Blum, an emissary sent by Frankfurt to negotiate an end to the siege of Vienna. Blum was a radical and a native of Cologne; and the *Neue Rheinische Zeitung* had produced a special black-lined front page to commemorate his passing. Thereafter, the paper had all but lost interest in Frankfurt and relegated its proceedings to the back page.

The refusal of the king and the dissolution of the Assembly had taken Karl and the other radicals by surprise. This helps explain why at the moment when the Prussian Assembly endorsed the imperial constitution and demanded the lifting of martial law in Berlin, Karl was out of town fund-raising. Belatedly, the *Zeitung* got involved in the Rhineland resistance. Engels offered his services to the revolt in Elberfeld, and subsequently fought in the German Imperial Constitution Campaign, while Karl, who had kept clear of the conflict, nevertheless found himself placed under an expulsion order. He was told to leave Prussia on 16 May, and departed after publishing the last issue of the *Neue Rheinische Zeitung* three days later. This final edition, of 19 May, was printed in red. Its last message was to urge the 'emancipation of the working class', but it kept its distance from the campaign over the imperial constitution and warned workers not to get involved in any attempt at a 'putsch'.

Between the Malmo crisis in September 1848 and January 1849, Karl ran the *Neue Rheinische Zeitung* almost alone; of the original staff only Georg Weerth was left to assist him. After Worringen, and the protest meetings in Cologne, warrants had been issued for the arrest of Schapper, Moll, Wilhelm Wolff, Bürgers, Engels, Dronke and others. Moll went to London, where he began to make clandestine plans for the resurrection of the Communist League. Schapper was released on 15 November and returned to Cologne, where he provided crucial support for Karl in the continuing conflict with Gottschalk.

Engels first returned to the family home in Barmen, where he burnt incriminating papers, then left for Brussels. After being expelled from Belgium, he travelled by foot from Paris to Berne. On his way he took leave from politics and enjoyed the wine harvest in Burgundy. He offered a thumbnail sketch of the different kinds of female charm the traveller might encounter on this itinerary, confessing that he preferred 'the cleanly washed, smoothly combed, slimly built Burgundian women from Saint-Bris and Vermenton' to 'those earthily dirty, tousled, young Molossian buffaloes between the Seine and the Loire'. He saw no sign of the incipient republican sentiment which in some areas was to connect the peasantry with the democratic-social programme of *La Montagne* in the following year. For him, 'the peasant in France, as in Germany, is a barbarian in the midst of civilisation'.[61]

Engels only returned to Cologne in January, once the danger of imprisonment had passed. His role in Karl's circle remained contentious, just as it had been four years earlier. Ewerbeck, D'Ester and, not surprisingly, Hess still wished to oust him from his privileged position. But it was clear that Karl had no intention of abandoning such a prolific and dependable friend. As Ewerbeck remarked to Hess, Karl 'is completely crazy about Engels, whom he commends as excellent intellectually, morally and with respect to his character'.[62]

The problems faced by the *Neue Rheinische Zeitung* were considerable, quite apart from the enforced departure of so many members of its editorial team. As a result of the imposition of martial law in Cologne on 26 September, the problem of funding once again became acute. Martial law was lifted on 3 October, but the paper did not reappear until 12 October. Uncertainty about how long martial law would last coincided with the period set aside for quarterly renewals and this led to a sharp drop in the number of subscribers. At the same time, the recruitment of the poet Freiligrath to the editorial team was expected to increase circulation.

Some money was also raised in the form of 'loan certificates', but the response to this promotion was mixed. According to Lassalle, writing from Düsseldorf, 'men of decidedly radical views accused the said newspaper of perfidy and would like to see some other democratic organ founded in its place'.[63] On previous occasions, Karl's fund-raising trips had enjoyed some success. Over the summer of 1848, he had journeyed to Vienna and Berlin and soon after received 2,000 thalers from Vladislav Koscielsky in thanks for the paper's support to the Polish cause. But in its last months raising funds became ever more difficult. From 14 April through to 9 May, Karl attempted to fund-raise in Westphalian towns and later in Bremen and Hamburg. But he returned with only 300 thalers, just enough to pay off immediate debts. And then the paper was forced to cease publication.

During this period, radicalism in Cologne was weakened once more by the unseemly row between the supporters of Gottschalk and the group around Karl. Gottschalk was acquitted on 23 December 1848 and, had the authorities allowed it, would have been accompanied from court through the streets in a triumphal torchlight procession.[64] On 16 October 1848, Karl was temporarily made President of the Workers' Association during Gottschalk's absence. But when Gottschalk and Anneke were released, Karl did not relinquish the post. Seeing no chance of ousting Karl and his supporters from their now controlling position within the Association, Gottschalk left Cologne, first to tend to his sick sister in Bonn, and on to Brussels and Paris. His supporters remained in charge of the Association's newspaper, *Freiheit, Brüderlichkeit, Arbeit* (*Freedom, Brotherhood, Labour*) and were determined to contest the takeover.

Conflict initially focused upon a specific political issue. Having dissolved the previous Prussian Assembly, the Brandenburg ministry in Berlin had issued a new constitution and decreed elections on 22 January 1849 for a new Assembly. Democrats had to determine whether to accept a constitution bestowed upon the people by the king as an act of grace. All male citizens except those on poor relief were eligible to vote, but elections were indirect, in two stages: electors would vote for delegates, who in turn would vote for representatives. Karl and his circle campaigned for the democratic candidates, Franz Raveaux and Schneider II. But in the Workers' Association Anneke proposed that independent worker candidates should stand; democrats should be supported tactically only where worker candidates stood no chance. Against this Karl argued it was too late to put up separate candidates. In the *Neue Rheinische Zeitung* on 21 January, he contended that 'workers and the petty bourgeois' would do 'better to suffer in modern bourgeois society, which by its industry creates the material means for the foundation of a new society that will liberate you all, than to revert to a bygone form of society, which, on the pretext of saving your classes, thrusts the entire nation back into medieval barbarism'.[65] In the ensuing elections, Cologne democrats, who refused the terms of the new constitution, did extremely well. But this was no constitutional crisis, since the Rhineland was outvoted by other parts of Prussia where opinion was more conservative.

The supporters of Gottschalk denounced the whole strategy. Wilhelm Prinz, now the editor of *Freiheit, Brüderlichkeit, Arbeit*, attacked the democratic candidates, and despite attempts to discipline him went on to attack Karl directly. On 25 February 1849, the battle culminated in an anonymous denunciation by Gottschalk himself of Karl's linkage between the democratic position and the necessity of a bourgeois revolution. Gottschalk attacked intellectuals for whom 'the hunger of the poor has only a scientific doctrinaire interest' and derided the political strategy of the *Neue Rheinische Zeitung*, according to which the outbreak of revolution in Germany depended upon the outbreak of revolution in France, and the outbreak of revolution in France was made dependent upon the outbreak of revolution in England.

By then, the conflict had reached the stage in which two different versions of the newspaper, with almost identical logos, the one *Freiheit, Brüderlichkeit, Arbeit* and the other *Freiheit, Arbeit*, competed to express the purported position of the Workers' Association. Under the leadership of Karl Schapper, the Workers' Association was reorganized in such a way that Gottschalk's supporters were marginalized. In place of the 7,000 or more members of the previous summer, a much smaller and more tightly organized Association was created. Organization by trade was discontinued, members paid fees and a far more pedagogic approach was adopted. Members were now enjoined to study Karl's 'Wage Labour and Capital' and directed to read up on the themes discussed in the editorials of the *Neue Rheinische Zeitung*. But, despite all this, support for Gottschalk did not diminish. A month after his attack on Karl, Gottschalk wrote to Hess, expressing his satisfaction that the attack on Karl and Raveaux had made 'a powerful sensation', and that a banquet in the Gürzenich had been packed out because of Gottschalk's expected presence.[66]

In the early months of 1849, the *Neue Rheinische Zeitung* was strengthened by the return of most of the former editorial team, mainly as a result of the unwillingness of Rhineland juries to support the prosecution of radicals by state authorities from Berlin. The two trials in which Karl was involved benefited from this attitude. At the first trial Karl made masterly use of the Napoleonic penal code to accuse prosecutors of falling back upon the extra-legal assumptions of an absolutist state.[67] In the second Karl provided the jury with his theory of the bourgeois revolution in Prussia, building on the contrast between the still feudal United *Landtag* and the bourgeois National Assembly. On that basis, he argued that the laws he was supposed to have transgressed no longer existed.[68]

Most striking in the first few months of 1849 was how extraordinarily optimistic Karl and his group remained, despite Bonaparte's victory, the fall of Vienna, and Friedrich Wilhelm's triumph over the Prussian National Assembly. In an article in the *Neue Rheinische Zeitung*, published on New Year's Day 1849, he declared, 'the table of contents for 1849 reads: Revolutionary rising of the French working class, world war'. This was the speculative prophecy mocked by Gottschalk: 'The liberation of Europe' depended upon 'the successful uprising of the French working class'. But this was likely to be 'thwarted' by the English bourgeoisie. The toppling of this bourgeoisie could only be accomplished by a 'world war'; 'Only when the Chartists head the English government, will the social revolution pass from the sphere of utopia to that of reality.'[69] In an image repeatedly used by the two friends from 1844 onwards, Engels was equally convinced of the revolutionary transformation of Europe, once 'the Gallic cock crowed'. In Central and Eastern Europe, this would ensure the victory of the three nations which represented the cause of revolution: the Germans, the Poles and the Magyars. Conversely, those who belonged to the cause of counter-revolution – the Czechs, Moravians, Slovaks, Croats, Ruthenians, Rumanians, Illyrians and Serbs – were 'destined to perish before long in the revolutionary world storm'. Engels expected that 'The next world war will result in the disappearance from the face of the earth not only of reactionary classes and dynasties, but also of entire reactionary peoples.'[70]

Through the mid-century revolutions, Karl stuck in formal terms to the goal of democratic revolution. But within that framework hopes of a progression across Europe towards a second wave of revolution led Karl and his friends in 1849 to place growing emphasis upon the role of the proletariat, while adopting an ever more dismissive attitude to the role of the democrats. After concluding that 'constitutional monarchy' was 'impossible' in Germany, Karl's treatment of the democratic beginnings of the revolution itself became increasingly contemptuous.[71] There had been no events 'more philanthropic, humane and weak than the February and March Revolutions'.[72] Similarly, the *Neue Rheinische Zeitung* distanced itself from the democratic deputy from Breslau, Julius Stein, who had attempted to subject the army to parliamentary control. The paper declared that it had never 'flirted with a parliamentary party' and that in the struggle against the existing government 'we ally ourselves even with our enemies'.[73] In a similar spirit, the paper denounced the March Association, which had been founded in Frankfurt in November 1848 and had acquired over 900 branches. It was committed to the establishment of a constitutional monarchy and the defence of the gains of the March Revolution by all legal means. Sticking doggedly to the French revolutionary script, Karl compared the Association with 'the Feuillants', the liberal constitutional reformers who had opposed the dethroning of Louis XVI and 'had to be got out of the way before the outbreak of the real revolution'; they were 'the *unconscious tool of counter-revolution*'.[74]

Finally, on 14 April 1849, Karl, Schapper, Anneke and Wilhelm Wolff announced their resignation from the Democratic District Committee in Cologne, proposing instead a closer union of Workers' Associations, and calling for a Congress of Workers' Associations to meet on 6 May. Simultaneously, the Workers' Associations it reached were sent copies of 'Wage Labour and Capital' and the revised statutes of the Cologne Workers' Association.

There have been various subsequent attempts to justify this abandonment of the Democratic Society, ranging from the appropriateness of the foundation of a proletarian party at this stage, to Karl's disappointment at the activities and aspirations of the *Kleinbürger* (lower middle class), to his desire to join together with the recently created Workers' Brotherhood (*Arbeiterverbrüderung*) initiated by Stefan Born and by then active in Berlin.[75] But none of these interpretations are especially convincing. This was a moment of large-scale protests on the part of liberal constitutionalists as well as democrats and socialists against the king's rejection of the imperial throne and constitution, together with another dissolution of the Prussian National Assembly and the imposition of martial law in Berlin. This was hardly an auspicious moment to plan the formation of a separate proletarian party. As for the desire to link up with Born's Workers' Brotherhood, there was no reason why such a step should have precluded continued membership of the Democratic Association. More likely, it was a move designed to placate Gottschalk supporters within the Cologne Workers' Association.[76]

In a larger sense, this was a continuation of the stance Karl had adopted in Brussels: the attempt both to support the democratic or so-called 'bourgeois' revolution and at the same time to fast-forward to the development of a 'social-republican revolution' beyond. This zigzag between the two scenarios continued through the revolutionary period. In August 1848, Karl had insisted against Weitling that the democratic revolution must contain a coalition of 'the most heterogeneous elements' just like the French Provisional Government of February.[77] But in April 1849 his justification for leaving the 'Democratic Associations of the Rhine Province' was 'the conviction that, in view of the heterogeneous elements in the Associations in question, there is little to be expected from them, that would be advantageous for the interests of the working class or the great mass of the people'.[78] In February, he had supported the democratic candidates; now he considered it urgent 'firmly to unite the homogeneous elements'. Similarly, on the anniversary of the March Revolution in Berlin, the *Neue Rheinische Zeitung* dismissed it as 'that feeble echo of the revolution in Vienna' and declared that the anniversary which the paper would celebrate would be that of 25 June (the Paris uprising).[79] Yet in June he travelled to Paris as the representative of the 'Democratic Central Committee' of the Palatinate.[80]

Seen from the perspectives of other democrats – the many enrolled in the March Associations for example, or the liberals and radicals pushing for a constitutional monarchy – the precise location of Karl and his friends, whether in the Democratic Society or the Workers' Association, was of purely scholarly interest. For what Karl meant by democracy, in the context of a 'bourgeois' revolution, was a re-enactment of the activities of the indivisible republic, the Convention and the Committee of Public Safety in 1793. Even in August 1848, when he had argued for the necessity of a coalition of 'heterogeneous elements', his attitude towards putative allies had remained ungenerous, even cantankerous. Carl Schurz, who attended the Democratic Congress from Bonn, recalled many years after:

> Everyone who contradicted him, he treated with abject contempt; every argument that he did not like he answered either with biting scorn at the unfathomable ignorance that had prompted it, or with opprobrious aspersions upon the motives of him who had advanced it. I remember most distinctly the cutting disdain with which he pronounced the word 'bourgeois'; and as a 'bourgeois' – that is, as a detestable example of the deepest mental and moral degeneracy – he denounced everyone who dared to oppose his opinion.[81]

Flaubert wrote of the 1848 February Revolution in France: 'in spite of the most humane legislation ever seen, the bogy of 1793 reared its head and every syllable of the word "republic" vibrated like the thud of the blade of the guillotine'.[82]

Horrific though the memory of the Terror remained, at the time it had possessed justification, and as a result significant support. The Terror of 1793 had not been inaugurated as an act of will. It had been introduced, and justified, as a reluctant response to wartime emergency – '*La patrie en danger*' – since France had been invaded and the Vendée was in revolt. This had been an appeal to the political wisdom of the ancients – *Necessitas non habet legem* (Necessity knows no laws). Those who had carried out the Terror had not imagined that the politics of emergency could be wilfully invented, irrespective of whether or not an emergency existed. For this reason, it was not simply the 'bourgeoisie' who found the constant allusions to the watchwords of 1793 either frightening or indeed tiresome.

Although the *Neue Rheinische Zeitung* was successful in establishing itself as the voice of a distinctively caustic form of radicalism in 1848, the extent of its understanding of the events – and therefore the quality of its journalism – was limited by its dogmatic tone and its reductive conception of politics. The position it occupied at one extreme of the political spectrum was too marginal to have much impact upon the general course of development in the second half of 1848. But insofar as it possessed the ability to affect the political situation, its impact was mixed. When opportunities arose, it made the aim of securing a united front more difficult. When it articulated the authentic and widely held local hostility towards Prussian rule and the military occupation which sustained it, it provided a powerful and uncompromising expression of popular sentiment in the Rhineland.

8. THE AFTERMATH

From Cologne, Karl and Engels proceeded to Baden and the Palatinate, where they expected to find an insurrection under way. They hoped to persuade the left in Frankfurt to summon armed assistance from Baden and the Palatinate. But the Frankfurt representatives were reluctant to assume responsibility for an armed insurrection, and the troops in Baden and the Palatinate were loath to fight beyond their frontiers. Around 3 June, Karl therefore went on to Paris now as the accredited representative of the Palatinate Democratic District Committee.

Paris was very different from the city he had left fourteen months earlier. Hope of revolution had given way to fear of disease. Alexander Herzen recorded in his *Memoirs*: 'The cholera raged in Paris; the heavy air, the sunless heat produced a languor; the sight of the frightened, unhappy population and the rows of hearses which started racing each other as they drew near the cemeteries – all this corresponded with what was happening . . . The victims of the pestilence fell nearby, at one's side.' Nevertheless, Karl found on his arrival excitement among revolutionaries about what they considered an imminent and transforming event. In May 1849, to please the church, Bonaparte had sent the French army to Rome to expel Mazzini and the republicans, and to restore the exiled Pope. In the National Assembly, Ledru-Rollin denounced Bonaparte and the ministry, claiming that they should be impeached for violating the terms of the new constitution. He and the party of *La Montagne* called for a public demonstration to be held on 13 June. The left hoped that this protest might topple the government.

On 12 June, Herzen's friend Sazonov came to see him. 'He was in the greatest exaltation: he talked of the popular outbreak that was impending, of the certainty of its being successful, of the glory awaiting those who took part in it, and urgently pressed me to join in reaping the laurels.'[83]

When 13 June dawned the government was well prepared and the meeting attracted only a few participants. Soldiers drove the *Montagnards* off the streets; some of their deputies were arrested, Ledru-Rollin went into hiding and then fled to England. Karl later affected to believe that this failure was due to the deficiencies of the 'petite bourgeoisie'. More likely, as Maurice Agulhon has suggested, the Parisian crowds were less preoccupied with foreign affairs than with questions of economic well-being.[84]

As a result of the failure of 13 June, the 'Party of Order' took full control of the National Assembly and the scale of repression increased. Germans in Paris were particularly subject to police attention, and it was only a matter of time before Karl's address was discovered. On 19 July, he was told to leave Paris and was given the option of moving to Morbihan, an especially unhealthy coastal region of Brittany. So he decided instead to cross the Channel to England on 24 August 1849. Jenny and the family followed on 15 September.

During the summer of 1849, the last pockets of revolutionary resistance were eliminated across Europe. The Hungarians surrendered to the Russians, while Prussian armies destroyed remaining centres of resistance in the German Confederation, most spectacularly the insurrection in Dresden between 3 and 9 May. Yet despite this string of defeats Karl and the left remained ebullient. Like Herzen, Karl noted that Paris was *'morne'* (dreary) and that 'the cholera is raging mightily'. But his reaction was similar to that of Herzen's friend Sazonov: 'For all that,' Karl wrote on 7 June, 'never has a colossal eruption of the revolutionary volcano been more imminent than it is in Paris today.'[85]

At the end of July, Karl was undaunted. He wrote to Freiligrath that 'with each reactionary measure' the French government 'alienates yet another section of the population', while Cobden and 'the English bourgeoisie's attitude to continental despotism' offered another source of hope.[86] His rejoicing sounded like *Schadenfreude*. Around the same time, he wrote to Weydemeyer that he was among 'the *satisfaits*. *Les choses marchent très bien* [things are going very well] and the Waterloo suffered by official democracy may be regarded as a victory: "Governments by the grace of God" are taking it upon themselves to avenge us on the bourgeoisie and to chastise them.'[87] Two weeks later he awaited the expulsion of 'the Barrot-Dufaure clique' from the French cabinet, and 'as soon as this comes about you can look for an early revolutionary resurrection'. In England, he was hopeful for an alliance of Chartists and free traders: 'Consequences of this economic campaign against feudalism and Holy Alliance incalculable.'[88]

During the whole period between early 1849 and the summer of 1850, Karl was preoccupied with the strategy and activities of the Communist League. The League had been disbanded in the summer of 1848, but as the forces of reaction gained the upper hand in the autumn and winter of that year, pressure grew to restore it. At the Second Democratic Congress in Berlin, Ewerbeck, the representative from Paris, had met with other former members and agreed to summon a meeting in Berlin, at which new officers could be appointed. The December crisis in Berlin, caused by Brandenburg's dissolution of the Assembly, prevented this meeting from taking place, but arrangements for re-constituting the League went ahead anyway. The initiative was carried forward mainly by the London branch, where former members were still active, notably Joseph Moll after fleeing from Cologne, Heinrich Bauer and Johann Georg Eccarius. At the beginning of 1849, Karl Schapper had set up a branch in Cologne, and attempts had been made to persuade Karl and other members of the *Neue Rheinische Zeitung* to rejoin. According to one report, a meeting to discuss the issue was held in Cologne at the beginning of 1849, and was attended by Karl, Engels and Wilhelm Wolff, together with Joseph Moll and other members. Karl remained opposed since he considered a secret society unnecessary as long as there remained freedom of speech and freedom of the press.[89] But at some point later in the spring – perhaps around 16 April, when Karl resigned from the Democratic Society – he and Engels evidently rejoined.

Some commentators have treated Karl's political activity in the Communist League in 1849–50 as a regrettable lapse of political judgement, provoked by 'the breakdown of his immeasurable hopes'.[90] It makes more sense, however, to relate his behaviour not to psychology, but to the inherent volatility of his theoretical position. His attempt to combine politics and a preset notion of development led to a continued impression of zigzagging, which disconcerted friends and enemies alike. In the light of his advocacy of 'revolutionary terror', his emphatic rejection of the existence of any 'legal basis' and his denunciation of the 'bourgeois' revolution towards the end of 1848, what was there to distinguish his position from that of insurrectionary intransigents like Willich?[91] The main point of difference was Karl's insistence upon dividing the revolution into a series of distinct 'stages', for the moment a purely academic point. If Karl no longer believed a 'bourgeois revolution' to be possible in Germany, why should workers accept their subordination to a democratic 'petite bourgeoisie'? Karl was not only prepared to rejoin the Central Committee of the reconstituted Communist League, but was active in pushing its position further to the left. This is strongly suggested by his collaboration with August von Willich during the autumn and the winter after he arrived in London in August 1849.

Willich was a former artillery officer from an aristocratic family and had been deprived of his rank for writing to the king in defence of his fellow officer Fritz Anneke, who had publicly proclaimed his support for socialism. Having left the army and become a carpenter, Willich joined the Cologne Communist League and met and befriended Andreas Gottschalk, with whom he had headed a demonstration which invaded the Cologne Council Chamber on 3 March 1848. Willich was imprisoned, and then released at the outbreak of the March Revolution; so he proceeded to Baden, where he participated in a failed insurrection. He appealed through Anneke for financial assistance for those who had taken part in the insurrection. Karl and the Democratic Society rejected the appeal, but it was supported by Gottschalk and the Workers' Association. During the campaign over the imperial constitution, Engels had served under his command, and when Willich came to London in the autumn of 1849, it was with a strong recommendation from Engels. As President of the Central Authority, Karl proposed the co-option onto the Committee, not only of Engels, but also of Willich. Later on, Schapper was co-opted as well on his return from Germany. He too favoured an insurrectionary position.

Willich was not therefore an unknown quantity and the fact that he was welcomed by Karl suggests a substantial political convergence. This is suggested by three clues. The first was Karl's role in what came to be called the Social Democratic Support Committee for German Refugees. This committee was set up by the German Workers' Educational

Association at 30 Great Windmill Street, the centre of a maze of streets adjoining Leicester Square and Soho. In 1849, the Association became the destination for the large numbers of German political exiles and refugees who had streamed into London. Many were in distress, without a job, away from their families and lacking other contacts. But providing help was not straightforward, not simply because of the shortage of money, but also because of the fierce political disagreements among the exiles and refugees themselves. At a general meeting of the Workers' Educational Association on 18 September to discuss the plight of refugees, Karl was elected to a committee in charge of charitable relief. Collaboration between communists and democrats was difficult, and these divisions became even sharper when, on Karl's initiative, Engels and Willich joined the committee, and its title was changed to the Social Democratic Support Committee for German Refugees.

The second clue was to be found in the direction followed by the Central Authority of the Communist League itself. The Authority also co-opted Engels, Willich and Schapper; and this was followed up by an effort in 1850 to reactivate branches in Germany. The shoemaker Heinrich Bauer was sent on a tour of German centres, and Karl sent a letter to the cigar-maker Peter Röser, urging him to re-establish a branch in Cologne and other Rhineland cities.

The third and most obvious indication of this emerging alliance was indicated by the League's policy pronouncements. These adopted a strikingly aggressive tone towards democrats. During the last few weeks in Cologne, divergence from the democrats was of little practical importance, but in England Karl and his allies behaved as if democrats had been solely responsible for the failure of the Revolution. The new position was clearly spelled out in 'Address of the Central Authority to the League' of March 1850, signed among others by Karl, Engels and Willich, and almost certainly written by Karl. It began with an uncompromising criticism of the position adopted in 1848, arguing it had been wrong to imagine that the time for secret societies was over and therefore to dissolve the League. It had also been a mistake not to have put up independent worker candidates in the elections of January/ February 1849. As a result, the working class was now under the domination of the petite bourgeoisie.[92]

In the future, the proletariat in France and Britain should be engaged in a direct struggle for state power. In Germany, on the other hand, bourgeois revolution was to be completed and then succeeded by a second revolution headed by the proletariat and the petite bourgeoisie. In this second revolution, the petite bourgeoisie would probably triumph, but while 'the democratic petty bourgeois wish to bring the revolution to a conclusion as quickly as possible, it is our interest and our task to make the revolution permanent … until all more or less possessing classes have been forced out of their position of dominance, the proletariat has conquered state power' and 'competition among proletarians all over the world has ceased'.[93]

The Address's vision became even more surreal; thus 'alongside the new official governments [of petit bourgeois democrats] they [the workers] must immediately establish their own revolutionary workers' governments'. In order to do so, they would have to be armed. If victorious, the revolutionary government would not distribute the feudal lands to the peasants as free property. Such land would remain state property 'and be converted into workers' colonies cultivated by the associated rural proletariat'. Workers should oppose a federal republic and strive not only for 'a single and indivisible German republic, but also within this republic for the most determined centralisation of power in the hands of the state authority'. If the democrats were to propose 'moderately progressive taxation, the workers must insist on a taxation with rates that rise so steeply that big capital will be ruined by it'. The workers' 'battle cry must be: The Revolution in Permanence'.[94]

This Address was reinforced by another in June, stressing the need for 'a strong secret organisation of the revolutionary party'. Once again, a strenuous effort was made to establish clear boundaries between the League and the 'petty bourgeois' democrats, particularly in Baden, the Palatinate and Switzerland. It surveyed the situation in various other countries. In relation to England, it applauded 'the breach' between the 'revolutionary independent workers' party' and 'the more conciliatory faction led by O'Connor'. It also claimed that 'of the French revolutionaries the really proletarian party, led by Blanqui, has joined forces with us'. The Address concluded with the prediction that 'the outbreak of a new revolution can no longer be very far away'.[95]

The reference to the 'Blanquist secret societies' and 'the important tasks' entrusted to League members 'in preparation for the next French Revolution' was underlined by the participation of the League in the future formation of the Universal Society of Revolutionary Communists.

This society was dedicated to 'the downfall of all privileged classes' and 'the submission of those classes to the dictatorship of the proletarians by keeping the revolution in continual progress until the achievement of communism, which shall be the final form of the constitution of the human family'.[96] This international association of secret societies was made possible by the contacts established within the Fraternal Democrats. The declaration was signed by the Blanquist exiles Vidil and Adam, Julian Harney for the Chartists, and Karl, Engels and Willich for the Communist League.

As it began to dawn on Karl that the prospects of revolution were receding, his previous emphasis on 'stages' returned. Already in early summer rumours of squabbles in the Central Authority had reached German League members. According to Röser's evidence, based on a letter from Karl in July 1850, Karl had given a series of lectures to the Workers' Association in the previous winter, and argued in them that there would be no prospect of communism for a good number of years and that in the meantime the main task of the League would be education and propaganda. The letter added that Willich had violently opposed these ideas, insisting that the coming revolution would be communist. By August, Karl was openly ridiculing Willich's 'communist reveries', while Willich's supporters – the majority of the London branch – attacked 'journalists and semi-learned men' in whose eyes 'the workers are zeros'. At a meeting of the Workers' Association, at which Willich resigned from the Refugee Committee, supporters of the two sides practically came to blows, while at a meeting of the Central Authority in late August Willich accused Karl of lying. Conrad Schramm, one of Karl's strongest admirers at the time, challenged Willich to a duel, which was fought in Belgium and left Schramm slightly wounded.[97]

Knowing that most members of the Communist League's London branch backed Willich and that a general assembly was imminent, on 15 September Karl hastily called a meeting of the Central Authority, on which he possessed a majority. Conveniently forgetting his endless strictures on Camphausen for not displaying revolutionary will in the summer of 1848, Karl declared that for the minority on the Central Authority (Willich and Schapper) revolution had been seen 'not as the product of realities of the situation, but as a result of an effort of *will*'. Instead of telling the workers: 'you have 15, 20, 50 years of civil war to go through in order to alter the situation and to train yourselves for the exercise of power', the minority claimed 'we must take power *at once*'. Karl and the majority voted that the Central Authority be transferred from London to Cologne and that the existing League Rules become null and void. Schapper declared these proposals unconstitutional, while Willich and his supporter Lehmann walked out.[98] The breach was made final when the minority elected their own Central Authority. Karl 'adjourned indefinitely' his London section and dissolved it in November 1852. There is a danger of devoting disproportionate attention to the scholastic disputes which took place within what at the time was a tiny sectarian grouping, unable to comprehend that the moment of revolution in reality had passed, and that its vision of what had happened had in any case been hopelessly obscured by myth. Karl could not be compared with prominent revolutionary leaders of 1848 – Mazzini, Kossuth, Blanqui and others. He was virtually unknown outside Cologne, and remained so throughout the 1850s and 1860s. His followers during this period amounted at most to a few dozen. It was only in the 1870s, after his notorious defence of the Paris Commune and after people began to read *Capital*, in German, French or Russian editions, that Karl began to acquire global fame.

Karl's engagement with insurrectionary communism came to an end in the autumn of 1850, but this was not quite the end of his dealings with the Communist League.

In May 1851, a tailor named Nothjung was arrested by the Saxon police. He was found to be in possession of papers relating to the League in Cologne. Police searches in Cologne revealed more documents. Particularly valuable in the police's eyes were intemperate letters sent by Willich to the Cologne communists. Prussian police were keen to prosecute, in the aftermath of an assassination attempt on Friedrich Wilhelm IV in the spring of 1850. Government fears of revolutionary conspiracies had become endemic, and in London, especially, an army of spies – serving the Austrians, the German states, the French, the Belgians, the Dutch and the Danes – competed to supply information about the revolutionary diaspora and their real or alleged plans. The tiny 'Marx party' was a favourite target.

By the summer of 1851, eleven of its members were in prison awaiting trial. The evidence of criminal intent was very flimsy. The accused for the most part rejected Willich's argument and shared the position expressed by Peter Röser in his interrogation: that the purpose of the League was education and propaganda. The authorities were worried that the case as it stood was insubstantial and unlikely to be accepted by a Rhineland jury. Therefore, between the end of 1851 and beginning of the trial, on 4 October 1852, the police forged documents to incriminate the 'Marx party'. Karl conversely threw himself into the task of exposing forgeries, establishing defence committees, writing to newspapers and raising funds. Jenny provided indispensable assistance. At the end of October, she wrote to Adolf Cluss in Washington: 'A complete office has now been set up in our house. Two or three people are writing, others running errands, others scraping *pennies* together so that the writers may continue to exist and prove the old world of officialdom guilty of the most outrageous scandal. And in between whiles my three merry children sing and whistle, often to be harshly told off by their papa. What a bustle!'[99] As a result of these efforts, four of the accused were acquitted. The rest served terms of imprisonment ranging from three to six years. Karl wrote a polemical account of the prosecution, in a pamphlet, *Revelations Concerning the Communist Trial in Cologne*, published in Basle in January 1853, but all but a few copies were confiscated at the Baden frontier.

Karl's other preoccupation in his first year and a half in London was to produce a new version of the *Neue Rheinische Zeitung*. To restart the paper was to keep together his 'party', especially while the Revolution was temporarily in abeyance. During this period, the term 'party' could refer to a political entity – the 'communist party', the 'Girondin party', the 'Whigs'. But it could also, and that is the sense in which Karl used it, refer to something more intimate, a group of like-minded individuals who operated together on a newspaper and built up a following in the wider society. Once again, France was probably the model. For there, republicanism was divided between the followers of *Le National* and the followers of *La Réforme*. This had also been the way in which Karl had thought of those who worked with him on the *Deutsch-Französische Jahrbücher*, on *Vorwärts!*, and on the *Neue Rheinische Zeitung*. For this reason, his first priority in London was to re-establish the *Neue Rheinische Zeitung* in some form.

Just before he left Paris for London, Karl wrote to Engels that 'in London, there is a *positive* prospect of my being able to start a German newspaper. I am *assured* of part of the funds.'[100] As soon as he reached London, he also wrote to Freiligrath, using the address Peterson's

Coffee House, Grosvenor Square, that there were 'excellent prospects of my being able to start a monthly review here', and in January 1850 he was still talking of its transformation 'into a fortnightly and weekly and if circumstances permit, back into a daily paper'.[101] Finally, in mid-November, and with the help of Theodor Hagen, a member of the Communist League, an agreement was reached with a Hamburg publisher, Schuberth, for the publication of a monthly, *Neue Rheinische Zeitung – Politisch-Ökonomische Revue*.

As in other publications set up by Karl, the financial and administrative arrangements were unsatisfactory. It was planned that Conrad Schramm would travel to the United States with financial support from the Chartists and Blanquists in London to raise funds from well-wishers. But none of this happened. Publication should have started on 1 January, but the manuscript was not ready and Karl was ill so publication was postponed to early March 1850. By May, three numbers were published, and then nothing until a final double number in November. Sales were poor, and contributors few. Some idea of the frustrations surrounding the project was evident in a letter from Jenny to Weydemeyer in May 1850. In it she begged for whatever money had come in from sales of the *Revue*: 'We are in *dire need of it.*' Jenny reproached friends in Cologne for not helping in return for all the sacrifices Karl had made for '*Rh.Ztg*'. 'The business has been utterly ruined by the negligent slovenly way in which it was run, nor can one really say which did most harm – the bookseller's procrastination, or that of acquaintances and those managing the business in Cologne, or again the whole attitude of the democrats generally.'[102] The project ended with Karl intent upon suing the publisher and continuing the *Revue* from Cologne or Switzerland.

Once again, none of this was realized. The *Revue* contained some important essays, including Engels' account of 'The Campaign for the German Imperial Constitution' and a series of essays by Karl entitled '1848 to 1849', later published by Engels under the title *The Class Struggles in France, 1848 to 1850*. It also included a critical discussion of conspiracy, particularly interesting since it coincided with the participation of Karl, Engels and Willich in the Blanquist Universal Society of Revolutionary Communists. But the project was doomed. Demand for the journal was low, not least because of its belligerent treatment of democrats. In large parts of Germany democrats and communists were few and they saw no reason not to continue to collaborate. A particularly ill-chosen example was Karl's sneering attack on the speech made by Gottfried Kinkel, before a military court at Rastatt. Kinkel was a democratic hero who had fought in Baden under Willich, and his trial was followed with great sympathy by the public.[103]

More positive was the attention which the *Revue* devoted to global economic development. The prospectus written on 15 December 1849 stated that the *Revue* would provide 'a comprehensive and scientific investigation of the *economic* conditions which form the foundation of the whole political movement'.[104] In the final number a justification was provided for the *Revue*'s move away from the revolutionary line of the Communist League. After examining the economic upswing, which had taken place since 1848, it stated:

> With this general prosperity, in which the productive forces of bourgeois society develop as luxuriantly as is at all possible within bourgeois relationships, there can be no talk of a real revolution. Such a revolution is only possible in the periods when *both these factors*, the *modern* productive *forces* and the *bourgeois forms of production*, come *in collision* with each other . . . *A new revolution is possible only in consequence of a new crisis. It is, however, just as certain as this crisis.*[105]

In June 1850, Karl was able to secure a ticket to use the library of the British Museum. This was the beginning of the years of study that culminated in the writing of *Capital*. On 15 November, Engels left for Manchester to take up employment in his father's company. On 30 July, Karl had received a friendly letter from Charles Dana, editor of the *New-York Daily Tribune*, whom he had first met in Cologne. Dana invited Karl to write for the paper.[106] On 17 November 1852, on Karl's suggestion, the Communist League was dissolved. Karl's life was entering a new phase.

9. THE MEANING OF 1848

In two works written in London, Karl attempted to produce an interpretation of the mid-century revolutions, focusing in particular upon France. '1848 to 1849', later retitled by Engels *The Class Struggles in France, 1848 to 1850*, was written between January and October 1850, and published in successive numbers of the *Neue Rheinische Zeitung – Politisch-Ökonomische Revue*. The next essay, *The Eighteenth Brumaire of Louis Bonaparte*, was written between December 1851 and March 1852.[107]

While he was composing the *Eighteenth Brumaire*, Karl wrote to Joseph Weydemeyer that 'the *existence of classes*' was connected with '*certain historical phases in the development of production*'.[108] How well did this approach relate to what happened in 1848? Throughout most of the twentieth century, Karl's notion of 'class struggle' received little critical attention. It was treated as a dramatization of the self-evident socio-economic facts of industrialization. During the last thirty years, however, it has become increasingly clear that there were no self-evident economic facts of the kind presupposed in this socio-historical interpretation.[109] Furthermore, historians have come to understand class no longer as the expression of a simple social-economic reality, but as a form of language discursively produced to create identity.[110] Consciousness of class, so far as it existed, was inseparable from a plurality of the ways it was experienced and expressed. It is therefore not surprising to discover that the language of class that Marx attempted to take over in 1845–6, that of French socialists and republicans, possessed quite different premises and aspirations from those which arose from theoretical debate among German radicals of 1843 and 1844.

Underlying Karl's approach to class was the attempt to merge two very different forms of discourse. On the one hand there was the teleological account of the place of labour in the transformation of the world, a product of the development of the Young Hegelian movement in Germany. On the other hand he used the language of 'bourgeoisie' and 'proletariat' originating in republican, socialist and even Legitimist opposition to the 'bourgeois' monarchy of Louis Philippe in France.

The language imputed by Karl to bourgeoisie and proletariat was part of his attempt to reformulate his philosophical stance in the light of Stirner's criticism of Feuerbachian humanism. 'Communism', as he and Engels presented it between 1845 and 1848, no longer expressed the realization of 'man'. It was now 'the *real* movement which abolishes the present state of things', while communists, as the *Manifesto* put it, 'merely express, in general terms, the actual relations springing from an existing class struggle'.[111]

In his earlier writings of 1843–4, Marx had stressed the estrangement of human activity in a world created by private property. His picture of the proletariat was that of *dehumanization*, of man bifurcated by the post-classical division between the 'political state' and a market fuelled by private interests. According to the argument put forward in the *1844 Manuscripts*, in producing the proletariat, private property produced a class 'driven by the contradiction between its human *nature* and its condition of life, which is the outright, resolute and comprehensive negation of that nature ... The proletariat is compelled as proletariat to abolish itself and thereby its opposite private property.'[112]

This picture, built out of the degradation produced by private property, was extra-political. Karl's hostility towards the modern representative state continued, with consequent belittlement of the significance of manhood suffrage and the democratic republic. A similar disregard for political forms informed Engels' account of proletarian class formation in England. In an analysis of the political and legal system in England at that time, he had concluded that the constitution was 'nothing but a big lie'. The Chartist battle against the undemocratic state was therefore in reality not a political battle, but a social battle against the rule of property: 'the struggle of democracy against the aristocracy in England is the struggle of the poor against the rich. The democracy towards which England is moving is a *social* democracy.'[113]

This disregard of political and legal forms continued, but from 1845 onwards the terminology changed. In place of private property, the proletariat were now engaged in class struggle with the 'bourgeoisie'. This was a new conception of the historical significance of labour, combined with Karl's principal aim during these years, the critique of political economy. This approach had originally been inspired by Engels' contention that political economy was largely 'the elaboration of private property'. But with the shift towards an emphasis upon human activity and the material transformation of the world, the terms of this critique also shifted. The picture was no longer of a suffering class in need of illumination by philosophy, facing private property as an impersonal entity. A critique of the relationship between labour and capital within political economy was now combined with the French political vocabulary of bourgeois and proletarian; and this produced an extraordinary amplification of the active roles assigned to these classes in the *Communist Manifesto*.

As argued before (see p. 235), the *Communist Manifesto* freed the picture of the bourgeois from local limitations. It now embodied the supposed rational political capacities of Guizot's *classe moyenne* as well as the productive proclivities of Thierry's *industriels*, in addition to the reputed economic dynamism of the Lancashire cotton master.[114] Similarly, the *proletarian* incorporated both the 'communist' militancy of the Parisian followers of Blanqui or Raspail and the membership of a mass movement such as Chartism. In sum, Guizot's belief that the July regime had ushered in the rule of the most able and rational of the citizenry, the *classe moyenne*, denounced by the opposition as the rule of the 'bourgeoisie', was now transmuted by Karl's alchemy into the global sociological destiny of capitalism itself, even if it as yet incorporated only one fraction of that class – 'the stock exchange kings'.[115] The imagined political trajectory of the French 'Third Estate' had fused together with the economic trajectory of English industrial capital.

The attempt to merge this global historical vision with day-to-day empirical history explains the strangeness of the account of the 1848 revolution in *The Class Struggles in France*. Despite a wealth of descriptive details, there is scarcely any reference to the political context in which the struggles took place. In particular, the promise asserted by the February Revolution that the 'social question' could be resolved by 'the democratic and social republic' through its commitment to 'the right to work' and the acknowledgement of the value of 'association' was barely mentioned.

Equally striking is the absence of more than a cursory reference to the social-economic context in which the February Revolution originally occurred. French socialist analysis of the capitalist crisis had concentrated on the phenomenon of overproduction. This had originally been highlighted by Sismondi in reaction to the post-war crisis of 1819.[116] Karl's understanding of economic crisis had followed this line of reasoning. But the mid-century crisis was not of this type. It started from the potato blight, poor wheat harvests and a poor cotton crop, which occasioned mass unemployment in Lancashire. Harvest crises raised the price of bread and lowered the demand for industrial goods, not only in the towns but in large parts of Northern Europe, where linen production as a rural by-industry in many places faced terminal collapse. It precipitated the first large wave of emigration to America from Ireland, south-west Germany and to a far lesser extent France.[117] The crisis in the 1840s was not simply a combination of industrial depression and exceptional dearth. It represented a more secular turning point in the history of the Western European economy. It inaugurated the de-industrialization of the countryside and the pastoralization of extensive areas that until then had combined agriculture and domestic industry, though it did not in England or anywhere else diminish the importance of small workshop production in the towns.[118]

The most direct connection between this crisis and the revolutions of 1848 was its creation of mass unemployment, exacerbated by an unprecedented scale of migration to the cities. This may not have been the prime factor producing the collapse of the regime in France in February 1848. But it was certainly the prime factor in provoking the establishment of the *Ateliers Nationaux* (National Workshops) in Paris and the political debate about their future.

Karl's text virtually ignored this material economic context, even though it centred upon the Paris insurrection in June 1848, following the decision of the National Assembly to close down the National Workshops. The participants were led for the most part by those discharged from the Workshops. The June Insurrection was described by Karl as class war between the bourgeoisie and the proletariat: 'the first great battle . . . fought between the two classes that split modern society'. But neither the proletariat nor the bourgeoisie were defined and their identity in terms of the Marxian conception of 'relations of production' remained unclear.[119] References to the 'proletariat' occasionally slipped back into that of 'the people', while references to the 'bourgeoisie' were ubiquitous, but could easily be exchanged for the term 'republic'. In reality, the executive of the new Republic was not composed of employers, industrial or otherwise; nor were the insurgents by any means exclusively composed of wage workers as many small employers were also involved. Most blatantly, Karl rearranged his depiction of the social combatants engaged in the insurrection to disguise the fact that those engaged in its suppression were no more or less 'proletarian' than the combatants themselves. There was no meaningful social difference to justify Karl's distinction between the June Insurgents (the proletariat) and the *Garde Mobile* (the *Lumpenproletariat*).[120] It is also important to remember that the insurrection, although clearly of major significance, only mobilized a minority of the Parisian working classes, 40,000–50,000 out of 200,000–300,000.[121]

More fundamentally, no account was given of what primarily

prompted the resistance of the insurgents – the threat of destitution following the closing down of the National Workshops – nor of their principal political grievance – the Republic's failure to keep its promise of 'the right to work'. What caused the rebellion was not the action of the employing class, but the decisions of members of the National Assembly, motivated by a dislike of what they feared as 'communism'.

Karl also made no reference to the financial and organizational difficulties of the Republic, faced with the practical need to provide for 150,000 unemployed workmen, and mindful of the dangers of huge numbers of unoccupied and politically volatile working men clustered on the streets. Throughout the four-month existence of the National Workshops, 90 per cent of their members – 140,000 – remained without work; the workers were scattered across the city to while away their time drinking, womanizing or playing cards until 4 p.m. when they could collect a 'demeaning dole'. If they were given work, one of their organizers argued, 'you will see, you self-satisfied critics, if we are lazzaroni asking no better than to live off public funds'.[122] Unsurprisingly, the fact of having to support one third of the Parisian labour force without any appreciable result aroused resentment – not just from 'the bourgeoisie', but from large numbers of the Parisian working population too.

The insurgents in June possessed no nationally recognized leaders. Nor did they make any demands beyond the insistence that the 'democratic and social' Republic honour the promises it had made at the time of the February Revolution. Karl did not provide a concrete account of the precipitants or of the character of the June battle. Instead, he veered off into an unfounded fantasy about the Parisian proletariat: 'In place of its demands, exuberant in form, but petty and even bourgeois still in content, the concession of which it wanted to wring from the February Republic, there appeared the bold slogan of revolutionary struggle: Overthrow the bourgeoisie! Dictatorship of the working class.'[123]

Karl was right to view the events between 1789 and 1848 as a series of social and political struggles of a potentially revolutionary nature. This was an exceptional period in England and France because, in both countries, political organizations and social movements, sometimes on a national scale, did seek to bring down the existing political order in the name of a *true* republic or a *true* constitution based upon universal manhood suffrage. But Karl misunderstood both the causes and the remedies for this exceptional phase of political antagonism.

In the first half of the nineteenth century, the first appearance, both in England and in France, of movements and organizations which claimed to speak in the name of the 'working class' or 'working classes' was *not* the result of the *economic* advance of modern industrial capitalism; it was rather the *political* effect of the demolition of the *Ancien Régime* in France, and in England of the unprecedented political mobilization of the population following the American and French Revolutions, the prolonged wars against France and the economic distress following the defeat of Napoléon.

During these years, the 'bourgeoisie' or 'middle classes' were also conjured into political existence. The languages of class, which became prevalent in France around 1830 and in England around 1832, were closely connected with the need to reform the constitution and the political system in a rational and secular way, *without* allowing an opening to *popular sovereignty*, which was still greatly feared from the years of Robespierre and the Terror. What Karl and his 'party' failed to understand was that the character of politics in this period was not simply an expression of the nature of class. Just as important, especially in the juxtaposition of 'bourgeois' and 'proletarian', or 'middle' and 'working' classes, was the fact that these languages of class were a particular product of the politics of the representative state.

It was not the activities or strategy of a fictive 'bourgeoisie', but the attempt around 1830 to construct a political system based upon the political *exclusion* of wage-earners that created the 'struggle' of the 'working class' and the 'middle class'. In England, the vote was defined on the basis of property holding and hence those who earned wages were excluded. Class-consciousness, whether among the Chartists in England or 'democratic and social Republicans' in France, was not for the most part the result of *dehumanization* or proletarianization, but political exclusion. Indeed, exploitation was seen by the leaders of these radical workers' movements as the consequence of exclusion. Given his hostility to representation and the 'political state', Karl was in a poor position to understand these political determinants of working-class action.

Karl's form of political myopia was widely shared in 1848. Far from being ahead of his times in his conception of class, Karl shared the general perception of the propertied classes in Western Europe who, while they purported to sympathize with them, failed to listen to the discourse of workers themselves, whether in Britain or in France during the 1830–50 period.[124] In the light of Thomas Carlyle's distinction between the 'distracted incoherent embodiment of Chartism' and 'its living essence, the bitter discontent grown fierce and mad', the tendency to discount what workers actually said was general.[125] Propertied and educated observers found it hard to think of workers or proletarians as other than wild, predatory and levelling. The point was put clearly by Thomas Macaulay in his speech in Parliament rejecting the Chartist Petition of 1842. To accept the Petition would be to commit government to a class which would be induced 'to commit great and systematic inroads against the security of property . . . How is it possible that, according to the principles of human nature, if you give them this power, it would not be used to its fullest extent?'[126] A similar fear was expressed by de Tocqueville writing about the Mobile Guard, even after it had fought for the Republic against the insurrection: 'it would have taken very little to make them decide against us instead of for us . . . They went to war as to a festival. But it was easy to see that they loved war in itself much more than the cause for which they fought.'[127]

A combination of memories of the Terror, gothic nightmares about the criminal and dangerous classes, and the 'spectre of communism' haunted the political imagination in 1848. It was one of the reasons why the middle classes both in France and in Germany were so insistent upon keeping within the limits of legality. Karl was unusual, only in thinking about the conflict of classes not as a reason for fear, but as a source of hope. This deep fear according to Daniel Stern was a major reason why the Republic of 1848 did not rest on true foundations:

> The principal cause is to be found in the ignorance in which the lettered and opulent classes have remained with regard to the people, and the false idea they have conceived of the necessities of the proletariat. Troubled by a vague awareness of the duties which they have failed to perform during the last two reigns, they have attributed to them pitiless resentments and insatiable appetites. The ghost of 1793 has appeared to their souls in distress.[128]

The ideals and aspirations of the working classes in 1848 were not mysterious. They involved the desire for political inclusion and association. But their speech was discounted. It was ignored or replaced by quite different forms of discourse conjured up by the fervid imagination of writers from the propertied classes.

The fact that exclusion and lack of recognition rather than exploitation were the prime precipitants of the insurrectionary sentiments of the peoples in 1848 was borne out by the subsequent history of Western Europe. With manhood suffrage and a representative system established in France after the fall of the Second Empire, and renewed talk of Reform in England, the working classes were progressively reincorporated back into the political system.[129] Thus the political and extra-constitutional significance of the 'class struggle', as it had been invoked by the *Manifesto*, faded away.

9

London

1. FIRST YEARS: 'I AM AS TORMENTED AS JOB, THOUGH NOT AS GOD-FEARING'

Dean Street, where the Marx family lived, together with their servant, Lenchen, between 1850 and 1856, was in the heart of Soho. On 13 May 1850, they had moved into two rooms in 64 Dean Street belonging to a Jewish lacemaker and occupied by Heinrich Bauer, the treasurer of the Refugee Committee. At the end of the year, they moved from 64 Dean Street to number 28.

In a London that had become 'the great city of refuge for exiles of all nations', Soho was the favoured centre for Germans, particularly for democrats, republicans and socialists. While the unskilled Germans working in bakeries lived in the East End, and the genteel frequented the drawing rooms of St John's Wood, for radicals – especially artisans – Soho, with its German Workers' Educational Association in Great Windmill Street, was an obvious point of attraction. According to the journalist George Augustus Sala, these Germans were particularly to be found 'in the purlieus of Oxford Street, near Leicester Square, or in the centre of that maze of crooked streets between Saint Martin's Lane and Saint Anne's church, Soho'.[1]

In his satirical sketch of 'Herr Brutus Eselskopf' (donkey-head), a publican and in his time 'general of brigade', Sala depicted the manners and way of life of these Germans. Eselskopf wore 'a Turkish cap, with blue tassels, and a beard and moustaches of prodigious magnitude'. His 'little back parlour' was 'filled morning, noon and night, with foreigners under political clouds of various degrees of density, and in a cloud of uniform thickness and of strong tobacco, emitted in many-shaped fumes from pipes of eccentric design'. Among the customers 'by the fire reading the *Allgemeine Zeitung* or the *Ost-Deutsche Post*, and occasionally indulging in muttered invectives against the crowned heads of Europe', Sala picked out 'that valiant republican Spartacus Bursch, erst PhD. of the University of Heidelberg'. He was 'then on no pay, but with brevet rank, behind a barricade formed of an omnibus, two water-carts and six paving stones at Frankfort . . . afterwards of Paris, Red Republican, manufacturer of lucifer matches, *affilié* of several secret societies, chemical lecturer, contractor for paving roads, usher in a boarding school' and 'ultimately . . . promoter of a patent for extracting vinegar from white lead, keeper of a cigar shop, professor of fencing, calisthenics, and German literature; and latterly out of any trade or occupation'. Others included 'enthusiastic young advocates, zealous young sons of good families, patriotic officers, who have thrown up their commissions under despot standards to fight for liberty, freedom-loving literary men, republican journalists, socialist workmen . . . hunted from frontier to frontier on the Continent like mad dogs'.

Sala also alluded to the interminable conflicts between moderate and intransigent exiles. These refugees, or at least the great majority, were 'the quiescent ones'. But there were also 'the incandescent ones, the roaring, raging, rampaging, red-hot refugees; the amateurs in vitriol, soda water bottles full of gunpowder, and broken bottles for horses' hoofs; the throwers of grand pianofortes from first floor-windows on soldiers' heads, the cutters off of dragoons' feet, the impalers of artillery men'. These were no longer welcome at Herr Eselskopf's and met instead at the little *Gasthaus* in Whitechapel, formerly known as the *Schinke-nundbrot* (the ham sandwich) and now rechristened 'The Tyrants' Entrails'.

Soho of the 1850s was overcrowded with an average of fourteen inhabitants per house, and was particularly unhealthy since the water supply was in some parts contaminated. It was, as Karl noted, 'a choice district for cholera' and the site of an isolated outbreak in London in 1854. 'The MOB is croaking right and left (e.g. an average of 3 per house in Broad Street) and "victuals" are the best defence against the beastly thing.'[2]

Karl and Jenny had not planned to live in Soho. After pawning her silver in Frankfurt, selling her furniture in Cologne, and being forced to leave Paris, Jenny had arrived in London with three children and a fourth expected within a month. When she arrived, she was met by one of the *Neue Rheinische Zeitung* group, Georg Weerth, who put her up in a boarding house in Leicester Square. But, as she noted in her auto-biography, 'the time was approaching when I would need a quiet roof over my head', and they had therefore looked in haste for a larger lodg-ing house in Chelsea. The baby was born on 5 November, 'while the people outside were shouting "Guy Fawkes for ever!"' and 'small masked boys were riding the streets on cleverly made donkeys . . . We called him Little Fawkes, in honour of the great conspirator.'[3]

The family had come to England expecting their stay to be brief. They expected the revolution to regain its momentum, and for the *Neue Rheinische Zeitung* team to be reassembled in London, in the meantime, ready to return to Cologne. This was the aim which under-pinned the *Neue Rheinische Zeitung – Politisch-Ökonomische Revue*, set up at the beginning of 1850. But the paper was dogged by problems from the beginning. It never attracted the readership once enjoyed by its predecessor, and by the end of the year the project had foundered.

The halting and half-hearted circulation of the *Revue* meant unan-ticipated penury for the Marx family. Evidence of their desperation was to be found in an angry letter of 20 May from Jenny to Joseph Weyde-meyer in Frankfurt. After apologizing for not being in touch before, she declared that 'circumstances' now 'compelled' her to take up her pen: 'I beg you to *send us as soon as possible any money that has come in or comes in* from the *Revue*. We are in *dire need of it*.'[4]

Like other radicals, Karl and Jenny were unwilling to accept that the revolution was over. The failure of the *Revue* was therefore blamed upon 'the bookseller's procrastination, or that of . . . those managing the busi-ness in Cologne', but especially upon 'the whole attitude of the democrats generally'. She reminded Weydemeyer that while her husband would not 'demean himself by passing around the democratic begging-bowl', he 'was entitled to expect of his friends', especially in Cologne, 'active and energetic concern for his *Revue*, especially among those who were aware of the sacrifices he had made for the *Rh.Ztg*'. Her husband had 'been all but crushed by the most trivial worries of bourgeois existence', while she, unable to afford a wet-nurse, struggled to cope with 'agonising pain in my breast and back' brought about by an infant who was 'always ailing and in severe pain by day and by night'.[5]

In these circumstances, the expense of living in Chelsea proved unsustainable and ended in eviction. On 24 March, as a result of their inability to pay the £5 rent arrears, their possessions were placed under distraint by two bailiffs.

> The following day we had to leave the house, it was cold, wet and overcast, my husband went to look for lodgings; on his mentioning 4 children no one wanted to take us in. At last a friend came to our aid, we paid and I hurriedly sold all my beds so as to settle with the apothecaries, bakers, butchers, and milkman who, their fears aroused by the scandal of the bailiffs, had suddenly besieged me with their bills. The beds I had sold were brought out onto the pavement and loaded on to a barrow – and then what happens? It was long after sunset, English law prohibits this, the landlord bears down on us with constables in attendance, declares we might have included some of his stuff with our own, that we are doing a flit and going abroad. In less than five minutes a crowd of two or three hundred people stands gaping outside our door, all the riff-raff of Chelsea. In go the beds again; they cannot be handed over to the purchaser until tomorrow morning after sunrise; having thus been enabled, by the sale of everything we possessed, to pay every farthing, I removed with my little darlings into the two little rooms we now occupy in the German Hotel, 1 Leicester Street, Leicester Square, where we were given a humane reception in return for £5.10 a week.[6]

But their stay there did not last long. According to Jenny 'one morning our worthy host refused to serve us our breakfast and we were forced to look for other lodgings'.[7] They had then moved to the Soho apartment, 28 Dean Street, in which they lived from December 1850 through to 1856. This was graphically described in a spy report in 1853. There were two rooms:

> The one looking out on the street is the living room, and the bedroom is at the back. In the whole apartment there is not one clean and solid piece of furniture. Everything is broken down, tattered and torn, with a half inch of dust over everything and the greatest disorder everywhere. In the middle of the living room there is a large old-fashioned table covered with an oilcloth, and on it there lie his [Karl's] manuscripts, books and newspapers, as well as the children's toys, and rags and tatters of his wife's sewing basket, several cups with broken rims, knives, forks, lamps,

an inkpot, tumblers, Dutch clay pipes, tobacco ash – in a word, everything
topsy-turvy, and all on the same table . . .[8]

In the years that followed, the imbalance between income and expenditure which had first led them to choose an expensive apartment in Chelsea
continued. On 6 January 1851, Karl wrote to Engels, asking for money by
return. 'My landlady is VERY POOR, this is the second week she has not
been paid, and she is dunning me with dreadful determination.' Engels
sent him £1. He was unable to send him the whole amount, but promised
the rest in early February.[9] Once again oppressed by debt in March 1851,
he asked Jenny to procure some money from his mother-in-law, but learnt
that the 'remainder of *Jenny's money*' had been sent to Mexico with her
brother Edgar. He had then written to his own mother threatening to
draw bills on her. But she had written back 'full of moral indignation',
addressing him 'in the most *insolent* terms' and 'declaring *positivement*
that she will protest any bill I draw on her'. He complained that he did not
have a farthing in the house, so that 'tradesmen's bills – butcher's, baker's
and so forth – keep mounting up'.[10] The problem seemed temporarily to
have been resolved by a post office order sent by Engels.[11] At the end of
July, Karl complained, 'I haven't written for a fortnight because during
such time as I haven't spent at the library, I've been harried from pillar to
post.' The promise to discount a bill for him had been put off from month
to month and had now been refused.[12] In October, he was pressed by the
county court to pay back the £5 which had been lent to him by Carl
Göhringer, a friend of Willich. Engels sent him £2 and advised him that
there was nothing to do except pay up.[13]

In 1852, although he had begun to work for the *Tribune* and had
added a third room to the apartment, the situation seemed even more
desperate. On 20 February, Karl wrote to Weydemeyer declaring that
he could not send his promised instalment of the *Eighteenth Brumaire*,
because 'for a week or more I have been so beset by money troubles
that I have not been able to pursue my studies at the Library, let alone
write articles'.[14] The situation got even worse in the following week. 'A
week ago I reached the pleasant point where I am unable to go out for
want of the coats I have in pawn, and can no longer eat meat for want
of credit.' He was afraid that this might at some point 'blow up into a
scandal'. The one hope was that Jenny's 'indestructible uncle' was ill.
'If the cur dies now I shall be out of this pickle.'[15]

Perhaps the lowest point came on 14 April, with the death of his one-year-old daughter, Franziska. He had not been thrilled by her arrival in the first place: 'My wife, alas,' he had written to Engels on 2 April 1851, 'has been delivered of a girl, and not a *garçon*. And, what is worse, she's very poorly.'[16] But he sounded more affected when he wrote to Engels on 14 April 1852, 'only a couple of lines to let you know that our little child died this morning at a quarter past one'. Engels wrote to tell Weydemeyer that Karl's youngest child had died 'the second already in London. As you can imagine, his wife is greatly afflicted by it.'[17] Jenny wrote that 'little Franziska had a severe bronchitis.

> For three days, she was between life and death. She suffered terribly. When she died we left her lifeless little body in the back room, went into the front room and made our beds on the floor. Our three living children lay down by us and we all wept for the little angel whose livid lifeless body was in the next room. Our beloved child's death occurred at the time of the hardest privations, our German friends being unable to help us just then . . . Anguish in my heart, I hurried to a French emigrant who lived not far away and used to come to see us, and begged him to help us in our terrible necessity. He immediately gave me two pounds with the most friendly sympathy. That money was used to pay for the coffin in which my child now rests in peace.[18]

On 8 September in the same year, Karl wrote to Engels:

> Your letter today found us in a state of great agitation . . . My wife is ill. Little Jenny is ill. Lenchen has some sort of nervous fever. I could not and cannot call the doctor because I have no money to buy medicine. For the past 8–10 days I have been feeding the FAMILY solely on bread and potatoes, but whether I shall be able to get hold of any today is doubtful . . . I have not written any articles for Dana because I didn't have a PENNY.[19]

The pattern was repeated in the following year. On 27 April, Jenny wrote to 'Mr Engels' telling him that she had already written 'to Hagen in Bonn, to Georg Jung, to Cluss, to my mother-in-law, to my sister in Berlin. Ghastly letters! And so far not a word from a single one of them . . . I cannot describe what things are like here.' Throughout August and through to October, there were repeated complaints about how shabby the family had become, how all had been pawned and how 'there hasn't been a sou in the house'.[20] In 1854–5 there was more of the same. In 1855, Karl wrote to Moritz Elsner of the Breslau-based *Neue Oder-Zeitung*, excusing himself for not writing in the previous week, explaining that he had been forced to leave London to avoid Jenny's Dr Freund, who had been pursuing him for the settlement of unpaid medical bills, dating back to the previous year.[21] He had first gone to stay in the house of Peter Imandt in Camberwell and then proceeded to Manchester, where he stayed with Engels through to December.

The chronic ill-health of Karl and Jenny was in large part the result of living in an overcrowded and ill-kept apartment situated in narrow and insanitary streets. But Karl's habits made things worse: 'When you enter Marx's room, smoke from the coal and fumes from the tobacco make your eyes water, so much that for a moment you seem to be groping about in a cavern, but gradually, as you grow accustomed to the fog, you can make out certain objects, which distinguish themselves from the surrounding haze. Everything is dirty and covered with dust, so that to sit down becomes a thoroughly dangerous business.'[22] Upon a family with a hereditary predisposition towards tubercular and respiratory illness the effects of such conditions were devastating. Three of the children died in Dean Street, two in infancy and one before the age of ten.[23] It was the death from 'convulsions' of the sickly one-year-old Guido, who, as Jenny told Weydemeyer, 'since coming into the world . . . never slept a whole night through', that led the family to move from 64 to 28 Dean Street.[24] But there was no significant improvement. Particularly sad was the case of the one little boy in the household, the eight-year-old Edgar, or 'Musch', as he was called. At the beginning of 1854, he showed 'the first symptoms of the incurable disease which was to lead to his death a year later'.[25] The following March, Karl reported to Engels that 'Musch has had a dangerous gastric fever which he has still not shaken off (this is the worst of all).'[26] For a couple of weeks it seemed as if the boy was getting better. But, on 16 March, Karl confessed that 'I do not believe that the good Musch is going to get over his illness . . . My wife once again altogether DOWN.'[27] On 27 March, Karl again reported that there were some signs of improvement, but could write no more than a few lines: 'I am dog-tired from the long night vigils, since I am Musch's nurse.'[28] But on 30 March he had become resigned to the worst: 'Latterly . . . the illness has assumed the character, hereditary in my family, of an abdominal consumption, and even the doctor seems to have given up hope.'[29] The end came a week later. 'Poor Musch is no more. Between 5 and 6 o'clock today, he fell asleep (in the literal sense) in my arms.'[30] In her memoirs, Jenny wrote, 'had we been able to give up our small unhealthy flat then [in 1854] and take the child to the seaside, we might have saved him. But what is done cannot be undone.'[31]

Karl's tendency to respiratory illness and a tubercular condition had been clearly noted when he was exempted from military service. From 1849 onwards he was afflicted by complaints of liver and gall. As Jenny told Lassalle in April 1858, Karl was incapable of writing to him at that time, because 'the liver complaint from which he was already suffering at the time – unfortunately it recurs every spring – had got so much worse that he has had to dose himself constantly'.[32] When Karl finally got round to writing to Lassalle, on 31 May, he explained:

> having been totally incapable of writing – not only IN A LITERARY, BUT IN THE LITERAL SENSE OF THE WORD – for several weeks, and striven in vain to rebel against my illness . . . In itself the illness wasn't dangerous – enlargement of the liver – but on this occasion the accompanying symptoms were particularly revolting; moreover in my family it has nasty implications in that it was the starting point of the illness which led to my father's death.[33]

Symptoms included headaches, eye inflammation, neuralgia, piles and rheumatic pains. Karl's irregular way of life made things worse. According to the 1852 spy report:

> He leads the existence of a real bohemian intellectual. Washing, grooming and changing his linen are things he does rarely, and he likes to get drunk. Though he is often idle for days on end, he will work day and night with tireless endurance, when he has a great deal of work to do. He has no fixed times for going to sleep and waking up. He often stays up all night, and then lies down fully clothed on the sofa at midday and sleeps till evening, untroubled by the comings and goings of the whole world . . .

Karl's eating habits, given his liver trouble, were also noxious. According to Blumenberg, he liked highly seasoned dishes, smoked fish, caviar and pickled cucumber together with Moselle wine, beer and liqueurs.[34]

Later in the 1850s, his work routine became more regular, but no more healthy. He continued to study or write *Tribune* articles in the day and write at night, pushing himself excessively from around 1857 in an effort to write up his political economy in response to the arrival of a fresh economic crisis. On 18 December, he told Engels, 'I am working enormously, as a rule until 4 o'clock in the morning', while he reported to Ferdinand Lassalle on 21 December, 'I am forced to fritter away . . . my days earning a living. [Only] the nights remain free for *real* work and that is disrupted by ill-health . . . The present commercial crisis', he explained, 'has impelled me to set to work seriously on my outline of political economy and also to prepare something on the present crisis.'[35]

Not surprisingly, his body was unable to cope with the strain. At the end of April 1858, he wrote to Engels:

> Never before have I had such a violent *attaque* of liver trouble and FOR SOME TIME there was a fear that it might be sclerosis of the liver. The doctor wanted me to travel but *d'abord* that was incompatible with the STATE OF FINANCE, and secondly I hoped from day to day to be able to start work again. The persistent urge to get down to work coupled with inability to do so helped aggravate my condition . . . Whenever I sit down and write for a couple of hours I have to lie quite fallow for a couple of days. I hope to heaven that this state of affairs comes to an end next week. It couldn't have happened at a more inconvenient time. Obviously I overdid my nocturnal labours last winter.[36]

In 1859, Karl suffered intermittently from liver trouble and in the first three months of 1860 was continuously ill. Around Christmas 1860, having helped Lenchen nurse Jenny through smallpox, he reported, 'last Wednesday, I got a cold and cough accompanied by a stabbing pain, so that not only coughing, but turning my carcass from one side to the other, caused me physical PAINS'. Given a 'hair-raising' doctor's bill, he decided to treat himself – 'no smoking, CASTOR OIL, drink only lemonade, eat little, no spirits whatever, stay at home'. But ten days later, he reported a 'relapse' and was back under medical treatment. The doctor recommended riding and a 'CHANGE OF AIR . . . Writing means that I have to stoop, which hurts, and so I keep putting it off. As you see, I am as tormented as Job, though not as God-fearing.'[37]

In 1863, Karl developed carbuncles on his feet, another symptom of his liver trouble. In November of that year, Jenny Marx wrote to Wilhelm Liebknecht in Berlin that for three weeks Karl had been

'*desperately ill*' with a carbuncle on his back. He had already been 'ailing for months', found it intensely difficult to work, 'smoked twice as
much as usual and took three times as many pills of various kinds'. He
developed a boil on his cheek, which he got rid of with 'the usual household remedies'. But once that was gone, another erupted on his back,
which could not be treated with 'poultices'. 'At last, when the swelling
was of the size of my fist and the whole of his back misshapen, I went
to [Dr] Allen.' While Lenchen held Karl, the doctor 'made a deep, deep
incision' from which blood poured out. Then he began to apply a round
of hot poultices, applied night and day, while 'at the same time, the
Doctor ordered 3–4 glasses of port and half a bottle of claret daily and
four times as much food as usual. The object was to restore the strength
he had lost.' Lenchen also fell ill from worry and exertion.[38] Karl supplemented this prescription with the daily addition of one and a half
quarts of 'the strongest London STOUT', and combated the pain with
large doses of opium.[39]

The liver problems thereafter did not leave him. On 30 November
1863, Karl's mother died, and he felt obliged to travel to Trier to settle
the question of his inheritance. Dr Allen gave him 'two enormous bottles of medicine' to take with him. After settling his affairs in Trier, he
went on to see his uncle, Lion Philips, in Zaltbommel. 'My uncle, a
splendid old BOY, applies my poultices and cataplasms with his own
hands, while my charming and witty cousin with the dangerously dark
eyes nurses and cossets me in exemplary fashion.'[40] But the trouble did
not go away and would afflict him almost uninterruptedly through
1864. 'In loathsome pain' and too sick to move on, he stayed in the
Philips household until the end of February.

Jenny's illnesses were both physical and psychological. Living in
Dean Street caused repeated bouts of bronchitis, which led her frequently to retire to bed. But she was also prone to what was referred to
as 'nervous excitement'. Her maladies were as much the product of
depression or despair as of physical illness. Remedies again generally
involved the use of alcohol. On 15 July 1852, Karl reported to Engels
that Jenny had a cough and was losing weight. The doctor had in addition to medicine prescribed 'plenty of porter'.[41] But things did not
improve. On 18 September, Karl reported, 'Physically, my wife is lower
than ever before, i.e. sheer debility. On doctor's orders she has been
taking a spoonful of brandy every hour for the past 3 days. There is

however some improvement inasmuch as she at least got up today.'[42] In 1854, Jenny had again become 'very unwell' probably as a result of night vigils and nursing the ailing Musch. On this occasion, she refused to consult the doctor: 'she is dosing herself – on the pretext that two years ago when she was similarly indisposed, Freund's medicines only made her worse'.[43] In the winter of 1860, Jenny went down with small-pox, despite, as Karl wrote, being vaccinated twice. 'For many weeks my wife had been in an exceptionally nervous state owing to our many TROUBLES and was thus more liable to CATCH the contagion in an omnibus, shop or the like.' Once again, alcohol seems to have been the main remedy. 'The doctor has allowed my wife claret, taken in small doses, as she is exceptionally weak', while at the beginning of December the doctor cancelled the claret, and prescribed port instead.[44]

Jenny's 'nervous state' was a constant concern. In June 1850, Karl apologized to Weydemeyer for his wife's 'agitated letters. She is nursing her child [Guido], and our situation here is so extraordinarily wretched that an outburst of impatience is excusable.'[45] In November, after Guido died, Karl wrote to Engels that 'she's in a really dangerous state of exci-tation and exhaustion'.[46] A few months later, on 31 March, after the birth of another child, Franziska, Karl wrote that, though the confine-ment had been an easy one, 'she is now very ill in bed, the causes being domestic [bürgerlich] rather than physical'.[47]

Perhaps this referred to the awkward and potentially explosive situ-ation in the Dean Street apartment and the toll it took upon Karl and Jenny's relationship. 'In the early summer 1851', Jenny wrote in her 'Short Sketch', 'an event occurred which I do not wish to relate here in detail, although it greatly contributed to increase our worries, both personal and others.'[48] This was the birth of Lenchen's son, Henry Frederick Demuth, later known as Freddy, on 23 June 1851 at 28 Dean Street.[49] There seems little doubt that Karl was the unacknowledged father. The births of Freddy and Franziska were within three months of each other. The atmosphere in a tiny two-room flat occupied by two heavily pregnant women – both with children sired by him – can only be imagined. Freddy was put out to nurse and subsequently brought up in East London by working-class foster parents.[50]

In the surviving correspondence, there are no obvious references to this situation. The family were led to believe that Engels was the father. After Engels' death, Karl's daughter Laura went carefully through his correspondence to remove any material which could be damaging or hurtful to him or to Marx. But a few oblique remarks would appear to hint at the situation. Around the time that Jenny gave birth to Franziska, Karl wrote to Engels about a '*mystère*', which he was about to reveal, but was then called away to help nurse his wife. Two days later, he stated that he would not write about the *mystère* since he would be coming to see him at the end of the month – 'I must get away from here for a week.'[51] The arrival of Lenchen's baby, whatever was said to allay suspicions, clearly increased tensions within the household. At the end of July, Karl wrote to Engels, apologizing for the slow progress of his political economy:

> I should have finished at the library long ago. But there have been too many interruptions and disturbances and at home everything is always in a state of siege. For nights on end, I am set on edge and infuriated by floods of tears. So I cannot of course do very much. I feel sorry for my wife. The main burden falls on her and, *au fond* [deep down], she is right. *Il faut que l'industrie soit plus productive que le mariage.* For all that, you must remember that by nature I am *très peu endurant* [not very patient] and even *quelque peu dur* [a little rough], so from time to time I lose my equanimity.[52]

Two days later, oppressed both by lack of resources and by gossip about the apartment and its two resident mothers, Karl wrote to Weydemeyer in resigned despair. 'As you can imagine, my circumstances are very dismal. My wife will go under if things continue like this much longer'; not only 'the constant worries', but on top of that 'the infamies of my opponents . . . casting suspicions on my civil character'. The word in the street was that Marx was '*perdu*', while 'My wife, who is poorly and caught up from morning till night in the most disagreeable of domestic quandaries, and whose nervous system is impaired, is not revived by the exhalations from the pestiferous democratic cloaca daily administered to her by stupid tell-tales.'[53]

Jenny was an intelligent woman. It is hard to believe that she was taken in by the face-saving formula which attributed paternity to Engels. But, whatever the reasoning, it is clear that the underlying relationship between Karl and Jenny remained strong enough, while Lenchen's help continued to be seen as indispensable.[54] In Karl's case, some anxiety was perhaps revealed in an over-eagerness to reassure, suggested by the effusive and hyper-romantic imagery in some of the subsequent letters to Jenny.[55] In Jenny's case, the tension may have emerged in her frequent changes of mood and tendency to retire to bed. But during these years she seems fully to have shared her husband's politics and wholly to have accepted his right to lead. In particular, she enjoyed acting as Karl's secretary, making neat copies of his illegible scripts. She appears to have done this job particularly from the time of the Cologne treason trial. At first that role was played by Karl's enthusiastic but incompetent admirer Wilhelm Pieper. But soon Jenny took over this secretarial role. In her 'Short Sketch', she stated that 'the memory of the days I spent in his little study copying his scrawly articles is among the happiest of my life'.[56]

Whatever the tensions within the household, surviving accounts also suggest a strong and happy family life. According to 'the Prussian spy', writing in 1852, 'as a husband and father, Marx, in spite of his wild and reckless character, is the gentlest and mildest of men'. A particular friendship developed between the Marx family and Wilhelm Liebknecht and his wife.[57] When Jenny went down with smallpox in the autumn of 1860, the children were looked after by the Liebknechts. Wilhelm Liebknecht in his later recollections offered a vivid account of Sunday family expeditions to Hampstead Heath during the time that the Marx family lived in Soho:

> Those walks to Hampstead Heath! Were I to live to a thousand I would never forget them . . . The children used to speak about it the whole week and even the adults young and old used to look forward to it. The journey there was a treat in itself.
>
> The walk took place as follows. I generally led the way with the two girls, entertaining them with stories or acrobatics or picking wild flowers, which were more abundant then than now. Behind us came a few friends and then the main body: Marx and his wife and one of the Sunday visitors who was deserving of special consideration. In the rear came Lenchen and the hungriest of our party, who helped her carry the hamper.
>
> When we arrived at the Heath we first of all chose a place to pitch our tent, taking tea and beer facilities into consideration as much as possible.
>
> Once food and drink had been partaken of, both sexes went in search of the most comfortable place to lie or sit. Then those who did not prefer a nap got out the Sunday papers bought on the way and spoke about politics. The children soon found playmates and played hide-and-seek among the gorse bushes.[58]

2. AT THE FOOT OF THE HAMPSTEAD HILLS

In the mid-1850s, there was an improvement in the family's situation. Jenny proudly recorded that from 1853 Karl gained a regular income from writing his two articles a week for the *New-York Daily Tribune*. 'This steady income enabled us to pay off our old debts to a certain extent and to live a less anxious life . . . Christmas that year was the first merry feast we celebrated in London.'[59]

Between August 1851 and September 1852, Karl supposedly contributed an extensive account of the Revolution in Germany – eighteen articles on 'Revolution and Counter-Revolution in Germany'. But these were in fact written by Engels.[60] In 1852 Charles Dana asked Karl to contribute articles which threw light on 'the coming revolutionary crisis'. Karl's first article appeared in August 1852. His English was not yet proficient. So it was written in German and translated by Engels. But by February 1853 Karl was able to write in English. Dana was impressed by the articles and in 1853 increased Karl's payment from £1 to £2 per article.

Dana exercised his editor's prerogative, sometimes incorporating articles into editorials, sometimes sub-editing to ensure that articles were in accord with the overall editorial line. Occasionally, his articles were signed, other times not. But in 1855 it was agreed that all his pieces should remain unsigned.

Demand for Karl's (and Engels') articles fluctuated with American interest in Europe. In 1853 and 1854, the *Tribune* published around eighty of his articles. This amounted to an income of £80 in 1853 and £160 in 1854. While the amount dipped in 1855–6 – with Dana only publishing forty articles in 1855, and twenty-four in 1856 – the shortfall was in large part filled by earnings of £50 from the *Neue Oder-Zeitung*. But in 1857 Dana agreed to pay Karl for one article per week, irrespective of whether it was printed.[61]

The second way in which the fortunes of the Marx family improved was the result of Engels' growing prosperity. Engels had started back in Manchester at a salary of £100 per year, together with £200 as an 'expenses and entertainment' allowance. In the mid-1850s, he was in addition accorded a 5 per cent profit share, rising to 7.5 per cent by 1860. In 1856, this profit share amounted to £408, by 1860 £978. This meant that his earnings amounted to well over £1,000 per year in 1860, or over £110,000 per year in today's money.[62] In 1860 also, Engels' father died, enabling Friedrich to make possible freer disposal of his funds. The Marx family could therefore rely upon the ever more regular and generous support derived from Engels' position in the cotton thread enterprise of Ermen and Engels.

Finally, the family benefited from two bequests in 1856. In May, Jenny received an inheritance of £150 from a ninety-year-old uncle, and following her mother's death in Trier a further £120 in September.[63] As a result, on 29 September 1856, the family moved from Dean Street to 9 Grafton Terrace, Haverstock Hill, Kentish Town. Engels, who had helped pay for some of the furnishings for the house, wrote to Jenny, 'you really are right out in the country, at the foot of the Hampstead Hills ... in a highly romantic district'. The reality was more prosaic. Kentish Town, still semi-rural in the 1840s, thanks to railway development was rapidly built over in the 1850s and 1860s. According to Jenny, the new house was difficult to get to: 'There was no smooth road leading to it. Building was going on all around, one had to pick one's way over heaps of rubbish and in rainy weather the sticky red soil caked to one's boots so that it was after a tiring struggle and with heavy feet that one reached our house.'[64]

Grafton Terrace with eight small rooms on four floors was 'a princely dwelling compared with the holes we lived in before'.[65] But despite the apparent increase in comfort and resources, illness, debt and financial penury soon returned. By December 1856, Jenny was again unwell. Karl reported that she was 'still dosing herself continually' and that the house was always in 'such disarray that it is difficult for me to settle down and write'. In January 1857, he wrote to Engels:

> So here I am without any prospects and with growing domestic liabilities, completely stranded in a house into which I have put what little cash I possessed and where it is impossible to scrape along from day to day as we did in Dean Street. I am utterly at a loss what to do, being, indeed, in a more desperate situation than 5 years ago. I thought I had tasted the bitterest dregs of life. *Mais non!* And the worst of it is that this is no mere passing crisis. I cannot see how I am to extricate myself.[66]

Jenny also was ill at ease in adjusting to the new house. 'It was a long time before I could get used to the complete solitude ... I often missed the long walks I had been in the habit of making in the crowded West End Streets, the meetings, the clubs and our favourite public house and homely conversations which had so often helped me to forget the worries of life for a time.'[67]

Later in the year, in a show of desperation, Karl had sent a detailed letter to Engels itemizing his income and expenditure. It was all to demonstrate that their situation was 'absolutely untenable'. He argued that his 'abstract thinking' was no longer a match for 'domestic miseries', that 'the general unpleasantness has made a nervous wreck of my wife'; Dr Allen had not ruled out 'brain fever or something of the sort unless she is sent to a seaside resort for a longish stay'. He alleged that 'I for my part wouldn't care a damn about living in Whitechapel', provided he could secure peace to get on with his work, even if it meant a 'wholly working-class lodging', getting rid of the maids and living on potatoes. But in view of his wife's 'condition', this would be impossible. 'The SHOW of RESPECTABILITY which has so far been kept up has been the only means of avoiding a collapse.'[68] Engels did what he could to stave off disaster. But at the end of the year the situation was again bad. On 11 December 1858, Karl complained that 'in this house things look MORE DREARY AND DESOLATE THAN EVER'. Jenny was beset by debts and 'running errands to the pawnshop in town ... My wife is quite right', Karl continued, 'when she says that, after all the *misère* she has had to go through, the revolution will only make things worse and afford her the gratification of seeing all the humbugs from here once again celebrating their victories over there. Women are like that.'[69]

Although in the 1860s material circumstances changed for the Marx family and its reliance upon the accoutrements of a middle-class existence – private schools, piano lessons, better clothes, two servants – increased, the basic disproportion between income and expenditure persisted. The early 1860s were difficult years. For, while Engels' financial support gradually increased, other and more independent sources of income fell away. In April 1857, Dana had asked Karl to contribute to the *New American Cyclopaedia*. He counted on Karl 'to furnish the military articles' at $2 a page, and stressed that entries on politics, religion and philosophy should have 'no party tendency whatever'.[70] This meant that most of the sixty-seven entries published in the *Cyclopaedia* were written by Engels, who contributed fifty-one items. It is not clear why the agreement broke down, but no further contributions were published after 1860.

Contributions to the *Tribune* similarly came to an end. Back in 1857, Dana had written to Karl that 'European affairs dull enough in themselves, have been quite crowded out of our attention by the superior interest and moment of events in this country'. At the beginning of the 1860s, with the onset of the American Civil War, and pressure from the proprietor, Horace Greeley, for Karl's dismissal, Dana asked that the publication of Karl's articles be suspended for several months. Finally, in March 1862, Dana wrote announcing his own imminent withdrawal from the *Tribune* and requesting that Karl not send further contributions.[71]

Jenny's ups and downs also continued. In December 1861, Karl reported to Engels that his wife was 'in a dangerous nervous condition' and that for a few days Dr Allen had been 'most alarmed'.[72] Ten days later, when he informed Jenny of an attempted loan negotiation, it brought on 'a kind of paroxysm'.[73] He told Engels that he didn't yet know 'how I am to weather this crisis'. At the end of February 1862, his seventeen-year-old daughter Jenny, who was ill and old enough 'to feel the full strain and also the stigma of our circumstances', had made enquiries about going on the stage. 'Taken all in all,' he told Engels, 'leading such a dog's life is hardly WORTH WHILE'. And a few months later, the situation had hardly changed. The family were awaiting the arrival of wine from Engels: 'the house is otherwise very forlorn'.[74] A month later, Karl apologized for 'pouring out my *misère*', but '*que faire?* Every day my wife says she wishes she and the children were safely in their graves, and I really cannot blame her, for the humiliations, torments and alarums that one has to go through in such a situation are indeed indescribable.'[75] At the end of the year, one misfortune followed another. With creditors clamouring for repayment, Jenny went on a fund-raising trip to Paris, only to find that the would-be donor had just suffered a stroke. During her absence, Lenchen's sister, Anna, who had become a second servant in the household, died of a heart attack. On 7 January 1863, Engels wrote to say that his partner, Mary, had just died. 'The poor girl loved me with all her heart.' Karl was clearly too preoccupied to respond to the gravity of the event. On 8 January, after a cursory reference to how 'good-natured, witty and closely attached to you' she was, he went on to bemoan his own 'ill-luck'. Everything was in pawn; the children could not go out because they lacked shoes and clothes. He excused his self-absorption by claiming it was 'a homeopathic remedy' and presumed to comfort Engels with the thought that 'instead of Mary, ought it not to have been my mother [*who should have died*], who is in any case a prey to physical ailments and has had her fair share of life . . . ?' He then had second thoughts: 'you can see what strange notions come into the heads of "civilised men" under the pressure of certain circumstances'.[76]

Engels was deeply hurt by 'the frosty view' that Karl had taken of his 'misfortune', even 'his friends, including philistine acquaintances', had 'given me proof of greater sympathy and friendship than I could have looked for'. He explained that he was not in a financial position to 'raise the largish sum of which you speak' and advised him to explore the possibilities of loans, life assurance or a limited bill which he would be prepared to sign; failing that, he should approach his uncle, Lion Philips, in Holland.[77] About ten days later, Karl made a not entirely convincing effort to excuse his behaviour by attributing it to momentary rage against his wife, and her refusal to accept the impossibility of indefinitely 'keeping up false appearances'. He proposed a declaration of bankruptcy; the two elder children might become governesses, Lenchen would enter service elsewhere, while he and Jenny would go to a 'CITY MODEL LODGING HOUSE'.[78] Perhaps that letter was designed to frighten rather than announce a serious declaration of intent. In any event, Engels was relieved to find that in losing Mary he had not also lost his 'oldest and best friend'. Even so, 'that letter, I tell you, obsessed me for a whole week'.[79]

From March 1863, the financial pressure on the Marx family eased thanks to the efforts of Engels and Ernst Dronke, and through much of August Karl was able to send the family to holiday in Ramsgate. On 30 November, Karl's mother, Henriette, died. He asked Engels for money to travel to Trier and wind up the estate, adding the somewhat cryptic comment: 'I myself have already had one foot in the grave. Circumstances being what they were, I, presumably, was needed more than my mater.'[80] Afflicted once more by liver trouble, Karl stayed with his uncle in Zaltbommel and did not return to London until the end of February. In May 1864, Wilhelm Wolff – 'Lupus' – Karl's close friend, died in Manchester, and Karl was the main beneficiary of his will.[81] Together with what he had inherited from his mother, Karl therefore received bequests of around £1,500 (around £170,000 in today's terms).

But even with this change of fortune, the habits of the Marx family did not change. On returning from Holland, the family moved before the end of March into 1 Modena Villas, in Maitland Park. The three-year lease cost £65 per year plus rates of £4-8 shillings: an 80 per cent increase over the expenses of Grafton Terrace. Jenny spent £500 on furniture and fittings, including a 'sturdy CARVING KNIFE AND FORK' for Engels.[82] But by a year later the familiar pattern had reasserted itself. On 31 July 1865, Karl wrote to Engels, explaining his prolonged silence:

> For two months I have been living solely on the pawnshop which means that a queue of creditors has been hammering on my door, becoming more and more unendurable every day. This FACT won't come as any surprise to you when you consider: 1. that I have been unable to earn a FARTHING the whole time and 2. that merely paying off *the debts* and furnishing the house cost me something like £500 . . . I myself found it unbelievable how the money disappeared.[83]

How was this recurrent descent into poverty to be explained? Londoners were accustomed to irregular and uncertain incomes. Henry Mayhew in the 1850s concluded that:

> out of four million five hundred thousand people who have to depend on their industry for the livelihood of themselves and families, there is . . . barely sufficient work for the *regular* employment of half of our labourers, so that only 1,500,000 are fully and constantly employed, while 1,500,000 more are employed only half their time, and the remaining 1,500,000 wholly unemployed, obtaining a day's work *occasionally* by the displacement of some of the others.[84]

Nor was this solely a problem for manual labour and the working classes; one need only think of Captain Hawdon or 'Nemo' of *Bleak House*, a former army officer, who made a living as a casual law-writer.

But in the case of the Marx family, this was not poverty in the ordinary sense of the word. In 1862, Lassalle's well-meant suggestion that one of Karl's daughters might take paid work with Countess von Hatzfeldt, his partner, was regarded as an unspeakable disregard of their social status and occasioned some of Karl's ugliest racist abuse.[85] 'Just imagine! This fellow, knowing about the American affair, etc. [the loss of earnings at the *Tribune*], and hence about the state of crisis I'm in, had the insolence to ask me whether I would be willing to hand over one of my daughters to *la* Hatzfeldt as a "companion".' One justification of their behaviour was to suggest that it was governed by the need to secure the future of the children. In July 1865, Karl admitted, 'It is true my house is beyond my means, and we have, moreover, lived better this year than was the case before. But it is the only way for the children to establish themselves socially with a view to securing their future.' He believed that Engels would agree with him that 'even from a merely commercial point of view, to run a purely proletarian household would not be appropriate in the circumstances, although that would be quite all right, if my wife and I were by ourselves or if the girls were boys'.[86]

The last point may be doubted. There had never been any question of running a 'purely proletarian household'. When Jenny had originally arrived in London, the family had rented a flat in Chelsea, twice as expensive as the later cost of Grafton Terrace. Similarly in 1854, despite the debts, a considerable amount was spent on a new outfit for Jenny when she would be visiting her mother, 'since she could naturally not arrive in Trier looking shabby'.[87] It also emerged at the time of the death of Lenchen's half-sister, Marianne, that the family had been employing two servants during the previous five years. Nor was it solely Jenny who insisted upon living out the appearance, if not always the reality, of a bourgeois standard of life. According to Werner Blumenberg, Karl liked to give visitors, especially foreigners, the impression that he was living in comfortable bourgeois circumstances.[88] To his Dutch relatives, and in particular his uncle, Lion Philips, he liked to pretend that despite his political beliefs he was not averse to the occasional shrewd flutter on the stock market. In the summer of 1864, rather than admitting to his receipt of the Wilhelm Wolff legacy, he claimed to have made a £400 killing in American funds and English stocks.[89]

But in Karl's case it was not solely an insistence upon gentility and the need to keep up appearances which explained his behaviour. There was also the respect due to him even during the darkest years in Soho as the head of a 'party'. David McLellan has calculated that in the year previous to his employment on the *Tribune*, Karl received £150 in gifts (the equivalent, he estimates, of the income of a lower-middle-class family) and that amount only included sums specifically mentioned; it probably amounted to considerably more.[90] Gifts and support came not only from Engels, but from his Cologne friends Daniels and Weerth, from Lassalle, and from one of Jenny's cousins and, at least during her time in Chelsea, from her mother, Caroline.

The end of the 1848 Revolution and the failure of another to break out again left Karl frustrated and angered. His testiness was sharpened by a sense of unrecognized notability. He was incensed by the pretensions of 'the Great Men of the Exile' – Mazzini, Kossuth, Ledru-Rollin – and the plaudits they received, but particularly irritated by his fellow countrymen Gottfried Kinkel, Karl Heinzen or Arnold Ruge, against whom he poured forth all his bile. After 1852, Karl had withdrawn from any organized grouping, but 'the party', as he conceived it, remained, and would continue to play its privileged role in the unfolding historical drama. By 'the party' he did not mean the Communist League. 'The "League", like the *société des saisons* in Paris and a hundred other societies, was simply an episode in the history of a party that is everywhere springing up naturally out of the soil of modern society.'[91] It was 'the party' in the world-historical sense that remained. In more mundane terms, it was a group – probably no more than a dozen or two – held together by deference to Karl, by ties of friendship and political solidarity, and by a commitment to keep the Marx family financially afloat.

3. BONAPARTE AND BONAPARTISM

The Revolution had been brought to an end by the return of economic prosperity. This had been the verdict of the final double number of the *Neue Rheinische Zeitung – Politisch-Ökonomische Revue*, which had appeared in November 1850. But a year later, what remained to be explained was why the revolution in France had come to such a grotesque end. Its final act did not consist in the renewed polarization of opposing forces – of a Parisian proletariat, now recovered from the defeat of June, facing a party of order, now harnessing the combined strengths of Orléanists, Legitimists and conservative republicans. Instead there had been the triumph of an imposter, Louis-Napoléon, apparently able to soar above the predictable path of the class struggle. What needed to be explained, therefore, was 'how the class struggle in France created circumstances and relationships that made it possible for a grotesque mediocrity to play a hero's part'. This was the theme of the series of essays written between December 1851 and March 1852, detailing the lead-up to Bonaparte's coup d'état.

Like other writers of the time, notably Victor Hugo, Karl was struck by the ridiculous aspects of the contrast between the uncle (Napoléon I) and the nephew, Louis Bonaparte. As a way of underlining the point, Engels suggested a comparison between Bonaparte's coup of 2 December 1851 and Napoléon's original 'Eighteenth Brumaire' seizure of power in 1799. The day after the coup, he wrote to Karl, recalling Hegel's idea that World Spirit caused 'everything to be re-enacted twice over, once as grand tragedy and the second time as rotten farce'. Karl took over the idea; hence the title of the text, *The Eighteenth Brumaire of Louis Bonaparte*.[92]

This was a more finished and considered document than *Class Struggles*. The bulk of the text consisted of a detailed blow-by-blow account of the conflict between Bonaparte and the National Assembly. Bonaparte had been elected President of France on the basis of manhood suffrage by a massive majority on 10 December 1848. The two successive forms of the National Assembly had also been elected on the basis of universal manhood suffrage. The first, the 'Constituent National Assembly', had been the product of the period of the constitution of the Republic, which ran from 4 May 1848 to 28 May 1849. The second, the constitutional republic, or the 'Legislative National Assembly', covered the period from 28 May 1849 to 2 December 1851, the moment of Bonaparte's coup d'état.

The famous opening lines, which depicted the contrast between the stories of the two Napoléons as that between tragedy and farce made for an arresting beginning. But in other respects the treatment of the mid-century crisis as a form of comedy was inappropriate. It missed what was important in the sequence of events: above all, the emergence of a novel form of democratic politics resulting from the direct participation of 'the people' (or at least, adult males) in the electoral process. The creation of a constitution, based not only upon manhood suffrage in the election of the National Assembly, but also (following the example of the United States) in the election of an independent presidential executive, wholly changed the form and content of French politics. In place of 'the bourgeois republic' anticipated by the political class, an untried electorate chose an outsider, whose power and legitimacy did not depend upon the National Assembly, but directly upon the ballot. Furthermore, the new constitutional arrangements developed by the Assembly required both that the President should serve a four-year term and that he should not be eligible for re-election when his current term came to an end.

Bonaparte was adroit in exploiting the possibilities of his new position. The February Republic had been experienced by conservative France as a frightening shock; its social-democratic rhetoric seemed to justify all the fears about the spectre of communism which had been endlessly reiterated during the July Monarchy, and had apparently been confirmed by the June Insurrection in Paris. The elections in May 1848 had produced a generally moderate Assembly, but one divided between Legitimists, Orléanists and conservative republicans. As Karl emphasized, it was only the existence of the 'parliamentary republic' which enabled the supporters of the rival royal houses to combine in the 'Party of Order'. However, the situation remained unstable. When the threat from the social-democrat left – *La Montagne* – looked imminent, pressure for unity within the Party of Order increased. When it receded, the Party tended to break down into its component parts. To the outside world, these tensions and rivalries looked either tiresome or dangerous. The Party of Order in the National Assembly also forfeited support by imposing substantial restrictions upon the right to vote.[93]

As President, Bonaparte possessed privileged access both to the army and to the large number of central and local government officials, which had grown under the French absolutist monarchy and Napoléon. In addition, he possessed both considerable executive power and ample ideological space in which to manoeuvre. Bonaparte's innovation was to accept popular sovereignty and to restore universal suffrage – hitherto, the nightmare of all conservatives – but to set them within a strongly conservative and nationalist framework. He appealed over the heads of the National Assembly to all classes – to the middle classes as much as to the peasantry, requiring order and tranquillity, and to the working classes through his restoration of universal suffrage and his vague promise to address the social question.[94] The idea that not only representative government, but also political democracy, could be appropriated for the populist politics of the right was wholly new. It was one of the ways in which 1848, far from signifying farcical or comic repetition, represented a huge innovation in nineteenth-century politics.

Karl's hostility towards political democracy and universal suffrage was in no way lessened by the experience of 1848. In *Class Struggles*, he had rejoiced that 'universal suffrage did not possess the magic power which republicans of the old school had ascribed to it'. Its one great merit had been in 'unchaining the class struggle', of taking away from the middle classes 'their illusions' and from all sections of the 'exploiting class' their 'deceptive mask'.[95] His position remained unchanged in *Eighteenth Brumaire*. After referring to the 'Holy Grail of Universal Suffrage', he wrote that 'universal suffrage seems to have survived only for a moment in order that with its head, it may make its last will and testament before the eyes of all the world and declare in the name of the people itself: all that comes to birth is fit for overthrow, as nothing worth'.[96]

In place of the democrats' view that the whole period of the Constituent and Legislative Assemblies could be considered a 'simple struggle between republicans and royalists', Karl attempted to present the sequence of events as the result of class struggle or the contradictory relationship between forces and relations of production. The results were mixed. Looked at more closely, Karl contended, 'the superficial appearance, which veils the *class struggle* and the peculiar physiognomy of this period, disappears'. The clearest example was the conflict between the Legitimists and the Orléanists. What divided the 'lily and the tricolour' was 'not any so-called principles, it was their material conditions of existence, two different kinds of property, it was the old contrast between town and country, the rivalry between capital and landed property ... Upon the different forms of property,' he continued, 'upon the social conditions of existence, rises an entire superstructure of different and distinctly formed sentiments, illusions, modes of thought and views of life. The entire class creates and forms them out of its material foundations and out of the corresponding social relations.'[97]

This was not an especially controversial claim for, as Karl himself acknowledged, the depiction of the relationship between bourgeoisie and aristocracy as a form of class struggle between town and country had been common to historians since the work of Guizot, Thierry, Thiers and others in the 1820s.[98] But why should one section of the bourgeoisie support a republic rather than a dynastic party? Karl had no 'materialist' interpretation to offer, only a tautology: 'it was not a faction of the bourgeoisie held together by great common interests and marked off by specific conditions of production. It was a clique of republican-minded bourgeois writers, lawyers, officers and officials.'[99] The proletariat was not discussed since it had supposedly been put out of action by the repression of the June Insurrection. In the case of 'petit bourgeois' democrats and republicans, it was claimed that this group did not wish 'to enforce an egoistic class interest' but tended to associate the special conditions of their own emancipation with the general conditions for the emancipation of society. Their main concern was to harmonize the interests of labour and capital. Within the term 'petty bourgeoisie', strongly differing occupational categories were combined – on the one hand democratic writers, on the other shop-keepers, for example. But in a brave attempt to suggest and explain their shared position, it was argued that, 'In their education and indi-vidual position, they may be as far apart ... as heaven and earth. What makes them representatives of the petty bourgeoisie is the fact that in their minds they do not get beyond the limits which the latter do not get beyond in life.'[100] Finally, in the case of the bourgeoisie itself, the difficulty – it was suggested – was that it could no longer conceal its rule beneath the crown, as it had done during the July Monarchy. The Revolution created the form in which bourgeois rule, combined within the Party of Order, was plainly revealed. 'The revolution had first created the form in which the rule of the bourgeois class received its broadest, most general and ultimate expression and could therefore also be overthrown, without being able to rise again.' 'Out of enthusi-asm for its purse, it [the bourgeoisie] rebelled against its own politicians and men of letters.'[101]

In attempting to explain why France seemed to have escaped 'the despotism of a class only to fall back beneath the despotism of an indi-vidual, and what is more, beneath the authority of an individual without authority', Karl pinpointed two putative social groups.[102] The first was the peasantry, of whom Karl claimed that 'the identity of their interests begets no community, no national bond'. They were like pota-toes in 'a sack of potatoes'. They were 'incapable of enforcing their class interests in their own name ... They cannot represent themselves, they must be represented. Their representative must at the same time appear as their master, as an authority over them, as an unlimited governmental power that protects them against other classes ... The political influence of the small-holding peasants therefore finds its final expression in the executive power subordinating society to itself.'[103]

What was omitted from this sociologically ingenious account was firstly the fact that Bonaparte's electoral victory in 1848 owed as much to Paris and the towns as it did to the countryside.[104] Secondly, in an important qualification, Karl conceded that 'the Bonaparte dynasty represents not the revolutionary, but the conservative peasant'; not 'the enlightenment, but the superstition of the peasant'.[105] He could hardly do otherwise in a situation in which the one major rebellion against Bonaparte's 1851 coup d'état was predominantly a rebellion of peasants and of small-town France.

In Karl's account, the other major promoter of the Bonapartist cause was the so-called *Lumpenproletariat*. This was a claim very much of its time. In the first half of the nineteenth century, anxiety about the size and anonymity of large cities took the shape of a frequently expressed fear of the uncertain and invisible boundaries between poverty and criminality; or, in the language of the day, between *la classe laborieuse* and *la classe dangereuse*. By the 1840s, these preoccupations had produced a large and popular literary genre ranging from Dickens's *Oliver Twist* to Eugène Sue's *Les Mystères de Paris* and Henry Mayhew's *London Labour and the London Poor*.

Karl appears to have subscribed to this urban myth, and his description of the components of this 'class' was typical:

> Alongside decayed *roués* with dubious means of subsistence and of dubious origin, alongside ruined and adventurous offshoots of the bourgeoisie, were vagabonds, discharged soldiers, discharged jailbirds, escaped galley slaves, rogues, mountebanks, *lazzaroni*, pickpockets, tricksters, gamblers, *maquereaus*, brothel keepers, porters, *literati*, organ-grinders, rag-pickers, knife-grinders, tinkers, beggars – in short, the whole indefinite, disintegrated mass, thrown hither and thither, which the French term *la bohème*.[106]

Like others, Karl believed this group capable of conspiracy. In his account, the Paris *Lumpenproletariat* was organized into 'secret sections' and was at the behest of Bonaparte. 'This Bonaparte, who constitutes himself *chief of the lumpenproletariat*,[107] who here alone 'rediscovers in mass form the interests which he personally pursues, who recognises in this scum, offal, refuse of all classes the only class upon which he can base himself unconditionally, is the real Bonaparte'.[108]

So far as this melodrama touched upon a social reality, it referred to the extent of marginalization and underemployment found not just among the labouring poor, but in every class from the illegitimate progeny of the aristocracy through the discharged military and bankrupt businessmen down to Joe, the orphan crossing-sweeper described in Dickens's *Bleak House*. A similar picture was conjured up by Mayhew in his description of the London docks in the 1850s:

> Those who are unable to live by the occupation to which they have been educated, can obtain a living there without any previous training. Hence we find men of every calling labouring at the docks. There are decayed and bankrupt master-butchers, master-bakers, publicans, grocers, old soldiers, old sailors, Polish refugees, broken-down gentlemen, discharged lawyers' clerks, suspended government clerks, almsmen, pensioners, servants, thieves – indeed, every one who wants a loaf, and is willing to work for it.[109]

But there was no obvious similarity between the 10,000 'rogues' or the members of the so-called 'Society of 10 December', described in the *Eighteenth Brumaire*, and the Mobile Guard, also allegedly lumpenproletarians, who were described in *Class Struggles in France*. No doubt Bonaparte's following included its proportion of adventurers of different kinds, but to describe this assortment of individuals as a 'class' was far-fetched.

Because of Karl's insistence upon depicting Bonaparte's triumph in class terms, the main point seems to have been missed. As Karl himself realized, 'Bonaparte would like to appear as the patriarchal benefactor of all classes.' He managed to present himself both as a friend of the middle class and as a protector of the peasants against the threat of the bourgeoisie. By restoring manhood suffrage, which the Party of Order in the National Assembly had abolished, he could also present himself as a friend of the working class. He practised what would later be called populism. It was not so much 'enthusiasm for its purse' as a generalized fear of anarchy and the threat of socialist triumph in the elections of 1852 that enabled him to appeal to all classes as the friend of order and strong executive government.

Both at the beginning and at the end of the text, Karl drew upon

Benjamin Constant to place Bonaparte in a larger frame. Constant had written in the first two decades of the nineteenth century about the revolution of 1789–1814, which 'draped itself alternately as the Roman Republic and the Roman Empire'. Karl drew upon Constant's criticism of the Jacobins' confusion of ancient and modern liberty. With modern commercial society, Constant maintained, came a corresponding theory of liberty. Commerce and peace had replaced the ancient reliance upon plunder, slavery and war. How then was it possible that the supposedly peaceful imperatives of commercial society – '*doux commerce*', as its eighteenth-century admirers had called it – could throw up a despot and a warrior like Napoléon? Constant declared that 'the prolonged practice of despotism is impossible today', that despotism like usurpation and conquest was 'an anachronism'.[110]

Karl did not attack Louis-Napoléon Bonaparte for his warrior role as Constant had done, since the emperor had no military reputation to defend. But in emphasizing his relative detachment from the main classes of civil society and his relationship with the army and the peasants, Karl followed Constant in accusing him of 'anachronism': 'One sees: *all "idées napoléoniennes" are ideas of the undeveloped smallholding in the freshness of its youth*; for the smallholding that has outlived its day they are an absurdity. They are only the hallucinations of its death struggles.'[111]

Even though he now expected that the return of revolution would depend upon the trade cycle, the note of apocalyptic optimism remained: 'The parody of empire was necessary to free the mass of the French nation from the weight of tradition and to work out in pure form the opposition between state power and society. With the progressive undermining of smallholding property, the state structure erected upon it collapses.'[112] 'The revolution', he comforted himself, 'is thorough. It is still journeying through purgatory. It does its work methodically . . . First it perfected the parliamentary power, in order to be able to overthrow it. Now it was perfecting 'the *executive power*', reducing 'it to its purest expression . . . in order to concentrate all its forces of destruction against it. And when it has done this second half of its preliminary work, Europe will leap from its seat and exultantly exclaim: Well burrowed, old mole!'[113]

As in *Class Struggles*, the most prominent feature of Karl's new conception of history was his refusal to accord independent space to the people's political concerns. Universal suffrage was treated as a form of illusion akin to the notion of the equality of exchanges in the economy or the apparent naturalization of economic categories in what he was later to call 'the fetishism of commodities'. The illusion of political democracy was yet another symptom of the alienating power of commercial society. But his refusal to think of universal suffrage as anything other than a pathological symptom imposed serious limitations upon his understanding of the sequence of events. It led him to underestimate the ways in which the suffrage issue pushed the revolution in directions different from anything encountered in 1789 or 1830.

As a result, his reading of the sequence of events which had culminated in the implementation of universal suffrage, Bonaparte's massive electoral majority and finally his coup d'état was wilful and perverse. He claimed that these events signified the ripening of the 'party of insurrection' into 'a really revolutionary party', and the establishment of the Second Empire was not a defeat of the bourgeoisie, but a new form of bourgeois rule. But he had little to say about what was to be its more obvious consequence – that, as a result of the political demand for universal male suffrage in France in 1848, and again in Germany in the 1860s, both the liberals and the more traditional parties of order found themselves defeated, not by radical democrats on the left, but by the demagogic manoeuvres of maverick post-Legitimist leaders on the right – Bonaparte and Bismarck.

If Karl had hoped that the *Eighteenth Brumaire* would make a splash among German radical exiles in London and New York, he was disappointed. The text was originally meant to appear as a series of articles in *Die Revolution*, a new weekly set up by Karl's friend Joseph Weydemeyer in New York. But the newspaper folded after two issues, and Karl's essay arrived too late for inclusion. Weydemeyer published the work as the first issue of another 'non-periodical' journal, also called *Die Revolution*, in May 1852. But, much to Karl's annoyance, he got the title wrong, entitling it *The Eighteenth Brumaire of Louis-Napoléon*, whereas throughout the text Karl had emphatically referred only to 'Louis Bonaparte', part of his determination to deny Bonaparte the legitimacy bestowed upon him by the name of 'Napoléon'. Weydemeyer could not afford to recall the issue. Very few copies reached Europe, so the text remained virtually unknown. The first accessible edition appeared only in 1869.[114]

Maybe this helps to explain the sour and sardonic tone of *The Great Men of the Exile*, his next essay, co-written with Engels, partly in London and partly in Manchester, over May and June 1852. If this essay began as a witty attack on the German democratic exiles, the underlying bitterness soon showed through. The essay began with a satirical account of Gottfried Kinkel, poet and pastor, whose sentimental search for his 'authentic inner being' and a true partner was couched in terms of 'Heinrich von Ofterdingen' and his search for 'the blue flower'.[115] Due to his redoubtable wife Joanna, Kinkel had been released from his Prussian prison after being captured at Rastatt at the end of the Baden campaign. Once in London, he was treated as a hero and lionized in London society, even invited to meet Dickens. He was variously presented as 'the Democratic Christ' or 'the German Lamartine'.

In this first section, the tone remained light, but thereafter the attack became crude and unbounded.[116] This was the description of Gustav Struve, one the leaders of the Baden uprising in 1848–9: 'At the very first glimpse of his leathery appearance, his protuberant eyes with their sly, stupid expression, the mat gleam on his bald pate and his half Slav, half Kalmuck features, one cannot doubt that one is in the presence of an unusual man.'[117] But an even worse treatment was reserved for their erstwhile mentor, Arnold Ruge, who was described as 'the Swiss guard of German philosophy':

> Paris acquaintances were wont to sum up his Pomeranian-Slav features with the word 'ferret-face' . . . This is the gutter in which the contradictions of philosophy, democracy and phrase-mongering in general all strangely merge; such a man is moreover richly endowed with all the vices, the mean and petty qualities, with the slyness and stupidity, the avarice and the clumsiness, the servility and the arrogance, the untrustworthiness and the bonhomie of the emancipated serf, the peasant: philistine and ideologist, atheist and slogan worshipper, absolute ignoramus and absolute philosopher all in one – that is Arnold Ruge as Hegel foretold him in 1806.[118]

Like the *Eighteenth Brumaire*, *Great Men of the Exile* was originally meant to appear in Weydemeyer's *Die Revolution*. When this journal folded, it was necessary to look elsewhere. In July 1852, Colonel Bangya, a Hungarian exile and confidant of Kossuth, with whom Karl had become friends, promised to get it published in Germany and to pay a £25 fee. Bangya did not deliver on his promise, and turned out to be a spy in the pay of the Austrian, French and Prussian police. The essay was not published until the twentieth century.[119]

4. THE *NEW-YORK DAILY TRIBUNE* AND THE JOURNALISM OF THE 1850S

Insofar as Karl earned his living in the years from 1852, it was as a European correspondent writing for the *New-York Daily Tribune*. It is estimated that the *Tribune* published 487 articles from Karl, 350 written by him, 125 by Engels, and 12 jointly. This far exceeded what he wrote for the *Neue Rheinische Zeitung* or his contributions in the 1850s to the Chartist journal of Ernest Jones, the *People's Paper*, or the Turkophile David Urquhart's *Free Press*. Only in 1855 in his 220 or more contributions to the *Neue Oder-Zeitung* did he briefly exceed his productivity on the *Tribune*. The work on the *Tribune* was exceptional also because it continued over such a long period of time: the first contribution dated from August 1852, the last at the beginning of 1862, nearly ten years later. Work for the *Tribune* was valuable not merely because it provided a source of income. In the long years following 1848, it was a way of addressing new developments in the world. As Jenny wrote after she had moved away from the bustle and vitality of Soho, 'luckily I still had the article for the *Tribune* to copy out twice a week and that kept me in touch with world events'.[120]

In 1850, the editor of the *Tribune*, Charles Dana, who had been impressed by Karl when they met in Cologne in 1848, invited him to become a correspondent. Previously, along with Nathaniel Hawthorne, Emerson and others, Dana had been a member of the Fourierist Phalanstery at Brook Farm in 1842. After a fire destroyed the Phalanstery in 1846, Dana had become a journalist under the aegis of Horace Greeley, and in 1848 as European correspondent witnessed the June Insurrection in Paris and revolutionary developments in Berlin. As a result of American interest in the European revolutions, the *Tribune*'s circulation had shot up and by the 1850s reached around 200,000, the largest circulation in the world at the time. Under Dana, the paper retained an interest in Fourierism, and opposed slavery and the death penalty, while favouring protection and prohibition.

So many contributions over such a long period of time suggest that, despite some obvious political differences, Karl's contributions were of value to the *Tribune*, to such an extent that in certain years up to one third of his output was published in the *Tribune*'s editorial leaders. An important view of Karl's value to the *Tribune* was provided by Dana. In March 1860, he was asked by Karl to supply a testimonial to support his case against the scientist and Bonapartist supporter Carl Vogt. Dana applauded Karl's work: 'Nearly 9 years ago I engaged you to write for the New York Tribune, and the engagement has continued ever since. You have written for us constantly, without a single week's interruption, that I can remember, and you are not only one of the most highly valued, but one of the best paid contributors attached to the journal.' But what makes Dana's letter particularly interesting is that the praise he offered was not unqualified: 'The only fault I have had to find with you has been that you have occasionally exhibited too German a tone of feeling for an American newspaper. This has been the case with reference both to Russia and to France. In questions relating to both Czarism and Bonapartism, I have sometimes thought that you manifested too much interest and too great anxiety for the unity and independence of Germany.'[121] Dana rightly perceived that there was an obsessive dimension to Karl's discussion of 'Czarism and Bonapartism' in the *Tribune* and it was found even more strongly in his other writings during the period. Many revolutionaries in 1848 called for an all-out war against Russia since that was most likely to galvanize the revolutionary energies of the people. Russia for its part was fully committed to preserving the Vienna settlement of 1815 and was active in its name in driving forward the counter-revolution in 1848–9. It had reversed the Prussian intervention in Schleswig-Holstein and Posen; revolutionaries quite rightly focused upon the fact that the Prussian king was the czar's brother-in-law. Russia had propped up the bankrupt Austrian Empire by massively intervening against the revolution in Hungary in the summer of 1849. A Slavophile position had also begun to make headway on the left, attracting in particular those dismayed by the disenchanting story of revolution in the West. Karl, along with other revolutionaries, had reacted fiercely against this phenomenon and denounced the Pan-Slavist initiatives of Bakunin, Herzen and Bruno Bauer.[122]

Among the political classes in Britain and France, there was also concern about Russia, not so much as the protector of the European counter-revolution, but more as an expansionist military power with designs upon the failing Ottoman Empire and an ambition to control access to the Black Sea. In the spring of 1853, these tensions culminated in the Crimean War between Russia and the Ottomans, who were supported by the British and the French.

In Britain, Karl's visceral Russophobia found local expression in the conspiracy theories of the maverick Romantic Tory MP David Urquhart. Urquhart, once a fighter for Greek independence and now an ardent enthusiast for the Ottomans, had for a number of years pursued a tireless campaign against the foreign policy of Lord Palmerston. In early 1853, Karl was drawn towards Urquhart's writings after Engels had directed his attention to 'the mad MP, who denounces Palmerston as being in the pay of Russia'.[123] By the autumn of 1853, Karl in a series of eight articles on Palmerston had accepted much of Urquhart's line. 'Whom was the Czar indebted to for occupying Constantinople by his troops, and for transferring by virtue of the Treaty of Unkiar-Skelessi, the supreme seat of the Ottoman Empire from Constantinople to St Petersburg? To nobody else but the Right Honourable Henry John Viscount Palmerston.'[124] In December 1853, after Palmerston had resigned, Karl declared that as a result of Urquhart's revelations, both in speeches at anti-Russian meetings and in print, Palmerston had 'been found out'.[125] By this time, Urquhart's *Free Press* had published 15,000 copies of Karl's pamphlet *Palmerston and Russia*, while the *Sheffield Free Press*, another Urquhart publication, reprinted a number of his other articles around the same theme.

In relation to the connection between Britain and Russia, Karl always tried to present himself as the fair-minded enquirer who did not share Urquhart's single-minded obsession. 'Urquhart's writings on Russia and against Palmerston had interested but not convinced me,' he claimed. But if that had been his initial stance, it did not remain so. In order to verify Urquhart's claims, 'I undertook the laborious analysis of *Hansard's Parliamentary Debates* and the diplomatic Blue Books from 1807 to 1850.' This allegedly 'demonstrated Palmerston's involvement with the St. Petersburg Cabinet on the basis of his transactions with Poland, Turkey, Circassia, etc.'.[126] Even the fact that Britain was now supposedly at war with Russia did not diminish belief in this collusion. For the current war in the Crimea was just an appearance. The whole of English diplomacy between 1830 and 1854 could be reduced to one principle – 'to avoid war with Russia at all costs'. 'War with Russia', Karl declared at the end of 1854, 'has hardly broken out.'[127]

Two years later, in 1856–7, he examined diplomatic documents in the British Museum going back to the beginning of the eighteenth century. There he discovered 'continuous secret collaboration between the Cabinets of London and St. Petersburg' starting from the time of Peter the Great, who 'coupled the political craft of the Mongol slave with the proud aspiration of the Mongol master, to whom Genghis Khan had, by will, bequeathed his conquest of the earth'.[128] As an introduction, he published *Revelations of the Diplomatic History of the Eighteenth Century*.

In the 1850s, just as concern about the expansionist ambitions of czarist Russia was common among the British political class, so was anxiety about the adventurism of Napoléon III; and in both cases these worries were largely endorsed by public opinion. Suspicion of Russian designs on the Ottoman Empire was sufficient to provoke the Crimean War from 1853 to 1856, while hostility towards Napoléon III brought about the fall of Palmerston's government in 1858 when, at the instigation of the French, he had attempted to introduce a bill limiting the right of asylum, following the attempt by a revolutionary nationalist, Felice Orsini, to employ a British-made explosive to assassinate the French emperor.

As in the case of his writings about Russia, there was towards Bonaparte an extra dimension to this hostility fuelled by bitterness and disappointment about the defeats of 1848 and 1851. Bonaparte was always pictured both by Karl and by others as an adventurer, a gambler, and this led to continuous speculation about his next allegedly desperate move. From the time of Bonaparte's 1851 coup and throughout the 1850s, the most immediate hope was that Bonaparte's dependence upon army support, probably in alliance with Russia, would lead him into a military adventure, which might spark off a European war. Whom he might fight was a secondary matter. He could attempt to please French Catholics as he had done in launching the expedition to Rome to restore the Pope. He could seek to avenge the humiliation of Waterloo, which would suggest a conflict with England. Or he could attempt to champion 'the principle of nationality' and therefore foment war with Austria over Italy. The main point was to strengthen support within the army. As Engels wrote to Karl a few weeks after the coup, 'that the good Louis-Napoléon must go to war is clear as day and, if he can come to an understanding with Russia, he will probably pick a quarrel with England'.[129] In the bleak years of reaction between 1848 and the beginning of the Italian war of 1859, what fuelled the remaining revolutionary hopes of Karl, Engels and the 'party' was either the possibility of a European war, or else the prospect of a world economic crisis.

In February 1856, Karl speculated on Bonaparte's economic difficulties; he claimed that for 'the first time in their history, the French people have shown themselves indifferent to their old hobby "la gloire"'. This meant 'that the epoch of Bonapartism has passed its climax'.[130] But in June of that year he had to concede that, for the moment, Bonaparte had resolved his problem. His coup had been based upon 'two diametrically opposite pretences: on the one hand proclaiming it was his mission to save the *bourgeoisie* and "material order" from the Red anarchy to be let loose in [the election of] May 1852; and on the other hand, to save the working people from the middle-class despotism concentrated in the National Assembly'. Now he had discovered a means of simultaneously satisfying both of these contradictory demands. The success of the innovative methods devised by one-time Saint-Simonians engaged in the *Crédit Mobilier* had for the moment led to the belief that 'all the antagonism of classes must disappear before the creation of universal wealth by some new-fangled scheme of public credit'.[131]

In 1858, Karl was again speculating upon the approaching end of the Bonapartist regime since the prosperity upon which it rested had been battered by the commercial crisis of 1856–7. Only 'another military adventure' could postpone 'the end of his strange, wicked and pernicious career'. Everywhere in the summer of 1858, war was believed to be imminent. 'Louis Napoleon has no other means of escaping speedy destruction.'[132] More precarious than ever, and even more dependent upon army support, Karl claimed in early 1859, 'his last trump, in an extreme danger, is a war, and a war for the reconquest of the left bank of the Rhine'. This would be his last move in a war which he would commence in Italy.[133]

Even more nightmarish visions of a Europe divided up between Russia and France were conjured up in *Herr Vogt* (to be dealt with in the next section) and other writings in 1860. 'The natural frontier of the

Slav Empire', according to *Herr Vogt*, would encompass Bohemia and Moravia.[134] Furthermore, in the light of an allegedly secret treaty at Breslau in October 1859, relations between Russia and France had grown 'more ostentatiously intimate'. As a result, after seizing Savoy, Bonaparte was threatening Switzerland, and throwing out hints upon some unavoidable 'rectification of the Rhenish frontiers'.[135] It is no wonder that confronted by even more extravagant versions of these speculations, Dana had sent back fourteen or fifteen articles (by Engels) on Pan-Slavism from the first half of 1856.[136] But while on questions of Bonapartism and Pan-Slavism Dana clearly distrusted the tendency of Karl and other European radicals to go over the top, in other areas there was a remarkable match.

In his coverage of English politics, Karl relied heavily on the reports of parliamentary speeches in Hansard and *The Times*. On the state of the economy, he based himself on the *Economist*, amplified by Manchester business gossip regaled by Engels, while on the development of factory industry and the condition of the workers he consulted the reports of the factory inspectors and the medical investigations of the *Lancet*. When Karl embarked upon a series requiring knowledge of a larger historical background, as was the case in his series on Russell, Palmerston, Spain, India and the opium trade, he consulted everything he could find in the British Museum. He also perused a wide range of newspapers. In addition to *The Times*, he made frequent use of the Whig *Examiner*, the pro-Disraeli *Press* and the Chartist *People's Paper*. As a result, his *Tribune* articles on British politics, industrial development and world trade were both well written and well informed – winning at one point lavish praise from John Bright in the House of Commons.[137]

Not surprisingly, his choice and coverage of themes were similar to those found in the rest of the press. In the 1852 elections in Britain, for example, like other columnists he thought that the political battle being fought out by two aristocratic parties scarcely concealed the fact that both parties could only survive by pleasing the urban middle classes. Similarly, the idea that Napoléon III was a parody of his uncle was widely found in the English press. He was distrusted as someone who, in order to further his own advancement, did not scruple to flout the constitution. Concern about Bonaparte's methods around the mid-1850s led to the suspicion that Palmerston's ambitions and tactics resembled those of the French emperor. Like Bonaparte, Palmerston from 1855 to

1858 appealed over the heads of an elected assembly to the nation at large. In addition, the Indian Mutiny presented him with an excuse to increase still further his powers of patronage, both civil and military. In 1857, everyone from Gladstone to the Chartist Ernest Jones believed that the election of that year could be seen as a coup d'état, in which England would become a Palmerstonian dictatorship and Parliament its obedient tool.[138]

Karl arrived in England with little knowledge of the English class system beyond what he had read in Guizot and Engels.[139] He gradually elaborated a more subtle picture of British politics with the help of the parliamentary speeches and writings of Benjamin Disraeli and of the *People's Paper* of Ernest Jones. He considered Disraeli 'the ablest member' of the House of Commons, and followed him in his scornful treatment of the Whigs and their 'Venetian constitution' as too patrician any longer to hold in check the more democratic aspirations of the northern middle classes. He also adopted Disraeli's sardonic depiction of the free-trade followers of Cobden and Bright as 'the Manchester School'.

From Ernest Jones in the *People's Paper*, on the other hand, Karl elaborated what he thought to be the emerging shape of industrial class struggle. In 1852, he reported:

> While the Tories, the Whigs, the Peelites . . . belong more or less to the past, the Free Traders (the men of the Manchester School, the Parliamentary and Financial Reformers) are the *official representatives of modern English society*, the representatives of that England which rules the market of the world. They represent the party of the self-conscious Bourgeoisie, of industrial capital striving to make available its social power as a political power as well, and to eradicate the last arrogant remnants of feudal society . . . By Free Trade they mean the unfettered movement of capital, freed from all national or religious shackles.[140]

The 'unparalleled growth' of commerce and manufacture in the following few years appeared to reinforce this conclusion. In relation to Britain's social development, Karl felt able to reiterate, almost word for word, his description of the development of modern industry in the *Communist Manifesto*:

> In no other country have the intermediate stations between the millionaire commanding whole industrial armies and the wages slave living only

from hand to mouth so gradually been swept away from the soil. There exist here no longer, as in continental countries, large classes of peasants and artisans almost equally dependent on their own property and their own labour. A complete divorce of property from labour has been effected in Great Britain. In no other country, therefore, the war between the two classes that constitute modern society has assumed so colossal dimensions and features so distinct and palpable.[141]

In contrast to past revolutions, Karl was pleased to claim that: 'The so-called revolutions of 1848 were but poor incidents . . . Steam, electricity, and the self-acting mule were revolutionists of a rather more dangerous character than even Barbès, Raspail and Blanqui.'[142]

Karl was also keen to demonstrate that the impersonal brutality of laissez-faire Britain was as visible in the countryside as in the towns. Of particular interest to American readers were the evictions, which were forcing so many of the Scots and the Irish off the land and across the Atlantic. Unlike the Continent, in which executioners were 'tangible and hangable beings', in England, 'there acts . . . an invisible, intangible and silent despot, condemning individuals, in extreme cases to the most cruel of deaths and driving in its noiseless, every day working, whole races and whole classes of men from the soil of their forefathers, like the angel with the fiery sword who drove Adam from paradise. In the latter form the work of the unseen social despot calls itself *forced emigration*, in the former it is called *starvation*.'[143] Moreover, the activity of this 'silent despot' was fully authorized by the teachings of political economy: 'Begin with pauperising the inhabitants of a country, and when there is no more profit to be ground out of them, when they have grown a burden to the revenue, drive them away, and sum up your Net Revenue! Such is the doctrine laid down by Ricardo, in his celebrated work, *The Principle of Political Economy*.'[144]

This emerging society was not only heartless, but built upon the contrast between unheard of wealth and unlimited poverty, in which 'A matter of a million paupers in the British workhouses is as inseparable from British prosperity, as the existence of eighteen to twenty millions in gold in the Bank of England.' It was driven forward by a commercial cycle, which would first enter 'the phase of *excitement*, in order thence to pass over to those of over-speculation and convulsion'.[145] In 1852, Karl predicted that the crisis would assume a far more dangerous character than in 1847. The effects of 'industrial over-production' would hit 'the *manufacturing* districts' and recall 'the unequaled stagnation of 1838–'42'.[146] But the advent of this crisis was apparently halted by gold finds in California and Australia.

In May 1853, Karl was once again warning of the unprecedented extension of factories in England. In France, the whole state machinery had been turned into a swindling and stock-jobbing concern, while Austria was on the verge of bankruptcy.[147] Two years later, Karl warned again of *'the crisis in trade and industry*, which since last September is growing more violent and more universal every day'. The first houses to collapse had been the cotton spinners, followed by the shipowners, the Australia and California merchants, then the Chinese houses and finally the Indian. 'A few more months, and the crisis in the factory districts will reach the depth of 1842.' Then 'the political movement', which had been 'dormant over the past six years', would return.[148]

In 1856, Karl discerned a monetary crisis, akin to 1847, but moving from East to West rather than from West to East. What all 'far-sighted politicians' now feared was 'an enlarged edition not only of the crisis of 1847 but also of the revolutions of 1848':

> The anxiety of the upper classes in Europe is as intense as their disappointment . . . A general bankruptcy is staring them in the face, which they know to be coincidental with the settlement-day of the great pawning shop at Paris . . . In 1848 the movements which more immediately produced the Revolution were of a merely political character, such as the reform banquets in France, the war of the Sonderbund in Switzerland, the debates at the United *Landtag* at Berlin, the Spanish marriages, the Schleswig-Holstein quarrels, &c; and when its soldiers, the workingmen of Paris, proclaimed the social character of the Revolution of 1848, its generals were as much taken by surprise as the rest of the world. Now, on the contrary, a social revolution is generally understood, even before the political revolution is proclaimed; and a social revolution brought about by no underground plots of the secret societies among the working classes, but by the public contrivances of the Crédits Mobiliers of the ruling classes. Thus the anxiety of the upper classes in Europe is embittered by the conviction that their very victories over revolution have been but instrumental in providing the material conditions in 1857 for the ideal tendencies of 1848.[149]

For the *Tribune*, all this was grist to the mill. The politics of Dana and of Horace Greeley, the proprietor of the *Tribune*, were protectionist. Free trade, championed by England – especially after the Repeal of the Corn Laws – was, they argued, the means by which England dominated world commerce, and through its enforcement of the gold standard acted as the world's banker. The economic basis of the *Tribune*'s protectionism was most clearly articulated by the American economist Henry Carey, who like his father, a successful Philadelphia publisher, had developed Alexander Hamilton's argument for the protection of infant industries in the face of British commercial superiority. Carey attacked the gold standard and advocated instead a cheap money fiscal policy. He denounced free trade because it inhibited national economic development. Free trade promoted an international division of labour, which privileged Britain's status as the workshop of the world, while forcing other countries to continue to specialize in agriculture. The social effects of free trade were also denounced as harmful. Free trade accentuated the gulf between wealth and poverty and it did not benefit the English working man. Carey argued that factory slavery in Britain strengthened and perpetuated plantation slavery in the United States. According to Carey, 'from year to year the small proprietor was seen to pass into the condition of a day-labourer, and the small employing mechanic or tradesman to pass into a receiver of wages, and thus did the whole people tend more and more to become divided into two great classes, separated from each other by an impassable gulf, the very rich and the very poor, the master and the slave'.[150]

If these were the policies which defined the editorial line of the *Tribune* and the emergent Republican Party in the 1850s, it is not difficult to understand why Karl was considered such a valuable European correspondent. Karl's emphasis upon the anachronistic character of British party politics, upon the industrial causes of commercial crises and upon the failure of free trade, either to remove crises or to improve the condition of the workers, derived from his conception of 'the economical' basis of 'bourgeois society'. In the eyes of the *Tribune*, on the other hand, these were above all the effects of free trade. But, however different the supposed causes of Britain's position, Karl's depiction of the condition of 'modern English society', converged closely with the *Tribune*'s depiction of the consequences of free trade.

Dana's decision to recruit Karl as a European correspondent was also based upon his personal sympathy and familiarity with the European revolutions of 1848 and his interest in socialism. He was a one-time Fourierist, whose social and political sympathies were clear. In the first surviving letter he had written to Karl in July 1850, he had stated that although he could not 'anticipate any immediate explosion of the great volcano ... the play is not yet over, thank God'.[151] In 1852, as the publication of the 'Letters on Germany' (unbeknown to Dana, written by Engels) drew to a close, Dana was very happy to accept Karl's proposal to write on 'English current affairs'.[152]

Karl, on the other hand, when he embarked upon his own first article for the *Tribune* at the beginning of August 1852, seemed only to have been vaguely aware of the political stance of the paper. In a letter to Engels, he was unsure whether Dana might take offence at his attack on the Whigs in Britain, given the *Tribune*'s support for American 'Whig' candidates in the forthcoming American election.[153] Three days later, he was assailed by further anxieties. What about the competition from other European contributors to the *Tribune*, including his old enemies Heinzen, Ruge and Bruno Bauer? And 'what is even more unfortunate, I see from today's *Times* that the *Daily Tribune* is protectionist. So it's all VERY OMINOUS.'[154] In the years before 1848, Karl had offered a paradoxical endorsement of free trade as the most developed form of bourgeois society leading it down the path to revolution, while in 1845, in an unpublished essay, he had ridiculed the protectionist position of Friedrich List's *National System of Political Economy*, in large part on the grounds that the time of the nation-state was over.[155]

Engels was reassuring. There was no need to worry about other European competitors. Their presence was the result of the *Tribune*'s desire to ensure 'an "all-round" character ... As for protectionism,' he went on, 'it does no harm. American Whigs are all industrial protectionists, but this by no means implies that they belong to the landed aristocracy. Derby variety. Nor are they so stupid not to know just as well as does List that FREE TRADE suits English industry better than anything else. By the way, I could at a pinch insert a word here and there to that effect with the FREE TRADERS, which you could cross out if not to your liking. But there's really no need for it.'[156] Karl took some notice of Engels' letter. In one of the first articles he sent to the *Tribune*, the 'Free Traders' were treated as representatives of 'that England which rules the market of the world'.[157] But the full import of what that meant only struck him the following June, after Henry Carey had sent Karl a copy of his *Slavery at Home and Abroad*, which cited Karl repeatedly as 'a recent English writer' or *Tribune* correspondent. In this book, according to Karl in a letter written to Engels, 'All ills are blamed on the centralising effect of big industry. But this centralising effect is in turn blamed on England, who has made herself the WORKSHOP of the world and has forced all other countries to revert to brutish agriculture divorced from manufacturing.' So this 'ULTRA-FREE-TRADER finally recommends *protective tariffs*'. He also noted irritably that the *Tribune* was 'puffing Carey's book for all it's worth' and concluded that both Carey and the *Tribune* could be identified: 'in the guise of Sismondian-philanthropic-socialist anti-industrialism, they represent the protectionist, i.e. industrial, bourgeoisie of America'. This was the reason why 'the *Tribune*, despite all its "isms" and socialist flourishes, manages to be the "LEADING JOURNAL" in the United States'.[158]

Despite his irritation with Carey, there is nothing to suggest that in subsequent articles Karl did much to distinguish his approach from that of the Republican protectionists. If anything, the opposite seemed to be true. For his articles thereafter referred far more to 'free trade' than to 'bourgeois society'. Similarly, his discussions of commercial crisis made frequent and explicit reference to the deficiency of free trade and monetarist interpretations of the fluctuations of the economy. On 9 September 1853, he highlighted the fallacies of Peel's 1844 Bank Charter Act, maintaining that the Act would aggravate the severity of the approaching crisis.[159] In 1855, he argued that the crisis in trade and industry had 'shut up the mouths of those shallow Free Traders who for years had gone on preaching that since the Repeal of the Corn Laws in 1846, glutted markets were impossible'. Furthermore, 'the glut' had been made more acute by the attempt to dump goods in newly developing extra-European markets: 'India and China, glutted though they were, continued to be used as outlets – as also California and Australia. When the English manufacturers could no longer sell their goods at home, or would not do so rather than depress prices, they resorted to the absurd expedient of consigning them abroad, especially to India,

China, Australia and California.'[160] In 1857, after the suspension of the Bank Charter Act as a result of its failure to alleviate the commercial crisis, he once again observed, 'we were told that British Free Trade would change all this, but if nothing else is proved it is at least clear that the Free-Trade doctors are nothing but quacks.'[161] In a lead article in August 1858, he repeated his attack upon the monetarist approach. 'The idea that banks had unduly expanded the currency, thus producing an inflation of prices violently to be readjusted by a final collapse' was 'too cheap a method of accounting for every crisis'.[162] Once again, the stated, the real root of the crisis was industrial overproduction.

Such an analysis was central to the Republican election campaign of 1857. So it was not surprising that Dana decided that the *Tribune* should continue to retain Karl, despite 'the unexampled ruin now pervading the commercial system in this country', which 'compels us all to retrenchment', and the dropping of all other foreign correspondents. He urged Karl to confine his articles to 'the most important topics such as the Indian War and the commercial explosion which I suppose will now take place in England as well as on the continent'.[163]

In practice, the one area in which a clash between his own position and that of the *Tribune* might have occurred was in the treatment of Asia. For while the *Tribune* believed that India, like the United States, was a victim of the global free-trade system, created by the British, Karl considered the disruption of traditional India by the British a necessary world-historical development. In June 1853, Karl congratulated Engels on his article on Switzerland as 'a direct swipe at the *Tribune*'s "LEADERS" (anti-centralization etc.) and *their* man Carey'. And he went on: 'I continued this clandestine campaign in my first article on India, in which England's destruction of native industries is described as *revolutionary*. This they will find very SHOCKING. Incidentally the whole administration of India by the British was detestable and still remains so today.'[164] Marx's writings on India during the 1850s in large part repeated the critique of empire found in English radicalism in the first half of the nineteenth century.[165] Imperial administration and the East India Company were lambasted as a form of 'old corruption', but colonization in social and economic terms was often considered progressive. In one of Karl's earliest articles on India, in June 1853, it was stated that the East

India Company dated back to an agreement between constitutional monarchy and 'the monopolising monied interest' after the 1688 Revolution. Originally, its treasures were gained less by commerce than by 'direct exploitation'; and colossal fortunes were extorted and transmitted to England. After the Seven Years War, 'oligarchy absorbed all of its [the Company's] power which it could assume without incurring responsibility'.[166] In India under the East India Company, there was 'a permanent financial deficit, a regular over-supply of wars, and no supply at all of public works, an abominable system of taxation and a no less abominable state of justice and law'.[167] The Court of Directors itself dispensed each year appointments of the value of nearly £400,000 among the upper classes of Great Britain. It was also attended by a large and exceedingly slow-moving bureaucracy. As Karl summarized the situation: 'The oligarchy involves India in wars, in order to find employment for their younger sons; the moneyocracy consigns it to the highest bidder; and a subordinate Bureaucracy paralyse its administration and perpetuate its abuses as the vital condition of their own perpetuation.'[168]

But, for all this, the British presence in India and British incursions elsewhere in Asia were seen ultimately as progressive. Karl inherited from writers of the first half of the nineteenth century as diverse as James Mill, Hegel and Jean-Baptiste Say an image of Asia as stationary and without a history. His writings of the 1850s and 1860s reproduced these images of the passive immobility of the extra-European world. In his first article on India for the *Tribune* in early June 1853, he wrote, 'However changing the political aspect of India's past must appear, its social condition has remained unaltered since its remotest antiquity . . . Indian society has no history at all, at least no known history. What we call its history, is but the history of the successive intruders who founded their empires on the passive basis of that unresisting and unchanging society.'[169]

Throughout the following decade, his view of Asian empires did not fundamentally change. In 1862, he described China as 'that living fossil', and explained that 'the Oriental empires demonstrate constant immobility in their social substructure, with unceasing change in the persons and clans that gain control of the political superstructure'.[170] Karl, in line with his rationalist and Enlightenment predecessors, expressed distaste for the orientalist fantasies of what Heine had termed 'the Romantic school': 'we must not forget that these idyllic village communities, inoffensive though they may appear, had always been the solid foundation of Oriental despotism, that they restrained the human mind within the smallest possible compass, making it the unresisting tool of superstition, enslaving it beneath traditional rules, depriving it of all grandeur and historical energies.' Not only were these little communities 'contaminated' by caste and slavery, but, as Karl noted, following Hegel, India's religion was 'at once a religion of sensualist exuberance and . . . self-torturing asceticism'. Above all, these communities 'subjugated man to external circumstances, instead of elevating man [to be] the sovereign of circumstances'. It was this 'brutalising worship of nature' which accounted for the worship of 'Kanuman the monkey, and Sabbala the cow'.[171] The only real question to be resolved was how the supposedly 'unchanging' character of 'oriental despotism' was to be reconciled with Karl's picture of historical development as a progressive sequence of 'modes of production'. In 1853, encouraged by Engels, Karl thought the unchanging character of Asia could be explained, firstly, by 'the leaving to central government the care of great public works', especially irrigation, and secondly, a 'village system' based upon the 'domestic union of agricultural and manufacturing pursuits' agglomerated in small centres.[172] In the late 1850s, he came to emphasize the absence of private property in land as its crucial feature, and on the basis of his researches on 'pre-capitalist economic formations' in 1857–8 he felt confident enough to write of an 'Asiatic' mode of production as the first stage in the 'economic development of society'.[173]

What part, then, would be played by the extra-European world in the revolution which would result from the ever more far-reaching intrusion of global capitalism? Or, as Marx saw it in 1853, 'can mankind fulfil its destiny without a fundamental revolution in the social state of Asia?'[174] Marx agreed with the writers of the 1820s that change in Asia must come from outside. In *The Communist Manifesto*, he firmly placed his confidence in 'the bourgeoisie', 'the cheap prices' of whose 'commodities are the heavy artillery with which it batters down all Chinese walls . . . It compels all nations, on pain of extinction, to adopt the bourgeois mode of production; it compels them to introduce what it calls civilisation into their midst.'[175] This was the thought which he elaborated in one of his *Tribune* articles on India in 1853. The age-old 'village system' based upon the 'domestic union of agricultural and manufacturing pursuits' was being 'dissolved', 'not so much through the brutal interference of the British tax-gatherer and the British soldier, as to the working of English steam and English free trade'. British rule was bringing the advantages of political unity, European science, a European trained army, a free press, British-trained civil servants, the abolition of the old system of common-land tenure and a shorter passage between India and England. If the revolution depended upon the social transformation of Asia, England 'was the unconscious tool of history in bringing about that revolution'.[176]

Despite what Dana called 'the Indian War', Karl's thinking was not deeply affected by the Indian Mutiny. The Indian revolt did not begin with the Ryots, who were 'tortured, dishonoured and stripped naked by the British', but with 'the Sepoys, clad, fed, petted, fatted and pampered by them'. He therefore compared the Sepoy revolt with that of the French nobility against the monarchy on the eve of the fall of the *Ancien Régime*.[177] His reports dwelt mainly upon the cruelties inflicted by both sides and details of the fighting. It was only after a speech by Disraeli that he was prepared to concede that the insurrection might not simply be 'a military mutiny', but 'a national revolt'.[178] His attitude to the Taiping Rebellion was even more distant and poorly informed. It fitted perfectly his belief in the unchanging structures of Oriental empires. As for the rebels, 'they are aware of no task except changing the dynasty. They have no slogans . . . they seem to have no other vocation than, as opposed to conservative stagnation, to produce destruction in grotesquely detestable forms, destruction without any nucleus of new construction'.[179]

In his first contributions to the *Tribune* in 1852–4, Karl accepted that the 1848 revolutions were over. But he remained confident that in Britain the modern class struggle between the 'bourgeoisie' and 'the politically active portion of the British working class' was imminent. This was the struggle between 'the Manchester School' and the Chartists. For the moment, the central importance of this struggle was obscured by the party battles at Westminster. But 'the Tories, the Whigs, the Peelites' all belonged 'more or less to the past'. 'The *official representatives of modern English society*' were the free traders, the men of the 'Manchester School', 'led on by the most active and most energetic portion of the English Bourgeoisie – the *manufacturers*'; and they were faced by the Chartists, for whom 'Universal Suffrage is the equivalent for political power for the working class of England, where the proletariat forms the large majority of the population, where, in a long, though underground civil war, it has gained a clear consciousness of its position as a class and where even the rural districts know no longer any peasants, but only landlords, industrial capitalists (farmers) and hired labourers.'[180] For the representatives of the 'Manchester School' since their victory in 1846 with the Repeal of the Corn Laws, 'the aristocracy' was 'their vanishing opponent', 'the working class' 'their arising enemy'. For the moment, as Karl admitted, they preferred to compromise with 'the vanishing opponent':

> but historical necessity and the Tories press them onwards. They cannot avoid fulfilling their mission, battering to pieces Old England, the England of the Past; and the very moment when they will have conquered exclusive political dominion, when political dominion and economical supremacy will be united in the same hands, when, therefore, the struggle against capital will no longer be distinct from the struggle against the existing Government – from that very moment will date the *social revolution of England*.[181]

In the following year, there was a large-scale strike movement in the industrial districts. In 1853, Karl wrote in his still stilted English, 'there have waned away the false pretenses on the part of the masters and the silly illusions on the part of the men. The war between those two classes has become unmitigated, undisguised, openly avowed and plainly understood . . .' The question was no longer one of *wages* but one of *mastership*: 'The Manchester liberals, then, have at last thrown off the lion's skin. What they pretend at – is mastership for capital and slavery for labour.'[182] In September of that year, Karl was excited by a panic on the London Stock Exchange and expectant that, should the resultant depression prove lasting, the activity of the work-people 'will soon be carried over to the *political field*'.[183] In 1854, Karl was optimistic about a Chartist revival. Through the initiative of the Chartist leader, Ernest Jones, a 'Labour Parliament' met in Manchester and this was followed in the summer by one of Jones's speaking tours through the manufacturing districts, attracting large crowds.

In 1855, depression loomed. In March, Karl predicted that after a few more months 'the crisis in the factory districts will reach the depth of 1842. Once the effects of this crisis began to be felt among the working classes:

> the political movement which has been more or less dormant among these classes over the past six years, leaving behind only the cadres for a new agitation will spring up again. The conflict between the industrial proletariat and the bourgeoisie will flare up again at the same time that the conflict between the bourgeoisie and the aristocracy reaches its climax. Then the mask, which has so far hidden the real features of Britain's political physiognomy from foreigners, will drop.[184]

Later that summer, he got carried away witnessing the mass demonstration in Hyde Park – swelling from 50,000 to 200,000 – against the Bill, proposed by Evangelicals, to outlaw Sunday trading. It was according to Karl the largest demonstration in London since the death of George IV in 1830. 'We saw it from beginning to end and do not think it is an exaggeration to say that the *English Revolution began in Hyde Park yesterday.*'[185]

The 1850s was the period of Karl's maximal faith in the global unfolding of the 'bourgeois system of production'. 'The devastating effects of English industry' in relation to India were 'the organic results of the whole system of production as it is now constituted ... Bourgeois industry and commerce create those material conditions of a new world in the same way as geological revolutions have created the surface of the earth.'[186]

> There is one great fact, characteristic of this our 19th century, a fact which no party dares deny. On the one hand, there have started into life, industrial and scientific forces, which no epoch of the former human history had ever suspected. On the other hand, there exist symptoms of decay, far surpassing the horrors recorded of the latter times of the Roman Empire.

However:

> On our part, we do not mistake the shape of the shrewd spirit that continues to mark all these conditions ... the new-fangled forces of society ... only want to be mastered by new-fangled men – and such are the working men. They are as much the invention of modern times as

machinery itself. In the signs that bewilder the middle class, the aristocracy and the poor prophets of regression, we do recognise our brave
friend, Robin Goodfellow, the old mole that can work in the earth so
fast, that worthy pioneer – the Revolution. The English working men are
the first-born sons of modern industry. They will then, certainly, not be
the last in aiding the social revolution produced by that industry, a
revolution, which means the emancipation of their own class all over the
world, which is as universal as capital-rule and wages-slavery.

The moment of social redemption was at hand. In the Middle Ages,
there had existed in Germany a secret tribunal called the 'Vehmgericht'
to revenge the misdeeds of the ruling class; it had placed a red cross on
every house doomed by the 'Vehm': 'all the houses of Europe are now
marked with the mysterious red cross. History is the judge – its execu-
tioner, the proletarian.'[187]

However surreal this extraordinary vision, it was a product of the
unquiet spirit which for nearly a decade seethed beneath the artificial
calm produced by the burial of the Revolution of 1848. There could be
no doubt that the 1850s had inaugurated a new era in the economy. The
extraordinary energy of the economic boom which took hold not only
in Britain, but also in important manufacturing regions across the
Continent, was now no longer held back by institutional obstacles and
reactionary political authority. No state could afford to be without railways and the new forms of enterprise which went with them.

But the subterranean political developments which emerged into the
light at the end of the decade were not those anticipated by the revolutionaries of the 1840s. When commercial crisis came, it bore no
resemblance to 1842. Chartism did not return. The leaders of the
'Manchester School', Cobden and Bright, were defeated in the election
of 1857. Tories abandoned protection and redefined themselves under
Disraeli as an urban as much as a rural party. Whigs and Peelites did
not simply disappear, but together with Irish MPs and the remnants of
'the Manchester School' formed the Liberal Party in 1859. Even Ernest
Jones, the editor of the People's Paper and Karl's only friend and ally in
the Chartist movement, allied himself with middle-class radicals in
1857. From 1858, Karl's writing in the Tribune had little to say about
English working-class politics. It mainly drew upon parliamentary proceedings or focused upon European news. At the end of the 1850s, Karl

was an increasingly isolated figure, even among his German 'party' friends. The strains of continuing to maintain a common front were beginning to show.

5. THE ITALIAN WAR AND THE END OF THE 'PARTY'

After the Cologne communist trial and the dissolution of the Communist League in 1852, followed by the breakup of the Willich–Schapper faction amid a welter of accusations and exposure of spy intrigue, political activity among revolutionary German exiles in London went into abeyance. In 1853, neither democrats nor socialists believed any longer in the imminence of revolution. Membership of radical political clubs dwindled, while increasingly large numbers emigrated to either the United States or Australia.

Not surprisingly, the change in the political climate also affected Karl's 'party'. The band of brothers who had once gathered around Karl – in some cases going back to *Vorwärts!* and Paris in 1844 – became increasingly depleted, both for political and for personal reasons. Of Karl's Cologne friends, the physician Roland Daniels, who had been arrested in 1851 but acquitted in the communist trial of 1852, emerged from prison terminally afflicted by tuberculosis and died in 1855. Conrad Schramm, who had miraculously survived a duel with Willich on Karl's behalf in 1850, died of consumption in Jersey in 1858. George Weerth, who had acted as the feuilleton editor on the *Neue Rheinische Zeitung* in 1848–9, became a travelling agent for a German commercial firm and died of 'jungle fever' in Havana in 1856.

Heinrich Bürgers, another of Karl's Cologne friends, was imprisoned for six years. This, according to Karl, had 'a very moderating effect on him', and in the 1860s he gravitated towards the *Nationalverein* (the liberal pro-Prussian National Association) and the Progress Party.[188] Wilhelm Pieper, a sort of secretary to Karl in the early 1850s, had come to be regarded as increasingly tiresome. He stayed with the Marx family over Christmas 1857. Karl reported that 'he arrived in a state of alcoholic remorse and was more vapid and boring THAN EVER'.[189] According to Jenny writing to Louise Weydemeyer a few years later, Pieper had become a schoolmaster in Bremen, 'has come down badly in the world and has become a slovenly flibbertigibbet'. Like Bürgers, he had joined the National Association. Peter Immand had left Camberwell for a job in Scotland, while Ferdinand Wolff, 'Red Wolff', became a teacher in 'some Godforsaken spot', got married, had three children, and 'turned philistine *aussi*'.[190] 'Little' Ernst Dronke, as Karl and Jenny contemptuously called him, started a business in Glasgow. By 1865, according to Jenny, he had become 'an all-out philistine, boastful and repulsive'.[191] Already, when Conrad Schramm had died at the beginning of 1858, Engels lamented, 'Our old guard is rapidly dwindling away during this long spell of peace!'[192]

When political interest revived around 1858, with the advent of what the Prussian king declared to be a 'new era', political debate was no longer determined by discussion among exiles.[193] Political differences among the Germans in London were now shaped by public discussion in Germany. The social question was no longer predominant. Politics was no longer defined by the supposed imminence of revolution, but by questions about Prussian leadership and the future of Germany. Rival conceptions of national unification in turn shaped differing reactions to the new wars and conflicts engendered by the opportunist adventurism of Napoléon III, to fears about Russian expansion, and more generally to the 'Eastern Question' and the future of the Ottoman Empire. In the face of these developments, it was not surprising that Karl's idea of the 'party' did not survive the pressure of events.

The important test came in 1859 with the Italian War. Despite a twenty-year struggle, the Italian national movement found it impossible to dislodge the Austrians occupying Lombardy and Venetia. Foreign assistance was needed and was most likely to come from France. In 1858, Cavour, the Prime Minster of Piedmont, signed a treaty with Bonaparte, committing both states to war with Austria. Austria was in a weak and isolated position. It had alienated Prussia at the Treaty of Olmutz in 1850 by reconstituting the German Confederation and forcing the withdrawal of Prussian troops from Schleswig-Holstein. It had alienated Russia by siding against it in the Crimean War of 1853–6.

But for radicals, particularly in Germany, help for Italy from the French emperor was considered problematic. It was widely believed that Bonaparte had designs on the Rhineland and was counting on Russian support against Austria. France under Bonaparte had already intervened in Italy in 1849, at that point to please French Catholics, by restoring the Pope to Rome and ending Mazzini's Roman Republic. Among Germans, there was division between a majority who believed that support should be given to Austria in opposing the expansionist ambitions of France and an influential minority, including Bismarck, who believed that Prussia should take advantage of the war to hasten the exclusion of Austria from the German Confederation. The Austrians, keen to build up support within Germany, played upon the fear of French expansionist designs by recalling memories of the first Napoléon and the French revolutionary occupation of the Rhineland. To this end, they coined the slogan that the Rhine must be defended along the Po – or, more plainly, that Austrian rule in Upper Italy was a vital national concern for Germany – and by this means managed to win over public opinion in Germany in support of Austria against the threat of France.

In early 1859, Engels intervened with a pamphlet entitled *The Po and the Rhine*. He argued that although Austria had no claim to Lombardy and Venetia, militarily the Austrian occupation of Upper Italy was essential to the security of Germany. The main point was to combat the Bonapartist threat, since, as Engels argued, Napoléon's real ambition was to establish the French frontier at the Rhine, and thus to win back the glory which France had lost at the Congress of Vienna. Karl thought the pamphlet 'EXCEEDINGLY CLEVER', although he admitted the 'political side' was 'damned difficult'.[194]

Lassalle disagreed. In a pamphlet entitled *The Italian War and Prussia's Task*, he considered that the Italian War was no threat to Germany, that a war between France and Germany was undesirable and that democracy should oppose it. German support for the Austrian position in Italy was a mistake. It would strengthen Austria's position in Lombardy and Venetia; similarly, if Germany attacked France, Napoléon's standing in France would be strengthened.

Karl reacted angrily. 'Lassalle's pamphlet is an ENORMOUS BLUNDER. The publication of your "anonymous" pamphlet', he told Engels, 'made him envious . . . We must now absolutely insist on party discipline.'[195] In November 1859, Karl attempted to correct Lassalle on Bonaparte and Italy:

So far as I can see, the Italian war has temporarily strengthened Bonaparte's position in France; betrayed the Italian revolution into the hands of the Piedmontese doctrinaires and their henchmen; made Prussia

exceptionally popular with the liberal *vulgus* by virtue of her Haugwitz-
ian policy; increased *Russia's* influence in Germany; and, finally, propagated
demoralisation of an unprecedented kind – a most repulsive combination
of Bonapartism and drivel about nationalities.[196]

So much for the *Risorgimento*![197] He went on to berate Lassalle from
the viewpoint of the 'party'. 'Either no one speaks for the party without
prior consultation with the others, or everyone has the right to put forward his views without any regard for the others'. Public polemic, he
insisted, would in no way benefit such a small party, 'which, I hope,
makes up in vigour for what it lacks in numbers'.[198] But Lassalle did not
change his position.

The question of the meaning of 'party' arose again in 1860, this time
in relation to the answer Karl attempted to construct in relation to Carl
Vogt.[199] The Vogt affair arose out of differences between the exiles in
London. The majority were prepared to go along with Prussian leadership in Germany at least until the constitutional conflict of 1861–2. This
was the position adopted by Gottfried Kinkel, who founded *Hermann*,
the most successful German-language paper in London. *Hermann* under
Kinkel aligned itself with the National Association. But in July 1859 the
editorship of *Hermann* changed hands and the paper moved towards a
strongly pro-Austrian position. In this connection, it gave support to
Karl Blind, who had been associated with Struve in 1848. Blind was
inspired by Mazzini, had attacked pan-Slavism and supported a republican, anti-Prussian position in Germany. He also wrote a sharp attack
on Bonapartism and its expansionist ambitions. He was convinced that
political discussion was being influenced by Bonapartist agents, in particular Carl Vogt, a professor of geology and zoology at the University
of Geneva.

The renewal of political interest in 1858–9 found expression not
only in the growth of the liberal *Nationalverein*, but also in the revival
of the CABV (the *Communistischer Arbeiter-Bildungsverein*, or Communist Workers' Educational Association). The majority of its members
were followers of Weitling or Cabet and former members of the
Willich–Schapper faction. But there were also some followers of Karl,
notably Wilhelm Liebknecht, a philosophy graduate from Giessen and
former activist in the Communist League,[200] and the tailors Johann Georg
Eccarius and Friedrich Lessner. Liebknecht had become important

in the organization; he provided a weekly political survey and was chairman of the West End branch. One of the results of the Association's renewed political interest was the foundation in 1859 of a radical rival to *Hermann*: *Das Volk*, whose first number appeared on 7 May.

Karl was not a member of the Association, and he was cross with Liebknecht for allowing Bruno Bauer's brother, Edgar, to join. Nevertheless he was eager to re-establish his political renown. In the autumn of 1859, he gave 'private lectures' on political economy on the premises of the CABV to '20–30 picked men'. The first instalment of his *Contribution to the Critique of Political Economy* had just appeared in Germany, but he was resigned to poor sales since, as he told Lassalle, it had been 'utterly ignored' by critics.[201] He had also set his hopes upon the impact which would be made by Engels' *Po and Rhine* as a riposte to 'those dogs of democrats and liberal riff-raff . . . stultified by the ghastly period of peace'.[202] Karl's main hope was that the revival of the Association and the launching of *Das Volk* would provide an opportunity to re-establish the political hegemony of the 'party'. For this reason, from the beginning he offered covert help to the paper. His efforts to take control of the policy of the paper did not succeed, but when this ambition became known, it occasioned widespread resentment within the CABV and its disavowal of any further connection with the paper. A sharp decline in the readership followed, and despite considerable efforts on the part of Karl and Engels to save the paper it collapsed in August.

Karl's contributions to *Das Volk* were mainly concerned with the question of combating Bonaparte. His interest in the Italian War was virtually confined to this issue. He repeated his view that Bonaparte was in secret alliance with Russia, and that his involvement in the Crimean and Italian wars was dictated by the fact that 'War is the condition on which he keeps the throne.'[203] He even speculated that 'Mr. Bonaparte could not lead his praetorian hordes to any enterprise that could be more popular in France and a large part of the continent of Europe than an invasion of England.' And he concluded that 'Mr. Bonaparte is just the man to stake all on invasion. He must play *va banque* [go for broke]; sooner or later, but play he must.'[204] Karl's involvement in the affairs of *Das Volk* mattered because it led to his legal and political conflict with Carl Vogt, a battle which preoccupied Karl from the summer of 1859 through to December 1860, when he published his 300-page polemic *Herr Vogt*.

In *Herr Vogt*, Karl recounted that at a public meeting on 9 May 1859, arranged by David Urquhart to discuss the Italian War, he had been approached by Karl Blind – an ex-member of the Communist League, turned Mazzinian – who told him that he suspected that Carl Vogt was in the pay of Bonaparte. Vogt had been on the radical wing of the Frankfurt National Assembly in 1848–9 and had been prominent enough to be chosen as one the five 'imperial regents' when the Parliament was dissolved. He had developed a strongly anti-Austrian position and more recently argued that the support of Bonaparte was necessary to destroy Austrian hegemony and clear the way for successful liberal and national development in Germany.

Carl Vogt was one the most famous natural scientists of the age. He was a student of the famous chemist Liebig, and became professor of geology, physiology and zoology at the University of Geneva. In his early career, he achieved fame through his investigation of the mechanism of apoptosis – programmed cell death – which he identified in his study of the development of toad-tadpoles. He was acknowledged by Darwin as one of the foremost champions of the theory of evolution in *The Descent of Man*.[205] In his later career, he had developed a variant of evolutionary theory, entitled 'polygenism'. In this approach, the existence of different races was ascribed to the fact that each race had evolved from a different type of ape. This meant that the 'white race' belonged to a different species from 'the negro'.

Politically, what particularly attracted suspicion was Vogt's 1859 pamphlet, *Studies on the Present Situation of Europe*. The purpose of this work was to reassure German public opinion that Bonaparte's attitude towards the Italian Question fully respected 'German unity and nationhood' and should inspire 'the greatest sense of security in Germany'. But some of the phrases used appeared to be direct translations of French Bonapartist propaganda. As Karl wrote, 'his *Studien* are nothing but a *compilation* in German of *Moniteur* articles'.[206] In an anonymous article in Urquhart's *Free Press*, Blind directed suspicion at Vogt without actually naming him, but did name him in an anonymous flysheet, *Zur Warnung*.

Having heard the rumours from Karl, Liebknecht and the editor of *Das Volk*, Elard Biscamp, reprinted the allegations in *Das Volk*, claiming in addition that they had proof that Vogt had attempted to bribe a Baden democrat on France's behalf. In response, Vogt sued, not *Das Volk*, but the pro-Austrian Augsburg *Allgemeine Zeitung*, which reported the claim. The editors of the *Allgemeine Zeitung* turned to *Das Volk* for evidence to back up the allegations. *Das Volk* turned to Karl, and Karl turned to Karl Blind. Blind, however, denied authorship of *Zur Warnung*. It therefore looked as if Karl was the originator of the story. Karl repeatedly attempted to get Blind to admit to his authorship. But he refused.

From there, the story became even more complicated. In the print shop which published *Das Volk*, Liebknecht discovered the original proofs of *Zur Warnung* with corrections in Blind's handwriting. Eventually, this led to the admission that the author of *Zur Warnung* was a friend of Blind, Karl Schaible. Karl was therefore able to rebut the accusation that he had been responsible for the original allegation. But in the meantime, in December 1859, Vogt had published his own lengthy self-defence, *My Action against the Allgemeine Zeitung*, in which he attributed his persecution not to Blind, but to 'the web of intrigue woven by London Communists'. As Karl noted, Vogt had cleverly manoeuvred the evidence to make it seem as if it were a dispute between liberals and communists. As he told Lassalle, 'it was very clever of Vogt to make me out to be the source of the denunciation . . . Mr Vogt knew that Germany's vulgar democrats regard me as their *bête noire*.'[207]

Biographers have generally treated Karl's book-length self-defence, *Herr Vogt*, either as an example of his inability to distinguish between the important and the trivial or else as an unfortunate diversion from *Capital*, which he was supposed to be preparing at the same time. But given the gravity of Vogt's accusations, this charge seems unreasonable. Vogt charged that communists in London sent appeals to workers in Europe, who by responding identified themselves; thereafter they were either blackmailed or fell into the hands of the police. This unscrupulous activity had allegedly originated in Switzerland. Its original members had been connected with the attempted republican putsch of Gustav Struve in September 1848. Forced into Switzerland after the defeat of the Imperial Constitution Campaign, its members formed one or more gangs, the 'Brimstone Gang' and the 'Bristlers' (or maybe these were two names for the same organization). They moved to London, where they became active in one of the refugee committees. Vogt paid no attention to the 1850 split within the Communist League between the Marx faction and the Willich–Schapper faction. Both, according to Vogt, were branches of the Brimstone Gang.

With the renewal of political activity in 1858–9 and the founding of *Das Volk*, the Brimstone Gang were again said to have become active and were intent upon 'tearing to pieces the democratic party'. Vogt claimed that the gang was now said to be led by Karl, Liebknecht and Biscamp, the editor of *Das Volk*. At first, Vogt had believed that they were the unconscious tools of reaction. But today 'I have come to the conviction that they do so deliberately, that the persons mentioned are knowingly the instruments of reaction, that they maintain the closest connection with it . . . Everybody who enters into any kind of political dealings with Marx and his comrades will sooner or later fall into the hands of the police.' Clearly, the core accusations – the charges of blackmail and betrayal – were absurd. In response, Karl presented his own account of the history of the Communist League, starting from its activities before 1848. But, despite his best efforts, it was practically impossible to provide a clear and straightforward alternative account of communist activity in the aftermath of 1848 to the mixture of lies, half-truths and genuine facts presented by Vogt. It was a time in which far-fetched rumours and insurrectionist fantasy were too easily believed in exile circles, and in which every organization or grouping was vulnerable to the activities of spies and agents provocateurs. Edgar Bauer, who had himself become a Danish spy, claimed that the German emigration and the political police were 'two branches growing on the same tree'.[208] This activity of spies and double agents was at its height around the lead-up to the Cologne treason trial in 1852 and the manufacture of forged evidence to support the prosecution. Such activity made particularly deep inroads into the credibility of the Willich–Schapper faction, in which the doings of police agents such as Cherval, Gipperich, Hirsch and Fleury seriously compromised the reputation of Willich. But Karl was also implicated, having been flattered into writing *The Great Men of the Exile* at the behest of the secret agent 'Colonel Bangya'.

In the light of this somewhat grey history, it is perhaps not surprising that Karl's own interpretation of the exile in the 1850s was uncharacteristically mild: 'Except for a few persons, the emigration can be reproached with nothing worse than indulging illusions that were more or less justified by the circumstances of the period, or perpetrating follies which arose necessarily from the extraordinary situation in which it unexpectedly found itself.'[209] In the rest of the book, Karl recapitulated his belief in an unholy alliance between Bonapartism and Pan-Slavism, and that the arguments for such an alliance were to be found in Vogt's *Studies*. He also summarized the interpretation of Bonaparte he had put forward in the *Eighteenth Brumaire* and the allegations made in *Revelations of the Diplomatic History of the Eighteenth Century* that there had been 'continuous secret collaboration between the cabinets of London and St Petersburg' since the time of Peter the Great, a parallel but much more grandiose set of conspiracy theories to match those of Vogt. According to Karl, 'the Russian Pan-Slavist' Vogt supported the establishment of the 'natural frontier' of a Slav empire, and in support of this ambition had suggested that 'Russia annex Austria, Salzburg, Styria and the German parts of Carinthia'. In relation to Bonapartism, Karl explained why it was necessary for Napoléon to mount a limited war in Italy in response to the parlous state of the French economy and as a way to bolster the faltering loyalty of the army. He then went on to detail Bonaparte's designs on Switzerland, following his acquisition of Savoy.[210]

After reading *Herr Vogt*, Engels wrote to Karl: 'This is, of course, the best polemical work you have ever written; it's simpler in style than the Bonaparte [the *Eighteenth Brumaire*] and yet just as effective, where this is called for.'[211] Liebknecht also placed *Herr Vogt* together with *Capital* and *Eighteenth Brumaire* in a 'Trinity', each 'the unit of a great personality expressing itself differently on different topics'.[212] Edgar Bauer was more measured. He agreed that Karl had refuted Vogt's allegations against him. But although he had mounted a plausible case against Vogt on the basis of his writings, he had not succeeded in proving Vogt was a Bonapartist agent and was unable to do more than repeat Blind's original allegation.[213]

In Karl's own estimation, the battle with Vogt was 'crucial to the *historical vindication* of the party and its subsequent position in Germany'.[214] But, if anything, the argument with Vogt and the larger argument about the role of Bonaparte in Italy attested to the fading relevance of the 'party' at the end of the 1850s and the beginning of the 'new era'. The Vogt affair began as an argument among democrats, the allegations made by Blind against Vogt. The issue was not about revolution or the proletariat, but about the significance of Bonaparte's actions in Italy in relation to the prospect of national unification in Germany. This was not an issue which pitted socialists against democrats. It was an issue which divided socialists, just as it divided democrats. The inability to reach an agreed 'party' position on Italy was made apparent by the different approaches of Engels and Lassalle.

The fading relevance of 'party' was also made clear when Karl tried to enlist the support of the poet Freiligrath in the legal battle over Vogt. Although Freiligrath was happy to reiterate his personal friendship with Karl, and to affirm, like Karl, his continuing dedication to Saint-Simon's *'classe la plus laborieuse et la plus misérable'*,[215] he refused to be drawn into the Vogt battle as an issue of 'party'. He replied to Karl, 'when towards the end of 1852, the League was dissolved as a result of the Cologne trial, I severed all links that bound me to the party as such'. He had been 'a poet of the Revolution and the proletariat' long before he had joined the League or joined the editorial board of the *Neue Rheinische Zeitung*. As a poet, he needed freedom, but the party was 'a kind of cage'. Finally, another consideration had reinforced him in his determination never to regret his distance from the party. That was its association with the two-faced and base elements – like Tellering, Bangya, Fleury, etc. – who despite every precaution had been able to impose themselves upon the party. He was delighted whenever he recalled the feeling of cleanliness produced by not belonging to an organization which could bring him again into contact with such elements.[216]

Freiligrath's activities in the 1850s aptly illustrated the forces leading to the breakup of the 'party' in the second half of the 1850s. Despite his radical convictions, poetry and German literary culture drew Freiligrath closer to the affluent literary circle around the aspiring poet Gottfried Kinkel and his talented composer wife, Joanna, in affluent St John's Wood. In 1858, the newly founded radical democrat London paper *Die Neue Zeit*, aiming at a radical working-class audience, published an anonymous article by Karl ridiculing Kinkel's proposal to read German poetry to a select party touring the English lakes. Kinkel's weekly liberal-national journal *Hermann* was prepared to downplay republican and democratic politics in favour of a Prussian-led national unification. In the summer of 1858, Kinkel had also made renewed appearances to read his poetry at the Workers' Educational Association, leading to what Karl called a 'Kinkel Revival'.

In the autumn of 1858, Joanna Kinkel fell out of a window and was killed. For her funeral, Freiligrath wrote a poem, praising her faith in freedom, love and poetry and saluting her as a martyr fallen on the battlefield of exile. Karl was apoplectic at the apostasy of Freiligrath, whom he referred to in private as 'the fat philistine', for having participated in the 'melodramatic' funeral organized by Gottfried for 'the death of the 'NASTY acrimonious shrew'.[217] He was further offended the following year, when the attention of most Germans in London was focused upon the Schiller Festival to be held at Crystal Palace.[218] As poets, Kinkel together with Freiligrath were the most prominent members of the preparatory committee. Karl was angry that Freiligrath had made no attempt to insist that any of 'his party friends' be invited to the committee ('though he knew perfectly well that I wouldn't attend'). Kinkel's *Hermann* gave extensive publicity to the event, and virtually the entire German colony in London participated in the event.

Freiligrath's letter about the Vogt affair a few months later forced Karl to relinquish the convenient ambiguity that had attached to his notion of 'party' in the 1850s. Since he felt that he could not afford to alienate Freiligrath, his reply was placatory. By 'party', Karl explained, he did not mean the Communist League or the *Neue Rheinische Zeitung*, but 'party in the broad historical sense'.[219]

APPENDIX: FREDERICK DEMUTH

It is unlikely that much was seen of Frederick Demuth, 'Freddy', during Karl's lifetime. But he is said to have become a regular visitor to the surviving household, once Lenchen became Engels' housekeeper after Karl's death in 1883. At this point, Freddy was a skilled fitter and an active member of the King's Cross Branch of the Amalgamated Society of Engineers. Karl's daughters certainly knew him and considered that they had an obligation towards him. The accepted family story was that Freddy was Engels' son. But if that were true, the daughters thought Engels' treatment of him had been shabby. At the time of Lenchen's death in 1890, Eleanor Marx wrote to her sister, Laura, 'Freddy has behaved admirably in all respects and Engels' irritation against him is as unfair as it is comprehensible. We should none of us like to meet our pasts, I guess, in flesh and blood. I know I always meet Freddy with a sense of guilt and wrong done.'[220]

But a few days before Engels' death in August 1895, Eleanor first learnt from his close friend Samuel Moore that in fact Karl was

Freddy's father. He revealed the fact to give the lie to the gossip that Engels had disowned his son. It is likely that Laura already knew or strongly suspected this to be true. But Eleanor was shocked and upset. She went to get confirmation from Engels himself. Engels was dying from oesophageal cancer and too weak to speak, but wrote down the fact on a slate. He had told Moore, 'Tussy [Eleanor] wants to make an idol of her father.'[221]

Details of this deathbed scene first came to light as a result of the discovery in Amsterdam by Werner Blumenberg in 1962 of a letter of 2 August 1898 from Louise Freyburger to August Bebel. Freyburger, formerly the wife of Karl Kautsky, was Engels' housekeeper from 1890 until his death in 1895. Although she accepted Karl's paternity, Yvonne Kapp in her biography of Eleanor Marx launched a strong attack upon the credibility of the Freyburger letter. She claimed it was written in 'a vein of high fantasy' and she demonstrated the unlikelihood of several of the claims made in the letter.[222] Given the fact that only a typewritten copy of the letter existed and that its discovery provided useful anti-communist ammunition at the height of the Cold War, some like Terrell Carver believed the letter to be a forgery 'possibly by Nazi agents'.[223] In my entry on Engels in *The Dictionary of National Biography*, I also accepted this interpretation, and more recently this approach has been continued in the study by Paul Thomas.[224]

I now believe that although the Freyburger letter contained a number of far-fetched claims, these were garbled memories of what she might have heard from Engels rather than deliberate untruths. As for the idea that the document was a forgery, evidence confirming that several prominent German Social Democrats in the 1890s were aware of Freddy's paternity was collected by David Riazanov, but hidden in Soviet Communist archives after Riazanov was purged. This evidence came to light after the fall of Communism in the 1990s. From this, it also emerged that Freddy himself, who was a toolmaker and who died in 1929, was aware that Karl was his father.[225]

10

The *Critique of Political Economy*

1. KARL'S *OUTLINES OF THE CRITIQUE OF POLITICAL ECONOMY* IN 1857–8: THE SO-CALLED *GRUNDRISSE*[1]

In 1857, faced with the prospect of a global economic crisis and the possibility of another period of revolution, Karl finally pulled together the components of the 'critique of political economy', upon which he had first embarked in Paris in 1844. 'I am working like mad all night and every night collating my economic studies', he informed Engels, 'so that I at least get the outlines clear before the *déluge*.'[2] As he wrote to Lassalle in February 1858, he had 'been at work on the final stages for some months' and was 'at last ready to set to work after 15 years of study'. He wanted to publish the work in instalments without any 'rigid datelines', and hoped Lassalle might help him by finding 'someone in Berlin' prepared to undertake this form of publication. As Karl described the work to Lassalle:

> The work I am currently concerned with is a *Critique of Economic Categories* or, IF YOU LIKE, a critical exposé of the system of the bourgeois economy. It is at once an exposé and, by the same token, a critique of the system . . .
>
> The whole is divided into 6 books: 1. On Capital (contains a few introductory CHAPTERS). 2. On Landed Property. 3. On Wage Labour. 4. On the State. 5. International Trade. 6. World Market. I cannot, of course, avoid all critical consideration of other economists, in particular a polemic against Ricardo in as much as even he, *qua* bourgeois, cannot but commit blunders *even from a strictly economic viewpoint*. But generally speaking

the critique and history of political economy and socialism would form
the subject of another work and, finally, the short *historical outline* of the
development of economic categories and relations yet a third.[3]

The story narrated in what later became known as the *Grundrisse* was
that of man's loss and historical recuperation, of his 'social' or 'human
nature'. This nature had been concealed beneath the external and
abstract form which it had assumed in civil society. The attempt to
recount this development took the form of a 'critique of political economy', because economic categories – trade, competition, capital, money,
etc. – were 'only the theoretical expressions, the abstractions, of the
social relations of production'.[4]

But Karl's work did not go smoothly. Some months later, exasing his
delay in sending off the manuscript, he explained to Lassalle that this
was caused by illness; he also had to carry on with his journalistic
'"bread and butter" work'. It was not so much that he needed to do
more research – 'the material was to hand and all that I was concerned
with was the form'. But, he continued, 'the style of everything I wrote
seemed tainted with liver trouble'; and he was determined that 'the
product of 15 years of research, i.e. the best years of my life' should not
be 'spoiled on medical grounds'. Furthermore, he added, reasserting his
conception of himself as head of the 'party', 'In it an important view of
social relations is scientifically expounded for the first time. Hence I
owe it to the Party that the thing shouldn't be disfigured by the kind of
heavy, wooden style proper to a disordered liver.'[5]

The exposition of Karl's argument in the *Grundrisse* was clumsy and
disjointed. The presentation was chaotic. He did not follow the plans
which he had laid out to Lassalle, and there was little or no sign of the last
three books. The manuscript consisted of around 800 pages; an unfinished introduction, and two chapters, the first on 'Money', amounting to
120 pages, the second on 'Capital', amounting to around 690 pages. Most
of the text related to part 1, on 'Capital', and this was subdivided into
three subsections – 'The Process of Production of Capital', 'Circulation
Process of Capital' and 'Capital as Bearing Fruit. Interest. Profit. (Production Costs, etc.)'. Major themes jostled with preoccupations arising
from the events of 1848, or from his *New-York Tribune* journalism.
Although the text abounded with unresolved intellectual questions, it
is wrong to interpret this disorganization in a wholly negative light. In

part, it was the result of a period of intense creativity marked by desperate attempts to jot down thoughts which properly belonged to much later stages in the argument than the topics supposedly to be covered in the initial volume. As Jenny wrote to 'Mr Engels' in April 1858, Karl's 'bile and liver are again in a state of rebellion ... The worsening of his condition', she went on, 'is largely attributable to mental unrest and agitation which now, of course, after the conclusion of the contract with the publisher, are greater than ever and increasing daily, since he finds it utterly impossible to bring the work to a close.'[6] Six weeks later, Karl himself wrote asking whether Engels could write something general about the British forces in India for the *Tribune*, 'Since reading over my own manuscript will take me the better part of a week. The damnable part of it is that my manuscript (which in print would amount to a hefty volume) is a real hotchpotch, much of it intended for much later sections. So I shall have to make an index briefly indicating in which notebook and on which page to find the stuff I want you to work on first.'[7]

2. 1844–57: THE DEVELOPMENT OF KARL'S CRITICISM OF POLITICAL ECONOMY

In 1844, when Karl had first begun to criticize political economists, there had been no internal critique or detailed engagement with political economy and there was nothing which could be depicted as a contradiction specific to the modern 'bourgeois economy'. The only reality described was that of private property, whose effect had been to make man dependent upon competition and to turn the worker into a commodity whose creation or destruction depended upon changes in demand. Karl followed Proudhon in maintaining that where private property existed, objects cost more than they were worth, and goods were sold for more than their value. Exchange, as Engels maintained, was the result of 'mutual swindling' and its only law was 'chance'. The overall contrast was between the miseries attributable to private property and the true destination of 'man'. The 'man' delineated here was not the empirical man invoked by political economy, but man as he was essentially: 'a human natural being', whose meaning was to be found not in his natural beginnings, but in his historical destination.

Similarly, the 'forces' and 'relations' of production mentioned in Karl's writings of 1845 and 1846 were not linked to the internal workings of any specific economic system. Although the terminology may have been new, the ideas themselves were not original. Ideas that linked private property to higher degrees of productivity, or suggested an affinity between forms of production and forms of government, were already to be found in the seventeenth century: for example, in contrasts between European landed property and the nomadic hunting-and-gathering practices of American tribes, or between the property-based regimes of Europe and 'oriental despotism'.[8]

Only in *The Poverty of Philosophy* did Karl begin to focus upon 'the bourgeois economy', and even then only in a cursory manner.[9] Engaged in a denunciation of Proudhon, Karl drew upon Ricardo's *Principles of Political Economy and Taxation* to provide an alternative theory of value.[10] Proudhon had objected that Ricardo's assumption of the equivalence of values and prices in exchange was a mere idealization. The main problem of the bourgeois economy was that products did not sell at their value. To remedy this failing, Proudhon proposed various measures including the abolition of money, which he saw as the main obstacle to the establishment of true and just relations of exchange.

Karl replied with a defence of Ricardo: 'the determination of value by labour time – the formula M. Proudhon gives us as the regenerating formula of the future' was 'merely the scientific expression of the economic relations of present-day society'. He then drew upon his reading of English political economists to argue that Proudhon's practical proposals were similar to those of John Francis Bray and others, put forward twenty years earlier. These Owenite socialists had believed that problems of deflation and credit restriction could be solved by the introduction of a system of labour notes to replace money.[11] Beyond such arguments, there had been no sustained examination of Ricardo's economic theory. In *The Poverty of Philosophy*, Karl had simply treated Ricardo's work as the 'completion' of the science of political economy at its moment of triumph, the expression of an epoch, now passed.

Settled in London in 1850–51 in the aftermath of the revolutions, Karl resumed his economic studies and again consulted Ricardo.[12] He began to think that Ricardo's conception of value might be employed both to provide a measure of bourgeois wealth and to explain how the 'bourgeois economy' – or what he increasingly called 'capital' or the 'value form' – drove forward the forces of production. It reinforced the emphasis that he was now placing upon the power and centrality of the development of productive forces. In 1847, he had argued that the 'productive forces' had been driven forward by a 'system of class antagonisms', especially that between 'accumulated labour and immediate labour' (capital and labour).[13] Yet in his writings up to and including *The Class Struggles in France*, productive forces played a relatively modest and indeterminate role in Karl's thought. In the early 1850s, however, he could not miss their power and dynamism in the world-wide boom and return to prosperity that had killed off the revolution in Europe. He now placed his hopes in the cyclical character of the growth of the productive forces. The volatile development of modern industry associated with steam power and the factory system was accompanied by recurrent bouts of overproduction. This would soon bring about renewed unemployment, the re-emergence of the workers' movement and the return of revolution.

Karl attempted to employ Ricardo's concept of value in the elaboration of a theory quite remote from anything which had concerned Ricardo himself. Ricardo's theory related value to socially necessary labour time, and was intended to be valid only in aggregate; he placed qualifications upon its validity. His notion of value was not intended to be generally applicable. Its purpose was limited: to make possible an account of changing distribution, once complicating factors like the heterogeneity of products had been removed.

Unlike Ricardo himself, Karl saw Ricardo's value simply as 'bourgeois wealth in its most abstract form'.[14] He wanted to make the value of labour measurable and applicable to the individual enterprise. He wanted it to explain the source of unpaid labour and show why a system ostensibly resting upon equal and fair exchange could consistently yield a surplus to one of the parties to the exchange. If, as he believed, the source of inequality was not to be discovered in the process of exchange, but in the process of production, a focus upon the hours of labour worked in value terms in contrast to the notional number of hours necessary to enable the labourer to subsist and reproduce his kind would provide a way of substantiating the argument.

Around 1857, Karl drew together into one argument a number of propositions from previously unconnected sources. From the French radical economic literature of the 1830s and 1840s, he adopted the idea that what the labourer sold was not his labour, but his ability to labour, his 'labour power'. This idea was already to be found in Buret and Proudhon. He now attempted to connect this insight with his reading of Ricardo, in which the value of a commodity was determined by socially necessary labour time and the value of labour was that necessary to sustain and reproduce the labourer. He also added in the belief, popular among radicals and socialists, that labour was the sole source of wealth ('the labour theory of value'), and that therefore profit could only be derived from living labour.

Karl's approach offered a new way of demonstrating the exploitative character of capital. In purchasing labour power, the labourer's capacity to work, the capitalist was motivated to increase the value created by labour beyond that necessary to sustain and reproduce the labourer (Ricardo's subsistence theory of wages); in other words, to extract 'surplus value' from the workers. The way this had been done was by lengthening the working day, what Karl called 'absolute surplus value'. But with the growing use of machines and steam power, the emphasis was moved towards increasing the productivity of the labourer during each hour of work, by using machines to determine the speed at which labourers were compelled to work. This was called 'relative surplus value'.

According to Karl, the great advantage of the value theory was that it made possible the development of a theory of crisis which was specific to the 'bourgeois economy'. In place of broad references to private property, polarization and immiseration, it pointed to contradictions specific to modern industry and capital; and it was particularly relevant as a counter to bourgeois public opinion that still accepted the popular Malthusian approach, which attributed problems of poverty and unemployment to overpopulation and the workers' lack of self-restraint: 'Since the condition of production based on capital is that the worker produces an ever greater quantity of surplus labour, it follows that an ever greater quantity of *necessary labour* is set free. The chances of his sinking into pauperism therefore increase. The development of surplus labour implies that of surplus population.'[15]

With the development of modern industry and increasing investment in labour-saving machinery, the trend was accentuated in two ways. First, the productivity, and hence intensity, of exploitation of labourers was increased. As Karl's reading of the works of Andrew Ure and Charles Babbage had revealed, increased productivity was not simply a matter of machine technology; it also involved the reorganization of the division of labour and of factory space such that work was no longer divided between workers, but between machines and their minders.[16] Secondly, the numbers of labourers from whom surplus value could be extracted was diminishing; or to put it in the terms Karl employed, the ratio of 'constant capital' (fixed capital investment) to 'variable capital' (wage labour) increased. Since, in Karl's view, profit could only be derived from living labour, this meant that the rate of profit was falling:

> the *rate of profit* depends on the ratio between the part of capital exchanged for living labour and the part of it existing in the form of raw material and means of production. So, as the portion exchanged for living labour declines, there is a corresponding decline in the rate of profit. In the same degree, therefore, in which capital as capital takes up more space in the production process relative to immediate labour, i.e. the greater the increase in relative surplus value – in the value creating power of capital – the more *the rate of profit declines*.[17]

'In every respect,' Karl wrote, 'this is the most important law of modern political economy, and the most essential one for comprehending the most complex relationships'; and it had never before been grasped, let alone 'consciously formulated'.[18] For what it proved, he thought, was that there was a mechanism inherent within capital itself which was productive of crisis.

Faced with this threat, capital would 'try everything to make up for the smallness of the proportion which surplus value, if expressed as profit, bore to "the pre-posited capital"'. The result would be that:

THE HIGHEST DEVELOPMENT OF PRODUCTIVE POWER TOGETHER WITH THE GREATEST EXPANSION OF EXISTING WEALTH WILL COINCIDE WITH DEPRECIATION OF CAPITAL, DEGRADATION OF THE LABOURER, AND A MOST STRAIGHTENED EXHAUSTION OF HIS VITAL POWERS.

These contradictions, he asserted, would lead to:

EXPLOSIONS, CATACLYSMS, CRISES

Capital's survival might be ensured through a:

MOMENTANEOUS SUSPENSION OF LABOUR

and

ANNIHILATION OF A GREAT PORTION OF CAPITAL ...
YET, THESE REGULARLY RECURRING CATASTROPHES
LEAD TO THEIR REPETITION ON A HIGHER SCALE, AND
FINALLY TO ITS VIOLENT OVERTHROW.[19]

The adoption of this value theory was combined with a picture of
human development, presented as the changing relationship between
matter and form. 'Matter' consisted of persons and things. Form consisted of the particular connections made between persons and things,
together with accompanying conceptions of the world. The advantage
of this terminology over the more frequently employed 'forces and relations of production' was that it highlighted the idea that value and the
production of commodities constituted a social *form*. At a certain point
in human development, there had been progressively superimposed upon
the relations between and within societies the primacy of a particular
social form. Assisted by the growth of monetary relations, the simple
exchange of useful products had increasingly given way to the exchange
of commodities as embodiments of exchange value. Thus the subsequent
growth of productive powers had taken place under the auspices of what
Karl called 'the value form': economic activity defined as the maximiza-
tion of exchange value.

Subsequent history was therefore the development of a dual process
of material production and of valorization. At the beginning, the process of material production and the process of valorization had been
relatively distinct. But 'by the incorporation of labour into capital, capital becomes process of production, but initially *material* process of
production; process of production in general, so that the process of production of capital is not distinct from the material process of production
in general. Its determinateness of form is completely extinguished.'[20]
This meant that capital was '*this unity of production and valorisation
not immediately*, but only as a process tied to certain conditions'.[21]

3. THE ORIGINS OF A SOCIAL FORM

Why and how did this social form come into being? At the beginning
of *The Wealth of Nations*, Adam Smith stated that the division of

labour was 'the necessary, though very slow and gradual, consequence of a certain propensity in human nature . . . the propensity to truck, barter, and exchange one thing for another'.[22] Similar assumptions were made in manuals of popular political economy, which Karl attacked at the beginning of his introduction to the *Grundrisse*. In them, economic life was imagined to have begun as it did in *Robinson Crusoe*, with an 'individual and isolated hunter and fisherman . . . They saw this individual not as a historical result, but as the starting point of history; not as something evolving in the course of history, but posited by nature, because for them this individual was the natural individual, according to their idea of human nature.'[23] Karl stressed the absurdity of believing that private property and the individual should be considered the appropriate historical starting points in accounts of political economy: 'It is not until the 18th century, in "bourgeois society"' that the various forms of the social nexus confront the individual as merely a means towards his private ends, as external necessity . . . Production by an isolated individual outside society', he continued, 'is just as preposterous as the development of language without individuals who live *together* and speak to one another.'[24]

In order to establish that capital or commercial society was not simply an expression of human nature, it was necessary to show that it was the product of a particular social form. The *Grundrisse* traced an elaborate history designed to demonstrate that 'the value form' was the product of a certain stage of productive development and was destined to be superseded once a higher stage was reached. Underlying Karl's alternative picture was the supposition of a world of aboriginal sociability, which had been disrupted, but also propelled into a particular trajectory of development, by the incursion of private property and the development of exchange relations. Man became 'individualised only through the process of history'. Originally, he was 'species being, a tribal being, a herd animal . . . The further back we go in history, the more does the individual and accordingly also the producing individual, appear to be dependent and belonging to a larger whole. At first he is still in a quite natural manner part of the family, and of the family expanded into the tribe, later he is part of a community, of one of the different forms of community which arise from the conflict and the merging of tribes.'[25]

Exchange was the major agent of individualization. It made 'herd-like existence . . . superfluous' and dissolved it. If, as he argued, 'the earth is the great workshop, the arsenal, which provides both the means and the material of labour', then:

> What requires explanation, is not the *unity* of living and active human beings, with the natural, inorganic conditions of their exchange of matter with nature, and therefore their appropriation of nature. Nor of course is this the result of an historical process. What we must explain is the *separation* between these inorganic conditions of human existence and this active being, a separation which is posited in its complete form only in the relationship between wage labour and capital.[26]

In historical terms, the form most frequently found in the earliest times was common property, as it had prevailed, for instance, among the Indians, Slavs and ancient Celts. But even where land was not common property, the individual was not a proprietor in a modern sense. 'An isolated individual could no more have property in land than he could speak.' His relation to the objective conditions of labour was 'mediated by his being a member of a community'.[27]

In time, increase in population and the beginnings of trade destroyed these conditions. The communal system decayed and died along with the property relations upon which it was based. But the process was a gradual one. 'Even where the land has become private property, it is exchange value only in a restricted sense. Exchange value originates in the isolated natural product separated from the earth and individualised by means of industry (or simple appropriation). This is the stage too, at which individual labour makes its first appearance.'[28] Exchange did not initially arise within communities, but at their borders. Trading peoples like the Jews and the Lombards were 'the intermundia of the ancient world' and could coexist with ancient communities, without disrupting them. But eventually, the impact of trade on communities was 'to subject production to exchange value and force immediate use value more and more into the background by making subsistence depend more upon the sale of the product than upon its immediate use'.[29]

The speed at which this happened varied. In Asia, the communal system was most long-lasting, still in existence, in part because of poor communications, in part because it rested upon a self-sustaining unity of manufacture and agriculture at village level. In these conditions, the individual did not become independent in relation to the commune. In Ancient Rome, on the other hand, and other small warring polities, the continuation of the commune was dependent upon 'the reproduction of all its members as self-sustaining peasants', whose surplus time belonged to the commune, 'the labour of war etc.'. In areas accustomed to communal production, where conquest in war meant that the producer was captured along with his land, systems of slavery or serfdom were established. 'Slavery and serfdom are therefore only further developments of property based on tribalism.'[30] These conditions were 'the result of a restricted historical stage of the development of the productive forces, both of wealth and the mode of producing it . . . The purpose of the community, of the individual – as well as the condition of production – was the reproduction of these specific conditions of production and of individuals, both singly and in their social groups and relations – as the living carriers of these conditions.'[31]

Ancient history was 'the history of cities, but cities based on landed property and agriculture'. 'Asiatic' history was a 'kind of indifferent unity of town and country'; really large cities were merely 'royal camps' and were 'an artificial excrescence on the actual economic structure'. A third form of development emerged in the Middle Ages, Hegel's 'Germanic period'. It began with 'the land as the locus of history', and its further development then proceeded 'through the contradiction between town and country'. Modern history was 'the urbanisation of the countryside, not as in ancient times, the ruralisation of the city'.[32]

The origins of modern bourgeois society were explained in terms of the breakdown of communal forms in the face of the development of forces of production and emergence of the value form. The attempt was to tell a two-fold story: on the one hand, of the development of man's essential capacities (industry, the forces of production), and on the other, of the sequence of social relations which punctuated the expansion of capital and the value form.

In his manuscript, Karl noted that in the first section, where exchange value, money and price were considered, 'commodities always appear as already in existence', they expressed 'characteristics of social production', even if their determinant role was not explicit.[33] As a result, in the published version of the work, *A Contribution to the Critique of Political Economy*, which appeared in 1859, Karl chose to begin with the commodity; and he retained this starting point in the eventual publication of *Capital* in 1867. The commodity was chosen because it represented both a concrete and useful object, a 'use value', and an abstract component of an economic system, based upon private property, an 'exchange value'.[34]

From the commodity it was possible to trace the emergence of money. Unlike the commodity, money as an abstract exchange value lacked any connection with the natural form of commodity. If exchange value represented man's externalized social relations, money embodied this relationship in its most abstract form; it was a pure abstraction of 'universal social qualities'. Karl was obliged to modify the unqualified condemnation of money which he had issued in 1844. Money in some of its forms – as a measure of value or as a medium of exchange – had coexisted with ancient communities. Hence, it was not money as such but money in its 'third determination', as abstract exchange value and its role as an externalized social relationship in civil society, which was incompatible with the existence of primitive pre-capitalist communities. The 'community of antiquity' had been shattered by the 'development of money in its third dimension'.[35] Its effect had been to dissolve tribes, clans and ancient peasant communities.

In this form, money enabled capital to emerge. Its emergence was to be traced in the transition between two cycles. The first cycle, in which money functioned solely as a medium of exchange – C–M–C (commodity–money–commodity) – and which did not presuppose the existence of capital, Karl called 'simple circulation'. But exchange value did appear in the following cycle, M–C–M (money–commodity–money), which Karl considered characteristic of merchant capital. But its presence on the periphery of society and its employment by the Lombards or the Jews did not involve the production of commodities and did not – at least in its early stages – disrupt the functioning of ancient communities.

The morally corrupting effects of money in its third dimension was condemned as vehemently in 1857 as it had been in 1844: 'The exchangeability of all products, activities, relationships for a third, *objective* entity, which can in turn be exchanged for everything *without distinction* – in other words the development of exchange values (and of monetary relationships) is identical with general venality, with corruption. General prostitution appears as a necessary phase ... Equating the incommensurate, as Shakespeare appropriately conceived of money.'[36] But the role of money was now linked in a more measured way with the larger pattern of economic development. While it was true that 'the prehistory of the development of modern industrial society' opened 'with a general greed for money on the part of individuals and states', that appetite had also provoked innovation. The search for gold had created new wants and led to the discovery of remote parts of the world. Furthermore, unlike Rome, where money was accumulated by plunder, and the wealth of individuals was fortuitous, money 'as a developed element' now presupposed the presence of wage labour. It pointed to the presence of the 'elementary precondition for bourgeois society', wage labour and capital as 'different forms of developed exchange value and of money as its incarnation'.[37]

This was of particular importance in the countryside, where the spread of monetary relations and the formation of modern capital was signalled by the transformation of the feudal lord into the recipient of money rent. Such a transition could not have happened simply through the movement of exchange values in the process of circulation. It was made possible through 'the dissolution of the old form of landed property'. Feudal retainers were dismissed, and, as Adam Smith noted, the landowner was instead enabled to exchange his corn and cattle for imported use values. Agriculture was converted into 'industrial agronomy', while cotters, serfs, villeins, copyholders and cottagers 'necessarily' became 'day labourers, wage labourers'. Thus *wage labour* in its totality' was first created by the action of capital upon landed property.[38]

In his account, Karl distinguished between 'the original [or 'primitive'] accumulation of capital' and the assemblage of large concentrations of resources by non-economic means from the regular process of circulation. Investment in new forms of manufacture and the commercialization of agriculture were made possible by the availability of concentrations of monetary wealth, acquired through usury, trade, urbanization and the development of government finance, together with enclosure and the appropriation of church property.[39] At the same time, in England, by means of wage legislation and other coercive measures, the Tudor state had forced those thrown off the land – beggars and 'sturdy vagabonds' – towards wage labour.

Once they were separated from their land, those who had originally combined the possession of a smallholding with spinning or weaving as ancillary activities found themselves increasingly dependent upon the domestic manufacture and sale of these products. Entanglement in a system of monetary relations, dominated by merchants and situated outside the towns, and therefore beyond the control of the guilds, led to increasing indebtedness and the eventual loss of their possession of instruments of labour. Finally, even the illusion that these workers were independent producers selling products evaporated. The final step was to remove the work performed at home into large workshops and eventually factories. What had begun ostensibly as a form of exchange ended as wage labour in a system resting upon 'the total separation of labour and property'.[40]

Capital now included not only the exchange of values, but also the production of exchange values, and this entailed the development of a labour process that bound together capital and wage labour. It also produced a cycle which possessed an inner dynamic. For now, at the point of departure:

> *Production* which creates, which posits exchange values . . . *presupposes circulation as a developed moment* and appears as a constant process positing circulation and continually returning from circulation back into itself, in order to posit it anew. Hence the movement which posits exchange values now appears in a much more complex form in that it is no longer only the movement of the presupposed exchange values or the movement which formally posits them as prices, but the movement which simultaneously creates, produces, exchange values as its own premiss.[41]

Such a self-sustaining cycle of production and circulation encroached upon landed property – the intended subject of Karl's Book III. It also constantly enlarged and extended the sphere of wage labour – the intended subject of Book IV.

Although Karl's historical examples were drawn overwhelmingly from England, England was only intended as an illustration of the development of a global organic system; one in which each entity followed the other along a predetermined path of development: or, as Karl put it, 'the anatomy of man is the key to the anatomy of the ape'.[42] Each circuit of capital entailed the return to its point of departure; capital thus created the social conditions for its continued reproduction and expansion through the increasing subversion of pre-capitalist forms, whether of peasant or craft production, and progressively installed in their place the continually renewed production of capitalists and wage labourers. Thus the global destiny of capital was 'to conquer the whole earth for its market'. Through circles of ever greater universality, the purport of the simple commodity at the beginning was linked to the development of the world market at the end. But, like other organisms, capital as a whole was characterized by a life cycle, which meant that its ultimate global conquest would at the same time mark the beginning of its dissolution.

4. BETWEEN HEGEL AND FEUERBACH

The mixture of elements put together to underpin this first full-scale 'critique of political economy' was the product of Karl's critical encounters with those who had most deeply shaped his philosophical formation: Hegel and Feuerbach. It is clear that when attempting to organize his material, Karl's first resort was Hegel. At points in the *Grundrisse*, Karl attempted to apply Hegel's dialectical organization of concepts.[43] But he also reminded himself that it would be necessary 'to correct the idealist manner of presentation which makes it appear as if it were merely a matter of the definitions of concepts and the dialectic of these concepts'.[44] Karl remained true to the original insight which he derived from his reading of Hegel's *Phenomenology* in 1844: that the essence of labour was to be understood as the creation of man as 'the outcome of man's *own labour*'.[45] But by 1857 this original emphasis upon man as producer had been transformed into a more grounded conception of the historical development of the forces of production.

In attempting to visualize this global pattern of productive development, Karl was also attracted by the circular image which he found in Hegel's *Science of Logic*. In a letter written to Engels in January 1858, he stated, 'What was of great use to me as regards *method* of treatment was Hegel's *Logic*, at which I had taken another look by MERE ACCIDENT, Freiligrath having found and made a present of several volumes of Hegel, originally the property of Bakunin.'[46] In his *Science of Logic*, Hegel had conceived the development of thought as a circular process, or rather as a spiral of concepts of increasing universality. In the *Grundrisse*, Karl similarly presented the growth of the value form as a series of cycles or of one great spiral embracing more and more universal forms of human interaction. Thus, in the depiction of the development from simple circulation to capital, Karl noted that 'Exchange value posited as the unity of commodity and money is *capital*, and this positing itself appears as the circulation of capital. (But this is a spiral line, an expanding curve, not a simple circle).'[47] In this way, the circular trajectory of the commodity proceeded from the simplest of beginnings through to its apogee in the world market.

Even so, the dialectic present in the *Grundrisse* was not that of Hegel. In both Hegel and the *Grundrisse*, a relationship is presented between form and matter or content (the *Grundrisse* text refers indifferently to *Stoff*, *Inhalt* or *Materie*). This relationship begins as one of seeming externality and indifference, but conceals and eventually reveals itself as one of reciprocal interdependence. In Hegel's thought, this contradiction, embodied in the exteriority of form and matter, would be surmounted as soon as the internal relations were revealed, and it became clear that the matter contained the form enclosed within it. In the *Grundrisse*, the relationship between use value and exchange value was similarly presented as the immanence of the one within the other. But while Hegel saw this relationship of contradiction and exteriority as ending in unity and synthesis, in the *Grundrisse* form and matter remained separate and irreducible to each other. The one was subordinate to the other, and their relationship remained that of hierarchy, in which the dominant moment was played by production.

In other words, the value form – economic relations – was unilaterally determined by the movement of productive forces embodied in the labour process. In the introduction to the *Grundrisse*, Karl stated this objection to Hegel: 'nothing is simpler for a Hegelian than to posit production and consumption as identical'. Production, distribution, exchange and consumption were not identical; they were all 'elements of a totality, differences within a unity'. But production was 'the dominant moment, both with regard to itself in the contradictory determination of production and with regard to the other moments'.[48] Distinguishing his own approach from that of Hegel later in the manuscript, Karl wrote, 'Considered *notionally*, the dissolution of a definite form of consciousness would be sufficient to destroy an entire epoch. In reality, this barrier to consciousness corresponds to a *definite degree of development of the material productive forces* and thus of wealth.'[49] In the introduction, Karl's 'point of departure' – 'individuals producing in a society – hence the socially determined production by individuals' – also defined his opposition to conventional political economy.[50] He considered its main defect to be the assumption of the priority of circulation and relations of exchange. This was his main objection to French political economy. He mocked what French radicals believed to be the original promise of the French Revolution: that equal citizenship would lead to equal exchange. There were some like Frédéric Bastiat who maintained that with the advent of free trade this promise was being realized. But Karl's main target was Proudhon, who, together with other socialists, objected that exchanges remained unequal and that the exchange process had been distorted by the banks. This was why the first twenty-five pages of the *Grundrisse*, Chapter One, was taken up with a critique of proposals for banking reform put forward by the Proudhonist Alfred Darimon.[51] Karl's acceptance of the Ricardian claim that products did exchange at their value obliged him not only to elaborate his conception of the primacy of production over exchange and circulation, but also to explain why the surface appearance was deceptive.

This association of capital with equality and freedom was understandable. Bourgeois society was not hampered by the explicit relations of hierarchy and subordination found in feudalism or slavery. The performance of labour was preceded by a freely made contract between the worker and the capitalist, who encountered each other in conditions of apparent equality. Furthermore, the commodities then produced were sold in a market governed by free competition. In bourgeois society, the worker also confronted the capitalist as consumer; 'he becomes one of the innumerable centres of circulation, in which his specific character as worker is extinguished'.[52] The legitimacy of capital was built upon these facts. The system of exchange, of the market, represented the public face of bourgeois society; society appeared to consist of exchangers. As Karl was later to put it in *Capital*, it was 'a very Eden of the innate rights of man. There alone rule Freedom, Equality, Property and Bentham.'[53]

But if exchanges were equal, how had capital accumulation taken place? Equal exchange implied the principle of identity, or non-contradiction. Without contradiction, there could be no movement. The simple movement of exchange values could never realize capital; '*circulation . . . does not contain in itself the principle of self-renewal*'.[54] Karl's solution was that circulation, seen as 'that which is immediately present on the surface of bourgeois society', was 'pure semblance'. It was '*the image of a process occurring behind it*'.[55] This process began when trade seized control of production and the merchant became a producer or the producer a merchant. It had been documented by Karl in his account of the transformation of the English rural economy, of expropriation from the land, of the emergence of the putting-out system and, as a result, the growth of a relationship between wage labour and capital, based upon 'the propertylessness of the labourers'.[56] The picture of exchange painted by Proudhon and other socialists was an anachronism. It meant applying the property and legal relationships corresponding to simple exchange to those of a higher stage of exchange value.[57] The socialists had been deceived by its surface appearance. It was true that 'an exchange of equivalents occurs . . . [But it] is merely the surface layer of [a system] of production which rests on the appropriation of alien labour *without exchange*, but under the *guise of exchange*. This system of exchange has *capital* as its basis. If we consider it in isolation from capital, as it presents itself on the surface, as an *independent* system, we are subject to a mere *illusion*, though a *necessary one*.'[58]

Reference to the illusory characteristics of exchange enabled Karl to restate an argument he had first sketched out in 1844. This was that the effect of the ascendancy of capital as a social form was akin to the emergence of religion. This approach was originally inspired by his encounter with Feuerbach in 1843–4. During his years in Brussels in 1846–7, Karl had criticized Feuerbach for the passivity of his image of man, but he had not distanced himself from Feuerbach's idea of abstraction or alienation. In Feuerbach's critique of religion and philosophy, human emotions or thoughts (concepts) were projected onto God, or, by extension, onto equally fictive impersonal beings, now endowed with independent movement and agency. Under the sway of capital and the value form, an analogous evacuation of human agency had taken place in the everyday conduct of economic life. Just as in religion, it no longer appeared that man had created God, but that God had created man, so in economic life humans no longer saw themselves as the authors of their social relationships, but as the creatures of impersonal economic forces endowed with independent will and power. In bourgeois society, 'the absolute mutual dependence of individuals, who are indifferent to one another, constitutes their social connection. This social connexion is expressed in *exchange value* . . . The activity, whatever its individual form of manifestation, and the product of the activity, whatever its particular nature, is *exchange value,* i.e. something general in which all individuality, all particularity, is negated and extinguished.'

These conditions superimposed upon social relations an 'objective illusion' and in particular a process of inversion or abstraction analogous to that discussed by Feuerbach in his analyses of Christianity or Hegel: 'The general exchange of activities and products, which has become the condition of life for every single individual, their mutual connection, appears to the individuals themselves alien, independent, as a thing. In exchange value, the social relationship of persons is transformed into a social attitude of things; personal capacity into a capacity of things.'[59] Capital as 'objectified labour' continued to be presented as a baleful Frankenstein's monster: 'The product of labour, objectified labour is endowed with a soul of its own by living labour itself and establishes itself as an alien power confronting its creator.'[60]

As the visible surface of society, behind which the process of production pressed forward, exchange or circulation represented the boundary or limit of capital as a social form. Value could only be 'realized' in an act of exchange, and money was the medium of this exchange. But there was no guarantee that such exchanges would take place. Overproduction or the disproportionality between sectors could easily disrupt the process. Capital was the 'dynamic unity of production and circulation'.[61] Circulation was 'an essential process of capital' since 'the process of production cannot be recommenced until the commodity has been transformed into money'. Thus, 'The *uninterrupted continuity* of that process, the unhindered and fluent transition of value from one form into the other, or from one phase of the process into the other, appears as a basic condition for production based on capital to a much greater degree than for all earlier forms of production.'[62] The continuity of this process depended on chance, even if this unpredictability was to an increasing extent reduced by the operation of credit. With the extension of credit, however, came over-trading, speculation and overproduction. The forces that drove capital on were also those that drove towards its dissolution: 'The universality for which capital ceaselessly strives, comes up against barriers in capital's own nature, barriers which at a certain stage of its development will allow it to be recognised as being itself the greatest barrier in the way of this tendency, and will therefore drive towards its transcendence through itself.'[63] What was becoming increasingly clear was that 'there is a limit, not inherent to production generally, but to production founded on capital'.[64]

The signs of approaching crisis were everywhere to be seen in their effects upon the worker: 'the activity of the worker, restricted to a mere abstraction of activity, is determined and governed in every respect by the movement of machinery, not vice versa'. Yet far from diminishing the intensity of labour, the pressure imposed by the falling rate of profit upon employed workers meant that 'the most developed machinery now compels the labourer to work for a longer time than the savage does, or than the labourer himself did when he was using the simplest, crudest implements'.[65] It was approaching the point where 'the relation of capital becomes a barrier to the productive forces of labour'. Once this point was reached, wage labour 'enters the same relation to the development of social wealth and the productive forces as the guild system, serfdom and slavery did, and is, as a fetter, necessarily cast off'.[66]

In the *Grundrisse*, there was little or nothing to indicate what the promised 'books' on the state, international trade and the world market might contain. Mention of wage labour was also sparse and unspecific. For labour, 'The recognition of the products as its own, and its awareness that its separation from the conditions of its realisation is improper and imposed by force, is an enormous consciousness, and is itself the product of the mode of production based on capital, and just as much the KNELL TO ITS DOOM as the consciousness of the slave that he cannot be the *property of another*, his consciousness of being a person, reduced slavery to an artificial lingering existence, and made it impossible for it to continue to provide the basis of production.'[67] The imminence of the end of wage labour was indicated by the direction taken by the productive forces. As Robert Owen had suggested, 'since the general introduction of inanimate mechanism into British manufactories, man, with few exceptions, has been treated as a secondary and inferior machine'. The worker now stood 'beside the production process rather than being its main agent'.[68]

This new foundation of production created by large-scale industry suggested a possible escape from the current 'miserable foundation' provided by 'the *theft of alien labour time, which is the basis of present wealth*'. Once labour in its immediate form ceased to be 'the great source of wealth', this would mean that the '*surplus labour of the masses*' would cease to be 'the condition for the development of general wealth, just as the *non-labour of a few*' would cease to be 'the condition for the development of the general powers of the human mind'. Then production based upon exchange value would collapse, and the immediate material production process itself would be 'stripped of its form of indigence and antagonism'.[69] In these conditions, man would achieve 'comprehension of his own history as a *process* and knowledge of nature (likewise available as practical control of nature) as his real body'.[70] Work would become pleasurable once it was no longer '*externally imposed, forced labour*'.[71]

It was in this context that Karl reflected upon his own neo-classical humanism and his love of Shakespeare: 'as regards art', how could it be that there were 'certain periods of its florescence' which by no means 'corresponded to the general development of society, or therefore to the material base, the skeleton as it were, of its organisation?' There was an obvious answer. Greek art and epic poetry presupposed Greek mythology; and all mythology 'subdues, dominates and fashions the forces of nature in the imagination and through the imagination; it therefore disappears when real domination over these forces is established'. But the real difficulty, he admitted, was that 'they still give us aesthetic pleasure and are in certain respects regarded as a standard and unattainable model'. Here he was forced back himself into an old-fashioned mythology about 'the childhood of man'. Not all mythologies were attractive. There were 'unbred children and precocious children'. But the Greeks were 'normal children', and therefore 'the charm their art has for us' did not conflict with 'the immature stage of society in which it originated'. And does not the child's 'naivety' and 'veracity' give pleasure to the adult?[72]

In another passage, however, he adopted a more determinedly modernist stance. He contrasted 'the old view . . . which seems very exalted', in which 'man always appears in however narrowly national, religious or political a determination as the end of production' with the 'modern world, in which production is the end of man, and wealth the end of production'. In fact, however, 'If the narrow bourgeois form is peeled off, what is wealth if not the universality of the individual's needs, capacities, enjoyments, productive forces, etc., produced in universal exchange; what is it if not the full development of human control over the forces of nature – over the forces of so-called Nature, as well as those of his own nature?'[73] The relationship between man and nature would change. The humanization of nature dreamt of in 1844 would become a fact. For the first time, nature would become 'purely an object for men, nothing more than a matter of utility'. It would cease to 'be acknowledged as a power for itself'.[74]

5. PRODUCTION AND ITS LIMITATIONS

In an essay entitled 'Bastiat and Carey', intended for inclusion in the *Grundrisse*, Karl wrote condescendingly about developments in political economy in the years following Ricardo or Sismondi.[75] Since the 1820s, economic literature had ended up either in 'eclectic, syncretic compendia', like the work of John Stuart Mill, or in the 'detailed elaboration of particular branches', like Thomas Tooke's *History of Prices*.[76] It was 'altogether derivative'. By contrast, the distinctiveness of Karl's position derived from the priority he ascribed to productive activity. This enabled him to construct a form of socialism that assigned an active political role to producers. They were no longer the victims of history or 'the suffering class', oppressed by force and fraud. Nor were they – as they were to become in the post-Darwin era – natural beings striving to rise above their simian origins and baser instincts or instinctively herding together in nature's competitive struggle.

But this focus on production had not proved an adequate guide either to a full understanding of the economy, or to the construction of a tenable politics based upon it. Other forms of radicalism and socialism were proving more flexible. In England, more attention was paid to inequalities of distribution, and the political domination of the landed class. The aim of Mill's Land Tenure Reform Association and of the Land and Labour League, both founded in 1869, was to contest this dominance.[77] In France, the Saint-Simonians had contested more broadly the right of inheritance. Among the socialists, the followers of Owen and Proudhon emphasized the defects of circulation, a system based upon 'buying cheap and selling dear'. They suggested a variety of measures ranging from cooperative production to a currency of labour-notes or, in more moderate and reform-minded versions, the full legalization of trade unions, an expansion of credit or reform of the banks.

The politics of producers, on the other hand, placed a particular emphasis upon the overthrow or capture of the state. Inspired originally by Jacobin politics, it aimed to re-create society and the state in its own image, and was prepared to employ violent or authoritarian means to accomplish this end. Such an approach in Karl's case was perceptive in its insight into the nature of work and what went on inside the factory. This was an emphasis shared with the American protectionists and factory reformers, who highlighted the dangerous domestic consequences of free trade, and campaigned to restrict child-labour and limit working hours. But the emphasis upon production ran the risk of replacing one half-truth – exclusive focus upon exchange – by another. Workers were not just producers, but also consumers and, even more importantly, workers also aspired to become citizens. This had been the inspiration offered by the French and American Revolutions. This was why, beyond the confines of socialism, exclusion from active participation in the polity – Chartism, republicanism, radicalism – was in practice a more potent activating creed than exploitation, a far more variable experience.

When Karl first formulated his approach in the mid-1840s, its great strength had been its focus upon the power and dynamism of the bourgeois economy. His intervention occurred at a moment when radical and socialist movements were entering a moment of defeat or uncertainty. Chartism was in decline, while the first socialist systems – Owenism, Fourierism and Icarianism – were in crisis. The failure of the more grandiose utopian visions of cooperative community in both Europe and the United States had become clear for all to see. But that was not the end of the story.

At the close of the 1850s, a new politics had begun to emerge, in which the radical and socialist ideas of the 1840s reappeared in a more modest and practical form. Ideals of cooperation had been reformulated; trade unionism was expanding and was seeking a more secure legal basis. Liberals and radicals had begun to collaborate in reform-minded suffrage movements, and there were signs of the renewal of a feminist movement which had first appeared in Britain and France in the 1830s. It is perhaps not surprising that, in comparison with earlier texts, the *Grundrisse* had so little to say about working-class movements. These were developments which Karl did his best to ignore.

Karl's condescension towards developments in political economy seems also to have been misplaced, especially when the defects of his own core arguments in the *Grundrisse* are considered. His own approach relied heavily upon his reading of Ricardo's labour theory of value, firstly because it purported to prove the reality of workers' exploitation behind the supposed equality of exchanges, and secondly because it claimed to identify a form of crisis peculiar to what he had begun to call 'the capitalist mode of production': the falling rate of profit. Karl's argument contained fundamental flaws, which he was never able to overcome. In the *Grundrisse*, his treatment of the value problem was obscure. In the first volume of *Capital*, he evaded the most difficult issues surrounding the question by confining his discussion to production, while his reluctant efforts to confront the problem in the unpublished second and third volumes were unsuccessful. Given the extraordinary volume of literature and the intensity of scholarly debate which subsequently came to surround the notion of value, it is worth retracing the origins of the question.

Confusion over the question of value did not begin with Karl, but went back to the original debate surrounding the reception of Ricardo's argument in the first edition of his *Principles of Political Economy and Taxation* of 1817. According to Ricardo, the exchange value of a commodity was its power of exchange against other commodities. It was measured by the number of commodities for which it could be exchanged under equilibrium conditions. Exchange value was a relative magnitude. Underlying the exchange value of a commodity was its value. Value was the absolute magnitude which underlay the relativities of equilibrium price. Ricardo suggested that the magnitude of value was determined by socially necessary labour time. According to his argument, when rates of profit and wages were uniform, commodities sold at their natural prices, their exchange value depending upon the quantities of labour expended upon them. But this no longer held when commodities were produced with unequal amounts of fixed and circulating capital. Where this happened, the relative prices of such commodities would vary 'in proportion to the quantity and durability of the fixed capital employed'.

In the period immediately following the publication of *The Principles*, Ricardo was flattered by the attention his book received. He seems to have been fairly relaxed about the status ascribed to his arguments and inattentive to the particular ways in which his hypotheses might be understood. This was particularly true of his reaction to a eulogistic review of *The Principles*, written in 1818 by one of his admirers, J. R. McCulloch. In McCulloch's review, the qualifications Ricardo made to his own argument were ignored.

Ricardo's first inclination was nevertheless to praise McCulloch's essay. But when his friend Hutches Trower pointed out the omission of the qualifications, Ricardo acknowledged 'the inaccuracy of the reviewer'.[78] The reason why this matters was because McCulloch stuck to his initial version of the theory in the 'Memoir' that formed the preface to the French edition of The Principles, which appeared in 1835. It was in this edition that Karl first read Ricardo. In the accompanying 'Memoir', McCulloch asserted that 'The fundamental principle maintained by Mr. Ricardo in this great work, is that the exchangeable value, or relative worth of commodities, as compared with each other, depends exclusively on *the quantities of labour necessarily required to produce them*.'[79] McCulloch dismissed Adam Smith's opinion that such principles only applied 'in the earliest and rudest stages of society', and argued that Ricardo had shown that the same principle held in the present.

When in 1850–51, Karl returned to his economic studies, he read the 1821 third edition of the Principles in English. But even at this stage he showed no interest in Ricardo's qualifications. Only in the Grundrisse did he finally cite the relevant passage from the Principles: 'The principle that the relative amounts of labour contained by commodities determine their value, becomes significantly modified by the application of machinery and other fixed and durable capital.'[80] Yet he did not treat this as a significant challenge to his approach. He observed that 'this has nothing to do with value determination; it comes under the heading of price'.[81] Later, in Capital, Karl's answer to the qualifications made by Ricardo was that the question did not concern the deviation of value from socially necessary labour time, but that of equilibrium price from value. But he had already defined value as socially necessary labour time. In other words, he had conceded Ricardo's point without appearing to do so.

A large part of the problem arose from Karl's conflation of two propositions which derived from quite separate forms of discourse. The first was Ricardo's tentative proposition that socially necessary labour time determined equilibrium price – a proposition which Ricardo was quite happy to qualify substantially, when he took into account variations in periods of production. The second proposition – similar in its form, but in fact completely unrelated – was the politically loaded assertion that only labour created value, and for this reason was resistant to qualification.[82]

The original proposition had arisen from a question about how markets operated. If commodities didn't exchange with each other randomly, but in definite proportions and in time and space, what then explained equilibrium prices? In 1867, in *Capital*, Karl arbitrarily ruled out the relative desirability or utility of commodities, what he called their 'use values'. Use values constituted 'the substance of all wealth, whatever may be the social form of that wealth'.[83] But in the particular social form constituted by 'the capitalist mode of production', use values were also 'the material depositories of exchange value'. Use values were of different qualities, but as exchange values they were 'merely different quantities'. If, therefore, use value was left aside, it was easy for Karl to single out his pre-chosen solution, that the 'one common property left' was that of 'being products of labour'. Labour must therefore be the value-creating substance. The 'magnitude of this value' was measured by 'the quantity of the value-creating substance, the labour, contained in the article'.[84]

The problem about this way of proceeding was that the original question posed – the relativities of equilibrium price in market exchange – had disappeared. For in market exchange, even if it were assumed that all commodities were the products of labour, it by no means followed that socially necessary labour time was the only determinant of equilibrium price.

There was also a further complication. Ricardo's theory derived the magnitude of value from socially necessary labour time and assumed that this magnitude was determined by *currently* necessary labour time. In a strict sense, what this meant was that past socially necessary labour time no longer had any bearing upon current value. This position contradicted the idea found in radical discourse which claimed that labour and only labour created value, irrespective of time and place. In an attempt to overcome Ricardo's qualification – that, given divergences in periods of production, equilibrium prices were not *always* determined by socially necessary labour time – Karl shifted between one position and the other without consistent awareness of their incompatibility.

Karl's fixation on production in the *Grundrisse* led him to identify exchange with just one of the properties of a commodity, that it was a product of labour, that it was 'labour objectified'. In Karl's approach, as in Adam Smith's original discussion, the value of a commodity was known before it was submitted to exchange. But Smith considered this situation only to have existed in primitive society. Karl tried to transform it into an objective process valid in the present. This, however, ignored the fact that, in market exchange, commodities only possessed a relative value, a value relative to other commodities. In Karl's approach, value first appeared as an individual quantity, as the objectification of a determinant quantity of labour. This was not deduced from the law of value, but preceded its expression as a relative expression in the law of value. Karl's approach made most sense not in a commercial society, but in a feudal one. The exploitation of the serf was manifest. What he produced went not to him, but to his feudal superior. In commercial society, there was no comparable process since the product was not divided between capitalist and worker. It wholly belonged to the capitalist but then had to be marketed.[85]

Finally, and most extraordinary considering the article of faith it subsequently became for Marx's followers, what of the lynchpin of 'the capitalist mode of production', what of 'surplus value' itself? According to the *Grundrisse*:

> If . . . only half a working day is needed to keep a worker alive for a whole working day, a surplus value of the product is the automatic result, because the capitalist has paid in the price [of labour] only half a working day and he has received a whole working day objectified in the product; therefore has exchanged *nothing* for the second half of the working day. It is not exchange, but a process in which he obtains without exchange *objectified labour time*, i.e. *value*, which alone can make him into a capitalist. Half the working day costs capital *nothing*; it therefore receives a value for which it has given no equivalent. And the augmentation of values can occur only because a value over and above the equivalent is obtained, hence *created*.[86]

If? . . . If? The idea of surplus value, however plausible it may have seemed at the time, was no more than a piece of unsupported speculation, a single paragraph in an 800-page manuscript.

6. 'GOOD FOR WHAT?'[87] THE 1859 *CRITIQUE OF POLITICAL ECONOMY*

At the beginning of 1858, Lassalle offered to try and find a publisher in Berlin for Karl's *Grundrisse* (*Outlines of the Critique of Political Economy*). But Karl's attempt to publish his findings in *A Contribution to the Critique of Political Economy: Part One* in 1859 was little short of a disaster. His liver complaint, as Jenny told Engels, was made worse by 'mental stress and excitement', but especially because 'he finds it utterly impossible to bring the work to a close'.[88] In the summer of 1858, his finances once again reached a point of apparently terminal crisis, only avoided by bail-outs from Engels. The Marx family's penury continued into the following year. In January 1859, 'the ill-fated manuscript' was ready, but couldn't be sent off, 'as I haven't even a farthing for postage or insurance'.[89] Jenny herself became 'a nervous wreck', haunted 'by the spectre of final and unavoidable catastrophe'. Their doctor could not rule out 'brain fever' unless she was sent to a seaside resort 'for a longish stay'.[90]

As if this were not enough, Karl's political authority in London was also under increasing threat. Edgar Bauer arrived in London in 1858, appointed as editor of *Die Neue Zeit,* and then worked on Gottfried Kinkel's journal, *Hermann.* Bauer was introduced into the Workers' Educational Association by Wilhelm Liebknecht. 'Watch him!' Karl warned. The 'philistine' Freiligrath wrote a moving poem on the death of Mrs Kinkel: 'nice of Freiligrath to give the signal for a Kinkel revival in Germany ... The canaille believed that we were both of us done for – the more so just now when Mr Clown "Edgar Bauer" had "supplanted" us "in the eyes of working men", as Gottfried Kinkel is telling all and sundry in the City.'[91]

When Karl first began to consider in what form to publish his *Critique of Political Economy,* he originally sought Lassalle's help in finding a publisher in Berlin. He hoped to 'bring out the whole work in instalments without any rigid deadlines', and so find a publisher more easily.[92] Three weeks later, he wrote to Lassalle putting forward a plan, identical to that later adopted in the three published volumes of *Capital*: 'Whatever the circumstances, the first instalment would have to constitute a relative whole and, since it lays the foundations for all that follows, it could hardly be done in under 5 or 6 sheets. But that is something I shall find out when I come to finish it off. It contains 1. Value, 2. Money, 3. Capital in General (the process of production of capital; process of its circulation; the unity of the two, or capital and profit; interest). This constitutes a pamphlet in its own right.'[93] In the course of March 1858, Lassalle managed to persuade the Berlin publisher Franz Duncker to go along with Karl's idea of publishing the work in instalments.[94] The intention was to have the first ready around the end of May.

On 2 April, Karl wrote to Engels outlining the plan of the first instalment, *Capital in General*, which would be composed of three parts: (i) value; (ii) money; (iii) capital. When, after outlining in reasonable detail his plans for 'value' and 'money', he reached the third section on 'capital', he informed Engels that this was 'really the most important part of the first instalment', and one on which he particularly needed Engels' opinion, 'but today I can't go on writing. My bilious trouble makes it difficult for me to ply my pen.' He promised it 'for next time'.[95]

Engels' reply on 9 April betrayed signs of alarm. He praised the division into six books and 'the development of the monetary business'; but 'the study of your ABSTRACT of the first half instalment has greatly exercised me; IT IS A VERY ABSTRACT ABSTRACT INDEED'. He hoped he would 'get a better idea of the DRIFT when I've had the last part of capital in general' and trusted that 'the abstract dialectical tone of your synopsis will, of course, disappear in the development'.[96]

But, throughout April, nothing more came, and on 29 April Karl wrote to explain his silence. Illness meant that he could not write, even in a physical sense – he dictated the *Tribune* articles to Jenny. Both Dr Allen and Karl's family agreed that he should be sent to Manchester, where he should 'drop all INTELLECTUAL LABOUR FOR SOME TIME and take up riding as his main therapy. He hoped Lassalle would explain the delay to Duncker.[97]

Karl returned to London, claiming to be 'fully restored'. But, whether because of his continuing health problems, his wife's shattered nerves, or his own financial desperation, he produced no new work over the summer. He resumed writing in August and at the end of November informed Engels that Jenny was now 'copying the manuscript', which was 'hardly likely to go off before the end of this month'. He explained that the first section was longer because the two initial chapters now started with 'The Commodity', which had not existed in the rough draft, while the second, 'Money, or Simple Circulation', he had treated at greater length. But he failed to mention the crucial third chapter on 'Capital'.[98]

Whether he was deceiving others or – more likely – deceiving himself about the reality or likelihood of the third chapter is unclear. Just over a fortnight before, when he had written to Lassalle explaining the delay in sending off the manuscript and asking him to put Duncker in the picture, he had added, 'There is a further circumstance which, however, you should not put to him until the arrival of the manuscript. The first section, *"Capital in General"*, is likely to run to two *instalments* since I have discovered while elaborating it that here, at the very juncture where the most abstract aspect of political economy is to be discussed, undue brevity would render the thing indigestible to the public.' In other words, the third chapter, on 'Capital', would not be there. But, confusingly, he went on, 'this second instalment must come out *at the same time* as the first. This is demanded by their intrinsic coherence, and the whole effect depends upon it.'[99]

Finally, in a letter to Engels around mid-January 1859, Karl divulged the contents of the manuscript he was sending to Duncker: 'The manuscript amounts to ABOUT 12 sheets of print (3 instalments) and – don't be bowled over by this – although entitled *Capital in General*, these instalments contain **nothing** as yet on the subject of capital, but only the two chapters: 1. *The Commodity*, 2. *Money or Simple Circulation*.'[100]

The book was entitled *Zur Kritik der politischen Oekonomie* (*A Contribution to the Critique of Political Economy*) and was published in Berlin in 1,000 copies in June 1859. In the preface, Karl announced the plan for his study of 'the system of bourgeois economy'. It was arranged under six headings and divided into two parts: the first concerned 'the economic conditions of existence of the three great classes into which modern bourgeois society is divided' – '*capital, landed property, wage-labour*'; the second examined their interconnections in relation to '*the State, foreign trade, world market*'. The first part of the first book, '*Capital*', would be divided into three chapters: (i) the commodity; (ii) money or simple circulation; (iii) capital in general. But this study would only deal with the first two of these topics. The book was relatively short – around 130 pages – and could be read as the first draft of what became the opening chapters of *Capital* in 1867. This tripartite division of the book was followed in all subsequent plans and announcements of *Capital* and provided the basis of Engels' posthumous publication of Volumes II and III of *Capital* in 1885 and 1894.

The first chapter of the 1859 *Critique* analysed in general terms the commodity, use value, exchange value and labour time in a way which had already been broached in the *Grundrisse*, but with none of the detail found there. It was an exposition to be repeated in more systematic form in *Capital*, Volume I. The chapter was followed by 'Historical Notes on the Analysis of Commodities', starting with seventeenth-century writers like Petty and Boisguilbert and ending with Smith and Ricardo. The second chapter, 'Money or Simple Circulation', examined the exchange value of commodities in the form of a general equivalent and, as a measure of this equivalence, price. Price represented the relation between commodities as expressed within the value form, while their 'real form' in circulation was comprised by their use value. It was followed by more detailed discussion of the various functions of money – as a measure of value and as a medium of exchange – together with sections on means of payment, hoarding, coins, precious metals and other items. There was no discussion of the subsequent development of exchange relations. As in the first chapter, a concluding section provided a historical account of money forms pertaining to the sequence of simple circulation described in the *Grundrisse*, C–M–C (commodity–money–commodity). That is where the book ended. There was no concluding summary or argument.

Without the third part on 'Capital in General', which Engels thought essential for a better idea of 'the drift', this was a very strange book. Even stranger, however, was how impervious Karl remained to the defects of the book, and his continuing fantasy about its importance. Whether because of illness, penury or the parlous state of family relations, Karl's judgements at this time were increasingly disordered, perhaps even touched by delusion, with mood changes ranging from unreal euphoria through uncontrolled paranoia to fantasies of revenge. In his letter to Engels, he maintained that the omission of the chapter on 'capital' was a 'good' thing, firstly, because, 'if the thing is a success, the third chapter on capital can follow very soon' and, secondly, because the book's restrictive coverage would prevent 'the curs' confining 'their criticism solely to tendentious vituperation . . . and since the whole thing has an EXCEEDINGLY serious and scientific air', he maintained, 'the canaille will later on be compelled to take my views on capital RATHER SERIOUSLY.'[101]

A fortnight later, he struck a similar note in a letter to Weydemeyer in Milwaukee. Excusing a year's delay in replying to Weydemeyer's original letter, Karl referred to his liver trouble and the fact that he had been 'overwhelmed with work'. But, 'now for essentials', he went on. He described the contents of his *Critique* and continued, 'you will understand the *political* motives that led me to hold back the third chapter on "Capital" until I have again become established'.[102]

Karl's hope was 'to win a scientific victory for our party'. As in the *Grundrisse*, one of his main ambitions in the published text appears to have been the scoring of yet another knock-out blow against his major antagonist of the 1840s, Proudhon. 'Proudhonist socialism now FASHIONABLE in France', he informed Weydemeyer, 'is demolished to its very foundations.'[103] Similarly, later in 1859, when attempting to persuade a somewhat reluctant Engels to review the book, he asked him to emphasize that 'it extirpates Proudhonism root and branch'.[104]

By this stage Karl was becoming aware that the book had not secured the recognition he had expected. Wilhelm Liebknecht, a day-to-day ally in London exile politics and a family friend, who lived just round the corner, stated that 'never has a book *disappointed* him so much', while Biscamp, the editor of *Das Volk*, could not see what the point of the book was.[105] Karl's own reaction was to revert once again to a conspiratorial view of the book's problems. It began with the delay in the manuscript reaching Duncker, which Karl suspected to be the work of the notorious Prussian police officer Wilhelm Stieber. But it was much intensified when Duncker decided to publish Lassalle's work before his *Critique*, and was slow in advertising Karl's book. Karl was furious and, despite the fact that it was Lassalle who had secured the publication of the *Critique* in the first place, was quick to blame him for the hold-up: 'I shan't forget the trick the little Jew has played.'[106]

Engels, always at his worst when he suspected a rival for Karl's attention, ascribed the darkest motives to Lassalle, who had also had the temerity to take a different line on the question of the war in Italy. Writing on the occasion of the Peace of Villafranca, which had brought to an end the Italian War of 1859, Engels wrote that all except the Russians and the revolutionaries had been discredited, but that 'His Excellency Ephraim Artful [Lassalle] is the most discredited of all.' Karl agreed. A few days later, he wrote urging Engels to review his book since this would 'set the tone for the correspondents down here', prevent the possibility of a review by Biscamp and 'likewise help frustrate Lassalle's plan to KILL me'.[107]

Engels loyally accepted Karl's request, but clearly did not feel comfortable in taking it on. On 3 August, he wrote, 'through lack of practice, I have grown so unused to this sort of writing that your wife will be greatly tickled by my awkwardness. If you can knock it into shape, do so.' He also wished that there could be 'a few convincing examples of the materialistic viewpoint'.[108] Every effort was to be made to promote the *Critique*. Engels urged him to make sure about translation rights and Karl had asked Dana whether he could find 'a Yankee' for an English edition.[109] Karl continued to convince himself of the book's future through to the autumn. He claimed that after the book's preface had been published in *Das Volk*, it had been variously commented on by German papers in America from New England to California; and he repeated this point to Lassalle as late as November, claiming that its first instalment had been discussed at length from New York to New Orleans. But with reference to Germany, as he now admitted to Lassalle, 'I expected to be attacked or criticised, but not to be utterly ignored, which, moreover, is bound to have a serious effect on sales.'[110]

Today the only thing remembered about the *Critique* is the preface, five pages introducing a strange book lacking a last chapter and without a conclusion. The preface was sent off to Duncker on 23 February 1859. Karl reprinted a version of it in *Das Volk* and Engels referred to it in his unfinished review, which appeared later in the same journal. But through the rest of the century the preface does not seem to have occasioned much comment.[111] By contrast, however, in the twentieth century, while the book was ignored, the preface, or more precisely one long paragraph within it, acquired canonical status. Here is the beginning of the key passage:

> In the social production of their existence, men inevitably enter into definite relations, which are independent of their will, namely relations of production appropriate to a given stage in the development of their material forces of production. The totality of these relations of production constitutes the economic structure of society, the real foundation, on which arises a legal and political superstructure and to which correspond definite forms of social consciousness. The mode of production of material life conditions the general process of social, political and intellectual life. It is not the consciousness of men that determines their existence, but their social existence that determines their consciousness. At a certain stage of development, the material productive forces of society come into conflict with the existing relations of production or – this merely expresses the same thing in legal terms – with the property relations within the

framework of which they have operated hitherto. From forms of development of the productive forces these relations turn into their fetters. Then begins an era of social revolution.[112]

This passage came to be considered a magisterial statement of the principles of what was later called 'historical materialism'. Similarly, among commentators there was an increasing tendency to separate themes like alienation or 'the fetishism of commodities', considered as relics of Karl's youthful philosophy, from the formulations of 1859, taken from the announcement of his 'mature', 'scientific' theory of history. But such readings took no account of the circumstances in which the text was composed or of the particular combination of presences and absences which shaped the language of this famous passage. When placed in relation to the *Grundrisse*, this point will become clearer.

In the *Grundrisse*, Karl had traced the emergence and development of the 'value form'. At the beginning of history, common property and communal forms characterized the social relations between human beings. But trade and population increase led to the spread of exchange relations and a process of individualization. Communal systems broke down and the relations both between communities and between individuals within communities were increasingly subjected to the domination of exchange value.

This history was conceived in terms of a complex dialectical interplay between matter and form, between processes of material production and 'valorization'. Capital, or the value form, was a social form which came into existence as a result of human productive development. This domination of the value form first spread across systems of circulation and then began to invade the labour process and systems of production. As it spread, it engulfed human beings and led to the loss of a human sense of mastery. Older systems of slavery or feudalism, where social relations were conceived in terms of hierarchy and subordination, gave way to a system in which products were sold in a free market and wages were the result of a contract freely entered into by masters and men. What emerged was a society based upon the universality of private exchange. Dependence was no longer between person and person, but upon a system perceived as alien and in no sense the product of the efforts of associated individuals. If the freedom and equality associated with exchange provided the 'public face of society', exchange itself was only a 'semblance', the image of a 'process occurring behind it'. It was a society in which humans conceived themselves to be the creatures of economic forces, and the relations between persons appeared to have been replaced by the relations between things.

The problem of the 1859 preface was that in the absence of the chapter on capital, Karl attempted to introduce the book without mentioning the value form. This meant that the complex dialectical relationship between matter and form was replaced by a crude and mechanical relationship of determination between base and superstructure. The illusions of consciousness in relation to the freedom and equality of exchange or the subjugation of persons to economic forces, which Karl considered comparable to those produced by religion, were reduced to 'the determination of consciousness by social being'. Human activity and creativity embodied in the term 'forces of production' were conflated with their coexistent social relations of production within the term 'mode of production'. History was composed of a succession of modes of production, made familiar by the work of the German Historical School and, in a larger sense, the whole tradition of natural law starting from the seventeenth century.[113] In turn, 'the mode of production of material life' was said to condition 'the general process of social, political and intellectual life'.

In the *Grundrisse*, the boundary between freedom and necessity set by the division of labour was seen as receding as human invention and productivity advanced. Productive advance made possible by the coming of steam power and machinery meant that the surplus labour of the masses would cease to be the condition of general wealth and the non-labour of the few. In the future, 'the theft of alien time', the basis of present wealth, would come to an end, and work would be free of externally imposed, forced labour.

In the preface, Karl stated that 'bourgeois relations of production' were 'the last antagonistic form of the social process of production'. But there was no mention of capital as a mode of production, of the struggle between the classes or of excessive labour involved in the extraction of surplus value. Nor was there any mention of politics or the state. Thus situated, the meaning of an 'antagonistic form' remained abstract and vague.

It is possible that the language of the preface owed something to Engels. Karl had stayed with Engels in Manchester in May 1858, and it is probable that Engels emphasized the ways in which Germany had abandoned any interest in Hegel and was now moving towards a form of materialism inspired by the natural sciences. In his *Das Volk* review, Engels claimed that while 'Hegelianism gradually fell asleep . . . Germany applied itself with quite extraordinary energy to the natural sciences', accompanied by 'a new materialism', inspired in particular by chemistry and physiology. 'The essential foundation of German political economy' was '*the materialist conception of history*, whose principal features' were 'briefly outlined in the "Preface"'.

Supposedly, this materialist conception had now been successfully combined with the Hegelian dialectic. Karl, he claimed, was 'the only one who could undertake the work of extracting from the Hegelian logic the kernel containing Hegel's real discoveries in this field and of establishing the dialectical method divested of its idealist wrappings, in the simple form in which it becomes the only correct mode of the development of thought'.[114] How far Karl took account of Engels' opinion in the mode of presentation of his ideas in the preface can only be a matter of conjecture. The changing intellectual climate had already begun to make his use of Hegel more guarded, especially as he addressed a new, post-1848 generation. But there was no fundamental change in Karl's viewpoint between 1857 and 1859. Even within the 1859 paragraph, he had been careful to distinguish between 'the material transformation of the economic conditions of production, which can be determined with the precision of natural science, and the legal, political, religious, artistic or philosophic – in short, ideological forms in which men become conscious of this conflict and fight it out'.[115] History was still the process through which man's essential social being would be realized, once the 'narrow bourgeois form' had been 'peeled off'. But it had become increasingly clear that the apparent simplicity of the world-historical trajectory, which had led from the breakdown of man's original sociality to its restoration at the end of the process, was not as straightforward as it had originally looked. That is why Karl now spent eight years in what amounted to an attempt to reformulate the missing third chapter – 'Capital in General'.

7. WRITING *CAPITAL*

In August 1861, Karl resumed work on the third section of 'Capital in General' at the point at which the 1859 *Critique* had left off. He worked on a second draft of the whole text until March 1863. The manuscript began with a chapter on 'The Transformation of Money into Capital', which explained in greater detail how labour became 'objectified' in commodities. As in the *Grundrisse*, Karl distinguished between material production and the process of valorization. But now he was able to provide a more precise picture. He first defined the universal and elementary components of 'the labour process', found in any mode of production, and then examined its particular appropriation by capital, once money became capital by being exchanged for living labour capacity. Capital took control, according to Karl, not only of 'the labour process in general', but of the 'specific actual labour processes' as it found them 'in the existing technology', and in the form in which they had developed 'on the basis of non-capitalist relations of production'. He called this process the 'subsumption' (or subordination) of labour under capital.[116]

By using the notion of subsumption, it was possible to depict the progressive stages by which capital was able to take control over the labour process and exert pressure upon the productivity of wage labour. Historically, this was described in terms of a transition from the 'formal' to the 'real' subsumption of labour under capital. He described three historical stages in the increase of labour productivity – cooperation, the division of labour and machinery. Cooperation, the oldest means of increasing the productiveness of labour, was found as much among the ancients as the moderns. Division of labour, on the other hand, was more specific to the inception of capital, and the emergence of civil society. For division of labour presupposed the formal subsumption of labour under capital and the universal spread of commodity production. The third stage, machinery, corresponded to the full development of the capitalist mode of production and the growth of the 'real' subsumption of labour under capital.

'Formal subsumption' also described the conditions in which the Ricardian definition of value became applicable. For 'the general laws formulated in respect of the commodity, e.g. that the value of the commodity is determined by the socially necessary labour time contained in it, first come to be realised with the development of capitalist production, i.e. of capital';[117] 'the capitalist will make sure that the worker really works, works the whole time required, and expends *necessary labour time only*, i.e. does the normal quantity of work over a given time'. At this stage, capital only subsumed the labour process '*formally*, without making any changes in its specific technological character'. But in the course of its development, capital came 'not only formally [to] subsume the labour process but [to] transform it, [to] give the very mode of production a new shape and thus create the mode of production peculiar to it'.[118] This was the 'real' subsumption of labour under capital, which encompassed factory production and machine technology.

Formal subsumption was accompanied by major social changes. The nature of 'the compulsion' to labour altered. Worker and capitalist now formally met 'as commodity owners, as seller and buyer, and thus as formally free persons'. In urban manufacture, there was an important shift away from the hierarchy of guild master, journeyman and apprentice, towards the relationship between capitalist and wage-earner. 'The form of domination and subordination' was no longer 'politically or socially fixed'. Particularly important was the change of form which had taken place in agriculture, where 'former serfs or slaves' were transformed into free wage labourers. But the same transition in the case of formally 'self-sustaining peasants' or farmers meant that a 'relation of domination, of subordination' followed 'the loss of a previous *independence*'.[119]

But by far the largest part of the manuscript was devoted to a critical history of political economy: 'Theories of Surplus Value'. While the chapters on the 'Transformation of Money into Capital' and on 'Absolute Surplus Value' and 'Relative Surplus Value' amounted to around 350 pages, the draft notebooks devoted to the history of political economy amounted to over 1,200 pages. As in the *Grundrisse*, the main line of distinction was that between the original landmarks in the development of political economy as a science – ending with insights associated with Smith, Ricardo and Sismondi – which Karl defined as 'classical', and the later ones, defined as 'vulgar'. It was argued that after the 1820s political economy became evasive or apologetic. This shift was argued to have been the result of an inability to resolve mounting problems surrounding the acknowledgement and definition of surplus value in a period in which the development of the forces of production led to increasing class antagonism. Those categorized among the exponents of 'vulgar' political economy included not only free-trade propagandists like Bastiat, but also substantial theorists including Jean-Baptiste Say, John Stuart Mill, John McCulloch and William Nassau Senior.

This historical survey was intended by Karl to provide the concluding volume of his critique of political economy. It would eventually be published as *Theories of Surplus Value* in three volumes between 1905 and 1910 by Karl Kautsky.[120]

Getting back into work on 'Capital in General' proved very difficult. In April 1862, progress was 'very slow' and through that summer Karl remained in a state of depression, even wondering whether he should try to do something else in life; that autumn, he applied for a job as a railway clerk. In addition to domestic worries and acute financial problems, there was also the anxiety that Lassalle, who stayed for three weeks with the Marx family in July, might use some of Karl's ideas in producing a critique of political economy of his own.[121] It may be for these reasons that most of his time was spent working on his history of economic ideas rather than pushing forward with his own theoretical work. Illness was also becoming increasingly intrusive, preventing any creative work through the spring of 1863.

Nevertheless, at the end of 1862, Karl wrote to his admirer Dr Kugelmann in Hanover that the second part of the 1859 book was now finished, 'save for the fair copy and the final polishing . . . It is a sequel to Part 1, but will appear on its own under the title *Capital*, with *A Contribution to the Critique of Political Economy* as merely the subtitle.'[122] He had drawn up a plan for the fresh version of the first and third sections of 'Capital in General' around the same time, and this suggested that the order of exposition would largely follow that of the second draft.[123] Despite this, in July 1863 Karl embarked upon a fresh draft of the whole.

The only part of this third draft to survive was 'Chapter Six. Results of the Direct Production Process'. But this chapter was of particular importance, since it was designed to summarize and conclude the preceding account of production and lead into 'The Circulation Process of Capital'. The chapter began by stressing the centrality of 'the commodity' to capitalist production. 'Commodity circulation' and 'money circulation' were 'the *presupposition*, the *starting point*, *of capital formation* and the capitalist mode of production'. The capitalist mode of production had been the first 'to make the commodity the universal form of all products'.[124]

The account of the transition from pre-capitalist forms to 'formal' subsumption slightly enlarged upon what had been written in the second draft. One of its main features was an emphasis upon the increased scale of production. What had counted as a maximum of apprentices and journeymen in handicraft production 'hardly even forms a minimum for the capital-relation'. Attention was also paid to the effect of 'subsumption; upon rural and domestic occupations, originally pursued to meet the needs of the family, but progressively 'transformed into independent capitalist branches of labour'.[125]

Reiterating a theme which he had first encountered in the 1840s, Karl stated that the ability of 'objectified labour to convert itself into *capital* i.e. to convert the means of production into means of command over, and exploitation of, living labour, appeared under capitalist production as 'an inherent characteristic of the means of production' that was 'inseparable from them as a *quality* which falls *to them as things . . .* The social form assumed by labour in money expressed itself as the *qualities of a thing*.' In this perspective, 'The capitalist functions only as capital *personified . . .* just as the worker only functions as the personification of *labour . . .* Thus the rule of the capitalist over the worker is . . . the rule of the object over the human, of dead labour over living, of the product over the producer.' This, he claimed, was 'exactly *the same* relation in the sphere of material production, in the real social life process – for this is the production process – as is represented by *religion* in the ideological sphere, the inversion of the subject into the object and *vice versa*'.[126]

'Historically', Karl claimed, it was necessary 'to pass through this antagonistic form, just as man had first to shape his spiritual forces in a religious form, as powers independent of him'. This 'inversion' appeared 'at the point of entry, necessary in order to enforce, at the expense of the majority, the creation of wealth as such, i.e. the ruthless productive powers of social labour, which alone can form the material basis for a free human society'. Seen in relation to this 'alienation process', the worker stood 'higher than the capitalist from the outset'. For the capitalist is 'rooted in that alienation process and finds in it his absolute satisfaction, whereas the worker as its victim stands from the outset in a relation of rebellion towards it and perceives it as a process of enslavement'.[127]

Just as the production of absolute surplus value could be regarded as the material expression of formal subsumption, so the production of relative surplus value could be regarded as that of real subsumption of labour under capital. As this transition was effected, there took place a 'complete and constant, continuous and repeated revolution in the mode of production itself, in the productivity of labour and in the relation between capitalist and worker'. In the capitalist mode of production now fully in place:

> new branches of business are constantly called into existence, and in these capital can again work on a small scale and again pass through the different developments outlined until these new branches of business are also conducted on a social scale. This is a constant process. At the same time, *capitalist production* tends to conquer all *branches of industry* it has not yet taken control of, where there is as yet only *formal subsumption*. Once it has taken control of agriculture, the mining industry, the manufacture of the main materials for clothing, etc., it seizes on the other spheres where the subsumption is as yet only *formal* or where there are still even independent craftsmen.[128]

In sum, 'a complete economic revolution was taking place'. And here the scenario reverted to that of the *Communist Manifesto*. Capital:

> does not just produce capital, it produces a growing mass of workers, the material which alone enables it to function as additional capital. Hence not only does labour produce the conditions of labour on an ever increasing scale as *capital*, in opposition to itself; capital for its part, produces on an ever increasing scale the *productive wage labourers* it requires . . . Capitalist production is not only the reproduction of the relation, it is its reproduction on an ever increasing scale . . . along with the capitalist mode of production, the pile of wealth confronting the worker grows, as *wealth ruling over* him, as *capital*, and the world of wealth expands vis-à-vis the worker as an alienating and dominating world . . . The *deprivation* of the worker and the *abundance* of capital correspond with each other, they keep in step.

But the revolution had created the real conditions for a new mode of production, 'superseding the antagonistic form of the capitalist mode of production' and laying the basis 'for a newly shaped social life process'.[129]

The aim of Chapter Six was both to summarize the results of the study of the production process of capital and to provide a transition to the study of the circulation process, which would be analysed in the second part of the book. As Karl envisaged the work as a whole as late as October 1866, the text would deal both with production and with circulation within a single volume. In a letter to Dr Kugelmann, he outlined the following plan:

> The whole work is thus divided into the following parts:
> Book I. The Process of Production of Capital.
> Book II. The Process of Circulation of Capital.
> Book III. Structure of the Process as a Whole.
> Book IV. On the History of the Theory.[130]

The summary provided by Chapter Six drew upon previous drafts. The chapters on the 'Transformation of Money into Capital', on 'Absolute and Relative Surplus Value' and on 'The Accumulation of Capital' were connected more closely to the analysis of subsumption, which now incorporated its effects in agriculture, its relationship to the 'alienation' of the producers, and a discussion of its relationship with productive and unproductive labour. The historical excursions, which had occupied a substantial part of the 1859 *Critique*, were now to be moved to a separate volume.

At various points, Karl mentioned the relationship between production and circulation. Commodity circulation and money circulation were 'the *presupposition*, the *starting point, of capital formation* and the capitalist mode of production'; 'Commodities are the elements of capitalist production and they are its product, they are the forms in which capital reappears at the end of the production process.'[131] As in the *Grundrisse*, analysis of the expansion of capital through the circulation process focused upon its circular form: 'What appears first as its element is later revealed to be its own product . . . the commodity, as it emerges from capitalist production is determined differently from the commodity, as it was, as the element, the presupposition, of capitalist production.'[132]

Capitalist production had annihilated the original basis of commodity production: independent production and the exchange between owners of commodities, or the exchange of equivalents. This was the origin of the association between capital, freedom and equality. But it no longer pertained. A transition had occurred from 'simple circulation' (the conversion of commodities into money, and their reconversion into commodities) to a situation in which commodities were 'the repositories of capital', and in which at the same time 'they are capital itself, valorised, pregnant with surplus value'.[133]

The constant transformation of surplus value back into capital created new capital and new wage-earners. Therefore, the growth of capital and the growth of the proletariat were interconnected. As economic relations took on an increasingly capitalist character, the worker–capitalist relation was reproduced on an ever more extensive scale, incorporating more and more branches of production. In this way, the scale of the capitalist mode of production was reaching global proportions. Capital was now approaching its point of culmination, but also a terminal point of over-reach in its growing domination of the world market.

After completing Chapter Six in the summer of 1864, Karl returned to the draft of the whole, to the plan, which he would present to Dr Kugelmann in 1866. He began writing Book III, 'Forms of the Entire Process'. This was conceived as a simpler and more descriptive volume, itemizing how various forms of capital – profit, interest, ground rent – could all be understood as offshoots of surplus value. The overall design of Books I–III was to proceed from the abstract to the concrete, in line with his thoughts on method in his introduction to the *Grundrisse* in 1857. 'Book I: The Process of Production of Capital' would set in place the skeleton of abstract concepts required to demonstrate 'the laws of motion' of capital. Book III would analyse these developments in concrete and empirical terms. Book II on 'Circulation' would connect the beginning and end of the analysis by introducing the dimensions of time and space into the abstract depiction of the development and expansion of capital which had been posited in Book I.

By 1865, an almost final draft of the first part of Book III was ready. It was followed by a series of notes and fragments, since Karl interrupted his work on Book III in order to prepare a draft of Book II. The bulk of the writing of the unfinished Book III was completed before that year and published in more or less unamended form by Engels in 1894. It discussed the conversion of surplus value into profit and attempted to account for the discrepancy between prices and values by arguing that value constituted the centre of gravity around which prices would fluctuate. The volume also reiterated Karl's conception of the falling rate of profit.

Engels' published edition of Volume III in 1894 soon encountered fundamental criticism, notably from Eugen von Böhm-Bawerk.[134] The solution to the question of the conversion of surplus value into profit was found to be cursory and superficial. Thirty years earlier, however, the problem that seemed to have troubled Karl more was how to connect the production of capital with its supposed circulation and extended reproduction. This was why he had left its drafting until last.

As in the *Grundrisse*, the starting point of Karl's depiction of circulation in the draft of Volume II was that of the circular or spiral progression of capital, which through its own momentum dissolved previous economic forms and produced workers and capitalists on an ever-increasing scale. The particular aim of the analysis was to connect the emergence of commodity production in Book I with the transition from feudal or other pre-capitalist forms of land tenure to capitalist ground rent in Book III. But how could a necessary connection be established between the abstract depiction of the extended reproduction of capital and the actual historical expansion of capitalist relations? The version of Volume II which Engels published in 1885 presented Karl's writings on this question as a series of consecutive chapters. But the material itself suggested repeated attempts to draft a satisfactory solution to the same problem. For the discussion of circulation and expanded reproduction never got beyond abstractions. Karl wrote eight drafts of the section on circulation between 1865 and 1880, and this suggests that he had not given up hope of finding a solution to the problem. But the fact that he reached no solution at the time of preparing *Capital* for publication helps to account for the peculiar shape of *Capital*, Volume I, when it was published in 1867.

8 THE PUBLISHED VOLUME OF *CAPITAL*, 1867

Capital: A Critique of Political Economy was published in 1867. It was not the three-volume work that Karl had envisaged in his letter to Dr Kugelmann as late as October 1866, but a single volume entitled *The Process of Production of Capital*. In March 1863, with the help of Wilhelm Strohn, a former member of the Communist League and regular visitor to Hamburg, Karl had secured a contract with Meissner, a Hamburg publisher of school textbooks and medical books.[135] The original deadline had been set for May 1865, but in July Karl wrote to Engels that he still had three chapters to write in order to complete the theoretical part: 'I cannot bring myself to send anything off until I have the whole thing in front of me. WHATEVER SHORTCOM-INGS THEY MIGHT HAVE, the advantage of my writings is that they are an artistic whole, and this can only be achieved through my practice of never having things printed until I have them in front of me IN THEIR ENTIRETY.'[136]

In response, Engels had evidently made fun of 'the work of art to be', but in August Karl was still sticking to the idea of simultaneously pub-lishing the whole work.[137] He changed his mind in early February 1866. Engels wrote, warning Karl to 'give over working at night for a while and lead a more regular life ... If your brain is not UP TO THE MARK for the theoretical part, then do give it a bit of a rest from the more elevated theory ... Can you not so arrange things that the first volume at least is sent for printing first and the second one a few months later?' A few days later, Karl agreed to 'get the first volume to Meissner as soon as it is ready'.[138] In the light of Karl's physical condition, this was a sensible decision. On 26 February, Jenny wrote to Dr Kugelmann:

> For four weeks now, my poor husband has been laid low again with his old, very painful and dangerous complaint . . . Right at the beginning of January he had begun to prepare his whole book for printing, and he was making wonderfully rapid progress with copying, so that the manuscript piled up most impressively. Karl felt in the best of 'SPIRITS' and was happy to be so far on at last, when a carbuncle suddenly erupted, soon to be followed by 2 others. The last one was especially bad and obstinate and furthermore was so awkwardly placed that it prevented him from walking or moving at all. This morning it has been bleeding more strongly, which has brought him some relief. Two days ago we began the arsenic cure, of which Karl expects a good effect. It is really dreadful for him to be interrupted again in the completion of his book, and in his delirium at night he is forever talking of the various chapters going round and round in his mind.[139]

The illness was menacing and real enough. What was less clear was whether the illness was the cause or effect of his difficulties in complet-ing the book. For, as his own remarks implied, its most ferocious assaults appeared to occur whenever he was compelled to encounter 'the more elevated theory'.

Evidently, the decision to defer the publication of the two subsequent volumes was beneficial. By November 1866, he had sent off the first batch of manuscripts to the publisher, and by the end of March 1867 the whole of Volume I was completed. In the middle of April, Karl sailed to Hamburg, and after spending three or four days dealing with last-minute corrections and revisions, he moved on to Dr Kugelmann in Hanover, where he stayed until 14 May. The first proofs did not begin to arrive until 5 May. Ten days later he had to return to England, and the last proofs were not sent until the end of August. The book was published in late September.

Capital contained eight parts:

I. Commodities and Money, pp. 1–156
II. The Transformation of Money into Capital, pp. 157–86
III. The Production of Absolute Surplus Value, pp. 187–316
IV. Production of Relative Surplus Value, pp. 317–508
V. The Production of Absolute and Relative Surplus Value, pp. 509–34
VI. Wages, pp. 535–63
VII. The Accumulation of Capital, pp. 564–703
VIII. The So-Called Primitive Accumulation, pp. 704–61

These parts were redrafted versions of the material found in the *Grundrisse* and the second draft of 1861–3, but with substantial additions of empirical material, not used before. There were also significant changes made between the published volume and what remained from the third draft (the material which was summarized in 'Chapter Six').

The opening part, on 'Commodities and Money', started with the commodity. It first distinguished between use value and exchange value – a distinction which went back to Aristotle – and then explained how a single commodity in the course of exchange could become the equivalent of all other commodities; in other words, perform the function of money. It was argued that money and the commodity in the form of exchange value described a logical circle, whose conclusion was also a return to its point of departure. In the 'value form', use values appeared as abstract representations of universal exchange value. As a particular and distorted reflection of underlying social relations, the value relation was also responsible for the objective illusion, conveyed by Karl's notion of 'the fetishism of commodities', in which relations between people appeared as relations between things.

Engels raised questions about the obscurity of the argument in the first part of the book about 'the form of value' for a post-Hegelian generation. 'The *populus*, even the scholars, just are no longer at all accustomed to this way of thinking, and one has to make it as easy for them as one possibly can.'[140] Karl conceded that his first chapter was of 'the greatest difficulty' and in answer both to Engels and to Kugelmann, who had raised a similar question, he produced an appendix on the 'value form' which aimed to help 'the non-dialectical reader'.[141] But it is doubtful how much this appendix helped, since in later editions it was dropped. Much of the difficulty could have been avoided had the argument simply begun with exchange. But for Karl the point of starting with 'the commodity' was to move forward from his original approach, in which exchange value in the form of money had been the corrosive agent responsible for the destruction of ancient communities. That, in turn, had been linked with his notion of the transition from 'C–M–C' to 'M–C–M'. But now the destruction of ancient communities was scarcely mentioned. Instead, he hoped to infer the emergence of the 'value form' by a process of deduction. This would demonstrate that money as such was not the agent responsible for the development of the exchange values and the production of commodities; any other commodity could have played the role of the universal equivalent.

Karl made little attempt to address the difficulties attending the theory of socially necessary labour time. He only considered the criticism that 'Some people might think that if the value of a commodity is determined by the quantity of labour spent on it, the more idle and unskilful the labourer, the more valuable would his commodity be, because more time would be required in its production'.[142] He summarily dismissed this objection by stating that the labour in question was 'homogeneous human labour', and that the theory referred to 'one homogeneous mass of human labour power, composed though it be of innumerable individual units . . . The whole mystery of the form of value', he claimed, was concealed in the equation, 20 yards of linen = 1 coat. Once this mystery was removed, it became clear that 'it is not the exchange of commodities which regulates the magnitude of their value; but, on the contrary, that it is the magnitude of their value which controls their exchange proportions'.[143]

The problem remained, however, that 'man's reflections on the forms of social life' did not proceed in step with historical development. They began '*post festum*' (after the event). Reflection started from the point where 'the characters that stamp products as commodities, and whose establishment is a necessary preliminary to the circulation of commodities, have already acquired the stability of natural self-understood forms of social life'. Therefore, despite the discovery of the underlying determinant of the magnitude of value, everyday practice and belief carried on as before. For 'this ultimate money form of the world of commodities' concealed rather than disclosed 'the social character of private labour, and the social relations between the individual producers'. Such forms of concealment or inversion were characteristic of 'the categories of bourgeois economy', which consist of 'such like forms'. They were 'forms of thought expressing with social validity the conditions and relations of a definite and historically determined mode of production, viz., the production of commodities'. But 'The whole mystery of commodities, all the magic and necromancy that surrounds the products of labour as long as they take the form of commodities, vanishes . . . so soon as we come to other forms of production.'[144]

The second part, on 'The Transformation of Money into Capital', examined how surplus value was extracted from the worker in the production process and then transformed into capital in circulation. This argument followed preceding drafts from the *Grundrisse* onwards in presenting the distinction between the sale of labour and the sale of labour power as the solution to the riddle of how inequality could result from a process of equal exchange. At the end of Part 2, both the riddle and its solution were revealed with an artfully contrived rhetorical flourish, as if no one previously had thought of the answer: 'Money-bags, who as yet is only an embryo capitalist, must buy his commodities at their value, must sell them at their value, and yet at the end of the process must withdraw more value from circulation than he threw into it at starting. His development into a full-grown capitalist must take place both within the sphere of circulation and without it. These are the conditions of the problem. *Hic Rhodus, hic salta!*'[145] But, as in previous drafts, once the possibility of the extraction of surplus value in production had been established, the division of the working day into periods of necessary and surplus labour – the putative rate of surplus value – was simply assumed.

The change which was to make the biggest impact upon the understanding of *Capital* was the decision not to include discussion of circulation and expanded reproduction in the published volume. In the *Grundrisse*, capital had been defined as the dynamic unity of production and circulation. In Volume I, however, 'detailed analysis' was reserved for the following volume; while in the meantime it was simply assumed 'that capital circulates in its normal way'.[146] This decision was not simply the result of an inability to complete the text in time. It was also a way of avoiding questions posed by the approach adopted towards the circulation and extended reproduction of capital in the *Grundrisse*. The lack of such a discussion left essential questions unanswered. In what sense, for example, was capital a global phenomenon? What was the connection between 'the process of capitalist production' and the proclaimed imminence of capitalist crisis? Ideas about the falling rate of profit and the relationship between global capitalist crisis and ever more extended circuits of capital were deferred until a subsequent volume, and not in fact published in Karl's lifetime.

The effects of this change were particularly noticeable in Parts III and IV of the published volume. In Part III, on 'The Production of Absolute Surplus Value', the distinction between the production process and the valorization process was retained, but the 'subsumption' of labour under capital, which had played such a prominent role in the second draft, was all but eliminated. Similarly, in the part contrasting 'absolute' and 'relative' surplus value, there was only a brief mention of the transition from 'formal' to 'real subsumption', while most other references to 'subsumption' were removed. Thus the distinction between the three methods of increasing the productivity of labour – cooperation, division of labour and machinery – were no longer presented as progressive stages in the subsumption of labour under capital.

In earlier versions of the work, the narrative was propelled by the advance of the 'value form'. Its spread and development had been presented as responsible for the destruction of ancient communities. Its trajectory had been depicted as one in which historical development and the growth of the value form formed part of a single process. Overall development was depicted in the guise of a complex dialectic between matter and form, between human activity and its unintended consequences. Human beings entered a process, first of exchange and later of production, which had increasingly come to dominate their activity and their relations with each other. They came to believe themselves the victims of a process in which relations between persons appeared as relations between things. As a result, they increasingly lost the sense of their own agency in the creation of the situation by which they were confronted: 'the product of labour, objectified labour, was endowed with a soul of its own' and established itself as 'an alien power confronting its creator'.[147] 'Fetishism of commodities' was a product of the 'value form'.

Alongside the desire to avoid problems raised by circulation, there was also a noticeable retreat from the picture of capital as a continuous and unstoppable progression, as a developing organism from its inception in ancient times through to its global triumph in the world market followed by its collapse and dissolution. Just as there was now an attempt to present value as a logical deduction rather than an organic development, so subsequent chapters were placed side by side in the form of a classificatory arrangement rather than a developmental sequence. Therefore, although there remained an underlying historical logic to the arrangement of the book, this was not made explicit. It seems as if the intention in the published volume was to avoid an arrangement of the material which might too easily be identified with a Hegelian schema.

This might help explain why, unlike in the earlier drafts of *Capital*, there was no general account of the destruction of ancient communities through the process of 'subsumption'. In the final version, the only example of such destruction was reserved for the explicitly historical Part 8 – 'The So-Called Primitive Accumulation' – which discussed the expropriation of peasants and independent producers in Britain from the fifteenth century to the nineteenth. But as this process was described in *Capital*, these communities were destroyed not by capital, but by conscious action on the part of royal authorities. Similarly, the emancipation of the serfs in Russia, which Karl originally saw as another example of the corrosive impact of capital upon traditional agrarian communities, was also soon to be revealed in the subsequent Russian debate around the issue as the product of political force.

Beneath the new arrangement of the material, fragments of the original design survived. But now, without the support of historical or philosophical analysis, such fragments appeared as mere dogmatic assertions. Thus it was claimed without further elaboration that 'as soon as capitalist production stands on its own feet, it not only maintains this separation [between labour and means of production], but reproduces it on a constantly expanding scale'.[148] Similarly, of the global expansion of capital it was stated in the preface that 'Intrinsically it is not a question of the higher or lower degree of development of social antagonisms that spring from the natural laws of capitalist production. It is a question of these laws themselves, of these tendencies winning their way through and working with iron necessity. The country that is more developed industrially only shows, to the less developed, the image of its own future.'[149] There was also little in the preceding text to justify the famous peroration at the conclusion of the book, in which 'the knell of capitalist private property sounds' and 'the expropriators are expropriated'.[150] Instead, there was only a reiteration of themes found in *The Communist Manifesto* and the *Grundrisse*. Finally, the effect of the removal of developmental sequences was the weakening of a sense of the dialectic of form and matter. Although there was a reference to 'the revolt of the working class', the overall picture of the end of capital was of the conjunction of impersonal and inevitable processes, detached from the actions of human agents.

This difference of position between the published version of *Capital* and its earlier drafts was accentuated still further in the 'Afterword to the Second German Edition', which Karl wrote in 1873.[151] This cited with apparent approval a Russian review of *Capital* from 1872. According to this review, what mattered in his work was: 'the law of the phenomena with whose investigation he is concerned' and still more, 'the law of their variation, or their development i.e. of their transition from one form into another'. This law demonstrated 'both the necessity of the present order of things, and the necessity of another order into which the first must inevitably pass over'; and this was the same 'whether men are conscious or unconscious of it'. According to the reviewer, 'Marx treats the social movement as a process of natural history, governed by laws, not only independent of human will, consciousness and intelligence, but rather on the contrary determining that will, consciousness and intelligence'. In the history of civilisation, 'consciousness' played a 'subordinate part. That is to say, not the idea but the material phenomenon alone can serve as its starting point'. 'Social organisms differ among themselves as fundamentally as plants and animals'. 'The scientific value' of such an enquiry lay 'in the disclosing of the special laws that regulate the origin, existence, development, death of a given social organism and its replacement by another and higher one'. 'What else is he picturing', wrote Karl, 'but the dialectic method?'[152]

The change in Karl's approach was initially necessitated by the need to move from the original project to the publication of a single volume, dealing only with 'the production process of capital'. But in making the choice to postpone the discussion of the process of circulation and global expansion of capital, he was arguably motivated not only by his inability to meet unrealistic deadlines, but also by his increasing awareness of how far the intellectual climate had changed since the 1840s. In his preparation of the single volume he had eliminated as far as possible the concepts designed to bridge the gap between production, circulation and expansion of capital, not least because these were the areas in which the philosophical derivation of his original conception was most obvious. In 1867, the reduction in scope of his theory may have seemed an unfortunate necessity. But by 1872 he appeared to accept the single volume as a sufficient statement of his theory as a whole.

This is also suggested by the changing place assigned to the notion of 'subsumption'. It was given a prominent place up to the penultimate draft of *Capital*, and then was all but dropped. The idea of 'subsumption' had originally appeared in the philosophies of Schelling and Hegel. In his attempt to draw together the modern state and commercial society, Hegel in his early writings had contrasted 'ethical life' with inorganic nature as components of an organism. The attributes of his later conception of the state were also those of 'an organism'. These attributes were expounded most clearly in the section on 'the living being' in the first book of his *Encyclopaedia*, the *Logic*. 'The living being', Hegel wrote, was 'the syllogism whose very moments are inwardly systems and syllogisms' or 'the process of its own con-cluding with itself, which runs through three processes'. The first and most relevant process was 'of the living being inside itself'; 'in this process it sunders itself and makes its corporeity into its object, or its inorganic nature'. In addition, Hegel – like Schelling – cited the poet and biologist A. von Haller, in dividing this process of 'the living being inside itself' into the forms of 'sensibility, irritability and reproduction'; 'as sensibility, the living being is immediately simple relation to itself, the soul which is everywhere present in its body, so that the mutual

426

externality of the bodily parts has no truth for it. As irritability, the living being appears sundered within itself, and, as reproduction, it is constantly reestablishing itself out of the inner distinction of its members and organs. It is only as this constantly renewed inner process that the living being is.'[153] Or, as Hegel put it in the first version of *The Philosophy of Right*, 'a living organism is the first and the last because it has itself as the product of its activity'.[154]

However remote this account of 'living being' might at first seem, it provided the template for Hegel's picture of the state. It was a product of philosophical speculation that had accompanied the late-eighteenth-century proto-Romantic fascination with the growth of life sciences. The state was an organism encompassing a relationship between the particular and the universal, the inorganic and the organic, civil society and the state, the economic and the political. 'Subsumption' was the means by which the particular was related to the universal, by constantly renewing the process of incorporating the one within the other.[155] In earlier drafts from the *Grundrisse* onwards, Karl attempted to adapt this approach to his own purposes.

The effective removal of 'subsumption' turned *Capital* into a far more descriptive work, now relying more upon statistical and empirical data than upon dialectical progression. The original dialectic between matter and form had preserved a notion of human agency, even if the results of its activity confronted it in alien form. By contrast, to make 'the ideal ... nothing else than the material world reflected by the human mind and translated into forms of thought' was to make speech a reflection of action, and action, whether 'conscious or unconscious', the product of necessity.[156] The ambiguity of these formulations opened the way back to the understanding of man as a natural being governed by impulse and the dictates of nature, and forward to the conventional understanding of 'Marxism' in the twentieth century.

Why Karl accepted this interpretation of his work is not entirely clear. But it seems likely that he was impressed by Engels' point that a new generation would know little about Hegel and would be unlikely to grasp – let alone accept – the original premises of dialectical reasoning. In his afterword to the German edition of 1873, it is noticeable that despite paying tribute to Hegel's greatness as a thinker, Karl was at pains to distance himself from Hegel's philosophy. He did so by claiming that 'my dialectic method is not only different from the Hegelian, but is its direct opposite', and by conceding only that he had occasionally 'coquetted with the modes of expression peculiar to him'.[157]

9. *CAPITAL* AND THE WRITING OF HISTORY

Yet to focus solely upon the philosophical status and problems surrounding *Capital* is to miss its most distinctive and lasting qualities. Two thirds of the book was devoted to a fact-based depiction of the development and current state of the relations between capital and labour, mainly in England. The precondition of the emergence of the capitalist mode of production was 'the expropriation of the agricultural producer, of the peasant from the soil'. This was 'the basis of the whole process'. England was chosen because, while 'the history of this expropriation, in different countries, assumes different aspects, and runs through its various phases in different orders of succession, and at different periods . . . in England alone, which we take as our example, has it the classic form'.[158]

Part 7 on 'The Accumulation of Capital' provided a detailed account of the condition of wage-workers in sectors of the British economy in the 1860s. It described conditions in agriculture and in branches of industry. The extraordinary wealth of statistics, official reports and pieces of press reportage, from which his overall picture was composed, remains impressive. Extensive use was made of the reports of factory inspectors, medical officers of health and government commissions of enquiry. These were used to demonstrate a number of facets of this economy from pressures to lengthen the working day or increase the speed of work to the extensive use of child-labour. Karl surveyed not only cotton textiles, where the battles over hours of work had been most fiercely fought, but also the making of military clothing, pottery, wool manufacture, baking, dyeing and bleaching. Special attention was paid to the diet, housing and health of workers in agriculture. Capitalist development had not only increased the ratio of 'constant' to 'variable' capital, but in so doing had put many smaller capitalists out of business and produced the growth of a 'reserve army of labour' that moved in or out of employment as dictated by fluctuations in the trade cycle.[159]

Away from the complexities of value and the falling rate of profit, in this part Karl came nearest to a concrete assessment of the prospect of crisis and revolt. He was particularly struck by the development of agriculture, in which increasing productivity combined with the misery of agricultural workers was leading to an ever-increasing exodus to the towns: 'The dispersion of the rural labourers over larger areas breaks their power of resistance while concentration increases that of the town operatives.'[160]

The final part, on 'The So-Called Primitive Accumulation', provided a historical account of the development of a capitalist economy in Britain from the dissolution of feudal relations at the end of the fourteenth century through to its triumph in the mid-Victorian period. It demonstrated the ambiguity of the notion of 'freedom' in the case of the early-modern peasant or artisan, freed from serfdom, but also free in the sense of being deprived of any independent access to the means of production. Possessing nothing therefore, except their labour power, these once independent peasants and artisans were compelled constantly to resell their labour power in order to survive. It traced how the separation of labour from means of production was maintained and reinforced by the process of primitive accumulation: 'the spoliation of the church's property, the fraudulent alienation of the State domains, the robbery of the common lands, the usurpation of feudal and clan property, and its transformation into modern private property, under circumstances of reckless terrorism, were just so many idyllic methods of primitive accumulation. They conquered the field for capitalistic agriculture, made the soil part and parcel of capital, and created for the town industries the necessary supply of a "free" and outlawed proletariat.'[161] Once more, the narrative was enriched by an array of sources, which stretched from Holinshed, Thomas More and Francis Bacon to Richard Price, William Cobbett, Thomas Macaulay and James Thorold Rogers.

If *Capital* became a landmark in nineteenth-century thought, it was not because it had succeeded in identifying the 'laws of motion' of capital. Karl had produced a definitive picture neither of the beginning of the capitalist mode of production, nor of its putative end. He had made some cogent criticisms of specific tenets of political economy. He mocked Nassau Senior's defence of 'the last hour' against the advocates of factory hours limitation, the conception of a 'wage fund' and

Malthus's idea of overpopulation, which he showed to be related to means of employment rather than means of subsistence.[162] But he did not succeed in producing an immanent critique of political economy as a whole. Similarly, while he produced a powerful picture of the misery and wretchedness of child-labour, of the degrading conditions to be found among agricultural workers, and of the poor diet and housing of a large proportion of English workers, he did not succeed in establishing a logically compelling connection between the advance of capitalist production and the immiseration of producers.

Karl's achievement was precisely in the area for which he affected to have least regard. That was the work which had developed from his writing and research for the *New-York Daily Tribune* and for the various lectures delivered from the late 1840s onwards. He was able to connect critical analysis of the current capitalist economy with its longer term historical roots. The foregrounding of production led him to uncover unfamiliar tensions within the modern workshop or the automatic factory. Through his determination to trace the progress of the capitalist economy as a whole, and in particular the consequences of new forces of production, he became one of the principal – if unwitting – founders of a new and important area of historical enquiry, the systematic study of social and economic history.[163] He inaugurated a debate about the central economic and social landmarks in modern history which has gone on ever since.

Any analysis of Karl's critique of political economy which simply treated the resulting volume as an intellectual defeat would also be untrue to the recasting of his hopes and expectations around 1867. Although he was unable to admit it, the original approach had failed. He had not been able to sustain his original depiction of capital as an organism whose continuous and unstoppable spiral of growth from inconspicuous beginnings in antiquity to global supremacy would soon encounter world-wide collapse. Examination of the global development of capitalist relations in Britain showed that economic development had been decisively assisted by political intervention during the period of 'primitive accumulation'. But, by the same token, what this examination implied was that the triumph of capitalist production in areas outside Western Europe could be resisted or avoided.

Nearer home, the changes made to the sequence of chapters prior to publication might also be seen as a response to the new political situation in England after 1864. The growth of trade societies, the foundation of the International, the success of the factory movement, the growing strength of cooperative production and, above all, the increasing popular agitation for (political) reform all enabled Karl to imagine new and possibly non-violent ways of precipitating revolutionary change. In the 1850s, imagination of a global crisis on the horizon had been abstract and remote. Pictures of revolutionary change were still overwhelmingly derived from the great Revolution in France. But in the mid-1860s, in place of the peremptory replacement of one social order by another, as had occurred in France in 1792–3, another vision of transition had begun to take shape. In this picture, change could be envisaged not as a rapid succession of revolutionary *journées*, but as a cumulative process composed of both political and social developments and occurring over a much longer period of time. In this sense, the transition from capital to the rule of the 'associated producers' might be more akin to the transition from feudalism to the rule of capital between the fourteenth and nineteenth centuries. To aid such a comparison was one of the reasons why in 1867, in place of the *Grundrisse*'s speculative account of the destruction of ancient communities by the value form, Karl chose to substitute as his final chapter the more memorable long medieval and early-modern history of the 'So-Called Primitive Accumulation' of capital.

11

Capital, Social Democracy and the International

PART I

1. COMING TO TERMS WITH THE NEW ERA

After the failures of 1848 and the triumph of reaction across mainland Europe through the 1850s, the 1860s witnessed not only a revival of democratic hopes, but some real democratic gains. In Germany in 1862–3, there developed an independent workers' movement, and in France the beginnings of a veiled workers' opposition to Bonaparte. In England, three developments were particularly important. Without them, the International Working Men's Association (IWMA) would never have come into existence, let alone have made the impact it did. The first was the popular response to republican transnationalism in the form of identification with the stirring and heroic national struggles in Italy, Poland and elsewhere against the Hapsburg, Bourbon and Russian autocracies.[1] The second and equally important development was the growth of popular support for the abolition of slavery and the cause of the North in the American Civil War. The fact that Lancashire cotton workers were prepared to endure the unemployment deriving from the resultant 'cotton famine' without abandoning the abolitionist cause helped to convince many in the propertied classes that workers were entitled to the full rights of citizenship and contributed to the success of the agitation for political reform in 1867. But none of these campaigns would have made such an impact without a third and fundamental development, the transformation in the capability and political presence of trade unions.

Karl was slow to discern the importance of these developments. Until 1863, he appears to have remained fixated upon a renewal of 1848. But once he began to understand and accept the new shape of politics, he became excited by the new opportunities which it opened up. The years between 1864 and 1869 were the most fruitful and successful in Karl's life. During this period he made an enduring contribution both to an understanding of the history and anatomy of capitalism, and to the development of the European labour movement. *Capital* was published in 1867, while his most lasting and valuable work on the General Council of the IWMA took place in the years before the Franco-Prussian War of 1870–71. These were achievements which transcended the narrow world of exile groups and sectarian politics, and they were recognized beyond his immediate circle. It was also in these years that Karl initially became personally acquainted with a spectrum of British radicals at first hand – Owenites, Positivists, pacifists, ex-Chartists, feminists, trade unionists, Irish nationalists and others.

Participation in the IWMA and the publication of *Capital* had been preceded by four or five years of anxiety and frustration. Karl had not been successful as a theorist or as a political leader. As a theorist, the exaggerated hopes he had invested in his *Contribution to the Critique of Political Economy* in 1859 had proved wholly unrealistic. There was more interest in his polemic, *Herr Vogt*. But as a means of affirming the political solidarity of a group, this book was unsuccessful. The mixed reactions to *Herr Vogt* underlined what had already become obvious in the disagreement over Italy. The 'party', as Karl still liked to imagine it, no longer existed.

The one area in which he had made his mark had been as a journalist – an occupation which he sometimes affected to despise. The largest constituency for Karl's writings around the end of the 1850s had been the English-speaking readers of the *New-York Daily Tribune*. The *Tribune* had also provided a lifeline to the Marx family. It had been the nearest thing to a real earned income that Karl had experienced, and for Jenny it had been a source of considerable pride. But with the onset of the American Civil War, the *Tribune*'s demand for his contributions declined. In February 1861, his employment was reduced to one article per week, and in 1862 it was discontinued.

It was in these years as well that Karl's health problems became acute. What is remarkable is not that Karl failed to complete *Capital*, but that he managed to publish a version of some kind. For it was particularly the anxiety surrounding the attempt to write up his critique of political economy that appeared to bring on his illness. Writing around November 1863, when Karl had remained 'tied to the sofa' by boils and carbuncles, Jenny wrote to 'Mr Engels': 'You can imagine, too, how depressed this business makes him. It seems as though the wretched book will never get finished. It weighs like a nightmare on us all. If only the LEVIATHAN were launched!'[2] The ups and downs in his health in the following year were characteristic. After Karl's convalescence at his uncle's in Zaltbommel from December 1863 through to the end of February 1864, his condition improved. He and his family moved to Modena Villas, Maitland Park, Haverstock Hill, but in June and July he was ill again. Being 'utterly incapable of work', he read books on anatomy and physiology.[3] In late July and the beginning of August, together with his daughters, he attempted to recuperate in Ramsgate. But the illnesses continued into the winter. On 4 November, Karl informed Engels that all had gone well until two days before, when another carbuncle had appeared. 'If the thing does not clear up quickly and others appear, I intend to use Gumpert's arsenic remedy this time.' On 14 November, Karl reported that although the carbuncle was now 'clearing up' he had had to stay in bed for almost a week. Two days later, Engels replied that he was glad that it was getting better. 'Let us hope it is the last. But do take arsenic.' On 2 December, he reported that another carbuncle was appearing on his hip. He was scared that his local doctor, who had not approved the arsenic cure, would give him 'a most dreadful dressing down' for attempting self-medication behind his back.[4]

The politics of the early 1860s were also disappointing. Developments in the 1850s had not conformed to Karl's expectations. The world-wide economic depression of 1857–8 had not brought about a new sequence of revolutions. In France, the Bonapartist police state had successfully stifled the public expression of opposition. Boosted by exceptional economic growth, Bonaparte had succeeded in strengthening support for his regime, particularly in the countryside. In a plebiscite as late as 1870, he managed to win 7.4 million votes over an opposition of 1.6 million.

In Paris itself, changes in the city made the chances of revolution look increasingly slim. During the 1850s and 1860s, the population almost doubled. Migrant workers attracted by a spectacular building boom crowded into the new industrial suburbs or into the dilapidated and overcrowded centre. The authorities were well aware of the dangers of a vast new city, a quarter of whose inhabitants were classified as 'indigent'. From 1853 onward, the emperor, with assistance of his Prefect of Paris, Baron Haussmann, rebuilt much of central Paris. Replacing many of the closely packed lanes of the ancient city by wide boulevards, lined with brightly lit cafés, bars and the first department stores, reduced the possibilities for building barricades and mounting insurrections. The accompanying improvements in sanitation and transport combated cholera and speeded up economic activity.

Displays of opposition in Paris were further limited by a new administrative structure; the city lacked a mayor, and the city's twenty municipal councils were appointed rather than elected. In addition, the opposition itself was divided. But despite all these obstacles, the threat to the regime did not disappear. The police stored information on 170,000 potentially subversive Parisians, while a small but more visible grouping continued to identify with the revolutionary politics of the imprisoned Auguste Blanqui.[5]

This was of little comfort to Karl. For all the trouble he had taken in the 1840s to make known his views to the French, his work had gone unread. *The Poverty of Philosophy*, his criticism of Proudhon, published in France and specially written in French, had remained unknown even to political activists. Similarly, his 1848 writings on *The Class Struggles in France* and the *Eighteenth Brumaire* remained untranslated.

Karl believed that the emperor's dependence upon the military would ultimately end in his downfall. And so, in the end, it did; but not before France had been provoked into war with Prussia in the summer of 1870. In the meantime, from 1859 onwards the regime employed a number of stratagems to move forward from the straightforward repression of the early 1850s. In an effort to create a more liberal image of empire, the emperor courted workers as a counterweight to the liberal opposition. He proclaimed an amnesty in 1859, legalized strikes in 1864 and relaxed press censorship in the later 1860s.

435

As part of this tactic, Bonaparte sponsored an elected delegation of French workers to visit the London Exhibition of 1862. The meeting of this delegation with workers in London proved to be of real significance in the events leading to the formation of the IWMA in 1864. But this became clear only in retrospect. Not surprisingly, at the time, Bonapartist support for a workers' delegation was viewed by radicals with considerable suspicion.

In England, despite – or perhaps because of – the large-scale development of industry and trade, Chartism as a mass movement faded away. Karl found it hard to adjust to the changed political environment. The Tory Party had abandoned Protection, but the depression of 1857 had not brought back Chartism; nor had it resulted in a triumph for the radical members of the 'Manchester School'. On the contrary, in the 1857 general election the former leaders of the Anti-Corn League, Cobden and Bright, lost their seats, and in 1859 they joined together with Whigs, Peelites and Irish MPs to found the Liberal Party. Instead of the radical simplicity of a struggle between the bourgeoisie of the 'Manchester School' and the proletarian radicals of the Chartist movement, the reconstituted Liberal Party incorporated a new alliance between the middle and working classes.[6]

The impact of these shifts was evident in the political trajectory of a friend of Karl's, the former Chartist leader, Ernest Jones.[7] In the early 1850s, Jones had vainly attempted to revive the Chartist movement. Using his *People's Paper* (to which Karl had contributed several articles), he had conducted successive speaking tours in the North, and unsuccessfully fought a number of elections. But in 1857 Jones abandoned this strategy. He broke with most of the remaining Chartist leaders, and in February 1858 called a conference on parliamentary reform at St Martin's Hall in London, to which he invited every variety of 'reformer', from the veteran socialist Robert Owen to the leaders of middle-class radicalism, such as John Bright and J. A. Roebuck.

Seemingly oblivious to the failure of all Jones's previous attempts to revive Chartism, Karl still insisted that 'The ass should begin by *forming* a party, for which purpose he must go to the manufacturing districts. Then the radical bourgeois will come to him in search of compromise.'[8] While he continued to think of Jones as 'an honest man', he considered his new role 'inane'. Still resisting the idea that Chartism had disappeared, he persisted in the belief that the re-emergence of a proletarian party akin to that of the 1840s was only a matter of time. In April 1863, he attended a trade union meeting chaired by John Bright: 'The working men themselves spoke *very well indeed* without a trace of bourgeois rhetoric or the faintest attempt to conceal their opposition to the capitalists (who by the by, were also attacked by papa Bright).' He was not sure 'how soon the English workers will throw off what seems to be a bourgeois contagion'. But having looked again at Engels' 1844 book, *The Condition of the Working Class in England*, he confidently told his friend that: 'So far as the main theses in your book are concerned, by the by, they have been corroborated down to the very last detail by developments subsequent to 1844.'[9] Engels did not agree. He thought a new edition of his book at this point would not be appropriate: 'This is not a suitable moment . . . now that the English proletariat's revolutionary energy has all but completely evaporated and the English proletarian has declared himself in full agreement with the dominancy of the bourgeoisie.'[10]

2. LASSALLE AND THE END OF THE 'PARTY'

In Germany, the 'new era' opened up political opportunities once more after a decade of reaction. But, for Karl, the upshot was again frustrating and disappointing. In the early 1860s, an independent working-class politics did emerge. But it developed not as a result of Karl's 'party', but in spite of it.

Like Karl, many of the most active revolutionaries in Germany in 1848 had gone abroad to the United States, England or Switzerland. In Germany itself, Karl's earlier writings were for the most part either unknown or forgotten. At most, the *Communist Manifesto* was familiar to a few hundred veterans from 1848. It was only when it was republished in 1872 as the result of a quirk in the law that it became well known.[11]

Karl had been infuriated not only by the independent political line adopted by Lassalle on Italy – 'no one speaks for the party without prior consultation with the others' – but equally by his refusal to toe the line on Vogt.[12] In the course of this quarrel, he had become increasingly officious, referring in unspecific terms to Lassalle's alleged misbehaviour. While denying any personal involvement in the accusation, he wrote about reasons for 'mistrust' of Lassalle and referred to an unfounded letter from Baltimore denouncing Lassalle. 'The official allegations against you . . .', he went on, 'are in the League's files, which are neither in my possession nor am I authorised to use them.'[13] Lassalle reacted angrily. What virtue was Karl claiming by dissociating himself from this patently absurd 'trickery'? For him, it was just proof of Karl's inclination unhesitatingly to believe the worst of every person, while considering it some sort of virtue in this particular case not to have given credence to it.[14]

Karl's behaviour was particularly perverse, since at the end of the 1850s Lassalle was his only important political contact in Germany. Lassalle had been a member of the Communist League in 1848 and had been lucky to get away with a light prison sentence after urging the citizens of Düsseldorf to prepare for armed resistance in response to the Prussian government's dissolution of the National Assembly. He had become famous in the 1850s for his legal defence of Countess Sophie von Hatzfeldt in protracted divorce proceedings, which ended in 1854, leaving Lassalle with a comfortable annual income of 5,000 thalers.

If Karl himself had once dreamt of his destiny as a great poet, a great critic or a born leader, in Lassalle he met his match. Lassalle not only aimed to make a substantial contribution to legal theory, but also to be recognized as a classical scholar, a dramatist and a political leader. Among his many projects was the ambition to produce his own critique of political economy: a project which Karl found profoundly threatening.[15] As a follower of Hegel and a radical activist with 'a desire to attain a speculative construction of things', Lassalle was an avowed admirer of Karl. Even his companion, Sophie von Hatzfeldt, so he professed, could not match him. Karl was his 'last manly friend': 'The countess so excellent though this lady is in every respect, and of infinite worth though her friendship is, nevertheless as a woman is not able to follow all the mysteries of a man's thought with truly creative understanding'.[16]

The extraordinary scale of Lassalle's ambition, his restlessness and unselfconscious conception of himself as the vehicle of a higher providence were clearly conveyed in one of the letters he wrote to Karl in March 1859. At the time, he was engaged in a work on pre-Socratic philosophy. The letter explained how towards the end of the time he had devoted to this two-volume study, *The Philosophy of Heraclitus*,[17] an unanticipated force impelled him to compose a drama. The story would concern the early-sixteenth-century imperial knight, defender of Luther and national hero, Franz von Sickingen: 'You will be astonished, when you see I have sent you a play. Almost as astonished, as I myself was when I came up with the idea of writing one, or in truth when the idea came to me. For my sense of what happened was not of a freely willed decision on my part to produce something, but rather of a force which took me over and which I was utterly unable to fend off.'[18]

Like others who had experienced 1848, and were frustrated by the contrast made famous by Hegel between the 'greyness of theory' and the vividness of life – 'those practical things which bring colour to our cheeks today' – he found it difficult to focus solely upon Heraclitus: 'Oh how often when some association of ideas brings me out of that world of ideas, in which I must perforce ruminate, to our burning contemporary issues, to the great questions of the day, which even when outwardly appearing to be at rest, continued to seethe inside me with boiling heat – how often did I have to jump up from my writing desk and throw away my pen. It was as if all my blood was up and only after struggling with myself half an hour or more did I regain my self-control and once more force myself back to my seat and devote myself to the hard concentration, which that work demanded.' It happened one night, when as a relief from *Heraclitus* Lassalle was perusing works from the Middle Ages, the Reformation and particularly the works of Ulrich von Hutten. He had just flipped through 'an extremely miserable modern drama' when he was struck by the thought that a play needed to be written, not about Hutten, another figure from the world of 'pure theory', but about Franz von Sickingen, 'the great dramatic hero': 'And scarcely had I had this thought, when as it were I had an intuition of the whole worked out plan and in the same moment a force not to be resisted commanded me: "you must also carry it out".' Now, he could 'write so much from the heart'. As he admitted to Karl, he considered the play to be 'very good', but he would never write another one: 'This one was inflicted on me from above like a fateful command and nothing more.'[19]

In the course of 1860, the quarrel over Italy was patched up. Lassalle still hoped that it would be possible to work with Karl, while Karl wanted Lassalle's help in dealing with the publisher of his *Contribution to the Critique of Political Economy*. During the rest of the year, the correspondence was friendly. Lassalle noted that events had proved his reading of Italy to be correct. Karl reiterated his position, but asserted that the past was no longer his concern and that what was now most important was that '*we* should come to an agreement on a programme'. He also thanked Lassalle for his praise of Karl's book on political economy.[20] Otherwise, they exchanged notes about Karl's ailments, Jenny's smallpox and Lassalle's gout.

On 11 March 1860, Lassalle again enquired whether Karl and Engels would consider returning to Prussia when the old king died and an amnesty would be declared.[21] A year later, the old king, Friedrich Wilhelm IV, by then incapable and demented, finally died. He was succeeded by his brother, Wilhelm I, who immediately declared a political amnesty. In 1861, Lassalle reiterated his invitation and proposed a revival of the *Neue Rheinische Zeitung*. The countess was prepared to invest 20,000–30,000 thalers in the paper, and it would be edited jointly by Karl and Lassalle, with Engels as well, if Karl insisted.

Karl was not keen to return to Prussia. As he told Engels: 'I would, circumstances being what they are, clutch even at this straw, but the tide in Germany hasn't risen high enough yet to bear our ship. The thing would prove abortive from the very outset.'[22] Set against this, however, the loss of earnings from the *Tribune* was alarming. It was, as he told Lassalle, a 'financial crisis'. He therefore decided that having visited his uncle, Lion Philips, in Zaltbommel to 'put his financial affairs in order', he would proceed to Berlin 'in order to discuss with you, personally, the possibility of joint politico-literary enterprises'.[23] He also used the opportunity to draw upon Lassalle a bill for £20, which he promised to repay from Holland before the expiry date or else 'bring it to Berlin in person'.[24]

Between around 16 March and 13 April 1861, Karl stayed with Lassalle in Berlin. He gave a detailed account of his stay to his Dutch cousin, Antoinette Philips. From Lassalle, he received 'a most friendly welcome' and was also at once introduced to the Countess of Hatzfeldt, 'who, as I soon became aware, dines every day in his house at 4 o'clock p.m. and passes her evenings with him'. Karl provided a detailed and not particularly flattering account of her physical appearance, but conceded that she was 'A very distinguished lady, no blue-stocking, of great natural intellect, much vivacity, deeply interested in the revolutionary movement, and of an aristocratic *laissez aller* very superior to the pedantic grimaces of professional *femmes d'esprit*.'[25]

The possibility of combining together with Lassalle on a newspaper depended upon the possibility of Karl reacquiring Prussian citizenship.

For since Karl had abandoned his citizenship voluntarily, he was not covered by the terms of the amnesty. Lassalle vigorously lobbied the highest government officials on his behalf and, while the negotiations were proceeding, he, together with the countess, saw to it that Karl was shown the best that the city had to offer. But Karl was not impressed: 'On Tuesday evening Lassalle and the countess led me to a Berlin theatre where a Berlin comedy, full of Prussian self-glorification, was enacted. It was altogether a disgusting affair. On Wednesday evening, I was forced by them to be present at the performance of a ballet in the Opera House. We had a box for ourselves at the side – *horribile dictu* – of the king's "loge". Such a ballet is characteristic of Berlin. It forms, not as at Paris, or at London, an *entrejeu* or the conclusion of an opera, but it absorbs the whole evening . . . It is in fact deadly – dull.'

He was also the guest of honour at a dinner party which included General von Pfuel, the historian, Hofrath Förster and Ludmilla Assing, the niece of Varnhagen von Ense and editor of the Varnhagen correspondence.[26] Karl's account of Fräulein Assing, who was seated next to him, was gratuitously nasty: 'This Fräulein, who really swamped me with her benevolence, is the ugliest creature I ever saw in life, a nastily Jewish physiognomy, a sharply protruding thin nose, eternally smiling and grinning, always speaking poetical prose, constantly trying to say something extraordinary, playing at false enthusiasm, and spitting at her auditory during the trances of her ecstasis.' But there were some moments of real relaxation. He looked up his old friend from his student days, the orientalist Friedrich Köppen. 'I went out on a spree with him twice and it was a real treat for me.'[27] His intention was to stay in Berlin until he received the official answer to his petition for naturalization.[28]

In the event, Karl had to leave before any decision had been made. He set off from Berlin around 14 April and made his way back to London through the Rhineland, stopping off for two days in Trier with his mother, who cancelled some of his old IOUs.[29] He then proceeded to Zaltbommel, where his inheritance from his uncle gave him £150 in cash to pay bills due at the beginning of May. Money was evidently his overwhelming preoccupation. Back in London, he wrote to Lassalle that 'conditions in America' – meaning his employment prospects – would probably mean that 'even if nothing comes of the newspaper enterprise, I may move to Berlin for a semester or thereabouts'. This would depend upon the outcome of his application for naturalization. But, even so, he would much rather stay in London: 'London, I CAN'T DENY IT, possesses an extraordinary fascination for me, although, to a certain extent, I live a hermit's life in this gigantic place.'[30]

On 18 June, Karl heard from the Countess von Hatzfeldt that his application for naturalization had been turned down. From the start, the whole scheme had suffered from an air of unreality. Engels, whose attitude towards Lassalle had been much more negative from the start, had no intention of abandoning his position in Manchester. It would mean suffering 'severe financial loss' and 'falling into the clutches of Prussia's common law'. He also thought that circumstances were 'not yet ripe for the setting up of a newspaper'.[31]

As for Jenny, she had been appalled by the idea. At the beginning of April, she had written to Engels, reassuring him that, contrary to rumours in the press, it had not 'ever occurred to Karl that the family might move to and settle down in Berlin'. It was true that Karl was interested in renaturalization, but, as she admitted, she did not understand why. Nor was she tempted by the prospect of setting up a newspaper. 'What a risky venture for Karl – a daily paper, and on the countess's own ground, too!' Jenny herself felt 'small longing for the fatherland, for "dear", beloved, trusty Germany', and 'as for the girls!', 'The idea of leaving the country of their precious Shakespeare appals them; they've become English to the marrow and cling like limpets to the soil of England.'[32]

Karl's attitude remained more equivocal. On 11 June, he wrote to Lassalle stating that whether or not he was granted Prussian nationality, he was still considering travelling to Berlin together with his family on a foreign passport and spending the winter there. He also encouraged Lassalle by providing a generally commendatory response to Lassalle's latest work, a two-volume study on the law of inheritance.[33] He perhaps still believed that a crisis in Prussia might enable him both to find a new source of income and to recapture some of the political prominence he had enjoyed in 1848. While in Berlin, he had witnessed from the press gallery a meeting of the Prussian Second Chamber. With few exceptions, as he had told Engels, it was a 'gathering of pygmies'. But the political situation in Berlin had not been without hope: in 'bourgeois circles' there had been discontent about the tax exemption of landowners and the position of the military.[34] As he had told Antoinette Philips: 'The state of things here is ill-boding for the powers that be. The Prussian Exchequer labours under a deficit, and all the old parties are in a movement of dissolution. The chamber of deputies will have to be re-elected during this season, and there is every probability that, during the process of its reconstitution, a great movement will pervade the country.' He also believed that 'this may, as my friend Lassalle thinks, be the proper moment for starting a newspaper here in the Prussian capital . . . I have not yet come to a firm resolution,' Karl concluded.[35] Despite the letter from the countess, he still believed in July that his 'Berlin affair' had 'not yet been brought to a definite issue', and that for the coming year he would be able to travel on his existing passport, while after that 'things will perhaps have so altered in Prussia, that I shall not want their permission'.[36]

These hopes were almost certainly a product of his financial anxieties. Whether dependable or not, Lassalle was not only his most important political ally in Germany, but also one of the few in a position to help him financially. Hence the panicky tone of his letter to Lassalle in April 1862. Despite a promise of rapid repayment dating back to the months before he had visited Berlin in 1861, he had still not been able to find the £10 owing, and now a further disaster had struck. The *Tribune* had finally dismissed all its foreign correspondents: 'So, I now find myself in a complete vacuum. I have no intention of treating you to a tale of woe of any sort; it's a wonder I haven't actually gone *mad*. If I mention the beastly mess at all, it's simply so that my other misfortunes should not be compounded by a misunderstanding with you.'[37] During the next few months, Karl's financial desperation continued. Jenny wished she and the children were in their graves. The gap left by the *Tribune* was filled in part by articles for the Viennese paper *Die Presse*, but the payment was poor and fewer than one in three of his contributions were published. Political disagreement brought the arrangement to an end and his last contribution was published in November.

The situation was made still worse by Lassalle's announcement of his intention to stay with them when he came to visit the International Exhibition in South Kensington in the summer of 1862.[38] After he had been entertained so regally in the previous year in Berlin, Karl could on no account lose face by not reciprocating. His reply to Lassalle was welcoming. Politically, he declared, 'we are, indeed, but few in numbers – and therein lies our strength', while, in social terms, he unwittingly revealed the family's isolation in its new suburban setting:

'We shall all be very glad to see you over here. It will greatly please my family, not to mention myself, as they hardly ever see a "human being" now that my English, German and French acquaintances all live *outside* London.'[39] The girls were particularly looking forward to seeing Lassalle after receiving the fine cloaks he had sent them as presents from Berlin, while Jenny declared herself delighted by the impression that the girls' new clothes could make upon 'the philistines of the neighbourhood and earn us respect and credit'.[40]

But putting Lassalle up placed an almost unbearable strain on family life, both financially and psychologically. Lassalle arrived on 9 July and proposed to stay for several weeks. 'In order to keep up certain *dehors* [appearances] vis-à-vis the fellow, my wife had to put in pawn everything that wasn't actually nailed or bolted down.'[41] But Karl had already written telling Lassalle about the loss of his American earnings, so it was difficult to conceal the family's real situation. Lassalle's well-intentioned response was resented. Karl wrote indignantly that Lassalle had had 'the insolence to ask me whether I would be willing to hand over one of my daughters to *la* Hatzfeldt as a "companion"'. 'The fellow has wasted my time and, what is more, the dolt opined that, since I was not engaged upon my "business" just now, but merely upon a "theoretical work", I might just as well kill time with him.' As he warmed to his theme, Karl's abuse plumbed the depths of what he imagined to be the lowest form of racist insult: 'It is now quite plain to me – as the shape of his head and the way his hair grows also testify – that he is descended from the Negroes who accompanied Moses' flight from Egypt ... The fellow's importunity is also niggerlike.'[42] In her *mémoire*, Jenny's description bristled with sarcasm: 'The laurel wreath was fresh on his Olympian brow and ambrosian head or rather on his stiff bristling Negro hair.' But she left a memorable description of his presence in the house: 'As on the wings of the wind he swept through our rooms, perorating so loudly, gesticulating and raising his voice to such a pitch that our neighbours were scared by the terrible shouting and asked us what was the matter. It was the inner struggle of the "great" man bursting forth in shrill discords.'[43] The nastiness of Karl and Jenny's attitude towards Lassalle in 1862 was undoubtedly inflamed by their financial desperation. As Karl admitted, 'Had I not been in this appalling position and vexed by the way this parvenu flaunted his money bags, he'd have amused me tremendously.'[44] Karl also thought Lassalle had changed since he had seen him in Berlin. He'd gone 'quite mad' and Karl found it intolerable to have to put up with his 'incessant chatter in a high falsetto voice, the aesthetic histrionic gestures, the dogmatic tone'. He was incensed that Lassalle, who had 'happily lost another 5,000 talers in an ill-judged speculation', 'would sooner throw his money down the drain than lend it to a friend'.[45]

When, at the end of his stay, Karl told Lassalle about his desperate financial plight, Lassalle lent him £15 and also advanced him a further £60, provided Engels guaranteed the loan. Karl drew upon Lassalle's £60, but reacted angrily when Lassalle insisted upon receiving a written guarantee from Engels, and did not make the requisite arrangements to ensure its return. Lassalle expressed his annoyance and also reproached Karl for not sending him the copy of Wilhelm Roscher's *System of Political Economy*, as he had promised.[46] In response, Karl acknowledged Lassalle's 'rancour' and offered a half-hearted apology for his behaviour. But he immediately went on to reproach Lassalle for not taking into account Karl's own state of mind as 'a man on a powder barrel' who 'would have liked nothing better than to blow my brains out'. He therefore trusted that, despite everything, their old relationship would 'continue untroubled'.[47] Thereafter, however, their personal correspondence ceased.

There was more at issue in this breakdown of relations than Lassalle's histrionics or Karl's parlous financial plight. It was not until he came to stay with Karl in London in the summer of 1862 that Lassalle became fully aware of the distance that separated him from Karl, both in politics and in philosophy. What had brought their disagreement to the surface was the changed situation in Prussia. In the winter of 1861, Lassalle had gone to Italy, where he had attempted to persuade Garibaldi to launch an attack on the Austrians. This, he had hoped, might provoke a revolutionary situation in Germany. The project failed. But in December 1861 in the election for the Prussian Assembly, the Constitutional Party was defeated by the Progressives. The conflict between the government and the Assembly over taxes and the role of the military now reached a critical stage.

Lassalle believed that the Progressives were too timid to provoke a revolutionary situation. They defined the conflict as one between force and right, but had no plans to act. According to Lassalle, only in a democratic state could there be a claim of right. In a quasi-academic lecture, Lassalle argued that attention should be paid not to the paper constitution, but to the real constitution – the relations of power; and March 1848 showed the power of the nation to be greater than that of the government and the army.[48] Practically, this meant that the Assembly should defy the government by proroguing itself indefinitely. In the spring of 1862, he went further. He defined the existing three-class suffrage system in Prussia as a bourgeois regime reliant upon free trade and indirect taxation. But, he argued, the French Revolution had inaugurated a new epoch, in which the working class was called upon to form society on a new basis. As he went on to argue, the true task of the state was not, as the bourgeoisie believed, to act as a night-watchman, but to form the unity of individuals into a moral whole.[49]

Like Karl, Lassalle had originally been inspired by Hegel. But he was seven years younger than Karl and had therefore largely missed the radical controversies fought over Hegel's conception of the state in the mid-1840s. Practically, this meant that he did not believe, like Karl, that the state was a creature of civil society. As in Hegel's *Philosophy of Right*, Lassalle believed that civil society was subsumed within the state as the larger social, political and spiritual whole. The crucial objective therefore was to transform the character of the state, and thereby perfect society. The fundamental improvement in the workers' condition would not come about through the practice of self-help, as liberals like Schulze von Delitzsch proposed, or even through the agency of trade unions. Fundamental improvement could only come about through the activity of a transformed state built upon universal suffrage and able to replace the vagaries of the market by state-aided cooperative production.

It was not until Lassalle stayed with the Marx family in July 1862 that the extent of their differences became clear. At one level, Lassalle's programme represented a summary of radical social democracy, as it had existed in 1848. As Karl later recalled, his programme linked Buchez's demand for state-aided producer associations, a French demand which dated back to 1834, with the Chartist call for manhood suffrage. But that was to ignore the particular implications of such a programme in Prussia. For, as Karl pointed out, by emphasizing the 'practicality' of his programme, the 'state' became 'the Prussian state'. According to Karl, he had 'proved' to Lassalle that 'direct *socialist* intervention by a *Prussian* state was an absurdity'.[50] It would have meant, as he later wrote to Johann Baptist von Schweitzer, that Lassalle would have been forced to make concessions to the Prussian monarchy, to Prussian reaction ('the feudal party') and even to 'the clericals'.[51] According to Karl, 'all this I predicted to Lassalle, when he came to London in 1862, and called upon me to place myself, with him, at the head of the new movement'. But, as he told one of his followers, Dr Kugelmann, 'as soon as he had become convinced in London (at the end of 1862) that he could not play his game *with* me, he resolved to set himself up as workers' dictator *against* me and the old party'.[52]

In May 1863, thanks to the inspired campaigning of Lassalle, an independent workers' party, the General German Workers' Association (*Allgemeiner Deutscher Arbeiterverein*, henceforth ADAV), came into being. Karl and Engels reiterated the position that they had adopted in 1848. In an essay on 'The Prussian Military Question', Engels argued that the constitutional conflict between the liberals and the government, now led by Bismarck, was just a further expression of the struggle between aristocratic feudalism and bourgeois liberalism. The ADAV should push the liberals forward against the government, and only turn against bourgeois forces once feudalism was finally defeated.[53]

Lassalle by contrast adopted an anti-liberal strategy which focused upon the reluctance of the liberals to challenge the government and their refusal to support the enfranchisement of manual workers. Manhood suffrage, the principal demand of the new Association, neatly undercut the aims of the liberal constitutional movement, but also suggested the disturbing possibility of an implicit alliance between the crown and the workers against the middle class. Karl witnessed Lassalle's success with a mixture of admiration, irritation and distrust. Liebknecht reported to Karl on Lassalle's vanity and the danger of getting too close to him.[54] Karl agreed with Liebknecht's caution: 'while we consider it politic to give Lassalle a completely free rein for the time being, we cannot identify with him in any way'.[55]

Karl's attitude towards Lassalle had veered between paranoia and grudging admiration. But when, at the beginning of September 1864, Freiligrath came round to tell him of Lassalle's death from peritonitis as the result of a duel, he was deeply shocked. However mean so many of Karl's remarks about Lassalle had been, he admitted to Engels that 'during the last few days my thoughts have been damnably preoccupied with Lassalle's misfortune'. He was 'the foe of our foes . . . It's hard to believe so noisy, STIRRING, PUSHING a person is now dead', he continued and he regretted that their relationship should have been 'clouded in recent years', though 'the fault lay with him'.[56] In his letter of condolence to Sophie von Hatzfeldt, he regretted that he had been out of touch with Lassalle, and diplomatically ascribed this to the effects of his illness, 'which lasted over a year and of which I only rid myself a few days ago'.[57]

But the distrust did not disappear. Initial relations with Johann von Schweitzer, editor of *Der Sozial-Demokrat* and Lassalle's effective successor, were cordial. The journal published a translation of Karl's inaugural address to the IWMA, and an obituary of Proudhon. But by the end of January 1865 Karl and Engels considered their deepest suspicions confirmed. On the basis of a report by Liebknecht, that Lassalle had planned to back Bismarck's annexation of Schleswig-Holstein in return for the introduction of universal suffrage, Karl wrote, 'we now know that Izzy [Lassalle] planned to trade off the workers' party to Bismarck'. A few weeks later, he and Engels withdrew cooperation with the *Sozial-Demokrat* and drafted a letter denouncing 'royal Prussian governmental socialism'.[58] Schweitzer replied that while he was happy to follow Karl in matters of theory, he was not prepared to accept his instruction in practical matters.[59]

The rupture with Lassalle and his new party followed by Lassalle's sudden death strengthened Karl's sense of isolation, which was further reinforced by his awareness of the passing of the 1848 generation. 'Our ranks are being steadily depleted', Karl lamented, 'and there are no reinforcements in sight.'[60]

3. TRANSNATIONALISM AND THE NEW POLITICS OF THE 1860s

A reluctance to abandon his original hopes caused Karl at first to underrate the importance of the new forms of social and political movement emerging in the 1860s. It was only once he had agreed to participate in the IWMA that he became fully aware not only that, after ten to fifteen years of political quiescence, political life had reawakened in Britain, Europe and North America, but that its character and ambitions were significantly different from those of 1848.

The most conspicuous manifestation of the new political climate of the 1860s was to be found in the widespread and enthusiastic support for the struggles of oppressed peoples for liberty and independence against the *ancien régimes* of Europe, especially Russia and Austria. Dating back as a cause to the beginning of the century, this dedicated transnational republicanism, inspired by the idea of sacrifice and a heroic ethos, was to remain the most serious alternative to the class-based transnationalism delineated in Karl's vision of the 'International'.

The origins of transnationalism as a facet of radical politics went back to the transformation of the European state system during the French Revolution and the Napoleonic Wars. Most important had been the way in which Napoléon had spread the promise of revolution across Europe. As a result, states had begun to be imagined no longer in dynastic terms, but as actual or potential nations. Napoléon's armies had been responsible for the transmission of a transnational ideal, in which the creation of the republic as the embodiment of a free and democratic people was the destiny of every nation. As Madame de Staël had remarked, Napoléon was 'Robespierre on horseback'.

The enduring potency of this republican ethos after 1815 became clear in the attempted conspiracies and revolts directed against the restored Europe of the Holy Alliance. Rebellion against Spanish rule resulted in the formation of republics throughout Latin America, while the Greek battle for independence from the Ottomans triumphed in 1832. In the 1820s, there were also attempts to topple Legitimist regimes in Spain, Naples, Piedmont and Russia. In France and Italy, the *Carbonari*, a secret society dedicated to the overthrow of the Bourbons and the Congress of Vienna, engaged in a number of plots, the most famous of which, that of the 'Four Sergeants of La Rochelle' in 1822, impelled the young Auguste Blanqui to commit the rest of his life to revolutionary struggle.[61]

Many of the leaders of these early plots and conspiracies had served in Napoléon's *Grande Armée*, not only in France and Spain, but also in Poland, where the uprising of November 1830 was led by Napoleonic veterans. As failed plots and uprisings followed each other, more and more clusters of activists were forced into emigration. The number of political exiles began to mount. Settled mainly in capital cities, living from hand to mouth, and generally without stable employment, these exiles formed unstable and volatile groups, numbers of whom were willing to fight for the republic wherever the battle was to be fought. At the time of the July Revolution in 1830, there were estimated to be over 5,000 political refugees living in Paris. The radical critic of German passivity Ludwig Börne, arriving in Paris just after the Revolution, noted the presence of 'the English, people from the Netherlands, Spanish, Portuguese, Indians, Poles, Greeks, Americans, even Negros, all excluding Germans', who 'fought for the liberty of France, which is certainly the liberty of all peoples'.[62] It was from such activists that Godefroi Cavaignac was able to form his 'sacred battalion' of 600 men to fight for the attainment of a Belgian republic in 1830.

In the two decades following 1830, the somewhat inchoate republicanism of the 1820s was refashioned by Mazzini and others into diverse forms of transnationalism aimed at the establishment of a Europe of free republics. In Mazzini's case, the struggle for the republic was imagined as a providential movement towards 'a Holy Alliance of the Peoples'.[63] The emphasis was upon voluntarism. Even among those who did not share Mazzini's sacral conception of 'the duties of man', the achievement of the republic was associated with an act of will. Mazzini's declared aim was to organize 'not thought, but action'. Action in turn was identified with the active practice of virtue. According to the oath sworn by members of Mazzini's Young Italy, 'virtue consists in action and sacrifice'.[64]

By 1848, enthusiasm for the republic had also spread to the 7,000 or so Germans resident in Paris, an assortment of political exiles and migrant artisans. From this group, the republican poet and one-time friend of Karl, Georg Herwegh, assembled a poorly organized legion of volunteers to cross the Rhine at Strasbourg, to join the uprising in Baden and declare the German Republic. But, as Karl warned at the time, the expedition was a disaster and the legion was scattered on its first encounter with Württemberg troops at the end of April.[65]

In Germany itself, republicanism made little impact in 1848.[66] The heroic image of the republic was associated rather with the Poles, the Hungarians and the Italians. The most impressive example was the Roman Republic, declared after Pope Pius IX had fled Rome in February 1849. It was governed by a 'Triumvirate' which included Mazzini, but was soon attacked by the Catholic powers of Europe, in response to an appeal from the Pope, the Austrians in the north, and the Neapolitans in the south. Most shocking was the invasion force sent by

France – supposedly a sister republic. The Roman Republic was supported by many volunteers from Italy and elsewhere, but eventually, despite the resistance organized by Garibaldi, succumbed to French troops.

In the 1850s, the career of Garibaldi as a transnational hero continued. After a spell as a sea captain, including a famous visit to Tyneside in 1854, in 1859 he became actively involved in the Second Italian War of Independence. In April 1860, there were uprisings in Messina and Palermo. Garibaldi and his 'thousand' volunteers landed in Sicily, and after a number of hard-fought battles succeeded in incorporating Naples and Sicily in the new kingdom of Italy. Although he felt compelled to compromise his republican ideal, by recognizing the Piedmontese monarch, Garibaldi in many ways embodied the transnational and heroic ideal of the republic, as it had developed from the early years of the century. He fought not only in Italy and South America, but also ten years later for the French Republic, when he together with a force of *francs-tireurs* in the Vosges mounted resistance against the Prussians after Bonaparte's defeat in the Franco-Prussian War. As he wrote in his *Autobiography*: 'the man who defends his own country or who attacks the country of others, is but a soldier, pious in the first hypothesis – unjust in the second; – but . . . the man who, making himself a cosmopolite, adopts the second as his country, and goes to offer his sword and his blood to every people struggling against tyranny, is more than a soldier: he is a hero.'[67]

In Britain, the heroic deeds of the 'Thousand' captured the popular imagination, and from 1863 excitement about political events in Europe and the wider world reached unprecedented levels. Karl remained suspicious or hostile towards national or transnational struggles, except where they forwarded his own notion of revolution. Revolts in Poland and Ireland could help destabilize Russia and Britain, but he dismissed republican revolts in Italy, Spain and other Slavic lands, especially when championed later in the decade by a returned Siberian exile, Michael Bakunin.

Such distrust found no resonance in popular sentiment. In the aftermath of 1848, inspired by the presence in London of exiled leaders of oppressed nations like Mazzini or Kossuth, republicans, democrats, socialists and many liberals considered radicalism and transnationalism to belong together.[68] When, in the spring of 1864, Garibaldi, the hero of the *Risorgimento*, visited London, half a million people turned out to meet him and a huge trade union procession escorted him into the City. The response to Garibaldi was the expression of a general upsurge of interest in politics and a feeling of solidarity with subject nations. Garibaldi was celebrated not only as a leader of a nation, but also as a 'man of the people', and this support soon turned into a campaign of protest when it became clear that an 'aristocratic government' had contrived to prevent him from touring the provinces.[69] This accusation was one of the precipitants of the campaign to reform the franchise, a movement which gathered full force with the foundation of the Reform League in 1865.

The upsurge in progressive sentiment in 1863 was also a response to President Lincoln's proclamation of the abolition of slavery in the United States at the beginning of that year.[70] In response to the suspicion that in ministerial, aristocratic and business circles there might be support for the slave-holding Southern Confederacy, a movement was formed under the leadership of John Bright to support the democratic North. Trade union leaders were again prominent in this movement, as they had been in the campaign to welcome Garibaldi. Karl later claimed that 'a monster meeting' in St James's Hall, chaired by Bright, had 'prevented Palmerston declaring *war on the United States*, which he was on the point of doing'. In the Marx household, Karl's youngest daughter, the ten-year-old Eleanor, wrote to Lincoln, appointing herself his political adviser.[71]

In the first months of 1863, there was an uprising in Poland against Russian rule. Among radicals, the revolt revived a concern about the plight of Poland, which went back to the revolt of 1830 and the declarations of the Fraternal Democrats in the years before 1848. In combination with the popularity of the *Risorgimento* and the enthusiasm for Lincoln, the Polish revolt further intensified the transnational preoccupations of politically engaged workers and middle-class radicals, both in England and in France.

As a result of the events in Poland, the originally innocuous and officially supported visit of French workers to the International Exhibition of 1862 bore fruit of an unexpected kind. When the French delegation had arrived, they had been invited to a tea party by the committee of the *Working Man*, a journal associated with the cooperative movement. Convened under the patronage of Shaftesbury and Palmerston, the meeting had not been designed to be of anything other than of cultural and philanthropic interest. But unbeknown to its patrons, the gathering had included radical French workers and political refugees – Tolain, Fribourg, Talandier and Bocquet – all to be active members of the future International. Similarly, on the English side, the meeting included G. E. Harris and Charles Murray, followers of the Chartist–feminist politics of Bronterre O'Brien. At the meeting, one of the French refugees, Bocquet, had proposed that 'a corresponding committee should be formed in London for the purpose of interchanging ideas with the workmen of France'.[72] In 1862, there had been no reason to suppose that anything of political consequence would follow from the proposal.

But the significance of such a committee was transformed by the outbreak of the Polish revolt against czarist rule at the beginning of 1863. Following correspondence between English and French workers, a mass meeting in support of the Poles was held at St James's Hall on 22 July 1863. It was attended by a five-member delegation from the Paris Working Men's Polish Committee. On the following day, English and French workers met at the Bell Inn and agreed to inaugurate a joint campaign on behalf of Poland. On 5 August, this resulted in the founding of the National League for the Independence of Poland together with an address to French workers drafted by George Odger, the Chairman of the London Trades Council. This address called for 'a gathering together of representatives from France, Italy, Germany, Poland, England and all countries where there exists a will to cooperate for the good of mankind'.

The National League represented an important moment in the re-emergence of an independent movement of politically engaged working men. As part of its agitation, a delegation of working men from Tower Hamlets met with Palmerston and urged him, if necessary, to wage war against Russia in support of 'oppressed nationality' in Poland. Similarly, at the July meeting, George Odger declared that 'if the government did not move in the matter, it was for the working people of the country to call upon them to take an active part in the question'.[73] The League drew upon the support of former Chartists, leading trade unionists and middle-class radical activists, including John Stuart Mill and Frederic Harrison.

The theme of transnational cooperation came up again in April 1864 at a meeting of the English Working Men's Garibaldi Committee, whose membership overlapped that of the National League, and also included a delegation of French working men. There, it was proposed that a 'congress of continental and English working men' be held in London, and on 27 August it was announced in the *Beehive*, the journal of the London Trades Council, that an international meeting would be held on 28 September. This was the first meeting of what was to become the IWMA. Around 19 September, Karl was invited to this meeting as a representative of Germany. He was also asked to choose a German worker, and put forward his old ally and former member of the Communist League, the tailor Johann Georg Eccarius.

A crowded meeting duly took place in St Martin's Hall, Long Acre, attended by a deputation from Paris, headed by an engraver, Henri Tolain. Karl was one of those elected a member of the General Council. But whether because of ill-health or preoccupation with his own work, it took some weeks before Karl began fully to appreciate the potential importance of the Association. Having been elected to the General Council and also appointed to the sub-committee responsible for drawing up a 'declaration of principles' and provisional rules, he was unable to attend either the following meeting of the General Council or the first two meetings of the sub-committee. It was only when Eccarius warned him that there was danger in delaying his appearance any longer, citing Livy, 'a case of *periculum in mora*' (danger in delay), that Karl went along to the sub-committee.

In early November, however, he wrote to Engels with enthusiasm about what had happened. The meeting of 28 September had been '*chock-full*'. It was an indication, according to Karl, that 'there is now evidently a revival of the working classes taking place', and, he went on, 'I knew that on this occasion "people who really count" were appearing, both from London and from Paris, and I therefore decided to waive my usual standing rule TO DECLINE ANY SUCH INVITATIONS'.[74]

4. TRADE SOCIETIES AND THE INTERNATIONAL WORKING MEN'S ASSOCIATION

The 'people who really count' were the trade unionists. What distinguished the IWMA from earlier international associations such as the

Fraternal Democrats was the presence and participation of the leaders of the most important London trade societies. The location of the International in London in the 1860s was not the result of its concentration of political exiles residing in the city – though this made it an obvious choice. Nor was it simply the result of Britain's liberal reputation. It was the consequence of an upsurge of new forms of trade unionism which had occurred in London at the end of the 1850s. The formation of the IWMA owed its inception to the expanding ambitions of the new London trade societies, themselves a response to the rapid increase in production which had occurred in Britain and elsewhere after 1848.

Between 1850 and 1890, industrial world production increased four-fold, world trade six-fold.[75] The most eye-catching aspects of this increase were to be found in the growth of railways, steamships, coal mines and factory towns. But striking changes also occurred in capital cities, whose rapid expansion was signalled by the building booms of the 1850s and 1860s. Kentish Town, where the Marx family settled, was one of the new areas of housing developed during this construction boom.

The boom was accompanied by even more striking changes in the production of consumer goods. In clothing, footwear and furniture, as well as building, a technological revolution occurred during the 1850s. The invention of the sewing machine in 1846 and the band saw in 1858, and the adoption of mass sewing and cutting from 1850, provided the basis for the take-off of a large-scale ready-made clothing industry. The application of the sewing machine to shoe sewing in 1857 removed the production bottleneck imposed by hand-sewn shoemaking. At the same time, the use of steam power in sawmills, assisted by the use of wood-working machines from the end of the 1840s, enormously accelerated furniture production. In the building trades, mechanized brickmaking, automatic lockmaking and other innovations similarly accelerated the pace of production.[76]

The tensions generated by these changes in the pace of work and attendant losses in job control came to a head in the London building trades in 1859. In that year, metropolitan building workers demanded a maximum nine-hour day. In response, the employers demanded that workers sign a 'document' disavowing trade societies. The refusal of the men to comply led to a six-month lockout, involving 24,000 masons, bricklayers, joiners and labourers. The men on strike appealed nation-wide for financial help, and in response representatives from other London trades organized national support. The struggle ended in a draw. The workers withdrew their demand for a nine-hour day and the employers withdrew their 'document'.

One of the reasons why the building workers had been able to survive the lockout without capitulation had been the substantial financial support (£3,000) they had received from the Amalgamated Society of Engineers. This was another novel achievement of the post-Chartist era. The Amalgamated Society of Engineers (ASE), founded in 1850, embodied a new form of unionism. In place of the traditional practices of small and localized trade societies, the ASE built up a national organization with 21,000 members. It possessed a centrally organized financial organization and conducted disputes in accordance with strict and nationally agreed rules. The other London trade unionists reformed their own trade societies along the lines pioneered by the Engineers. While George Howell reorganized the Operative Bricklayers' Society, Randall Cremer and Robert Applegarth transformed the Carpenters into a nationally based 'amalgamated' union, whose membership rose from 949 to 10,475 between 1862 and 1871, with 207 branches. These 'new model unions' were able to offer greater benefits to their members. Their bargaining position was greatly strengthened, both by their size and by the effectiveness of their organization.[77] This was why, in Karl's words, their leaders were 'people who really count'.

Experience of the strike led the leaders of London trade societies to consider that new and more coordinated forms of labour organization had become necessary. In 1860, the representatives of the London trades formed a permanent body, the London Trades Council. Its members included a new generation of trade union leaders – George Howell of the Bricklayers, George Odger of the West London Shoemakers, Randall Cremer of the Carpenters and, a little later, Robert Applegarth, also of the Carpenters. These men, whom the Webbs were to call 'the Junta', were soon to become leading figures in the agitations over the American Civil War, Italy and Poland.[78] They encouraged the formation of trades councils in other towns, and in 1868 founded the Trades Union Congress with the ambition to advance the political as well as social aims of labour. This was stated in 1861 in the declaration of the aims of the London Trades Council, which were to: 'watch over the general interest of labour, both political and social, both in and out of

Parliament; to use their influence in supporting any measure likely to benefit trade unions'.[79]

The Council could recommend assistance for particular strikes, summon delegates and make pronouncements on issues of public interest. Its first Secretary was George Howell, between 1861 and 1862, and he was succeeded by George Odger, who remained Secretary through to 1871.

It was the trade union leaders who effectively brought the IWMA into existence. It was the 'Address to the French Working Classes', drawn up by Odger and co-signed by Cremer and others, which led to the foundation of the International. In the 'Address', which was published in the *Beehive* on 5 December 1863, it was stated that: 'A fraternity of peoples is highly necessary for the cause of labour, for we find that whenever we attempt to better our social condition by reducing the hours of toil, or by raising the price of labour, our employers threaten us with bringing over Frenchmen, Belgians, and others to do our work at reduced wages.' This had been the result of 'a want of regular and systematic communication between the industrious classes of all countries, which we hope to see speedily effected'.[80]

Similarly, it was George Odger's open letter to trade unionists appealing to them to agitate for the franchise which led to the formation of the Manhood Suffrage and Vote by Ballot Association, the precursor of the Reform League.

The creators of the IWMA did not make a sharp distinction between economic and political aims. They were as much inspired by transnational republican movements as other radicals. Thus, their 'first united effort' was to be 'for the freedom of Poland'. For Howell, Garibaldi was 'an idol', while both Howell and Cremer by the early 1860s were friends of Mazzini. At the foundation meeting of the International, Odger sounded an equally Mazzinian note. Workers were to lead a campaign for a foreign policy based on morality and justice and to head an alliance of subject peoples – Italians, Hungarians and Poles – against Austria and Russia.[81] Domestically, 'the enfranchisement of the masses of the people was to be the first object of the English Section'. This was the object achieved in the Reform Bill of 1867.[82]

In the economic sphere, the purpose of the Association was equally large-minded. The object was not simply to combat the use of continental labour as blacklegs: a new phenomenon resulting from commercial expansion and the growing ease of transport between Britain and the Continent.[83] The Trade Society leaders saw blacklegging as the symptom of a deeper disparity between the condition of labour in Britain and Europe. Therefore the fundamental aim of the IWMA, as it was conceived by the English Trade Society leaders, was to bring the benefits of British social legislation (limitation of working hours, restriction of juvenile employment) and the achievements of the new 'amalgamated' model of trade unionism to the other nations of Europe and the world.[84]

The IWMA was both organizationally heterogeneous and ideologically diverse. It was governed by a General Council, of whom the vast majority were English – 27 out of 34.[85] Conversely, each national section, except the English, was represented on the General Council; Karl and Eccarius were to represent Germany. The Association issued an 'Inaugural Address' and 'Provisional Rules' in November 1864. Its overall aims were to promote brotherhood and the end of war.[86] But the Association was, and remained, a very fragile institution. Contrary to rumours at the time, it was virtually without resources, and was at one point expelled from its premises for non-payment of rent. Furthermore, its membership through affiliation was notional. According to George Howell, 'The whole system of "affiliation", that is joining in a body or society, consisted simply of a vague agreement with certain undefined propositions by a formal resolution, the chief of which was the urgent need of an association which should embrace the workmen of all countries.' Therefore, while it was reported that the Council had obtained 18,000 adhesions, actual paying members in England did not exceed 500. There were more in France, Belgium and Switzerland, 'but in no country were the numbers formidable'.[87] The General Council met weekly in Greek Street in Soho, its main business being to accept the affiliation of new branches, whether of individuals or associations. The other task of the General Council was to prepare for annual congresses, which would vote on matters of policy. Karl played a central role in preparing the agenda of each congress, but only attended the congress at The Hague in 1872.

At a preliminary meeting in London in September 1865, the task was to set the agenda for the first congress, to be held in Geneva in September 1866. The main issue, which arose there, and again at Geneva, was Poland. The French and the Belgians did not consider the question of Poland to be relevant to an 'economic' conference; nor were they happy about the specific condemnation of Russian tyranny; if the resolution were to be admitted at all, it should be directed at tyranny in general. The question was resolved by a compromise amendment.

In Geneva, not surprisingly, the sixty delegates came mainly from France and Switzerland. Nevertheless, despite some French opposition to state intervention, the congress passed a number of resolutions in line with the aims of the English trade unionists, most notably the demand for an eight-hour day and restrictions on juvenile labour. A French demand, voiced by Tolain, that only workers should be admitted to congresses as delegates, was rejected by the English trade unionist Randall Cremer, but another motion recommending the prohibition of female labour was passed.

In September 1867, a second congress was held, in Lausanne. Once again, there was a large French presence, even though, as in the previous year, French delegates were harassed by the authorities. In England, the attention of members of the General Council was distracted by the agitation over the Reform Bill, while Karl himself was preoccupied with the publication of *Capital*. But that did not damp down a wider international interest in the congress in 1867. The combination of the Reform struggle in England and a series of prominent strikes in Europe – bronze workers in Paris, builders in Geneva, silk workers in Basle – heightened the growth of international attention to the aspirations of the working classes. The proceedings of the congress in Lausanne were reported in *The Times* and reproduced by the rest of the European press. The *Times* editorial stated, 'it will be nothing less than a new world, we really believe, when Englishmen and foreigners find themselves able to work together'. Thirty-three more trade societies affiliated to the International, and by the spring of 1868, the number had reached 120.

Two issues dominated the congress. The first was social ownership. Proposals of state responsibility for education and ownership of the railways were raised by Belgian delegates, but rejected or amended by the French. The question of ownership of the land, whether it should be based on peasant proprietorship or be socialized, was another issue between the French and the Belgians which was deferred until the next congress.

The second issue raised at Lausanne was the relationship of the International with the League of Peace and Freedom, whose founding congress was held in neighbouring Geneva. The League had the support of John Stuart Mill, Victor Hugo, Giuseppe Garibaldi, Louis Blanc, Alexander Herzen, Michael Bakunin and others. Six thousand supporters attended the congress and 10,000 people across Europe had also signed a petition promoting its aims. The League had changed the starting date of its congress, so that delegates from Lausanne would also be able to attend. On 13 August 1867, at a meeting of the General Council, Karl had argued that while 'it was desirable that as many delegates as could make it convenient should attend the Peace Congress in their individual capacity ... it would be injudicious to take part officially as representatives of the International Association. The International Working Men's Congress was itself a Peace Congress, as the union of the working classes of the different countries must ultimately make international wars impossible.'[88] At Lausanne, the majority of delegates favoured cooperation with the League, but added a motion proposed by Tolain that war could only be stopped by a new social system based upon a just distribution of wealth. This did not hinder the enthusiasm of the League, which happily accepted the amendment. However, no further action was taken.

The Brussels Congress of 1868 attracted ninety-one delegates, not only twelve from Britain, but also delegates from Spain, Italy and Germany. There was a large Belgian delegation and the congress began with a Belgian resolution. It was inspired by Bonaparte's ill-fated imperial expedition to Mexico, and declared that the root of wars was to be traced to the economic system, in which what was unleashed was a war between producers – in reality, therefore, a civil war. A declaration of war should therefore be countered by a general strike. There was general agreement about the need to assist strikes, when they were justified. Trade unions were to be supported, not merely in themselves, but as 'a means to a higher idea – that of cooperation'. A tribute was paid to Karl's recently published *Capital* and his analysis was used in a discussion of machinery led by Eccarius. But despite the increased numbers of the English delegation, it was noted that 'In England the unsettled state of politics, the dissolution of the old parties, and the preparation for the coming electoral campaign have absorbed many of our most active members, and to some degree, retarded our propaganda.'[89] Proposals for free credit and state education were referred back for further discussion. A controversial resolution, advocating the collective ownership of land, railways, mines and forests, was passed, but only in a small ballot: 9 to 4 in favour, with 15 abstentions.

The final congress before the outbreak of the Franco-Prussian War was held in Basle in September 1869. It was composed of seventy-eight delegates, including a twelve-man delegation from the newly formed Eisenach Social Democratic Party in Germany led by Wilhelm Liebknecht. In Britain, with the success of reform and hopeful indications of improvement in the legal status of trade unions, interest in the International had continued to decline, and in the Annual Report the country was barely mentioned. In Basle, unlike Brussels, commitment to public ownership of the land was strongly reaffirmed. But the conditions under which the land should be held remained a matter of controversy. Opinions also differed about English-supported proposals for compulsory, secular and inspected state education. Bakunin again raised the originally Saint-Simonian demand for the abolition of inheritance, but failed to achieve the required two-thirds majority.[90] The next congress was planned for Paris, but two weeks before it was due to take place, Napoléon declared war on Prussia, and the congress was cancelled.

The earliest account of the history of the International was written by Edward Beesly, a Positivist professor at University College, London, who had chaired the International's founding meeting in 1864. He declared that an 'account of the political and economic principles advocated by the International' was of 'very little importance in comparison with the practical work done by the association'.

Five months after the Geneva Congress, at the beginning of February 1867, 5,000 Parisian bronze workers were locked out by their employers. An appeal was made to the General Council, which in turn passed on the request for aid to its affiliated societies, and this produced sufficient promises of assistance to force a defeat of the employers. In the ensuing years, the Association helped the resistance to lockouts and supported a number of strikes, notably those of London bookbinders and tailors. In the spring of 1868, Genevan 'master builders' locked out their men for refusing to renounce their connection with the International. But international aid from relevant trade societies forced the masters to withdraw their demand and make concessions on wages and hours of work. This resulted in a great increase in the International's reputation in Switzerland. In the years 1868–9, it was said that 'industrial war raged over Europe'.[91] Most of these conflicts were in fact unconnected to the International, but were nevertheless associated with it in the public mind.

In the late 1860s, industrial disputes directly connected with the International began to include some industrial workers, notably weavers and spinners in Rouen and the Norman textile district.[92] But the struggles of the International for the most part took place in workshops or on building sites, and were related to the concern of skilled artisans that the import of cheaper labour from Europe should not become the norm. A characteristic example of its success in that sector concerned the basketmakers of Bermondsey:

> During the London basket-makers' dispute, in 1867, information was received that six Belgians were at work under the railway arches in Blue Anchor Lane, Bermondsey. They were as strictly guarded against contact with the outside public as a kidnapped girl in a nunnery. By some stratagem a Flemish member of the Council succeeded in obtaining an interview, and upon being informed of the nature of their engagement, the men struck work, and returned home. Just as they were about to embark a steamer arrived with a fresh supply. The new arrivals were at once communicated with; they too repudiated their engagement and returned home, promising they would exert themselves to prevent any further supplies.[93]

However limited the economic reach and effectiveness of the International Association, its impact and legacy were far broader. The greatest achievement of the IWMA was to forge and spread across Europe and the Americas a new and lasting language of social democracy. European socialism was an invention of the 1860s. Terms like 'solidarity', 'strike', 'meeting' or 'trade union' were adopted in countries where their previous use had been unknown. British radicals and trade unionists were perceived as role models across Europe. Some of their leaders – George Odger, Benjamin Lucraft, George Howell – were seen as standard-bearers for what had formerly been known as Chartist ideas of political participation. The picture of the new British trade unions as established and well-funded contrasted strongly with the situation of unions in France, fragmented between different regions and lacking recognized or protected union rights. Finally, the success of the Reform League in pressing for the Reform Bill of 1867 was perceived as a demonstration that political emancipation could be achieved through 'pressure from without'.

5. THE AIMS OF THE INTERNATIONAL: THE 'INAUGURAL ADDRESS'

When Karl became involved in the International, his political views were virtually unknown as he had played little or no part in the emergence of the new politics of the 1860s. Furthermore, as his own account made clear, the opportunity to play such a central part in highlighting the condition of the working classes and in formulating the aims of the International Association came about largely as a matter of chance. Karl had been appointed to a sub-committee delegated to produce 'a declaration of principles and provisional rules'. Preliminary drafts of the 'declaration' had been prepared by an Owenite manufacturer, John Weston, and of the rules by Mazzini's secretary, 'Major' Luigi Wolff.

Weston, according to Karl, had drawn up 'a programme full of extreme confusion and of indescribable breadth'; Wolff's rules had been lifted directly from the statutes of Italian Workers' Associations, which in reality, according to Karl, were benefit societies. Karl was absent from the first two meetings of the sub-committee; during this period, a redraft had been prepared by a Jersey-born French republican refugee, Victor Le Lubez. At the following meeting, which Karl had finally been able to attend, the redraft was read out to the full committee. Karl was really 'shocked'. It was 'A fearfully cliché-ridden, badly written and totally unpolished preamble, pretending to be a declaration of principles, with Mazzini showing through the whole thing from beneath a crust of the most insubstantial scraps of French socialism.' He was equally scornful of the Italian-inspired rules, which he thought referred to 'something quite impossible, a sort of central government of the *European* working classes (with Mazzini in the background, of course)'.

According to his own account, Karl 'remonstrated mildly' and, as a result, the drafts were sent back to the sub-committee for further editing, but with the instruction that 'the sentiments' expressed in the Le Lubez Declaration should be retained. Two days later, on 20 October, a meeting of the sub-committee at Karl's house lasted until one o'clock in the morning, but only succeeded in reformulating one of forty rules. Cremer called the meeting to a close with the hope that a reformulated document could be agreed by the sub-committee on 27 October. The 'papers' were 'bequeathed' to Karl for his perusal.[94]

In order to accommodate the 'sentiments' of Le Lubez, while tactfully detaching them from their Mazzinian framework, Karl replaced the 'Declaration of Principles' by an 'Inaugural Address' which recounted the development of the working classes from the mid-1840s. This declared that, despite the rapid growth of the world economy, the misery of the working masses had not diminished between 1848 and 1864. Drawing upon Parliamentary Public Health Reports, he pointed to the virtually starvation wages existing among groups of workers as diverse as agricultural labourers, silk and stocking weavers, needlewomen and others.[95] He also quoted the announcement of the Chancellor of the Exchequer, William Gladstone, that between 1853 and 1861 the taxable income of the country had increased by 20 per cent. 'This intoxicating augmentation of wealth and power', Gladstone had added, was 'almost entirely confined to classes of property'.[96] Everywhere in Britain and Europe, according to the 'Inaugural Address', 'the great mass of the working classes were sinking down to a lower depth, at the same rate at least that those above them were rising in the social scale'. Only a minority 'got their wages somewhat advanced'. Contrary to the promises of industrialization and free trade, it appeared that 'no improvement of machinery, no appliance of science to production, no contrivances of communication, no new colonies, no emigration, no opening of markets, no free trade, nor all these things put together, will do away with the miseries of the industrious masses.'[97] But the situation was not hopeless. The period also possessed 'compensating features'. Firstly, there had been the success of the Ten Hours Bill (limiting factory hours). This was 'the first time that in broad daylight the political economy of the middle class succumbed to the political economy of the working class'. Secondly, there was the cooperative movement, 'a still greater victory of the political economy of labour over the political economy of property'.

Of course, 'the lords of land and lords of capital' would always use their 'political privileges' to defend 'their economical monopolies'. As the Prime Minister, Lord Palmerston, had 'sneered', when defeating the advocates of the Irish Tenants' Right Bill, 'the House of Commons' was 'a house of landed proprietors'. For this reason, 'to conquer political power has ... become the great duty of the working classes'. Their 'fraternal concurrence' was also required in combating the foreign policy of the ruling classes in pursuit of criminal designs, whether for the preservation of transatlantic slavery or the support of 'heroic Poland' against 'that barbarous power, whose head is at St Petersburg and whose hands are in every cabinet in Europe'. At that stage, a Mazzinian point was added. In foreign policy, the aim was to 'vindicate the simple laws of morals and justice, which ought to govern the relations of private individuals, as the rules paramount of the intercourse of nations'. But the concluding sentence reiterated the words of the *Manifesto*: 'Proletarians of all countries, Unite!'[98]

The strategy adopted in the 'Provisional Rules' was the same as that found in the 'Inaugural Address'. Concessions were made to the Mazzinian standpoint, but 'these are so placed that they can do no harm'. Members of the International Association were to 'acknowledge truth, justice, and morality, as the bases of their conduct towards each other, and towards all men, without regard to colour, creed, or nationality'. But the first and fundamental point was that 'the emancipation of the working classes must be conquered by the working classes themselves'. Karl was also pleased that he had managed to forefront Russian tyranny and to refer to 'countries' rather than 'nationalities'. He lamented the fact that he was unable to employ 'the old boldness of language', and was compelled to 'frame the thing so that our view should appear in a form that would make it ACCEPTABLE to the present outlook of the workers' movement'.[99]

But, in truth, that was a large part of the document's strength. Not only did it conceptualize the emancipation of the working classes as a global project and articulate a transnational community of workers' interests, but it did so in a language with which politically aware working men at the time could identify. Similarly, the discussion of the workers' condition during the preceding fifteen years took care to mirror what trade unionists like Howell and Applegarth considered to be their own understanding of the period. It also addressed conventional notions of justice and respectability by emphasizing that what was being discussed was not 'the deserved poverty of idleness', but 'the poverty of working populations'.

With one or two minor amendments, Karl's reformulation of the drafts of Weston, Wolff and Le Lubez was accepted unanimously by the General Council. According to Edward Beesly, 'The Address thus issued is probably the most striking and powerful statement of the workman's case against the middle class that has ever been compressed into a dozen small pages.'[100] What particularly impressed contemporaries were its deployment of official sources and the confining of its claims to historical fact. As the Secretary of the Reform League, George Howell, put it, with understandable exaggeration, 'a Gladstone or a Bright could have accepted it with a good conscience'.[101]

6. *CAPITAL* AND THE POLITICS OF THE 1860s

It was in the formulation of this new social-democratic language in the mid-1860s that Karl made his greatest contribution to the International, both in the definition of the aims of the Association and in a global diagnosis of the workers' condition. These were also the years – between 1863 and 1867 – in which Karl was writing up *Capital*. The pronouncements in the 'Inaugural Address' and the 'Rules' of the International were closely related to the analysis he was currently developing in his book. But before this proximity can be fully recognized, it is necessary to dismantle the standard twentieth-century reading of Karl's theory of revolution.

The turbulent history of the twentieth century from 1917 through to the 1970s created an almost indelible association between Karl and a 'Marxist' language of revolution. 'Marxism' was identified with the violent overthrow of capitalism and the leading role of the revolutionary party. The leaders of revolutionary parties constructed their strategies upon what they conceived to be the correct reading of a small number of prescribed Marxian texts. Particular emphasis was placed upon *The Communist Manifesto*, the 1859 preface to *A Contribution to the Critique of Political Economy*, *The Civil War in France* and *The Critique of the Gotha Programme*. Significantly, this canonical list contained no more than dutiful mention of Karl's works during the period of his greatest achievement, the years 1864–9. This period included his publication of *Capital* and his formulation of the aims of the International Working Men's Association.

Twentieth-century associations have obscured Karl's conception of revolutionary change during the 1860s. What excited him was not the expectation of an apocalyptic event, some revolutionary doomsday, in which 'the knell of capitalist private property sounds' and 'the expropriators are expropriated'.[102] Rather, his assumption was that the process of a transition from the capitalist mode of production towards the society of associated producers had already begun.

The existence of such an assumption has been obscured by Karl's failure to publish *Capital* as a single work in 1867. The delay in publishing the second volume was never envisaged. On 7 May 1867, Karl wrote to Engels that Meissner, his publisher, was demanding the second volume by the end of the autumn at the latest: 'I shall therefore have to get my nose to the grindstone as soon as possible, as a lot of new material relating especially to the chapters on credit and landed property has become available since the manuscript was composed. The third volume must be completed during the winter, so that I shall have shaken off the whole *opus* by next spring.'[103] Engels thought it 'obvious' that after completing the first volume 'you must have a 6 week rest'. But in the following August, having 'read the thing through to the end', he 'definitely' thought that 'the second volume is also *indispensable*, and the sooner you finish it the better'.[104]

In the event, the manuscripts of the unfinished volume were only published by Engels in 1885 and 1894, between twenty and thirty years after their original composition. Furthermore, Engels' introductions, which focused upon preoccupations of the 1880s and 1890s – Karl's alleged plagiarism of the political economy of Rodbertus, and Engels' suggested solution to the problem of relating surplus value to profit – deadened any connection there might have been with the original political intention of the book. In particular, this posthumous publication dulled any sense of an immediate connection between the 'Inaugural Address' and the allusions to the transition from bourgeois society to the society of associated producers found in the unpublished part of *Capital*.[105]

The most distinctive feature of Karl's conception of revolution in the 1860s was that its focus was not upon event, but upon process. It was for this reason that in the 1867 preface to *Capital* he could write about the actuality of 'the process of revolution' in England.[106] The picture of revolutionary change presented there was not of revolution as theatrical event – the fall of the Bastille, the storming of the Winter Palace. Successful revolution meant rather the political ratification of changes which were already occurring or had already occurred in civil society.

The greater the extent of these preceding social changes, the less the violence likely to accompany the process of political change. It was for this reason that Karl believed that workers in England might 'by peaceful means' conquer 'political supremacy in order to establish the new organisation of labour'.[107] In January 1867, in a speech in support of Polish independence, he suggested that the struggle between workmen and capitalists might be 'less fierce and bloody than the struggles between the feudal lord and the capitalist proved in England and France. We will hope so.'[108] The picture was not of the violent seizure of power associated with twentieth-century communism, but of a social-democratic process propelled by 'pressure from without'.[109] It was in the same spirit that Karl concluded his chapter on 'The Working Day' in *Capital*: 'In place of the pompous catalogue of the "inalienable rights of man" [of 1789] comes the modest Magna Charta of a legally limited working day . . . *Quantum mutatus ab illo!*'[110]

The picture of the transition from capitalism to socialism was analogous to that from feudalism to capitalism. The depiction of the emergence and ascent of the capitalist mode of production in *Capital* showed that crucial changes in the development of civil society preceded both the achievement of a bourgeois state and the technological triumphs of the industrial revolution. In accordance with his organic vision of the development of modes of production, Karl maintained that 'the economic structure of capitalistic society' had 'grown out of the economic structure of feudal society' and that 'the dissolution of the latter' had 'set free the elements of the former'.[111] In feudal times, 'The money capital formed by means of usury and commerce was prevented from turning into industrial capital, in the country by the feudal constitution, in the towns by guild organisation. These fetters vanished with the dissolution of feudal society, with the expropriation and partial eviction of the country population.' Global developments further assisted this capitalist development: 'The discovery of gold and silver in America, the extirpation, enslavement and entombment in mines of the aboriginal population, the beginning of the conquest and looting of the East Indies, the turning of Africa into a warren for the commercial hunting of black-skins, signalised the rosy dawn of the era of capitalist production. These idyllic proceedings are the chief momenta of primitive accumulation.'[112] Heralded by the communal movements in late medieval towns, freeing urban corporations from feudal structures, together with the expansion of international trade and the discovery of new continents, civil society had developed alongside new forms of commodity production. Assisted between the fifteenth and eighteenth centuries by the 'expropriation of the agricultural population from the land', new legal and institutional arrangements made possible the accumulation of capital. This process of social change found political and legal ratification in the 'bourgeois revolution' of 1688, which removed remaining restrictions on the inheritance of property.[113]

Parallel examples of the transition from bourgeois property to that of the 'associated producers' were to be found in Karl's picture of the 1860s. In the third, unpublished volume of *Capital*, Karl wrote of the transformation of stock companies: 'the stock company is a transition toward the conversion of all functions in the reproduction process which still remain linked with capitalist property, into mere functions of associated producers, into social functions.'[114] This, he continued, 'is the abolition of the capitalist mode of production within the capitalist mode of production itself, and hence a self-dissolving contradiction, which *prima facie* represents a mere phase of transition to a new form of production.'[115] But the most impressive of these examples was the development of cooperative factories which 'represent within the old form the first sprouts of the new . . . the antithesis between capital and labour is overcome within them, if at first only by way of making the associated labourers into their own capitalist, i.e., by enabling them to use the means of production for the employment of their own labour.' They showed how 'A new mode of production naturally grows out of an old one, when the development of material forces of production and of the corresponding forms of social production have reached a particular stage.'[116]

In the 'Inaugural Address', he developed the same thought, but with a sharper political edge. Cooperative factories 'by deed instead of argument' had shown that 'Production on a large scale, and in accord with the behests of modern science, may be carried on without the existence of a class of masters employing a class of hands; that to bear fruit, the means of labour need not be monopolised as a means of dominion over, and of extortion against, the labouring man himself.' This demonstrated that 'Like slave labour, like serf labour, hired labour is but a transitory and inferior form, destined to disappear before associated labour plying its toil with a willing hand, a ready mind, and a joyous heart.' The advent of cooperative production performed by associated labour had been the central issue not only in the development of Owenism in England, but also the rational core of schemes for the emancipation of labour in 1848: 'In England, the seeds of the cooperative system were sown by Robert Owen; the working men's experiments, tried on the continent were, in fact, the practical upshot of the theories, not invented, but loudly proclaimed, in 1848.'[117]

7. CREATING THE POLITICS OF A CLASS: KARL'S WORK IN THE GENERAL COUNCIL

Karl regularly attended the weekly meetings of the General Council and played an intellectually leading role within it. Uniquely positioned to act as a mediator between British and European currents of thought, he was able to give shape and meaning to the development of events at home and abroad. He was also able to draft coherent responses to the unfolding of events. It was therefore not surprising that in the years before the Franco-Prussian War, his services to the Council were highly appreciated. Their value was pointed out at the Geneva Congress by the trade unionist Randall Cremer in opposition to a French motion declaring that only workers should be eligible as delegates to congresses of the International. Cremer pointed out that the movement in Britain owed much to members of the Council who were not manual workers. 'Among those members, I will mention one only, Citizen Marx, who has devoted all his life to the triumph of the working classes.'[118] Contemporaries were particularly struck by his economic and statistical erudition. According to Edward Beesly, 'While the practical English element prevents it from splitting to pieces on economic and political theories, the foreign members, in whose hands the continental correspondence necessarily lies are men of great ability and information, who have devoted themselves to the International from its foundation. To no one is the success of the *Association* so much due as to Dr Karl Marx, who, in his acquaintance with the history and statistics of the industrial movement in all parts of Europe, is, I should imagine, without a rival.'[119]

Karl's intellectual authority in this area was demonstrated in a running debate on the General Council in the spring and summer of 1865, sparked off by 'Citizen' Weston's 'proposition' on wages. Weston questioned the value of trade unions since wage increases merely resulted in higher prices; only producer-cooperatives could increase workers' standard of living. Drawing upon his current work in *Capital*, Karl argued over two meetings that wage rises might bring about a fall in the rate of profits, but would leave the value of commodities unaltered. The general tendency of production, however, was to lower wages. Trade unions were valuable in counteracting, even if only temporarily, falls in wage rates, and in limiting the working day. But, above all, their value lay 'in organising the working class as a class'. They failed generally by 'accepting the present relations of capital and labour as permanent instead of working for their abolition'.[120] In response to Weston, Randall Cremer, at that point the General Secretary of the Council, thought that 'Citizen Marx had given two or three practical illustrations or rather facts which completely destroyed the positions affirmed by Citizen Weston.'[121]

On the General Council, Karl's strategy was to align himself as closely as possible with the positions of the new trade union leaders. The Association, as he wrote to Dr Kugelmann at the end of November 1864, was 'important because the leaders of the London Trade Unions belong to it'.[122] Over a year later, his views remained unchanged: 'We have succeeded in attracting into the movement the only really big workers' organisation, the English "*TRADE UNIONS*", which previously concerned themselves *exclusively* with the wage question.'[123] Twentieth-century assumptions about the centrality of the Party have obscured the extent to which this was *not* Karl's assumption in the 1860s. His confidence in the merits of a party as the vehicle of revolution had been undermined by the developments of the preceding fifteen years. His hope that Chartism might be revived had finally had to be abandoned, while his efforts to preserve his own 'party' in exile had been destroyed by the emergence of what he called 'governmental socialism' under Lassalle and Schweitzer in Germany. Throughout the 1860s, Karl put his faith in trade unions as the means of the formation and consolidation of class identity and activity. In Hanover, in 1869, Karl told a delegation of Lassallean metal workers, 'All political parties, whatever they may be, without exception, inspire the masses of the workers only temporarily, the unions, however, mesmerise the masses of the workers for good, only they are capable of truly representing a workers' party and being a bastion against the power of capital.' Trade unions, he continued, were 'the schools of socialism'. In trade unions, workers were formed as socialists, since 'there daily the struggle against capital was played out before their eyes'.[124]

Writing to Dr Kugelmann early in 1865, after explaining why it was now impossible for him to participate in Prussian politics, he went on, 'I prefer my agitation here through the *International Association* a 100 times. The effect on the *English* proletariat is direct and of the greatest importance.'[125] Pushing the International Association towards a conventional socialist agenda was not his primary concern. As he later emphasized, the General Council had not been 'responsible' for the decision of the 1868 Brussels Congress to demand the nationalization of mines, railways and forests. That initiative had come from the Brussels delegates. As he explained to Dr Kugelmann, in relation to the programme of the 1866 Geneva Congress, his objective was rather to confine it 'to points which allow direct agreement and combination of efforts by the workers and give direct sustenance and impetus to the requirements of the class struggle and the organisation of the workers into a class'.[126] The ambition to steer clear of issues that might spark off divisive political struggles was clear in the 'Instructions for the Delegates of the Provisional General Council', which he drafted for the Geneva Congress. The 'Instructions' concentrated upon statistical enquiries about conditions of labour, the limitation of the working day, juvenile and children's labour, producer cooperatives and trade unions. On controversial questions about international credit or religion, he recommended, 'initiative to be left to the French'.[127]

In order to make class formation a priority and to avoid sectarian squabbles, which might distract from it, Karl was prepared to make whatever compromises might be necessary. His willingness to incorporate Mazzinian formulations within the 'Inaugural Address' was a good example of his approach. Another was his preparedness in the face of liberal and Nonconformist opposition to accept the removal of his protégé, Johann Georg Eccarius, from the editorship of *The Commonwealth*, briefly the International's official newspaper. In January 1866, Karl had hoped that Eccarius's appointment could counter the influence of the paper's liberal, Nonconformist backers. But in March, while Karl was away in Margate on a prolonged health trip, the Editorial Supervision Committee dismissed Eccarius. Whatever the rebuff, Karl thought that 'good understanding with the English must, of course, be more important to us than satisfying Eccarius' more or less justified ambition'.[128] On international questions as well, he attempted to avoid involvement in intra-party quarrels. He made every effort to remain neutral in the arguments between republicans and Proudhonists in France, and between the Lassallean and Eisenach parties in Germany.

In the first few years of the International, there was practical agreement between Karl and the English trade unionists on major issues, both on the General Council and in the annual congresses. In particular, in the 1865 London Conference and in the Geneva and Lausanne Congresses of 1866 and 1867 there was consensus in opposing a variety of French positions. These included the refusal to condemn Russian actions in Poland (according to the French, this was not the business of an 'economic' association), indifference towards trade unionism (the aim should not be to encourage strikes, but to remove the wage system altogether), opposition to the eight-hour day or state education (these would imply approval of state interference with freedom of contract) and the French demand for the exclusion of women from the labour force.

The success of Karl's approach, particularly on issues where the English approach faced a challenge from abroad, led him to an increasingly enthusiastic identification with the Association. In early 1865, now referring to himself as part of the General Council, he had informed Dr Kugelmann: 'We are now STIRRING the GENERAL SUFFRAGE QUESTION here.'[129] Around the same time, he wrote to Engels about the setting up of the new Reform League, 'the *whole leadership* is in our hands'.[130] The great achievement of the International Association was to have created in the Reform League a movement which could transform European politics: 'The REFORM LEAGUE is OUR WORK ... The WORKINGMEN are ALL MEMBERS OF OUR COUNCIL ... WE HAVE BAFFLED all attempts by the middle class TO MISLEAD THE WORKING CLASS ... If we succeed in re-electrifying the POLITICAL MOVEMENT of the ENGLISH WORKING CLASS, our ASSOCIATION will already have done more for the European working class, WITHOUT MAKING ANY

FUSS, than was possible IN ANY OTHER WAY. And there is every prospect of success.'[131]

At the beginning of 1866, his confidence in the capacity of the General Council to channel workers' activity in the right direction remained undiminished. In January 1866, he informed Dr Kugelmann: 'The English society we founded to achieve UNIVERSAL SUFFRAGE (half of its Central Committee consists of members – working men – of our Central Committee) held a giant meeting a few weeks ago, at which only working men spoke.'[132] At this time, Karl liked to imagine that he was playing a controlling role: a result, he claimed, of *acting* behind the scenes, while retiring in public'. He saw this as a contrast with the 'democrats' habit of puffing themselves up in public and DOING NOTHING'.[133] On 9 October 1866, Karl reported to Dr Kugelmann that 'The Reform movement here, which was called into being by our Central Council (*quorum magna pars fui* [in which I played a large part]), has now assumed enormous and irresistible dimensions.'[134] On 13 October, he announced that the London Trades Council was conidering declaring itself the British section of the International. 'If it does so,' he confided to Kugelmann, 'the control of the working class here will IN A CERTAIN SENSE pass into our hands and we shall be able to give the movement a good "PUSH ON".'[135]

In the summer of 1867, Karl was too preoccupied with the publication of *Capital* to pay much attention to domestic political events. He continued to be optimistic. In the case of England, he remained confident that 'pressure from without' could result in a revolutionary transformation and that such a revolution need not be violent. In September 1867, he wrote to Engels: 'When the next revolution comes, and that will perhaps be sooner than might appear, *we* (i.e., you and I) will have this mighty ENGINE *at our disposal*. COMPARE WITH THIS THE RESULTS OF MAZZINI'S ETC. OPERATIONS SINCE 30 YEARS! And with no money to boot! And with the intrigues of the Proudhonists in Paris, Mazzini in Italy and the jealous Odger, Cremer, Potter in London, with the Schulze-Delitzsch and the Lassalleans in Germany! We can be well satisfied.'[136] Early successes had led Karl both to overestimate the importance of the IWMA in British radical politics, and his own importance within the Association. But he had begun to notice that as a result of a growing preoccupation with the suffrage and a parallel need to defend the legality of trade union action in industrial disputes, union leaders were now devoting most of their time to the Reform League and parliamentary lobbying. Their attendance of the General Council had fallen off. In October 1866, Karl claimed that he had to run the whole Association himself.[137]

Furthermore, from 1866–7, he found it increasingly difficult to sustain an ecumenical position. Different positions were emerging within the Council, in particular over the agitation for political reform and the reappearance of a republican independence movement in Ireland. Both issues raised questions about the political role of the IWMA and that of the most important trade union leaders within it. Should the Association aim to maintain an independent position? Or should it aim to work alongside other progressive political forces allied to the Liberal Party, now under the charismatic leadership of Mr Gladstone?[138]

8. THE SECOND REFORM BILL AND REBELLION IN IRELAND

The preface to *Capital* was written in July 1867 towards the end of a year of mounting political agitation around the issue of manhood suffrage. The campaign for reform had been pursued by the Reform League, a radical and predominantly working-class organization, supported by trade unions and the International. At its height, it possessed over 600 branches. The campaign had begun in 1865 and had proceeded in parallel with a modest parliamentary Reform Bill proposed by the Liberal government of Russell and Gladstone. But popular interest in the question only gathered pace after the fall of this government and its replacement in June 1866 by the Tory ministry of Derby and Disraeli. In the following month, a series of increasingly large Reform meetings in Trafalgar Square culminated in the decision to hold a demonstration in Hyde Park – crown property and, until then, largely the preserve of the horse-riding gentility of Rotten Row. Although the meeting was forbidden and the park guarded by the Metropolitan Police backed up by the military, the crowd pulled down the railings, broke into the park and for three days engaged in minor skirmishing with the forces of law and order. Finally, the League met the Home Secretary, Spencer Walpole, and offered to clear the park, provided the police and military withdrew. The Home Secretary accepted the offer and was said to have wept with gratitude. This supposedly shameful climb-down by the government greatly enhanced the power and prestige of the League.

But however laughable Walpole's refusal to use the military might first have seemed – Karl called him 'the weeping willow' – this was a sign of the strength, rather than the weakness, of the English polity. As the Positivist Frederic Harrison observed:

> A centralised bureaucratic system gives a great resisting force to the hand that commands the Executive. Our Executive has nothing to fall back upon . . . A few redcoats may be called upon to suppress a vulgar riot; but the first blood of the people shed by troops in a really popular cause, as we all know, makes the Briton boil in a very ugly manner . . .
>
> The fact is that our political organism of the constitutional type was based on a totally different theory from that of force at all. The governing classes never pretended to rely on force. They trusted to maintain their supremacy by their social power, and their skill in working the machine. Local self-government, representation of the people, civil liberty, was all the cry, until at last the tone of English public life became saturated with ideas of rule by consent, and not by force . . . The least suggestion of force puts the governing classes in an outrageously false position, and arrays against them all the noble sentiments of liberty on which they based their own title to rule.[139]

This was also the sentiment that restrained the leaders of the Reform League from pushing their advantage to the limits. At a meeting of radical MPs and leaders of the Reform League, John Stuart Mill urged the League not to occupy the park and 'produce a collision with the military', while in the following months John Bright, who was leading a series of Reform demonstrations in Glasgow, Leeds, Birmingham and Manchester, warned about the possibility that further demonstrations in London might attract armed volunteers: it 'would place the peace of the country on a soil hot with volcanic fire'.[140]

It is not clear how Karl expected the existing situation to develop. He was well aware that Britain was not France. Back in April 1866, writing from Margate, he had complained to Engels that 'The accursed traditional nature of all English movements is manifesting itself again in the REFORM-MOVEMENT. The same INSTALMENTS which but a few weeks ago were rejected with the utmost indignation by the people's party – they had even refused Bright's ultimatum of HOUSE-HOLD SUFFRAGE – are now treated as a prize worthy to be fought for. And why? Because the Tories are screaming blue murder.' But he was encouraged by the course of events over the summer. On 7 July, he was excited to report that 'The Workers' demonstrations in London are fabulous compared with anything seen in England since 1849, and they are solely the work of the *INTERNATIONAL*. Mr Lucraft, FI, the captain in Trafalgar Square, is ONE OF OUR COUNCIL.' He had mixed feelings about Walpole's dealings with the League in the Hyde Park railings affair. 'The government has almost caused a mutiny here.' But, he continued, 'Your Englishman first needs a revolutionary educa-tion.' If the military had had to 'step in, instead of merely parading . . . then things would have got quite jolly . . . This much is certain', he went on, 'These stiff-necked John Bulls . . . will accomplish nothing without a really bloody clash with those in power.'[141]

The possibilities remained open. But from the beginning of the agi-tation Karl had been made aware that the priorities of the leading trade unionists on the General Council were not the same as his own. At the time of the Hyde Park railings affair, he had lamented that the leaders of the Reform movement lacked 'the METTLE of the old Chartists'.[142] His failure to establish Eccarius on the editorial board of the *Common-wealth* showed that his hostility to the participation of middle-class radicals in the Association was not generally shared. It was also far from clear that the leaders of the Reform League would stick to their original demand for 'manhood suffrage' rather than accept some form of household suffrage, which would allow agreement with radical liberals. At the end of August 1866, he complained to Johann Philipp Becker, one of the International's most energetic supporters in Geneva, that 'Cremer and Odger have both *betrayed* us in the Reform League, where they came to a *compromise with the bourgeoisie* against our wishes.'[143]

If there had been any serious possibility of political crisis in England, by the spring of 1867 it was already passing.[144] It had been doused by Parliament itself. In the first few months of 1866, the moderate reform proposals of Russell and Gladstone had been opposed both by the

Tories and by the so-called Adullamites within Liberal ranks. The incoming Tory administration of Derby and Disraeli had had no initial plans for reform. But in the winter of 1866–7, against a background of economic depression and the return of cholera, with Reform demonstrations continuing with undiminished intensity, and the dangers of an uprising in Ireland, the government's priorities fundamentally changed.[145] As Disraeli put it, 'we might take a step which would destroy the present agitation and extinguish Gladstone and Co.'.[146]

In January 1867, Disraeli introduced reform proposals and, whether as the result of a change in party calculation or of continuing pressure from outside, was prepared to accept increasingly radical amendments to the Bill. This culminated in Hodgkinson's amendment, which extended household suffrage to include the large urban lodger population. It was a concession scarcely dreamt of months before, and even Ernest Jones was eager to convince Karl that the amended Bill deserved support. The result was a franchise four times larger than originally intended, or, in Jonathan Parry's words, 'the most unintended revolution in the history of British politics'.[147]

One of the reasons why both parties were anxious to settle the question of reform was mounting anxiety about Ireland.[148] The Irish Republican Brotherhood, or the Fenians, as they were popularly known, originated among Irish expatriates in America. It began planning an insurrection in 1865 that it hoped would be reinforced by veterans from the American Civil War. The Fenians collected around 6,000 firearms and claimed the support of up to 50,000 volunteers. But in September of that year the government closed down the Fenian newspaper, *The Irish People*, and arrested most of its leaders. Despite this, the Fenians attempted to launch an insurrection in early 1867. They proclaimed a republic based upon universal (male) suffrage, dispossession of the ascendant landed oligarchy, religious freedom and the separation of church and state. There was an unsuccessful insurrection in County Kerry, followed by failed risings in Cork, Limerick and Dublin. Even more ominously, the organizers hoped to draw upon the support of the Irish living in England. Their plans included the capture of arms in Chester Castle and the appropriation of rail and shipping links to Dublin. But the uprising was poorly planned and undermined by informers.

On 18 September 1867, the prison van transporting two of the arrested leaders to the Manchester courthouse was attacked by armed

Fenians. The prisoners escaped, but a policeman was killed in the struggle. A trial in November led to the execution of three of the Fenians involved on the 23rd. On 13 December, a bomb designed to aid the escape of imprisoned Fenian leaders in Clerkenwell prison resulted in twelve deaths and 120 wounded. In this instance, unsurprisingly, much of the support for the Fenians drained away. As Karl wrote to Engels, 'This latest Fenian exploit in Clerkenwell is a great folly. The London masses, who have shown much sympathy for Ireland, will be enraged by it and driven into the arms of the government party. One cannot expect London proletarians to let themselves be blown up for the benefit of Fenian emissaries. Secret melodramatic conspiracies of this kind are in general, more or less doomed to failure.'[149]

The unrest in Ireland and Fenian violence in Manchester and Clerkenwell transformed the character of political debate. Quite apart from Fenianism, discontent among the middle class in Ireland had led to the formation of the National Association, which demanded the disestablishment of the Irish (Anglican) church, tenant rights on the land and the establishment of a Catholic university. Although deeply disturbed by the activity of the Fenians, it was to these demands that Gladstone explicitly responded in the general election of 1868. His move to disestablish the church not only addressed a major grievance of Catholics in Ireland, but also gained enthusiastic support from English Dissenters. Through the winter of 1867–8, discussion was dominated by the question of Ireland and Gladstone's proposal to disestablish the Irish church. As Karl reported to Dr Kugelmann in April 1868, 'The Irish question predominates here just now. It has naturally only been exploited by Gladstone and consorts to take over the helm again and particularly to have an ELECTORAL CRY at the next elections, which will be based on HOUSEHOLD SUFFRAGE.'[150]

Like the rest of the nation, Karl's family was drawn into discussion of the Irish question. In the case of the Engels household, commitment to the cause of Ireland was long-standing, and enthusiasm for the Fenians immediate. Lizzie Burns had always been a fierce supporter of Irish independence. Engels himself had also long been deeply engaged and in the winter of 1869–70 was to embark upon an ambitious, but never completed, plan to write *The History of Ireland*.[151] Five days after the Fenian armed rescue in Manchester, he took Laura Marx's companion, Paul Lafargue, to show him the railway arch 'where the great Fenian liberation battle was enacted . . . The affair was splendidly organised and executed', he wrote to Dr Kugelmann, but unfortunately, 'the ringleaders were caught'.[152]

Karl needed to be more cautious. He had sought 'by every means at my disposal to incite the English workers to demonstrate in favour of FENIANISM', and he certainly would not keep 'entirely silent'. 'But', he argued, 'under no circumstances do I want the fellows, when criticising my book, to confine themselves to the statement that I am a demagogue.'[153] The execution of three of the Fenians involved in the Manchester rescue attempt was felt as a tragedy by both households. 'Jenny goes in black since the Manchester execution,' wrote Karl, 'and wears her Polish cross on a green ribbon.' 'I need hardly tell you', Engels replied the next day, 'that black and green are the prevailing colours in my house too.'[154]

Feelings of outrage about the sentences passed on the Fenians were shared by the General Council of the International. At its meeting to discuss Fenianism on 19 November 1867, the tone was set by Hermann Jung, a Swiss watchmaker. He argued that although he was 'no abettor of physical force movements . . . the Irish have no other means to make an impression.' The Reform League had accomplished much by 'moral force', but it was only 'under a threat that physical force might be resorted to on the occasion of the Hyde Park meetings that the Government gave way . . . Garibaldi is held up as a great patriot; and have no lives been sacrificed in Garibaldi's movements? The Irish have the same right to revolt as the Italians . . . (Loud cheers.)'[155] At meetings of the Reform League, feelings ran equally high. Odger even declared that had he been born an Irishman, he would also have been a Fenian.[156]

Karl arrived late for the 19 November meeting of the General Council. He was still suffering from a fever, and was relieved not to have to speak, since the press was present. He prepared a speech for the following meeting on 26 November, but in the event was happy to make way to enable another member, Peter Fox, to speak instead; government treatment of the Irish should be condemned first and foremost, he thought, by the English, and not just by European members of the Council. Thereafter, recurrent bouts of illness meant that he did not attend Council meetings from January through to the summer of 1868. The speech he would have given to the Council, he delivered more discreetly on 16 December to the German Workers' Educational Association.[157]

No doubt, as he had already indicated, he was anxious not to let his views on Ireland deflect attention from the publication of *Capital*. But there were also other reasons for caution. The view he now developed on Ireland also formed part of a more basic revision of his conception of the possibilities of British politics as a whole. On Ireland, he conveyed the gist of his new approach in a couple of letters to Engels in November. On 2 November, he referred to forcible methods of 'driving thousands from their homes', including 'well-to-do tenant farmers', and to the confiscation of their 'improvements and capital investments . . . In no other European country', he wrote, 'has foreign rule assumed this form of direct expropriation of the natives', and he concluded, 'I once believed the separation of Ireland from England to be impossible. I now regard it as inevitable, although *Federation* may follow upon separation.'[158] In a further letter to Engels on 30 November, he elaborated his argument. He claimed that since 1846 the economic content and political purpose of English rule had 'entered an entirely new phase'. Ireland had lost its monopoly of the English corn market. It had therefore exchanged tillage for pasture. This meant 'the clearing out of the estates of Ireland', and the driving out of the Irish 'by means of sheep, pigs and oxen'. For these reasons he believed that 'Fenianism is characterised by socialist (in the negative sense, as directed against the APPROPRIATION of the SOIL) leanings and as a LOWER ORDERS MOVEMENT.' English workers, he concluded, should declare their support for Repeal of the Union (the Union of the English and Irish Parliaments in 1801). What the Irish needed were 'self-government and independence', 'agrarian revolution' and protective tariffs against England.[159]

His new view of Ireland went together with a fading of the hopes he had initially entertained about the Reform League and the London trade unionists. In April 1868, he wrote to Dr Kugelmann that '*At the moment*, this turn of affairs is detrimental to the workers' party, because the intriguers among the workers, such as Odger, Potter, etc. who want to get into the next Parliament, have now found a new excuse for attaching themselves to the bourgeois liberals.'[160] He was particularly incensed by their enthusiasm for Mr Gladstone, a man who had refused clemency to the Fenian insurgents, and who as late as 1862 had expressed support for Jefferson Davis and the Confederate cause.

The chances of independent political activity on the part of workers were further diminished by the course of the 1868 election. The Reform

League did not field independent candidates of its own. Not only did it not possess the financial resources to do so, but there was little popular support for such initiatives. A lib–lab alliance was firmly in the ascendant. As Beesly argued, 'no workman would cast his vote against such men as Mr. Bright, Mr. Mill or Mr. Gladstone, let the opposing candidate promise what he would'.[161] Furthermore, the campaign to disestablish the Irish church was popular; even Karl himself thought that 'in the long run' it would benefit the English working class. For 'The overthrow of the Established church in Ireland would mean its fall in England, and the two will be followed (in their downfall) by LANDLORDISM, first in Ireland and then in England. And I have always been convinced that the social revolution must begin *seriously* from the ground, i.e. from landed property.'[162]

In 1869, the issue of Ireland surfaced again with the emergence of an Irish-based movement pressing for an amnesty for the Fenian leaders imprisoned in 1867. It scored a particular triumph with the victory of the imprisoned Jeremiah O'Donovan Rossa in the 1869 Tipperary by-election. Fenianism briefly captured the imagination not just of activists, but of Irish moderates willing to support the amnesty campaign and of a broad spectrum of sympathizers in England, ranging from the Marx family to Cardinal Newman. In September, 'Tussy' toured Ireland together with Engels and Lizzy Burns, and early the next year, using the pseudonym J. Williams, her sister, Jenny, wrote a series of supportive articles on the Fenians for *La Marseillaise*. In October, she wrote to Dr Kugelmann, describing a mass demonstration for the Fenian prisoners' release: 'As Tussy has returned from Ireland, a stauncher Irishman than ever, she did not rest until she had persuaded Moor, Mama and me to go with her to Hyde Park . . . This Park . . . was one mass of men, women and children, even the trees up to their highest branches had their inhabitants.'[163]

Karl hoped to use the amnesty campaign to make a frontal assault on Gladstone. He now thought it imperative to shift the attitude of the English working class towards Ireland, but if that were to happen, the trade unionists' infatuation with the Liberals would have to be challenged. On 16 November, he opened discussion in the General Council on 'the attitude of the British ministry to the Irish amnesty question'. He spoke for an hour and a quarter. In his reply to Irish demands for 'the release of the imprisoned Irish patriots', Karl contended, 'Mr

Gladstone deliberately insults the Irish Nation.' In support of his resolution, Karl claimed that 'during the election, Gladstone justified the
Fenian insurrection and said that every other nation would have
revolted under similar circumstances'. He also contrasted Gladstone's
support for 'the American Slave Holders' Rebellion' with his preaching
of 'passive obedience' to the Irish people.[164] In the following Council
meeting on 23 November, Odger, in defence of Gladstone, raised the
question of whether it was not 'impolitic' to employ such strong language, if the aim were to secure the prisoners' release, while Thomas
Mottershead of the weavers' union not only rejected any Irish demand
for independence, on the grounds that Ireland was needed as a defence
against France, but also strongly defended Gladstone's political record.
Finally, Odger suggested that the resolution could be passed unanimously, if the word 'deliberately' was omitted.[165]

'I have now attacked Gladstone,' Karl wrote to Dr Kugelmann on
29 November. The intention behind his resolution, he explained, 'naturally had other grounds than simply to speak out loudly and decidedly
for the oppressed Irish . . . I have become more and more convinced', he
went on, that 'The thing now is to drum this conviction into the English working class – that they will never be able to do anything decisive
here in England before they separate their attitude towards Ireland
quite definitely from that of the ruling classes, and not only make common cause with the Irish, but even take the initiative in dissolving the
Union.'[166] But, as it happened, Karl was unable to attend the meeting of
7 December, in which he was due to open the discussion about Ireland
and the English working class. 'My family did not allow me to go in
this FOG and in MY PRESENT STATE OF HEALTH.'[167]

Not only was Karl's resolution on Ireland and the English working
class not discussed on this occasion, but the matter was not discussed
again. The General Council was happy to support Irish demands for independence, but not prepared to go further. Trade unionists like Odger
backtracked on any endorsement of the use of force by the Fenians. They
were also reluctant to participate in an unqualified attack on Gladstone,
especially since they supported not only his Church Bill, but also his Land
Bill, which dominated the government's legislative programme.[168] Moreover, in 1870 the salience of Fenianism receded. The majority of the Fenians
themselves backed away from the politics of armed rebellion and in
1874 switched their support to a parliamentary campaign for home rule.

Throughout the 1870s, the General Council was happy to leave the matter to one side. The only evidence suggesting engagement on their part was a 'Circular' which was allegedly sent by the General Council to 'the Federal Council of Romance Switzerland', its ostensible purpose to reply to an attack upon its constitutional behaviour in the Geneva-based *Egalité*, a newspaper sympathetic to Bakunin.

The main aim of the Circular was to oppose the proposal to separate the General Council from a Federal Council, which would act as the English branch of the Association. In defence of the existing position of the General Council, the Circular developed an ambitious speculative analysis of the downfall of the British Empire and the world market. It was stated that while revolution might begin in France, 'England alone can serve as the lever for a serious *economic* revolution'. It was a country in which the great majority of the population were wage labourers, and where class struggle and the organization of the working class by the trade unions 'have acquired a certain degree of maturity and universality'. England dominated the world market; it was the world centre of landlordism and capitalism. Its weak point was Ireland.

The first concern of the Association was 'to advance the social revolution in England. To this end, a great blow must be struck in Ireland.' The power of English landlordism depended importantly upon absentee ownership of Irish land, while the English bourgeoisie had reinforced its power by forcing the immigration of poor Irish workers. This had divided the proletariat in Britain into two hostile camps: 'The average English worker hates the Irish worker as a competitor who lowers wages and the STANDARD OF LIFE. He feels national and religious antipathies for him. He regards him somewhat like the POOR WHITES of the Southern States of North America regarded black slaves.' By forwarding Irish independence and breaking the power of landlordism, the collapse of the ruling class became possible. Therefore it became imperative to move the English working class towards the Repeal of the Union. For Repeal was a *'precondition to the emancipation of the English working class* to transform the present *forced union* (i.e., the enslavement of Ireland) into *equal and free confederation* if possible, into *complete separation*, if need be'.

Written in French and defined as a 'confidential' document, the Circular escaped the elementary cautions that normally attend official documents. For whatever the merits of its reading of the relationship between the British working class and Ireland, discussion of how this political objective might be achieved resulted in an unbuttoned flight of pure fantasy, generally found only in private correspondence. Revolution could not be entrusted to the English: 'The General Council now being in the *happy* position *of having its hand directly on this great lever of the proletarian revolution*, what folly, we might say even what a crime, to let this lever fall into purely English hands! . . . The English', it went on, 'have all the *material* necessary for the social revolution. What they lack is the *spirit of generalisation and revolutionary ardour.*' This could be provided by the General Council, which could 'accelerate the truly revolutionary movement in this country, and consequently *everywhere*'.[169] The Circular purported to derive from the General Council. At the beginning of the Circular, it was stated: 'at its extraordinary meeting on 1 January 1870, the *General Council* resolved . . . ' But there is no evidence that such a meeting ever took place.[170] Nor is it at all likely that the members of the General Council would have approved of such a document.

In Karl's approach, the complexities of the Irish situation were wished away. His analysis was based upon the unreal premise that religious and sectarian divisions would quickly recede. Once the Irish church had been removed, Karl wrote to Dr Kugelmann in 1868, 'The Protestant Irish tenants in the province of Ulster will make common cause with the Catholic tenants and their movement in the 3 other provinces of Ireland, whereas so far LANDLORDISM has been able to exploit this *religious* antagonism.'[171] Through 1870, Karl persisted with this reading of Ireland as the key to the advent of social revolution, first in England and then, by extension, the world. In March 1870, he wrote to the Lafargues: 'To accelerate the social development in Europe, you must push on the catastrophe of official England. To do so, you must attack her in Ireland. That's her weakest point. Ireland lost, the British "Empire" is gone, and the class war in England, till now somnolent and chronic, will assume acute forms. But England is the metropolis of landlordism and capitalism all over the world.'[172] But without further evidence of the 'pressure from without', which had given some substance to the hopes of 1866–7, the analysis appeared abstract and doctrinaire.

The focus on Ireland was in part the result of frustration about the lack of further critical developments in England together with disappointment at the reluctance of trade unionists to move beyond their initial positions. Until 1871, Karl remained a respected, if somewhat isolated, figure on the General Council. Beyond indigenous traditions of radicalism, there were Mazzinians, but no Marxians. There were also Comteans: intellectuals, such as Mill, who grappled with Comte, or became Comtean Positivists like Edward Beesly or Frederic Harrison. Karl became notorious after the Paris *Commune* and the publication of *The Civil War in France* in 1871. But there was no wider interest in Marxian ideas until *Capital* appeared in French from the late 1870s. It is probable, as George Howell later claimed, that little was known about his larger views beyond the practical questions which concerned the Association. Karl's views and those of the trade unionists on the General Council had converged on a number of important issues – the limitation of factory hours and juvenile labour, secular education and the ownership of the land. But the language of class articulated by English trade unionists differed substantially from that imagined by Karl.

Karl, and Engels before him, only half understood this language as it was articulated in radicalism and Chartism. While Karl conceived of class as a purely social phenomenon, for English radicals class was inseparable from the political oppression which resulted from an unbalanced constitution. Socially, there were good and bad employers; so far as there was hostility towards employers, it had been political – their collusion in a state dominated by the landed aristocracy. The trade unionists were happy to collaborate with those who supported reform, with 'advanced liberals' like Miall. The trade unionists approved of arbitration, where possible, supporting strikes only where they were necessary. So far as there was a more visceral form of class hostility, it was directed against the landed aristocracy. Their position was based not upon work, but upon conquest. Land reform, whether in the shape of the abolition of primogeniture recommended by Mill's Land Tenure Reform Association or public ownership of the land as pursued by the Land and Labour League, had long belonged within the radical tradition.

The trade union leaders with whom Karl had to deal in the International – George Odger, George Howell, William Cremer, Robert Applegarth, Thomas Mottershead, John Hales and others – all belonged to a particular generation. Their attitude to industrial conflict had been shaped by the political climate of the 1850s. The turning point had been the great strike wave of 1853–4: in particular the strike in Preston, an event of sufficient importance to inspire Dickens to write *Hard Times*. The strike wave had marked the first revival of mass working-class activity after 1848. But attempts to connect this movement with Chartism failed. Both the radical press and its propertied counterpart spoke about the struggle in new terms. They spoke of the harmony or conflict of interests between 'capital' and 'labour', a new economic rhetoric quite distinct from that of the Chartist agitation between 1837 and 1842.[173] It marked the first step in the process by which the working classes came to be recognized as legitimate bargainers in the polity. The propertied press for the first time spoke of the working class as the 'Fourth Estate' with legitimate interests and grievances.[174]

The new attitude towards industrial relations was a product of the changed political climate after the demise of Chartism in 1848. After the drastic restructuring it had undertaken in the 1830s and 1840s, the state withdrew from the salient role it had played in the labour market. The conflict between 'capital' and 'labour' no longer possessed immediate political connotations. Chartism had been a struggle not against the wages system as such, but rather against its abuses, which were abetted and facilitated by a corrupt state. The change in the stance of the state in the 1850s and 1860s was accompanied by changing attitudes on the part of the working classes.

While Karl paid much attention to developments within the English economy between 1850 and 1870, he scarcely noticed the changing character of the state and the political system. In 1844, Engels had seriously underestimated the importance of England's 'birthrights', and Karl did not question Engels' position. As 1848 indicated, freedom of the press and freedom of association were not unimportant legitimizing features of the English political system at a time when they did not exist anywhere else in Europe.

In the following twenty years, the moral legitimacy of the state and the political system substantially increased. The excesses of 'old corruption' were reduced, Nonconformists were able to breach the Anglican monopoly of state employment and higher education, working hours were restricted, trade union funds were legally protected, strikes were increasingly tolerated and, in 1867, a significant proportion of the working classes was enfranchised. The differences in the political climate between Britain and the Continent were highlighted by Robert Applegarth, the leader of the Amalgamated Society of Carpenters and Joiners, who remarked at the Basle Congress of the International in 1869: 'fortunately, in England we have no need of creeping into holes and corners lest a policeman see us'.[175]

PART II

9. THE FRANCO-PRUSSIAN WAR

The 1870 Congress of the International was scheduled to take place in Paris, but continued harassment of the Association in France led to the decision to hold it in Mainz. On 19 July 1870, however, two weeks before it was due to take place, France declared war on Prussia, and the congress was cancelled. War was the product of dynastic ambition compounded with nationalist arousal. French fears of encirclement had been aroused by Bismarck's support of a Hohenzollern claim to the Spanish throne. In nurturing a bellicose mood in France (but not in initiating war himself), Bismarck's aim was to draw South Germany closer to the Prussian-dominated North German Confederation. The Hohenzollern claim had been withdrawn. But French opinion had been inflamed by the supposed snub to France delivered by the Prussian king in the course of withdrawing the claim (the famous Ems telegram). Given the triviality of the ostensible reason for war and Bonaparte's reputation for military adventurism, initial sympathy lay with the Prussians; they had supposedly been forced into a defensive war. As Karl's daughter, Jenny, wrote to Dr Kugelmann: 'We have not yet recovered from our surprise and indignation at the turn affairs have taken ... Instead of fighting for the destruction of the Empire, the French people are sacrificing themselves for its aggrandizement. This revival of chauvinism in the nineteenth century is indeed a hideous farce.'[176] Karl's initial support for the Prussians was emphatic: 'The French deserve a good hiding. If the Prussians win, then centralisation of the STATE POWER will be beneficial for the centralisation of the German working class. German predominance would then shift the centre of gravity of the West European workers' movement from France to Germany.'

From 1866, he continued, the German working class had been 'superior to the French both in theory and organisation'. Prussian victory would ensure 'the predominance of *our* theory over Proudhon's'. He also believed that Bonaparte's defeat was likely to provoke a revolution in France, while a German defeat would 'only protract the present state of things for 20 years'.[177]

On 23 July, Karl was empowered by the General Council to draft an 'Address' on the war. Bonaparte, the 'Address' declared, was engaged in a purely 'dynastic' war, which would be 'the death knell of the Second Empire'. The Germans, on the other hand, were engaged in 'a war of defence'. It would be disastrous, if the German working class were to 'allow the present war to lose its strictly defensive character', but 'the principles of the International' were 'too firmly rooted among the German working class to apprehend such a sad consummation'. In contrast to the 'old society, with its economic miseries and political delirium', the 'Address' concluded, a 'new society' was springing up, whose 'international rule' would be *Peace* and *Labour*.[178] In Britain, the 'Address' was very well received. At the meeting of the General Council on 2 August, it was reported that John Stuart Mill 'was highly pleased with the address. There was not one word in it that ought not to be there; it could not have been done with fewer words.'[179]

French mobilization was slow and German military superiority was rapidly established. Already by the first week in August, it was clear even to Karl, who understood 'nothing of military matters', that the French were heading for defeat. 'Rarely has a campaign been conducted in a more mindless, planless and mediocre manner than this campaign'. But hopes of the restraining influence of the labour movement were quickly dashed. Engels' assessment had been more sombre from the start: 'Louis Bonaparte realises how badly he has miscalculated.' The campaign could not possibly end well for him. Any hope of a 'pretend war' on the part of the Prussians was pointless. '*On ira au fond*' ('It will be fought through to the bitter end').[180] This was soon made clear by the Prussian war demands – the payment of an indemnity of 5,000 million francs, and the loss of Alsace and most of Lorraine.

Karl ascribed this change of ambition to 'the Prussian Camarilla' and 'South-German beer-patriots'. He also saw clearly enough that 'the lust for Alsace and Lorraine . . . would be the greatest misfortune that could befall Europe and above all Germany'.[181] The war, as Karl had foretold, also brought the Second Empire to an end. On 2 September, Bonaparte, together with an army of 120,000 men, surrendered at Sedan. On 4 September, the *Corps Législatif* declared the end of the Empire, while a group of republican deputies declared a Republic. The war was blamed on Bonaparte, but Bismarck's demands remained. War now meant the defence of the Nation and the Republic.

In response to what had happened, the General Council on 9 September issued a 'Second Address', also drafted by Karl. In that address Germany's switch towards a 'policy of conquest' was ascribed to the German liberal middle class, 'with its professors, its capitalists, its alderman, and its pen-man', irresolute since 1846 in its struggle for civil liberty, but now 'highly delighted to bestride the European scene as the roaring lion of German patriotism'. German military arguments for annexation, the so-called 'material guarantees', were derided. France must either become 'the *avowed* tool of Russian aggrandisement, or, after some short respite', would prepare for another war, 'not one of those new-fangled "localised" wars, but a *war of races* – a war with the combined Slavonian and Roman races'.[182]

In a letter Karl wrote to Friedrich Sorge around the same time, he was more explicit: 'What the Prussian jackasses do not see is that the present war is leading just as inevitably to a war between Germany and Russia as the war of 1866 led to the war between Prussia and France.' The 'best outcome' of such a war would be the end of 'Prussia' since 'Prussianism' could only exist 'in alliance with and in subjection to Russia'. Secondly, such a war would act as 'the midwife of the inevitable social revolution in Russia'.[183]

The 'Second Address' went on to salute the 'advent of the Republic in France' while cautioning at the same time that the new French government, composed of Orléanists and middle-class republicans, might serve as a 'mere stopgap' on the way to an Orléanist Restoration. But 'French workmen' should not attempt to disrupt the new administration: 'Any attempt at upsetting the new government in the present crisis, when the enemy is almost knocking at the doors of Paris, must be a desperate folly.' This seemed a real danger, given the increasing probability of French defeat. Even before Bonaparte's defeat at Sedan, the French army had appeared demoralized. After a string of defeats in August, a Prussian siege of Paris seemed inevitable. The appointment of the Conservative Louis-Jules Trochu as military governor of the Paris region and the refusal to pull back the French army under Bazaine to defend the capital led to the belief that the main concern of the emperor was not to protect Paris, but to check civil unrest in the city.

With the end of empire and Prussian armies moving towards Paris, the only serious force left to defend the capital was the National Guard. They were armed and in possession of the cannons to be employed in the defence of the city. Unlike the imperial armies and Trochu's 15,000 Mobile Guard, the National Guard during the war had become increasingly well organized. They had also become a militantly republican force. They had increased to 134 battalions comprising 170,000–200,000 men, and during the first week of September, with the addition of further battalions, the total came to number 340,000 men. National guardsmen elected their company commanders. They were predominantly workers or men from the lower middle class, unknown outside their particular *quartiers*, and they were paid 1.50 francs per day, with the payment of extras for spouses and children. This wage was of crucial importance, since with the cessation of peacetime economic activity, poorer Parisians had become increasingly dependent upon their daily '*30 sous*' to sustain their families.

The Germans decided not to bombard the city, but to starve it into submission. The siege began on 18 September 1870 and lasted until the armistice of 28 January 1871. Parisians hoped that they would be relieved by Bazaine's army at Metz. But on 31 October Metz fell and the army of 150,000 surrendered. At the same time, it appeared that attempts were being made to negotiate an armistice with the Prussians by the veteran conservative Adolphe Thiers. It now seemed only a question of getting the Parisians to accept defeat.

But this was not how Parisians understood the situation. Parisians had voted against Bonaparte since 1863 and resented the fact that they had been denied municipal self-government. The Haussmann building boom had resulted in phenomenal migration into the city, causing alarm among its richer inhabitants. Building workers now constituted 20 per cent of the city's population in what had become an increasingly unstable economy. An economic downturn in 1867–8 had been followed by a wave of strikes in 1869–70, with the result that large numbers of small masters had become bankrupt.

The working population was republican and anti-clerical. The alliance of Bonaparte and the Catholic church was particularly disliked.

After 1848, not only had the church blocked Italian unification by hanging on to its temporal possessions with French help; it had also officially promoted the purportedly miraculous happenings at Lourdes, and in its 'Syllabus of Errors' of 1864 had peremptorily rejected any compromise with liberalism or the Enlightenment.[184] In Paris, this reactionary turn on the part of the church was matched by the growth of a radical and militant secularism articulated by a generation of radical students, inspired by the atheism of Proudhon, the positivism of Auguste Comte and the religious criticism of Renan, together with the arguments of Darwinians and other natural materialists.

But, at least until the armistice with Prussia, the mood in Paris was not revolutionary. When Metz fell, a Blanquist attempt to overthrow the government failed for lack of support and, soon after, the government reinforced its position by holding a plebiscite, which it won by a large majority (221,374 to 53,585). The government also held municipal elections, in which revolutionaries were clearly defeated, even though they gained a significant foothold in some working-class districts.

Within Paris, cut off from the outside world by the siege, confidence in the city's ability to outlast the siege and break through to ultimate victory remained strong. Among radicals, the siege had engendered a new language of revolutionary patriotism, in which increasing appeal was made to the *Commune*. This was a reference to the 'revolutionary *Commune*' of Paris of August 1792, a moment in which a besieged France in an exceptional burst of patriotism had broken through to victory. That *Commune* had presided over the crucial turning point of the Revolution. It had overthrown the monarchy, transformed national defence by introducing the *levée en masse* (universal conscription) and provoked the killing of suspected enemies of the Revolution in the September Massacres. The potency of the term '*Commune*' derived from the fact that it concentrated within one word the idea of national defence, of local democracy and of revolution. This language encouraged the belief that dedicated republican citizens could overcome the demoralized armies of monarchy. Revolutionary leaders and National Guard commanders expressed 'practically daily in speeches, poems, pamphlets, posters and articles their utter determination to pursue *la résistance à outrance*, to die rather than surrender, to mount a *sortie torrentielle*'.[185]

On 30 November, a sortie of 60,000 men, which was intended to join up with the Army of the Loire, failed to break through German lines and suffered 10,000 casualties. In January 1871, Bismarck attempted to bombard the city into surrender, but without success. In response, Trochu, finally acceding to the arguments of republican patriots, employed combat units from the National Guard in a sortie intended to attack the Prussian headquarters at Versailles. But the attack by 90,000 French troops, including 42,000 National Guardsmen, was soon halted, leaving 4,000 men killed or wounded. Humiliated and angry, radical battalions of the National Guard pressed for further resistance. But the government, supported by most of the population outside Paris, now sought an armistice, which was accorded on 28 January 1871.

Paris had endured a four-month siege in vain. The government was blamed for the defeat. On 8 February, a national election was held to approve peace terms. Conservatives supported by rural voters campaigned for peace. Republicans based in urban areas, and above all Paris, pressed for a continuation of the war. The result was a National Assembly consisting of 400 Conservatives, for the most part royalists, and 150 republicans. Parisian hostility to this Assembly, dominated by *les ruraux* (country people), was intense. Their bigotry and hostility to the Republic, it was alleged, were maintained by the church through the use of the confessional.

Further developments threatened the status and position of Paris still more. The moderate republican Government of National Defence, now wholly discredited, was replaced by a new conservative government nominated by the National Assembly and headed by Adolphe Thiers. On 10 March, the National Assembly itself was moved from Bordeaux, not to Paris, but to Versailles, where it could remain at a safe distance from 'the mob'. The Assembly itself decided to phase in repayment of commercial bills of exchange, a move which caused alarm among small businessmen, especially in Paris. It was feared that this measure would be followed by legislation to enforce the repayment of rent arrears and to end the daily *30 sous* paid to the National Guard. It was also suspected that the National Assembly would move to re-establish a monarchy, as soon as it became possible to do so.

On 1 March, the Prussians held a victory parade on the Champs-Élysées. In response to the shame and perceived threat posed by Prussian soldiers within the city walls, the National Guard re-established itself as a Republican Federation in order to resist disarmament and prepare for the recommencement of the war. It held large patriotic and republican demonstrations, beginning on 24 February – the anniversary of the beginning of the 1848 Revolution. It also began collecting rifles and ammunition lest these fell into the hands of the Germans. Finally, it moved 300–400 cannons (which it claimed belonged to the people of Paris and not to the government) away from official gun parks and up to the heights of Montmartre, Belleville and eastern Paris.

The hostility towards Paris revealed by the measures of the National Assembly hampered government attempts to negotiate the handover of the cannon. But a handover was essential, for as long as the National Guard remained in possession of sufficient means of defence, government control of the city could not be enforced. To end this impasse, Thiers decided to take back the weaponry by surprise. Before dawn on 18 March, regular troops were dispatched to scale the heights of Montmartre and to bring back the cannon. But thousands of National Guardsmen, women and children turned out to obstruct them. Finding their progress blocked, soldiers ignored the orders of their officers to disperse demonstrators by force, and fraternized with the crowd. Two unpopular generals, one an unpopular appointee to command the National Guard, the other thought responsible for ordering troops to fire on the demonstrators, were taken away and shot. Barricades went up across the city. Paris was out of control. The government and army high command retreated with all available troops to Versailles. Paris was now left in the hands of the National Guard, whose Central Committee of the Republican Federation established itself the as *de facto* ruler of Paris in the *Hôtel de Ville*.

10. THE *COMMUNE* AND THE CIVIL WAR IN FRANCE

It is impossible to understand the *Commune* except as the product of the virtually unique circumstances produced by the siege and the war. To imagine a world city suddenly obliged or enabled to construct its own form of law and government from scratch was unprecedented and inimitable. It was also a freedom framed by tragedy. The *Commune* ended in one of the most notorious massacres of the nineteenth century. This happened in large part because both sides were armed and the slaughter was understood as an act of war. The bitterness produced by

17. A view of Trier in the nineteenth century

DEUTSCH-FRANZÖSISCHE

JAHRBÜCHER

herausgegeben

von

Arnold Ruge und Karl Marx.

———

1ste und 2te Lieferung.

PARIS,
IM BUREAU DER JAHRBÜCHER. } RUE VANNEAU, 22.
AU BUREAU DES ANNALES.

—

1844

18. The title page of the *Deutsch-Französische Jahrbücher*, first edition, Paris, 1844

19. The bodies of those killed during street fighting in February 1848 are paraded by torchlight through the streets of Paris

20. A Session of the *Commission des travailleurs* in spring 1848, at the Palais de Luxembourg, Paris

21. The barricade at Cologne Town Hall, 19 March 1848

22. The scene in the courtyard of the royal palace in Berlin in March 1848 as the corpses from the street battle are presented to Friedrich Wilhelm IV, King of Prussia

23. The Chartist meeting on Kennington Common, 10 April 1848

24. The masthead of the first edition of the *Neue Rheinische Zeitung*, 1 June 1848

25. The barricade in the rue Saint-Maur-Popincourt after the attack by General Lamoricière's troops, Monday 26 June 1848

26. Insurgents in custody in Paris, July/August 1848

27. The opening of the International Exhibition in South Kensington, London, in 1862

28. *Ramsgate Sands (Life at the Seaside)*, by William Powell Frith, 1851–4

29. *Civil War* by Edouard Manet, 1871

巴黎公社就是工人阶级夺取政权。 马克思

巴黎公社万岁

纪念巴黎公社一百周年

30. A poster from the Chinese Cultural Revolution of 1971 celebrating the centenary of the Paris Commune of 1871

the polarization of positions in the months following the collapse of the Empire built upon an antagonism which was of much longer standing. The Republican Federation increased its support with commemorations of 24 February 1848 and the foundation of *La République démocrate et sociale*. Versailles and rural France, on the other hand, were for the most part erstwhile supporters of Bonaparte, who had come to power in the presidential vote of December 1848 as the leader of the country against revolutionary Paris, and had triumphantly reaffirmed this mandate in the plebiscite of 1870.

In the days immediately following 18 March, there was a reluctance to employ the term '*Commune*'. The sudden and complete evacuation of Paris by the government was greeted with astonishment. There was little desire on the part of the Central Committee of the National Guard to hold on to the power which had been dropped into its lap. The hope in the press and among the National Guard was that an agreement could be reached with the government. The best way to secure this, it was agreed by local mayors, by Parisian deputies to the National Assembly and by the Central Committee itself, was to hold elections for a city council which could negotiate a settlement.

The elections were held on 26 March. But the plan backfired: the Versailles government would not recognize the legitimacy of the poll, and this meant that many conservatives either left the city or boycotted the elections. As a result, there was a massive increase in electoral support for the radical republican left. The new Council, which consisted of seventy-three radicals and only nineteen moderates, promptly adopted the name '*Paris Commune*'. What had begun as a defence of the National Guard had turned into a revolution. But, as Benoît Malon put it, 'never has a revolution so surprised revolutionaries'.[186] Elections which had been intended to pave the way for negotiations had resulted in an even sharper confrontation. But, in fact, it had been unclear from the beginning what sort of compromise could have been reached. Demands for municipal autonomy and recognition of the Republic by the National Assembly were tantamount to the demand for a state within a state. Thiers insisted that the *Commune* possessed no legitimacy, and therefore that there was nothing to negotiate. The *Communards* must simply give up their weaponry and surrender.

Finding themselves unexpectedly in government, the *Commune* belatedly produced 'A Declaration to the French People' on 19 April, setting out the 'Programme of Paris'. The demands included 'the recognition and consolidation of the Republic' and the extension of 'the absolute autonomy of the *Commune*' to all localities in France. France would become a federation of *Communes*, each with absolute control over economy, administration, security and education. It would mark the inauguration of 'a new era of experimental politics, positive and scientific . . . It is the end of the old governmental, priest-ridden world, of militarism, of bureaucracy, exploitation, market-rigging, monopolies, privileges, to which the proletariat owes its serfdom and the fatherland its sufferings and its disasters.'[187]

What little chance there had remained of negotiation with Versailles was ended by the first military skirmishes in the western suburbs of Paris on 2 April. Thiers's troops engaged a concentration of National Guardsmen at Courbevoie and won a victory. Thirty *Communards* were taken prisoner and condemned to summary execution. In response, the *Commune* assembled up to 20,000 men, and sent out four columns in the direction of Versailles, one of them under the command of Jenny's friend Gustave Flourens. A colonel who observed the National Guardsmen leaving Paris for Versailles noted their state of disorder: each was carrying some sausage, bread and a litre of wine. Some were drunk and singing, while resourceful merchants plunged into their ranks selling strong eau de vie.[188]

The leaders of the *Commune* had reassured the National Guardsmen that the Versailles soldiers would not fight, that they would point their rifles to the ground, as they had done on 18 March. But this proved not to be true. The sortie faced incessant shelling, and only one column had some success, but then had to fall back because of lack of support. Flourens, an able and energetic commander, was captured, and brutally butchered by a gendarme. Other commanders, who had surrendered, were also shot, despite an original indication that they would be spared. On 4 April, the Versailles troops launched a counter-attack, capturing various strongpoints around the city. The *Commune* had lost about 3,000 fighters, killed or captured. But, for the moment, the mood within the strongly fortified city remained optimistic.

The task of improvising a new system of government within a few days left many issues unresolved, in particular the boundaries between authorities and the division between functions. The Central Committee of the National Guard supposedly handed over power to those elected to the governing Council of the *Commune* on 26 March. But in fact the Central Committee not only remained in existence throughout the subsequent duration of the *Commune*, but continued to exercise independent authority as 'the guardian of the revolution'. This was only one of many instances in which the activities of overlapping authorities hampered the efficiency of the whole. The *Commune* Council met almost daily at the *Hôtel de Ville*, but its authority was limited by the *mairies* of each of the component *arrondissements*. In place of a conventional distinction between legislative and executive, the *Commune* established executive 'commissions', each headed by a 'delegate'. These 'commissions' convened twice a day at the *Hôtel de Ville*. But the consequence of democratic answerability was the incessant convening of lengthy and often unproductive meetings, in which much time was spent discussing irrelevant issues.

The enforcing of the decisions was also a problem. The Council depended on the goodwill of mayors, deputy mayors, policemen and National Guardsmen in each *arrondissement*. While most of these officials were cooperative, some were inefficient or obstructive. Despite these obstacles, however, the *Commune* was supported by the great majority and was able to act effectively in the interests of ordinary Parisians. The *Commune* prohibited eviction of tenants unable to pay rent arrears, rephased repayment of debt over three years (rather than the three months decreed by the National Assembly) and suspended the sale of items due for redemption at municipal pawnshops. It also banned night work in bakeries – a measure seen by some as 'socialist', but scarcely more radical than the limitation upon factory hours imposed by English Parliaments. Finally, on the basis of a loan negotiated with the Bank of France, the *Commune* was able to maintain the payment of the daily *30 sous* to National Guardsmen.

Most *Communards* were skilled workers in long-established and small-scale craft industries, together with small employers, white-collar employees, women (active as *ambulancières* and *cantinières*) and radical students. They were 'proletarian' according to the contemporary French usage of the term: those who worked for their living. The salient political distinction was not between 'bourgeoisie' and 'proletariat', but between 'producers' and 'idlers'. As republican and revolutionary papers declared in 1871, 'while the Second Empire had fomented hatred' between 'our brave proletarians' and 'our good bourgeois', under the Republic, 'the people and the hardworking bourgeoisie are one'. That part of the bourgeoisie who were not part of the people were those who had taken advantage of the corrupt political system of the Second Empire, speculators and exploiters of the people.

Above all, the *Communards* were champions of *La République démocrate et sociale*. 1789 had emancipated the bourgeoisie, 1848 had aimed to emancipate the proletariat. The enemy had been the state, especially the authoritarian state of the Second Empire – the soldier, 'the policeman believed on oath', the tax-gatherer, the unaccountable official and the 'unsackable magistrate'.[189] The ideal was 'federation'. Political power would be devolved to democratic communities; exploitation would be abolished by placing production in the hands of workers' cooperatives. But there would still be a place for the small masters and employers of Paris, who formed an important part of the support for the *Commune*.

These ideals were above all associated with the name of Proudhon, who according to the painter Gustave Courbet was 'the Christ' of *Communard* socialism. But it would be a mistake to demarcate too precisely the supposed boundaries between the various forms of republicanism, mutualism and socialism which emerged in the 1860s. The leaders of the *Commune*, generally those who had become politically engaged during the three or four years before the war, were eclectic in their beliefs. Allowing for withdrawals, among the 79 members of the *Commune* Council, 25 were Freemasons, 34 belonged to the International and 43 were past or present members of the Central Committee of the National Guard.[190] While Proudhon's name was revered by many activists, by the late 1860s most of the leaders had rejected Proudhon's exclusion of women's work outside the home, his dismissal of strikes and his refusal to accept the efficacy of political revolution. Typical was the ethos of the Paris branch of the International, which in the years leading up to the war had become a mixture of socialist, syndical and cooperative ideas. But one common point of agreement was the statement found in the preamble to the statutes of the International that 'the emancipation of workers ought to be the work of workers themselves'. On this basis, faith was placed in worker-controlled organizations (co-ops, *chambres syndicales*), together with general opposition to the centralized and authoritarian state.[191]

In the late 1860s, there had been convergence between the different groups (Mutualists, Collectivists, anti-authoritarian communists and even Blanquists). But in the course of April 1871 the increasingly endangered position of the *Commune* produced a split between the Jacobins and Blanquists, on the one hand, and the federalist, democratic socialists and Proudhonists on the other. From 2 April, the *Versaillais* had begun a bombardment of Paris and the shelling increased in intensity from then on. By the end of April, the military situation became more desperate. After Cluseret failed in his attempt to reorganize the National Guard, it was proposed that a Committee of Public Safety be established: once again an attempt to replicate the achievement of 1793. While the majority of the *Commune* supported this Jacobin–Blanquist proposal by thirty-four to twenty-eight, the minority of federalists, secularists and middle-class activists denounced it as dictatorial and, after 15 May, ceased to attend *Commune* meetings. Once more, however, the course of events reminded *Communards* that 1871 was not 1793, and after little more than a week the Committee had to be replaced.

The reason why Thiers had so dramatically pulled the government and armed forces out of Paris was that he had realized that he lacked sufficient forces to crush the insurrection. More than 300,000 soldiers and officers who had surrendered at Sedan and Metz were interned in German states. By early April, the troops at the disposal of Versailles amounted to 55,000, but Thiers estimated that at least 100,000 would be needed to retake Paris. In the meantime, he could do no more than intimidate parts of the city through bombardment, and recapture some important outposts beyond the city walls. It was only after 10 May and the signing of the Treaty of Frankfurt with Prussia that the defeated French army was free to return. Its troops were to form one quarter of the 130,000 men whom Thiers employed in the final assault on the city.

In the interim, during the ten weeks that the *Commune* lasted, the majority of Parisians enjoyed an unreal sense of freedom. The most visible change in everyday life concerned the place of religion. Education was secularized and anti-religious theatre was performed on the streets. Women's clubs were formed, and women themselves addressed as '*Citoyenne*' rather than '*Madame*'. Much music was performed, including huge concerts in the Tuileries and the public recitation of poems in aid of the wounded. The atmosphere on the street was noted with distaste by Goncourt: 'you cannot imagine the suffering caused by the despotism exercised in the streets by the riff-raff disguised as soldiers'. But although there were festive occasions in which the working classes from Belleville and Montmartre 'descended' on the city and complaints were made about drunken behaviour among the National Guard, the general standard of behaviour appears to have been good, even prim. Concerts were decorous: no more Offenbach. No more street crime: instead a culture of self-improvement and stern control of prostitutes.

The city was lost on the evening of 22–23 May. *Versaillais* troops invaded from the south-west across ramparts which had been abandoned by the National Guard. The *Commune* called for a *levée en masse*, but got little response. Most were only prepared to defend streets in their own neighbourhoods, and generally retired after a few shots had been fired. *Communards* set fire to public buildings and tried to divest themselves of their weapons, uniforms and any other incriminating material. But they were soon engulfed in the mass slaughter that attended what became known as '*La Semaine sanglante*' (the bloody week). The soldiers were often ignorant countrymen who had been told by their officers that the *Communards* were lawless insurgents and criminals. Many were therefore encouraged to believe that they could kill captured insurgents with the blessing of their officers. Anyone stopped and found carrying weapons or suspected of fighting was shot on sight, as were the so-called *pétroleuses* – females suspected of setting fire to houses. On the *Communard* side, the few acts of massacre were mainly the responsibility of Blanquists. Darboy, the Archbishop of Paris, was arrested, and after the failure of attempts to exchange him for the imprisoned Blanqui he, together with three others, was executed on 24 May. On 25 May, there was a massacre of Dominican priests, and on 26 May fifty hostages in Belleville were shot, again on the initiative of Blanquists. Against this, however, it is estimated that between 1,500 and 4,000 *Communard* combatants were executed.[192] 40,000 were rounded up and transported to New Caledonia.

On the General Council, the *Commune* was first discussed on 21 March, when Engels and a French shoemaker, Auguste Serraillier, endeavoured to correct misrepresentations in the press about the battle over the cannons.[193] Thereafter, it became increasingly clear that the Council must make a public statement about the situation. But the difficulty, as the Chairman, Hermann Jung, explained on 18 April, was that 'wanting direct communications from Paris, we had only false newspaper reports'.[194] Karl concurred: only a general resolution was possible, an address should be issued afterwards. Privately, he was pessimistic about the *Commune*'s chances of survival. In a letter to Dr Kugelmann on 12 April, he had claimed that crucial mistakes had been made early on. The Central Committee had surrendered its power to the *Commune* too soon, and had lost precious time in electing its members. He blamed the *Communards* for their 'decency' and maintained that 'they should have marched at once on Versailles'.[195]

At the Council meeting of 25 April, Karl continued to complain about the absence of up-to-date letters and papers, while a week later, on 2 May, he was absent. Engels announced that the *Address* was not quite ready and that Karl had been advised to leave town on account of his health. His absence continued through 9 and 16 May. But on 23 May he reappeared. He feared 'the end was near', but reported that the *Address* should be ready the following week. Finally, on 30 May, Karl completed the *Address*, which he read out to the Council. It was adopted unanimously. But by then the *Commune* was over.

The Civil War in France, a pamphlet of around forty pages, was composed with some care. In addition to the published version, there still survive two rough drafts. It was divided into four sections. The first contained a portrait of the Thiers government, presented in the form of a rogues' gallery, a villainous cabal supposedly conducting the war against Germany, but primarily engaged in a conspiracy to put down the Paris working class. Thiers himself was depicted as a 'monstrous gnome', for fifty years 'the most consummate expression' of the 'class-corruption' of the French bourgeoisie. Equally demeaning was the portrait of Jules Favre, the Foreign Minister responsible for the peace treaty with Germany and for the crusade against the International. Other ministers portrayed included Ernest Picard, the Finance Minister, presented as the close confrère of his brother, Arthur, a convicted thief and financial swindler.

According to the next section, which examined the immediate circumstances leading up to the *Commune*, the Versailles battle against Paris was not only animated by hatred, but fuelled by corruption. The republican government had negotiated a loan of two milliards. Out of that loan, newspapers alleged, ministers were to receive 300 million francs as a commission, but only provided that the resistance in Paris had been crushed.[196] Karl argued that Thiers's untruthful claim that the Paris cannonry was state property provided the required pretext for re-establishing control over the city.

In the third part of the essay, an attempt was made to depict the political character of the *Commune*. The *Commune* was not a reaction against state power in general, but against the French state, which had originated 'from the days of absolute monarchy, serving nascent middle-class society as a mighty weapon in its struggle against feudalism'. It was obvious that 'ready-made State machinery' of such a kind could not be simply taken over by the working class and 'wielded for its own purposes'. Thus 'the centralised State power, with its ubiquitous organs of standing army, police, bureaucracy, clergy and judicature', was removed.[197] The standing army was turned into a people's army; legislative and executive were combined; this body would be elected by universal suffrage, and its members were to be paid workmen's wages to be 'responsible and revocable in short terms'. Church would be separated from state; education would be free and no longer subject to clerical interference. Judges and magistrates would be elected by the people.

It would be wrong to treat this list as a factual description of the *Commune*'s constitutional structure or of its day-to-day proceedings. This was not an account of what the *Commune* was, but of what it might have become. The discrepancies between fact and putative intention were made clear enough by the use of the subjunctive mood.[198] As a matter of fact, delegates and officials were not paid workmen's wages, nor were judges and magistrates elected by the people. Nor was it the recorded intention of any of its actual participants that the *Commune* should 'serve as a lever for uprooting the economical foundations upon which rests the existence of classes, and therefore of class rule'.[199]

What was listed was in part an actual depiction of the *Commune*, in part an imaginary projection of the changes that might accompany a transition towards the rule of associated producers, in which 'every man becomes a working man, and productive labour ceases to be a class attribute'.[200] As for the 'social' measures identified with the *Commune* (for example, the oft-cited prohibition of night work for bakers), these, as Karl wrote in one of the drafts, were of a kind undertaken by any government under siege, and were 'principally confined to the military defence of Paris and its *approvisionnement*'.[201]

The final pages completed Karl's account of 'the conspiracy of the ruling class to break down the Revolution by a civil war carried on under the patronage of the foreign invader'. It ended with 'the entrance of MacMahon's praetorians through the gate of St Cloud' and 'the carnage of Paris' that followed. It recounted the difficulties Thiers had experienced in the country in attempting to raise a provincial National Guard against Paris and the disappointing results of new elections for the National Assembly. Finally, it described the 'ineffable infamy' of Thiers, a modern-day 'Sulla', whose 'glorious civilisation' had first to 'get rid of the heaps of corpses it made after the battle was over'.[202]

The Civil War in France was not only written in English, but for the English. It was Karl's most impressive effort to express himself in colloquial terms. Earnest translators at the end of the century must have puzzled over the precise rendition of 'ticket-of-leave men', 'gentlemen's gentlemen', 'parson-power', 'natural superiors', 'shoddy men', and must have wondered who 'Joe Miller' was. Had they delved into the drafts they might also have wondered what was meant by 'turtle-soup guzzling aldermen', by 'the circumlocution office', 'the upper ten thousand', 'servants' hall' or 'Billingsgate'.

The ambition was not simply to capture the cadences of popular speech, but also to juxtapose in moral terms the Paris of Versailles and the Empire against the Paris of the *Commune*. Imperial Paris was presented as the immoral *other* of Victorian England. Karl may have particularly disliked Jules Favre as one of the 'bourgeois' republicans, responsible for the suppression of the June Uprising in 1848, but in the text he was pilloried for 'living in concubinage with the wife of a drunkard resident at Algiers', and for securing a succession for the offspring of his adultery. Thiers was similarly impugned for ingratiating himself with Louis Philippe by 'acting the minister-spy upon, and the jail-*accoucheur* of the Duchess de Berry', Jules Ferry as Mayor of Paris was said to have made 'a fortune out of famine'. The Paris of these men was a 'phantom Paris':

> The Paris of the Boulevards, male and female – the rich, the capitalist, the gilded, the idle Paris, now thronging with its lackeys, its blacklegs, its literary *bohème* and its *cocottes* at Versailles, Saint-Denis, Rueil, and

Saint-Germain; considering the civil war but an agreeable diversion, eyeing the battle going on through their telescopes, counting the rounds of cannon, and swearing by their own honour and that of their prostitutes, that the performance was far better got up than it used to be at Porte St-Martin. The men who fell were really dead; the cries of the wounded were in good earnest; and, besides, the whole thing was so intensely historical.[203]

But with the coming of the *Commune*, while the *cocottes* followed the scent of their protectors – 'the absconding men of family, religion and, above all, of property' – there appeared in their place 'the real women of Paris . . . heroic, noble and devoted, like the women of antiquity'.[204]

From the time of the fall of the Empire, Karl had feared that some foolish attempt would be made to overthrow the newly established Republic. On 6 September, he noted that the entire London-based French branch of the International was setting off for Paris 'to commit all sorts of follies there in the name of the International'. 'They' intended 'to bring down the Provisional Government' and 'establish a *commune de Paris*'.[205] In Lyons, Bakunin and his supporters attempted something similar. Describing the event in a letter to Edward Beesly, Karl wrote that in Lyons at first 'everything went well' and a republic had been proclaimed there before Paris. But then 'the asses, Bakunin and Cluseret', had arrived and 'spoiled everything . . . The Hôtel de Ville was seized – for a short time – and most foolish decrees on the *abolition de l'état* and similar nonsense were issued. You understand that the very fact of a Russian – represented by the middle class papers as an agent of Bismarck – pretending to impose himself as the leader of a *Comité du Salut de la France* was quite sufficient to turn the balance of public opinion.'[206] The actual *Commune* had been the result of an accident – 'the presence of the Prussians right before Paris' – a 'decisively unfavourable "accident"', which had presented Paris with 'the alternative of taking up the fight or succumbing without a struggle'. The city's prospects had looked bleak, and in a letter written to Vienna a few days later Karl had considered that the course taken 'had precluded all prospects of success'. The best that could be hoped for was an honourable peace between Paris and Versailles.[207] But a month later his tone had changed. He now wrote that, whatever the immediate results, 'the struggle of the working class against the capitalist class and its state' had 'entered upon a new phase' and that 'a new point of departure of world-historic importance has been gained'.[208] What accounted for this change of mind?

It was not the social content of the insurrection. The *Commune* remained a purely political event. It had been generated as much by the anxieties and anger of shopkeepers and small masters, threatened by the resumption of debt payments, as by workers.[209] Furthermore, through the agency of the *Union Républicaine*, these groups were just as active in the leadership of the movement. Although *The Civil War in France* claimed that the *Commune* was 'essentially a working class government, the produce of the struggle of the producing against the appropriating class', this was only true in the non-Marxian sense that, both in England and in France, the primary political distinction was not that between workers and employers, but between producers and idlers.[210] It was 'the working classes' in this broad sense, whose aim as in 1848, was to realize *La République democrate et sociale*. This was clearly recognized by Karl himself. As he wrote to the Dutch socialist Domela Nieuwenhuis in 1881, 'the majority of the *Commune* was in no sense socialist, nor could it have been ... A socialist government does not come into power in a country unless conditions are so developed that it can immediately take the necessary measures for intimidating the mass of the bourgeoisie sufficiently to gain time – the first *desideratum* – for permanent action.'[211]

What excited Karl about the *Commune* was 'its own working existence'. This was its 'great social measure'.[212] In practical terms, this meant a revolution not only *for* the working masses, but also a revolution *by* the working masses. As he explained in the 'First Draft':

> That the revolution is made in the *name* and confessedly *for* the popular masses, that is the producing masses, is a feature this Revolution has in common with all its predecessors. The new feature is that the people, after the first rise, have not disarmed themselves and surrendered their power into the hands of the Republican Mountebanks of the ruling classes, that by the constitution of the *Commune*, they have taken the actual management of their Revolution into their own hands and found at the same time, in the case of success, the means to hold it in the hands of the People itself, displacing state machinery, the governmental machinery of the ruling classes by a governmental machinery of their own.[213]

The *Commune* excited Karl because it provided an unanticipated demonstration of what had been the starting point of his political criticism: the priority which he had accorded as early as 1843–4 to self-activity as the distinguishing feature of human history. Karl's theory of history had started out from what he had considered to be Hegel's greatest achievement in *The Phenomenology of the Spirit* – to have grasped 'the self-creation of Man as a process'. Man was not merely a natural being, but 'a human natural being' whose point of origin was not nature, but history; a being who was able to make his activity 'the object of his will'. But Hegel had also obscured the force of this insight by moving away from a vision of the *polis*, in which human powers were fully expressed, to a conception of the modern state based upon the division between state and civil society. It was to challenge this division that Karl had embarked upon his first full-scale work of political criticism, his *Contribution to the Critique of Hegel's Philosophy of Right* in 1843.

The unreal situation created by the temporary removal of the army, police, bureaucracy, clergy and judiciary from Paris in 1871 enabled Karl to return to his starting point and to imagine a polity in which the distinction between state and civil society had disappeared. Particularly exciting was the fact that the *Commune* had not emerged merely by default. The *Commune* had come into existence through its own agency. As he put it in his 'First Draft', 'Whatever the merits of the single measures of the *Commune*, its greatest measure was its own organisation, extemporised with the Foreign Enemy at one door, and the class enemy at the other, proving by its life its vitality, confirming its thesis by its action.' In this situation, it was possible to conceive the abolition of the distinction between legislative and executive, and of the role formerly played by Parliament being taken over by a democratically elected working body, cheaply and efficiently performing its function on workmen's wages. He elaborated his idea:

> The *Commune* – the reabsorption of the State power by society, as its own living forces instead of as forces controlling and subduing it, by the popular masses themselves, forming their own force instead of the organised force of their suppression – the political form of their social emancipation, instead of the artificial force (appropriated by their oppressors) (their own force opposed to and organised against them) of society wielded for their oppression by their enemies. The form was simple like all great things.[214]

The character of the *Commune* also enabled him to make a distinctive contribution to the post-1848 discussion about the form of society and polity to be attained in the future. He didn't reiterate the formulations of the *Communist Manifesto*, which could easily look like the authoritarian state forms associated with the Second Empire. Nor did he reproduce the parliamentarism which, in the case of Bismarck's *Reichstag*, at least, maintained the subordination of a weak legislative to an all-powerful executive.[215] He went a long way towards accommodating the federalist ideals espoused by the leaders of the *Commune*: 'In a rough sketch of national organization, which the Commune had no time to develop, it clearly states that the Commune was to be the political form of even the smallest country hamlet ... The rural communes of every district were to administer their common affairs by an assembly of delegates in the central town and these district assemblies were again to send deputies to the National Delegation in Paris, each delegate to be at any time revocable and bound by the *mandat impératif* (formal instructions) of his constituents.'[216] But he was also careful to emphasize that 'The few but important functions which still would remain for a central government were not to be suppressed, as has been intentionally mis-stated, but were to be discharged by Communal, and therefore strictly responsible agents. The unity of the nation was not to be broken, but, on the contrary, to be organized by the Communal constitution.'[217]

As in his writings of the 1860s, he was also anxious to stress that the transition to a situation in which 'united cooperative societies' would 'regulate national production upon a common plan' – what he called 'possible communism' – would be a long-drawn-out process. 'The working class did not expect miracles from the Commune.' They had 'no ready-made utopias to introduce'. 'They know that in order to work out their own emancipation, and along with it that higher form to which present society is irresistibly tending by its own economical agencies, they will have to pass through long struggles, through a series of historic processes, transforming circumstances and men.'[218]

In publishing terms, *The Civil War in France* was a great success. It ran through three editions in two months, the second edition selling 8,000 copies.[219] Suddenly, Karl had become a famous person. As he wrote to Dr Kugelmann on 18 June: 'The *Address* is making the devil of a noise and I have the honour to be at this moment the best calumniated and the most menaced man of London. that really does one good after a tedious twenty years' idyll in the backwoods.'[220] His fame – or rather notoriety – had preceded the publication of the *Address*. On 19 March, a day after the *Commune* began, a right-wing Versailles newspaper, *Journal de Paris*, had reported an alleged letter sent by Karl – 'the Red Doctor' – to the members of the International in Paris, instructing them to start an insurrection. Karl believed this forgery to have been the work of Wilhelm Stieber, chief of the Prussian political police, German adviser to Versailles and, twenty years earlier, chief prosecution witness in the Cologne communist trial.

This allegation was taken up by most of the continental and British press. But it was accompanied by various lurid embellishments. In the *Times* report, the International was conflated with Bakunin's 'Alliance' and cited as demanding the abolition of religion and marriage.[221] By contrast, the Bonapartist press believed that the real author of the *Commune* was Bismarck and that Karl was his agent. On 2 April, *Le Soir* announced that Karl Marx, one of the main leaders of the International, had been Secretary to Count Bismarck in 1857, and remained in his service. But the Versailles government preferred the Stieber story. On 6 June, the Versailles Foreign Minister, Jules Favre, sent a circular letter to foreign governments, declaring the *Commune* to be the work of the International and calling upon all governments to cooperate in its suppression. Thereafter, the story was variously orchestrated by the French, Austrian and German governments.

In the light of these allegations, when Karl's authorship was made public on 20 June, some of the more vulnerable or questionable formulations in the *Address* were subjected to concerted attack. Most vulnerable was the reference at the end of the *Address* to the relationship between the *Commune* and the International. It was stated: 'Wherever, in whatever shape, and under whatever conditions the class struggle obtains any consistency, it is but natural that members of our Association should stand in the foreground.'[222] In earlier drafts, the claim for the role of the International had been even greater, and it was perpetuated by Engels. But, in actual fact, the role of members of the International had been marginal – the efficiency of the Bonapartist police had resulted in the closure of the Paris International Branch in 1869; and as Karl repeatedly tried to point out, the International was not a secret society with a hierarchy of command.[223] But in the light of the assertions of Favre and the hostility of most of the press, it proved virtually impossible to rebut the picture of the *Commune* as an International plot. As Karl observed to Dr Kugelmann, 'The daily press and the telegraph, which in a moment spreads its inventions over the whole earth, fabricate more myths in one day (and the bourgeois cattle believe and propagate them still further) than could have previously been produced in a century.'[224]

The second area in which the *Address* was particularly subject to attack was its handling of *Communard* violence. In the light of the hundreds or perhaps thousands of people shot down by *Versaillais* troops, it was perhaps unreasonable of hostile commentators to make so much of *Communard* atrocities. But Karl's defence of *Communard* actions in this instance was inept. In a passage about the conflict over the cannons on 18 March and the shooting of the generals, Thomas and Lecomte, which shortly followed, Karl offered a singularly implausible defence of this extra-judicial killing. The *Commune* was not really responsible, or rather, 'The Central Committee and the Paris working men were as much responsible for the killing of Clément Thomas and Lecomte as the Princess of Wales was for the fate of the people crushed to death on the day of her entrance into London.'[225] Similarly, because the execution of Archbishop Darboy came after a refusal by Versailles to exchange him for the veteran revolutionary Auguste Blanqui, the *Address* maintained that 'the real murderer of Archbishop Darboy is Thiers'.[226] The shooting of other priests was not mentioned. Similarly, the resort to incendiarism was defended as if it were purely a question of necessary defence. Whatever might be said about these arguments, they failed to convince. It would have been preferable to apologize in the case of indefensible actions and thereby make it possible to redirect scrutiny towards the much more extensive and indiscriminate slaughter committed by Versailles.

Positivists, such as Frederic Harrison and Edward Beesly, bravely tried to defend the *Commune*. There were also working men who sympathized with the *Communards*, not 'upon strictly Communist grounds', but because 'they believed [the *Communards*] to be thorough patriots and true republicans' who supported the International's aim to secure 'the fusion of interests among the working classes throughout the world'.[227] But these were a minority. Even among radicals, the issue was very divisive. To cite only the more prominent, the *Commune* was attacked by Tolain, Mazzini, Holyoake and Bradlaugh. In an irascible exchange at the meeting of the General Council on 20 June, George Odger, one of the most prominent of trade unionist founders of the International, said that he had not been present when the *Address* was read out and that it should have been submitted to everyone whose signature was to be attached. After Karl had reminded him of the standing orders, Odger replied that 'he wouldn't be dictated to, if the Satellites of Dr Marx liked, they could, but he wouldn't'. He stated that he had not come to resign, but since 'there was no reason on the Council', he would do so. As a leading republican activist, he identified the republican cause with the Orléanist government of Favre and Thiers. Secondly, as he stated elsewhere, the main purpose of the International was to promote peace and higher wages in Europe. Another prominent member of the General Council, Benjamin Lucraft, a cabinetmaker and a member of the London School Board, also resigned. Referring to the *Address* at the meeting of 20 June, he stated, 'There was a great deal in it he objected to. The International defended Ruffians who had done deeds that he abhorred, ruffians that did not belong to the International, he would not sanction murder and Arson.'[228]

The Civil War in France did not succeed in stemming the hostile tide of public opinion. Over twenty years later, Karl's daughter Eleanor vividly recalled the climate: 'the condition of perfectly frantic fury of the whole middle class against the *Commune*'. So strong was the animosity towards the *Commune* and the *Communard* refugees that an attempt to book a hall to mark its first anniversary was cancelled by the landlord. He 'preferred to return the deposit and pay a penalty for breach of contract to allowing such a set of "ruffians" in his highly respectable Hall . . . Saddest of all', she continued, was 'the fact that in England the workers also, with rare exceptions (just as there were some middle class exceptions among the Comtists) were as bitterly hostile to the *Commune* as their exploiters.'[229]

I I. THE BATTLE OVER FEDERATION AND THE END OF THE INTERNATIONAL

In England, the government took no action against *Communard* refugees. But hostility towards the *Commune* was pervasive. Among radicals, it was highlighted by the resignation of leading members of the General Council and the lack of any demonstrations in the *Commune*'s support. Six months after the *Commune*, Eleanor's sister, Jenny, who had been helping *Communard* refugees, reported on their miserable condition in London:

> Employers will have nothing to do with them. The men who had succeeded in obtaining engagements under borrowed names are dismissed, so soon as it is found out who they are.
>
> As the refugees cannot find employment, you can imagine to what straits they are reduced. Their sufferings are beyond description – they are literally starving in the streets of this great city – the city that has carried the *chacun pour soi* [each for oneself] principle to its greatest perfection. It is not to be wondered at that Englishmen, who consider starvation cases to be part and parcel of their own glorious constitution . . . are not much impressed by the nameless misery of foreigners for whom they have no sympathies whatever.[230]

By contrast, for republicans and socialists from Spain and Italy through to Switzerland and Belgium, the *Commune*'s defiance of one of the most centralized and heavily policed regimes of post-1848 Europe was a source of inspiration. The Europe imagined by the *Communards* was a Europe of federations, freed from the oppressive weight of police and bureaucracy. The Republic proposed by Paris had entailed 'The absolute autonomy of the Commune extended to all localities in France, assuring to each the integrality of its rights . . . The autonomy of the Commune, only limited by the equal right to autonomy of all the other Communes adhering to the contract, whose association is to assure French unity.'[231] At first glance, *The Civil War in France* had appeared to give full support to the federalist position: 'the Commune was to be the political form of even the smallest country hamlet'. This was the assumption of Bakunin's ally and leader of the domestic craftsmen in the Jura, James Guillaume: 'Marx appeared to have abandoned his own programme in order to rally behind federalist ideas.'[232] But not only was Karl careful to retain the existence of 'central government', but in his account of the government of communal France, he had been careful to avoid employing the term 'federation'.[233]

The ideal of federation had been most influentially articulated in the later writings of Proudhon, especially, his *De la capacité politique des classes ouvrières* (*The Political Capacity of the Working Classes*) of 1865.[234] In this work, Proudhon had qualified the 'Mutualist' position which he had put forward in his *General Idea of the Revolution of the Nineteenth Century*: free credit, a drastic reduction of the political functions of the French state, and its eventual replacement by economic contracts and social agreements. His experience of the Second Empire had led him to conclude that democratic constitutions and universal suffrage were preferable to arbitrary decrees and electoral disfranchisement; and in the immediate future, at least, a federal state was the most viable solution. In his last writings he had also advocated, as a protest against the Bonapartist regime, electoral abstention. Workers should form their own cooperatives and mutual-aid societies, acquire predominance, whether in workshop, factory or farm, and eventually replace the existing political and economic system with a democratic federation of their own. But his followers in Paris, while still inspired by his larger vision, dissented from the argument about electoral abstention, considering the self-emancipation of the working class to mean active participation in the electoral process.[235]

In the early congresses of the International, nearly one third of those attending were broadly followers of Proudhon. But as early as 1867, at the Lausanne Congress, divisions were opening up within Proudhonist ranks. The strict Proudhonist position represented by Tolain (anti-social legislation, anti-trade union, anti-political engagement) was challenged by a grouping around a Parisian bookbinder, Eugène Varlin, and a Belgian compositor turned physician, César De Paepe.[236] The leaders of this group, while still subscribing to 'Mutualist' ideals, had moved towards an espousal of what De Paepe was one of the first to call 'collectivism', the collective ownership of the means of production and endorsement of trade unions.[237] While Varlin continued to agree with Tolain that strikes were economically self-defeating, he now maintained that they could at the same time increase solidarity among workers and provide means of moral protest.[238]

The strict Proudhonist position associated with Tolain and his followers was defeated at the Congress of Basle in 1869. The collectivist resolutions, put forward earlier at Brussels, passed overwhelmingly, alongside a motion calling for the immediate social collectivization of the land. The resolutions were careful to specify 'social' or 'public' ownership, and not 'state ownership'. The victory of the French and

Belgian group around Varlin and De Paepe over Tolain and his supporters was amplified by the energetic advocacy of Bakunin, together with a dozen followers. During the debate, Bakunin had emerged as one of the congress's leading exponents of collectivism. Tolain and Fribourg complained that Bakunin and Karl's allies on the General Council had wrested control from Paris Mutualists and produced a triumph for 'Russo-German communism'.[239]

But while the congress's rejection of Proudhon's hostility to political engagement and trade unionism marked an important step forward, the involvement of Bakunin posed a different but ultimately more ominous threat to Karl's vision of the International. At the end of 1861, Bakunin had escaped from Siberia after twelve years' imprisonment by the czar. He made his way to San Francisco and then on to Europe, where he arrived at Herzen's house in London at the beginning of 1862. Herzen wrote in his journal:

> Into our work, into our closed shop of two, a new element had entered, or rather an old element, perhaps a risen shade of the 'forties, and most of all of 1848. Bakunin was just the same; he had grown older in body only, his spirit was as young and enthusiastic as in the days of the all-night arguments with Khomyakov in Moscow. He was just as devoted to one idea, just as capable of being carried away by it, and seeing in everything the fulfilment of his desires and ideals, and even more ready for every experience, every sacrifice, feeling that he had not so much life before him, and that consequently he must make haste and not let slip a single chance ... The fantasies and ideals with which he was imprisoned in Königstein in 1849 he had preserved, and had carried them complete across Japan and California in 1861. Even his language recalled the finer articles of *La Réforme* and *La Vraie République*, the striking speeches in *La Constituante* and at Blanqui's club. The spirit of the parties of that period, their exclusiveness, their personal sympathies and antipathies, above all their faith in the second coming of the revolution – it was all here.[240]

Mikhail Bakunin, four years older than Karl, was from a Russian aristocratic household. He was initially an artillery officer, became an enthusiast for Hegel in the mid-1830s and went as a student to Berlin in 1840. While in Berlin, he frequented left Hegelian circles and became close to Arnold Ruge. Hegel was and remained a formative influence upon his thinking. Among his Russian contemporaries, he was considered to possess 'to a superlative degree a facility for dialectics, so indispensable if one is to infuse life into abstract logical formulas and to obtain conclusions from them applicable to life'.[241] Like others in the 1840s, he was deeply and lastingly impressed by Feuerbach's critique of religion as the source of human alienation; real freedom was to be found in Hegel's organic state as the formation of an inclusive ethical community, but not 'the tutelary state' of Prussia, let alone the oppressive Russian autocracy of Nicholas I. In his early 1842 essay 'The Reaction in Germany', he advocated a 'religion of democracy', a secular translation of the Christian ideal of brotherhood put forward by the French socialist Pierre Leroux.

The second formative moment in Bakunin's political thought was his experience of 1848. Enthusiasm for the democratic revolution in the spring of 1848 gave way to the disillusion of the autumn. He came to associate the bourgeoisie with reactionary politics, exemplified by the record of the Frankfurt Parliament, which showed that democracy in itself was not sufficient. By 1849, he had come to support a second popular revolution to establish a 'red republic'. In the Dresden insurrection, he fought on the barricades alongside Richard Wagner. He was captured and imprisoned, first in Königstein in Saxony, and then he was transferred to Russia.

Before that, however, in the summer of 1848, he had participated in the first Slav Congress in Prague. Conservative Slavophilism, which lauded Russia's past before the reforms of Peter the Great, was given a radical twist in the light of the failures of 1848. Building upon the observations of August von Haxthausen's 1846 *Studies of the Interior of Russia*, it was argued that the peasant *commune* in Russia possessed a natural morality and was inherently 'socialist' in its assumptions. In the light of the failure of revolution in the West, hopes of revolutionary change were increasingly placed in Russia. An endorsement of a radical version of the Slavophil position brought with it a belief in the self-sufficiency of the peasant *commune* and a rejection of the centralizing activity of czarist state power inaugurated by Peter the Great. In Bakunin's case, a left-Hegelian conception of the organic nature of the state was ascribed to the peasant *commune*. These were the Russian roots of Bakunin's federalism.[242]

Back in Europe in 1861–2, having missed more than a decade of its intellectual and political development, Bakunin, as Herzen observed, started exactly where he had left off in 1849. His aim was to throw himself into preparations for a Polish insurrection. As he wrote to Herzen from San Francisco on his way back to Europe in October 1861, 'as soon as I arrive I shall set to work; I shall work with you on the Polish-Slavonic question, which has been my *idée fixe* since 1846 and was in practice my speciality in 1848 and 1849.'[243] In 1862, he still believed that natural Slav socialism contained more promise than that of the French or the Germans, or the utopian communism of the working classes. But the failure of the Polish revolt in the summer of 1863 led him to rethink his position. He broke with Pan-Slavism and began to criticize the peasant *Commune* as a patriarchal institution based on injustice and inequality. In 1864, in his *Letters from a Democrat*, his hopes centred once more upon Europe, while in his political thinking he returned to his radical Hegelian critique of the 'tutelary' state with religion as its foundation. His programme concluded with a utopian vision of the abolition of the right of inheritance, free marriage, equal rights for women and the upbringing of children by society. But the abolition of the 'tutelary' state did not entail the abolition of politics. Provinces would be made up from *Communes*, and the nation would be made up from provinces, while nations themselves would join a voluntary international federation. In 1865, he wrote in more practical terms, contrasting the religion-based official morality imposed by Napoléon III and other European countries with the 'real liberty' existing in Britain and the United States, and citing the United States as one possible model of federal government.

These positions were pushed further in 1866 in his *Revolutionary Catechism*. He called for 'the radical dissolution of the centralised, tutelary and authoritarian state, together with the military, bureaucratic, governmental, administrative, judicial and civil institutions'.[244] In previous texts, he had extolled 'real democracy' as a fundamental sentiment which came from 'within the people'. Now he also added in labour, not only as the primary component of human dignity, but also as the basis of the solidarity which he had previously identified with the peasant *Commune*. A year later in a text explaining his disagreement with Pan-Slavists, he stated that they associated Slav emancipation with the expansion of the czarist empire, while he associated it with its destruction. He then added that there was another 'great difference': 'They are unitary at all costs, always preferring public order to liberty, while I am anarchist and prefer liberty to public order, or rather, in order not to credit the case of my enemies too easily, I am federalist from head to toe.'[245]

Bakunin, both in body and in personality, was a charismatic figure, as attested by so many contemporaries. He was 6 feet 5 inches tall and reported to be massively strong. As an irrepressible activist, whose political expectations had been formed in the years before 1848, Bakunin was one of the last major representatives of the transnational republicanism which had accompanied the development of Europe between the age of Napoléon and the Franco-Prussian War. But the experience of 1848 and the inadequacies of Pan-Slavism had convinced him that republics, democratic constitutions, representative govern-ments or national liberation were not enough. Social revolution was the only means by which the oppressed peoples of Europe would achieve emancipation. It went without saying, as he had emphasized up to 1864, that the freedom of Europe required the breakup of the military despotisms of Austria, Prussia and Russia. But it had also become clear that national unification by no means necessarily brought with it social or political liberation. In early 1864, Bakunin had moved to Italy, where disillusion, particularly in the south, with trade liberalization and Piedmontese taxation had grown apace. In Italy, he became one of the first to respond to this disenchantment by criticizing Mazzini's idea of the moderate political republic.[246]

In 1867, having moved from Italy to Switzerland, he attended the inaugural Congress of the League of Peace and Freedom, based in Geneva. By that time, he was famous across Europe. As he rose to speak, 'The cry passed from mouth to mouth: "Bakunin!" Garibaldi, who was in the chair, stood up, advanced a few steps and embraced him. This solemn meeting of two old and tried warriors of the revolu-tion produced an astonishing impression . . . Everyone rose and there was a prolonged and enthusiastic clapping of hands.'[247] Bakunin gave a rousing speech endorsing internationalism, socialism, anti-statism and federalism, and in the subsequent year attempted to persuade the League to adopt a socialist programme and to link itself to the Inter-national, whose Geneva branch he had just joined. At the second conference, held in Berne in 1868, when Bakunin attempted to initiate a debate on the 'equalization of classes', he was accused of 'commun-ism'. In response, he argued that the advocacy of 'collective property' along with the congress of 'the workers' in Brussels, was not 'communism', but 'collectivism': 'I hate communism because it is the negation of liberty . . . I am not a communist because communism concentrates and causes all the powers of society to be absorbed by the state . . . I want the abolition of the state . . . I want the organisation of society and collective or social property from the bottom up, by way of free association, and not from the top down by means of any authority whatsoever.'[248]

Rejected by the League, Bakunin and his followers founded the International Alliance of Social Democracy. The Alliance considered itself from the outset to be a branch of the International and undertook to accept its rules and statutes. In December 1868, it applied for formal membership. The application was refused on the grounds (drafted by Karl) that the General Council did not accept '"International" branches' and that 'the presence of a second international body working within and outside the International' would be 'the most infallible means of its disorganization'.[249]

In February 1869, the Alliance put in a second and successful bid for membership. It agreed to dissolve itself as an 'international body', while its branches in Switzerland, Spain and Italy would enrol as individual sections. In other words, a form of dual membership was permitted, a dangerous concession given Bakunin's ambition since 1864 to form a secret society. Such an organization inhabiting a space within larger and more broadly based societies could hasten the pace of change. What was needed, as Bakunin explained in 1872, was 'a secret society in the heart of the International, to give it a revolutionary organization, to transform it and all the popular masses which exist outside it into a power sufficiently organized to destroy the politico-clerico-bourgeois reaction, and the economic, juridical, religious and political institutions of the state.'[250] It is unlikely that this plan was ever more than a fantasy. But what was undeniable was the growing power and influence of Bakunin's revolutionary vision of federalism and collectivism within the International. One sixth of the Basle Congress consisted of Bakunin's delegation; furthermore, Bakunin had managed to defeat the General Council on the question of inheritance, even if not by the required two-thirds majority.

More generally, after 1867 in England and Germany, membership and participation in the International were static or declining, while elsewhere journals in Geneva, Le Locle, Lyons, Naples and Barcelona were spreading Bakunin's ideas. By the beginning of 1870, 2,000 members had joined the International in Madrid, and by June 150 sections from thirty-six regions had formed a regional federation and adopted a Bakuninist programme in Spain.[251] His appeal was not confined to what Engels considered 'backward' peasant regions, but was also strong in France and industrialized Belgium. The Franco-Prussian War and its aftermath, which destabilized relations in France and in neighbouring countries, led to a major increase in Bakunin's support in Spain, where it was one of the factors accounting for a major strike wave in 1871. Its impact was also felt in Italy, where Mazzini's condemnation of the *Commune* was vigorously combated by Bakunin and Garibaldi.

The appeal of Bakunin's federalism and collectivism in Southern Europe was not surprising in regions where freedom of speech and of association was absent, where there were no labour organizations and where, therefore, open propaganda was not tolerated. In these areas, not surprisingly, the Carbonari, the Freemasons and other secret societies were thought more effective. But the appeal of Bakunin was not confined to the allegedly backward and non-industrialized South. The appeal of federalism was an expression of the deep-rooted hostility across Europe towards the militarized and undemocratic states which had taken over after the suppression of the revolutions of 1848.

There was little sympathetic understanding of these developments on Karl's part. For Karl, the whole original point of involvement in the affairs of the International had been the possibility of acting in a pivotal role in relation to the English working class in the only country in which a transition towards a society of associated producers appeared a realistic possibility. What happened in Spain or Italy was of marginal interest.

In 1864, when he had met Bakunin again for the first time since 1848, he was impressed. 'I must say I liked him very much, more so than previously . . . one of the few people, whom after 16 years I find to have moved forwards and not backwards.' A few months later, they were also agreed upon the need to combat Mazzini's attempt to control the International.[252] But once Bakunin left Italy for Geneva and joined the League of Peace and Freedom, Karl's suspicions – dating from 1848 – returned.[253] Peace and disarmament would leave Europe at the mercy of Russian armies. Therefore, as he wrote to Engels, 'the Peace

Congress in Geneva was, of course, a fabrication of the Russians, which is why they sent along their WELL WORN OUT AGENT, Bakunin'.[254] In the case of the Alliance, Bakunin tried flattery and protestations that he was Karl's 'disciple' and now understood 'how right you were in following and inviting all of us to follow the great road of economic revolution'.[255] But Karl was unmoved. He sent the Rules of the Alliance to Engels with the comment, 'Mr Bakunin is condescending enough to wish to take the workers' movement under *Russian* leadership.'[256]

In the areas in which Bakunin's federalist and collectivist message had found a response, and thus a growth of support for the International, it was simply mocked. The shift in the political character of Europe around the end of the 1860s had largely passed Karl by. Referring to a document produced by members of the Alliance, Karl ironized:

> Their 'revolutionary' programme had had more effect in some weeks in Italy, Spain, etc., than that of the International Working Men's Association had in years. If we should reject their 'revolutionary programme' we would [produce] a *separation* between the countries with a '*revolutionary' workers' movement* (these are listed as *France*, where they have all of 2 correspondents, *Switzerland*(!), *Italy* – where the workers apart from those who belong to us, are simply a tail to Mazzini – and *Spain*, where there are more clerics than workers) and those with a *more gradual development* of the working class (viz., England, Germany, the United States and Belgium) . . .
>
> That the Swiss should represent the revolutionary type is really amusing.[257]

But the problem posed by Bakunin could not be ignored. For the growth of the International in these new areas was likely to lead to a Bakuninist majority at the next congress and this might mean the abandonment of a strategy based upon social-democratic growth in England and other advanced areas of Western Europe. Furthermore, this problem was becoming acute, because interest in the International was fading among English trade union and working-class leaders.

After the General Council permitted individual sections of the Alliance to enrol, the Geneva section attempted to join. But this was blocked by the pre-existing Geneva Federation, which was hostile and had rejected its application. For this reason, at the Basle Congress,

Bakunin voted in favour of wider powers for the General Council, including the right to accept or refuse the admission of new sections. The General Council could then override the Geneva Federation's veto.

But by the time the issue came up for decision, the attitude of the General Council had changed. In pressing the Basle Congress to vote for the abolition of inheritance, Bakunin had secured a majority rejection of Karl's position. This marked the beginning of the battle which pitted Bakunin against Karl and his allies. Soon after Basle, Liebknecht denounced Bakunin as a Slavophil and an enemy of the International, while Moses Hess reported the conflict between Bakunin and the General Council as a contest between civilization and barbarism. Bakunin retorted with an attack upon German Jews. He now foresaw a 'life and death struggle' with Karl and his supporters. In late 1869, Bakunin himself left Geneva. But the pro-Bakuninist Geneva journal *L'Égalité* continued with an attack upon the General Council, which Karl attributed to 'the insolence' of Bakunin, especially the way in which he and his 'Cossacks' posed as the 'guardian of true proletarianism'. At Karl's instigation, the General Council followed up the attack, and in March 1870 sent a confidential circular to German sections, denouncing Bakunin as 'this most dangerous intriguer'.

In spring 1870, the Geneva section of Bakunin's Alliance once again applied for admission to the local Genevan Federal Council, the *Fédération Romande*. In accordance with the rules of the International, this was granted at its annual congress of the *Fédération* at Chaux-les-Fonds, but only by a majority of three. This led the anti-Bakunin minority to secede and hold its own conference. Each now claimed to be the true representative of the *Fédération Romande*. But in June 1870 the General Council found in favour of the anti-Bakunin minority. It decreed that the majority should adopt another name, a clear breach of its constitutional powers.

The Genevan Bakuninists changed their name to that of the Jura Federation in the summer. But the Swiss and other federations reacted with indignation to this high-handed action by the General Council, especially since in March it had admitted another Genevan Russian section, organized by Karl's ally and leader of anti-Bakuninist Russians, Nicholas Utin. Support for federalism and Bakunin – or, at least, hostility to the arbitrary proceedings of the General Council – grew, particularly among the 'Latin' sections in Spain, Italy, Southern France and Switzerland. Faced with this mounting resistance, Karl planned to stage the next congress in Mainz, away from these pressures. But the war put paid to these plans.

Karl's *Civil War in France* was an attempt to draw Federalist supporters nearer to the position of the General Council. But its unwanted effect was to further accentuate the decline of English participation in the International. By the summer of 1871, political 'apathy' among the English working classes had become obvious. At a meeting of the General Council on 8 August, Engels vented his frustration: 'The Working Classes in England had behaved in a disgraceful manner, though the men of Paris had risked their lives, the working men of England had made no effort either to sympathise with them or assist them. There was no political life in them.'[258] In an attempt to prevent the organization falling into the hands of a Bakuninist majority, on 25 July 1871 Engels had urged the summoning of a 'private Conference of the Association' in London later that summer, while Karl specified that it 'would be confined to questions of organisation and policy'.[259] The conference was held in a pub off Tottenham Court Road in the middle of September. It contained no one from Germany, two representatives from England, some *Communard* refugees from France, two former supporters of Bakunin from Switzerland (including Utin) and a six-man delegation from Belgium. The Jura Federation was not invited, on the specious grounds that it had never relinquished the title *Fédération Romande*.

The conference attempted to transform the International Association from a forum for discussion into a political party. Resolutions were made binding on all sections. Political action, originally a 'means for social emancipation', was now made mandatory, since in the militant activity of the working class 'its economic movement and its political action are indissolubly united'. Such action would progress 'peaceably where it is possible and by force of arms when it may be necessary'.[260] The General Council was authorized to choose the time and place of the next congress, and the new powers given to the General Council at Basle to affiliate or disaffiliate sections of the International were now used to deny the affiliation of the Bakuninists in Switzerland by equating the congress decision with a General Council opinion. Through this subterfuge, Bakuninism was turned into a heresy. Karl also attempted, but failed, to associate Bakunin with the criminal activities of Nechaev. He tried to secure a condemnation of the Alliance, but was reminded that this was unnecessary, since the Alliance had already dissolved itself. In both cases, it was the Belgian delegation, led by De Paepe, which played a restraining role. Overall, Karl considered the conference a great success. He wrote to Jenny that 'it was hard work ... but more was done than at all previous congresses put together because there was no audience in front of which to stage rhetorical comedies'.[261]

Federalists, however, were right to consider this conference a stitch-up. In November 1871, the Jura Federation convened a congress at Sonvilliers, and issued a circular to all the other federations, demanding that another congress be called, since the meeting in London was invalid. That meeting had arrogated to itself unconstitutional powers and its decisions were unrepresentative.[262] The rules of the International did not allow for a 'secret conference' like that held in London. The International Working Men's Association had been constituted as 'a free federation of autonomous sections', not a hierarchical and authoritarian organization, composed of disciplined sections under the control of the General Council. The General Council should return to its original purpose, which was to act as 'a simple correspondence and statistical bureau'. The circular concluded by asking, 'how can a free and equal society arise from an authoritarian organisation?'

Nominally written on behalf of the General Council, Karl's response, jointly composed with Engels, appeared in March 1872 and was called 'Les prétendues scissions dans l'Internationale' ('Fictitious Splits in the International'). This document purported to trace the history of 'the persistent efforts of certain meddlers to deliberately maintain confusion between the International and a society which has been hostile to it since its inception'. This society (the Alliance) had been 'fathered by the Russian, Mikhail Bakunin', whose ambition, it was alleged, was to use it as his instrument, and to replace the General Council by his personal dictatorship.[263] Once again, the authors attempted to discredit Bakunin, both by revealing that two of his supporters were Bonapartist spies and by linking him with the criminal activities of Nechaev.

Sergei Nechaev was the son of a village priest. He was especially notorious for two reasons.[264] Firstly, he had attempted to set up a revolutionary secret society in Russia composed of five-person groups whose only link with each other was through Nechaev himself. In Moscow, a student called Ivanov, belonging to one of these groups, had questioned Nechaev's authority. So, in order to quell any possibility of mutiny and to bind the group together by making it jointly complicit in a common crime, Nechaev organized Ivanov's murder on the pretext that he was about to denounce the group to the authorities. It was this murder, on 21 November 1869, which provided the plot for Dostoyevsky's novel *The Devils*.

Secondly, in January 1870, Nechaev had found Bakunin in Locarno, engaged in a Russian translation of *Capital*. Perpetually short of money, Bakunin had signed a contract to translate the book for 1,200 roubles, of which 300 roubles had been paid as an advance. He had soon tired of the task and was pleased when Nechaev promised to persuade the publisher to release him from his contract. Thereafter, Nechaev demanded that the publisher leave Bakunin in peace, threatening in the name of the secret committee of People's Justice that unless the publisher withdrew his request for the return of the advance, unpleasant consequences would follow. Perhaps aware of Ivanov's fate, the publisher duly complied.

For some time in the late 1860s Bakunin had clearly been entranced by Nechaev's revolutionary picture of himself. But there was no evidence, nor was it in any sense likely, that Bakunin was involved in, or even aware of, Nechaev's crimes. Thus the repeated references made by Karl to Bakunin and Nechaev's foundation of a 'secret society among the students' in Russia was an unsubstantiated smear.[265]

The main weakness of this counter-circular was that it failed to respond to the main point made at Sonvilliers: that the General Council in 1871 had arrogated to itself certain powers *not* covered by its own original 'rules'.[266] As a result, Engels' 'organizational' initiative, far from placating Federalist opponents, widened still further the divisions within the International Association.

The next congress had been arranged to take place from 1 to 7 September 1872 in The Hague. This was a place that Bakunin would find it difficult, if not impossible, to reach. Furthermore, the vetting of delegates to the congress would be in the hands of Karl's allies. In a letter to César De Paepe, Karl made an estimate of the forces ranged for and against him:

> England, the United States, Germany, Denmark, Holland, Austria, most
> of the French groups, the northern Italians, Sicily and Rome, the vast

majority of the Romance Swiss and the Russians in Russia (as distinct from certain Russians abroad linked with Bakunin) are marching in step with the General Council.

On the other hand, there will be the Jura Federation in Switzerland (in other words the men of the Alliance who hide behind this name), Naples, possibly Spain, part of Belgium and certain groups of French refugees ... and these will form the opposing camp.[267]

Just before the congress, Karl urged Dr Kugelmann to attend, arguing that it was a 'matter of life and death' for the International and that the aim was to preserve it 'from disintegrating elements'.[268] Both sides competed to send delegates, but the supporters of Bakunin needlessly deprived themselves of vital support when the Italians, indignant about the claims made in 'Les Prétendues Scissions', decided to boycott The Hague and hold a rival congress at Neuchâtel.

At the congress itself, following the scrutiny of the credentials of delegates, particularly potential supporters of Bakunin, Karl was assured of majority support from the start and did not hesitate to exploit his advantage. The congress defeated the Bakuninist proposal that the General Council become simply a central office for correspondence and the collection of statistics. It also succeeded in incorporating the decisions of the London Conference into the rules of the Association. Furthermore, a committee of enquiry, chaired by Engels' friend Theodor Cuno, found Bakunin to be the head of a secret organization and recommended that he and Guillaume be expelled. Karl, anxious to besmirch Bakunin further, produced a letter allegedly implicating Bakunin in the intimidation of his publisher.

Finally, Engels, backed up by Karl, Charles Longuet and others, put forward the surprise proposal that the General Council be moved to New York. There was silence and then confusion, particularly among the Germans and the French Blanquists, who up until then had been happy to support the battle against Bakunin. But the proposal was narrowly carried by 26 to 23 with 9 abstentions. The justification was that if the proposal had not been carried, the International Association would have ended up in the hands of either the Blanquists or the Bakuninists. It would have become a discredited conspiratorial organization, without larger social or political importance.

A year later, in *Statism and Anarchy*, Bakunin put forward his own picture of the conflict which had engulfed the International. His book powerfully expressed the shock to Europe produced by Bismarck's triumphant wars against Denmark, Austria and France, and by the proclamation of the new German Empire in the Versailles Hall of Mirrors. Since the time of Louis XIV, and onward through the Napoleonic Wars, France had always been considered the most powerful state on the European mainland. *Statism and Anarchy* dwelt upon 'the shattering of the historical supremacy of the French State' and its replacement by 'the even more odious and pernicious supremacy of state-supported Pan-Germanism'.[269] Its analysis of 1848 in Germany in some ways prefigured Lewis Namier's *1848: The Revolution of the Intellectuals*.[270] It stressed the learned character of the Frankfurt Assembly, its unjust treatment of the Poles and the Czechs and the inability both of Frankfurt and of the Prussian Parliament to challenge the state. This was not least, according to Bakunin, because the desire that prevailed 'in the consciousness or instinct of every German' was 'the desire to expand far and wide the boundaries of the German Empire'.[271]

'The propagation of this Germanic idea', according to Bakunin, was also 'now the chief aspiration of Marx, who . . . tried to resume within the International, to his own advantage, the exploits and victories of Prince Bismarck'.[272] Bakunin did not mention the centrality of England in Karl's theory or his work on the General Council. He made no reference to the place accorded to federalism in *The Civil War in France*, but instead equated Karl's approach solely with that of the *Communist Manifesto*. He acknowledged Karl's gifts as a theorist, and agreed with his critique of Proudhon. But Germans could not make revolutions. They lacked 'character'. They proceeded not from life to thought but, like Hegel himself, from thought to life. Even the 'school of materialists or realists', such as Karl or the natural materialist Ludwig Büchner, 'could not and cannot free themselves from the sway of abstract, metaphysical thought'.[273]

Karl's thought was roughly coupled with that of Lassalle. Not only were they both advocates of representative democracy, but Lassalle's practice was built upon Karl's theory. The fundamental point of Lassalle's programme was 'the liberation (imaginary) of the proletariat *solely by means of the state*'. This was what Lassalle had taken from 'the communist theory created by Marx'. It was also suggested that Karl himself was a 'direct disciple of (Louis) Blanc' and therefore (inaccurately) that he, like Lassalle and Blanc before him, advocated making available 'unlimited credit' to 'producers' and consumers' associations of workers'.[274]

Theoretically, *Statism and Anarchy* was rather thin, consisting largely of assertions rather than reasoned evidence. It was argued that 'the passion for social revolution' could only be satisfied when the state's power of coercion, the last bulwark of bourgeois interests, collapses. For any state entailed 'domination and consequently slavery':

> That is why we are enemies of the state . . . No state, howsoever democratic its forms . . . is capable of giving the people what they need: the free organisation of their own interests from below upward, without any interference, tutelage or coercion from above. That is because no state, not even the most republican and democratic, not even the pseudo-popular state contemplated by Marx, in essence represents anything but government of the masses from above downward, by an educated and thereby privileged minority which supposedly understands the real interests of the people better than the people themselves.[275]

Later on in the book, it was asked, if the proletariat were to be the ruling class, whom would it rule? Bakunin speculated that if it were a question of 'cultural levels', it might be 'the peasant rabble', while if the question were considered from a national viewpoint, it might be the Slavs. Finally, there was also the question raised by a sentence in the *Communist Manifesto*: 'the proletariat raised to a governing class'. Would 'the entire proletariat head the government? Will all 40 million be members of the government?' The answer by Karl and others that 'there would be government of the people by a small number of representatives elected by the people' was a lie behind which the 'despotism of the ruling minority' was 'concealed', the expression of a 'sham popular will'.[276]

Not surprisingly, Bakunin also attacked Karl's character:

> A nervous man, some say to the point of cowardice, he is extremely ambitious and vain, quarrelsome, intolerant, and absolute, like Jehovah, the Lord God of his ancestors, and, like him, vengeful to the point of madness. There is no lie or calumny that he would not invent and disseminate against anyone who had the misfortune to arouse his jealousy – or his hatred, which amounts to the same thing. And there is no intrigue so

sordid that he would hesitate to engage in it if in his opinion (which is for the most part mistaken) it might serve to strengthen his position and his influence or extend his power. In this respect, he is a thoroughly political man.[277]

But as a 'political man', who aspired to lead the International, Karl was presented as a failed Lassalle. Although strong on theory, he lost 'all significance and force in the public arena'. According to Bakunin, 'He proved it in his hapless campaign to establish his dictatorship in the International and through the International over the entire revolutionary movement of the proletariat of Europe and America.' Just as at Basle, the 'integrity' of the International's programme had been defended against the Germans and their attempt to introduce 'bourgeois politics into it', so in 1872 'Marx had suffered a total and well-deserved defeat'. This, according to Bakunin, was how the schism within the International had begun.[278]

Karl wrote out some notes and commentary on Bakunin's book between April 1874 and January 1875. His notes were either taken directly in Russian or translated into German. His main criticism concerned Bakunin's inability to understand that 'a radical social revolution is bound up with definite historical conditions of economic development; these are its premises'. Bakunin, he claimed, 'understands absolutely nothing of social revolution, only its political rhetoric'. He therefore imagined 'that *radical revolution* is equally possible in all (social) formations'. In common with other Romantic representatives of the transnational radical tradition, Bakunin believed that 'willpower, not economic conditions', was 'the basis of his social revolution'.[279]

Karl also took him up on his criticism of the representative principle. In response to Bakunin's question, would 'the entire proletariat stand at the head of the government?', Karl answered, 'in a trade union, for example, does the entire union form its executive committee?' Similarly, in answer to the question about whether 40 million Germans could rule, Karl replied, 'Certainly! For the system starts with the self-government of communities.' He also went on to explain that only when the proletariat was victorious in its struggle to 'abolish its own character as wage labour' would 'the distribution of general functions' become a 'routine matter which entails no domination' and elections would 'lose their present political character'.[280] In that situation, the assignment of functions, as in a cooperative factory, would simply be according to suitability; and all Bakunin's 'fantasies about domination would go to the devil'. Harking back to his own polemics thirty years earlier, Karl observed, 'Mr Bakunin has only translated Proudhon's and Stirner's anarchy into the barbaric idiom of the Tartars.'[281]

Both Bakunin and Karl put forward what they conceived to be critiques of 'parliamentarism'. But neither was wholly successful in presenting a convincing alternative. The main difficulty of Bakunin's criticism of the representative principle, and the conception of power 'from the bottom up', was the problem of embodying it in any stable or sustainable institutional form. For this reason, belief in federalism, so strong at the end of the 1860s, faded in the course of the subsequent decade. It was displaced by the growing attraction of social-democratic parties, adhering to representative principles.

Karl's attempted synthesis of state and civil society in *The Civil War in France* took the form of an elected assembly, formed on the basis of democratic and representative principles. Once the proletariat was victorious, he argued, there would be a 'distribution of general functions, assigned as in a cooperative factory according to suitability'. This image of representatives chosen according to particular skills, as an employer might search out the best worker to perform a particular task, was recurrent in Karl's writings from the 1840s onwards. What was lacking in this conception was a social and political space in which a plurality not merely of functions, but also of opinions, might be expressed. In this sense, it was open to an authoritarian interpretation. The challenge of socialism in the years after 1848 was, as John Stuart Mill argued, 'To unite the greatest individual liberty of action with an equal ownership of all in the raw material of the globe and an equal participation in the benefits of combined labour.'[282] On this issue, Karl had nothing to say.

It is difficult to arrive at a fair judgement of Karl's behaviour in relation to Bakunin in the years following the Basle Congress. Bakunin's operatic attempt at revolution in Lyons in the autumn of 1870 and his predilection for secret societies were two good reasons to distrust him. Furthermore, however appropriate such organizations were in areas where freedom of association was absent, the statutes of the International Association committed it to open organization and propaganda. On the other hand, it was clear that the calling of the secret conference in London in the autumn of 1871 and its promulgation of new rules and objectives were a breach of the original statutes, which the London Conference did not possess the constitutional authority to amend.

The major political reason for bringing the International Association to such a hasty and inglorious end at the Hague Congress was that Karl could no longer look to any significant support from English trade union leaders on the General Council. Replacing these trade unionists with French refugees did nothing to strengthen the standing of the International Association as a representative institution. Karl's fear was that the Association would become a mere sect, remote from English politics, and riven by an esoteric struggle between Blanquists and Bakuninists. Two years earlier, at the beginning of 1870, his confidence in the potentiality of the International had been strong. When attempting to mobilize continental sections of the International against the Bakuninist complaints of *L'Égalité*, he had considered it vital to keep the English representation in the hands of the General Council. England, he had argued, was the only country where 'the great majority of the population consists of wage labourers and where class struggle and organisation of the working class by the trade unions have acquired a certain degree of maturity and universality ... The English,' he went on, 'have all the material conditions for the social revolution. What they lack is the spirit of generalisation and revolutionary ardour.' Luckily, however, the General Council was in 'the happy position of having its hand directly on this great lever of the proletarian revolution'.[283] For this reason, it was vital to keep English representation in the hands of the General Council.

Yet less than two years later he had abandoned this idea, and at the London Conference of 1871 made no objection to the separation of the English Federal Council from the General Council. At the beginning of that year, Karl had believed that the Gladstone government would fall and that another period of crisis was imminent. His optimism was based upon his hopes of a conflict with Russia. According to the Treaty of Paris, which had concluded the Crimean War in 1856, the Black Sea was to become a demilitarized area, not open to Russian warships. But during the Franco-Prussian War Russia, with the connivance of Prussia, took advantage of the prostration of France to remilitarize the Black Sea. The London middle classes, led by the *Pall Mall Gazette*, were incensed by the infringement of the Treaty, and demanded war.

Gladstone had been a member of the Whig–Liberal government which in 1854 had declared war on Russia. He had no intention of going to war with Russia, especially in the absence of European allies. But he could not ignore the breach of the Treaty. Government indecision was interpreted by many as a national humiliation which would not have happened in Palmerston's time. The Liberal government, it seemed, was incapable of defending national interests. Karl was right to the extent that Gladstone's failure to force the Russians to back down was one of the factors which led to his defeat in the 1874 election. But it did not bring the working classes onto the streets, let alone precipitate a social crisis of the kind imagined by Karl.

The working classes, as Engels complained, had remained stubbornly 'apathetic'. Not only did they not become engaged in the agitation over Russia, but they offered little or no support to the Paris *Commune*. At the time of the London Conference in September 1871, Karl exploded in fury against those whom he had previously regarded as his allies: 'The Trade Unions . . . are an aristocratic minority – the poor workers cannot belong to them; the great mass of workers whom economic development is driving from the countryside into the towns every day – has long been outside the trade unions – and the most wretched mass has never belonged; the same goes for the workers born in the East End of London; one in ten belongs to trade unions – peasants, day labourers never belong to the societies.' Defiantly, he continued: 'The Trade Unions can do nothing by themselves – they will remain a minority – they have no power over the mass of proletarians – whereas the International works directly on these men.'[284]

In the Hague Congress of 1872, his anger was no less immoderate. He joined forces with the maverick Conservative journalist Maltman Barry, who somehow managed to get himself appointed to represent a German-speaking section from Chicago. When the English trade unionist and former Chartist Thomas Mottershead quite reasonably questioned Barry's credentials as a representative of English working men, Karl launched into a tirade. If Barry was not 'a recognised leader of English working men . . . that was an honour, for almost every recognised leader of English working men was sold to Gladstone, Morley, Dilke, and others'.[285] Six years later, his bitterness towards 'the Gladstones, Brights, Mundellas, Morleys, and the whole gang of factory owners' remained. On 11 February 1878, Karl wrote to Liebknecht:

'The English working class had gradually become ever more demoralised as a result of the period of corruption after 1848, and had finally reached the stage of being no more than an appendage of the great Liberal Party, i.e. of its *oppressors*, the capitalists. Its direction had passed completely into the hands of the venal Trades Union leaders and professional agitators.'[286]

Much better, therefore, to bring the International – or at least his own involvement in it – to a close. On the last day of the Hague Congress, Barry's report explained why the General Council needed to move from London: 'The time and thought which the affairs of the General Council exacted of Marx, when added to his labours of translating the various editions of his great book, and the general supervision of the Association, were found exhausting and injurious to his health. During the last year or so, since the accession to the Council of a number of "representative" Englishmen, it has taxed all his efforts (and these have sometime failed) to keep the Council to its legitimate work.'[287]

For Karl himself, the end of the International came as liberation. Three months before the Hague Congress, Karl wrote to De Paepe: 'I can hardly wait for the next Congress. It will be the end of my slavery. After that I shall become a free man again; I shall accept no administrative functions any more, either for the General Council or for the British Federal Council.'[288] Throughout the period in which the International had attempted to engage with the Franco-Prussian War and the *Commune*, he had continued to be dogged by ill-health. On 17 August 1870, he complained to Engels: 'I have not slept a wink the fourth night running because of the rheumatism, and all that time fantasies about Paris, etc., run through my mind. I shall have Gumpert's sleeping potion prepared for me this evening.'[289] On 21 January 1871, he wrote to his ally Sigfrid Meyer in New York: 'My health has again been abominable for months on end, but who can give thought to such trivia at a time of such momentous historical events!'[290] Illness interrupted his attendance on the General Council during the *Commune* and resulted in a delay in his completion of *The Civil War in France*. But on 13 June he was able to tell his daughters that 'after a 6 weeks' illness I am all right again, so far as this is possible under present circumstances'.[291]

With the *Commune* came other anxieties, this time for the family. On 1 May, Jenny and Eleanor had travelled to Bordeaux to help Laura, whose third baby had been born in February and had become danger-ously ill. Laura's husband, Paul Lafargue, had returned from Paris with 'full powers' to organize a revolutionary army in Bordeaux. But once the *Commune* was destroyed by Versailles, Paul became a wanted man, so the family moved to Bagnères-de-Luchon, a remote small town in the Pyrenees, where they laid low, hoping to escape attention. On 13 June, Karl wrote a coded letter warning Paul of imminent arrest. The letter advised the family to move to a better climate on the Spanish side of the Pyrenees and advising that Paul's health in particular 'will deteri-orate and may even incur great danger, if he any longer hesitates to follow the advice of medical men'.[292] Paul remained for another six weeks in Luchon because of the baby's sickness. But on 26 July the baby died, and soon after Paul crossed the frontier into Spain. On 6 August, the three sisters and Laura's little son, Schnappy, went to visit him. Jenny and Eleanor then attempted to make their return to England, but were stopped on the French frontier, where they were searched and cross-examined. Jenny was in particular danger because she had with her a letter from Gustave Flourens, the assassinated *Com-munard*. Fortunately, in the police station she was able to hide the letter, and the two sisters returned home on 26 August.[293]

In other ways, Karl remained surprisingly ebullient in the summer of 1871. He enjoyed the scandal created by *The Civil War in France* and relished his reputation as 'the best calumniated and most menaced man of London'. At the end of July, his mood was still upbeat. He wrote to Dr Kugelmann: 'The work for the International is immense, and in addition London is overrun with refugees whom we have to look after. Moreover, I am overrun by other people – newspaper men and others of every description – who want to see the "MONSTER" with their own eyes.'[294]

There was also some healthy relaxation to be obtained away from the sooty and smog-ridden city at the seaside. Karl was fond of Brighton, but his favourite resort was Ramsgate. Engels described Ramsgate to his mother as 'The most important resort I know, extremely informal, very pretty firm beach immediately beneath the steep chalk cliffs; the beach is full of fake Negro-minstrels, conjurers, fire-eaters, Punch-and-Judy shows and nonsense of that sort. The place is not very fashionable, but cheap and easy going. The bathing is very good.'[295] In the summer of 1870, despite his rheumatism and his sleepless nights, Karl had writ-ten of Ramsgate: 'The family is amusing itself here royally. Tussy and

Jennychen never come out of the sea and are building up a good stock of health.'[296]

This optimistic mood carried through into the London Conference, which Engels had organized for the second half of September. But in the autumn and winter that followed, it became increasingly clear that the apparent victories achieved in London were fairly hollow. The followers of Bakunin had not accepted defeat. Bakunin himself counter-attacked with the accusation that the General Council was dominated by 'Pan-Germanism (or Bismarckism)'. His followers were publishing a newspaper in Geneva, and trying to form a French section in London and a German section in New York.[297] Parallel tensions were developing between the General Council and the English Federal Council. Former allies, like Johann Georg Eccarius and John Hales, were becoming uncompromising opponents.

In the face of these developments, Karl's tone became wearier and he increasingly complained about overwork. To Liebknecht, he complained that he and Engels were 'overwhelmed with International work' and that no efforts had been made to ensure the presence at the Conference of German delegates, thus lending credence to rumours being spread that 'Marx has lost his influence even in Germany!'[298] On 24 November, he wrote to De Paepe, referring publicly for the first time to the possibility of his resignation, half jokingly as a response to the charge of 'Pan-Germanism'.[299] In the spring of 1872, 'overburdened with work' to the extent that he had not been able to write to Laura or 'Dear Schnappy', he explained to Paul Lafargue that 'Indeed, the International impinges too greatly on my time and, were it not my conviction that my presence on the Council is still necessary at this period of strife, I should have withdrawn long since.'[300] Moving the General Council to New York was the means by which his withdrawal could be achieved and this was not announced until the Hague Congress itself. But he could already state by the end of May, both to his Russian translator, Nicolai Danielson, and to César De Paepe that his withdrawal from the Association was imminent and that his 'slavery' would come to an end.

The International Association in 1872 was very different from the organization which had been founded eight years earlier. But so was the world in which it operated. The constitutional upheavals of the 1860s were at an end. Many of the cohort of transnational republicans who had fought for the *Commune* had died in combat. Garibaldi's guerrilla campaign on behalf of the French Republic had had to be abandoned. The era of barricades was over. They were of little use in withstanding the onslaught of *Versaillais* soldiers, some newly equipped with machine guns. With the fall of the *Commune*, the transnational republican legacy had reached an ending.

Transnationalism had lost much of its point once the formation of states was no longer synonymous with the ambition to establish republics. Nationalism and republicanism were now separate. The nation-states formed in Italy and Germany came with hereditary monarchies and powerful aristocracies. Free trade had also begun to be challenged, culminating in Germany in a protective tariff, allying land and industry in an anti-liberal 'marriage of iron and rye'. The consolidation of states had also begun to impinge more directly upon the daily lives of citizens, whether in the form of elementary education or of military conscription. Conversely, the economic basis of cross-border trade union solidarity had shrunk in the face of depression.

In England, the political climate had also changed. According to *The Way We Live Now*, Trollope's bilious depiction of England around 1872, the self-confidence and liberality of the Palmerston era had gone. The 'honourable' traditions of the countryside had been submerged in a world dominated by the sordid machinations of international finance. Cosmopolitan adventurers of unknown origins, a plutocracy personified by Augustus Melmotte, dominated London society.

Karl's priorities had also changed. In the mid-1860s, he had fully expected both volumes of *Capital* to appear together. But a host of difficulties, both practical and theoretical, had obstructed this project. Certainly, his work for the International had occupied a large proportion of his time. But it also appeared that the nature of the project itself changed significantly in the years between 1867 and 1872. While he still stated that he 'must, after all, finally have done with *Das Kapital*', there was no mention of the accompanying second volume. In part, this was because the argument as originally conceived could no longer be sustained, but it was also because his thoughts about the global character of capitalism were changing. Perhaps the development of capitalism in Western Europe was a special case. Perhaps its expansion across the rest of the world could be avoided. That at least appeared to be the thought that governed his increasing interest in what might happen in Russia and other parts of the as yet pre-capitalist world.

12

Back to the Future

I. THE SECOND VOLUME OF *CAPITAL*[1]

With the ending of the political reform movement in Britain and the consolidation of an alliance between liberals and trade union leaders, pressure to get out the second volume ceased. The Irish troubles subsided. The response to the publication of the first volume was sluggish, and the only really enthusiastic response was that from Russia by followers of Chernyshevsky, who were not primarily interested in the crisis in the West. In France, after the disaster of the *Commune*, in the French translation of *Capital* Karl was keen to soften the edges of the English-based *Critique*. Not least, he was also relieved that the publication of the second volume could be deferred, since the intellectual problems which had inhibited him from bringing out the whole work originally had only increased.

In 1870, Karl succeeded in recasting almost half the manuscript of what became Volume II of *Capital*, but the treatment remained confined to abstractions, and thereafter little more was added beyond minor revisions.[2] In November 1871, Meissner, his Hamburg publisher, informed him that Volume I had almost sold out, and asked him to prepare a cheaper second edition. Between then and 1873, Karl did just that, spending most of his time preparing a revised second edition, including an attempt to simplify the argument of the first chapter. In 1872, admirers in St Petersburg embarked upon a Russian edition. The translation was begun by Hermann Lopatin and completed by Nicolai Danielson, and it proved a great success. At the same time, Karl signed a contract with Maurice Lachâtre to produce a French edition. It was to appear in instalments. In this form, Karl thought it would be 'more

accessible to the working class' and 'for me that consideration out-
weighs any other'.[3] The task was undertaken by Joseph Roy, the
translator of Feuerbach, and Karl initially wrote to his daughter that he
considered him 'a man perfectly suited to my purpose'. But the process
was very slow; Roy was compelled to work from Karl's handwritten
manuscript of the second German edition, and Karl found many passages unsatisfactory. He wrote to his Russian translator, Nicolai
Danielson, in May 1872 that 'Although the French edition – (the translation is by Mr. Roy, the translator of Feuerbach) – has been prepared
by a great expert in both languages, he has often translated too literally. I have therefore found myself compelled to re-write whole passages
in French, to make them palatable to the French public. It will be all the
easier later on to translate the book from French into English and the
Romance languages.'[4] Karl spent much time in the following two years
rewriting passages for the French translation, which only began to
appear in 1875. Slowness in correcting the translation together with
tasks left over from the removal of the International to New York
would anyway have caused delay in the appearance of the French edition. But these problems were compounded in the spring of 1873 by a
serious breakdown in Karl's health.

Alarm about Karl's condition became public at the end of June in
that year, when Maltman Barry, a radical Conservative and a supporter
of Karl, reported in the *Standard* that Karl was dangerously ill. Engels
had to reassure Karl's admirer Dr Kugelmann, who had read the news
in the *Frankfurter Zeitung*, that the report was an exaggeration. Nevertheless, the situation sounded serious enough. As Engels explained,
'from time to time, but to an increasing extent over a period of years
now, Marx has suffered from insomnia which he has always tried to
explain away with all sorts of unconvincing reasons e.g. a persistent
cough in the throat . . . he could not be brought to stop overworking
himself until finally a conspicuous pressure at the top of the head and
the insomnia increased to an unbearable point where even very powerful doses of chloral had no effect.'[5] It was a frustrating return to chronic
illness after a period in which he seemed to be on the road to recovery.
Back in April 1871, Engels had also tried to convince Kugelmann that
Karl's situation should not be seen 'in altogether too gloomy a light'. So
far as the insomnia, the cough, and his liver were concerned, Engels
had written then, 'you will understand that there can be no speedy cure

for an illness that, to my knowledge, has been more or less permanent for the last 26 years'. But he took cheer from the fact that the source of Karl's cough was 'solely in the larynx' and not in the lungs.

Engels was optimistic in 1871 because he believed that Karl was changing his way of life. While the excitement generated by the war and the *Commune* continued, Engels wrote, 'he has given up work on heavy theoretical matters and is living fairly rationally'. He even took one-and-a-half- to two-hour walks 'without my forcing him to' and sometimes did not 'drink a drop of beer for weeks on end'. A walk via Highgate to Hampstead, he concluded, 'is about 1½ German miles and involves going up and down several steep hills. And up on the top, there is more ozone than in the whole of Hanover.'[6]

It seems clear that it was not so much lack of physical exercise, but rather the need to confront theoretical difficulty that brought on headache attacks, insomnia and liver disease.[7] As Karl wrote to Friedrich Sorge on 4 August 1874, 'That damned liver complaint has made such headway that I was positively unable to continue the revision of the French translation (which actually amounts almost to complete rewriting).'[8] And on 12 August, writing to Nicolai Danielson, he added, 'I have since months suffered severely, and found out myself, for some time, even in a dangerous state of illness, consequent upon overwork. My head was so seriously affected, that a paralytic strike was to be apprehended, and even now I am not yet able to work more than a few hours.'[9] Most accounts have simply accepted that it was illness which prevented Karl from completing his life's work. It cannot be denied that during the last decade of Karl's life, he spent much of his time in pursuit of one health cure after another. But what this leaves out of account was the nightmare occasioned by Karl's desire to substantiate a theory which, without the Hegelian props he had employed in the 1850s, was impossible to prove.

In the *Grundrisse* in the 1850s, Karl had put forward the idea of 'the declining rate of profit' in relatively simplistic terms. But when he tried to write up the theory around 1864–5 (the manuscripts used by Engels for his edition of Volume III in 1894), doubts were already crowding in upon him. The supposedly simple operation of this 'law' was now so hedged in by 'counteracting tendencies' that it was unclear how it could exercise any terminal effect. All that could be claimed was that 'the law and its counteracting tendencies . . . breed overproduction, speculation crises and surplus capital alongside surplus population'.[10] It was also apparent that the processes of circulation and extended reproduction, which Karl had originally imagined in a form akin to the circular and spiral motions found in Hegel's *Science of Logic*, could no longer be employed without substantiation. Nor had he succeeded in refashioning and inserting these motions into an empirical narrative.

This failure touched centrally upon the question that *Capital*'s first serious readers were asking themselves. Was *Capital* the enunciation of a universal theory of development, which would affect all countries, or was it a historical account, whose relevance was primarily confined to Britain and Western Europe?[11] Karl could not find a way of reiterating his original theoretical position, but was equally resistant to any straightforward admission that he had changed his mind. For this reason, the furtive shifts of position he made had to be disinterred from the qualifications found in the text of the German second edition or the French translation.

Karl was relieved to evade or postpone explicit discussion of these questions for as long as possible. But they would have to be addressed when the second volume was published. Moreover, the problem grew worse as time went on. When *Capital* was originally being composed in the 1860s, it might have been enough to point to ways in which the capitalist mode of production was already being superseded and place reliance upon an imminent political moment, which for a short time seemed to be developing in the mid-1860s. But now that moment was definitely passed, and increasing pressure would therefore have to be placed upon some grandiose structural contradiction in the overall functioning of the capitalist mode of production. During the 1870s, he preferred to spend his time revising the text of Volume I or assisting Eleanor with her translation of Lissagaray's *History of the Commune of 1871*. No doubt the sicknesses were genuine, but it is clear too that they also provided protective cover for postponement of the day of reckoning.

This is suggested as well by Karl's irritation whenever he was asked directly about the contents of the second volume, as happened in the case of his most persistent admirer, Dr Kugelmann. Karl had stayed with Kugelmann in Hanover when Volume I was being prepared for publication in 1867. Kugelmann's daughter, Franziska, recalled that her father thought Karl 'one hundred years ahead of his time'. So his impatience to see what was in the second volume was not surprising. Karl's reaction had become increasingly defensive. In May 1874, for example, after thanking Kugelmann and his family for their interest in his progress, he continued, 'But you do me an injustice if you ascribe my failure to write to any other cause than a shaky state of health, which continually interrupts my work, then goads me up to make up for the time lost by neglecting all other duties (letters included) and finally puts a man out of humour and makes him disinclined to activity.' Karl looked forward to meeting Kugelmann in Carlsbad, where his doctor, Gumpert from Manchester, had recommended that he go for a cure. But in the meantime, on the question of the book, he wrote that 'While I was unable to write, I worked through a lot of important material for the second volume. But I cannot start on its final composition until the French edition is completed and my health fully restored'.[12]

Later that summer, Kugelmann arranged for Karl and Eleanor to join his family at the Hotel Germania in Carlsbad. But the holiday was not a success. Karl found 'unbearable' the way Kugelmann 'incessantly pours out his solemn long-winded balderdash in his deep voice' and was incensed by 'this arch-pedant' who constantly railed against his wife for her 'failure to comprehend his Faustian nature with its aspiration to a higher world outlook'. More prosaically, Eleanor was shocked by the way in which Gertrude Kugelmann was berated every minute by her husband as a woman without money ungrateful for all his *Wohltaten* (kindnesses) to her. According to Eleanor's account, Karl became 'the unwilling listener of a most abominable scene (for the rooms are only separated by a door)' and was compelled to request to be moved to the floor above.[13]

There is no reason to doubt this account. But there was also another side to the story, of particular note given Kugelmann's interest in the progress of *Capital*. Recalling her holiday as a seventeen-year-old, Franziska Kugelmann wrote in 1926 that during a long walk Karl and Kugelmann had quarrelled in a way 'which was never smoothed down'. Kugelmann had tried to persuade him to refrain from all political propaganda and complete the third book of *Capital* before anything else.[14]

A year later, in October 1875, Engels wrote to Wilhelm Bracke that Karl had returned from Carlsbad 'a completely different man, strong, invigorated, cheerful and healthy, and will soon be able to get down seriously to work again'.[15] In the following year, Engels informed Dr

Kugelmann that 'work on the second volume will be started again in the next few days'.[16] In 1878, Karl wrote to Danielson, his Russian translator, promising him the manuscript of the second volume as soon as it was ready, but that would 'hardly be before the end of 1879'.[17] In April 1879, however, Bismarck's anti-socialist laws provided Karl with an official reason for indefinite postponement: 'I am obliged to tell you (*cela est tout à fait confidentiel* [this in strict confidence] that I have been informed from Germany, my second volume *could not be published* so long as the present régime was maintained in its present severity.'[18] From time to time, Karl made attempts to return to the second volume. In July 1878, he started a fair copy, but after seven pages he gave up and never seems to have returned to the task.

In the last seven years of his life, Karl became increasingly secretive about his intellectual preoccupations. He stopped talking to Engels about his work, even though his friend had moved to London and now lived round the corner. In 1883, just after Karl's death, Engels was shocked to discover how little further work had been done on the second volume. At the end of August, later that year, he wrote to Bebel: 'As soon as I am back I shall get down to Volume 2 in real earnest and that is an enormous task. Alongside parts that have been completely finished are others that are merely sketched out, the whole being a *brouillon* [sketch] with the exception of perhaps two chapters.' Engels went on to complain about the disordered jumble of quotations and the handwriting, 'which certainly cannot be deciphered by anyone but *me*, and then only with difficulty'. He also posed the obvious question: 'You ask why I of all people should not have been told how far the thing had got. It is quite simple; had I known, I should have pestered him night and day until it was all finished and printed. And Marx knew that better than anyone else.'[19]

2. THE FORTUNES OF A FAMILY

In 1874, Karl's involvement in the winding-up of the International came to an end. Around the same time, Engels reported that there was no further reason for concern about French refugees from the *Commune*: 'we are now almost entirely rid of them'.[20] The Marx home was no longer a refuge or gathering point for radical exiles. In 1875, the family moved to a smaller house, 41 Maitland Park Road in Kentish Town. Sundays were still a time when friends were welcome to visit.

Karl himself kept mainly to his study. Life was quieter and less fraught with political tension. The change came as a great relief to Jenny. Three years earlier, in a letter to Liebknecht and his wife, she had expressed her admiration for their 'fortitude, tact and skill' in standing up to the public outcry in response to their rejection of the Franco-Prussian War and their recognition of the Paris *Commune*. She had gone on to describe her own experience, and to express her frustrations as a politically engaged woman:

> In all these struggles we women have the harder part to bear, because it is the lesser one. A man draws strength from his struggle with the world outside, and is invigorated by the sight of the enemy, be their number legion. We remain sitting at home, darning socks. That does nothing to dispel our fears and the gnawing day-to-day petty worries slowly but surely sap our spirit. I can say this from over thirty years' experience and can certainly claim that I am not one to lose heart easily. Now I have grown too old to hope for much and the recent terrible events have completely shattered my peace of mind.

The Paris *Commune* had placed a colossal strain on their lives:

> You cannot imagine what we have had to endure here in London since the fall of the Commune. All the nameless misery, the suffering without end! And on top of that the almost unbearable work on behalf of the International.

She was bitter about the fate that Karl had endured. As long as Karl had covered up the quarrelling between the sections and kept them apart, he spared the International from ridicule, kept himself out of the limelight, and in consequence 'the rabble remained silent'.

> But now that his enemies have dragged him into the light of day, have put his name in the forefront of attention, the whole pack have joined forces, and police and democrats alike all bay the same refrain about his 'despotic nature, his craving for authority and his ambition!' How much better it would have been, and how much happier he would be, if he had just gone on working quietly and developed the theory of struggle for those in the fight.[21]

With these strains behind her, she was able to find her own voice. Her passion was the theatre, and she was particularly enthusiastic for Henry Irving and his productions of *Hamlet* in October 1874 and *Macbeth* in September 1875. Her reviews and a number of smaller pieces appeared in the *Frankfurter Zeitung* from 1875. Jenny's interest in drama also found an outlet in the Dogberry, a private Shakespeare reading club, whose subscriptions provided front-row seats at Irving first nights. The club often met at the Marx house, where members joined in play-readings. On occasion, Karl and Engels also took part.

While the relations between Jenny and Engels always remained awkward, as is suggested by the formal terms in which they continued to address each other, an unlikely friendship developed between Jenny and the illiterate Lizzie Burns, after the Engels household moved to London. Lizzie's health was declining – she died of a tumour in 1878 – and Engels' main solution was to expose her as much as possible to sea air and different places. Jenny proposed that she and Lizzie go together on a seaside holiday in 1873, and in 1875 they went together to Shanklin in the Isle of Wight and then on to Ramsgate. Each morning, Engels took the two ladies to the railway station bar, where he treated them to a small glass of port before leaving them to themselves for the rest of the day.[22]

In 1877, Jenny's own health began to deteriorate. She went to Manchester, stayed with Engels' friend Sam Moore, and consulted Dr Gumpert, who diagnosed a carcinoma. In the winter of 1878–9, her condition became worse. But perhaps because she also felt more self-fulfilled in this period, accounts of her in her last years stress her capacity for self-mockery, her 'bright spirit and great heart'.[23]

The relationship between Jenny and her daughters, particularly Eleanor, appears to have been intense but intermittent. Most of the day-to-day management of the household had been left to Lenchen. Jenny was troubled by the fact that all her actual or prospective sons-in-law were French, and further that as a result of the student radicalism of the last years of the Empire of Napoléon III, followed by the war and the *Commune*, there were many sources of potential conflict between them. Laura had married Paul Lafargue in April 1868. Jenny became engaged to Charles Longuet in March 1872 and married him on 9 October. Writing to Liebknecht in May 1872, Jenny had admitted that 'I cannot contemplate their union without great uneasiness and would really have preferred it if Jenny's choice had fallen (for a change) on an Englishman or a German, instead of a French man, who of course possesses all the charming qualities of his nation, but is not free of their foibles and inadequacies ... I cannot help being afraid that, as a political woman, Jenny will be exposed to all the anxieties and torments inseparable from it.'[24] Nevertheless, she wrote, 'he is a very gifted man and he is good, honest and decent'. She also considered that 'the harmony of opinions and convictions between the young couple (i.e. their lack of religious affiliations) is certainly a guarantee of their future happiness'.[25] Engels agreed that he was a 'very kindly companion'.[26]

Longuet had been a fellow student with Lafargue, although three years older. Born in Caen in 1839, of a conservative bourgeois landowning family, he had become active in the French branch of the International, and edited its anti-Bonapartist student paper, *La Rive gauche*, and was imprisoned for eight months in 1866. He translated into French Karl's 'Inaugural Address' to the IWMA, and his *Civil War in France*. In the *Commune*, he had served as a member of its Labour Committee and as editor of its official journal, only narrowly managing to escape in the repression that followed. Arriving as a penniless refugee in London, he was unsuccessful in the attempt to secure private tutoring in Oxford, but in 1874 was appointed an Assistant Master in French at King's College, University of London. Jenny, despite her pregnancy, worked as a governess to the Manning family in 1873, and advertised lessons in singing and elocution. Her health had always been precarious and her first child died in 1874. But in the following years she produced five more children, the last barely a year before her death at the age of thirty-eight in 1883.

During their years of exile in London, the relationship between the Marx family and Paul and Laura Lafargue was a source of anxiety. But in this case, the burden was mainly borne by Engels. In the first years of their marriage in Paris, Laura had borne three children, but only Étienne ('Schnaps') had lived to the age of three, the other two dying in their first year. Despite gaining relevant medical qualifications, Paul refused to practise as a doctor. Much to the disappointment of the Marx parents, once in England, after activity in Bordeaux on behalf of the *Commune* and in Spain on behalf of the International, Paul devoted himself to a series of business ventures, which failed largely because of his impatience and inattention to detail. In various partnerships, he attempted to establish a business in photolithography using new techniques. Jenny Marx remarked in a letter to Sorge in 1877 that he should have stuck to being a doctor. 'Their business, printing by the *procédé* Gillot hasn't been doing very well.' There had been some improvement. But 'Lafargue, who always sees everything through rose-tinted spectacles, is now hoping for a big JOB.'[27] Needless to say, once again the venture failed and they were bailed out by Engels. Engels himself two years before – perhaps with the Lafargues in mind – had directed his criticism at the French refugees: 'The French refugees are in utter chaos. They have fallen out with each other and with everyone else for *quite personal reasons*, money matters for the most part and we are now almost entirely rid of them. They all want to live without doing any real work, their heads are full of imagined inventions which would bring in millions if only someone would enable them to exploit their discoveries, a matter of just a few pounds. But anyone who is naïve enough to take them at their word will be cheated of his money and denounced as a bourgeois into the bargain.'[28] Childless and always particularly indulgent to members of the Marx family, Engels never refused their requests, which went on to the end of his life. Between 1874 and 1880, Engels responded to almost forty Lafargue requests, which became increasingly frequent as the years went by.[29] Even Engels was sometimes taken aback by their importunity. 'How can I advise you on business', he wrote to Lafargue in 1880, 'if you give me all the information afterwards?'[30]

If there was a crisis in the Marx family in the years after the International, it was occasioned not by the two elder girls, but by their younger sister. It also seems clear that it was this family crisis, rather than simple overwork, which induced in Karl headaches and insomnia, together with his perennial liver sickness, in the spring of 1873. The crisis concerned the ambitions and desires of Karl's youngest daughter, the eighteen-year-old Eleanor, or 'Tussy', and her parents' determination to oppose them. Whatever their reservations about the marriages of Laura and Jenny, the Marx parents had not actively obstructed these unions.

In Tussy's case, their attitude was different. Around the spring of 1872, she had become engaged to Prosper-Olivier Lissagaray, another French exile living in London. Lissagaray was a radical journalist and ardent supporter of the democratic and social republic. Already thirty-three years old, he was famed as a heroic combatant in the Paris

Commune and a flamboyant personality. He was not, however, attached to any party and saw no reason to become so. This may have been one of the reasons why he and Paul Lafargue so greatly disliked each other.[31] Eleanor complained to Jenny Longuet that when the Lafargues coincided with Lissagaray on a visit to the Marx household, the Lafargues refused to shake hands.[32] Both Karl and Jenny disapproved of the match. Jenny avoided referring to Lissagaray in her correspondence, while, except on one occasion, Karl mentioned him only in connection with his *History of the Commune* of 1877.

In the spring of 1873, Karl and Eleanor spent three weeks in Brighton. When Karl returned to London, Eleanor stayed in Brighton and with the help of Arnold Ruge, Karl's old antagonist now living there, secured a job in a 'seminary' for young ladies run by the Misses Hall. Jenny Marx worried that Eleanor would not be strong enough for 'the treadmill of a boarding school', as her chest was weak, her back ached and her appetite was 'wretched'. Karl in the meantime, on Engels' advice, had gone to Manchester to consult Gumpert. The doctor diagnosed his problem as a 'certain elongation of the liver', and suggested a visit to Carlsbad as the best cure.

While Karl was in Manchester, Jenny travelled to Brighton and found that Lissagaray had been visiting Eleanor there. She decided not to tell Karl. From Manchester, Karl wrote to both Eleanor and Lissagaray. What he said is not known since many of these letters were destroyed. But in a letter to Engels Karl concluded that 'for the moment, Mr. L. will have to make the best of a bad job'.[33] In the meantime, Engels showed Karl's letter to Eleanor to Jenny Marx. It was clear that in relation to Eleanor's fate, husband and wife were not straightforwardly confiding in each other. Karl fretted that 'the damnable thing is that for the child's sake I have to tread very considerately and cautiously'. On the other hand, Mrs Marx had shocked Miss Hall, by proposing that Eleanor leave her teaching job mid-term and accompany Lenchen to Germany on a visit to her dying sister.

Eleanor resisted the pressure and remained in Brighton until the end of term. But she was back in London by September, and in November father and daughter travelled together for a three-week cure in what Jenny described as 'aristocratic German Harrogate'. Eleanor was prescribed complete rest and the use of 'Kissingen water', Karl was to take vigorous exercise. Since Gumpert had forbidden any work, he filled up the hours of inaction by playing chess with Tussy and reading Sainte-Beuve's book on Chateaubriand, 'an author I have always disliked'.[34]

In the following year, all the tensions returned. On 19 January 1874, while making light of 'my occasional illness', Karl reported to Kugelmann that the carbuncles had reappeared.[35] This, together with the return of headaches and insomnia, compelled him to spend around three weeks in Ramsgate in April and May.[36] At the same time, Eleanor's desire to see Lissagaray remained as powerful as ever. On 23 March 1874, she wrote to her father requesting permission to see 'L.' again. 'When I was so very ill at Brighton (during a week I fainted two or three times a day), L. came to see me, and each time left me stronger and happier; and the more able to bear the rather heavy load on my shoulders.'[37] In July 1874, Tussy was once more seriously ill for three weeks, and was tended by Elizabeth Garret Anderson, the first woman to have qualified as a physician in Britain. By 14 August, Karl reported that she was feeling 'much better; her appetite is growing in geometric PROPORTION'. But, he went on, 'it is the characteristic feature of these women's ailments, in which hysteria plays a part; you have to pretend not to notice that the invalid is again living on earthly sustenance. This too becomes unnecessary once recovery is complete.'[38]

A visit to Carlsbad was arranged and elaborate preparations were made, including an (unsuccessful) application on Karl's part for British nationality. Therefore, from the middle of August until 21 September, he and Tussy stayed in Carlsbad's Hotel Germania. The stay was spoilt by Karl's quarrel with Kugelmann, but he was pleased with Carlsbad and repeated the trip for a month alone in the following year. On that occasion, he was fortunate to meet a Russian aristocrat and land historian, Maxim Kovalevsky. Kovalevsky lived in London, and remained in frequent contact with Karl thereafter. In 1876, Karl travelled to Carlsbad once more with Eleanor. The journey was attended by a number of misadventures, in particular an involuntary stay-over in Nuremberg, where the town was full, not only on account of a millers' and bakers' convention but because of 'people from all over the world who were on their way to state musician Wagner's Festival of Fools at Bayreuth'. He reported that 'Tussychen' had been rather unwell on the journey, but was visibly recovering.[39]

In 1877, the choice was Neuenahr, a cheaper resort in the Black Forest. As Karl explained to Engels, 'As you know, my wife suffers from serious digestive disturbances and since I shall in any case be taking Tussy, who has had another nasty attack, my wife would take great exception to being left behind.'[40] On arrival, both he and his wife were under the care of Dr Schmitz, who reassured Karl that his liver was no longer enlarged: 'the digestive apparatus is somewhat disordered. But the actual trouble is of a nervous kind.' Jenny was required to take medicine before 'her trouble got worse', while 'Tussychen's appetite is improving, which is the best sign with her'.[41]

When her mother's decline became palpable in the summer of 1881, Tussy collapsed again. Alone in London, since Karl had taken his sick wife to visit their grandchildren at the Longuets in Argenteuil, Tussy was not only unable to sleep, but had also stopped eating. The situation became so alarming that her friend Dollie Maitland summoned Karl back from France. Karl reported to Jenny Longuet in Argenteuil that Tussy was looking 'pale and thin, since weeks she eats almost nothing'. Her 'nervous system' was 'in a state of utter dejection; hence continuous sleeplessness, trembling of the hands, neuralgic convulsions of the face, etc.'[42] The impending death of her mother brought about a breakdown. She was twenty-seven, uncertain whether she could make a career as an actor, and without a partner, since Lissagaray had returned to France after the amnesty of 1880. As she later wrote to her friend, Olive Schreiner, this turning point in her life finally prompted her to break off an engagement which after 'long miserable years' had become a burden. It had distanced her from her father and she felt guilt about the possibility that her mother died thinking her 'hard and cruel'. Her sorrow was mixed with anger at the thought that her mother had never guessed that 'to save her and father sorrow I had sacrificed the best, freshest years of my life'.[43]

A month after Jenny Marx's death, Karl and Tussy went for a rest to Ventnor. But the visit was not a success. Karl wrote to Laura that 'My companion (this *strictly between ourselves*) eats practically nothing; suffers badly from nervous tics; reads and writes all day long . . . She is very taciturn and, INDEED, seemingly endures staying with me simply out of a sense of duty, as a self-sacrificing martyr.'[44] Many aspects to this sad saga remain unclear, since much of the relevant correspondence was destroyed. Why did the Marx parents so disapprove of Lissagaray? Was it just because of his age? That might have explained Karl's prohibition in 1873, when Tussy was still eighteen, but that does not explain why the prohibition apparently continued and (but we don't really know) seems to have been accepted by Eleanor.

Political difference does not offer a solution either. Karl didn't feel comfortable with either of his sons-in-law. In November 1882, he exclaimed, 'Longuet is the last Proudhonist and Lafargue is the last Bakuninist. *Que le diable les emporte!* [May the Devil take them!].'[45] Longuet never abandoned his Proudhonism, but supplemented it with 'Marxist' ideas. In the 1880s, when he returned to France after the amnesty, he joined his friend Clemenceau and they worked together on the radical republican journal *La Justice*. Made conscious by his background of the strength and conservatism of the peasantry in France, his socialism became ever more moderate and he rejected the need for an independent workers' party.

Lafargue appeared much closer in outlook to Karl; he was self-avowedly 'Marxist'.[46] Yet the mixture of left-bank anti-religious materialism, the *Communist Manifesto* and Engels' *Anti-Dühring* was only nominally similar to Karl's approach. As Engels wrote to Bernstein in 1882, 'Marxism' in France was 'an altogether peculiar product'. It was in that context that Karl had once said to Lafargue, 'if anything is certain, it is that I myself am not a Marxist'.[47]

Conversely, Karl not only admired Lissagaray's book on the *Commune*, but spent much of 1877 and 1878 assisting Tussy in her translation of the book into English, and supervising its German translation and publication. Tussy apparently acceded to this appropriation of her relationship and, in the English-language edition, stated that she was 'loth to alter the work in any way' since 'it had been entirely revised and corrected by my father. I want it to remain as he knew it.'[48]

Whatever Lissagaray's original desires, he like Tussy acceded to Karl's pressure, and by the time of his return to France in 1880 the relationship was over. Eleanor was not only unable to confront her father on occasion, but remained a wholly uncritical admirer. That was why it was so upsetting when she eventually learnt that Freddy Demuth was Karl's unacknowledged son. She refused to believe it and maintained that Engels was lying. But the dying Engels stuck to his statement. She was shattered and wept bitterly. But Engels turned to his friend Sam Moore and said, 'Tussy wants to make an idol of her father.'[49]

3. THE ADVENT OF SOCIAL DEMOCRACY IN GERMANY

During the 1870s, Karl's intellectual reputation as the author of *Capital* steadily increased. The argument that capital was based upon the buying and selling of labour power explained how the equality in exchange highlighted by the apologists of commercial society was nevertheless compatible with the exploitation of wage-workers and the growth of inequality. *Capital* presented a graphic, yet sober-minded analysis of the conflict within the factory, and a horrific picture of the condition of workers in different industries. It was supported by a well-documented account of the historical development of the capitalist mode of production. At last, it seemed, the socialist condemnation of prevailing economic conditions depended on more than moral denunciation or utopian speculation alone; it was now based upon economic analysis and historical prediction. In Germany, the first edition sold well; a second edition appeared in 1872, and a third was prepared for 1883. French and Russian editions appeared in 1872 and 1875. The Russian edition, with a print run of 3,000 copies, sold exceptionally well. According to Karl, it was 'an extraordinary success' and he expected a second edition in 1873.[50]

Few, however, were attracted to Karl's politics. His original fixation on the activities of the Revolutionary Convention of 1792–3 belonged to the decades before 1848. He still dreamed of a Manichaean battle between emancipation and reaction engulfing the whole of Europe; in such a war, one of the major states, forced to the left in a war with Russia, would become enmeshed in a process of revolutionary turmoil and begin the process of emancipation. Until the late 1870s, he continued to hope for a European war. In August 1874, he wrote to Friedrich Sorge in Hoboken: 'General European conditions are such as to increasingly wage a *general European war*. We shall have to pass through it before there can be any thought of decisive overt activity on the part of the European working class.'[51] The only other political groupings still intent on replaying the political struggles of the French Revolution were the Blanquists, many of whom were exiles in London. But once the French Republic granted an amnesty to ex-*Communards* in 1880, support for their position declined precipitously.[52] Younger revolutionary activists were no longer drawn to the idea of a centralized state, however revolutionary. They were attracted instead to communal, federal or anti-state visions of socialism associated with Proudhon or Bakunin.

In the 1870s, Karl's reputation as an analyst of capital sat uneasily beside his notoriety as an advocate of what was considered as an outdated and unacceptable form of politics. Whatever his subsequent clarifications, he was stuck with the fame that he had acquired as the alleged 'Chief' of the International and the instigator of the *Commune*. But such fame had its costs. Henry Hyndman recalled that in 1880 'It is scarcely too much to say that Marx was practically unknown to the English public, except as a dangerous and even desperate advocate of revolution, whose organisation of the "International" had been one of the causes of the horrible Commune of Paris, which all decent, respectable people shuddered at and thought of with horror.'[53] In his book *England for All*, Hyndman, who had read *Capital* in French and had adopted its picture of the suffering of the working people 'under our present landlord and capitalist system', did not refer to Karl by name. He wrote instead about 'the work of a great thinker and original writer, which will, I trust, shortly be made accessible to the majority of my countrymen'.[54] Similarly, in France in 1880, when Karl's son-in-law Paul Lafargue, together with Jules Guesde, drew upon Karl for a preamble to the founding programme of the *Fédération du Parti des Travailleurs Socialistes*, Guesde asked Benoît Malon to take responsibility for its authorship.[55]

In the *Eighteenth Brumaire* Karl had dismissed the 1848 revolutions as 'comedy', no longer the true bourgeois revolution of the past, nor yet the proletarian revolution of the future. He saw them as a farcical replay of the past. He was therefore slow to recognize how 1848 had changed the character of popular political participation on the European mainland. He was suspicious about demands for manhood suffrage and showed little awareness of its capacity to mobilize new types of political engagement. This was another aspect of his difficulty in according any independence to the political sphere, except where there was a majority working-class population. He was still prone to dismiss universal suffrage as an illusion comparable to, or even produced by, the notion of the equality of exchanges in the economy.

Living in London, writing for the *New-York Daily Tribune* and interacting with British trade unionists in the IWMA had led Karl to revise this position, especially in relation to England after 1867. In an interview published in an American journal in 1871, Karl had stated that universal suffrage might enable English workers to achieve political power without a violent revolution.[56] Similarly, at the conclusion of the Hague Congress of the International in September 1872, Karl stated, 'We know that the institutions, customs and traditions in the different countries must be taken into account; and we do not deny the existence of countries like America, England, and if I knew your institutions better I might add Holland, where the workers may achieve their aims by peaceful means.' But that did not apply to 'most countries on the Continent'. There 'It is force which must be the lever of our revolution; it is force which will have to be resorted to for a time in order to establish the rule of the workers.'[57]

Following the 'comedy' of 1848, Karl had been suspicious of the political developments in Central and Southern Europe at the end of the 1850s. He dismissed the Italian *Risorgimento* and was sceptical about the beginning of the 'new era' in Germany. Yet the 'new era' indicated how 1848 had changed political expectations. In Germany, its starting point was neither a secret society born in exile like the League of the Just, nor a clearly defined revolutionary party like the Communist League. Instead, a new movement had grown out of the Workers' Educational Associations (*Arbeiterbildungsvereine*), which had flourished in 1848 and were revived again after 1858, together with various liberal and democratic organizations ranging from the National Association (*Nationalverein*) to the German People's Party (*Deutsche Volkspartei*).

The pro-Prussian liberal National Association had counted on the adhesion of these Workers' Associations. But it was not prepared to concede demands for their political representation. In response to this rejection, Ferdinand Lassalle urged the Workers' Educational Associations in 1862–3 to reject collaboration with liberal and even democratic parties, and instead to form a party of their own: the General German Workers' Association (*Allgemeiner Deutscher Arbeiterverein*), the first independent workers' party in Europe.

Outside Prussia, and particularly in South Germany, most of the associations felt a stronger affinity to the German People's Party, in its opposition to German unification under Prussian dominance, and pressed for a federal and democratic state. They formed the Union of German Workers' Educational Associations (*Verband Deutscher*

Arbeitervereine), which remained closely allied to the People's Party. In 1868, however, Wilhelm Liebknecht and August Bebel urged the Union's congress to affiliate with the International Working Men's Association. This led to a break with the People's Party and the formation of the Social Democratic Labour Party (*Sozialdemokratische Arbeiterpartei*) at Eisenach in 1869. By the end of the 1860s, therefore, there were two competing workers' parties – the Lassalleans and the Eisenachers – both with a socialist orientation. These parties shared the liberal and democratic principles of 1848, including parliamentary government, universal suffrage, a people's militia, free association and the separation of church and state. One indication of this shift was the disappearance of the word 'communism' and its replacement by the terms 'socialism' or 'social democracy'.

Lassalle was seven years younger than Karl, and his formative political experience had been the German revolutions of 1848, in which he had been imprisoned for six months. While Karl mocked the February Revolution, Lassalle proclaimed 24 February 1848 to be the dawn of a new historical epoch.[58] There had been three epochs in the history of the world, he argued, each governed by a ruling idea, expressed in all the social and political arrangements of the time, and embodied in a particular class or estate. In the Middle Ages, the idea of possession of landed property had been the precondition of feudal rule and this had permeated all its institutions. That epoch ended in 1789, replaced by the supremacy of bourgeois property and the rule of capital.

1789 had been the revolution of the 'Third Estate'. But 1848 was the revolution of the 'Fourth Estate'. The 'Third Estate' had claimed to represent the claims of humanity, but in fact represented the political ambitions of the bourgeoisie, satisfied by free competition and 'the night-watchman state'. Any claim to universality by the feudal nobility or the 'Third Estate' was contradicted by their sectional self-interest. The claims of the workers, on the other hand, were universal. Lassalle drew upon the *Communist Manifesto* (to Karl's annoyance): workers, unlike the higher classes, had no particular privileges to defend. But what this meant was not so much that they had 'nothing to lose but their chains', as that workers embodied a moral as well as a material principle. The concerns of workers were the concerns of humanity. This was why the fundamental principle underpinning the formation of an independent workers' party was the demand for *universal* manhood suffrage, accompanied by direct and secret elections.

Lassalle's case for the formation of an independent workers' party was fuelled by his distrust of the liberal middle class. The middle classes had betrayed the 'Fourth Estate' in 1848; in 1862, in the constitutional battle over control of the military, they had again shown themselves incapable of breaking the power of the Prussian absolutist regime. Despite the urgings of political economists and social reformers like Friedrich Bastiat and Hermann Schulze-Delitzsch, the economic as well as the political case for a middle-class liberal alliance was weak. The interests of workers and employers were not identical. Aided by savings banks, consumer cooperatives and providence societies, individuals might benefit from self-help, but this could not be true of the working classes as a whole. For, at a collective level, the efforts of workers to better themselves would always be thwarted by what Lassalle called 'the iron law of wages' – an argument drawn from Ricardo to the effect that wages could never advance much beyond subsistence.

This was another reason why nothing short of universal suffrage would suffice; and it could succeed, if it were pushed forward by a vigorous and large-scale campaign, like that waged by the Anti-Corn League in England. Once this was achieved, a state based upon universal suffrage and dependent upon workers' support could lead the way to workers' emancipation, implemented by state-supported producer-cooperatives. Such a state would eliminate the distinction between employers and employed and open the way to universal education and cultural flourishing. *Universal* suffrage would be the means by which this state would be brought into being. Anything short of this would be a 'lie', a form of 'pseudo-constitutionalism, in which the state declared itself to be a constitutional state, but in reality remained an absolutist state'.[59] Lassalle was elected leader of the ADAV for a five-year term, and the Party recruited 4,600 members, but in August 1864 he was mortally wounded in a duel.

Whatever the complexity of his feelings of animosity towards Lassalle (a mixture of apprehension, envy and contempt), Karl could not but acknowledge Lassalle's achievement. In 1868, he wrote to Lassalle's successor, Johann Baptist von Schweitzer, that the Lassallean Association was 'formed in a period of reaction ... After fifteen years of slumber, Lassalle – and this remains his immortal service – re-awakened the workers' movement in Germany.' But he went on to criticize the split with Schulze-Delitzsch, the advocacy of state-aided cooperatives, the conflation of 'the state' with the existing Prussian state and the adoption of the Chartist call for universal suffrage.[60]

The Eisenach Party was more acceptable, both because it was resolutely anti-Prussian and because Wilhelm Liebknecht, a London friend of Karl's family from the 1850s, was one of its leaders. But even in London he was not an altogether reliable political ally. In 1865, Engels complained to Karl that 'Liebknecht simply cannot help putting his foot in it' whenever he had to act on his own initiative. But he admitted that 'grumbling will not help matters' since 'at the moment he is the only reliable link we have in Germany'.[61]

In other words, throughout the 1860s and 1870s, Karl's German contacts were few and his influence upon the internal development of either of these parties was slight. The Eisenach Party had affiliated to the IWMA after its split from the Saxon People's Party in 1868. But this did not affect its continued commitment to the ideals of the *Volksstaat* (people's state). Both the Lassalleans and the Eisenachers believed that workers' emancipation would be brought about by the democratization of the state, and that this would be achieved through the ballot box. Similarly, although the Eisenachers were not committed to Lassalle's 'iron law of wages', both parties advocated state-supported cooperatives.

The major disagreement was that between supporters and opponents of a Prussian-dominated Bismarckian *Reich*. Lassallean support for Bismarck's national policy was countered by the bitterly anti-Prussian politics of the Eisenachers. The argument came to a head during the Franco-Prussian War of 1870–71. Was this a war of national defence? In the *Reichstag* of the North German Confederation, Schweitzer of the Lassalleans and Fritzsche of the Eisenachers voted in favour of the war loan, while Liebknecht and August Bebel, the future leader of the Social Democratic Party, abstained.

The course of the war itself, however, brought about a gradual abatement of hostility between the two parties and helped to prepare the path towards their unification at Gotha five years later. For whatever their initial positions, following the defeat and abdication of Napoléon III, and the proposed annexation of Alsace and Lorraine, both Eisenachers and Lassalleans turned against the war.

Both parties also declared their solidarity with the Paris *Commune* on 18 March 1871. In this situation, they briefly converged with Karl, who, whatever his reservations, in his capacity as Secretary of the IWMA declared the *Commune* to be 'the form at last discovered under which to work out the economical emancipation of labour'.[62] At the end of May 1871, reacting to the week of massacres which accompanied the suppression of the Parisian revolt, August Bebel in the *Reichstag* expressed his solidarity with the *Communards*, and declared that 'before many decades have gone by the battle-cry of the Parisian proletariat – "War on palaces, peace to cottages, death to poverty and idleness!" – will be the battle-cry of the entire European proletariat.'[63] As a result of socialist support for the *Commune*, the distance between the social-democratic and liberal parties in the new *Reich* increased. Lurid pictures of the excesses of the *Commune* shocked the propertied classes, and were exploited by Bismarck to strengthen his alliance with National Liberals. But solidarity with the Paris *Commune* at the moment of its suppression – however shocking to the propertied classes – did not impinge immediately upon the domestic strategy of German socialism. The question of unification between the two parties was raised by the Lassalleans in 1872. But the dissension between the two parties over the national question and the role of the state remained too great. As Bebel wrote, however, 'what did not ensue as a result of friendly negotiations was finally achieved by persecution'.[64]

The establishment of the Bismarckian *Reich* was now a *fait accompli*. The scale of the repression of socialists, whether Lassalleans or Eisenachers, was greatly increased and Lassallean hopes of state socialism correspondingly diminished. Potential friction between the two parties was further reduced by the resignation of Schweitzer, Lassalle's successor as President of the ADAV. Finally, with the onset of economic depression from 1873 pressure for more concerted action in strikes, and housing agitation, increased among the rank and file. As a result, it was possible for the two parties to unite behind a single programme at Gotha in May 1875.

Karl reacted with fury to the agreement, which he considered to be an abject surrender to the Lassalleans. It was true that crucial passages in the programme were not clearly thought out or were ambiguously expressed – though this was due more to Liebknecht than the Lassalleans themselves. Karl assailed the loose formulation of a labour theory of value, attacked its use of 'labour' instead of 'labour power', and interrogated the ambiguity of its use of the term 'free state' and its designation of non-proletarian classes as 'one reactionary mass'. He also reiterated his objections to the familiar Lassallean nostrums: state-aided producer-cooperatives, the 'iron law' of wages and the fail-ure to mention trade unions. He wrote to Wilhelm Bracke that once the Congress of the Union of German Workers' Educational Associa-tions was over, he and Engels would 'entirely disassociate' themselves from the 'programme of principles' and would 'have nothing to do with it'.[65]

These were reasonable objections. But in a larger political sense, they failed to confront the point of the exercise, which was no longer to enunciate the doctrine of a revolutionary sect like the Communist League, but to construct a credible electoral programme for a mass-based parliamentary social-democratic party. Karl made no attempt to understand the aspirations of post-1848 social democracy on the Conti-nent. Instead, he dismissed discussion of 'the old democratic litany familiar to all – universal suffrage, direct legislation, popular rights, a people's militia, etc.' as if, in the Bismarckian *Reich*, these demands had 'already been implemented'.

Finally, instead of discussing the democratic transformation of the state, he leapt forward to a notional period of revolutionary transition between capitalist and communist society, in which 'the state can be nothing but *the revolutionary dictatorship of the proletariat*'.[66] Later on, Engels similarly attempted to redefine the democratic republic as a 'specific form of the dictatorship of the proletariat', a proposal which also suggested an ambition quite remote from the social-democratic ideals or political realities of the 1860s and 1870s.[67] Not surprisingly, both the harsh criticism and threats to withdraw were ignored.[68]

4. THE STRANGE GENESIS OF EUROPEAN 'MARXISM'

Nothing could underline more strongly the marginality of Karl's ideas about politics and party in the new social-democratic constellation of the 1870s. Yet only ten years later the dominant discourse of the leader-ship of the Social Democratic Party had become a form of 'Marxism'.

Furthermore, between the end of the 1870s and the beginning of the 1890s, there sprang up in every major European country groups and embryonic parties that modelled themselves on the German Social Democratic Party, and identified with the ideas of 'Marxism'. The French Workers' Party (*Parti Ouvrier Français*) in 1879, the Russian Group of the Liberation of Labour in 1883, the English Social Democratic Federation in 1884, the Belgian Workers' Party (*Parti Ouvrier Belge*) in 1885, the Austrian and Swiss Social Democratic Parties in 1888, and the Italian Socialist Party in 1892. In 1888, Engels claimed with understandable exaggeration that 'the Marxist world outlook has found adherents far beyond the boundaries of Germany and Europe and in all the literary languages of world'.[69] What had brought about this remarkable change?

The most obvious reason for the founding of German-style social-democratic parties in other countries was the desire to replicate the astonishing electoral success of the German Social Democratic Party. In the *Reichstag* election of 1871, 124,000 voted for the two socialist parties. In 1877, the united party received 493,000 votes. In 1881, under the impact of Bismarckian repression, the vote fell back to 312,000. But by 1884 it had risen again to 550,000. In 1887, it amounted to 763,000 and in 1890 to 1,429,000.

These gains seemed all the more remarkable when set against the changes in the German *Reich* between the mid-1870s and the 1880s. By the end of the 1870s, both the strategies originally entertained by the Social Democratic Party had come to nothing. Lassalle's vision of a path to universal suffrage and the abolition of the 'iron law', built upon opposition to the bourgeois liberals and tactical alliance with monarchy and aristocracy, quickly stalled. Bismarck briefly toyed with the idea in 1863 as one means of escape from the constitutional crisis. But he took no further interest after the Prussian triumph over Austria at the Battle of Sadowa in 1866, and after the *Commune* of 1871 it became unthinkable. Bebel's speech, Bismarck subsequently claimed, had alerted him to the perils of socialism and the need for anti-socialist laws to combat social democracy, both as a social danger and as a threat to the state.

The Eisenach strategy had looked more promising. Bismarck founded the Second *Reich* in alliance with the most powerful fraction of the liberal bourgeoisie, the National Liberals. He had been careful to ensure that the political constitution of the Empire left all the essential mechanisms of absolutism in place, including crown control of the army and bureaucracy, the absence of ministerial responsibility to the *Reichstag*, the retention of the three-class suffrage in Prussia, and Prussian domination of the federal system through the *Bundestag*. But he also incorporated into its economic foundations all the leading demands of the liberals: above all free trade together with freedom of movement, the end of the usury laws, and the abolition of guild regulation and of state regulation of joint-stock companies.

Liberals were opposed to universal suffrage, but their identification with Bismarck's *Kulturkampf* (the legislative attack on German Catholics) found support among many Social Democrats. In particular, Social Democrats could identify with the promotion of secular education, centralization and rationalism over clericalism, particularism, ultramontanism and 'medieval' superstition. Liberals themselves still hoped that an alliance with Bismarck against *Reichsfeinde* (enemies of the *Reich*) might result in a constitutional state. This was also the hope which justified the Social Democrats' commitment to the *Freistaat* (free state) in the Gotha Programme.

Whatever the basis of these expectations, the events of the late 1870s dashed hopes of constitutional change through to the First World War. Prime among these were the political and economic effects of the Great Depression of 1873–96. After the boom of the early 1870s came the spectacular crash of 1873. There was a dramatic fall in wholesale prices, in coal, steel and cotton textiles. The situation was made worse by the annexation of Alsace and Lorraine, and so in these industries the first protection societies emerged in 1873–4.

In 1876, however, the falling prices hit agriculture too. Cheap American corn began flooding into England, depriving Prussian producers of their traditional export market. At the same time, cheap Russian and Hungarian corn began pouring into the home market. To the horror of farmers, bad harvests in 1875 and 1876 did not halt the continuing fall in agricultural prices, which brought a wave of bankruptcies in its wake. Protection now gained favour across the Prussian Corn Belt, and the terms were set for the 1879 tariff, based on the celebrated 'marriage between iron and rye': what some historians have called 'the second founding of the Empire'.

The repercussions of these developments extended far beyond the economy. The abandonment of free trade brought about the end of the liberal alliance. The social basis of liberalism had already been fractured by the growing distance between the values and way of life of the traditional middle class (teachers, small merchants, lesser officials) and those of a new and spectacularly wealthy industrial elite, keen to assimilate into the traditional ruling class. The consolidation of a new conservative bloc drawn from army, bureaucracy, landlords and industrialists was also greatly reinforced by alarm about the Paris *Commune* and fear of the growing workers' movement. Bismarck was particularly perturbed by 'the red menace'; already in the early 1870s he had attempted to change the press laws and the penal code to assist the prosecution of socialists. In 1878, on the pretext of two attempts to assassinate the emperor, he dissolved the *Reichstag*, fought an anti-socialist campaign, and passed an anti-socialist law which effectively outlawed the Social Democratic Party.[70]

Once reassured that the threat of a Catholic French–Austrian alliance had been removed by the arrival of the anti-clerical Third Republic in France, the government dropped its anti-Catholic campaign. The basic parameters of the new direction followed by the government included tariff protection against England and Eastern Europe, the introduction of measures of social security, an Austrian alliance, rapprochement with the Pope and acceptance of the Catholic Centre Party (the other large mass party apart from the Social Democrats). Liberalism never recovered from 1879. An openly conservative authoritarian state had come into being, in which for liberals, democrats and socialists a constitutional road to power was permanently blocked.

In these new circumstances, hopes of a constitutional struggle for a *Volksstaat* or a *Freistaat*, however remote, became wholly unrealistic. For the Social Democratic Party, recognition of Bismarck's *Reich* was out of the question. On the other hand, a strategy of extra-constitutional or revolutionary activism would simply invite complete repression. These were the circumstances in which a form of 'Marxism' came to offer an opportune solution to the Party's problems.

The turning point can be dated to the appearance of Engels' polemic *Herr Eugen Dühring's Revolution in Science*, popularly known as *The Anti-Dühring*, in 1878. Dühring had been a popular *Privatdozent* (untenured lecturer) at the University of Berlin. He had been dismissed as a result of a dispute with the university. He had a popular following among young socialists, including Eduard Bernstein, Johann Most and, briefly, August Bebel. His plight attracted special sympathy since he had gone blind during the course of his work. Dühring wrote extensively on philosophy, and in economics was a follower of the protectionist arguments of List and Carey. Karl had considered his critical, but respectful, review of *Capital* 'very decent'; he was 'the first expert who has said anything at all'.[71] But Dühring accepted the 'free state' ideal, rejected the Darwinian principle of struggle for existence and, following Carey, believed in the ultimate harmony of the interests of capital and labour.

Engels' attack on Dühring, begun at the behest of Liebknecht, initially encountered considerable resistance from the Social Democrats. The Party Conference at Gotha in May 1877 attempted to ban the serialization of Engels' book in *Vorwärts!*, the Party paper. But just how much the political climate had changed in a few years was indicated by the impact it subsequently made. According to David Riazanov, *Anti-Dühring* 'was epoch-making in the history of Marxism. It was from this book that the younger generation, which began its activity during the second half of the 1870s, learned what was scientific socialism, what were its philosophical premises, what was its method . . . all the young Marxists who entered the public arena in the early eighties – Bernstein, Kautsky, Plekhanov – were brought up on this book.'[72] Or, as Karl Kautsky put it, 'Judging by the influence that *Anti-Dühring* had upon me, no other book can have contributed so much to the understanding of Marxism. Marx's *Capital* is the more powerful work, certainly. But it was only through *Anti-Dühring* that we learnt to understand *Capital* and read it properly.'[73]

Engels' arguments were distilled in three chapters, from which the detailed polemic against Dühring had been removed, and published as *Socialism: Utopian and Scientific*. It appeared in French in 1880, followed by a German edition in 1882. This pamphlet thereafter became the most popular source for the understanding of 'Marxism' for the following twenty years.

Anti-Dühring was successful in large part because it transformed 'Marxism' into a *Weltanschauung*, a world philosophy, but not least because it answered the need for a new Party strategy in the late 1870s. *Anti-Dühring* managed to preserve a vision of the revolutionary collapse of the Bismarckian *Reich*, together with the dismantling of its repressive state, yet to keep these developments remote from the agency of the Party. Instead, these developments were presented as part of the increasingly crisis-ridden development of capitalism, as observed by 'scientific socialism'. This 'science', according to Engels, was built upon 'two great discoveries' made by Karl Marx: 'the materialistic conception of history' and 'surplus value' as 'the secret of capitalist production'.[74] Analysed in these terms, 'socialism was no longer an accidental discovery of this or that ingenious brain, but the necessary outcome of the struggle between two historically developed classes – proletariat and bourgeois'.[75]

According to Engels, the analysis found in *Capital* had revealed how 'modern large-scale industry' had 'called into being, on the one hand, a proletariat', which 'for the first time in history' could demand the abolition of class society, and was in such a position 'that it must carry through this demand'; and on the other, 'the bourgeoisie, a class which has a monopoly of all the instruments of production and means of subsistence, but which in each speculative boom period and in each crash that follows proves that it has become incapable of any longer controlling the productive forces, which have grown beyond its power; a class under whose leadership society is racing to ruin like a locomotive whose jammed safety valve the driver is too weak to open.' The downfall of the *Reich* and other repressive states in Europe would come about not as the result of the activities of this or that subversive party, but because the productive forces created by the capitalist mode of production had come into 'crying contradiction' with that mode of production itself: 'To such a degree that if the whole of modern society is not to perish, a revolution in the mode of production and distribution must take place'.[76]

Engels also offered an opportune criticism of the 'ultimate scientific insufficiency' of the ambition to create 'a free people's state'.[77] The bourgeoisie through its transformation of productive forces had replaced the means of production of the individual by social means of production only workable by 'a collectivity of men'. In effect the means of production had already begun to be socialized to such an extent that the state had already begun to take over 'the great institutions for intercourse and communication – the post office, the telegraphs, the railways'.[78] In this way, the bourgeoisie, having transformed 'the great majority of the population into proletarians', was itself 'showing the way to the accomplishing of revolution'. As a result, '*the proletariat seizes political power and turns the means of production in the first instance into state property'*.[79] But, 'The first act by virtue of which the state really constitutes itself the representative of the whole of society – the taking possession of the means of production in the name of society – this is, at the same time, its last independent act as a state. State interference in social relations becomes, in one domain after another, superfluous and then dies out of itself; the government of persons is replaced by the administration of things, and by the conduct of processes of production'. The state, Engels proclaimed, is not '"abolished". *It dies out.*' Or, in previous translations, *'It withers away.'*[80]

The impact of Engels' arguments was clear in the case of August Bebel, the foremost leader of the Social Democratic Party. In the first edition of his popular work *Woman and Socialism* in 1879 Bebel still used the idea of *Volksstaat*. But in the 1883 edition he replaced it with an account of Engels' doctrine of 'the withering away' of the state. Most striking was the shift in the imagination of the revolution itself. One way of removing the atmosphere of menace which surrounded the word was to associate it with gradualism and the avoidance of violence. This was the approach increasingly employed by Liebknecht. Another way was for the Party to develop a more 'passive' conception of its role if a revolution occurred. A striking example of this belief was to be found in a report by radical Party members on the Party's Conference in Copenhagen in 1883. The report began by declaring itself true to 'the principles of its great master, Marx'. But this meant that 'we are not a parliamentary party . . . but also we are not makers of revolutions . . . we are a revolutionary party . . . but the manner in which it will be achieved does not depend on us'.[81]

Bebel also believed that capitalism would collapse as a result of its own internal contradictions. The task of the Party was to enlighten the masses about the inevitability of collapse. When that moment came, the Party had to be ready to step in and undertake the task of social rebuilding. He did not appear to think that a violent class struggle would ensue, since, once catastrophe arrived, the ruling classes would succumb to some sort of 'hypnotic state' and submit to everything almost without resistance.[82] This vision of revolutionary crisis was also inscribed in the new programme of the Party, the Erfurt Programme, drafted by Karl Kautsky in 1891. In the first part, a Marxian picture of capitalism was presented: 'The number of proletarians becomes ever greater, the army of surplus workers becomes ever more massive, the contrast between exploiters and exploited becomes ever sharper and the class struggle between the bourgeoisie and the proletariat which divides modern society into two hostile camps and is the common feature of all industrialised countries, becomes ever more vehement.'[83] This struggle of the working class against capitalist exploitation was a 'political struggle'; it could not be accomplished 'without political rights'. What followed in the second part of the Programme, therefore, was a reiteration of the political demands to be found in the Eisenach and Gotha Programmes.

The 'Marxism' of the 1880s was not simply a picture of class struggle and the end of the bourgeois mode of production. In the *Anti-Dühring*, Engels provided an all-encompassing vision of nature and existence: 'In nature, amid the welter of innumerable changes, the same dialectical laws of motion force their way through as those which in history govern the apparent fortuitousness of events; the same laws which similarly form the thread running through the history of the development of human thought and gradually rise to consciousness in thinking men.'[84] Now nature was 'the proof of dialectics', and that proof had been furnished by 'modern science'.[85] Karl's breakthrough in the human sciences had been paralleled by Charles Darwin's breakthrough in the sciences of nature. In his speech at Karl's graveside in March 1883, Engels declared, 'Charles Darwin discovered the law of the development of organic nature upon our planet. Marx is the discoverer of the fundamental law according to which human history moves and develops itself, a law so simple and self-evident that its simple enunciation is almost sufficient to secure assent.'[86] The frontier between humanity and animality had been shifted. In 1844, Karl had started from the distinction between the 'natural being' and the 'human natural being'; unlike a purely 'natural being', man had a history. But in the *Anti-Dühring* man like nature was subject to the Darwinian struggle, which only came to an end with the disappearance of class society: 'The struggle for individual existence disappears. Then for the first time man, in a certain sense, is finally marked off from the rest of the animal kingdom, and emerges from mere animal conditions into really human ones.'[87]

The merger between Marxian theory and that of Darwin was promoted even more emphatically by Karl Kautsky. Kautsky was the editor of *Die Neue Zeit*, founded in 1883 as the Party's theoretical journal, and in the years from 1889 through to 1914 *Die Neue Zeit* remained the leading journal of the Second International. Drawing upon the writings of Thomas Buckle, Kautsky believed that history could become a science akin to the sciences of the natural world. From the writings of Darwin, he inferred man was 'a social animal' and that social instincts were the basis of group solidarity, whether of groups, classes or nations. This he conjoined with the assumption that history was the history of class struggle, and that all states were class states, ruled by the 'dominant economic class'. In Kautsky's writings, there was no question of any separation from the laws of nature. For socialism was precisely the creation of a new social system according to those laws, building upon his premise that the social instinct had become more and more concentrated in the movement of the oppressed class. For, as Kautsky later put it, organic instincts and drives underlay what philosophers had defined as ethics. 'What appeared to a Kant as the creation of a higher world of spirits is the product of the animal world . . . An animal impulse and nothing else is the moral law . . . The moral law is of the same nature as the instinct for reproduction.'[88]

5. KARL'S PLACE IN THE EMERGENCE OF 'MARXISM'

How far was Karl's theory responsible for what became known as 'Marxism' in the 1880s and after? How far was 'Marxism' a joint product of Karl and Engels in the years after 1867? Karl's contribution was substantial, but it was only one of the sources upon which the new doctrine was built. In 1867 and even in the preface to *A Contribution to the Critique of Political Economy* of 1859, Karl had appeared to open himself up to a much more determinist view of man than had been evident before; and this seemed to be reinforced by the significant theoretical statement with which he was prepared to associate himself in his afterword to the second German edition of *Capital* in 1873.[89]

Karl published little in the 1870s. Following Gladstone's campaign against Bulgarian Atrocities in 1875–6, and the lead-up to the Russo-Turkish War, Karl, with the aid of Maltman Barry, made some anonymous attacks in the Conservative press against Gladstone's Russian policy. In

1877, he apparently approved the whole of *Anti-Dühring*, which Engels read out to him, and even contributed an erudite chapter, criticizing Dühring's *Kritische Geschichte der Nationalökonomie* (*Critical History of Political Economy*).[90]

Does this mean that in the final decade of his life there was an effective convergence between the views of Karl and Engels? Not entirely. The evidence suggests that, in poor health and with diminished energy, Karl was prepared to allow Engels to act for him. At the same time, Karl's failure to find satisfactory solutions to the problems posed by the second volume of *Capital* resulted in a growing, if unacknowledged, divergence in their interests.

Karl no longer talked much about his work to Engels, yet to express disagreement during these years would have been increasingly difficult. No longer capable of producing the journalism once commissioned by the *New-York Daily Tribune*, and with no expectation of further legacies, the dependence of the Marx family upon Engels' largesse became ever more acute. Nor was dependence confined to Karl himself: Engels also provided for the girls, especially Laura, as already described. Little evidence of the strains caused by this dependence has survived, especially since Laura went through her parents' correspondence after their deaths to remove any reference to Engels that might be hurtful. But some hints survive. There is no reason, for example, to disbelieve the testimony of Hyndman, who saw Karl and his family fairly frequently in 1880–81, that 'Marx was, to put it in the common form, "under considerable pecuniary obligations" to Engels. This, Mrs Marx could not bear to think of. Not that she did not recognise Engels' services to her husband, but that she resented and deplored his influence over his great friend. She spoke of him to my wife more than once as Marx's "evil genius" and wished that she could relieve her husband from any dependence upon this able and loyal but scarcely sympathetic coadjutor.'[91]

On three issues at least, it is possible to discern a significant difference between the assumptions of the newly developing 'Marxism' of the 1880s and Karl's own views. The first of these concerned Karl's ideas about the collapse of capitalism. From the 1880s well through to the 1920s and 1930s, there was a widespread assumption among Second International socialists, and especially Bebel, that capitalism would come to an end not so much as a consequence of working-class revolt and an 'epoch of revolution', but rather as a result of systemic economic failure. These ideas of the *Anti-Dühring* and Bebel were reiterated in the 1891 Erfurt Programme, which stated that 'the forces of production have got beyond the control of present-day society' and that 'the class struggle between bourgeoisie and proletariat' was becoming 'ever more vehement'.[92] What was there in Karl's theory to authorize this idea of collapse? *Capital*, Volume I, was disappointing, offering nothing to suggest when and how capital would fall, except one purple passage, which spoke about 'the negation of the negation' and 'the expropriation of the expropriators'. Bebel along with others was expecting a real denouement in the second volume. After Karl's death, Engels, now editing the work, did his best to keep Bebel in a state of excited anticipation. In April 1885, he wrote to Bebel:

> 25 sheets (out of 38) of *Capital*, Book II have been printed. Book III is in hand. It is quite extraordinarily brilliant. This complete reversal of all previous economics is truly astounding. Our theory is thereby provided for the first time with an unassailable basis while we ourselves are enabled to hold our own successfully against all comers. Directly it appears, the philistines in the party will again be dealt a blow that will give them something to think about. For it will again bring general economic questions to the forefront of the controversy.[93]

Engels evidently became frustrated by the absence in the manuscript (untouched since 1864) of any punchline of the kind that the Party was looking for. The place to look was the concluding chapter of 'The Law of the Tendency of the Rate of Profit to Fall'. In the *Grundrisse* and elsewhere in the 1850s, this had been the focal point of Karl's expectation of capitalism's approaching demise. But in the manuscripts of Volume III, while Karl listed various factors which might lead to a fall in the rate of profit, in each case there were complicating counter-factors producing no clear end result. The most that Karl had assembled were a cluster of antagonistic circumstances, in which capital might be *erschüttert* (shaken). Engels was generally a scrupulous or even timid editor, but in this case he substituted the word '*zusammengebracht*' (collapsed).[94] Here was the origin of what became known between the 1890s and 1930s as '*Zusammenbruchstheorie*'.

The second area in which there was an appreciable divergence between Karl's views and those of Engels concerned the significance of Darwin. At Karl's graveside in 1883, Engels did his best to associate

Karl's work with that of Darwin. He proclaimed that 'just as Darwin discovered the law of development of organic nature, so Marx discovered the law of development of human history'.[95] And the notorious partner of Eleanor Marx, Edward Aveling, even invented the story that Karl had wished to dedicate *Capital* to Darwin.[96]

This argument was forced. Karl's objection to Darwin was that he regarded progress as 'purely accidental'.[97] Darwin did not believe that history possessed any unilinear meaning or direction: 'I believe in no fixed law of development.'[98] Karl, on the other hand, maintained that man was not simply a creature of his environment, as the Owenites and later 'Marxists' believed. Man's point of origin as '*human* natural being' was history, and history was 'a conscious self-transcending act of origin . . . the true natural history of Man'.[99] History was the process of the humanization of nature through man's 'conscious life activity'.[100]

There is no evidence that Karl ever renounced this view. While later admirers thought Karl started precisely where Darwin left off, Karl himself did not accept the fundamental continuity between natural and human history, as argued by the Darwinists. Karl considered that Darwin's book 'suits my purpose in that it provides a basis in natural science for the historical class struggle'.[101] But Darwin's theory could not accommodate Karl's belief that the first form of human society preceded private property and patriarchy, and, therefore, class struggle too. Class struggle and competition were not the results of nature-driven necessity, but consequences of man making his history in alien circumstances. Man remained not just a 'natural being', but a '*human* natural being', whose engagement in social struggle was a product of distinctively man-made social and cultural institutions. Class struggle and competition were not therefore to be regarded as resulting from the inherent animality of humans, but from heteronomy, the shaping of their behaviour by alien forces. It was private property and patriarchy, reinforced by religion, which had reduced man to the animal condition, of which class struggle and competition were the expression.

Like others, of course, Karl accepted Darwin's importance. In the face of Engels' enthusiasm, he could hardly do otherwise. But his acknowledgements were somewhat backhanded. He was mainly struck by the similarities between Darwin's portrayal of the animal kingdom and the world of competitive struggle depicted by Malthus and other political economists.[102] Moreover, when the opportunity arose, Karl was keen to belittle the esteem in which Darwin was held; for example, in 1864 he discovered 'a very important work' by Pierre Trémaux, *Origin and Transformation of Man and Other Beings*. He recommended it to Engels as 'a *very significant* advance over Darwin'.[103] Engels dismissed it in the most withering terms, 'utterly worthless, pure theorising in defiance of all the facts'.[104] But Karl was not wholly convinced, and even after receiving Engels' strictures wrote to his admirer Dr Kugelmann, still recommending the Trémaux book, despite its faults, as 'an advance over Darwin'.[105]

6. THE VILLAGE COMMUNITY: A NINETEENTH-CENTURY PHANTASM

Karl was respectful of Darwin's work, but not excited by it. What did excite him – and this was the third area in which Karl's interests and assumptions diverged from those of the 'Marxism' of the 1880s – was the new research of the 1850s and 1860s into the history of man, as it appeared not in biology, but in anthropology, philology and global pre-history. These interests came to the fore in the aftermath of the publication of *Capital*, Volume I in 1867.

In *The Communist Manifesto*, Karl had firmly placed his confidence in 'the bourgeoisie', who compelled 'all nations, on pain of extinction, to adopt the bourgeois mode of production'.[106] In the case of India, he had applauded what he thought would be the effect of steam power and free trade in bringing about the dissolution of the age-old 'village system' based upon the 'domestic union of agricultural and manufacturing pursuits'.[107]

On this basis, in 1859 he had also attacked the 'absurdly biased view' that '*primitive* communal property is a specifically Slavonic, or even an exclusively Russian phenomenon'. He pointed out that such forms could also be found 'among Romans, Teutons and Celts' and still survived in a disintegrated form in India. The passage was repeated, almost word for word, and with the same examples, in the first edition of *Capital*.[108] As Karl wrote to Engels in 1868, Russian village institutions, far from being unique, were a survival of a mode of production once found in Europe as well as Asia. 'The whole business *down to the smallest detail* is absolutely identical with the *Primeval Germanic* communal system.' But he went on specifically to align 'the Russian case' with 'part of the Indian communal systems', highlighting in particular 'the *non-democratic*, but *patriarchal* character of the commune leadership' and 'the *collective responsibility* for taxes to the state'.[109]

Karl's target was the Slavophil theory which identified the Slavic spirit with the church, popular traditions and the *obshchina* (the communal institutions of ownership in the Russian village). Particularly alarming to Karl was the fact that this theory appeared to have been accepted not simply by Romantic and conservative nationalists, but also by liberals and socialists, hence his outburst against Herzen at the end of the first German edition of *Capital*. Herzen was accused of prophesying the rejuvenation of Europe through 'the knout' and 'the forced mixing with the blood of the Kalmyks . . . This Belle Lettrist', he went on, 'has discovered "Russian" communism not inside Russia but instead in the work of Haxthausen, a councillor of the Prussian government.'[110]

But from the mid-1870s there was a remarkable change in Karl's general outlook, accompanied by subtle but noticeable changes in the character of his theory as a whole. This appears to have resulted from a combination of difficulties, both conceptual and practical. The theoretical changes have already been discussed. The mounting theoretical problems he had encountered can be detected by a comparison between the unmistakeably unfinished character of the published volume of 1867 and the various plans and manuscript drafts which had preceded it.

The inclusion of 'circulation' would have required a discussion of the expansion of capitalist relations across the world, what Karl called 'expanded reproduction', and this process was supposed to be distinct from 'primitive accumulation' (the origins of capitalism). How, then, did 'expanded reproduction' 'dissolve' earlier modes of production, and how did it refashion pre-existing societies along capitalist lines? In particular, how did the subordination of agriculture to capital occur? That was to be the topic covered in what Karl called 'the genesis of capitalist ground-rent', the main theme of *Capital*, Volume II. Furthermore, just as England had provided the basis for the discussion of capitalist production, so, it was planned, Russia, particularly after the Emancipation of the Serfs in 1861, would provide the basis for the discussion of the genesis of 'capitalist ground-rent'.[111]

But these plans were not realized. The 1867 volume of *Capital* did not include the intended analysis of circulation. Instead, the volume ended with 'primitive accumulation', a historical account of 'the expropriation of the agricultural population from the land' by means of enclosure and 'bloody legislation' in medieval and early-modern Britain.[112] Therefore, the question arose: was this British story to be understood as part of an inevitable and universal global process in which communal ownership died out? Many readers of the first edition of *Capital* certainly assumed so. But Karl himself had begun to back away from this position. Instances in which peasant communal production was 'dissolved' in a purely economic process had proved extremely hard to find. Conversely, researches into the history of landholding suggested that peasant communal ownership was far more resilient than had previously been supposed, and in some areas had survived until recent times. Peasant communal ownership, it seemed, did not simply 'dissolve' in the face of capitalist exchange relations; rather, as in Britain, it was destroyed by force or by destructive forms of taxation designed by the state.

If this were true, it suggested the need for a different approach to the question of the survival of the peasant commune in Russia, and the effect upon it of the emancipation of the serfs by the Russian government in 1861. It also suggested the need to examine the history of the peasant commune or village community elsewhere, especially the supposed universality of its existence as a primitive social form. For this reason Karl became interested in the works of Georg von Maurer in the year after the publication of the first volume of *Capital*. Maurer's work was one of the most important contributions to a debate which had begun in Germany in the second half of the eighteenth century, spread to other countries in Northern Europe after 1815 and by the 1860s, through the work of Henry Maine, been extended to the village system in Asia.

The village community was a German idea, which in its nineteenth-century forms was associated with what was called the Teutonic *Mark*. It went back to the writings of the eighteenth-century conservative patriot Justus Möser, who in his famous history of Osnabrück argued that the agrarian system in his native Westphalia, a pattern of isolated farmsteads, was 'still like that of the earliest times', by which he meant the times of Caesar and Tacitus.[113] In Möser's account, that early period was 'a "golden" age of free German farmers, associated with each other for purposes of self-government under an elected magistrate', an arrangement which lasted until the time of Charlemagne.[114] Each separate homestead, Möser claimed, was privately owned, but the 'common use of forest, pasture, moor, or mountain, where no one could fence off his own share, first united a few of these men in our part of the world. We call such common preserves Marks; and perhaps the earliest tribes who settled in isolated communities were members of a Mark-association (*Markgenossen*)'.[115] The division of the countryside into *Marken*, it was claimed, was dictated by nature; the *Mark* was therefore the oldest form of association in Westphalia.

In the Restoration Germany of 1815, fresh from the final defeat of Napoléon and intent upon the extirpation of Jacobin ideas from the public sphere, the attractions of this patriotic conservative combination of liberty, democracy and antiquity were irresistible. The alleged customs of the *Mark* were soon incorporated into histories of law and extended outwards from Westphalia to the rest of Germany. Karl Friedrich Eichhorn, a legal historian badly wounded as a volunteer at the Battle of Leipzig in 1813, took the lead. His foundation of the *Zeitschrift für geschichtliche Rechtswissenschaft* (*Journal of the History of Jurisprudence*), together with Karl Savigny and other leading representatives of the German Historical School of Law, was intended in part as a patriotic celebration of the expulsion and defeat of the French. In 1815, he declared that it was a 'known and proven' fact that 'according to German ideas all law proceeded from the whole body of full citizens, by means of which they preserved their life, their honour and their property'.[116]

But the *Mark* could also be placed in a more liberal and cosmopolitan setting. Following on from his claim that the Indo-European family of languages contained affinities not only of words and grammatical forms, but of mythology and culture, Jacob Grimm moved on to the ancient German *Mark*. It was identified with what had once been a widespread type of European folk community: the original village unit, both patriarchal and democratic, in which land was held and worked in common, and the elements of the polity formed.[117]

It was not long before the ancient village community was discovered in other nations beyond Germany. In 1849, John Mitchell Kemble, the translator of *Beowulf*, who had studied with Jacob Grimm, introduced the *Mark* into English historiography. In his two-volume study *The*

Saxons in England, Kemble considered it 'the original basis up on which all Teutonic society rests'.[118] It had been brought over to England at the time of the invasions of the Angles, Saxons and Jutes.

Prominent historians of the mid-Victorian period soon took up the idea. According to Bishop Stubbs, the Teutonic liberties of the *Mark* formed 'the primeval polity of the common fatherland', and he further elaborated this theme in 1866, when as Regius Professor in Oxford he delivered his inaugural lecture course on 'Constitutional History from Tacitus to Henry II'.[119] Edward Freeman, an enthusiast for the democratic traditions of 'the Aryan race', expressed the idea with characteristic extravagance. Commemorating the ancient German victory over the Romans at Teutoburg Wood, he proclaimed that Arminius, the German leader, was but 'the first of a roll which goes on to Hampden and to Washington'.[120] According to Freeman, signs of ancient Teutonic custom were visible everywhere, not least in 'what is undoubtedly a trace of the Teutonic *comitatus*, the fagging of our public schools'.[121] As in Germany, much of the attraction of this Teutonic liberties tradition, which, in the words of J. R. Green, stretched back from Westminster to the 'tiny moots, where the men of the village met to order the village life and the village industry', derived from its contrast with the absolutist ideas of Roman lawyers, or with the revolutionary abstractions of Jacobins and socialists.[122]

English historians were more interested in the evidence of ancient liberty and democratic government than in the form in which the land of the *Mark* had been owned or cultivated. But in this area there had been a growing identification of the *Mark* with communal ownership. Already in the later work of Eichhorn, private property in arable land, a prominent feature of Möser's original conception, was restricted to a right of usufruct, which was regulated by the community.[123] Möser's emphasis upon individual units and private property in his account of the origins of land ownership had been challenged from a number of quarters in the 1820s and 1830s. In 1821, a Danish study by Olufsen criticized Möser's picture on the basis of existing field divisions. In 1835, Georg Hanssen had argued that individual landownership had not existed among the German tribes. He elaborated his case on the basis of an 1831 study by J. Schwarz of the household communities (*Gehöferschaften*) of the Hunsrück district of Trier, claiming that these were survivals of the ancient communal system once existing among the German tribes.[124]

Hanssen's approach was very close to that which had been employed in 1829 by August von Haxthausen, in *On the Agrarian Constitution in the Principalities of Paderborn and Corvey*.[125] His study of this region's common-fields (*Gewannflur*) system presented it as a relic of an agrarian community going back to the time of Charlemagne and 'reaching back into mythical times' with originally equal allocation of holdings between companions (*Genossen*) and periodic redivision of the land. Haxthausen was honoured for his work by the Prussian king, and went on to discover, or rather project the same basic system onto, the character of the Russian *mir* (peasant community). This, he argued, was the legacy of a pre-agricultural epoch whose roots stretched back beyond the settlement of land with common usufruct (*Gemeinde-weise*) to the older, patriarchal family community with communal use of meadows.[126]

This change of perspective in turn helped to inspire the work of Georg von Maurer, formerly a key adviser in the setting up of the independent Greek kingdom with a member of the Bavarian Wittelsbach family as its first king. His most cited book was the *Introduction to the History of the Constitution of the Mark, Farmstead, Village and Town, and of the Public Power*, which appeared in 1854.[127] In opposition to Möser, Maurer claimed that 'the first cultivation of the land in Germany had not been carried out by individuals, but by whole families and tribes'. Originally nomadic, 'somewhat like [tribes] in Africa still today', Germanic tribes wandered to and fro, settling permanently only when they ceased to be attacked and continuing to retain elements of their tribal structure, as found in the peasant communities of the Dithmarsch in Schleswig-Holstein down to the present.[128] Maurer also instanced 'samples of ancient Teutonic agricultural customs and ancient forms of property in land' found in 'the more backward parts of Germany'.[129] It was claimed by his followers that 'the *Mark*, through a great part of Germany, has stamped itself plainly on land-law, on agricultural custom, and on the territorial distribution of landed property'.[130]

In the 1860s, the credibility of the Teutonic *Mark* as the universal starting point of a shared Indo-European culture was amplified still further by claims made on behalf of what was called the 'comparative method', an extension of the new nineteenth-century science of 'comparative philology'. Deriving from the discovery that the Germanic languages were related to Greek, Latin and Sanskrit, comparative philology assumed that a genetic relationship could be established between them, leading to the possibility of reconstructing the original form from which such variants developed. This in turn would make it possible to situate the range of Indo-European societies within a developmental sequence. The boldest example of the application of this approach was to be found in the writings of Sir Henry Maine, notably *Ancient Law* in 1861. According to Maine, 'we take a number of contemporary facts, ideas and customs, and we infer the past form of those facts, ideas and customs, not only from historical records of that past form, but from examples of it which have not yet died out of the world, and are still to be found in it'.[131] To confirm his point, Maine cited Freeman's field trip – 'democratic fossil hunting', as John Burrow has called it – to Switzerland in 1863–4.[132] Freeman had discovered that Kemble's *Mark* community, notably the solemn 'Ding or court' of the *GÐ*, or shire, at which 'thrice in the year the markmen assembled unbidden', was one of 'the fragments of Teutonic society, organised on its primitive model . . . an archaic *political* institution which has survived to our day' and was alive and well, and to be found in 'the Forest Cantons of Switzerland'.[133] Maine wished to emphasize that European writers were 'obviously unaware of the way in which Eastern phenomena confirmed their account of the primitive Teutonic cultivating group, and may be used to extend it'. The causes which had transformed the *Mark* into the feudal manor in the West, had barely impinged upon 'the Indian Village Community', which therefore remained 'a living, and not a dead, institution'.[134]

Maine shared none of the English historians' nostalgic celebration of the Teutonic past. *Ancient Law* depicted the transition from ancient to modern society as a 'movement of the progressive societies . . . a movement *from Status to Contract*'.[135] Maine saw the village community as the inverse of modern individualism, a sombre warning about what the renewed threat of communism and the tyranny of custom would portend. The modern territorial state based on private property, written laws, individual freedom and economic innovation was contrasted with a static and custom-bound archaic community, based upon collective ownership and the ascriptions of kin.

The Teutonic *Mark* was just a step beyond the aboriginal condition of mankind, in which corporate groups ruled by despotic patriarchs had occupied the land. It was originally an assemblage of co-proprietors, of families connected with one another by ties of kinship, real or imagined. The historical existence of this community could be inferred from the character of the feudal manor that succeeded it. For the manor contained 'characteristic and curiously persistent marks', which could be traced 'backwards to an earlier social form, a body of men democratically or rather aristocratically governed, in which the free tenants had as yet no lord'.[136]

Maine considered the displacement of the *Mark* community by the feudal manor to be a positive phenomenon. For modernity could only be attained by way of the social differentiation entailed in the breakup of the *Mark*. In this process, one cultivating family became dominant; common ownership of agricultural land was turned into feudal tenures through enclosure of the commons; free villagers became feudal villeins; the village assembly became the baronial court. As a result, the ascribed status bestowed by kin or blood relationships was replaced by feudal tenures recorded in contracts. The individual, whether as lord or tenant, was progressively freed from customary laws and archaic forms of collective ownership. It was this loosening of social ties which made possible the growth of individual freedom and economic innovation.

Just as the Historical School of Law had been concerned to combat rationalist proposals for legal codification in Germany in the aftermath of the Napoleonic Wars, so Maine designed *Ancient Law* as a riposte to Benthamite schemes of legal rationalization in post-Mutiny India.[137] Maine considered that Bentham's idea of law as the command of the sovereign ignored the stubborn existence of ancient custom in the interior of India. He attacked the assumption that a perfect social order could be evolved from the simple consideration of the natural state. He associated this idea with Bentham and Rousseau. It was an idea of a 'social order wholly irrespective of the actual condition of the world and wholly unlike it'. Maine proposed instead to apply 'the Historical Method of inquiry' in order to establish 'the rudiments of the social state'.[138]

In this enquiry, Maine considered Maurer's work to be of central importance. 'For many years past', he wrote in *Village-Communities*, 'there has been sufficient evidence to warrant the assertion that the oldest discoverable forms of property in land were forms of collective property'. In the Western world the only 'forms of collective property which had survived and were open to actual observation were believed to be found exclusively in countries peopled by the Sclavonic race'. It was not until Maurer published a series of works, Maine continued, 'that the close correspondence between the early history of Teutonic property and the facts of proprietary enjoyment in the Germany of our own day was fully established'.[139] Furthermore, Erwin Nasse had recorded similar findings 'concerning the plain and abundant vestiges of collective Teutonic property which are to be traced in England'.[140] By 1875, therefore, Maine felt confident enough to assert that 'The collective ownership of the soil by groups of men either in fact united by blood-relationship, or believing or assuming that they are so united, is now entitled to take rank as an ascertained primitive phenomenon, once universally characterising those communities of mankind between whose civilisation and our own, there is any distinct connection or analogy'.[141]

Like Maine, Karl was impressed by the importance of Maurer's work. On 14 March 1868, he wrote to Engels about studying Maurer's writings. 'Old Maurer's books (from 1854 and 1856, etc.) are written with real German erudition.' Maurer was praised for completely refuting 'the idiotic Westphalian squirearchical opinion', associated with Möser, that 'the Germans settled each by himself, and only afterwards established villages, districts, etc. . . . It is interesting just now that the *Russian* manner of redistributing land at certain intervals (in Germany originally annually) should have persisted in some parts of Germany up to the eighteenth century and even the nineteenth.' In this letter, Karl's references to Maurer were still overshadowed by the settling of old scores. Unbeknown to Maurer, his studies simply offered a further proof of 'the view I put forward', that 'the Asiatic or Indian property forms everywhere mark the beginning in Europe'. Similarly, in relation to Karl's long-standing irritation with the claims of Herzen and Haxthausen about the peasant commune in Russia, Maurer's work had vindicated Karl's position.[142] 'For the Russians, there disappears the last trace OF ORIGINALITY even in THIS LINE.'[143]

Karl wrote to Engels again ten days later on 25 March, with further thoughts about Maurer, this time of a more revealing and far-reaching kind. The letter contained a new assessment of Maurer's work: 'His books are extremely significant. Not only the primitive age but also the entire later development . . . get an entirely new character . . . The history of mankind', he goes on, 'is like palaeontology. Owing to A CERTAIN

JUDICIAL BLINDNESS, even the best minds fail to see, on principle, what lies in front of their noses. Later, when the time has come, we are surprised that there are traces everywhere of what we failed to see.' After admitting that 'we are all very much in the clutches of this JUDICIAL BLINDNESS', he cited the example of the Hunsrück: 'right in *my own* neighbourhood, on the *Hunsrück*, the old Germanic system survived until the *last few* years. I now remember my father talking about it to me from *a lawyer's point of view*.' Then, after blaming Grimm for mistranslating the relevant passages of Tacitus under the influence of Möser, Karl went on to claim that 'such Germanic primitive villages, in the form described [by Tacitus], still exist here and there in Denmark.' Scandinavia will become 'as important for German jurisprudence and economics as for German mythology . . . Only by starting from there will we be able once again to decipher our past.'[144]

This letter was not a flash in the pan. Thirteen years later, in one of the drafts of his reply to Vera Zasulich on the future of the peasant commune in Russia, Karl spelled out its implications in further detail. The ancient commune, he speculated, 'perished in the midst of incessant wars, foreign and internal; it probably died a violent death. When the Germanic tribes came to conquer Italy, Spain, Gaul, etc., the commune of the archaic type no longer existed.' But, he continued, 'its *natural viability* is demonstrated by two facts'. Firstly, there were 'sporadic examples which survived all the vicissitudes of the Middle Ages and have been preserved into our own day', and specifically Trier, 'in my native country'. Secondly, Karl put forward his own version of comparative philology and 'the comparative method'. For 'more importantly', this anterior social form 'imprinted its own characteristics so effectively on the commune which replaced it – a commune in which the arable land has become private property, whereas forests, pastures, common lands, etc., still remain communal property – that Maurer, when analysing this commune of secondary formation, was able to reconstruct the archaic prototype'. Lastly, Karl, like all the other admirers of the Teutonic *Mark*, reiterated its connection with a tradition of liberty and democracy that stretched back to ancient times: 'Thanks to the characteristic features' borrowed from 'the archaic prototype', 'the new commune introduced by the Germanic peoples in all the countries they invaded was the sole centre of popular liberty and life throughout the Middle Ages'.[145]

Unlike his attachment to communism or his ambition to merge state and civil society, Karl's enthusiasm for Maurer and the primeval village community was part of a mainstream development which had occurred in German and Anglo-Saxon culture, reaching the peak of its appeal in the 1860s and 1870s. In the middle decades of the nineteenth century, scholars, politicians and writers attached importance to questions about the historical existence and social character of the ancient village community for a variety of reasons. In Karl's case, his major preoccupation in his last years was related to his attempt to discover another and less vulnerable starting point from which to defend his vision of history and human nature.

Karl's letters of March 1868 can be regarded as a serious turning point. Why did he regard Maurer's books as 'extremely significant'? It is true that Maurer had endorsed the communism of the ancient German folk community, but mainly in the spirit of Grimm and the English constitutional historians. Maurer himself wrote that knowledge of the history of a people and its institutions was indispensable for those who led states: 'For he who would guide a state, must know above all the ground upon which he will operate . . . not only the physical properties of the land, but also above all its spiritual properties, therefore its historical foundations.' For what turning away from the past – breaking wholly with it – meant was revealed by 'the abyss' confronting 'a great neighbouring state on the other side of Rhine'.[146]

As a would-be poet, Karl had once been touched by such Romanticism himself. Yet since 1838 he had moved to the anti-Romanticism of Hegel, and had accepted the satire of Heine's *Romantische Schule*, and the anti-Romantic polemic of Ruge's *Hallische Jahrbücher*. Karl's writings from the early 1840s through to the publication of *Capital* in 1867 were resolutely modernist and anti-Romantic in tone. They were of a piece with his critique of political economy, and his identification of socialism with a post-capitalist future, which would be heralded by a revolt of the new industrial working class. But in the 1868 letter he modified his judgement: 'The first reaction to the French Revolution and the Enlightenment bound up with it was naturally to regard everything as medieval, Romantic, and even people like Grimm are not free from this.' But, he went on: 'the second reaction to it is to look beyond the Middle Ages into the primitive age of every people – and this corresponds to the socialist tendency, though these learned men have no idea that they are connected with it. And they are then surprised to find what is newest in what is oldest, and even EGALITARIANS TO A DEGREE which would have made Proudhon shudder.'[147] In a context in which previous assumptions about the displacement of communal or other traditional forms of agriculture did not work, arguments about the viability and longevity of the village community – not least those found in Maurer's work – seemed attractive. Starting from Maurer, it was not difficult to see how Karl's new-found enthusiasm for the discovery of 'what is newest in what is oldest' could find reinforcement in the political case for the support of the Russian *mir*: the communal ownership and periodic redivision of land in the Russian village community.

It was in this spirit – like Freeman's rediscovery of the *Mark* in the Swiss forest cantons and Maine's picture of the 'Indian village community', 'a living, and not a dead, institution' – that the *mir* provided yet another example of future regeneration by building upon the survivals from the archaic communal past. Haxthausen's claims were similar. He had conceded that over 1,500 years, with the introduction of agriculture, of Christianity, of the European concept of monarchy, and modern civilization, Russia had acquired 'a political organism' nearly identical to 'the other agricultural peoples of Europe'. But, he went on, 'the fundamental principles of the original nomadic society are still manifest in the character, the customs and the entire history of the Great Russians'.[148]

Before the mid-1870s, Karl found it hard to accept anything of value in the work of Haxthausen. But when radically reformulated from a socialist perspective, without homilies to the czar and the Russian church, by Nicolai Chernyshevsky, Karl found the argument irresistible. For Chernyshevsky had argued in 1858 that private property was only an intermediate stage in the development of property relations, that the ultimate stage would entail the return of communal production, and therefore that in the interim everything should be done to ensure the survival of the existing peasant commune.

It would seem that Karl's praise of Maurer and the beginnings of his interest in the Russian debate on the peasant commune developed around 1868. Karl first came to learn about Chernyshevsky in 1867 through N. A. Serno-Solovevich, one of his admirers based in Geneva. His reflections on Maurer were written in March 1868. He was first contacted by Nicolai Danielson, the leader of a group of Chernyshevsky enthusiasts in St

Petersburg, and future translator of the Russian edition of *Capital*, in September of the same year.[149]

In Karl's writings of the 1850s and 1860s, this form of communal property appeared inseparable from despotic rule. Nowhere was there any indication that the culture or politics of these regions contained – in however camouflaged a form – some germ of a different future. On the contrary, what stood out most sharply was the imprisonment of these forms in an irrational and despotic past. As Karl wrote of 'the ancient Asiatic and other ancient modes of production' in *Capital*, 'Those ancient social organisms of production are, as compared with bourgeois society, extremely simple and transparent. But they are founded either on the immature development of man individually, who has not yet severed the umbilical cord that unites him with his fellow men in a primitive tribal community, or upon direct relations of subjection.'[150] If in Asiatic and other pre-capitalist societies, communal ownership came coupled with despotism or 'lordship and bondage', it clearly had no place in a communist future.[151]

But after 1870 Karl discarded the assumption that communal property and despotic rule necessarily went hand in hand. The change was most obvious in his references to Russia. In 1881, Vera Zasulich from the Geneva group around Plekhanov requested Karl to make clear his position on the Russian village commune.[152] After the emancipation of the serfs in 1861, she asked, would the commune inevitably disappear as Russian capitalism developed? Or could it, before capitalist development became unstoppable, become 'the direct starting point' or 'element of regeneration in Russian society'? In reply, Karl conceded that 'isolation', even if not 'an immanent characteristic', was a weakness of the commune that, 'wherever it is found, has caused a more or less centralized despotism to arise on top of the communes'. Yet despite this he now argued that 'it is an obstacle which could easily be eliminated', that it would be 'an easy matter to do away with ... as soon as the government shackles have been cast off', or even that 'it would vanish amidst a general turmoil in Russian society'.[153]

Once again, this change in his evaluation of the village commune went back to the work of Nicolai Chernyshevsky, particularly an essay on the community ownership of land in Russia, and his review of Haxthausen. Chernyshevsky argued that Slavophil mysticism was a symptom of the nation's backwardness. But he had then gone on to argue that this backwardness could now be an advantage. For 'the development of certain social phenomena in backward nations, thanks to the influences of the advanced nation, skips an intermediary stage and jumps directly from a low stage to a higher stage'.[154] If this was correct, Chernyshevsky believed, it would be possible for Russia to proceed straight from the village commune to socialism.

Karl accepted Chernyshevsky's claim. In 1873, in the second German edition of *Capital*, he dropped the sneering reference to Herzen, and instead introduced a glowing tribute to Chernyshevsky, 'the great Russian Scholar and critic'.[155] Acceptance of this claim also meant abandoning the universal terms in which Karl had originally framed his argument in *Capital*. From the first edition in 1867, one sentence in particular stood out. It stated – and added an exclamation mark for further emphasis – that 'the country that is more developed industrially only shows, to the less developed, the image of its own future!' In the 1870s, Karl stealthily backed away from this claim. In the second German edition of 1873, the exclamation mark was dropped, and in the French translation of 1875 the chapter on 'The Secret of Primitive Accumulation' was amended to imply that the story of the dispossession of the English peasantry from the land applied only to the path followed by Western Europe. This enabled Karl two years later to dissociate himself from the idea that *Capital*'s depiction of the process of 'primitive accumulation' necessarily applied to Russia.[156]

With this shift also came the endorsement of the politics of Populism. That is, Karl now agreed that following the emancipation of the serfs in 1861, a socialist revolution must be made *before* capitalist development in the countryside destroyed the village commune. In one of the drafts of the letter to Vera Zasulich in 1881, Karl declared, 'to save the Russian commune, a Russian revolution is needed', and went on to argue that 'if the revolution comes at the opportune moment, if it concentrates all its forces so as to allow the rural commune full scope, the latter will soon develop as an element of regeneration in Russian society and an element of superiority over the countries enslaved by the capitalist system'.[157] At the same time, Karl strongly repudiated those of his social-democratic followers who believed that a socialist revolution would only be possible in the aftermath of capitalist development. In another of the drafts of the Zasulich letter, presumably referring to other members of Plekhanov's group, Karl wrote, 'The Russian

"Marxists" of whom you speak are quite unknown to me. Russians I hold "diametrically opposed views".[158]

Karl's vision of the village community in the 1870s entailed more than a shift of position on Russia.[159] It went together with other changes, both political and theoretical. Politically, the prospect of anti-capitalist revolution in the industrialized nations was becoming remote. This had become clear in the aftermath of the Franco-Prussian War, the defeat of the *Commune* and the growth of moderate and constitutionally oriented labour movements in Western Europe and North America. Conversely, the future of czarist Russia looked increasingly unstable. This looked particularly to be true at the outset of the Russo-Turkish war in 1877, when, intoxicated by the prospect of Russian defeat and revolution, an excited Karl wrote to Sorge in September 1877: 'this crisis is a *new turning point* for the history of Europe . . . This time the revolution will begin in the East, hitherto the impregnable bastion and reserve army of counter-revolution.'[160] But, in this war, the Russians were victorious.

More generally, Karl had also begun to adopt a different attitude towards empire and the fate of the extra-European world. In 1853, Karl had confided to Engels that he was waging a 'clandestine' campaign against the editorial line of the *New-York Daily Tribune*, which he described as the 'Sismondian-philanthropic-socialist anti-industrialism' of 'the protectionist, i.e. industrial bourgeoisie of America'. He had therefore hailed 'England's destruction of native industries' in India as 'revolutionary'.[161] But in the late 1870s Karl no longer praised the breakdown of traditional and often communal social structures by European merchants and colonizers. The main difference between Russia and India or China was that 'it is not the prey of a foreign conqueror, as the East Indies, and neither does it lead a life cut off from the modern world'.[162] Karl now appeared to believe that, as in Russia, primitive communal structures left to themselves were resilient enough to survive in the modern world, and in favourable political conditions could even develop.

In India, Africa and China, countries had been prevented from doing so by European colonization. He agreed with much of the account of the impact of colonization upon communal forms of property provided by his friend Maxim Kovalevsky, particularly in the case of the French conquest of Algeria. Underlining Kovalevsky's analysis, Karl noted that 'to the extent that non-European, foreign law is "profitable" for them, the Europeans recognise it, as here they not only recognise the Muslim law – immediately! – but "misunderstand it" only to their profit, as here'.[163] Similarly, in the case of the East Indies, it was not true, as Maine claimed, that the destruction of the communes was the result of 'the spontaneous forces of economic laws ... Everyone except Sir Henry Maine and others of his ilk, realises that the suppression of communal landownership out there was nothing but an act of English vandalism, pushing the native people not forwards but backwards.'[164]

Political disappointment was compounded by theoretical difficulty. Karl's critique of political economy had resulted in an inconclusive account of capitalist crisis. Similarly, there was nothing in his theory to account for the different politics of different capitalist states.[165] Ill-health was no doubt in part to blame. But that did not prevent the growth of other interests, notably his Russian researches and an increasing preoccupation with the early history of man.[166] The character of these interests also suggested a distancing from his previous perspectives. References to bourgeois society, so expansive in the 1850s, became cursory and dismissive. The Russian rural commune could by-pass the capitalist mode of production, Karl argued, because it could appropriate its 'positive acquisitions without experiencing all its frightful misfortunes'. But the 'acquisitions' mentioned were purely technological – the engineering industry, steam engines, railways, the 'mechanism of exchange'.[167] There was no mention of the changes in productivity and the division of labour which this technology presupposed. Capitalist production was 'merely the most recent' of a succession of economic revolutions and evolutions which had taken place since 'the death of communal property'. Although it had resulted in 'a wondrous development of the social productive forces', 'it has revealed to the entire world except those blinded by self interest, its purely transitory nature'.[168]

Conversely, capitalism's communal ancestor was endowed with a *natural viability*. It had survived in certain places, like the area around Trier, and had 'imprinted its own characteristics ... on the commune which replaced it'. Therefore, as noted earlier (see p. 577), Maurer, the historian of ancient Germany, when 'analysing this commune of secondary formation, was able to reconstruct the archaic prototype'.[169] 'The vitality of primitive communities', Karl claimed, 'was incomparably greater than that of Semitic, Greek, Roman, etc. societies, and *a forti-ori* that of modern capitalist societies.'[170] Or, as he noted of the work of the American anthropologist Lewis Henry Morgan, both on the Grecian gens and on the character of the Iroquois, 'unmistakeably . . . the savage peeps through'.[171] Karl was inspired by Morgan's depiction of the gens as that form of primitive community which preceded patriarchy, private property, class and the state. Morgan inferred the existence of the gens, both from his contemporary researches on the tribes of North America, especially the Iroquois, and from his classical study of Greece and Rome.[172]

Excited by the new world which prehistory had opened up, Karl now had a vision that encompassed not 'merely' bourgeois society, but the whole trajectory of 'civilization' since the downfall of the primitive community. Remarkably, Karl had come to agree with the French 'utopian' socialist Charles Fourier that 'the epoch of civilization is characterised by monogamy and private property in land' and that 'the modern family contained within itself in miniature all the antagonisms which later spread through society and its state'.[173] 'Oldest of all', he noted, primitive community contained 'the existence of the horde with promiscuity; no family; here only mother-right could have played any role'.[174]

One of the most interesting features of Karl's new focus upon the durability and 'viability' of the archaic village community was the way in which it invited the restatement of the conception of human nature so eloquently spelled out by him in 1843 and 1844 during his time in Paris. This conception had not, as many commentaries assume, been discarded as the unwanted juvenilia of 'the young Marx'. But it had been rendered virtually invisible during the twenty years between his Paris writings of 1844 and the publication of Volume I of *Capital* in 1867, as Karl focused upon the estranged character of human interaction under the domination of private property and exchange relations. If it were true, as Karl had claimed in 1844, that man's social nature could only be expressed in estranged form once human relations were inverted by the advent of private property, then – *conversely* – archaic communal forms, in the era preceding private property, expressed the true character of human nature in its spontaneous and pre-alienated form.[175] This is why the late writings and Karl's notebooks contain a larger number of relatively straightforward pronouncements upon human nature and human attributes.

It also explains why Karl became so incensed by Sir Henry Maine, 'the donkey' or 'block-headed John Bull', now nominated as the supreme representative of 'civilization', and English civilization in particular. Archaic communist society was on no account to be equated with primitive patriarchal despotism. Maine was accused of being unaware of descent through the female line in 'gentile society' and of transporting 'his "patriarchal" Roman family into the very beginning of things'.[176] Karl had become acquainted with Bachofen's *Mother-Right* of 1861, reinforced by McLennan's *Primitive Marriage* of 1865 and Morgan's *Ancient Society* of 1877.[177] Maine could only understand the primitive as 'the despotism of groups over the members composing them'.[178] He did not realize, as Karl did, that primitive community had preceded the subjection of women, and had embodied 'economic and social equality'. Kingship and private property in land – the political realm as such – both arose from the gradual dissolution of 'tribal property and the tribal collective body'.[179] Maine did not understand that the state was 'an excrescence of society'. Just as it had only appeared at a certain stage of social development, so it would disappear again, once it reached another stage yet to be attained: 'First, the tearing away of individuality from the originally not despotic chains (as the blockhead Maine understands it), but satisfying and comforting bonds of the group, of the primitive commune – then the one-sided spreading of individuality.'[180] 'Civilization', however, was now approaching its term. Capitalism was now in a 'crisis', which will only end in its 'elimination' and 'in the return of modern societies to the "archaic" type of communal property'.[181]

Karl's pressing, if unavowed, political expectations no longer wholly hinged upon the point at which the urban and industrial working classes of Western Europe might force a revolution against bourgeois society; neither the French, the British nor the Germans were showing any desire to embark upon an aggressive course of class struggle.[182] Karl's attention was directed rather to the point at which primitive communal systems of cultivation might be displaced by a transition to private property. In the reply Karl finally sent to Vera Zasulich about the future of the peasant commune in Russia, he stressed that 'the basis

of the whole development', 'the *expropriation of the agricultural producer*', had nowhere been 'accomplished in a radical fashion . . . except
in England' and that 'the "historical inevitability" of this process is
expressly limited to the *countries of Western Europe.*' In Western
Europe '*private property*, based on personal labour' was being supplanted by 'wage labour': in other words, one form of private property
was being replaced by another. But, Karl emphasized, 'In the case of
the Russian peasants, *their communal property* would, on the contrary, have to be *transformed into private property.*'[183]

7. THE END OF A LIFE

Karl's last three years were darkened not only by his own incurable
bronchitis, but also by the death of his wife and of his eldest daughter,
Jenny Longuet. It was a period entirely dominated by anxieties about
health, both his own and that of various members of the family. From
1879, it became clear that Mrs Marx was suffering from cancer of the
liver. Karl took her to see Dr Gumpert in Manchester, but nothing
much could be done, and in June 1881 it became clear that she was
dying. She was occasionally able to manage a visit to the theatre, and
in July Karl took her to Eastbourne, where she spent three weeks per-
ambulating the front in a wheelchair. Life had also become lonelier
without the presence of grandchildren, once the Longuet family had
returned to Argenteuil in France in February 1881. At the same time,
Eleanor was assailed by acute depression, while Jenny Longuet had to
suffer prolonged bouts of asthma.

The autumn and winter of that year were especially cruel. Karl's
bronchitis was so serious that he was unable to leave his bed, even to
see his wife in the adjoining room. Eleanor together with Lenchen
tended to both, but Jenny's pain became more and more acute. She
spent the last few days of her life helped by morphine, and died in her
sleep on 2 December 1881. Karl was devastated by her loss but too ill
to attend the funeral. As Engels observed, 'Moor is dead too' (Karl's
nickname within the family).

In 1882, there was a slight improvement in Karl's health. He was
able briefly to attend to political matters and agreed to a short preface
to the Russian edition of *The Communist Manifesto* co-authored with

Engels in early 1882. The preface contained an ambivalent formulation which concealed the extent of their differences on the Russian peasant commune: 'If the Russian Revolution becomes the signal for a proletarian revolution in the West, so that both complement each other, the present Russian common ownership of land may serve as the starting point for a communist development.'[184]

After this, he and Eleanor went to Ventnor on the Isle of Wight. But the stay brought little relief. Karl's cough continued unabated, and Eleanor remained on the verge of a breakdown, connected with the ending of her relationship with Lissagaray, but also despair about her lack of success on the stage. Her friend Dolly Maitland came to help, but this irritated Karl, who could not understand what his daughter's problem was and why she should seek help from a friend. Back in London with neither of his other daughters at that moment able to accommodate him, Karl was persuaded to stay for ten weeks in Algiers. But this bid to escape the European winter was a failure. Algiers was wet and cold: 'I have been frozen to the marrow . . . landed at Algiers on 20 February . . . February cold, when not also damp. I struck the 3 coldest days of the said last month . . . no sleep, no appetite, a bad cough.'[185]

From Algiers, Karl travelled to Monte Carlo, but still ailing with bronchitis and pleurisy. In June, he went to stay for three months with Jenny at Argenteuil. Although it was enjoyable to see the grandchildren, it was not a restful place. Jenny was expecting a baby, and her husband was bad-tempered and unwilling to help. In September, Karl prevailed upon Laura to accompany him to Vevey in Switzerland. There he encouraged her to undertake the English translation of *Capital* and promised her the archives of the International, so that she could write its history. In October, Karl returned to his London home, where not only Lenchen and Eleanor, but also Jenny Longuet's son, Johnny, were at hand. Karl once more set off for Ventnor, this time on his own.

Jenny herself was unwell. From April 1882 she developed cancer of the bladder. With four children, a resentful and uncooperative husband, and a mother-in-law who blamed her for the family debts, Jenny's decline was rapid. When the Lafargues went to see her in early January 1883, they found her 'sunk in torpor broken by nightmares and fantastic dreams'.[186] She became delirious and died on 11 January 1883 aged thirty-eight.

For Karl, whose thoughts over the past year had been haunted by memories of his wife, the death of 'the daughter he loved most' was an insupportable blow.[187] With chronic bronchitis and confined to his room by frost, snow and a bleak north-east wind, he was not up to reading more than the occasional light novel by Paul de Kock. He was looked after with customary loving care by Lenchen, but his health worsened. Karl developed an ulcer on the lung and on 14 March 1883 died of a haemorrhage.

Epilogue

The historical and philosophical themes which preoccupied Karl in his last years did not long outlast his death. Neither the scholarship underlying claims for the archaic village community nor the politics which accompanied them survived into the twentieth century.

In the period after the French Revolution and the Napoleonic Wars, the French showed little sympathy for claims about the Teutonic origins of liberty. Their preference was not for the aristocratic and militarist Franks, but for the industrious Gauls, the ancestors of the 'Third Estate'. Guizot in his 1823 *Essays on the History of France* made no reference to the *Mark*, but dwelt upon the Franks' aversion to work and their enjoyment of drinking and games.[1] Not surprisingly, the course of the Franco-Prussian War sharpened the edge of this hostility, and led to an all-out attack upon the scholarly credentials of Maurer by Fustel de Coulanges in 1889.[2]

Fustel's attack was devastating. The *Mark* theory received no support in the writings of Caesar or Tacitus. Without the slightest justification, Maurer had understood the word *ager* to mean *ager publicus*, although the word *publicus* does not appear in Tacitus' text. The word *Mark* in early German law simply meant 'boundary' (Latin *terminus*) and usually referred to private property, especially villas. In fact early German law was based upon the presupposition of private property in land, held by individuals or families, but never by larger groups. The only evidence of periodic redistribution of the land was based upon the blunder of a copyist. The term 'common' referred to a customary right of use enjoyed by tenants over land belonging to a lord. There was no evidence that these tenants were once joint *owners* of the land. Nor was there any evidence of *Mark* assemblies or *Mark* courts.

Instead, the earliest German law codes suggested a land to a large extent occupied by great estates, and cultivated by slaves or semi-servile tenants.

Evidence on England assembled by Frederic Seebohm, William Ashley and Paul Vinogradoff pointed in the same direction.[3] In 1883, Seebohm's *The English Village Community* demonstrated the uniform spread of the manorial system across the greater part of England. He argued that the origins of the feudal manor were not to be found in the disintegration of the free *Mark* community, but in the slave-worked villa of the late Roman Empire. The invading Anglo-Saxons had either already adopted the Roman estate system, or adopted what they found on arrival. Seebohm's work effectively demolished the existence of the *Mark*. The economist Alfred Marshall attempted in the 1870s to develop Maine's picture of the original 'Aryan' village and the Teutonic *Mark* community as the starting points of a philosophy of history to accompany his *Economic Principles*. It would have depicted the progress from custom-bound community to modern innovation and individual liberty. But after reading Seebohm's demonstration that village communities 'were not often "free" and ultimate owners of the land', he relegated what was left of the historical section to an appendix and dropped all mention of the *Mark*.[4]

Other evidence put forward by Fustel de Coulanges undermined the claims of the *Mark* in Switzerland, Serbia and Scotland.[5] Even Karl's cherished piece of evidence for the survival of communal property arrangements, the *Gehöferschaften* of Trier and the Hunsrück, were shown to be a later communal arrangement forced upon the people, and seigniorial in origin.[6] Finally, the historical credentials of the Russian *mir* were also effectively dismantled. Chicherin demonstrated that the existence of the *mir* only dated back to 1592 and was instituted by 'an act of despotic government', by a ukase of the Czar Fedor Ivanovitch. As Fustel de Coulanges admitted in 1889, 'the question is still warmly discussed', but on the basis of the evidence produced so far, the *mir* only came into existence with the feudal period and 'far from being collective ownership, the *mir* is collective serfdom'.[7]

The political life of Karl's new conception proved no less short. He had been less than straightforward in making public his shift in position after the publication of *Capital*, Volume I. So it was not surprising that most of his followers continued to equate Karl with the modernizing vision of the *Communist Manifesto*. They were also encouraged to do so by Engels, who had never been enthusiastic about Karl's latter-day interest in the village community. In 1882, Engels had criticized Maurer's 'habit of adducing, indiscriminately and side by side documentary proof and examples from any and every period'.[8] In 1894, he similarly questioned the merit of Chernyshevsky for encouraging 'a faith in the miraculous power of the peasant commune to bring about a social renaissance'. The fact was that the Russian commune had existed for hundreds of years 'without ever providing the impetus for the development of a higher form of common ownership out of itself; no more so than in the case of the German Mark system, the Celtic Clans, the Indian and other communes with primitive, communistic institutions'.[9] Engels was happy to hand over all Karl's Russian material to his friend Lavrov, and he made no attempt to integrate Karl's later thoughts into his editing of Volumes II and III of *Capital*. Nor did he object when, in the 1890s, Plekhanov, Struve and their follower Lenin depicted Russian Marxism as a battle between 'historical materialism' and 'Narodism', a Romantic belief in the uniqueness of Russia and its peasant commune: therefore, a rerun of earlier battles between Westernizers and Slavophils. This effectively ensured that Karl's views were forgotten in the one place where the significance of the peasant commune was an immediate political issue.

Engels remained hostile to the Romantic investment in the *obshchina*. He denied that ancient communal beliefs had much bearing upon modern collective institutions. In 1894, he brought out a new edition of the attack he had made twenty years earlier against the Populist and Bakuninist Petr Tkatchev. Ostensibly the essay was written for 'all Russians concerned about the economic future of their country'. He pointed out that in Russia 'the few thousand people' who were aware of 'Western capitalist society with all its irreconcilable antagonisms and conflicts' did not live in the commune, while 'the fifty million or so, who still live with common ownership of the land . . . have not the faintest idea of all this . . . They are at least as alien and unsympathetic to these few thousand as the English proletarians from 1800 to 1840 with regard to the plans which Robert Owen devised for their salvation.' And, as Engels emphasized, the majority employed in Owen's New Lanark factory also 'consisted of people who had been raised on the institutions and customs of a decaying communistic gentile society, the Celtic-Scottish clan ... But nowhere', Engels emphasized, 'does he [Owen] so much as hint that they showed a greater appreciation of his ideas ... It is a historical impossibility', he concluded, 'that a lower stage of economic development should solve the enigmas and conflicts which did not arise, and could not arise, until a far higher stage.'[10]

There were also deeper reasons why Karl's position in the debate about the village community did not survive into the twentieth century – and indeed was already beginning to look outmoded by the time of his death in 1883. Karl belonged to a generation of writers whose work on the transition from ancient to modern society preceded the impact of Darwin. Maine, Bachofen, Morgan, McLennan and Karl were all born between 1818 and 1827. All were lawyers, for whom the study of early or primitive society was not a branch of natural history, but of legal studies – of which political economy in the nineteenth century was often considered part. The institutions upon which they focused – private property, the state, marriage and the family – were also primarily legal. They were neither travel writers, nor social anthropologists in a later sense, even if Morgan made contact with Iroquois and Maine became part of the Indian Administration. Their sources were mainly classical or biblical. They drew especially upon the Pentateuch, Roman Law and Greek mythology – from the patriarchal despotism of Abraham, through the Ten Commandments and the Twelve Tables, to Prometheus and the misdeeds of the gods of Olympus, or to the Rape of the Sabines and to the Caudine Forks. Fundamental to their concerns was an equation between history, development and progress, whether 'from status to contract', from private property to the end of 'human pre-history', or from 'societas' to 'civitas'. All in their different ways believed that history was a means by which progress could be measured, a progressive movement from lower to higher stages of development, whether of forms of property, modes of production, types of kinship relation or marriage, custom or law. The so-called 'comparative method' was employed in different ways to assist the drawing up of these developmental sequences.

The American Lewis Henry Morgan, whom Karl saluted in his last writings for prophesying 'the revival, in a higher form, of the liberty, equality and fraternity of the ancient gentes', was a good example of this combination of legal formation and classical inspiration.[11] He trained as a lawyer in Rochester, New York, and became fascinated by the practices of the neighbouring Iroquois, whom he represented in several land disputes. Although not a practising Christian, Morgan shared many of the values of the local liberal Calvinist congregation, led by his close friend the Reverend J. S. McIlvaine. While McIlvaine and his congregation welcomed evolution, which they could only understand as the unfolding of a divine plan, they were unable to accept Darwin's idea of the mutability of species – for many the unacceptable 'materialist' core of Darwinism.[12]

Morgan shared this position and in his study *The American Beaver and His Works* tried to demonstrate the superiority of Cuvier's idea of the separate creation of fixed species.[13] Species could change in the embryological sense in which tadpoles changed into frogs or in the longer term by fulfilling their potential. Morgan also spent much time classifying marriage, kinship and language groups, in support of the idea that in addition to the Indo-European and Semitic languages there also existed the 'Turanian', a group made up of nomadic peoples, stretching from the Finns to the Tamils.[14] Like others of his generation, he combined his specialized ethnographic knowledge of American tribes with a historical model built upon classical learning, in his case George Grote's *History of Greece*.[15] As far back as 1851, Morgan had believed that there was a strong similarity between the political institutions of the Iroquois and those of the tribes of ancient Greece. Indeed, the democratic practices of the Greek gentes and the Iroquois seemed not dissimilar from those associated with the Indo-European *Mark*. For Morgan, the whole process of the development of 'a barbarian out of a savage, and a civilized man out of this barbarian' had been 'a part of the plan of the Supreme Intelligence'.[16]

Far-fetched though it may first seem, it is worth pointing to an affinity of position between Morgan's approach and that of Karl. Karl of course would not have countenanced any notion of 'the Supreme Intelligence', but like Morgan he was unhappy about Darwin's view that 'progress' was purely 'accidental'. Like Morgan also, Karl had a high regard for Cuvier. Cuvier was 'a great geologist and for a naturalist also an exceptional literary-historical critic'. He warmed to Cuvier's mocking the ideas of 'German nature-worshippers' about the mutability of the species, but reluctantly agreed that in the end the Darwinists were right.[17] He may well have pondered, however, what the status of his own theory of history was, if the Darwinists' conception was correct. But there can be no doubt about his enthusiasm for Morgan's findings in *Ancient Society*.

In order to highlight the intellectual gulf between Karl's generation and that which came to dominate the *Marxist* socialist movement in the 1880s and 1890s, it is only necessary to cite one of the most prominent members of the Group for the Emancipation of Labour, Georgi Plekhanov, and his best-known work of theory, *In Defence of Materialism: The Development of the Monist View of History*, published in 1895. According to this study, far from humanizing nature through his activity, man's capacity for 'tool making' was to be regarded as '*a constant magnitude*', 'while the surrounding external conditions for the use of this capacity in practice have to be regarded as a constantly varying magnitude'.[18] In other words, the crucial variable was not human activity, but the external environment. To summarize his theory: 'Darwin succeeded in solving the problem of how there originate vegetable and animal species in the struggle for existence. Marx succeeded in solving the problem of how there arise different types of social organisation in the struggle of men for their existence. Logically, the investigation of Marx begins precisely where the investigation of Darwin ends'.[19] A generation brought up on evolutionary biology could not inhabit the dreams of a generation brought up upon classical literature, ancient mythology and radical idealist philosophy. Nature was no longer the passive and repetitive 'inorganic body of man'. It had now become the actively threatening and disruptive agent, forcing man at every new turn to adapt the conditions of the struggle for existence to the ever-changing demands of the external environment. In the new language of twentieth-century socialism, the dreams of those whose thought had been formed in the decade before 1848 had become, to an ever-increasing extent, incomprehensible.

Finally, a suggestive story: in the *Marx-Engels Archiv*, published in Frankfurt in 1928, the pioneer Marx scholar, and first editor of the *Marx–Engels Gesamtausgabe*, David Riazanov (later to disappear in the Stalinist purges), reported that going through the papers of Karl's son-in-law Paul Lafargue in 1911, he came across several drafts, full of insertions and erasures, of a letter written in French by Karl on 8 March 1881.[20] This was a response to a letter of 16 February from Vera Zasulich of the exiled Russian Group for the Emancipation of Labour in Geneva.[21] In line with the preceding drafts discovered in

1911, the letter Karl finally sent Zasulich on the question of the commune was positive. What impact did it make?

Riazanov wrote round to surviving members of the Group to ask if any reply from Karl had been received. Plekhanov, Zasulich and probably Axelrod all replied in the negative; and yet, as Riazanov himself recalled, he spent time in Geneva in 1883 and heard of this exchange, and even rumours of a personal confrontation between Plekhanov, who was said to have denied communal property, and Karl, who was said to have defended it.[22] In 1923, the missing letter from Karl turned up in Axelrod's papers. But, according to Riazanov, the present editors were unable to elicit 'the real reasons why this letter of Marx, which dealt with a question so passionately provoking to revolutionary circles, fell into oblivion'. As Riazanov remarked, 'we saw that Plekhanov, and even the addressee, Zasulich, had likewise thoroughly forgotten this letter. One must recognize that this lapse of memory, particularly given the special interest such a letter would have aroused, is very strange and probably would offer to professional psychologists one of the most interesting examples for the extraordinary deficiencies of the mechanism of our memory.'[23]

We cannot know why in 1923 the former leaders of the Group for the Emancipation of Labour *forgot* Karl's 1881 letter urging them to support the village community rather than follow the supposedly orthodox 'Marxist' strategy of building an urban-based workers' social-democratic movement. But this only reinforces the point that the Marx constructed in the twentieth century bore only an incidental resemblance to the Marx who lived in the nineteenth.

Notes and References

PROLOGUE

1. Eugen von Böhm-Bawerk, *Karl Marx and the Close of His System: A Criticism*, trans. Alice M. Macdonald, London, T. Fisher Unwin, 1898.
2. For an account of the development of the revisionist debate, see H. and J. M. Tudor (eds.), *Marxism and Social Democracy: The Revisionist Debate 1896–1898*, Cambridge, Cambridge University Press, 1998. For Bernstein's attack upon 'collapse theory', see especially, pp. 159–73.
3. Werner Blumenberg, *Portrait of Marx: An Illustrated Biography*, trans. Douglas Scott, New York, Herder & Herder, 1972, p. 2; August Bebel and Eduard Bernstein (eds.), *Der Briefwechsel zwischen F. Engels und K. Marx*, 4 vols., Stuttgart, Dietz, 1913; 'August Bebel to Karl Kautsky, 7 February 1913', in K. Kautsky Jr (ed.), *August Bebels Briefwechsel mit Karl Kautsky*, Assen, Van Gorcum & Co., 1971, pp. 278–9.
4. Isaiah Berlin, *Karl Marx: His Life and Environment*, Oxford, Oxford University Press, 4th edn, 1978 [1939], pp. 4, 14.

1 FATHERS AND SONS

1. See Michael Rowe, *From Reich to State: The Rhineland in the Revolutionary Age, 1780–1830*, Cambridge, Cambridge University Press, 2003, pp. 158–9, 188.
2. Heinz Monz, *Karl Marx und Trier: Verhältnisse, Beziehungen, Einflüsse*, Trier, Verlag Neu, 1964, pp. 38–9.
3. Heinz Monz, *Karl Marx: Grundlagen der Entwicklung zu Leben und Werk*, Trier, Verlag Neu, 1973, pp. 221–32; also Jan Gielkens, *Karl Marx und seine niederländischen Verwandten: Eine kommentierte Quellenedition*, Schriften aus dem Karl-Marx-Haus, Trier, no. 50, 1999.
4. Timothy Tackett, *Becoming a Revolutionary: The Deputies of the French National Assembly and the Emergence of a Revolutionary Culture (1789–1790)*, Princeton, Princeton University Press, 1996, p. 120.

5. Keith Michael Baker, 'Fixing the French Constitution', in *Inventing the French Revolution: Essays on French Political Culture in the Eighteenth Century*, Cambridge, Cambridge University Press, 1990, p. 303.

6. Ibid., p. 265.

7. Ibid., p. 305.

8. See François Delpech, 'La Révolution et l'Empire', in B. Blumenkranz (ed.), *Histoire des Juifs en France*, Toulouse, E. Privat, 1972, pp. 265–304.

9. Rowe, *From Reich to State*, pp. 21–3.

10. R. Liberles, 'From *Toleration* to *Verbesserung*: German and English Debates on the Jews in the Eighteenth Century', *Central European History*, 22/1, 1989, pp. 1–32.

11. See David Sorkin, *The Transformation of German Jewry 1780–1840*, Oxford, Oxford University Press, 1987, pp. 25–7; Christopher Clark, *Iron Kingdom: The Rise and Downfall of Prussia, 1600–1947*, London, Allen Lane, 2006, pp. 331–8.

12. On Grégoire's conception of regeneration, see Alyssa Goldstein Sepinwall, *The Abbé Grégoire and the French Revolution: The Making of Modern Universalism*, Berkeley, University of California Press, 2005, pp. 56–136. In 1769, Lavater had attempted to convert Mendelssohn to Christianity by sending him Charles Bonnet's proto-evolutionary *Palingénésie Philosophique*, and urging him either to refute Bonnet's argument or to convert.

13. On Karl's family see Jonathan Sperber, *Karl Marx: A Nineteenth-Century Life*, New York, Liveright Publishing Corporation, 2013, ch. 1, pp. 5–25.

14. Delpech, 'La Révolution et l'Empire', pp. 282–5.

15. See Rowe, *From Reich to State*, Part II.

16. Cited in John McManners, *The French Revolution and the Church*, London, SPCK, 1969, p. 142.

17. Delpech, 'La Révolution et l'Empire', p. 287; see also Robert Anchel, *Napoléon et les Juifs*, Paris, Presses Universitaires de France, 1928, pp. 62–75.

18. See Albert Rauch, 'Der Grosse Sanhedrin zu Paris und sein Einfluss auf die jüdische Familie Marx in Trier', in Richard Laufner and Albert Rauch (eds.), *Die Familie Marx und die Trierer Judenschaft*, Schriften aus dem Karl-Marx-Haus, Trier, 1975, no. 14, pp. 18–22; Anchel, *Napoléon et les Juifs*, pp. 187–226; Delpech, 'La Révolution et l'Empire', pp. 286–301.

19. Heinz Monz, 'Der Religionswechsel der Familie Heinrich Marx', in Monz, *Karl Marx: Grundlagen*, ch. 19, pp. 239–40.

20. Laufner and Rauch, 'Vorbemerkung', in *Die Familie Marx und die Trierer Judenschaft*.

21. Rowe, *From Reich to State*, pp. 253–4.

22. Clark, *Iron Kingdom*, p. 311.

23. Hagen Schulze, *The Course of German Nationalism: From Frederick the Great to Bismarck, 1763–1867*, Cambridge, Cambridge University Press, 1991, pp. 48–56; and see also Clark, *Iron Kingdom*, ch. 11.

24. Monz, *Karl Marx: Grundlagen*, pp. 245-8.

25. Ibid., p. 247.

26. Ibid., p. 248.

27. Wilhelm Liebknecht, *Karl Marx: Biographical Memoirs*, London, Journeyman Press, 1975 [1901], pp. 13-14; 'Eleanor Marx to Wilhelm Liebknecht', in David McLellan (ed.), *Karl Marx: Interviews and Recollections*, London, Macmillan, 1981, p. 163.

28. 'Heinrich Marx to Karl Marx', 12 August 1837, *Karl Marx/Friedrich Engels Collected Works*, 50 vols., Moscow, London and New York, 1975-2005 (henceforth *MECW*), vol. 1, p. 674.

29. 'Edgar von Westphalen to Friedrich Engels', 15 June 1883, *International Institute of Social History Amsterdam, Karl Marx/Friedrich Engels Papers*, Inv. nr. L 6312-6319 [L IX 233-240].

    For Lessing's situating Christianity as a stage in the progressive education of humanity, see 'The Education of the Human Race', in H. B. Nisbet (ed.), *Lessing: Philosophical and Theological Writings*, Cambridge, Cambridge University Press, 2005, pp. 217-40; for Kant, see 'Religion within the Boundaries of Mere Reason', in I. Kant, *Religion within the Boundaries of Mere Reason and Other Writings*, eds. Allen Wood and George di Giovanni, Cambridge, Cambridge University Press, 1998, pp. 31-191.

30. 'Heinrich Marx to Karl Marx', 18 November 1835, *MECW*, vol. 1, p. 647.

31. Monz, *Karl Marx: Grundlagen*, p. 252.

32. 'Heinrich Marx to Henriette Marx', 12-14 August 1837, *Karl Marx-Friedrich Engels Historisch-Kritische Gesamtausgabe* Berlin, 1927-35 (henceforth *MEGA*), III, i, p. 313.

33. See Monz, *Karl Marx: Grundlagen*, ch. 4; Rowe, *From Reich to State*, p. 274.

34. Karl Marx, 'Proceedings of the Sixth Rhine Province Assembly. Third Article. Debates on the Law on Thefts of Wood' (1842), *MECW*, vol. 1, pp. 224-63. Jonathan Sperber, *Rhineland Radicals: The Democratic Movement and the Revolution of 1848-1849*, Princeton, Princeton University Press, 1991, p. 77.

35. See Monz, *Karl Marx: Grundlagen*, p. 52.

36. Estates were broad social orders in a hierarchically conceived society and were the standard form of representation before 1789. Although they continued to be favoured by conservatives throughout the nineteenth century, their legitimacy was radically challenged in the French Revolution, when the 'Third Estate' was declared to be the 'Nation', and the other two estates, clergy and nobility, were abolished.

37. Rowe, *From Reich to State*, pp. 270-71.

38. H. Heine, *Ludwig Börne: Recollections of a Revolutionist*, trans. Thomas S. Egan, London, Newman, 1881, p. 51.

39. Rowe, *From Reich to State*, pp. 276-8.

40. Speech cited in Monz, *Karl Marx und Trier*, p. 88.

41. Monz, *Karl Marx: Grundlagen*, p. 135.

42. Ibid., pp. 135–6.

43. 'Heinrich Marx to Karl Marx', 18–29 November 1835, *MECW*, vol. 1, pp. 647–8.

44. 'Heinrich Marx to Karl Marx', 2 March 1837, *MECW*, vol. 1, pp. 672–3.

45. McLellan (ed.), *Karl Marx: Interviews and Recollections*, p. 163.

46. Rowe, *From Reich to State*, pp. 247–9; Sperber, *Rhineland Radicals*, pp. 47–9.

2 THE LAWYER, THE POET AND THE LOVER

1. Franz Mehring, *Karl Marx: The Story of His Life*, trans. Edward Fitzgerald, London, John Lane, 1936, p. 2. The original German edition appeared in Berlin in 1918.

2. Cited in Jan Gielkens, *Karl Marx und seine niederländischen Verwandten: Eine kommentierte Quellenedition, Schriften aus dem Karl-Marx-Haus, Trier*, no. 50, 1999, p. 33.

3. Heinz Monz, *Karl Marx: Grundlagen der Entwicklung zu Leben und Werk*, Trier, Verlag Neu, 1973, p. 251.

4. 'Karl Marx to Friedrich Engels', 30 April 1868, *MECW*, vol. 43, p. 24.

5. 'Henriette Marx to Karl Marx', early 1836, *MECW*, vol. 1, p. 652.

6. 'Henriette Marx to Henriette van Anrooji', 18 November 1851; cited in Gielkens, *Karl Marx*, p. 143.

7. 'Henriette Marx to Sophie Philips', 14 April 1853; Gielkens, *Karl Marx*, p. 154.

8. 'Henriette Marx to Karl Marx', 29 November 1836, *MECW*, vol. 1, pp. 648–9.

9. 'Heinrich and Henriette Marx to Karl Marx', early 1836, *MECW*, vol. 1, pp. 651–2.

10. 'Henriette Marx to Karl Marx', 16 September 1837, *MECW*, vol. 1, p. 683; ibid., 10 February 1838, p. 693.

11. Of Hermann, who was apprenticed to an Amsterdam merchant, Heinrich wrote, 'of his hard work, I expect much, of his intelligence all the less'. 'Heinrich Marx to Karl Marx', 9 November 1836, *MECW*, vol. 1, p. 663.

12. Ibid., 12 August 1837, p. 674.

13. 'Jenny Westphalen to Karl Marx', 11–18 August 1844, *MEGA*, III, i, p. 441.

14. Cited in Monz, *Karl Marx: Grundlagen*, p. 235.

15. See, for instance, Mehring, *Karl Marx*, p. 5.

16. Karl Marx, 'Reflections of a Young Man on the Choice of a Profession', *Gymnasium* essay, August 1835, *MECW*, vol. 1, p. 7.

17. 'Heinrich Marx to Karl Marx', early 1836, *MECW*, vol. 1, p. 650.

18. Ibid., May/June 1836, p. 654.
19. 'Karl Marx to Heinrich Marx', 10/11 November 1837, *MECW*, vol. 1, p. 18.
20. 'Henriette Marx to Karl Marx', 15/16 February 1838, *MEGA*, II, i, p. 330.
21. Monz, *Karl Marx: Grundlagen*, p. 233.
22. Nothing comparable was expected of Karl's younger brother, Hermann: born on 12 August 1818. In 1836, according to his father, Hermann went to Brussels to be trained as a merchant. His father wrote, 'Of his industriousness I expect much, of his intelligence all the less.' He died in Trier in 1842 from consumption. See Monz, *Karl Marx: Grundlagen*, pp. 233–4.
23. Institut Marksizma–Leninzma, *Reminiscences of Marx and Engels*, Moscow, Foreign Languages Publishing House, 1957, p. 251. According to Eleanor's account, the sisters put up with this treatment, as they liked the stories he told them in recompense.
24. 'Heinrich Marx to Karl Marx', 28 December 1836, *MECW*, vol. 1, p. 664.
25. Ibid., 9 November 1836, p. 661; ibid., 12 August 1837, p. 675.
26. Monz, *Karl Marx: Grundlagen*, pp. 297–319.
27. 'Karl Marx to Friedrich Engels', 17 September 1878, *MECW*, vol. 45, p. 322.
28. See Monz, *Karl Marx: Grundlagen*, pp. 147, 153, 161–2.
29. On the Hambach Festival, see Chapter 1, p. 26.
30. In 1835, the works of a number of writers, including Heinrich Heine, Ludwig Börne and Karl Gutzkow, were banned at Metternich's instigation owing to the authors' alleged membership of Young Germany, a branch of the Mazzinian revolutionary secret society Young Europe. In fact, the Confederation had confused two distinct groups sharing the same name (although it is questionable whether Metternich was really so naive). The literary 'Young Germany' was never more than a loose association of writers, united by shared journalistic ventures and the championing of a similar literary and political outlook. Their alliance, such as it was, only existed between 1833 and 1835. Persecution quickly broke the connections between them, and the movement ended in a fog of mutual recrimination, apostasy and vendetta, most notoriously an undignified attack by Heine upon the memory of Börne.

    Nevertheless, Metternich had not been wrong to scent in Young Germany an unwelcome eruption on the hitherto placid surface of nineteenth-century German literature. For Young Germany was quite clearly a literary response to the 1830 revolutions, and an explicit attack, both upon the medievalist conservatism of the Romantic Movement and upon the political detachment of Goethe and German classicism. Both Friedrich Engels and Jenny von Westphalen were momentarily enthused by it.
31. On the social and political tensions in Trier in the aftermath of the 1830 revolutions, see Chapter 1, pp. 26–8.
32. 'Certificate of Maturity for Pupil of the Gymnasium in Trier', *MECW*, vol. 1, pp. 643–4; Monz, *Karl Marx: Grundlagen*, p. 314.

33. Marx, 'Reflections of a Young Man on the Choice of a Profession', pp. 3–9.

34. 'Johann Hugo Wyttenbach to Karl Marx', August 1835, *MECW*, vol. 1, p. 733.

35. The Prussian government funding to the Protestant Theology Faculty in Bonn was twice that of the Catholic faculty, although it took far fewer students. See Michael Rowe, *From Reich to State: The Rhineland in the Revolutionary Age, 1780–1830*, Cambridge, Cambridge University Press, 2003, p. 251.

36. Once a supporter of the French, Joseph Görres, a prominent Catholic publicist, was dismissed as Director of Education in Coblenz and wrote an influential attack on Prussian bureaucratic rule in the Rhineland in *Deutschland und die Revolution*, Coblenz, 1819; Ernst Moritz Arndt was an outspoken nationalist. In 1814, he had been secretary to the former Prussian First Minister, von Stein, at the time when he was head of the Inter-Allied Central Administration in the Rhineland. Appointed a professor of history at Bonn, Arndt attacked the police. In 1819 he was suspended for alleged links with the subversive activities of the *Burschenschaften*, and only rehabilitated in 1840 by the new Prussian king, Friedrich Wilhelm IV.

37. 'Bruno Bauer to Karl Marx', 1 March 1840, *MEGA*, III, i, p. 340.

38. 'Certificate of Release from Bonn University', *MECW*, vol. 1, p. 658; *MEGA*, III, i, p. 727; 'Heinrich Marx to Karl Marx', May–June 1836, *MECW*, vol. 1, p. 653; ibid.; ibid.

39. 'Certificate of Release', *MECW*, vol. 1, pp. 657–8; two of the courses in the summer term could not be assessed due to the sudden death of the lecturer.

40. See David Lindenfeld, *The Practical Imagination: The German Sciences of State in the Nineteenth Century*, Chicago, Chicago University Press, 1997, pp. 11–17, 60–64, 70–80, 90–91.

41. 'Heinrich Marx to Karl Marx', early 1836, *MECW*, vol. 1, p. 650.

42. Under Chancellor Hardenberg in the early 1820s, it had been agreed that no new taxes could be raised except with the consent of a representative assembly. This meant that despite the large increase in the Prussian population, the numbers employed in the administration remained static. See Lenore O'Boyle, 'The Problem of an Excess of Educated Men in Western Europe, 1800–1850', *Journal of Modern History*, 42 (1970), 471–95; Reinhart Koselleck, 'Staat und Gesellschaft in Preußen 1815–1848', in H.-U. Wehler (ed.), *Moderne deutsche Sozialgeschichte*, 2nd edn, Cologne, Kiepenheuer & Witsch, 1968, pp. 55–85; Reinhart Koselleck, 'Staat und Gesellschaft in Preußen 1815–1848', in Werner Conze (ed.), *Staat und Gesellschaft im deutschen Vormärz 1815–1848*, Stuttgart, E. Klett, 1962 (Industrielle Welt, vol. 1).

43. 'Karl Marx to Heinrich Marx', 10/11 November 1837, *MECW*, vol. 1, p. 20.

44. Institut Marksizma–Leninzma, *Reminiscences of Marx and Engels*, p. 130; Wilhelm Liebknecht, *Karl Marx: Biographical Memoirs*, London, Journeyman Press, 1975 [1901], p. 14.

45. 'Heinrich Marx to Karl Marx', 18 November 1835, *MECW*, vol. 1, p. 647.

46. Ibid. In November 1837, Karl burnt his earlier poetic works, see below, pp. 42, 47. A selection of his love poems was published in 1977: see *Love Poems of Karl Marx*, eds. R. Lettau and L. Ferlinghetti, City Lights Books, San Francisco, 1977.

47. 'Heinrich Marx to Karl Marx', early 1836, *MECW*, vol. 1, pp. 650–51.

48. 'Karl Marx to Heinrich Marx', 10/11 November 1837, *MECW*, vol. 1, p. 11.

49. See *MECW*, vol. 1, pp. 22–4 and pp. 517–616.

50. See in particular S. S. Prawer, *Karl Marx and World Literature*, Oxford, Clarendon Press, 1976; Mikhail Lifshitz, *The Philosophy of Art of Karl Marx*, London, Pluto Press, 1973 [Moscow, 1933]; P. Demetz, *Marx, Engels and the Poets: Origins of Marxist Literary Criticism*, Chicago, University of Chicago Press, 1967 [Stuttgart, 1959].

51. One exception, especially significant in the Rhineland, was the attack on entail and primogeniture found in *Scorpion and Felix*, ch. 29. 'The right of primogeniture', he claimed, 'is the wash-closet of the aristocracy', *MECW*, vol. 1, pp. 624–5.

52. Demetz, *Marx, Engels and the Poets*, p. 50.

53. 'Feelings', cited in Prawer, *Karl Marx and World Literature*, p. 12.

54. 'Concluding Sonnet to Jenny', cited in Lifshitz, *Philosophy of Art*, p. 16.

55. 'Human Pride', *MECW*, vol. 1, p. 586.

56. 'Sir (G)luck's *Armide*', *MECW*, vol. 1, p. 540.

57. 'Epigrams', *MECW*, vol. 1, pp. 576–7, 579.

58. *Scorpion and Felix*, *MECW*, vol. 1, pp. 624–5, 628.

59. *Oulanem*, *MECW*, vol. 1, pp. 593, 600, 606.

60. Ibid., p. 599.

61. Demetz, *Marx, Engels and the Poets*, pp. 55–6; see also Nicholas Saul, 'Aesthetic Humanism (1790–1830)', in Helen Watanabe-O'Kelly (ed.), *The Cambridge History of German Literature*, Cambridge, Cambridge University Press, 1997, pp. 248–50.

62. *Oulanem*, *MECW*, vol. 1, p. 601.

63. Ibid.

64. 'Heinrich Marx to Karl Marx', 28 December 1836, *MECW*, vol. 1, p. 666.

65. 'Karl Marx to Heinrich Marx', 10/11 November 1837, *MECW*, vol. 1, pp. 17–19.

66. 'Heinrich Marx to Karl Marx', 16 September 1837, *MECW*, vol. 1, p. 680.

67. 'Karl Marx to Heinrich Marx', 10/11 November 1837, *MECW*, vol. 1, p. 18. The quotation comes from Heine's poetry cycle *The North Sea*.

68. *MEGA*, I, i (2), pp. 92–6. The collection is drawn in large part not from the most famous collection of the period, Arnim and Brentano's *Boy's Magic Horn* (*Des Knaben Wunderhorn*) but from a less altered and reworked collection by Erlach, Kretschmer and Zuccalmaglio. It is also

interesting that Marx included one item used by Byron in *Childe Harold's Pilgrimage*. See Prawer, *Karl Marx and World Literature*, p. 20.

69. Monz, *Karl Marx: Grundlagen*, p. 324. On the family history of the Westphalens, see Boris Nicolaievsky and Otto Maenchen-Helfen, *Karl Marx: Man and Fighter*, trans. G. David and E. Mosbacher, London, Allen Lane, 1973 [1933], pp. 23–7.

70. The term 'Westphalia' was misleading. Westphalia refers to the region of Germany situated between the Rivers Rhine and Weser, and north and south of the River Ruhr. The Kingdom of Westphalia, on the other hand, was created in 1807 by merging territories ceded by Prussia in the Peace of Tilsit. These included the region west of the River Elbe and parts of Brunswick, Hanover and Hesse.

71. The state had a written constitution, jury trials and equal rights before the law, and French-style central administration. In 1808, it was the first German state to grant equal rights to the Jews.

72. Monz, *Karl Marx: Grundlagen*, pp. 325–7.

73. See Heinz Monz, 'Politische Anschauung und gesellschaftliche Stellung von Johann Ludwig von Westfalen', in Schriften aus dem Karl-Marx-Haus, Trier, no. 9: *Zur Persönlichkeit von Marx' Schwiegervater Johann Ludwig von Westphalen*, 1973, pp. 5–19. It is significant that he urged his nephew to burn the letter after reading it.

74. Konrad von Krosigk, 'Ludwig von Westphalen und seine Kinder: Bruchstücke familiärer Überlieferungen' in Schriften aus dem Karl-Marx-Haus, Trier, no. 9: *Zur Persönlichkeit von Marx' Schwiegervater*, p. 47.

75. The testimony of Lutz Graf Schwerin von Krosigk, cited in Monz, *Karl Marx: Grundlagen*, p. 345.

76. 'Karl Marx to Friedrich Engels', 15 December 1863, *MECW*, vol. 41, p. 499.

77. Letter from Ferdinand to his father-in-law, 10 April 1831, cited in Monz, *Karl Marx: Grundlagen*, p. 344.

78. Testimony of Lutz Graf Schwerin von Krosigk, p. 345.

79. Ibid.

80. Von Krosigk, 'Ludwig von Westphalen und seine Kinder', pp. 71–2.

81. 'Karl Marx to Friedrich Engels', 16 August 1865, *MECW*, vol. 42, pp. 180–81.

82. *OED* online states of Auscultator: 'Title formerly given in Germany to a young lawyer who has passed his first public examination, and is thereupon employed by Government, but without salary and with no fixed appointment (now called *Referendar*). 'Ausser Diensten' means 'in retirement'.

83. 'Jenny von Westphalen to Friedrich Engels', 23–24 December 1859, *MECW*, vol. 40, pp. 574–5. The conflict was made worse by the fact that Jenny suspected this was part of a plan to cheat her part of the Westphalen family out of an anticipated legacy.

84. 'Eleanor Marx-Aveling to Wilhelm Liebknecht', 15 April 1896, cited in Monz, *Karl Marx: Grundlagen*, p. 342.

3 BERLIN AND THE APPROACHING TWILIGHT OF THE GODS

1. Ernst Dronke (1822–91), from Coblenz, studied at Bonn, Marburg and Berlin. As a result of his book on Berlin, in 1847 he was sentenced to two years' confinement. He managed to escape to Brussels, where he became acquainted with Engels and Marx and joined the Communist League. In 1848, he accompanied them to Cologne, where he played a prominent part in the editorial team which produced the *Neue Rheinische Zeitung*. He participated in the 1849 rising and then escaped, first to Switzerland and then to England, where he spent the rest of his life. In 1852, he withdrew from politics and became an agent for a copper-mining company.

2. Ernst Dronke, *Berlin*, Darmstadt, Neuwied Luchterhand, 1974 [Frankfurt am Main, J. Rütten, 1846], p. 67; Friedrich Sass, *Berlin in seiner neuesten Zeit und Entwicklung*, Leipzig, Koffka, 1846, pp. 12, 134; and see Robert J. Hellman, *Berlin, the Red Room and White Beer: The 'Free' Hegelian Radicals in the 1840s*, Washington, DC, Three Continents Press, 1990, pp. 5–25.

3. Henry Vizetelly, *Berlin under the New Empire: Its Institutions, Inhabitants, Industry, Monuments, Museums, Social Life, Manners, and Amusements*, 2 vols, London, Tinsley, 1879, vol. 1, pp. 14–16, cited in Hellman, *Berlin*, p. 22.

4. Edgar Bauer, *Bruno Bauer und seine Gegner*, Jonas, Berlin, 1842, pp. 80–81, cited in Hellman, *Berlin*, p. 14.

5. Vizetelly, *Berlin*, vol. 2, p. 314; Hellman, *Berlin*, p. 9.

6. As a result of defeat at Jena and Auerstadt, Prussia lost half of its territory and was made to pay a massive indemnity. In order to pay it, the state was compelled to undergo a radical process of rationalization; and this brought to the fore reformers eager to implement a programme of reforms, based upon Enlightenment ideals. Serfdom was abolished, guild monopolies were removed, the military and educational systems transformed, and Jews accorded partial emancipation, and city government was reorganized on a representative basis. The reforms were carried out under the direction of von Stein (1807–10) and subsequently von Hardenberg (1810–22). The period of reform came to an end in 1819 with a conservative reaction highlighted by the Carlsbad Decrees.

7. Berlin and other Prussian universities benefited from the remarkable expansion of educational provision during the 'Reform Era' (1807–22). Between 1816 and 1846, the percentage of children attending school between six and fourteen rose from 61 to 82 per cent. The population of elementary schools rose by 108 per cent, that of *Gymnasiums* by 73 per cent and that of universities by 40 per cent. Together with this went a

remarkable expansion of social mobility. In the 1830s, for example, it was estimated that one third of the students enrolled at Halle were the sons of peasants, artisans and lower officials. See John R. Gillis, *The Prussian Bureaucracy in Crisis, 1840–1860: Origins of an Administrative Ethos*, Stanford, Stanford University Press, 1971.

8. Eduard Meyen, in *Hallische Jahrbücher für deutsche Wissenschaft und Kunst*, Leipzig, Verlag von Otto Wigard, no. 193, 12 August 1840, p. 1542, cited in Hellman, *Berlin*, p. 10.

9. 'Karl Marx to Heinrich Marx', 10–11 November 1837, *MECW*, vol. 1, pp. 10–21. The following quotations are from the same source.

10. He eventually filled 168 notebooks, providing subsequent scholars with an in invaluable guide to his intellectual development and its sources.

11. 'Heinrich Marx to Karl Marx', 28 December 1836, *MECW*, vol. 1, p. 664; ibid., 12 August 1837, p. 674; ibid., 16 September 1837, pp. 682–3; ibid., 17 November 1837, p. 684; ibid., 9 December 1837, p. 689.

12. Ibid., 28 December 1836, pp. 664–5, 666; ibid., 3 February 1837, p. 668.

13. Ibid., 28 December 1836, p. 664; ibid., 2 March 1837, pp. 670, 671.

14. Ibid., pp. 675, 691.

15. Ibid., p. 688.

16. Ibid., pp. 680, 690, 692.

17. Ibid., pp. 674, 678, 691–3, 694.

18. Dronke, *Berlin*, pp. 19, 21.

19. Hellman, *Berlin*, pp. 11, 18–22.

20. The German Historical School of Law came into prominence as part of the conservative reaction to the universal language of the rights of man associated with the French Revolution. It had originated in Göttingen before 1789 as a riposte to the stylized quasi-histories of Roman Law, which assumed that private property was coterminous with human nature and human history. After 1815, it became a central issue in the debate about the elaboration of a uniform legal code in the German Confederation. Savigny attacked the (rationalist and Enlightenment) idea of a universal code and championed instead a gradual, peaceful and non-political path to the peasant emancipation from feudalism. Gans in contrast considered that the validity of law derived from its coherence as a system of relations and obligations. In 1838, he attacked Savigny's view, defending codification as a means of reinforcing the law's universality and of marginalizing the discretionary role played by a conservative professorial elite.

21. Now spelt Stralau. This is a tongue of land between the River Spree and the Rummelsburger Sea. Since 1920 it has been part of Greater Berlin, but in the middle of the nineteenth century it was a separate village, which in 1855 counted 143 inhabitants.

22. Hegel's concern was the conscious mind. He had no time for symbolic and poetic intimations of the Absolute supposedly made possible by Schelling's idea of 'Intellectual intuition'. It was perhaps for that reason that Karl had

first been repelled by 'the grotesque craggy melody'. In later years, Hegel had also come to consider that art was of subordinate importance. It was no longer capable of portraying freedom or the divine, as it once had when Greek art through the gods had produced a unique vision of human freedom. With the advent of Jesus, a man rather than a mythical god, religion supplanted art, while in the modern period, with the growth of freedom and rational institutions, Dutch paintings of bourgeois life and domesticity were 'the greatest truth of which art is capable'.

23. Insofar as terms like idealism and materialism impinged upon the outlook of the educated laity in the eighteenth century and the early nineteenth, materialism at least in the Anglo-French tradition was associated with various forms of naturalism, primarily with the notion that man was an animal who pursued pleasure and avoided pain and therefore should seek to create an environment in which the possibilities of happiness were maximized. This was the position pursued by Helvetius, Bentham and the followers of Owenite socialism. It was particularly important as a rejoinder to the Evangelical Christian emphasis upon original sin. Its drawback was the passivity of its conception of man as a creature governed by instincts and interest. On the other hand, idealism in the broadest sense emphasized the ability of man through the employment of reason to resist passions and instinctive drives. In Kant, an ethical employment of reason could be made universal through the use of an ethical injunction urged upon each individual – the categorical imperative ('act only on that maxim which you can at the same time will to be a universal law'). In Hegel, the advance of a rational ethics was conjoined with a notion of historical progress, in which ethical injunctions become progressively institutionalized in systems of law and religion, thus making possible ever more adequate conceptions of 'ethical life'. For the development of idealism in Kant, see below, pp. 71ff. For a more detailed discussion of the attempted actualization of these different positions in the respective theoretical approaches of Marx and Engels in the mid-1840s, see Chapter 6, section 5.

24. Friedrich Karl von Savigny, *The History of the Roman Law in the Middle Ages*, trans. E. Cathcart, Edinburgh, A. Black, 1829, pp. vi, xv.

25. Friedrich Karl von Savigny, *Von Savigny's Treatise on Possession, or The Jus Possessionis of the Civil Law*, trans. Erskine Perry, London, Sweet, 1848, p. 3.

26. Savigny, *Roman Law*, p. xii.

27. Herder's position originally derived from J. G. Hamann, who had attacked Kant's conception of reason in 1783. Reason, he had argued, had no autonomous existence, except insofar as it was embodied in language and action. Reason therefore could not be treated as if it existed beyond the constraints of time and space. Reason had a history and it was embodied in language and culture. Languages and cultures changed over time and differed across space. Thus reason could not be treated as a formal criterion of judgement,

but rather as something embodied in more or less developed form in the spirit of a particular people. In contrast to Savigny, however, Herder also believed that national communities existed alongside each other in a pre-existing harmony, and in this sense looked back to the rationalism of Leibniz. See Frederick Beiser, *The Fate of Reason: German Philosophy from Kant to Fichte*, Cambridge, Mass., Harvard University Press, 1987.

28. Friedrich Karl von Savigny, *Of the Vocation of Our Age for Legislation and Jurisprudence*, trans. Abraham Hayward, London, Littlewood & Co., 1828, p. 24.

29. Savigny, *Roman Law*, p. xiv.

30. It has often been assumed that Gans must have exerted a considerable impact upon the young Karl. The basis of this assumption is that in the early 1830s Gans had visited Paris, interested himself in modern poverty and 'the social question', and had written about the Saint-Simonians. But this is contested. While it is true that Gans was one of the first to produce a progressive reading of Hegel, and edited the posthumous publication both of *The Philosophy of Right* and of *The Philosophy of History*, the trajectory of his thinking was quite distinct from that of the principal Young Hegelians. While he was sympathetic to the Saint-Simonian critique of competition, he was hostile towards Saint-Simonian ideas about religion and Enfantin's notion of 'the rehabilitation of the flesh'. He contested the Saint-Simonian assumption of the primacy of society over the state. When combined with the Saint-Simonian slogan, 'to each according to his capacities', Gans considered that there was a real risk of creating a new 'slavery', a 'slavery of surveillance'. While it is highly likely that Karl respected Gans as a counterweight to the arguments of Savigny, even in his early years in Berlin there are no references to Gans in Karl's letters or writings; and there are few unambiguous traces of the influence of his ideas. By 1842–3, it is clear that (had Gans lived) there was a wide divergence between Gans's ideas and those of Karl. Karl criticized Hegel's *Philosophy of Right* precisely on the basis of the primacy of society over the state. He amended the Saint-Simonian formula from 'to each according to his capacities' to 'to each according to his needs', and used it both in *The Poverty of Philosophy* (1847) and much later in *The Critique of the Gotha Programme* (1875). But this change of wording, although important in other ways, would not have obviated Gans's objection, which was to the authoritarian implications of the Saint-Simonian proposal. On Gans's criticism of Saint-Simonianism, see Myriam Bienenstock, 'Between Hegel and Marx: Eduard Gans on the "Social Question"', in Douglas Moggach (ed.), *Politics, Religion and Art: Hegelian Debates*, Evanston, Ill., Northwestern University Press, 2011, pp. 164–79.

31. The term 'party of movement' was current in the 1830s and 1840s. It is particularly useful because it captures the fact that at the time liberals, radicals, republicans and to some extent even socialists were not clearly distinguished. On Gans's membership of the Friends of Poland, see Auguste

Cornu, *Karl Marx et Friedrich Engels: Leur vie et leur oeuvre*, Paris, Presses Universitaires de France, 1955, vol. 1, p. 87.

32. Saint-Simon (1760–1825), often thought of as one of the founders of socialism, considered that the French Revolution had failed because it had failed 'to combine the interests of men ... by opening a path common to the particular and to the general interest'. This was the path of science. He also agreed with conservative critics of the Revolution that the Revolution had not been able to establish a new form of *pouvoir spirituel* (spiritual power) capable of displacing the Catholic church. Religion was essential since it was the ultimate source of a law which could bind together a community. In his early writings, he believed that Christianity could no longer play this role since it was scientifically obsolete. He had therefore proposed 'the religion of Newton'. But with the return of the French monarchy after 1815, he modified his argument, and in his last major work, *New Christianity*, argued that the Christian religion could be reconciled with science, by boiling it down to two premisses – that all men must treat each other as brothers, and that all must concern themselves with the improvement of the lot of the poorest and most numerous class.

After his death in 1825, his followers formed themselves into a collective group, and in 1829 produced *The Doctrine of Saint-Simon*, with the ambition of establishing a Saint-Simonian church. This made a sensational impact upon European intellectuals and, theoretically, was one of the defining sources of all thought about the 'social question' after 1830.

33. Discussion of the 'social question' became current in Western Europe in the early 1840s. It originated in the debates which occurred in the aftermath of the 1830 Revolution in France and the 1832 Reform Bill in Britain. The prominent participation of workers on the barricades in Paris in the three days which led to the abdication of Charles X, and in the Reform crisis in Britain, raised the question both of their continued subordinate constitutional status and of the new forms of poverty that afflicted them. In Germany, the discussion was further complicated by the difficulty of placing the new urban workers and rural migrants into the official categories of estate society. Sismondi in his *New Principles of Political Economy* of 1819 had introduced the term 'proletariat' to describe this novel phenomenon. Hegel, in *The Philosophy of Right*, had referred to this grouping as *das Pöbel* (the mob). Gans had originally accepted this terminology, but in the light of his visits both to France and to England adopted the term 'proletariat'. See Norbert Waszek, 'Eduard Gans on Poverty and on the Constitutional Debate', in D. Moggach (ed.), *The New Hegelians: Politics and Philosophy in the Hegelian School*, New York, Cambridge University Press, 2006, pp. 24–50.

34. On Gans's position on the history and philosophy of law, see Michael H. Hoffheimer, *Eduard Gans and the Hegelian Philosophy of Law*, Dordrecht, Kluwer Academic Publishers, 1995.

35. Savigny, *Of the Vocation*, pp. iv, 9, 18, 20, 22.

36. See Hoffheimer, *Gans*, pp. 35, 46. It is important to note, however, that Savigny's position was that of a 'conservative reformist' rather than of a straightforward reactionary. In relation to the gradual shift from feudal relations to possessory interests in the countryside, he contended that Roman Law could be adapted to new situations. In his view, gradual reform of property relations in the countryside should be led by legal scholarship rather than by legislation. See James Q. Whitman, *The Legacy of Roman Law in the German Romantic Era: Historical Vision and Legal Change*, Princeton, Princeton University Press, 1990, pp. 183–5.

37. See Hoffheimer, *Gans*, pp. 42–6.

38. Ibid., pp. 19–21.

39. See Donald Kelley, 'The Metaphysics of Law: An Essay on the Very Young Marx', *American Historical Review*, 83/2 (1978), pp. 350–67; Warren Breckman, *Marx, the Young Hegelians, and the Origins of Radical Social Theory: Dethroning the Self*, Cambridge, Cambridge University Press, 1999, p. 261.

40. *MECW*, vol. 1, p. 679.

41. Within the state administration itself, political reforms once thought imminent, like the promise to summon a representative assembly, were not carried through. One of the king's closest advisers, the Huguenot preacher Jean Pierre Ancillon, was convinced that the summoning of such an assembly would spark off a sequence of events which would replicate the actions of the French National Assembly in 1789 and end in the abolition of the monarchy. Instead, the government had established a series of provincial Diets, summoned along the lines of the traditional estates and denied any power over taxation. See Christopher Clark, *Iron Kingdom: The Rise and Downfall of Prussia, 1600–1947*, London, Allen Lane, 2006, pp. 402–3.

42. G. W. F. Hegel, *Elements of the Philosophy of Right*, ed. A. W. Wood, Cambridge, Cambridge University Press, 1991 [1821], p. 20. For a less guarded statement of his political philosophy before the Carlsbad Decrees, see G. W. F. Hegel, *Lectures on Natural Right and Political Science: The First Philosophy of Right*, trans. J. Michael Stewart and Peter C. Hodgson, Berkeley, University of California Press, 1995. Hegel's position remained ambivalent. According to Heine, having listened to the lectures on *The Philosophy of Right*, and being shocked by Hegel's notorious claim about the identity of the 'rational' and the 'actual', Heine went up and asked him to explain the meaning of his statement. Hegel is alleged to have smiled furtively and said quietly, 'It may also be expressed thus: all that is rational must be.' See G. Nicolin, *Hegel in Berichten seiner Zeitgenossen*, Hamburg, F. Meiner, 1970, p. 235.

43. In Kant's analysis in the first *Critique*, human sensory intuitions became representations of objects of nature when combined with non-intuitive conceptual forms (categories of thought). These representations took the

form of judgements, which were structured by rules followed by all rational agents. Objects of which we could become conscious had to be objects of possible experience. They had to have an existence in space and time. This ruled out non-sensible entities such as God or the immortal soul, since these could not be forms of any possible intuition.

44. Kant's theory of moral autonomy required that we only submit to laws which we ourselves have made. Morality, the *moral law*, was articulated in the form of a categorical imperative whereby we only apply to others that which we would apply to ourselves as an act of universal legislation. The problem created by this position was that if as natural beings our behaviour is solely determined by our interests (the pursuit of 'happiness') how was morality to find a place?

45. Immanuel Kant, *Religion within the Boundaries of Mere Reason and Other Writings*, eds. Allen Wood and George di Giovanni, Cambridge, Cambridge University Press, 1998, pp. 105–12.

46. The final end was introduced as an extension of the moral law, brought about by 'the natural characteristic of man that, for all his actions, he must conceive of an end over and above the law'. See W. Jaeschke, *Reason in Religion: The Foundations of Hegel's Philosophy of Religion*, trans. J. Michael Stewart and Peter C. Hodgson, Berkeley, University of California Press, 1990, p. 80; and see also pp. 72–3, 76–7.

47. Ibid., p. 82.

48. This was the position adopted by Kant's most immediate successor, Fichte. As a result in 1798 he was accused of atheism. See Yolanda Estes (ed.) and Curtis Bowman (ed., tr.), *J. G. Fichte and the Atheism Dispute (1798–1800)*, Farnham, Ashgate, 2010.

49. Hölderlin was both a poet and a philosopher responsible for some of the earliest formulations of the idea of the 'Absolute'. Schelling was the most precocious and prolific pioneer of post-Kantian idealism. After Tübingen, he left for Jena, where he became a leading light in a famous circle of Romantic writers, which included the Schlegel brothers and Schleiermacher. In 1800, he invited Hegel to join him and for a number of years they jointly edited a philosophy journal. Their friendship was brought to an end by the publication in 1807 of Hegel's *Phenomenology of the Spirit*, in which Hegel sharply criticized Schelling's intuitional conception of the Absolute. In the 1830s and 1840s, radicals remained in awe of Schelling's youthful pantheism and his philosophy of nature, but heavily critical of his return to a form of Christianity and renunciation of his philosophical past.

50. In his *Education of the Human Race* of 1780, Lessing incorporated the revealed story of Christianity into a chapter in the larger story about the progress of humanity towards a state of moral perfection. See H. B. Nisbet (ed.), *Lessing: Philosophical and Theological Writings*, Cambridge, Cambridge University Press, 2005, pp. 217–40. Like Kant, Lessing had looked

forward to the advent of a new and more enlightened form of religion, in which morality was no longer tied to prudential calculations about life after death. Rousseau's conception of 'civil religion' was developed in his *Social Contract*. See J.-J. Rousseau, *The Social Contract and Other Later Political Writings*, ed. Victor Gourevitch, Cambridge, Cambridge University Press, 1997, pp. 150–51; on Hegel's conception of the ethical harmony of Ancient Greece, see G. W. F. Hegel, *Phenomenology of Spirit*, trans. A. V. Miller, Oxford, Clarendon Press, 1979, paras 699–704.

51. 'The Earliest System-programme of German Idealism' (Berne, 1796), H. S. Harris, *Hegel's Development: Toward the Sunlight, 1770–1801*, Oxford, Clarendon Press, 1972, pp. 511–12.

52. Self-consciousness did not mean individual self-awareness, but the conjunction of particular and universal consciousness in the development of spirit. For the use of the term by Marx and Bruno Bauer, see Chapter 4, pp. 92–3.

53. Hegel insisted that his conception of the Absolute was different from Spinoza's 'substance', *Deus sive Natura* (God or Nature). Whether imagined in mechanical or, following Herder, in organic terms, Spinoza's substance unlike the Christian God was not a person or a subject. Hegel's God, by contrast, was at the level of religion a person, and at the philosophical level 'the Concept'. Unlike Spinoza's notion of substance, therefore, Hegel's Absolute was not something underlying the phenomenal world, but the conceptual system embedded within it. This conceptual system was not static; it developed with the advance of human knowledge and development. For this reason, Hegel's Absolute claimed to be an advance from 'substance' to 'subject'.

54. See Warren Breckman, 'Ludwig Feuerbach and the Political Theology of Restoration', *History of Political Thought*, vol. 13/3, 1992, pp. 437–62; also Breckman, *Marx, the Young Hegelians*, chs. 2 and 3.

55. Hegel's conception of the world began with thought (logic). Schelling's refutation was considered to be the first proclamation of what became the existentialist assertion proclaimed by Jean-Paul Sartre that 'existence precedes essence'. Or, as Kierkegaard argued, Schelling had located in the original passage from nothing to being the inability of 'all purely rational systems' to include 'the empirical, the existent, the real'.

56. See Breckman, 'Ludwig Feuerbach', pp. 445–51.

57. Strauss's book was a turning point, not just in Prussian intellectual history, but in the history of nineteenth-century Europe. Its impact upon Christian belief was as momentous as that later made by Darwin's *On the Origin of Species*. In 1846, a three-volume English edition appeared, translated by Mary Ann Evans (later better known as George Eliot). According to the Evangelical social reformer the Earl of Shaftesbury, this book was 'the most pestilential book ever vomited out of the jaws of hell'.

58. The idea of the Gospels as composite mythical structures created by a later tradition out of sayings belonging to different times and circumstances owed nothing to Hegel, and was in fact closer to the earlier works of Schelling.

59. Clark, *Iron Kingdom*, pp. 419–22.

60. Karl's father, Heinrich, made his last attempt at a public intervention in the rough draft of a short article defending the action of the state in relation to the church. His point was that the actions taken by the crown were a political and not a legal matter. Any ruler, when confronted by a serious threat to the security of the realm, would act beyond the law, and this had nothing to do with the difference between constitutional and absolutist forms of rule. Confronted by an analogous threat, an English minister would not have hesitated to act in a similar fashion. Karl later edited the manuscript. See 'Entwurf einer Broschüre über den Kölner Kirchenstreit zur Verteidigung der Haltung des Königs von Preußen', *MEGA*, I, i (2), 1927, pp. 231–3.

61. See Hegel, *Elements of the Philosophy of Right*, para 270, pp. 290–304.

62. Arnold Ruge (1802–80) was an activist in the student movement, *Burschenschaft*, in the early 1820s, for which he was imprisoned for six years. In the 1830s, he taught as a *Privatdozent* at the University of Halle, where in 1837 he set up the *Hallische Jahrbücher*, followed from 1841 to 1843 by the *Deutsche Jahrbücher*, once censorship had forced him to move to Saxony. With the enforced closure of this journal in 1843 at the behest of the Prussian government, he moved to Paris. He broke with Marx over the question of socialism. In 1848, he was a radical member of the Frankfurt assembly, after which he stayed in exile in England, settling in Brighton. In later years, however, he was a strong supporter of the Bismarckian unification of Germany.

63. For an account of the political development of the *Hallische Jahrbücher* around the end of the 1830s, see, especially, James D. White, *Karl Marx and the Intellectual Origins of Dialectical Materialism*, Basingstoke, Macmillan, 1996, ch. 3.

64. Pietism was a German reform movement within Lutheranism, particularly strong in the seventeenth and eighteenth centuries. It had affinities with Methodism in eighteenth-century England.

65. On Köppen, see especially Helmut Hirsch, 'Karl Friedrich Köppen: Der intimste Berliner Freund Marxens', *International Review of Social History*, vol. 1, 1936, pp. 311–70; and see also Hellman, *Berlin*, pp. 121–31.

66. Karl Friedrich Köppen, 'Friedrich der Grosse und seine Widersacher. Eine Jubelschrift', in Heinz Pepperle (ed.), *Ausgewählte Schriften in zwei Bänden*, Berlin, Akademie Verlag, 2003, vol. 1, pp. 156–7.

67. Friedrich von Schlegel, *Kritische Friedrich-Schlegel-Ausgabe*, Munich, F. Schöningh, 1961, vol. vi, pp. 252–3, cited in White, *Karl Marx*, pp. 122–3.

68. Karl Marx, doctoral dissertation: 'Difference between the Democritan and Epicurean Philosophy of Nature', March 1841, *MECW*, vol. 1, p. 30.

The Epicurean, Stoic and Sceptic philosophies represented 'the nerve muscles and intestinal system of the antique organism whose immediate, natural unity conditioned the beauty and morality of antiquity, and which disintegrated with the decay of the latter': ibid., p. 735.

69. Ibid., pp. 30, 52–3.
70. Ibid., p. 106.
71. Karl Marx, 'Notebooks on Epicurean Philosophy', *MECW*, vol. 1, pp. 491, 492.
72. Marx, doctoral dissertation, p. 86.
73. Ibid., pp. 29, 52, 58, 71.
74. Ibid., pp. 50, 51, 52, 70, 71, 72, 73; Marx, 'Notebooks on Epicurean Philosophy', p. 414.
75. Marx, doctoral dissertation, pp. 66–7, 70, 30, 73.
76. G. W. F. Hegel, *Lectures on the History of Philosophy*, Lincoln, University of Nebraska Press, 1995, vol. 2, p. 234.
77. Marx, doctoral dissertation, pp. 45, 51, 62.
78. Ibid., pp. 73, 74–6, 417–18; on the challenge represented by Schelling and Stahl, see Breckman, 'Ludwig Feuerbach', pp. 438–42.
79. Marx, doctoral dissertation, pp. 85, 86; Marx, 'Notebooks on Epicurean Philosophy', p. 498.

4 REBUILDING THE *POLIS*

1. 'Jenny von Westphalen to Karl Marx', 24 June 1838, *MEGA*, III, i, pp. 332–3.
2. 'Henriette Marx to Karl Marx', 29 May 1840, *MEGA*, III, i, pp. 347–8.
3. 'Sophie Marx to Karl Marx', March 1841, *MEGA*, III, i, p. 351.
4. 'Bruno Bauer to Karl Marx', 12 April 1841, *MEGA*, III, i, pp. 358–9.
5. 'Karl Friedrich Köppen to Karl Marx', 3 June 1841, *MEGA*, III, i, p. 361.
6. 'Bruno Bauer to Karl Marx', early April 1841, *MEGA*, III, i, p. 356.
7. Her death in addition to that of Ludwig put the family under severe financial pressure, and as a result Jenny and her mother moved for a time to Kreuznach.
8. 'Karl Marx to Arnold Ruge', 9 July 1842, *MECW*, vol. 1, p. 389. In the middle of these troubles, Karl's sister Sophie married (12 July 1842). She had been close to Jenny, and had acted as a sort of go-between, and she also remained close to her mother, whom she later described as 'small, delicate and very intelligent'. Sophie's move to Maastricht during the middle of these family troubles may have made the conflict worse. See Jan Gielkens, *Karl Marx und seine niederländischen Verwandten: Eine kommentierte Quellenedition, Schriften aus dem Karl-Marx-Haus, Trier*, no. 50, 1999, p. 33.
9. 'Karl Marx to Arnold Ruge', 25 January 1843, *MECW*, vol. 1, p. 397.

10. See Gielkens, *Karl Marx*, pp. 36–7. The only concession she was prepared to make was to enable Karl to pay off old debts. In 1861, he reported to Lassalle that a visit to Trier had enabled him to destroy some IOUs. But, however estranged, channels of communication continued to exist. Henriette lived the last part of her life at Fleisch Street with Karl's sister Emilie Conradi and her family. It seems from the condolences Eleanor received on the death of her father that Emilie's family remained in regular touch with that of Karl. See Heinz Monz, *Karl Marx: Grundlagen der Entwicklung zu Leben und Werk*, Trier, Verlag Neu, 1973, p. 237.

11. 'Karl Marx to Ferdinand Lassalle', 8 May 1861, *MECW*, vol. 41, p. 283.

12. Preoccupied with his financial worries, Karl had expressed only the most cursory condolences to Friedrich Engels about the death of his companion, Mary Burns, before going on to complain about his need for money. But, in a bizarre attempt to commiserate, he then added, 'Instead of Mary, ought it not to have been my mother, who is in any case a prey to physical ailments and has had her fair share of life . . .? You can see what strange notions come into the heads of "civilised men" under the pressure of certain circumstances.' 'Karl Marx to Friedrich Engels', 8 January 1863, *MECW*, vol. 41, pp. 442–3.

13. 'Jenny von Westphalen to Karl Marx', n.d., 1839, *MECW*, vol. 1, pp. 697–8.

14. 'Jenny von Westphalen to Karl Marx', 13 September 1841, *MEGA*, III, i, p. 368.

15. Ibid., after 10 May 1838, p. 331.

16. 'Jenny von Westphalen to Karl Marx', n.d., 1839, *MECW*, vol. 1, pp. 696–7.

17. Ibid., p. 696.

18. 'Jenny von Westphalen to Karl Marx', 13 September 1841, *MEGA*, III, i, p. 366.

19. 'Jenny von Westphalen to Karl Marx', n.d., 1839, *MECW*, vol. 1, p. 698.

20. Ibid., 10 August 1841, pp. 707–8.

21. Ibid., p. 708.

22. 'Bruno Bauer to Karl Marx', 11 December 1839, *MEGA*, III, i, pp. 335–6; 1 March 1840, *MEGA*, III, i, p. 341.

23. Ibid., 12 April 1841, pp. 357–8.

24. The University of Jena retained great intellectual prestige in the aftermath of its association with Goethe, Schiller, Fichte and the early Romantics. But it remained small and poorly financed, and therefore interested in fees as a method of supplementing its income. According to its statutes of 1829, those intending to pursue a teaching career at either a university or a *Gymnasium* were required to be examined in person by the assembled faculty and to submit a dissertation in Latin, while those aspiring to the highest award, *Magister der freyen Künste* (Master of Liberal Arts), were required

in addition to submit themselves to a public examination. But if this higher status was not required, it was possible for the candidate to be examined *in bsentia*, provided that he submitted, together with the dissertation, a detailed curriculum vitae recording university courses previously attended, and certificates of competence in Latin and of good behaviour, together with a fee of twelve *Louis d'Or*. Despite frequent criticisms from Prussian authorities, standards in this neighbouring state, Saxe-Weimar-Eisenach, remained high. In the year previous to Marx, Robert Schumann secured a doctoral qualification by similar means. The second and higher qualification necessary for academic employment, the *Habilitation*, Marx intended to attain in Bonn. See Erhard Lange, *Die Promotion von Karl Marx, Jena 1841. Eine Quellenedition*, Berlin, Dietz Verlag, 1983, pp. 185 ff.; Joachim Bauer et al., *'Ich präsentiere Ihnen Herrn Carl Heinrich Marx aus Trier . . .'*, Kabinettausstellung an der Friedrich-Schiller-Universität Jena, 13–19 April 2011 (an exhibition item).

25. Karl Marx, doctoral dissertation: 'Difference between the Democritean and Epicurean Philosophy of Nature', March 1841, *MECW*, vol. 1, p. 30.

26. Originally part of the early Romantic circle and friend of Friedrich Schlegel, in 1810 Friedrich Schleiermacher became Professor of Theology at the newly founded University of Berlin and remained there until his death in 1834. He was politically liberal, and his basic theological idea was that religion could not be apprehended rationally. What mattered was not creed, scripture or philosophical rationalization, but feeling. Religious feeling was the sense of absolute dependence upon God, communicated through Jesus to the church. Antagonism between Hegel and Schleiermacher was already evident from the aftermath of the Kotzebue assassination and the persecution of 'demagogues' in 1819. But it was made irremediable by Hegel's introduction to Hinrichs's *Religion in Its Inner Relation to Science* in 1822. Hegel sarcastically observed about the association of religion with the feeling of absolute dependence – a position known by everyone to be associated with Schleiermacher – that this would mean that a dog would make the best Christian; furthermore, that 'a dog even has feelings of salvation, when its hunger is satisfied by a bone'. Schleiermacher himself was deeply offended, and his friends never forgave Hegel for this insult. See Terry Pinkard, *Hegel: A Biography*, Cambridge, Cambridge University Press, 2000, pp. 500–502. In the 1830s and 1840s there was considerable and sometimes acrimonious rivalry between the followers of Hegel and those of Schleiermacher. It was therefore a misfortune for Bauer when he was transferred from Berlin to Bonn in 1839, since Bonn was a stronghold of Schleiermacher supporters, who had no intention of granting him tenure there.

27. Cited in John E. Toews, *Hegelianism: The Path toward Dialectical Humanism, 1805–1841*, Cambridge, Cambridge University Press, 1980, pp. 292–3.

28. Bruno Bauer, *The Trumpet of the Last Judgement against Hegel the Atheist and Anti-Christ: An Ultimatum*, trans. Lawrence Stepelevich, Lewiston, Edwin Mellen Press, 1989 [1841], pp. 189–90.

29. Bauer was forced to sell his library, and to experience the humiliation of having to ask Hegel's widow for remuneration for his editorial work on the *Lectures on the Philosophy of Religion*. Frustration induced him to burn his correspondence with Altenstein and Schulze; and when in 1840 Friedrich Wilhelm III died, Bauer was forced to accept that his chances of paid academic employment were over. Toews, *Hegelianism*, pp. 308–9; Douglas Moggach, *The Philosophy and Politics of Bruno Bauer*, Cambridge, Cambridge University Press, 2003, p. 63.

30. See especially Moggach, *Bruno Bauer*, ch. 3.

31. On Friedrich Wilhelm IV, see David E. Barclay, *Frederick Wilhelm IV and the Prussian Monarchy 1840–1861*, Oxford, Clarendon Press, 1995.

32. Letter 22, *Briefwechsel zwischen Bruno Bauer und Edgar Bauer während den Jahren 1839–1842 aus Bonn und Berlin*, Charlottenburg, Verlag von Egbert Bauer, 1844, cited in Gustav Mayer, 'Die Anfänge des politischen Radikalismus im vormärzlichen Preussen', in Gustav Mayer, *Radikalismus, Sozialismus und bürgerliche Demokratie*, Frankfurt am Main, Suhrkamp, 1969, p. 20.

33. It is also true that, as a follower of Schleiermacher, he had no reason to continue Altenstein's policy. See Moggach, *Bruno Bauer*, pp. 80–82, 234.

34. Mayer, *Radikalismus*, pp. 54–6.

35. 'Bruno Bauer to Karl Marx', 11 December 1839, *MEGA*, III, i, p. 336; ibid., 1 March 1840, p. 341; ibid., 5 April 1840, pp. 345–6; ibid., 31 March 1841, p. 354.

36. Ibid., 28 March 1841, p. 353.

37. Ibid., 31 March 1841, p. 354.

38. 'Bruno Bauer to Arnold Ruge', 6 December 1841, in A. Ruge, *Arnold Ruges Briefwechsel und Tagebuchblätter aus den Jahren 1825–1880*, ed. Paul Nerrlich, vol. 1, Berlin, Weidmann, 1886, p. 239.

39. Bauer, *Trumpet*, p. 62.

40. Ibid., pp. 61, 94, 114.

41. Moggach, *Bruno Bauer*, pp. 114–15, 107–12.

42. Bauer, *Trumpet*, pp. 136, 137, 140.

43. Karl Marx, 'Comments on the Latest Prussian Censorship Instruction', January/February 1842, *MECW*, vol. 1, pp. 116, 117.

44. 'Karl Marx to Arnold Ruge', 10 February 1842, *MECW*, vol. 1, p. 381; 'Arnold Ruge to Karl Marx', 25 February 1842, *MEGA*, III, i, p. 370.

45. 'Karl Marx to Arnold Ruge', 5 March 1842, *MECW*, vol. 1, p. 382.

46. Ibid., 27 April 1842, p. 387.

47. For Karl's notes in preparation for his 'Treatise', see *MEGA*, I, ii, pp. 114–18.

48. See the book of verse Karl sent to his father in 1837, which included 'the first elegy of Ovid's *Tristia* freely rendered', *MECW*, vol. 1, pp. 548–57; Loers had written a treatise on Ovid.

49. Karl Marx, *Economic Manuscripts of 1857–58 (Grundrisse)*, *MECW*, vol. 28, pp. 47, 48.

50. Bauer, *Trumpet*, pp. 155–6.

51. Johann Winckelmann (1717–68) was a pioneer art historian and archaeologist, who in his *History of Art in Antiquity* for the first time clearly distinguished between Greek, Greco-Roman and Roman together with Egyptian and Etruscan art. Art was treated as an expression of a particular civilization (its climate, freedom, craft). His work was decisive in the rise of the neo-classical movement in the late eighteenth century and its adulation of the art and civilization of Ancient Greece. His admirers included Lessing, Goethe, Herder and Heine.

52. For Bauer's radical reshaping of Hegel's position, see Margaret Rose, *Marx's Lost Aesthetic: Karl Marx and the Visual Arts*, Cambridge, Cambridge University Press, 1984, pp. 59–60.

53. Bauer, *Trumpet*, p. 157.

54. Carl Friedrich von Rumohr, *Italienische Forschungen*, Berlin and Stettin, Nicolai'sche Buchhandlung, 1827, p. 124, cited in Mikhail Lifshitz, *The Philosophy of Art of Karl Marx*, London, Pluto Press, 1973 [Moscow, 1933], p. 35.

55. See Charles de Brosses, *Du culte des dieux fétiches*, Paris, 1760; citations from de Brosses in Lifshitz, *Philosophy of Art*, pp. 36–8. Charles de Brosses (1709–77) was born in Dijon and was a friend of the naturalist Buffon. De Brosses wrote numerous essays on ancient history, philology and linguistics, some of which were used by Diderot and D'Alembert in the *Encyclopédie*. His 1760 work provided a materialistic theory of the origins of religion based upon a comparison between the religion of Ancient Egypt and that current in the region of the Niger.

56. See Rose, *Lost Aesthetic*, pp. 65–8.

57. J. J. Grund, *Die Malerei der Griechen*, vol. 1, Dresden, 1810, p. 15, cited in Lifshitz, *Philosophy of Art*, p. 37.

58. See Rose, *Lost Aesthetic*, pp. 1–34.

59. In his dissertation, Karl described the attempt of Gassendi to reconcile Catholicism with the heathen philosophy of Epicurus, 'as though someone had tried to cast a Christian nun's habit around the gaily luxuriant body of the Greek Lais': Marx, 'Foreword' to doctoral dissertation, p. 29; and see S. S. Prawer, *Karl Marx and World Literature*, Oxford, Clarendon Press, 1976, pp. 30–31.

60. 'Karl Marx to Arnold Ruge', 20 March 1842, *MECW*, vol. 1, p. 385–6.

61. Ibid., p. 386. At the beginning of April, Karl tried moving to Cologne, since he found the proximity of the Bonn professors 'intolerable': ibid., p. 385. But he found the atmosphere too distracting and moved back to Bonn.

62. 'Bruno Bauer to Edgar Bauer', in *Briefwechsel zwischen Bruno Bauer und Edgar Bauer*, p. 192.

63. *The Catholic World*, vol. 6, issue 34, 1868, p. 504.

64. Daniel O'Connell (1775-1847) was often known as 'the Liberator' or 'the Emancipator'. He campaigned for Catholic Emancipation – the right of Catholics to sit in the Westminster Parliament – and for the repeal of the Act of Union, which combined Great Britain and Ireland. Due to the crisis situation in Ireland, Catholic Emancipation was conceded in 1829, thus bringing to an end 'the Protestant Constitution'. Possible parallels with the confrontation between the Catholic Rhineland and Protestant Prussia were not hard to make.

65. For details of the conflict, see Chapter 3, pp. 77-8.

66. Friedrich List (1789-1846) was one of the leading German economists of the nineteenth century. In his *National System of Political Economy* (1841), he developed a strategy of national economic development based upon the protection of infant industries as opposed to the 'cosmopolitan' political economy of Adam Smith. Karl wrote, but did not publish, an article on List's book around 1845.

67. For discussion between members of the government on how to handle the *Rheinische Zeitung*, see Mayer, *Radikalismus*, pp. 35-52.

68. 'Karl Marx to Arnold Ruge', 27 April 1842, *MECW*, vol. 1, p. 387.

69. Ibid., 5 March 1842, pp. 382-3. *Res Publica* literally meant 'public thing' and originated in reference to the Ancient Roman republic.

70. This was a major issue in the poor forest regions around the Moselle and the Hunsrück.

71. Karl Marx, 'Debates on Freedom of the Press', 12 May 1842, *MECW*, vol. 1, p. 154.

72. Karl Marx, 'The Leading Article in No. 179 of *Kölnische Zeitung*', 14 July 1842, *MECW*, vol. 1, p. 195.

73. But the process was partial and halting, especially in the years after the 'Reform Era'. The experience of Karl's father, Heinrich, and of his Professor of Law in Berlin, Eduard Gans, shows how contradictory the process could be in the case of law and the academy.

74. See Chapter 1, pp. 24-5.

75. Karl Ludwig von Haller (1768-1854) was a Swiss jurist from Berne and author of *Restoration of the Science of the State*, an uncompromisingly counter-revolutionary treatise. For this reason he was one of the chief targets of Hegel's *Philosophy of Right*. His book was also burnt at the Hambach Festival of May 1832.

76. According to Warren Breckman, Prussia during this time was characterized not so much by its 'feudal vestiges' as by 'its extreme social fragmentation' and this was rationalized by a philosophy, which Breckman calls 'personalism' and 'atomism'. See Warren Breckman, *Marx, the Young Hegelians,*

and the Origins of Radical Social Theory: Dethroning the Self, Cambridge, Cambridge University Press, 1999, ch. 7.

77. This was the point made by Karl in his 'Comments on the Latest Prussian Censorship Instruction', pp. 109–31.

78. Marx, 'Leading Article in No. 179 of the *Kölnische Zeitung*', 10 July 1842, *MECW*, vol. 1, p. 189.

79. Marx, 'Debates on the Freedom of the Press', 10 May 1842, *MECW*, vol. 1, pp. 145, 151.

80. Karl Marx, 'Proceedings of the Sixth Rhine Province Assembly. Third Article. Debates on the Law on Thefts of Wood', 3 November 1842, *MECW*, vol. 1, p. 262.

81. 'Karl Marx to Arnold Ruge', 20 March 1842, *MECW*, vol. 1, p. 384.

82. Marx, 'Debates on the Law on Thefts of Wood', 25 October 1842, *MECW*, vol. 1, p. 231.

83. Ibid., 3 November 1842, p. 262.

84. Gustav Hugo (1764–1844) was Professor of Law at Göttingen in the Anglophile Electorate of Hanover. In the 1780s in reaction against the stylized treatment of the history of Roman Law, Hugo issued a translation and commentary on the chapter on Roman Law in Gibbon's *Decline and Fall of the Roman Empire*. In place of its treatment as an unchanging corpus of law in Heineccius and other legal commentaries, Gibbon showed how the law had adapted itself to changes in Roman society.

85. Karl Marx, 'The Philosophical Manifesto of the Historical School of Law', 9 August 1842, *MECW*, vol. 1, pp. 204, 206.

86. Ibid., p. 209.

87. Marx, 'Leading Article in No. 179 of the *Kölnische Zeitung*', pp. 199, 192, 193; 'Debates on Freedom of the Press', p. 155.

88. 'Debates on Freedom of the Press', pp. 155, 162.

89. Marx, 'Leading Article in No. 179 of the *Kölnische Zeitung*', p. 202.

90. Karl Marx, 'On the Commissions of the Estates in Prussia', 20 December 1842, *MECW*, vol. 1, p. 299.

91. Ibid., 31 December 1842, p. 306.

92. Ibid.

93. See Chapter 6, n. 11.

94. The term 'civil society' existed before Hegel but at that point referred to society as a whole. For Hegel's redefinition of the term, see Manfred Riedel, *Between Tradition and Revolution: The Hegelian Transformation of Political Philosophy*, Cambridge, Cambridge University Press, 1984, ch. 7.

95. Throughout the early modern period, Aristotle's view survived in the presumed contrast between the political virtue embodied in the independent landowner as opposed to the self-interest which was likely to shape the pursuits of the ordinary subject; and it was still present in the implicit

distinction between man and citizen in the French Revolution's declaration of rights in 1789.

96. Breckman, *Marx, the Young Hegelians*, pp. 204–5.

97. Karl Marx, 'Renard's letter to Oberpräsident von Schaper', 17 November 1842, *MECW*, vol. 1, pp. 282–6.

98. 'Karl Marx to Arnold Ruge', 9 July 1842, *MECW*, vol. 1, p. 391.

99. Ibid., 30 November 1842, pp. 393–4.

100. 'Karl Marx to Dagobert Oppenheim', 25 August 1842, *MECW*, vol. 1, p. 392.

101. Marx, 'Debates on the Law on Thefts of Wood', p. 262.

102. 'Karl Marx to Dagobert Oppenheim', 25 August 1842, *MECW*, vol. 1, p. 392.

103. 'Karl Marx to Arnold Ruge', 9 July 1842, *MECW*, vol. 1, p. 390.

104. 'Georg Herwegh to the *Rheinische Zeitung*', 22 November 1842, *MEGA*, III, i, p. 379. Herwegh was the most popular of the radical poets at the time, especially on account of his *Gedichte eines Lebendigen* (*Poems of a Living Man*).

105. 'Karl Marx to Arnold Ruge', 30 November 1842, *MECW*, vol. 1, p. 381.

106. Ruge also complained about reports of fighting and drinking involving the 'Free'. He called the whole affair a 'calamity', which could compromise Bauer and his cause: ibid., 4 December 1842, pp. 381–3.

107. 'Bruno Bauer to Karl Marx', 13 December 1842, *MEGA*, III, i, p. 386.

108. The moderating of Strauss's position since 1835 meant that it could accommodate transcendent conceptions, both of God and of humanity.

109. 'Bruno Bauer to Karl Marx', 16 March 1842, *MEGA*, III, i, p. 371; 'Karl Marx to Arnold Ruge', 20 March 1842, *MECW*, vol. 1, p. 383.

110. 'The Insolently Threatened Yet Miraculously Rescued Bible or: the Triumph of Faith', 1842, *MECW*, vol. 2, pp. 313–52.

111. 'Karl Marx to Arnold Ruge', 30 November 1842, *MECW*, vol. 1, p. 394.

112. See Boris Nicolaievsky and Otto Maenchen-Helfen, *Karl Marx: Man and Fighter*, trans. G. David and E. Mosbacher, London, Allen Lane, 1973 [1933], pp. 62–4.

113. Mayer, *Radikalismus*, pp. 50–52.

114. 'Karl Marx to Arnold Ruge', 25 January 1843, *MECW*, vol. 1, pp. 397–8.

5 THE ALLIANCE OF THOSE WHO THINK AND THOSE WHO SUFFER

1. For a definition of 'communism' during the years of the July Monarchy, see pp. 135–9.

2. Georg Herwegh (1817–75), born in Stuttgart, proceeded to the University of Tübingen as a theology student, moved briefly to law and then to journalism. Called up for military service, he was insubordinate and forced to flee to Switzerland. In Zurich, 1841–3, he published *Gedichte eines Lebendigen* (*Poems of a Living Man*), combining a popular style with

revolutionary sentiment. He became an idol among the radical youth of the 1840s. His journey through Germany in 1842 attracted much attention and culminated in an audience with the Prussian king. In 1848, in Paris, he was one of the leaders of the Romantically conceived, disastrously amateur German Legion, which aimed to march into the Odenwald and proclaim the German Republic (see Chapter 8, pp. 250–51). In 1842, he had married Emma Siegmund, daughter of a Berlin Jewish merchant, but in 1848, having abandoned the Legion, he became passionately involved with Herzen's wife, Natalie. (See E. H. Carr, *The Romantic Exiles: A Nineteenth-Century Portrait Gallery*, London, Victor Gollancz, 1933.) In later life, he supported and wrote songs for the German Social Democratic Party, otherwise devoting himself to the translation of Shakespeare plays.

3. 'Karl Marx to Arnold Ruge', 25 January 1843, *MECW*, vol. 1, p. 397; ibid., 13 March 1843, p. 399. Jenny's 'pietistic aristocratic relatives' clearly referred to her brother, Ferdinand, and his sisters. The identity of the 'priests and other enemies of mine' has not been discovered, but it is clear that the family had not finally abandoned the attempt to entice Karl back to a more secure livelihood. At Kreuznach he was visited by Esser, a friend of Karl's father and a *Revisionsrat* (state official), with the offer of government work. See Boris Nicolaievsky and Otto Maenchen-Helfen, *Karl Marx: Man and Fighter*, trans. G. David and E. Mosbacher, London, Allen Lane, 1973 [1933], p. 71.

4. See Heinz Monz, *Karl Marx: Grundlagen der Entwicklung zu Leben und Werk*, Trier, Verlag Neu, 1973, p. 349. Jenny complained that Bettina had robbed her of the company of her betrothed to roam the area from early morning until late at night, and this despite the fact that she and Karl had not seen each other for six months.

5. Jenny Marx, 'A Short Sketch of an Eventful Life', in Institut Marksizma–Leninzma, *Reminiscences of Marx and Engels*, Moscow, Foreign Languages Publishing House, 1957, p. 19.

6. 'Arnold Ruge to Karl Marx', 1 February 1843, *MEGA*, III, i, pp. 390–91.

7. *Anekdota zur neuesten deutschen Philosophie und Publicistik* was published in two volumes. The collection also included Karl's unsigned essay on the censorship instruction and, in addition, contributions from all the major Young Hegelians, Bruno Bauer, Köppen, Nauwerck and Ruge himself.

8. Ludwig Feuerbach, *The Essence of Christianity* (*Das Wesen des Christentums*), trans. Marian Evans (later called George Eliot), London, J. Chapman, 1854.

9. Ludwig Feuerbach, 'Preliminary Theses on the Reform of Philosophy', in *The Fiery Brook: Selected Writings of Ludwig Feuerbach* (trans. with an intro by Zawar Hanfi), New York, Doubleday, 1972, p. 157.

10. See Ludwig Feuerbach, *Sämmtliche Werke*, vol. 2, Leipzig, Otto Wigand, 1846, pp. 280, 304. In German, this read '*entäussert und entfremdet*' –

terms whose meanings were often at issue in twentieth-century debates about 'alienation'.

11. Arnold Ruge, 'Hegel's *Philosophy of Right* and the Politics of our Times', in Lawrence S. Stepelevich (ed.), *The Young Hegelians: An Anthology*, Cambridge, Cambridge University Press, 1983, pp. 211–36.

12. Ruge, 'Hegel's *Philosophy of Right*', pp. 215, 223–4. In an image which recalled Heine's criticism of the political complacency of Goethe, Ruge mocked Hegel's 'Olympian repose', which in turn recalled the account in Genesis of God's creation of the world: 'he looked at everything that reason had made, and it was good'.

13. Ibid., pp. 211–36.

14. 'Karl Marx to Arnold Ruge', 13 March 1843, *MECW*, vol. 1, p. 400.

15. This remained one of the most enduring parts of Karl's debt to Feuerbach. It was not only employed in the section on the 'Fetishism of Commodities' in *Capital*, but also discussed in Karl's letters on Maurer and the interpretation of the 'mark' in 1868. See 'Karl Marx to Friedrich Engels', 25 March 1868, *MECW*, vol. 42, pp. 558–9.

16. Feuerbach, 'Preliminary Theses', p. 154.

17. Karl Marx, 'Contribution to the Critique of Hegel's Philosophy of Law', 1843, *MECW*, vol. 3, pp. 21–2. The translation of 'Recht' in *MECW* is 'Law' rather than 'Right'. Both are possible, but standard usage is 'Right'.

18. Ibid., pp. 29, 61, 75.

19. Ibid., pp. 14, 39, 10. Hegel's *Science of Logic*, which appeared between 1812 and 1816, is arguably best understood as an attempt to extend what Kant had intended in his 'transcendental deduction of the categories' in his *Critique of Pure Reason*. This consisted of an attempt to derive a list of those non-empirical concepts, the categories, which he believed were presupposed by all finite, discursive knowers like ourselves. Whether these categories are to be understood as ontological (the structure of being), as in Aristotle, or as revealing the necessary structure of thought, as in Kant, is a matter of dispute among philosophers. For an extended discussion, see George di Giovanni's Introduction in G. W. F. Hegel, *The Science of Logic*, trans. and ed. George di Giovanni, Cambridge, Cambridge University Press, 2010, pp. xi–lxii; see also Stanford Encyclopaedia of Philosophy, 2015, http://plato.stanford.edu/.

20. Karl Marx, 'Afterword to the Second German Edition', 24 January 1873, in *Capital*, vol. I, *MECW*, vol. 35, p. 19.

21. Marx, 'Contribution to the Critique of Hegel's Philosophy of Law', pp. 63, 33, 49, 31.

22. Ibid., pp. 32, 79–80.

23. Ibid., p. 29.

24. Ibid., pp. 32, 110–11.

25. Ibid., p. 31.

26. Ibid., pp. 42, 50, 98, 108, 106, 45.

27. Ibid., pp. 115–16.

28. Ibid., pp. 117–19.

29. Ibid., p. 121.

30. 'Karl Marx to Arnold Ruge', 13 March 1843, *MECW*, vol. 1, p. 400.

31. Karl Marx, 'On the Jewish Question', 1844, *MECW*, vol. 3, pp. 154, 151, 156.

32. Ibid., pp. 155, 152, 158.

33. Ibid., pp. 163, 164.

34. Ibid., p. 168.

35. Republicanism also gained some support among organizations of silk workers in Lyons, where the struggle between the silk merchants and the *canuts* – the weavers (both masters and journeymen) – culminated in insurrectionary strikes in 1831 and 1834.

36. The followers of Cabet were called 'Icarians', after the novel, and were the largest grouping of 'communists' in France. In November 1847, Cabet announced the migration of the Icarians to the Promised Land – next to the Red River in Texas; and in February 1848 an advance party set off from France, but the community ended in disarray at the end of 1848. Other branches, however, were formed in Nauvoo, Illinois; Cheltenham, St Louis; Corning, Iowa; and elsewhere. For the history of the Icarians in France in the 1840s, see Christopher H. Johnson, *Utopian Communism in France: Cabet and the Icarians, 1839–1851*, Ithaca, Cornell University Press, 1974.

37. Thomas Carlyle, *Chartism*, London, James Fraser, 1839, ch. 1.

38. See the anonymous contributions of Friedrich Engels, 'The Internal Crises', 9/10 December 1842, *MECW*, vol. 2, p. 374.

39. Johann Caspar Bluntschli, *Die Kommunisten in der Schweiz nach den bei Weitling vorgefundenen Papieren* (*Communists in Switzerland According to Papers Found in Weitling's Possession*), Glashütten im Taunus, Auvermann, 1973 [Zurich, Druck von Orell, 1843], p. 5.

40. On Stein and the reaction to his book, see Diana Siclovan, 'Lorenz Stein and German Socialism, 1835–1872', Ph.D. thesis, Cambridge University, 2014; see also David Lindenfeld, *The Practical Imagination: The German Sciences of State in the Nineteenth Century*, Chicago, Chicago University Press, 1997; Keith Tribe, *Governing Economy: The Reformation of German Economic Discourse 1750–1840*, Cambridge, Cambridge University Press, 1988.

41. Moses Hess, 'Sozialismus und Kommunismus' (1843), in Wolfgang Mönke (ed.), *Moses Hess: Philosophische und sozialistische Schriften 1837–1850. Eine Auswahl*, Vaduz, Topos Verlag, 1980, pp. 197–210.

42. The historical significance of Stein's book has generally been misunderstood. He has been described as a pioneer 'sociologist' and it has sometimes been suggested that Karl might have acquired his conception of the proletariat from Stein's book. This is extremely improbable, given Karl's

increasingly hostile attitude towards 'the political state'. It is far more likely that he shared the hostility expressed by Hess.

43. Moses Hess, 'Die europäische Triarchie', in Mönke (ed.), *Philosophische und sozialistische Schriften*, pp. 159–60.

44. Karl Marx, 'Communism and the *Augsburg Allgemeine Zeitung*', 15 October 1842, *MECW*, vol. 1, pp. 220–21.

45. Ibid.

46. Feuerbach, 'Preliminary Theses', p. 165.

47. 'Karl Marx to Ludwig Feuerbach', 3 October 1843, *MECW*, vol. 3, p. 349.

48. Moses Hess, 'The Philosophy of the Act' (1843), in Albert Fried and Ronald Sanders (eds.), *Socialist Thought: A Documentary History*, Edinburgh, Edinburgh University Press, 1964, pp. 261, 264, 266.

49. 'Karl Marx to Arnold Ruge', 13 March 1843, *MECW*, vol. 1, pp. 398–9.

50. 'Jenny von Westphalen to Karl Marx', March 1843, *MECW*, vol. 1, p. 728.

51. 'Arnold Ruge to Karl Marx', 11 August 1843, *MEGA*, III, i, pp. 409–10.

52. 'Letters from the *Deutsch-Französische Jahrbücher*', March–September 1843, *MECW*, vol. 3, pp. 133–4.

53. 'Arnold Ruge to Karl Marx', March 1843, *MEGA*, III, i, pp. 402–5.

54. Ibid.

55. By the nineteenth century, the term 'philistine' (originally the biblical enemies of the Israelites) came to refer in Matthew Arnold to 'ignorant ill-behaved persons, lacking in culture or artistic appreciation, and only concerned with materialistic values'. Its early modern usage derived from the German, *der Philister*, and began with town vs gown clashes in the University of Jena in 1689.

56. 'Letters from the *Deutsch-Französische Jahrbücher*', March–September 1843, *MECW*, vol. 3, pp. 134, 137, 140, 141.

57. Ibid., pp. 141, 143, 144.

58. For details of the Parisian workforce in the 1840s, see Mark Traugott, *Armies of the Poor: Determinants of Working-Class Participation in the Parisian Insurrection of June 1848*, Princeton, Princeton University Press, 1985, ch. 1; for details of the German migrant population in Paris, see Jacques Grandjonc, *Marx et les Communistes allemands à Paris, Vorwärts 1844: Contribution à l'étude de la naissance du Marxisme*, Paris, F. Maspero, 1974, pp. 9–18.

59. 'Letters from the *Deutsch-Französische Jahrbücher*', March–September 1843, *MECW*, vol. 3, p. 142.

60. Arnold Ruge, *Zwei Jahre in Paris: Studien und Erinnerungen*, Leipzig, W. Jurany, 1846, part 1, pp. 48–9.

61. *Le Globe* was founded in 1824, moved towards the liberal opposition in 1828, and became the official voice of the Saint-Simonians in 1830. It was the most famous French newspaper around the time of the 1830 Revolution.

62. P. Leroux, 'De l'Individualisme et du Socialisme', *Revue encyclopédique*, vol. LX, pp. 94–117, Paris, October 1833, reprinted in David Owen Evans, *Le Socialisme romantique: Pierre Leroux et ses contemporains*, Paris, M. Rivière, 1948, pp. 223–38.

63. See Edward Berenson, *Populist Religion and Left-Wing Politics in France, 1830–1852*, Princeton, Princeton University Press, 1984.

64. Ruge was an admirer of Louis Blanc and was preparing an edition of his *History of Ten Years*; see Lucien Calvié, 'Ruge and Marx: Democracy, Nationalism and Revolution in Left Hegelian Debates', in Douglas Moggach (ed.), *Politics, Religion and Art: Hegelian Debates*, Evanston, Ill., Northwestern University Press, 2011, pp. 301–20. Karl on the other hand puzzled one of his Cologne admirers, Georg Jung, by expressing his disapproval of Blanc. It may be that he was offended by Blanc's reference to Ruge as Karl's 'master' in the *Revue indépéndante*. See 'Georg Jung to Karl Marx', 31 July 1844, *MEGA*, III, i, p. 438.

65. Hess,'Philosophy of the Act', pp. 262–4.

66. Ruge, *Zwei Jahre in Paris*, pp. 137–8.

67. Despite his enthusiasm for Feuerbach, Karl never warmed to attempts to conceive humanism in religious terms. In this respect, his attitude towards religion remained much closer to Bauer than to Feuerbach.

68. 'Arnold Ruge', in McLellan (ed.), *Karl Marx: Interviews and Recollections*, p. 9.

69. F. Engels, 'Progress of Social Reform on the Continent', *New Moral World*, 4 November 1843, *MECW*, vol. 3, p. 399. Citing an account of a visit to a Parisian Communist Club almost a year later, he wrote that members of the Club, in reaction to attempts to persuade them of the merits of Feuerbach, had declared that the question of God was a secondary matter, that 'to all practical intents [they] agreed with us, and said, "*Enfin, l'Athéisme, c'est votre religion*" [so in the end, atheism is your religion]': F. Engels, 'Continental Socialism', 20 September 1844, *MECW*, vol. 4, p. 213.

70. See Marcel Herwegh (ed.), *Briefe von und an Georg Herwegh*, 2nd edn, Munich, A. Langen, 1898, p. 328.

71. 'Ludwig Feuerbach to Karl Marx', 6–25 October 1843, *MEGA*, III, i, pp. 416–17.

72. M. Hess, 'Über das Geldwesen', in Mönke (ed.), *Philosophische und sozialistische Schriften*, pp. 331–45.

73. Marx, 'On the Jewish Question', p. 174.

74. Hostility towards Jews was common among French socialists in the 1840s. Both Fourier and Proudhon suspected that indebtedness and pauperism had been made worse by the emancipation of the Jews during the French Revolution. Complaints about the financial power of the Jews despite the incompleteness of their emancipation were frequent, and were made an object of comment both by Karl and by Bruno Bauer. This form of socialist

anti-Semitism reached its peak in Alphonse Toussenel's *Les Juifs, rois de l'époque: histoire de la féodalité financière*, Paris, G. de Gonet, 1845. Toussenel was a one-time editor of the main Fourierist journal, *La Démocratie pacifique*, and this book attacked just as fiercely the English, the Dutch and the Genevans: 'For he who says Jew, says Protestant.' The attack was directed at the centres of high finance, which he compared to a congregation of vampires. After 1848, he applied Fourierism to the animal world. In his most famous work, *Le Monde des oiseaux*, he developed his theory that 'birds are the precursors and the revealers of harmony'; see Sarane Alexandrian, *Le Socialisme romantique*, Paris, Éditions du Seuil, 1979, pp. 226-35.

75. Marx, 'On the Jewish Question', p. 172.

76. Ibid., p. 173.

77. Ibid., p. 174.

78. Karl Marx, 'Introduction' to 'Contribution to the Critique of Hegel's Philosophy of Law', 1844, *MECW*, vol. 3, pp. 175, 176, 178, 182.

79. Ibid., pp. 176, 178, 179, 185.

80. Ibid., pp. 186-7.

81. Ibid., pp. 183, 187; the distinction between 'heart' and 'head' came from Feuerbach's 'Preliminary Theses', p. 165.

82. A. Ruge, *Arnold Ruges Briefwechsel und Tagebuchblätter aus den Jahren 1825-1880*, ed. P. Nerrlich, Berlin, Weidmann, 1886, p. 350.

83. Anon., 'Berichte über Heines Verhältnis zu Marx' ('Reports on Heine's Relationship with Marx'), *Die Neue Zeit*, XIV, pt 1 (1895-6). The author was probably Mehring or Kautsky: see McLellan (ed.), *Karl Marx: Interviews and Recollections*, p. 10.

84. Ibid.

85. Ruge, *Arnold Ruges Briefwechsel und Tagebuchblätter*, p. 343, cited in McLellan (ed.), *Karl Marx: Interviews and Recollections*, p. 8.

86. Ruge, *Zwei Jahre in Paris*, pp. 138-40.

87. Ruge, *Arnold Ruges Briefwechsel und Tagebuchblätter*, p. 346.

88. 'Karl Marx to Ludwig Feuerbach', 11 August 1844, *MECW*, vol. 3, p. 354.

89. For an account of *Vorwärts!*, and Karl's relations with it, see Grandjonc, *Marx et les Communistes allemands*.

90. Adalbert von Bornstedt (1807-51) was the son of a military family. In 1831 he joined the exile community in Paris, and took part in the conquest of Algeria, where he was badly wounded. In Paris, he worked as an editor or journalist on several publications, notably *Vorwärts!*, but was expelled from France in 1845. From Paris he went to Brussels, where in 1846 he founded the *Deutsche Brüsseler Zeitung*. In 1848, he moved back to Paris, where he was one of the leaders of the German Legion together with Georg Herwegh.

Heinrich Börnstein (1805-92) was born in Lemberg (now L'viv, Ukraine). After half-hearted study at Lemberg and Vienna he became a touring actor in Germany together with his wife, and then a successful theatrical entrepreneur. In 1842, he attempted to take a German Opera Company to Paris; he then managed an Italian opera company. He was a friend of Franz Liszt, Alexandre Dumas and Giacomo Meyerbeer. In 1844–5, he published *Vorwärts!*, originally intended primarily as a cultural journal, but it was closed down by the authorities at the beginning of 1845. He was correspondent for the *New York Tribune* and in 1848 helped to organize Herwegh's German Legion. He left for the United States in 1849, where he was active as a journalist in St Louis, a prominent supporter of Lincoln, and, during the American Civil War, the American consul in Bremen.

91. Heinrich Börnstein, *Fünfundsiebzig Jahre in der Alten und Neuen Welt. Memoiren eines Unbedeutenden*, cited in Boris Nicolaievsky and Otto Maenchen-Helfen, *Karl Marx: Man and Fighter*, trans. G. David and E. Mosbacher, London, Allen Lane, 1973 [1933], p. 89.

92. See Ruge, *Zwei Jahre in Paris*, pp. 142–6.

93. 'Jenny Marx to Karl Marx', *c.*21 June 1844, *MECW*, vol. 3, pp. 574–5, 577–8.

94. Ibid., pp. 574–7.

95. After the Paris insurrection and the capture of the Tuileries of 10 August 1792, the Legislative Assembly decided to elect a Convention, which would draw up a constitution on the basis of the abolition of the monarchy. The Convention met from 21 September 1792 through to 26 October 1795. It was a period which included revolt in the Vendée, organized defence of national frontiers and 'terror' in the interior. Revolutionary government was in the hands of the Committee for Public Safety.

96. Philippe-Joseph-Benjamin Buchez and Pierre-Célestin Roux-Lavergne, *Histoire parlementaire de la Révolution française*, 40 vols., Paris, Librairie Paulin, 1833–8. This was the standard left-wing account of the revolutionary events during this period. It was also one of the main sources of Thomas Carlyle's *The French Revolution*, London, James Fraser, 1837. See François Furet, *Marx et la Révolution française*, Paris, Flammarion, 1986, ch. 1.

97. These manuscripts are discussed in the following chapter.

98. This work, completed at the end of November, was published as *The Holy Family, or, Critique of Critical Criticism against Bruno Bauer and Company*. All but a few pages were written by Karl. The reasons for Karl's continuing preoccupation with Bauer are discussed in the next chapter.

99. For an account of the Silesian events, see Christina von Hodenberg, *Aufstand der Weber: die Revolte von 1844 und ihr Aufstieg zum Mythos*, Bonn, Dietz, 1997.

100. *Vorwärts!*, no. 54, 6 July 1844, and no. 55, 10 July 1844. Heine's curse on God, King and Country was an inversion of the Prussian national slogan of the patriotic war of 1813: 'With God for the King and the Fatherland'; see Grandjonc, *Marx et les Communistes allemands*, pp. 44–8, 131–5.

101. 'A Prussian', 'The King of Prussia and Social Reform', *Vorwärts!*, no. 60, 27 July 1844.

102. 'Jenny Marx to Karl Marx', 4–10 August 1844, *MECW*, vol. 3, p. 580.

103. 'Moses Hess to Karl Marx', 3 July 1844, *MEGA*, III, i, p. 434.

104. 'Karl Marx to Ludwig Feuerbach', 11 August 1844, *MECW*, vol. 3, p. 355.

105. Karl Marx, 'Critical Marginal Notes on the Article "The King of Prussia and Social Reform. By a Prussian"', *Vorwärts!*, no. 63, 7 August 1844, *MECW*, vol. 3, pp. 189–206.

106. 'Karl Marx to Arnold Ruge', 13 March 1843, *MECW*, vol. 1, p. 400.

107. Marx, 'On the Jewish Question', pp. 173–4.

108. 'Karl Marx to Friedrich Engels', 7 March 1861, *MECW*, vol. 41, p. 282; 'Karl Marx to Antoinette Philips', 24 March 1861, *MECW*, vol. 41, p. 271.

109. 'Karl Marx to Jenny Longuet', 7 December 1881, *MECW*, vol. 46, pp. 157–8.

6 EXILE IN BRUSSELS, 1845–8

1. 'Jenny Marx to Karl Marx', *MEGA*, I, v, p. 449.

2. Heinrich Bürgers, 'Erinnerungen an Ferdinand Freiligrath', *Vossische Zeitung*, 1876, cited in Boris Nicolaievsky and Otto Maenchen-Helfen, *Karl Marx: Man and Fighter*, trans. G. David and E. Mosbacher, London, Allen Lane, 1973 [1933], p. 105.

3. Jenny Marx, 'A Short Sketch of an Eventful Life', in Institut Marksizma–Leninzma, *Reminiscences of Marx and Engels*, Moscow, Foreign Languages Publishing House, 1957, p. 222; 'Jenny Marx to Karl Marx', 24 August 1845, *MECW*, vol. 38, p. 528.

4. 'Jenny Marx to Karl Marx', 24 August 1845, *MECW*, vol. 38, pp. 527–8. Clearly Max Stirner's *The Ego and Its Own*, which would replace duty or vocation by the pursuit of individual desire, was a topic of household banter. On Stirner's book and the critical response of Hess, Engels and Karl, see pp. 188–90.

5. Caroline died on 13 January 1847.

6. 'Sophie Schmalhausen to Karl Marx', 25 September 1846, *MEGA*, III, ii, pp. 311–12.

7. For the argument between Say and Sismondi about globalization and 'the industrial revolution' in the 1820s, see Gareth Stedman Jones, *An End to Poverty?: A Historical Debate*, London, Profile Books, 2004, ch. 4.

8. J.-C.-L. Simonde de Sismondi, *Nouveaux principes d'économie politique, ou de la richesse dans ses rapports avec la population*, 2 vols., Paris, Chez Delaunay, 1819, vol. 2, p. 262.

9. See M. Hess, 'Über das Geldwesen', in Wolfgang Mönke (ed.), *Moses Hess: Philosophische und sozialistische Schriften 1837–1850. Eine Auswahl*, Vaduz, Topos Verlag, 1980, pp. 329–48.

10. Karl Marx, *Economic and Philosophical Manuscripts of 1844*, *MECW*, vol. 4, p. 297.

11. The term political economy was first used in 1615. 'Economy' derived from the Greek *oikos*, meaning pertaining to the household, and *nomos*, meaning law. The term political economy initially explored the parallel between managing a household and managing a polity (Greek *polis*) or a state. From the later eighteenth century, following Adam Smith, the term referred in particular to the laws or regularities pertaining to a commercial society. Critics in the first half of the nineteenth century, like Engels, objected to the theory of human nature which supposedly underlay prevalent analyses of commercial society.

12. Friedrich Engels, 'Outlines of a Critique of Political Economy', *MECW*, vol. 3, p. 421.

13. Ibid., pp. 434, 436–7.

14. Robert Owen (1771–1858) was the founder and pioneer in Britain of what in the first half of the nineteenth century came to be called 'socialism'. He first became famous for the enlightened and innovatory reforms he introduced into the management of a textile mill co-owned with David Dale in New Lanark, just outside Glasgow. In particular, he reduced factory hours, provided new forms of education for the children employed there and transformed the sanitation and housing of employees. In 1817, in response to the post-war depression and unemployment, he proposed the establishment of 'villages of cooperation', which he also believed would inaugurate the transition to the millennium. In the 1820s, he spent most of his fortune in establishing the community of New Harmony in Indiana. The project failed. But in the meantime a movement had developed in support of his principles, gaining widespread support among artisans and sections of the middle class. In the early 1830s, the movement pioneered the development of labour exchanges, trade unionism and cooperative production. In 1839–45 he made a final but also unsuccessful attempt to establish a socialist community at Queenwood Farm in Hampshire.

   Much of Owenite practice was based upon an environmental theory of human behaviour. He admired the optimistic vision of development associated with William Godwin, and defended his approach against the attacks made by Malthus. In major cities, Owenites set up 'Halls of Science' with secular Sunday services. Lectures, demonstrating scientific progress, attended by Engels, were regularly held in Manchester, including a demonstration of the possibilities of soil chemistry delivered by Justus Liebig. The Owenites attacked the endorsement of competition associated with political economy, developed a systematic critique of political economy articulated by John Watts, but also built upon the criticism associated with Thomas Hodgskin, William Thompson and John Francis Bray.

15. Engels, 'Outlines of a Critique of Political Economy', pp. 420–24.

16. Friedrich Engels and Karl Marx, *The Holy Family, or, Critique of Critical Criticism against Bruno Bauer and Company*, *MECW*, vol. 4, p. 31. Sieyès attacked the categories employed in the calling of the Estates General in 1789. He proposed the abolition of the first two estates – the clergy and the nobility – while redefining the 'Third Estate' as 'the Nation', since the 'Nation' was composed of those who worked.

17. Karl Marx, *MEGA*, IV, ii, pp. 301–480. For a description and an analysis of the character of Karl's engagement with these economic texts, I am greatly indebted to Keith Tribe, 'Karl Marx's "Critique of Political Economy": A Critique', in *The Economy of the Word: Language, History and Economics*, Oxford, Oxford University Press, 2015, ch. 6.

18. Marx, *MEGA*, IV, ii, pp. 318–19. These reflections were written in German; the notes were taken in French.

19. On the debate on Ricardo and his own changes in reaction to it in relation to the labour theory of value, see Terry Peach, *Interpreting Ricardo*, Cambridge, Cambridge University Press, 1993, chs. 1, 4 and 5.

20. Marx, *MEGA*, IV, ii, p. 405; and see Tribe, *Economy of the Word*, p. 263.

21. Marx, *MEGA*, IV, ii, p. 453; Karl Marx, 'Comments on James Mill, *Élémens d'économie politique*', *MECW*, vol. 3, p. 217, but note that *MECW* misleadingly translates *fixiert* as 'defines' rather than 'fixates'.

22. Marx, 'Comments on James Mill', p. 219.

23. In *MECW*, vol. 3, pp. 235–70, and other editions of the 1844 *Manuscripts*, the columns dealing with wages, capital and rent are misleadingly presented as consecutive chapters. The falsity of this arrangement was first pointed out in Margaret Fay, 'The Influence of Adam Smith on Marx's Theory of Alienation', *Science and Society*, 47/2 (Summer 1983), pp. 129–51; for the complex history of the publication of the manuscripts, see Jürgen Rojahn, 'Marxismus – Marx – Geschichtswissenschaft. Der Fall der sog. "Ökonomisch-philosophischen Manuskripte aus dem Jahre 1844"', *International Review of Social History*, 28/01 (April 1983), pp. 2–49.

24. See Tribe, *Economy of the Word*, pp. 192–3. Antoine-Eugène Buret (1810–42) was a follower of Simonde de Sismondi, the first to highlight the broader national and international implications of industrialization and proletarianization in the years following 1815. His study of the condition of the working classes in England and France (2 vols., 1840) was the first to highlight many of the themes developed by Engels in his study of the working classes in England in 1844. His theoretical work is further discussed in Chapter 10, 'The *Critique of Political Economy*'.

25. Eugène Buret, *De la misère des classes laborieuses en Angleterre et en France*, Paris, Paulin, 1840, vol. 1, pp. 49–50, cited in Tribe, *Economy of the Word*, p. 193.

26. Marx, *MEGA*, IV, ii, pp. 551–79. As Keith Tribe points out, the first hundred pages of Buret were spent examining approaches to the wage contract,

but out of nearly thirty pages of notes, these issues merited less than one. See Tribe, *Economy of the Word*, 2015, ch. 6.

27. Marx, *Economic and Philosophical Manuscripts of 1844*, p. 270.

28. Engels and Marx, *The Holy Family*, p. 31; Marx, *Economic and Philosophical Manuscripts of 1844*, p. 241.

29. Marx, 'Comments on James Mill', p. 220.

30. Marx, *Economic and Philosophical Manuscripts of 1844*, pp. 275, 276, 278, 280.

31. What is called the 'Preface' and printed at the beginning of what twentieth-century editors called *Economic and Philosophical Manuscripts of 1844* (*MECW*, vol. 3, pp. 231–4) originally appeared without a title in the third notebook. However, it is reasonable to believe that by late summer 1844 Karl was beginning to think of this work as a book. He announced in this passage (p. 232) that 'in contrast to the *critical theologian* of our day' (Bruno Bauer) he intended that the 'concluding chapter of this work' could contain 'a critical discussion of *Hegelian dialectic* and philosophy as a whole'. What remains unclear is whether the notebooks were drafts of this book or simply preparatory notes. See Tribe, *Economy of the Word*, pp. 216–17.

32. The German title was *Kritik der Politik und National Ökonomie*. For details, see *MECW*, vol. 4, p. 675. Karl received an advance of 3,000 francs, the second half to be paid when the volume was printed. In March 1846, however, worried by the probability of censorship, Leske suggested Karl find another publisher, and if he did find one, to return the advance. He was unable to find another publisher or to deliver the book. The contract with Leske was therefore cancelled in February 1847, but the advance was not repaid.

33. Marx, *Economic and Philosophical Manuscripts of 1844*, pp. 231–4.

34. Ibid., p. 272. The origin of this motif was to be found in the Lutheran rendering of the term *Entäusserung*. Karl wrote that 'the human being had to be reduced to this absolute poverty in order that he might yield his inner wealth to the outer world' (ibid., p. 300). Its original usage stemmed from Luther's translation of St Paul's Epistle to the Philippians (2:6–9), in which Jesus, 'though he was in the form of God, did not count equality with God a thing to be grasped, but emptied himself [*sich geäussert*], taking the form of a servant, being born in the likeness of men. And being found in human form, he humbled himself and became obedient unto death, even death on the cross.' See Georges Cottier, *L'athéisme du jeune Marx: ses origines hégéliennes*, Paris, Vrin, 1969.

35. Marx, *Economic and Philosophical Manuscripts of 1844*, pp. 317, 217, 276, 307.

36. Ibid., pp. 322, 219.

37. On the difficulties besetting this argument, see Gareth Stedman Jones, 'Introduction', *Karl Marx and Friedrich Engels: The Communist Manifesto*, London, Penguin Books, 2002, pp. 120–39.

38. Marx, *Economic and Philosophical Manuscripts of 1844*, pp. 303, 293–4.

39. Engels and Marx, *The Holy Family*, p. 36.

40. This was the significance of what Engels, following French commentators like Jean-Baptiste Say and Adolphe Blanqui, called 'the industrial revolution'; see Gareth Stedman Jones, 'National Bankruptcy and Social Revolution: European Observers on Britain, 1813–1844', in Donald Winch and Patrick K. O'Brien (eds.), *The Political Economy of British Historical Experience, 1688–1914*, Oxford, Oxford University Press, 2002, pp. 61–92; Stedman Jones, *An End to Poverty?*, pp. 133–99.

Following on from the debate between Say and Sismondi in the 1820s, an increasing number of social critics, including Robert Owen, Charles Fourier, Thomas Carlyle, Moses Hess and Engels himself, all in different ways pointed out that the old conditions of famine and scarcity had given way to a new form of crisis. This was what Fourier called 'plethoric crisis', the crisis of 'overproduction'. For communists, this became a sign of the discordance between the new possibilities of abundance and outmoded forms of property ownership. During the 1820s and 1830s for the first time, contemporaries also became aware of the relationship between factory production and the trade cycle. Investment in factory production and automatic machinery created the possibility of crises of overcapacity. The trade crises of 1825, 1837 and 1842 were each accompanied by the conspicuous presence of large quantities of unsold goods. See R. C. O. Matthews, *A Study in Trade-Cycle History: Economic Fluctuations in Great Britain 1833–1842*, Cambridge, Cambridge University Press, 1954.

41. Friedrich Engels, *The Condition of the Working Class in England: From Personal Observation and Authentic Sources*, *MECW*, vol. 4, pp. 295–584.

42. Engels and Marx, *The Holy Family*, p. 36.

43. On Engels' life, see Tristram Hunt, *The Frock-Coated Communist: The Revolutionary Life of Friedrich Engels*, London, Allen Lane, 2009; and see also the still classic account, Gustav Mayer, *Friedrich Engels: Eine Biographie*, 2 vols., Berlin, Dietz, 1970 [1919, 1932].

44. F. Oswald, 'Siegfried's Home Town', December 1840, *MECW*, vol. 2, pp. 132–6. During this period, Engels used the pseudonym 'Frederick Oswald'.

45. The *Freien* (the 'Free') were a group which gathered around Bruno Bauer after his return to Berlin in 1842. They frequented particular cafés, took the anti-Christian argument to extremes and were associated with a Bohemian life style. The group included Max Stirner and Bruno's brother, Edgar.

46. Friedrich Engels, 'Über eine in England bevorstehende Katastrophe', *Rheinische Zeitung*, no. 177, 26 June 1842, in W. Mönke (ed.), *Moses Hess: Philosophische und sozialistische Schriften 1837–1850. Eine Auswahl*,

Vaduz, Topos Verlag, 1980, pp. 183–5; Friedrich Engels, 'The Internal Crises', *Rheinische Zeitung*, no. 343, 9 December 1842, *MECW*, vol. 2, pp. 370–72.

47. Friedrich Engels, 'The Progress of Social Reform on the Continent', October–November 1843, *MECW*, vol. 3, 406.

48. Ibid., pp. 393, 407.

49. Engels, 'Outlines of a Critique of Political Economy', pp. 418–44.

50. Friedrich Engels, 'The Condition of England: The Eighteenth Century', *MECW*, vol. 3, pp. 475–6.

51. Engels, 'Outlines of a Critique of Political Economy', pp. 423, 424; Engels, 'The Condition of England: The Eighteenth Century', pp. 476, 485.

52. Friedrich Engels, 'The Condition of England: The English Constitution', *MECW*, vol. 3, p. 513.

53. Engels, 'The Condition of England: The Eighteenth Century', pp. 475–6.

54. Ibid., p. 464; Friedrich Engels, 'The Condition of England: *Past and Present* by Thomas Carlyle', *MECW*, vol. 3, p. 487.

55. Engels, *The Condition of the Working Class in England* p. 526.

56. 'Karl Marx to Friedrich Engels', 18 April 1863, *MECW*, vol. 41, pp. 468–9. He went on: 're-reading your work has made me unhappily aware of the changes wrought by age. With what zest and passion, what boldness of vision and absence of all learned or scientific reservations, the subject is still attacked in these pages!'

57. Engels and Marx, *The Holy Family*, p. 7.

Eugène Sue (1804–57) was one of the most popular novelists of the nineteenth century, most famous for *Les Mystères de Paris* (*The Mysteries of Paris*), published as a weekly serial in 1842–3. Sue was inspired by socialist writing and highlighted the dark side of city life. The novel was built upon the contrast between the high life of the nobility and the rich and harsh existence of the underclass. The Chartist sympathizer and publisher G. W. M. Reynolds brought out an English version: *The Mysteries of London*. Sue followed up the *Mysteries* with another global success, *Le Juif errant* (*The Wandering Jew*), which appeared in ten volumes between 1844 and 1845.

58. 'Georg Jung to Karl Marx', 18 March 1845, *MEGA*, III, i, pp. 458–9.

59. 'Friedrich Engels to Karl Marx', 17 March 1845, *MECW*, vol. 38, p. 28.

60. Engels and Marx, *The Holy Family*, p. 41.

61. Friedrich Engels, 'The Rapid Progress of Communism in Germany', *MECW*, vol. 4, p. 235.

62. Friedrich Engels, 'Speeches in Elberfeld', *MECW*, vol. 4, pp. 243–65.

63. Max Stirner, *The Ego and Its Own*, ed. David Leopold, Cambridge, Cambridge University Press, 1995 [1845], p. 323.

64. 'Friedrich Engels to Karl Marx', 19 November 1844, *MECW*, vol. 38, pp. 11–12.

65. Moses Hess, 'The Recent Philosophers' (1845), in Lawrence S. Stepelevich (ed.), *The Young Hegelians: An Anthology*, Cambridge, Cambridge University Press, 1983, pp. 359–60, 373.

66. In 1844, he had written in the *Deutsch-Französische Jahrbücher* that 'the criticism of religion' ended with 'the teaching that *man is the highest being for man*, hence with the *categorical imperative to overthrow all relations* in which man is a debased, enslaved, forsaken, despicable being'. Karl Marx, 'Introduction' to 'Contribution to the Critique of Hegel's Philosophy of Law', 1844, *MECW*, vol. 3, p. 182.

67. 'Karl Marx to Heinrich Börnstein', late December 1844, *MECW*, vol. 38, p. 14; and see Jacques Grandjonc, *Marx et les Communistes allemands à Paris, Vorwärts 1844: Contribution à l'étude de la naissance du Marxisme*, Paris, F. Maspero, 1974, p. 94.

68. 'Friedrich Engels to Karl Marx', *c.*20 January 1845, *MECW*, vol. 38, p. 16. Moses Hess had already written to Karl noting their critical consensus on 17 January 1845; see *MEGA*, III, i, p. 450.

69. Jenny Marx, 'Short Sketch', p. 222.

70. As early as 1801, for example, Louis-Sébastien Mercier in his *Néologie, ou Vocabulaire de mots nouveaux* (Paris, Moussard) had noted in reference to the 'proletarians', 'Woe to a nation divided into two necessarily enemy classes, that of the property owners and that of the proletarians.' Cited in Pierre Rosanvallon, *Le Sacre du citoyen: Histoire du suffrage universel en France*, Paris, Gallimard, 1992, p. 257. Karl himself made no claim to originality in resorting to the notions of class and class struggle. As he wrote to Joseph Weydemeyer in 1852, 'long before me, bourgeois historians had described the historical development of the struggle between the classes, as had the bourgeois economists their economic anatomy'. His claim to originality was 'to show that the *existence of classes* is merely bound up with *certain historical phases in the development of production*'. 'Karl Marx to Joseph Weydemeyer', 5 March 1852, *MECW*, vol. 39, p. 62.

71. Karl Marx, 'Development of the Productive Forces as a Material Premise of Communism', 1845–7, *MECW*, vol. 5, p. 49. This passage was formerly considered to form part of what was called *The German Ideology*. But there are now strong reasons for doubting the existence of such a text. See below, n. 80.

72. See Frederick Beiser, 'Max Stirner and the End of Classical German Philosophy', in Douglas Moggach (ed.) *Politics, Religion and Art: Hegelian Debates*, Evanston, Ill., Northwestern University Press, 2011, pp. 281–301. Stirner did not, of course, directly answer Karl's criticisms, because Karl's polemic was never published.

73. Friedrich Engels, 'On the History of the Communist League', October 1885, *MECW*, vol. 26, p. 318.

74. Engels and Marx, *The Holy Family*, p. 7.

75. Engels' theoretical insufficiencies did not go unnoticed at the time. According to Karl's companion from Cologne, Heinrich Bürgers, Engels' 'aversion to philosophy and speculation derive much less from an insight into their nature than from the discomfort which they have produced in his not very persevering mind'. Bürgers claimed that he probably resolved to protect himself from this discomfort in the future by 'the exorcism of contempt' and setting himself a descriptive task. 'Heinrich Bürgers to Karl Marx', February 1846, *MEGA*, III, i, pp. 506–7.

76. Friedrich Engels, 'Ludwig Feuerbach and the End of Classical German Philosophy', 25 February 1886, *MECW*, vol. 26, p. 366.

77. G. Plekhanov [N. Beltov], *The Development of the Monist View of History*, Moscow, Foreign Languages Publishing House, 1956 [1895], ch. 1.

78. 'Learned' because Karl used his doctoral research on 'Difference between the Democritean and Epicurean Philosophy of Nature' to challenge Bruno Bauer's findings.

79. On David Riazanov, see 'Epilogue', p. 710, n. 20.

80. See Terrell Carver, 'The German Ideology Never Took Place', *History of Political Thought*, 31 (Spring 2010), pp. 107–27, and see further Terrell Carver and Daniel Blank, *A Political History of the Editions of Marx and Engels's 'German Ideology Manuscripts'*, London, Palgrave Macmillan, 2014. The so-called *German Ideology*, as it was published in 1932, consists of an assortment of unedited or partly edited manuscripts, some of which were originally intended for publication elsewhere. Much of the early parts was written or transcribed by Karl or Engels; some of the later essays ('volume two') were originally composed or transcribed by Joseph Weydemeyer or Moses Hess. For these reasons, I have avoided citing any references in a form that implies that there existed such a book or integral text as *The German Ideology*.

81. These were published by Engels as an appendix to the 1888 edition of his essay. He made various editorial alterations, and provided it with the more portentous title, 'Theses on Feuerbach'.

82. Karl Marx, '*Ad* Feuerbach', *MECW*, vol. 5, p. 3.

83. Ibid., pp. 39–40.

84. Not all the observations made by Karl were accurate. While a criticism of the association of 'sensuousness' with passivity was justified, to criticize Feuerbach's view of man as that of 'an abstraction inherent in each single individual' rather than as part of an 'ensemble of social relations' – a point once made much of by Louis Althusser – makes little sense, given that one of Feuerbach's principal claims was to have replaced 'the solitary ego' as the starting point in philosophy by 'the unity of I and Thou'.

Incidentally, it is also quite wrong to infer from Karl's criticisms that Feuerbach was in some sense apolitical. Feuerbach declared that 'in the region of practical philosophy' he remained an idealist. His model of a republic was not that of Ancient Greece, but a German version of the United States. He also remained practically engaged in politics throughout his life, from his youthful association with the *Burschenschaften* through to his membership of the Democratic Congress in June 1848. See David Leopold, *The Young Karl Marx: German Philosophy, Modern Politics and Human Flourishing*, Cambridge, Cambridge University Press, 2007, pp. 203–18.

85. Marx, '*Ad* Feuerbach', p. 3.

86. Karl Marx, 'The Fetishism of Commodities and the Secret Thereof', in *Capital*, vol. I, *MECW*, vol. 35, pp. 81–94; on abstraction see below and also p. 199.

87. 'Karl Marx to Pavel Annenkov', 28 December 1846, *MECW*, vol. 38, pp. 100, 102.

88. Karl Marx, 'Direct Results of the Production Process', *MECW*, vol. 34, p. 398.

89. 'Karl Marx to Friedrich Engels', 25 March 1868, *MECW*, vol. 42, p. 558.

90. In emphasizing Karl's relationship with the idealist tradition, I am deeply indebted to the insights of Douglas Moggach and his idea of 'post-Kantian perfectionism'. See D. Moggach, 'Post-Kantian Perfectionism', in D. Moggach (ed.), *Politics, Religion and Art*, pp. 179–203; and for Marx's relationship with this tradition, see in particular the essay by Douglas Moggach, 'German Idealism and Marx', in John Walker (ed.), *The Impact of Idealism: The Legacy of Post-Kantian German Thought*, vol. II: *Historical, Social and Political Thought*, Cambridge, Cambridge University Press, 2013.

91. Karl Marx, 'Critique of the Hegelian Dialectic and Philosophy as a Whole', *MECW*, vol. 3, pp. 332–3. Hegel had reached this position in his years at Jena (1800–1807). In his lectures from 1803 onwards, he reversed the classical priority of activity (*praxis*) over labour (*poiesis*); work was no longer presented as a subordinate component of practical philosophy, confined to 'the relativity of a working class', but now became a central moment in the constitution of 'Spirit'. Practical behaviour was no longer confined to the concept of interaction with others or, as in Kant and Fichte, to the inner workings of moral subjectivity in interaction with its own sensuousness as object. For Hegel, this interaction between the self and the not-self was now extended through a new concept of labour to incorporate the whole of mankind's struggle with nature. Work and development were brought together in a transcendental history of consciousness, activity was objectified in work. See Manfred Riedel, *Between Tradition and Revolution: The Hegelian Transformation of Political Philosophy*, Cambridge, Cambridge University Press, 1984, chs.1 and 5.

92. Karl Marx, 'Estranged Labour', *MECW*, vol. 3, p. 280.

93. Immanuel Kant, 'Conjectural Beginning of Human History' (1786), in Lewis White Beck (ed.), *Kant: On History*, Indianapolis, Bobbs-Merril, 1980, pp. 59–60.

94. As Karl later wrote in his initial draft of *Capital*, the so-called *Grundrisse*, 'Labour obtains its measure from outside, through the aim to be attained and the obstacles to be overcome in attaining it. But Adam Smith has no inkling whatever that this overcoming of obstacles is in itself a liberating activity – and that, further, the external aims become stripped of the semblance of merely external natural urgencies, and become posited as aims which the individual himself posits – hence as self-realization, objectifications of the subject, hence real freedom': Karl Marx, *Economic Manuscripts of 1857–58 (Grundrisse)*, *MECW*, vol. 28, p. 530.

95. 'Ethical life' is an imperfect rendering of the German, *Sittlichkeit*, because the German word not only refers to morality, but equally to custom. The German word *Sitte* means custom. Thus *Sittlichkeit* refers to a mode of conduct habitually practised by a social group such as a nation, a class or a family, and regarded as a norm of decent behaviour. See Michael Inwood, *A Hegel Dictionary*, Oxford, Blackwell, 1992, pp. 91–3.

96. Marx, '*Ad* Feuerbach', p. 4.

97. Ibid., pp. 294–5, 296–7.

98. Plekhanov, *Development of the Monist View*, p. 166.

99. Karl Kautsky, *Ethics and the Materialist Conception of History*, Chicago, C. H. Kerr & Company, 1914 [1906], pp. 96–7, 102.

100. G. W. F. Hegel, *The Science of Logic*, trans. and ed. George di Giovanni, Cambridge, Cambridge University Press, 2010, pp. 657–69. Karl's application of Hegel's treatment of 'external teleology' to an analysis of the labour process in the 1844 *Manuscripts* has been argued by Douglas Moggach in 'German Idealism', pp. 19–21.

101. Moggach, 'German Idealism', pp. 21–3.

102. Karl Marx, 'Production and Intercourse: Division of Labour', *MECW*, vol. 5, pp. 33–4. Apart from the 'Asiatic mode of production' this list was very similar to that employed by Karl in 1859 in his preface to *A Contribution to the Critique of Political Economy*, *MECW*, vol. 29, p. 263. For the use made of the historical and legal studies of the German Historical School of Law – Savigny, Niebuhr, Hugo and Pfister – see Stedman Jones (ed.), *Communist Manifesto*, pp. 153–7. See also N. Levine, 'The German Historical School of Law and the Origins of Historical Materialism', *Journal of the History of Ideas*, 48/3 (July–Sept. 1987), pp. 431–51.

103. Karl Marx, *MECW*, vol. 5, p. 50.

104. Ibid., p. 50.

105. 'Karl Marx to Pavel Annenkov', 28 December 1846, *MECW*, vol. 38, pp. 96–7.

106. In *The Poverty of Philosophy*, Karl berates Proudhon for mechanically attempting to apply Hegelian categories. 'Once [reason] has managed to pose itself as a thesis, this thesis, this thought, opposed to itself, splits up into

two contradictory thoughts – the positive and the negative . . . The struggle between these two antagonistic elements comprised in the antithesis constitutes the dialectic movement': Karl Marx, *The Poverty of Philosophy*, *MECW*, vol. 6, p. 164. This hints at the dialectical inspiration of Karl's own approach in the 1844 *Manuscripts*, where labour as property and non-property develops into the antagonism between bourgeoisie and proletariat.

107. Marx, *Poverty of Philosophy*, p. 132.
108. Stedman Jones (ed.), *Communist Manifesto*, pp. 222–3.
109. Ibid., p. 226.
110. Marx, 'Critique of the Hegelian Dialectic', pp. 332–3.
111. Engels and Marx, *The Holy Family*, p. 37.
112. Ibid.
113. Karl's first encounters with flesh-and-blood workers, more precisely 'communist *Handwerker*' (artisans), occurred after he arrived in Paris in October 1843. He witnessed meetings of workers, and was plainly stirred. In the so-called *Economic and Philosophical Manuscripts of 1844*, he wrote, 'the brotherhood of man is no empty phrase, but a reality, and the nobility of man shines forth upon us from their toil-worn bodies', *MEGA*, I, ii, p. 289; *MECW*, vol. 3, p. 313. But his account did not move beyond stylized generality; there was no sense of one-to-one encounters with individual workers in the way made famous by Henry Mayhew in *London Labour and the London Poor* between 1848 and 1851. The one worker with whom he became more than superficially acquainted was the tailor Wilhelm Weitling. After praising him lavishly in *Vorwärts!* in August 1844 – as part of the 'brilliant literary debut of the German workers', *MECW*, vol. 3, p. 201 – he rapidly became exasperated with him, and in March 1846, in Brussels, angrily denounced his approach – see Chapter 7, pp. 214–15.
114. Douglas Moggach, *The Philosophy and Politics of Bruno Bauer*, Cambridge, Cambridge University Press, 2003, pp. 44–5.
115. Ibid.

7 THE APPROACH OF REVOLUTION

1. *Vormärz* literally means 'before March', i.e. before the March Revolution of 1848 in the German Confederation (including the Austrian Empire as well as present-day Germany). The period of *Vormärz* referred to the years between 1815 and 1848, a period dominated by conservative restoration following the defeat of Napoléon. During this period, states in the German Confederation resisted liberal reform and managed to avoid the revolutionary upheavals in France and Belgium in 1830. Policies of internal political

repression were accompanied by a strongly anti-revolutionary external policy led by Metternich, the Chancellor of the Austrian Empire.

2. For an impressively broad analysis of this question, see Warren Breckman, 'Diagnosing the "German Misery": Radicalism and the Problem of National Character, 1830 to 1848', in David E. Barclay and Eric D. Weitz (eds.), *Between Reform and Revolution: German Socialism and Communism from 1840 to 1990*, New York/Oxford, Berghahn, 1998, pp. 33–61. And see also Dieter Langewiesche, 'Revolution in Germany: Constitutional State – Nation State – Social Reform', in D. Dowe, H.-G. Haupt, D. Langewiesche and J. Sperber (eds.), *Europe in 1848: Revolution and Reform*, New York/Oxford, Berghahn, 2001, ch. 5.

3. I. Kant, 'On the Common Saying: "This may be true in theory, but it does not apply in practice"' [1793], in Hans Reiss (ed.), *Kant's Political Writings*, Cambridge, Cambridge University Press, 1970, pp. 61–93; see also Jacques Droz, *L'Allemagne et la Révolution française*, Paris, Presses Universitaires de Paris, 1949.

4. Elizabeth M. Wilkinson and L. A. Willoughby (eds.), *F. Schiller: On the Aesthetic Education of Man, in a Series of Letters*, Oxford, Clarendon Press, 1982, p. 25.

5. See Michael Rowe, *From Reich to State: The Rhineland in the Revolutionary Age 1780–1830*, Cambridge, Cambridge University Press, 2003.

6. Madame de Staël, *De l'Allemagne*, Paris, Firmin Didot Frères, 1860, p. 18. On the shift away from politics among the early Romantics, see Frederick C. Beiser, *The Romantic Imperative: The Concept of Early German Romanticism*, Cambridge, Mass., Harvard University Press, 2003.

7. On the character of democratic nationalist sentiment in the *Vormärz* period, see Hagen Schulze, *The Course of German Nationalism: From Frederick the Great to Bismarck, 1763–1867*, Cambridge, Cambridge University Press, 1991.

8. Heinrich Heine, *On the History of Religion and Philosophy in Germany and Other Writings*, ed. Terry Pinkard, Cambridge, Cambridge University Press, 2007, pp. 111, 116; see also Harold Mah, 'The French Revolution and the Problem of German Modernity: Hegel, Heine and Marx', *New German Critique*, no. 50 (Spring–Summer 1990), pp. 3–20.

9. Cited in Breckman, 'Diagnosing the "German Misery"', p. 39. Ludwig Börne, a democratic writer and a lapsed Jew, went into exile in Paris at the same time as Heine. He was one of the heroes of the young Friedrich Engels, especially because of his attack on the anti-French German nationalism of Wolfgang Menzel, in his 1837 *Menzel der Franzosenfresser*. Heine fell out with him and denounced him after his death in *Ludwig Börne: Eine Denkschrift* (1840), a book which Engels regarded as 'despicable'.

10. See Christina von Hodenberg, *Aufstand der Weber: die Revolte von 1844 und ihr Aufstieg zum Mythos*, Bonn, Dietz, 1997, pt III.

11. It is important to get away from the twentieth-century connotations of the word 'communism'. According to Stefan Born, one of the organizers of the Workers' Brotherhood (the *Arbeiterverbrüderung*) in Berlin in 1848, and an associate of Karl in the 1845–8 period, 'communism and communists were not binding words. Indeed people hardly talked about them.' At the left end of the spectrum, the line between communism and democracy was quite blurred. Stefan Born, *Erinnerungen eines Achtundvierzigers*, Leipzig, G. H. Meyer, 1898, p. 72.

12. Karl Grün, *Ausgewählte Schriften*, 2 vols., ed. Manuela Köppe, Berlin, Akademie Verlag, 2005, vol. 1, p. 100.

13. See Diana Siclovan, 'The Project of *Vergesellschaftung*, 1843–1851', M.Phil. dissertation, Cambridge University, 2010, p. 21.

14. See Pierre Haubtmann, *Proudhon, Marx et la pensée allemande*, Grenoble, Presses Universitaires de Grenoble, 1981, pp. 70–73.

15. Ibid., pp. 32, 33, 41.

16. Karl Marx, 'Statement', 18 January 1846, *MECW*, vol. 6, p. 34.

17. 'Karl Marx to Pierre-Joseph Proudhon', 5 May 1846, *MECW*, vol. 38, pp. 39–40.

18. Karl Marx, 'Critical Marginal Notes on the Article "The King of Prussia and Social Reform. By a Prussian"', *Vorwärts!*, no. 60, 7 August 1844, *MECW*, vol. 3, p. 201.

19. On the changes of position within the London League of the Just, see Christine Lattek, *Revolutionary Refugees: German Socialism in Britain, 1840–1860*, London, Routledge, 2006, ch. 2. On Hess's communist humanism, see Moses Hess, 'A Communist *Credo*: Questions and Answers', in *Moses Hess: The Holy History of Mankind and Other Writings*, ed. and trans. Shlomo Avineri, Cambridge, Cambridge University Press, 2004, pp. 116–27.

20. 'Jenny Marx to Karl Marx', 24 March 1846, *MEGA*, III, i, p. 518.

21. Cited in Boris Nicolaievsky and Otto Maenchen-Helfen, *Karl Marx: Man and Fighter*, trans. G. David and E. Mosbacher, London, Allen Lane, 1973 [1933], p. 125.

22. Pavel V. Annenkov, *The Extraordinary Decade: Literary Memoirs*, ed. Arthur P. Mendel, Ann Arbor, University of Michigan Press, 1968, pp. 169–71.

23. 'Wilhelm Weitling to Moses Hess', 31 March 1846, in Edmund Silberner (ed.), *Moses Hess: Briefwechsel*, The Hague, Mouton, 1959, p. 151.

24. 'Karl Marx and Friedrich Engels, Circular against Kriege', 11 May 1846, *MECW*, vol. 6, p. 35. There was no Communist Party at the time.

25. 'Hermann Kriege to Karl Marx', 9 June 1845, *MEGA*, III, i, pp. 470–72.

26. 'Hermann Ewerbeck to Karl Marx', June 1845, *MEGA*, III, i, p. 477; 'George Julian Harney to Friedrich Engels', 30 March 1846, *MECW*, vol. 38, p. 537.

27. 'P.-J. Proudhon to Karl Marx', 17 May 1846, *MEGA*, III, ii, pp. 203–5.

28. 'Communist Correspondence Committee in London to Karl Marx', 6 June 1846, *MEGA*, III, ii, p. 223; 'Joseph Weydemeyer to Karl Marx', 14 May 1846, *MEGA*, III, ii, p. 193.

29. 'Hermann Ewerbeck to Karl Marx', 15 May 1846, *MEGA*, III, ii, pp. 202–3.

30. See Siclovan, '*Vergesellschaftung*', pp. 42–3.

31. 'Hermann Ewerbeck to Karl Marx', 31 August 1845, *MEGA*, III, i, pp. 482–3.

32. Pierre-Joseph Proudhon, *Système des contradictions économiques, ou Philosophie de la misère*, 2 vols., Paris, Guillaumin, 1846, vol. 1, p. 164, 166.

33. Cited in Keith Tribe, *The Economy of the Word: Language, History and Economics*, Oxford, Oxford University Press, 2015, p. 227.

34. Karl Grün, 'Einführung', in *Ausgewählte Schriften*, vol. 1 p. 508; see also Siclovan, '*Vergesellschaftung*', pp. 42–3.

35. 'Karl Marx to C. J. Leske', 1 August 1846, *MECW*, vol. 38, p. 51.

36. 'C. J. Leske to Karl Marx', 2 February 1847, *MEGA*, III, ii, p. 329.

37. Karl Marx, 'Karl Grün: *Die Soziale Bewegung in Frankreich und Belgien*, Darmstadt 1845', or 'The Historiography of True Socialism', *MECW*, vol. 5, pp. 484–530. Most of the essay is taken up with a recital of the alleged plagiarisms and shoddy translations committed by Grün in relation to the accounts of socialism found in Lorenz von Stein and Louis Reybaud. The most interesting point was Karl's contrast between the consequences of the adoption by Grün and Proudhon of 'consumption' as a starting point in contrast to his own insistence upon the primacy of production: ibid., pp. 516–19.

38. 'Karl Schapper to Karl Marx', 6 June 1846, in *Der Bund der Kommunisten*, Berlin, Dietz, 1983, vol. 1, p. 348.

39. Gareth Stedman Jones (ed.), *Karl Marx and Friedrich Engels: The Communist Manifesto*, London, Penguin Books, 2002, p. 244.

40. Within radical and socialist circles, this view seems to have been widely held. The Chartist leader, Julian Harney, wrote to Engels, 'I heard that *you* [the literary characters in Brussels] *had* formed a society confined to yourselves into which you admitted no working man.' It was already known and 'has excited prejudice among the good men'. 'George Julian Harney to Friedrich Engels', 30 March 1846, *MEGA*, III, i, p. 526.

41. 'A Circular of the First Congress of the Communist League to the League Members', 9 June 1847, *MECW*, vol. 6, p. 590.

42. Born, *Erinnerungen*, p. 49.

43. 'Friedrich Engels to Karl Marx', 25 October 1847, *MECW*, vol. 18, pp. 138–9.

44. For the general character of Karl's argument in the *Manifesto*, see the more detailed account of the construction of the *Manifesto* and its prehistory in Stedman Jones (ed.), *Communist Manifesto*, pp. 3–185.

45. A fuller discussion of the *Manifesto* is given in the next chapter.

46. Stedman Jones (ed.), *Communist Manifesto*, pp. 251 and 248–51.

47. 'Demands of the Communist Party in Germany', 21–24 March 1848, *MECW*, vol. 7, p. 3.

48. See Siclovan, '*Vergesellschaftung*', pp. 50–51.

49. 'Joseph Weydemeyer to his fiancée', 2 February 1846, cited in Nicolaievsky and Maenchen-Helfen, *Karl Marx*, pp. 140–41.

50. *Deutsche-Brüsseler-Zeitung*, 6 January 1848, cited in Luc Somerhausen, *L'Humanisme agissant de Karl Marx*, Paris, Richard-Masse, 1946, p. 157.

51. Born, *Erinnerungen*, p. 68.

52. Wilhelm Liebknecht, 'Reminiscences of Karl Marx', in David McLellan (ed.), *Karl Marx: Interviews and Recollections*, London, Macmillan, 1981, p. 115; Jenny Marx, 'A Short Sketch of an Eventful Life', in Institut Marksizma–Leninzma, *Reminiscences of Marx and Engels*, Moscow Foreign Languages Publishing House, 1957, p. 229.

53. Jenny Marx, 'Short Sketch', p. 222.

54. Perhaps Engels broke into French to convey more exactly the status he ascribed to himself in this conversation. In English, it reads, 'You can regard Monsieur Marx as the head of our party (i.e. the most advanced fraction of German democracy, which I represent in relation to him) and his recent book against Proudhon as our programme.' 'Friedrich Engels to Karl Marx', 25–26 October 1847, *MECW*, vol. 38, p. 143.

55. Annenkov, *Extraordinary Decade*, pp. 167–8.

56. 'Friedrich Engels to Karl Marx', 17 March 1845, *MECW*, vol. 38, p. 29.

57. 'Frau' H. referred to Hess's companion, Sybille. The sarcastic use of inverted commas referred to the fact that they were not married. According to Cologne police reports, Sybille, née Pesch, was a former prostitute turned seamstress, whom Hess rescued as an act of philanthropy. This may be why Engels referred to her in such insulting language. For an account of this affair in relation to Engels' activities in the 1840s, see Tristram Hunt, *The Frock-Coated Communist: The Revolutionary Life of Friedrich Engels*, London, Allen Lane, 2009, pp. 143–6 and passim.

58. 'Roland Daniels to Karl Marx', 7 March 1846, *MEGA*, III, i, pp. 513–14.

59. 'Heinrich Bürgers to Karl Marx', end of February 1846, *MEGA*, III, i, pp. 506–7.

60. Ibid.

61. 'Jenny Marx to Karl Marx', 24 March 1846, *MECW*, vol. 38, pp. 529–32. In writing that 'all cats are of the same colour', Jenny was alluding to Hegel's famous reproach against Schelling's conception of the Absolute in the preface to the *Phenomenology* as 'the night in which all cows are black'.

62. 'Moses Hess to Karl Marx', 29 May 1846, *MEGA*, III, i, p. 211.

63. 'Friedrich Engels to Karl Marx', 19 August 1846, *MECW*, vol. 38, p. 56.

64. 'Friedrich Engels to Karl Marx', 27 July 1846, *MECW*, vol. 38, p. 46; 'Engels to the Correspondence Committee', 16 September 1846, *MECW*,

vol. 38, p. 65; ibid., 23 October 1846, p. 81; 'Friedrich Engels to Karl Marx', 15 January 1847, *MECW*, vol. 38, p. 108.

65. 'Friedrich Engels to Karl Marx', 14 January 1848, *MECW*, vol. 38, p. 153.

66. 'Friedrich Engels to Karl Marx', November/December 1846, *MECW*, vol. 38, p. 91.

67. Ibid., 9 March 1847, p. 115.

68. 'Jenny Marx to Karl Marx', after 24 August 1845, *MECW*, vol. 38, p. 529; 'Hermann Ewerbeck to Karl Marx', 31 October 1845, *MEGA*, III, i, pp. 489–90.

69. 'Georg Jung to Karl Marx', 18 March 1845, *MEGA*, III, i, pp. 458–9.

70. 'Joseph Weydemeyer to Karl Marx', 30 April 1846, *MEGA*, III, i, p. 532.

71. 'Moses Hess to Karl Marx', 28 July 1846, in Silberner (ed.) *Moses Hess: Briefwechsel*, p. 165.

72. Shelved and modified, but not abandoned. He continued to consider 'the economic' as a distortion of 'the human', and to assume that 'abstraction' was the means by which humanity subjected itself to inhuman goals. These themes reappeared in explicit form in the *Economic Manuscripts of 1857–58*, the so-called *Grundrisse*.

73. Karl Marx, *The Poverty of Philosophy*, *MECW*, vol. 6, p. 125.

74. Ibid., p. 138.

75. On these theories, which generally had little to do with the theories of Ricardo, see Gareth Stedman Jones, 'Rethinking Chartism', in *Languages of Class: Studies in English Working Class History, 1832–1982*, Cambridge, Cambridge University Press, 1983, pp. 128–45.

76. Marx, *Poverty of Philosophy*, pp. 189–90.

77. Karl Marx, 'Wages', *MECW*, vol. 6, p. 419. These were notes made for the lectures he gave to the German Workers' Educational Association in the autumn of 1847.

78. Karl Marx, 'Wage Labour and Capital', *MECW*, vol. 9, pp. 212–13. Karl's intention to publish his lectures of 1847 was interrupted by the outbreak of the revolution. Most of them were published in the *Neue Rheinische Zeitung* in 1849.

79. Ibid., p. 214.

80. Ibid., pp. 219–20.

81. Ibid., pp. 215, 225–6.

82. Marx, 'Wages', p. 432.

83. 'From our German Correspondent [Karl Marx], the Free Trade Congress at Brussels', September 1847, *MECW*, vol. 6, p. 290; Karl Marx, 'Speech on the Question of Free Trade', 9 January 1848, *MECW*, vol. 6, p. 465.

84. Louis Blanc, *The History of Ten Years, 1830–1840*, 2 vols., London, 1845, vol. 1, pp. 27 and 33.

85. Alexis de Tocqueville, *Recollections*, ed. J. P. Mayer and A. P. Kerr, trans. G. Lawrence, London, Macdonald, 1970, pp. 52, 92.

86. Friedrich Engels, *The Condition of the Working Class in England: From Personal Observation and Authentic Sources*, *MECW*, vol. 4, p. 304. For international comparisons, see M. Riedel, 'Bürger, Staatsbürger, Bürgertum', in O. Brunner, W. Conze and R. Koselleck (eds.), *Geschichtliche Grundbegriffe: Historisches Lexikon zur politisch-sozialen Sprache in Deutschland*, Stuttgart, Klett-Cotta, 1972, vol. 1, pp. 672–725; R. Koselleck, U. Spree and W. Steinmetz, 'Drei bürgerliche Welten? Zur vergleichenden Semantik der bürgerlichen Gesellschaft in Deutschland, England und Frankreich', in Hans-Jürgen Puhle (ed.), *Bürger in der Gesellschaft der Neuzeit: Wirtschaft, Politik, Kultur*, Göttingen, Vandenhoeck & Ruprecht, 1991, pp. 14–58; Reinhart Koselleck and Klaus Schreiner, *Bürgerschaft: Rezeption und Innovation der Begrifflichkeit vom Hohen Mittelalter bis ins 19. Jahrhundert*, Stuttgart, Klett-Cotta, 1994; Jürgen Kocka, 'Das europäische Muster und der deutsche Fall', in Jürgen Kocka (ed.), *Bürgertum im 19. Jahrhundert: Deutschland im europäischen Vergleich*, 3 vols., Göttingen, Vandenhoeck & Ruprecht, 1995, vol. 1, pp. 9–75; Pamela M. Pilbeam, *The Middle Classes in Europe 1789–1914: France, Germany, Italy and Russia*, Basingstoke, Macmillan Education, 1990.
87. See Engels, *The Condition of the Working Class in England*, pp. 295–596.
88. See John M. Maguire, *Marx's Theory of Politics*, Cambridge, Cambridge University Press, 1978, p. 203.
89. 'Karl Marx to Ludwig Kugelmann', 28 December 1862, *MECW*, vol. 41, p. 435; and see my discussion in 'The Young Hegelians, Marx and Engels', in Gareth Stedman Jones and Gregory Claeys (eds.), *The Cambridge History of Nineteenth-Century Political Thought*, Cambridge, Cambridge University Press, 2011, pp. 579–85.
90. 'George Julian Harney to Friedrich Engels', 30 March 1846, *MEGA*, III, i, p. 523.
91. 'Hermann Kriege to Karl Marx', 9 June 1845, *MEGA*, III, i, p. 470.
92. 'Carl Bernays to Karl Marx', 7 April 1846, *MEGA*, III, i, p. 529.
93. 'Heinrich Burgers to Karl Marx', 30 August 1847, *MEGA*, III, ii, p. 351.
94. Friedrich Engels, 'The Movements of 1847', *Deutsche-Brüsseler-Zeitung*, 23 January 1848, *MECW*, vol. 6, pp. 521–9.
95. For a biography of von Bornstedt, see p. **629**, n. 90.
96. See this chapter, pp. **220–22**.
97. See this chapter, pp. **210–22**.
98. 'Friedrich Engels to Karl Marx', 23–24 November 1847, *MECW*, vol. 38, pp. 146–9.
99. 'New Year's Eve Celebration', 31 December 1847, *Deutsche-Brüsseler-Zeitung*, *MECW*, vol. 6, p. 639.
100. *Le Débat social*, 6 February 1848, cited in Somerhausen, *L'Humanisme agissant*, pp. 172–4.

101. Karl Marx, 'The *Débat social* of 6 February on the Democratic Association', *MECW*, vol. 6, pp. 536–9.
102. Marx, 'Speech on the Question of Free Trade', pp. 463, 465.
103. Karl Marx, 'Speech on Poland', 29 November 1847, *MECW*, vol. 6, pp. 388–9.
104. Karl Marx, 'On the Polish Question', 22 February 1848, *MECW*, vol. 6, p. 546.
105. Friedrich Engels, 'Speech on Poland', 29 November 1847, *MECW*, vol. 6, p. 389.
106. Somerhausen, *L'Humanisme agissant*, pp. 183–200.
107. Karl Marx, 'Letter to the Editor of *La Réforme*', 6 March 1848, *MECW*, vol. 6, p. 565.

8 THE MID-CENTURY REVOLUTIONS

1. On the events of the February Revolution in Paris, see below.
2. Hanna Ballin Lewis (ed.), *A Year of Revolutions: Fanny Lewald's Recollections of 1848*, Providence, RI/Oxford, Berghahn, 1997, p. 41.
3. At this time, Engels believed Ledru-Rollin and Flocon and 'the men of the *Réforme* . . . are communists without knowing it'. 'Friedrich Engels to Emil Blank', 28 March 1848, *MECW*, vol. 38, p. 168. In a letter to his lawyer in 1860, accounting for his political career in answer to the accusations of Karl Vogt, Karl wrote, 'Flocon offered to help myself and Engels finance the founding of the *N. Rh. Z.* We refused because, as *Germans*, we did not wish to take subsidies from a *French government*, even if *friendly*.' 'Karl Marx to J. M. Weber', 3 March 1860, *MECW*, vol. 41, p. 102.
4. Gustave Flaubert, *A Sentimental Education*, ed. and trans. Douglas Parmée, Oxford, Oxford University Press, 1989, p. 317.
5. Sebastian Seiler, *Das Komplott vom 13 Juni 1849, oder der letzte Sieg der Bourgeoisie in Frankreich*, Hamburg, Joffman und Campe, 1850, p. 21, cited in Boris Nicolaievsky and Otto Maenchen-Helfen, *Karl Marx: Man and Fighter*, trans. G. David and E. Mosbacher, London, Allen Lane, 1973 [1933], p. 160.
6. 'Report of the Speeches made by Marx and Engels at the General Meeting of the Democratic Committee in Cologne on 4 August 1848', *MECW*, vol. 7, p. 556.
7. 'Karl Marx to Joseph Weydemeyer', 5 March 1852, *MECW*, vol. 39, p. 62.
8. Alexis de Tocqueville, *Recollections*, ed. J. P. Mayer and A. P. Kerr, trans. G. Lawrence, London, Macdonald, 1970, p. 18.
9. The suffrage under the July regime was extremely narrow, 166,000 in 1831 rising to 241,000 in 1846. But the proposal to extend the suffrage was

insignificant in comparison with the manhood suffrage decreed by the February Revolution. 8,221,000 were entitled to vote in the election for the Constituent Assembly on 23 April 1848.

10. Cited in Georges Duveau, *1848: The Making of a Revolution*, London, Routledge & Kegan Paul, 1967, p. 8.

11. Habitually described as 'the worker Albert', stressing the novelty of a government including a worker, his real name was Alexandre Martin. He was a leader of a secret society, a mechanic and one of the members of the Luxembourg Commission (established to discuss solutions to the labour question), and was elected a member of the National Assembly. He was compromised by his participation in the attempted coup of 15 May and arrested.

12. Christopher Clark, *Iron Kingdom: The Rise and Downfall of Prussia 1600–1947*, London, Allen Lane, 2006, p. 469.

13. The dangers of misunderstanding or over-reaction on the part of the forces of order, when confronted by urban crowds, and the high fatality attending street battles, in France, Austria and Germany, pointed to the dangers of leaving crucial questions of crowd control in the hands of an armed military. In Britain, by contrast, a civilian police force had existed since the 1820s.

14. 'Roland Daniels to Karl Marx', 21 March 1848, *MEGA*, III, ii, pp. 403–4. According to Daniels, 'only bankers and merchants receive private newsletters, and Camphausen declared the day before yesterday in the city council that he could not divulge details from his newsletters, since it would arouse too much unrest among the people'.

15. 'Georg Weerth to Karl Marx', 25 March 1848, *MEGA*, III, ii, p. 414.

16. See Oscar J. Hammen, *The Red '48ers: Karl Marx and Friedrich Engels*, New York, Scribner, 1969, p. 218.

17. 'Andreas Gottschalk to Hess', 26 March 1848, in Edmund Silberner (ed.), *Moses Hess: Briefwechsel*, The Hague, Mouton, 1959, pp. 175–6.

18. 'Gottschalk to Hess', in Silberner (ed.), *Moses Hess: Briefwechsel*, p. 175; and see Karl Stommel, 'Der Armenarzt, Dr. Andreas Gottschalk, der erste Kölner Arbeiterführer, 1848', *Annalen des Historischen Vereins für den Niederrhein*, 166 (December 1964), p. 81.

19. Karl's friend George Weerth, writing from Cologne in March, had expressed the same thought. 'Although everything that is accomplished here is quite democratic, people nevertheless shudder at the mention of the word republic.' By contrast, he also noted, however, that towards Coblenz and the Upper Rhine 'opinion is said to be in favour of a republic'. 'Georg Weerth to Karl Marx', 25 March 1848, *MEGA*, III, ii, p. 414.

20. Friedrich Engels, 'Revolution and Counter-Revolution in Germany', August 1851–March 1853, *MECW*, vol. 11, p. 37. This collection of essays was originally written for the *New-York Daily Tribune*, under Karl's name.

21. Stommel, 'Der Armenarzt', pp. 84, 91.

22. 'Minutes of the Meeting of the Cologne Community of the Communist League', 11 May 1848, *MECW*, vol. 7, p. 542.

23. 'Friedrich Engels to Karl Marx', 25 April 1848, *MECW*, vol. 38, p. 173.

24. See editorial announcement, *Neue Rheinische Zeitung* (henceforward abbreviated to *NRhZ*), 1 June 1848, no. 1, p. 1.

25. How much of his own inheritance Karl put into the paper remains in doubt. Traditional accounts state that he put the whole sum of 6,000 thalers into the paper. But, for a more qualified assessment, see Hammen, *The Red '48ers*, p. 269.

26. 'The First Trial of the *Neue Rheinische Zeitung*', a speech by Karl Marx, 7 February 1849, *MECW*, vol. 8, p. 316. Also see below p. 291.

27. 'Statement of the Editorial Board', 1 June 1848, *MECW*, vol. 7, p. 15.

28. (Karl Marx) 'Camphausen's Statement at the Session of 30 May', *NRhZ*, no. 3, 2 June 1848, p. 2, *MECW*, vol. 7, p. 33.

29. Friedrich Engels, 'The Assembly at Frankfurt', *NRhZ*, no. 1, 1 June 1848, *MECW*, vol. 7, p. 16.

30. Karl Marx, 'The Programmes of the Radical-Democratic Party and of the Left at Frankfurt', *NRhZ*, no. 7, 7 June 1848, *MECW*, vol. 7, pp. 49, 50.

31. 'Deutschland', *NRhZ*, no. 18, 18 June 1848, *MECW*, vol. 7, p. 89.

32. 'The Downfall of the Camphausen Government', *NRhZ*, supplement no. 22, 22 June 1848, *MECW*, vol. 7, p. 106. There is no reason to believe that the Auerswald-Hansemann government which followed the fall of Camphausen was more pro-Russian than its predecessor. But German radicals were quite right to be suspicious of Russian intentions, especially since the czar was married to Friedrich Wilhelm's sister.

33. Charles Greville, *The Greville Memoirs. Second Part: A Journal of the Reign of Queen Victoria from 1837 to 1852*, London, Longmans, Green and Co., 1885, vol. 3, pp. 202–3. Mark Traugott argues that it was the use of the semi-military form of hierarchy and organization which had been developed within the National Workshops that was responsible for the disciplined character of the uprising. See Mark Traugott, *Armies of the Poor: Determinants of Working-Class Participation in the Parisian Insurrection of June 1848*, Princeton, Princeton University Press, 1985, esp. chs. 5 and 6.

34. See Henri Guillemin, *La Première Résurrection de la République: 24 février 1848*, Paris, Gallimard, 1967, pp. 346–7. Aloysius Huber, who declared the Assembly dissolved, was a secret agent.

35. Maurice Agulhon, *1848, ou L'Apprentissage de la République, 1848–1852*, Paris, Éditions du Seuil, 1973, p. 64.

36. Approximately 500 insurgents and 1,000 soldiers and guardsmen lost their lives in the fighting. But in its aftermath 3,000 more insurgents were hunted down in the city and killed in cold blood, 12,000 were arrested and around 4,500 of them imprisoned or deported to labour camps in Algeria. Peter N. Stearns, *The Revolutions of 1848*, London, Weidenfeld & Nicholson, 1974, p. 92.

37. Karl Marx, 'The June Revolution', *NRhZ*, no. 29, 29 June 1848, *MECW*, vol. 7, pp. 144, 147–8.

38. Ibid., p. 149.

39. 'Report of the Speeches made by Marx and Engels at the General Meeting of the Democratic Society in Cologne on 4 August 1848', pp. 556–7.

40. For Karl's attempt to contest this decision, see 'The Conflict between Marx and Prussian Citizenship', *NRhZ*, no. 94, 5 September 1848, *MECW*, vol. 7, pp. 407–10.

41. Louis-Napoléon Bonaparte (1808–73), nephew of Napoléon, believed himself destined to re-establish the glories of the First Empire. Brought up largely in Switzerland, in 1836 and 1840 he made two unsuccessful attempts to seize power. The principles of Bonapartism, as he understood them, were based upon two ideas: universal male suffrage and the primacy of the national interest. While in prison, he wrote his most famous book, *L'Extinction du pauperisme* (1844), saluting the virtues of the French working class, and proposing various reforms guided by ideas of association, education and discipline. In 1846, he escaped jail and lived in London through to the summer of 1848. His popularity was not simply based upon his name. His programme combined a strong commitment to order, the family and the church together with supposedly progressive ideas on the social question. The extent of his appeal was revealed in the presidential election of December 1848, in which he won 5,572,834 votes or 74.2 per cent of votes cast. Bonaparte's politics, invoking the army and the nation, and drawing upon ideas both from the right and from the left, was a novel phenomenon. It inaugurated what came to be called populism, combining democracy and authoritarian rule. It disconcerted radicals and socialists, and found important imitators on the post-Legitimist right.

42. *La Montagne* ('The Mountain') referred to those who sat on the high benches to the left of the chair in the newly elected Convention in 1792. Following the fall of the monarchy and declaration of a republic, the question that initially divided the *Montagnards* from the *Girondins* was the fate of Louis XVI. It was *Montagnard* pressure that resulted in the trial and execution of the king.

43. Martial law was lifted on 3 October, but financial difficulties prevented the paper resuming publication until 12 October.

44. 'German Foreign Policy and the Latest Events in Prague', *NRhZ*, no. 42, 12 July 1848, *MECW*, vol. 7, p. 212.

45. 'In respect of social development, we Germans had only now arrived at the point which the French had already reached in the year 1789.' 'Report of the Speeches made by Marx and Engels at the General Meeting of the Democratic Society in Cologne on 4 August 1848', p. 556.

46. Karl Marx, 'The Crisis and the Counter-Revolution', *NRhZ*, no. 102, 14 September 1848, *MECW*, vol. 7, p. 432. The Vendée in the west of

France was the area in which the most serious rebellion against the Revolution took place on the occasion of the call-up of 300,000 men by the Convention in 1793.

47. 'Friedrich Engels to Karl Marx', 8–9 March 1848, *MECW*, vol. 38, p. 160.

48. Karl Marx, 'The Crisis and the Counter-Revolution', *NRbZ*, no. 101, 13 September 1848, *MECW*, vol. 7, p. 428.

49. Karl Marx, 'The Government of the Counter-Revolution', *NRbZ*, no. 110, 23 September 1848, *MECW*, vol. 7, p. 448.

50. Karl Marx, 'The Downfall of the Camphausen Government', *NRbZ*, no. 23, 23 June 1848, *MECW*, vol. 7, p. 107.

51. Marx, 'The Crisis and the Counter-Revolution', *NRbZ*, no. 102, 14 September 1848, *MECW*, vol. 7, p. 431.

52. Clark, *Iron Kingdom*, p. 479.

53. Karl Marx, 'The Counter-Revolution in Berlin', *NRbZ*, no. 142, 14 November 1848, *MECW*, vol. 8, p. 19.

54. After the summoning of the Estates General by the (bankrupt) French government in May 1789, there were frequent disputes between the first two estates (clergy and nobility) and the 'Third Estate' (commoners), particularly on the question of whether voting should be by order or by head. On 17 June, the 'Third Estate' decided to break away from the Estates General and draw up their own constitution. As a result, on 20 June, they were locked out from their meeting place. They therefore made their way to a nearby tennis court, named themselves the National Assembly and resolved not to disperse until they had established a new constitution for France.

55. Karl Marx, 'The Counter-Revolution in Berlin', *NRbZ*, no. 141, 12 November 1848, *MECW*, vol. 8, p. 15.

56. In relation to the campaign for tax refusal, in an 'Appeal' sent out in the name of 'The Rhenish District Committee of Democrats' and signed by Karl Marx, Karl Schapper and Schneider II on 18 November 1848, it was stated that that 'forcible collection' of taxes had to be 'resisted everywhere and in every way'. It also enjoined that 'a people's militia must be organised everywhere'. 'Appeal', 18 November 1848, *MECW*, vol. 8, p. 41. But three days later the same committee appealed that 'you conduct yourselves calmly'. See the 'Appeal' sent out to 'Democrats of the Rhine Province' in the name of 'Karl Marx, Karl Schapper and Schneider II', *NRbZ*, no. 148, 21 November 1848, *MECW*, vol. 8, p. 46.

57. Karl Marx, 'The Counter-Revolution in Berlin', *NRbZ*, no. 141, 12 November 1848, *MECW*, vol. 8, p. 17.

58. Karl Marx, 'The Victory of the Counter-Revolution in Vienna', *NRbZ*, no. 136, 7 November 1848, *MECW*, vol. 7.

59. Karl Marx, 'The Bourgeoisie and the Counter-Revolution', *NRbZ*, no. 183, 31 December 1848, *MECW*, vol. 8, p. 178.

60. Jonathan Sperber, *Rhineland Radicals: The Democratic Movement and the Revolution of 1848–1849*, Princeton, Princeton University Press, 1991, p. 383.

61. Friedrich Engels, 'From Paris to Berne', unpublished in his lifetime, *MECW*, vol. 7, pp. 519, 528–9.

62. 'August Ewerbeck to Moses Hess', 14 November 1848, in Silberner (ed.), *Moses Hess: Briefwechsel*, p. 209.

63. Cited in Hammen, *The Red '48ers*, p. 316.

64. Stommel, 'Der Armenarzt', p. 99.

65. Karl Marx, 'Montesquieu LVI', *NRhZ*, no. 202, 22 January 1849, *MECW*, vol. 8, p. 266; in this essay, for once, instead of endlessly reiterating his denunciation of 'the bourgeoisie', Karl was prepared, like the Chartists in England and the Démoc-Socs in France, to distinguish between its different social and political components. Apart from 'the commercial and industrial sections of the bourgeoisie' who 'throw themselves into the arms of the counter-revolution for fear of the revolution', there were also 'financial magnates, big creditors of the state, bankers and rentiers, whose wealth increases proportionately to the poverty of the people, and finally men whose business depends on the old political structure': ibid., p. 267.

66. 'Gottschalk to Hess', 22 March 1849, in Silberner (ed.), *Moses Hess: Briefwechsel*, pp. 216–17.

67. 'The First Trial of the *Neue Rheinische Zeitung*', speech by Karl Marx, 7 February 1849, *MECW*, vol. 8, pp. 304–17.

68. 'The Trial of the Rhenish District Committee of Democrats', speech by Karl Marx, 8 February 1849, *MECW*, vol. 8, pp. 323–39.

69. Karl Marx, 'The Revolutionary Movement', *NRhZ*, no. 184, 1 January 1849, *MECW*, vol. 8, pp. 214–15.

70. Friedrich Engels, 'The Magyar Struggle', *NRhZ*, no. 194, 13 January 1849, *MECW*, vol. 8, pp. 230, 238.

71. Marx, 'Bourgeoisie and the Counter-Revolution', p. 178.

72. Marx, 'Revolutionary Movement', p. 213.

73. Karl Marx, 'Stein', *NRhZ*, no. 225, 18 February 1849, *MECW*, vol. 8, p. 390.

74. Karl Marx, 'The Frankfurt March Association and the *Neue Rheinische Zeitung*', *NRhZ*, no. 248, 17 March 1848, *MECW*, vol. 9, pp. 84–5.

75. Dieter Dowe, *Aktion und Organisation: Arbeiterbewegung, sozialistische und kommunistische Bewegung in der preussischen Rheinprovinz 1820–1852*, Hanover, Verlag für Literatur und Zeitgeschehen, 1970, pp. 221–4.

76. Sperber, *Rhineland Radicals*, pp. 351–3.

77. 'Report of the Speeches Made by Marx and Engels at the General Meeting of the Democratic Society in Cologne on 4 August 1848', pp. 556–7.

78. 'Report on the Convocation of the Congress of Workers' Associations', *NRhZ*, no. 282, 26 April 1849, *MECW*, vol. 9, p. 502.

79. 'The 18th of March', *NRhZ*, no. 249, 18 March 1849, *MECW*, vol. 9, p. 108.

80. 'Karl Marx to Friedrich Engels', 7 June 1849, *MECW*, vol. 38, p. 200.

81. David McLellan (ed.), *Karl Marx: Interviews and Recollections*, London, Macmillan, 1981, p. 15.

82. Flaubert, *Sentimental Education*, p. 322.

83. Alexander Herzen, *My Past and Thoughts: The Memoirs of Alexander Herzen*, trans. C. Garnett, New York, A. A. Knopf, 1968, vol. 2, pp. 671–2.

84. Karl Marx, *The Class Struggles in France, 1848 to 1850*, *MECW*, vol. 10, p. 106; what is true is that, given his ambivalent role in February and June 1848, Ledru-Rollin was not entirely trusted as a popular leader in Paris. See Agulhon, *1848*, pp. 93–5.

85. 'Karl Marx to Friedrich Engels', 7 June 1849, *MECW*, vol. 38, p. 199.

86. 'Karl Marx to Ferdinand Freiligrath', 31 July 1849, *MECW*, vol. 38, pp. 205–6.

87. 'Karl Marx to Joseph Weydemeyer', end of July 1849, *MECW*, vol. 38, p. 209.

88. 'Karl Marx to Friedrich Engels', 17 August 1849, *MECW*, vol. 38, p. 211.

89. This is based upon the testimony of the cigar-maker Peter Röser, who was a member of the Communist League in Cologne. But his testimony must be treated with some caution, since it was given in a police investigation, and Röser had every incentive to stress Karl's emphasis on education and propaganda rather than upon revolutionary action. See Nicolaievsky and Maenchen-Helfen, *Karl Marx*, pp. 414–17 (appendix III).

90. Nicolaievsky and Maenchen-Helfen, *Karl Marx*, p. 223.

91. Marx, 'Victory of the Counter-Revolution in Vienna', p. 506; Marx, 'Bourgeoisie and the Counter-Revolution', pp. 154, 178.

92. Karl Marx and Friedrich Engels, 'Address of the Central Authority to the League', March 1850, *MECW*, vol. 10, p. 277.

93. Ibid., p. 281.

94. Ibid., pp. 283, 284, 285–7.

95. Karl Marx and Friedrich Engels, 'Address of the Central Authority to the League', June 1850, *MECW*, vol. 10, pp. 371–2, 377. Unlike the March Address, it has been questioned whether this Address was written by Karl. See Christine Lattek, *Revolutionary Refugees: German Socialism in Britain, 1840–1860*, London, Routledge, 2006, p. 60.

96. 'Universal Society of Revolutionary Communists', mid-April 1850, *MECW*, vol. 10, p. 614.

97. See the letter of Friedrich Engels and the statement of Henryk Miskowsky (Schramm's second), in Karl Marx, 'The Knight of the Noble Consciousness' (a pamphlet attacking Willich), 28 November 1853, *MECW*, vol. 12, pp. 489–96; there is a lively account of the duel in Francis Wheen, *Karl Marx*, London, Fourth Estate, 1999, pp. 164–5.

98. 'Meeting of the Central Authority', 15 September 1850, *MECW*, vol. 10, pp. 625–30. The positions adopted by Willich and Schapper have often been treated as one. This is not true since, unlike Willich, Schapper was

generally very wary of insurrectionary politics. Schapper's main concern in the meeting of the Central Authority was to try to mediate between the two sides. But even more important, he considered, was the need to keep the Workers' Association united; see Lattek, *Revolutionary Refugees*, pp. 72–80.

99. 'Jenny Marx to Adolf Cluss', 30 October 1852, *MECW*, vol. 39, p. 578.

100. 'Karl Marx to Friedrich Engels', 23 August 1849, *MECW*, vol. 38, p. 213.

101. 'Karl Marx to Ferdinand Freiligrath', 5 September 1849, *MECW*, vol. 38, p. 216; 'Karl Marx to Ferdinand Freiligrath', 11 January 1850, *MECW*, vol. 38, p. 224.

102. 'Jenny Marx to Joseph Weydemeyer', 20 May 1850, *MECW*, vol. 38, p. 555. The familial life of Karl during these early years in London is discussed in Chapter 9.

103. Karl Marx and Friedrich Engels, 'Gottfried Kinkel', *NRhZ – Politisch-Ökonomische Revue*, no. 4, 1850, *MECW*, vol. 10, pp. 345–7; and see Lattek, *Revolutionary Refugees*, pp. 59–60.

104. 'Announcement of the *Neue Rheinische Zeitung. Politisch-Ökonomische Revue*', 15 December 1849, *MECW*, vol. 10, p. 5.

105. Karl Marx and Friedrich Engels, 'Review, May to October 1850', *MECW*, vol. 10, p. 510.

106. McLellan (ed.), *Karl Marx: Interviews and Recollections*, p. 25.

107. This text is discussed in detail in Chapter 9.

108. 'Karl Marx to Joseph Weydemeyer', 5 March 1852, *MECW*, vol. 39, p. 62.

109. See E. A. Wrigley, *Continuity, Chance and Change: The Character of the Industrial Revolution in England*, Cambridge, Cambridge University Press, 1988; Roderick Floud and Paul Johnson (eds.), *The Cambridge Economic History of Modern Britain*, vol. 1: *Industrialisation, 1700–1860*, Cambridge, Cambridge University Press, 2004.

110. See Gareth Stedman Jones, *Languages of Class: Studies in English Working Class History, 1832–1982*, Cambridge, Cambridge University Press, 1983, pp. 1–25, 90–179.

111. Karl Marx, 'The German Ideology', *MECW*, vol. 5, p. 49; Gareth Stedman Jones (ed.), *Karl Marx and Friedrich Engels: The Communist Manifesto*, London, Penguin Books, 2002, p. 235.

112. Karl Marx, *Economic and Philosophical Manuscripts of 1844*, *MECW*, vol. 3, p. 241.

113. Friedrich Engels, 'The Condition of England: The English Constitution', March 1844, *MECW*, vol. 3, pp. 512, 513.

114. For the discussion of the contrasting images of *industriels* or *classe moyenne*, see Shirley M. Gruner, *Economic Materialism and Social Moralism: A Study in the History of Ideas in France from the Latter Part of the 18th Century to the Middle of the 19th Century*, The Hague, Mouton, 1973, part III; Sarah Maza, *The Myth of the French Bourgeoisie: An Essay on*

the Social Imaginary, 1750–1850, Cambridge, Mass., Harvard University Press, 2003.

115. On Guizot's initial confidence in the reputed rational capacities of the *classe moyenne*, see Pierre Rosanvallon, *Le Moment Guizot*, Paris, Gallimard, 1985.

116. See J.-C.-L. Simonde de Sismondi, *Nouveaux principes d'économie politique, ou de la richesse dans ses rapports avec la population*, 2 vols., Paris, Chez Delaunay, 1819. Overproduction was seen as the result of mechanization and the growth of a world market. See Gareth Stedman Jones, *An End to Poverty?: A Historical Debate*, London, Profile Books, 2004, ch. 4.

117. Gareth Stedman Jones, 'The Mid-Century Crisis and the 1848 Revolutions: A Critical Comment', in *Theory and Society*, 12/4 July 1983; Mark Traugott, *Armies of the Poor: Determinants of Working-Class Participation in the Parisian Insurrection of June 1848*, Princeton, Princeton University Press, 1985, ch. 1.

118. See Peter Kriedte, Hans Medick and Jürgen Schlumbohn, *Industrialisierung vor der Industrialisierung: Gewerbliche Warenproduktion auf dem Land in der Formationsperiode des Kapitalismus*, Göttingen, Vandenhoeck & Ruprecht, 1977, esp. ch. 6.

119. Marx, *Class Struggles in France*, p. 66.

120. The *Garde Mobile* was a special force called into being by the Republic, both as a form of employment and as a protection for the regime. It was composed of young unemployed workmen, from exactly the same social strata as the workmen in the National Workshops. *Lumpen* means 'rag' or 'rags and tatters'. *Lumpenproletariat*, the rag-picking proletariat, was a pejorative term referring to the *classe dangereuse*, a semi-criminal class: riff-raff or beggars. For the use of the term around 1850, see Chapter 9's discussion of Karl's essay *The Eighteenth Brumaire* and the discussion of Bonapartism, pp. 334–44 onwards.

121. Cited in Traugott, *Armies of the Poor*, p. 30.

122. Ibid., pp. 150–51.

123. Marx, *Class Struggles in France*, p. 69.

124. In Engels' case, see Gareth Stedman Jones, 'Voir sans entendre: Engels, Manchester et l'observation sociale en 1844', *Genèses*, vol. 22 (1996), pp. 4–17.

125. Thomas Carlyle, *Chartism*, London, James Fraser, 1839, ch. 1.

126. Hansard, 3rd Series, vol. 63, 3 May 1842.

127. Tocqueville, *Recollections*, p. 199.

128. Daniel Stern, *Histoire de la Révolution de 1848*, Paris, André Balland, 1985 [1850–52], p. 241. 'Daniel Stern' was the pen-name of the Comtesse d'Agoult. Born of a German-French aristocratic family, she lost caste by running off with the composer Franz Liszt, with whom she lived for some years. Deserted by Liszt, she supported herself by becoming a journalist,

writing under the name 'Daniel Stern'. Her *Histoire* has been generally considered one of the best accounts of the Revolution in Paris in 1848.

129. Conversely, the continued exclusion of or discrimination against the working classes through the three-class suffrage provided an important reason why in Germany workers remained a class apart.

9 LONDON

1. G. A. Sala, *Gaslight and Daylight with Some London Scenes They Shine Upon*, London, Chapman & Hall, 1859, pp. 88–91. On the political character of the German 'emigration', see also Karl's description in 1852: 'this hotchpotch of former members of the Frankfurt Parliament, the Berlin National Assembly, and Chamber of Deputies, of gentlemen from the Baden campaign, giants from the comedy of the Imperial Constitution, writers without a public, loudmouths from the democratic clubs and congresses, twelfth-rate journalists and so forth'. Karl Marx and Friedrich Engels, *The Great Men of the Exile*, *MECW*, vol. 11, p. 259. For a more general account the 1848 German exiles and refugees, see Rosemary Ashton, *Little Germany: Exile and Asylum in Victorian England*, Oxford, Oxford University Press, 1986; and for an account focusing specifically upon revolutionary socialist organizations and groupings, see Christine Lattek, *Revolutionary Refugees: German Socialism in Britain, 1840– 1860*, London, Routledge, 2006.

2. 'Karl Marx to Friedrich Engels', 13 September 1854, *MECW*, vol. 39, p. 481.

3. Jenny Marx, 'A Short Sketch of an Eventful Life', in Institut Marksizma– Leninzma, *Reminiscences of Marx and Engels*, Moscow, Foreign Languages Publishing House, 1957, p. 225.

4. 'Jenny Marx to Joseph Weydemeyer', 20 May 1850, *MECW*, vol. 38, p. 555.

5. Ibid., pp. 555, 556.

6. Ibid., p. 557. Doing a 'moonlight flit' was a well-known way of evading the payment of rent arrears. One of the most celebrated songs of the famous music hall performer Marie Lloyd – 'My Old Man (Said Follow the Van)' – was the story of a 'moonlight flit'.

7. Jenny Marx, 'Short Sketch', p. 226.

8. 'Prussian Spy', in Institut Marksizma–Leninzma, *Reminiscences of Marx and Engels*, p. 35.

9. 'Karl Marx to Friedrich Engels', 6 January 1851, *MECW*, vol. 38, p. 257; 'Friedrich Engels to Karl Marx', 8 January 1851, *MECW*, vol. 38, p. 263.

10. 'Karl Marx to Friedrich Engels', 31 March 1851, *MECW*, vol. 38, pp. 323–4.

11. Ibid., 2 April 1851, p. 325; 'Friedrich Engels to Karl Marx', 15 April 1851, *MECW*, vol. 38, p. 335; ibid., 6 May 1851, p. 346.

12. 'Karl Marx to Friedrich Engels', 31 July 1851, *MECW*, vol. 38, p. 397.

13. 'Friedrich Engels to Karl Marx', 15 October 1851, *MECW*, vol. 38, p. 477.

14. 'Karl Marx to Joseph Weydemeyer', 20 February 1852, *MECW*, vol. 39, p. 40.

15. 'Karl Marx to Friedrich Engels', 27 February 1852, *MECW*, vol. 39, p. 50.

16. Ibid., 2 April 1851, vol. 38, p. 326.

17. Ibid., 14 April 1852, vol. 39, p. 78; 'Friedrich Engels to Joseph Weydemeyer', 16 April 1852, *MECW*, vol. 39, p. 79.

18. Jenny Marx, 'Short Sketch', p. 228.

19. 'Karl Marx to Friedrich Engels', 8 September 1852, *MECW*, vol. 39, p. 181.

20. 'Jenny Marx to Friedrich Engels', 27 April 1853, *MECW*, vol. 39, p. 581; 'Karl Marx to Friedrich Engels', 8 October 1853, *MECW*, vol. 39, p. 385.

21. 'Karl Marx to Moritz Elsner', 11 September 1855, *MECW*, vol. 39, p. 550; Dr Freund was said to have gone bankrupt with debts of £3,000. In 1858, Karl wrote to Engels that 'Dr Freund is said to be so down on his luck that he has allegedly approached people in the street for a shilling': 'Karl Marx to Friedrich Engels', 29 November 1858, *MECW*, vol. 40, p. 357.

22. 'Prussian Spy', in D. McLellan (ed.), *Karl Marx: Interviews and Recollections*, London, Macmillan, 1981, p. 36.

23. Jenny, the eldest child, survived into adulthood, and married Charles Longuet, but she died from tuberculosis at the age of thirty-eight in 1883.

24. 'Jenny Marx to Joseph Weydemeyer', 20 May 1850, *MECW*, vol. 38, p. 556.

25. Jenny Marx, 'Short Sketch', p. 229.

26. 'Karl Marx to Friedrich Engels', 3 March 1855, *MECW*, vol. 39, p. 524.

27. Ibid., 16 March 1855, p. 528.

28. Ibid., 27 March 1855, p. 529.

29. Ibid., 30 March 1855, p. 529.

30. Ibid., 6 April 1855, p. 530.

31. Jenny Marx, 'Short Sketch', p. 229.

32. 'Jenny Marx to Ferdinand Lassalle', 9 April 1858, *MECW*, vol. 40, p. 570.

33. 'Karl Marx to Ferdinand Lassalle', 31 May 1858, *MECW*, vol. 40, p. 315.

34. 'Prussian Spy', p. 35. Werner Blumenberg, *Portrait of Marx: An Illustrated Biography*, trans. Douglas Scott, New York, Herder & Herder, 1972, pp. 112–13.

35. 'Karl Marx to Friedrich Engels', 18 December 1857, *MECW*, vol. 40, p. 224; 'Karl Marx to Ferdinand Lassalle', 21 December 1857, *MECW*, vol. 40, p. 226.

36. 'Karl Marx to Friedrich Engels', 29 April 1858, *MECW*, vol. 40, pp. 309–10.

37. 'Karl Marx to Friedrich Engels', 8 January 1861, *MECW*, vol. 41, p. 243; ibid., 18 January 1861, p. 247.

38. 'Jenny Marx to Wilhelm Liebknecht', c.24 November 1863, *MECW*, vol. 41, p. 587.

39. 'Karl Marx to Friedrich Engels', 4 December 1863, *MECW*, vol. 41, p. 497. According to Yvonne Kapp, Karl's liver disease and his carbuncles could have been connected with a generalized staphylococcal infection which could not have been diagnosed as such until the late 1880s. Both complaints were aggravated by alcohol. Yvonne Kapp, *Eleanor Marx*, 2 vols., London, Lawrence & Wishart, 1972, vol. 1, p. 49.

40. 'Karl Marx to Friedrich Engels', 27 December 1863, *MECW*, vol. 41, p. 503.

41. Ibid., 15 July 1852, vol. 39, p. 131.

42. Ibid., 18 September 1852, p. 186.

43. Ibid., 3 June 1854, p. 457.

44. Ibid., 23 November 1860, vol. 41, p. 216; ibid., 12 December 1860, p. 228.

45. 'Karl Marx to Joseph Weydemeyer', 17 June 1850, *MECW*, vol. 38, p. 238.

46. 'Karl Marx to Friedrich Engels', 23 November 1850, *MECW*, vol. 38, p. 242.

47. Ibid., 31 March 1851, p. 324.

48. Jenny Marx, 'Short Sketch', p. 227.

49. Helene Demuth (1820–90) was the housekeeper and servant of Jenny and Karl. Born of peasant parents in the Saarland, as a teenage girl she was adopted into the von Westphalen household to work as a maid. After Karl and Jenny were married, and had moved to Brussels, Helene was sent by Jenny's mother, Caroline, to help in April 1845. She stayed with the Marx family through to Karl's death in 1883, and for a number of years in the early 1860s had been joined by her sister (see pp. 330 and 332). After Karl's death, she moved to Engels' home until her death from cancer in 1890. She appears to have been regarded by all members of the Marx and Engels household as an indispensable member of the family. In accordance with Jenny's wishes, she was buried in the Marx family grave.

50. See the appendix to this chapter, pp. 373–4.

51. 'Karl Marx to Friedrich Engels', 31 March 1851, *MECW*, vol. 38, p. 324; ibid., 2 April 1851, p. 325. Karl stayed with Engels in Manchester from around 17 to 26 April. When referring to sexuality or the physiological aspects of women, Karl would often employ French.

52. Ibid., 31 July 1851, p. 398.

53. 'Karl Marx to Joseph Weydemeyer', 2 August 1851, *MECW*, vol. 38, pp. 402–3.

54. In a letter to Louise Weydemeyer in 1861, Jenny wrote, 'in the domestic sphere "Lenchen" still remains my staunch, conscientious companion. Ask your dear husband about her, and he will tell you what a treasure she has been to me. For sixteen years now she has weathered storm and tempest with us': 'Jenny Marx to Louise Weydemeyer', 11 March 1861, *MECW*, vol. 41, p. 572.

55. See, for example, the letter he sent to her when she was visiting her ailing mother in Trier. The letter concluded by declaring that love, 'not for

Feuerbachian Man, not for Moleschottian metabolism, not for the proletariat, but love for a sweetheart and notably for yourself, turns a man back into a man again': 'Karl Marx to Jenny Marx', 21 June 1856, *MECW*, vol. 40, p. 55. According to the contested testimony of Louise Freyburger, for Marx 'the fear of a divorce from his wife, who was dreadfully jealous, was ever present'. See the appendix to this chapter, pp. 373–4.

56. Jenny Marx, 'Short Sketch', p. 228.

57. But Karl did not wholly trust Liebknecht, because he had remained in the *Communistischer Arbeiter-Bildungsverein* (Communist Workers' Educational Association), despite the fact that the dominant faction within it was now that of Willich and Schapper.

58. From Wilhelm Liebknecht, *Karl Marx: Biographical Memoirs*, London, Journeyman Press, 1975 [1901].

59. Jenny Marx, 'Short Sketch', p. 229.

60. Engels' authorship of these articles did not become known until the beginning of the twentieth century. Eleanor Marx had attributed them to her father in her collection of his articles, *The Eastern Question*, published in London in 1897. See Chushichi Tsuzuki, *The Life of Eleanor Marx, 1855–1898: A Socialist Tragedy*, Oxford, Clarendon Press, 1967, pp. 269–70.

61. See David McLellan, *Karl Marx: His Life and Thought*, London, Macmillan, 1973, pp. 286–7.

62. Tristram Hunt, *The Frock-Coated Communist: The Revolutionary Life of Friedrich Engels*, London, Allen Lane, 2009, pp. 193–4.

63. See McLellan, *Karl Marx: His Life and Thought*, pp. 264–5, 277–8.

64. Jenny Marx, 'Short Sketch', pp. 229–30.

65. 'Jenny Marx to Louise Weydemeyer', 11 March 1861, *MECW*, vol. 41, p. 570.

66. 'Karl Marx to Friedrich Engels', 2 December 1856 and 20 January 1857, *MECW*, vol. 40, pp. 85, 94.

67. Jenny Marx, 'Short Sketch', p. 230.

68. 'Karl Marx to Friedrich Engels', 15 July 1858, *MECW*, vol. 40, pp. 328–31.

69. Ibid., p. 360.

70. 'Charles Dana to Karl Marx', 6 April 1857, *MEGA*, III, viii, p. 384. Engels supplied the initial batch of military articles, leaving Karl with the embarrassing task of putting Dana off until Engels recovered: see 'Karl Marx to Friedrich Engels', 11 July 1857, *MECW*, vol. 40, p. 145. He pretended that the bulk of the contributions had 'gone astray'. See ibid., 26 August 1857, pp. 159–60.

71. 'Charles Dana to Karl Marx', 6 April 1857, *MEGA*, III, viii, p. 384. 'Charles Dana to Jenny Marx', 28 March 1862, *MEGA*, III, xii, p. 47. Dana explained, 'this they do, simply from the impossibility of making room for them in the paper, every column being required for domestic

news relating to the war'. See also 'Friedrich Engels to Karl Marx', 5 May 1862, *MECW*, vol. 41, p. 359.

72. 'Karl Marx to Friedrich Engels', 9 December 1861, *MECW*, vol. 41, p. 333.

73. Ibid., 19 December 1861, p. 335.

74. Ibid., 26 February 1862, pp. 340–41; ibid., 19 May 1862, p. 365.

75. Ibid., 18 June 1862, p. 380.

76. 'Friedrich Engels to Karl Marx', 7 January 1863, *MECW*, vol. 41, p. 441; 'Karl Marx to Friedrich Engels', 8 January 1863, *MECW*, vol. 41, pp. 442–3.

77. 'Friedrich Engels to Karl Marx', 13 January 1863, *MECW*, vol. 41, pp. 443–4.

78. 'Karl Marx to Friedrich Engels', 24 January 1863, *MECW*, vol. 41, pp. 445–6.

79. 'Friedrich Engels to Karl Marx', 26 January 1863, *MECW*, vol. 41, p. 447.

80. 'Karl Marx to Friedrich Engels', 2 December 1863, *MECW*, vol. 41, p. 495.

81. On Wolff's character and his life in Manchester, see Ashton, *Little Germany*, pp. 117–21.

82. 'Karl Marx to Friedrich Engels', 4 July 1864, *MECW*, vol. 41, p. 546.

83. Ibid., 31 July 1865, vol. 42, p. 172.

84. Henry Mayhew, *London Labour and the London Poor*, London, Griffin, Bohn, and Company, 1861, vol. 2, p. 323; and see Gareth Stedman Jones, *Outcast London: A Study in the Relationship between Classes in Victorian Society*, Oxford, Clarendon Press, 1971 (4th edn, London, Verso, 2013), part 1.

85. 'Karl Marx to Friedrich Engels', 30 July 1862, *MECW*, vol. 41, p. 389. Karl called him a 'Jewish Nigger' because of the way his hair grew, and speculated that he was descended from the negroes who accompanied Moses' flight from Egypt. 'The fellow's importunity is also niggerlike': ibid., p. 390.

86. Ibid., 31 July 1865, vol. 42, pp. 172–3.

87. Ibid., 22 July 1854, vol. 39, p. 469.

88. Blumenberg, *Portrait of Marx*, p. 121.

89. 'Karl Marx to Lion Philips', 25 June 1864, *MECW*, vol. 41, p. 543.

90. McLellan, *Karl Marx: His Life and Thought*, pp. 264–6.

91. 'Karl Marx to Ferdinand Freiligrath', 29 February 1860, *MECW*, vol. 41, p. 82.

92. 'Friedrich Engels to Karl Marx', 3 December 1851, *MECW*, vol. 38, p. 505.

93. Following by-election defeats in March 1850, conservatives became anxious about the possibility of losing mass support. They therefore introduced a new electoral law, in May 1850, which removed one third of the poorest voters from the rolls, with much higher proportions in large towns and industrial centres. In Paris, the electorate was reduced from 225,192 to 80,894: cited in Roger Price, *The French Second Empire: An Anatomy of Political Power*, Cambridge, Cambridge University Press, 2001, p. 20.

94. In his *Idées Napoléoniennes* of 1839, he wrote of a 'social idea' in place of war. In *L'Extinction du pauperisme* of 1844, he advocated social reform.

95. Karl Marx, *The Class Struggles in France, 1848 to 1850*, *MECW*, vol. 10, p. 65.

96. Karl Marx, *The Eighteenth Brumaire of Louis Bonaparte*, 1852, *MECW*, vol. 11, p. 108. In the *People's Paper* review of literature on the coup d'état, Karl had Eccarius write, 'French Democracy is not to be confounded with the English. In France it represents the small proprietors and tenants, but less their real wants than their imaginary wishes. In England, Democracy applies directly to the movement of the working class': see 'A Review of the Literature on the *Coup d'État*', *MECW*, vol. 11, p. 598.

97. Marx, *Eighteenth Brumaire*, pp. 127–8.

98. More generally, Karl's approach to modern French history had been shaped by the French historians of the 1815–30 period, especially the prolific historian and Orléanist Chief Minister, François Guizot. In order to explain the development of revolution in France and its displacement of semi-feudal rule by a new commercial society based on talent and moneyed wealth, these historians had employed an English model. They had drawn a historical parallel between 1640, Cromwell and 1688 on the one hand, and 1789, Napoléon and 1830 on the other. In both cases these sequences of revolution could be presented as conflicts between land and mobile capital, or between feudalism and commercial society. Such an approach had worked well for Restoration historians. But it offered little guidance in distinguishing between one political faction and another in 1848.

99. Marx, *Eighteenth Brumaire*, pp. 112–13.

100. Ibid., p. 130.

101. Ibid., pp. 183, 182.

102. Ibid., p. 185.

103. Ibid., pp. 187–8.

104. In the presidential election of 10 December 1848, Bonaparte gained 58 per cent of the vote, in Lyons 62 per cent. His support was highest in the popular *quartiers*, where there was much evidence of Bonapartist support even during the June days. See Price, *French Second Empire*, p. 18.

105. Marx, *Eighteenth Brumaire*, p. 188. Peasant political attitudes differed strongly according to region. In the Massif Central, Alps, Rhône-Saône, Alsace and pockets across the *Midi*, support was predominantly for the 'Démoc-Socs'.

106. Ibid., p. 149.

107. Ibid.

108. Ibid.

109. Mayhew, *London Labour and the London Poor*, vol. 3, p. 301.

110. Benjamin Constant, *The Spirit of Conquest and Usurpation and Their Relation to European Civilization* (1814), in B. Fontana (trans. and ed.), *Constant: Political Writings*, Cambridge, Cambridge University Press, 1988, pp. 54, 101, 105.

111. Marx, *Eighteenth Brumaire*, p. 193.

112. Ibid.

113. Ibid., p. 185. Karl was particularly fond of this Shakespearean metaphor. The idea of the 'old mole' was taken from *Hamlet*, Act 1, Scene 5.

114. In England, an attempt to publicize the text was made by Karl and Engels through a review article by Karl's follower and former member of the Communist League, the London tailor Johann Georg Eccarius. See 'A Review of the Literature on the *Coup d'État*', which appeared in the Chartist *People's Paper*, between September and December 1852 (*MECW*, vol. 11, pp. 592–620). The review closely follows the arguments of *Eighteenth Brumaire*, and was clearly closely subedited by Karl himself.

115. Heinrich von Ofterdingen was a quasi-fictional poet and minstrel mentioned in the thirteenth-century epic *Der Sängerkrieg* (*The Minstrel Contest*). The legend was taken up in an unfinished romantic novel by Novalis in 1799–1800, and published by Ludwig Tieck in 1801. It is a symbolic tale, in which poetry and life become one. In the first chapter, the hero recounts a dream, the vision of a blue flower, which Heinrich ultimately plucks. In the nineteenth century the blue flower became the symbol of romantic longing and re-uniting of the dream world and the real world. The name was used in Richard Wagner's *Tannhäuser*. On the brief life of Novalis, see the novel by Penelope Fitzgerald *The Blue Flower*, 1997.

116. The treatment of Kinkel may have been comparatively mild because the previous attack that they had made in *Neue Rheinische Zeitung – Politisch-Ökonomische Revue*, no. 4, in April 1850, had gone down badly even among their supporters: see 'Gottfried Kinkel', *MECW*, vol. 10, pp. 345–7.

117. Karl Marx and Friedrich Engels, *The Great Men of the Exile*, *MECW*, vol. 11, p. 261.

118. Ibid., pp. 265, 267, 268.

119. McLellan, *Karl Marx: His Life and Thought*, p. 287.

120. Jenny Marx, 'Short Sketch', p. 230.

121. 'Charles Dana to Karl Marx', 8 March 1860, *MEGA*, III, ix, p. 362.

122. Pan-Slavism, like German and Italian nationalism, originated as a cultural and political response to the challenge to dynastic Europe resulting from the French Revolution and the wars of Napoléon. The first Pan-Slav Congress was held in Prague in June 1848, after the Czechs had refused to send representatives to the Frankfurt Assembly, believing that the interests of the Slavs were distinct. Partly out of disappointment about the results of revolutions in Western Europe, the idea for some years attracted the

support of Herzen and Bakunin. But liberal and socialist supporters always had to be careful to distinguish their position from conservative czarist versions of the idea. Some of the most apoplectic denunciations of the movement were written by Engels in the *Neue Rheinische Zeitung*.

123. 'Friedrich Engels to Karl Marx', 10 March 1853, *MECW*, vol. 39, pp. 284–5.

124. Karl Marx, 'Lord Palmerston – Fourth Article', *People's Paper*, 12 November 1853, *MECW*, vol. 12, pp. 372–3.

125. Karl Marx, 'Palmerston's Resignation', 16 December 1853, *MECW*, vol. 12, p. 545.

126. Karl Marx, *Herr Vogt*, 1860, *MECW*, vol. 17, p. 117.

127. Karl Marx, 'In Retrospect', 29 December 1854, *MECW*, vol. 13, p. 556.

128. Marx, *Herr Vogt*, p. 117; Karl Marx, *Revelations of the Diplomatic History of the 18th Century*, *MECW*, vol. 15, p. 87.

129. 'Friedrich Engels to Karl Marx', 22 January 1852, *MECW*, vol. 39, pp. 11–12.

130. Karl Marx, 'The American Difficulty – Affairs of France', *MECW*, vol. 14, p. 604.

131. Karl Marx, 'The French Crédit Mobilier', 24 June 1856, *MECW*, vol. 15, pp. 14–15.

132. Karl Marx, 'The Attempt on the Life of Bonaparte', 5 February 1858, *MECW*, vol. 15, p. 458; Karl Marx, 'Political Parties in England – Situation in Europe', 11 June 1858, *MECW*, vol. 15, p. 569.

133. Karl Marx, 'The Money Panic in Europe', 1 February 1859, *MECW*, vol. 16, p. 164. In relation to Bonaparte and Italy, Dana wrote to Karl in 1860, 'I had as little confidence as you in the sincerity of the French emperor, and believed as little as you that Italian liberty was to be expected from him; but I did not think that Germany had any such ground for alarm as you, in common with other patriotic Germans, thought she had': 'Charles Dana to Karl Marx', 8 March 1860, *MEGA*, III, x, p. 362.

134. Marx, *Herr Vogt*, p. 150.

135. Karl Marx, 'Preparations for Napoleon's Coming War on the Rhine', 2 May 1860, *MECW*, vol. 17, p. 377.

136. 'Charles Dana to Karl Marx', 26 June 1856, *MEGA*, III, viii, p. 281; the flavour of these pieces might be inferred from an article by Engels on 'Germany and Pan-Slavism' published in the *Neue-Oder Zeitung*, 21 April 1855: 'Pan-Slavism has now developed from a creed into a political programme, with 800,000 bayonets at its service. It leaves Europe with only one alternative: subjugation by the Slavs, or the permanent destruction of the centre of their offensive force – Russia', *MECW*, vol. 14, p. 157.

137. For the speech of John Bright in relation to 'taxes on knowledge', i.e. the Stamp and Advertisement Duty on newspapers, see Karl Marx, 'The Turk-

ish War Question – The *New-York Tribune* in the House of Commons – The Government of India', 5 July 1853, *MECW*, vol. 12, pp. 175–6.

138. See Miles Taylor, 'The English Face of Karl Marx, 1852–1862', *Journal of Victorian Culture*, 1/2 (1996), issue 2. I have found this essay, which contains a detailed examination of Karl's relationship with English politics and the press, in particular its coverage in the *Tribune*, especially illuminating.

139. For example, initially, on the basis of what he had heard from Harney, he assumed that there was widespread republican hostility to the monarchy among the middle classes. See Karl Marx, 'The Chartists', *People's Paper*, 10 August 1852, *MECW*, vol. 11, p. 334.

140. Ibid., 25 August 1852, p. 333.

141. Karl Marx, 'Letter to the Labour Parliament', 9 March 1854, *MECW*, vol. 13, p. 57.

142. Karl Marx, 'Speech at the Anniversary of *The People's Paper*', *People's Paper*, 14 April 1856, *MECW*, vol. 14, p. 655.

143. Karl Marx, 'Parliamentary Debates – The Clergy against Socialism – Starvation', *New York Daily Tribune*, 25 February 1853, *MECW*, vol. 11, p. 527.

144. Karl Marx, 'Forced Emigration', 4 March 1853, *MECW*, vol. 11, p. 529.

145. Karl Marx, 'Pauperism and Free Trade – The Approaching Commercial Crisis', 15 October 1852, *MECW*, vol. 11, pp. 359, 360.

146. Ibid., p. 361.

147. Karl Marx, 'Revolution in China and in Europe', 20–21 May 1853, *MECW*, vol. 12, pp. 99–100.

148. Karl Marx, 'The British Constitution', 2 March 1855, *MECW*, vol. 14, pp. 54–6.

149. Karl Marx, 'The Monetary Crisis in Europe', 3 October 1856, *MECW*, vol. 15, pp. 113–14.

150. Henry Charles Carey, *The Slave Trade, Domestic and Foreign: Why It Exists, and How It May be Extinguished*, London, Sampson Low, Son & Co., 1853, p. 214.

151. 'Charles Dana to Karl Marx', 15 July 1850, *MEGA*, III, iii, p. 591.

152. Ibid., 20 April 1852, v, p. 327.

153. 'Karl Marx to Friedrich Engels', 2 August 1852, *MECW*, vol. 39, p. 145; Karl's unfamiliarity with the *Tribune* is less surprising than it might seem. The paper was not available in London except to private subscribers, and Karl was forced to ask Weydemeyer in New York to procure a run of back numbers.

154. 'Karl Marx to Friedrich Engels', 5 August 1852, *MECW*, vol. 39, p. 146.

155. Karl Marx, 'Draft of an Article on Friedrich List's Book, *Das Nationale System der politischen Ökonomie*', *MECW*, vol. 4, pp. 265–95.

156. 'Friedrich Engels to Karl Marx', 6 August 1852, *MECW*, vol. 39, p. 147.

157. Marx, 'The Chartists', p. 333.
158. 'Karl Marx to Friedrich Engels', 14 June 1853, *MECW*, vol. 39, pp. 345–6. This was to underestimate or ignore the extent to which protectionism was not simply a position associated with the 'industrial bourgeoisie'. It was also of interest to the republicanism of American labour at the time. See Adam Tuchinsky, *Horace Greeley's New-York Tribune: Civil War-Era Socialism and the Crisis of Free Labor*, Ithaca, Cornell University Press, 2009. See also Alex Gourevitch, *From Slavery to the Cooperative Commonwealth: Labor and Republican Liberty in the Nineteenth Century*, Cambridge, Cambridge University Press, 2015. The position adopted towards protectionism in the *Tribune* formed an important component of the free-soil, free-labour position espoused by radical American republicans. In the *Grundrisse*, Karl dwelt upon the ahistorical character of Carey's contrast between the harmonious development of bourgeois relations from itself in America and the distorting effect of the emergence of bourgeois relations of production from the antagonistic relations of feudalism in England and its projection onto the rest of the world through its domination of the world market. But he also praised him as 'the only original economist among the North Americans' and acknowledged 'the scientific value of his researches': Karl Marx, 'Bastiat and Carey', in *Economic Manuscripts of 1857–58* (Grundrisse), *MECW*, vol. 28, pp. 5–11. The affinity between the Marxian picture of the world market and that of the protectionists was evident in the one sympathetic view of *Capital*, singled out by Karl, when the book first appeared. It was written by the Berlin academic Eugen Dühring, who was a disciple of Carey (see pp. **559–60**). In the 1870s, Dühring's protectionist social analysis was popular among German Social Democrats at a time when German industry was facing mounting competition from the United States. It may be surmised that part of the purpose of Engels' *Anti-Dühring* was to smother the appeal of Dühring's approach beneath a grandiose elaboration of 'scientific socialism'.
159. Karl Marx, 'The Vienna Note – The United States and Europe – Letters from Shumla – Peel's Bank Act', 9 September 1853, *MECW*, vol. 12, pp. 296–7.
160. Karl Marx, 'The Crisis in England', 2 March 1855, *MECW*, vol. 14, pp. 60–61.
161. Karl Marx, 'The British Revulsion', 13 November 1857, *MECW*, vol. 15, p. 387.
162. Karl Marx, 'Commercial Crises and Currency in Britain', 10 August 1858, *MECW*, vol. 16, p. 8.
163. 'Charles Dana to Karl Marx', 13 October 1857, *MEGA*, III, viii, p. 496.
164. 'Karl Marx to Friedrich Engels', 14 June 1853, *MECW*, vol. 39, p. 346.
165. For a more detailed study of Marx's writings on empire and the extra-European world, see Gareth Stedman Jones, 'Radicalism and the

Extra-European World: The Case of Karl Marx', in Duncan Bell (ed.), *Victorian Visions of Global Order: Empire and International Relations in Nineteenth-Century Political Thought*, Cambridge, Cambridge University Press, 2007, pp. 186–214; see also Kevin. B. Anderson, *Marx at the Margins: On Nationalism, Ethnicity, and Non-Western Societies*, Chicago, University of Chicago Press, 2010.

166. Karl Marx, 'The East India Company – Its History and Results', 24 June 1853, *MECW*, vol. 12, pp. 149, 151, 154.

167. Marx, 'The Turkish War Question – The *New-York Tribune* in the House of Commons – The Government of India', p. 178.

168. Ibid., pp. 181, 184.

169. Karl Marx, 'The British Rule in India', 10 June 1853, *MECW*, vol. 12, p. 128; Karl Marx, 'The Future Results of British Rule in India', 22 July 1853, *MECW*, vol. 12, p. 217.

170. Karl Marx, 'Chinese Affairs', 7 July 1862, *MECW*, vol. 19, p. 216.

171. Marx, 'British Rule in India', pp. 125–6, 132.

172. Ibid., p. 128.

173. 'In broad outline, the Asiatic, ancient, feudal and modern bourgeois modes of production may be designated as epochs marking progress in the economic development of society': Karl Marx, 'Preface' to *A Contribution to the Critique of Political Economy*, *MECW*, vol. 29, p. 263. However, the search for common features shared by societies and states allegedly defined by this mode of production turned out to be in vain; and it is notable that after 1859 Marx never again explicitly referred to the concept.

174. Marx, 'British Rule in India', p. 132.

175. Gareth Stedman Jones (ed.), *Karl Marx and Friedrich Engels: The Communist Manifesto*, London, Penguin Books, 2002, p. 224.

176. Marx, 'British Rule in India', pp. 131–2.

177. Karl Marx, 'The Indian Revolt', 16 September 1857, *MECW*, vol. 15, p. 353.

178. Karl Marx, 'The Indian Question', 14 August 1857, *MECW*, vol. 15, p. 313.

179. Marx, 'Chinese Affairs', p. 216.

180. Marx, 'Chartists', pp. 333, 335.

181. Ibid.

182. Karl Marx, 'War – Strikes – Dearth', 1 November 1853, *MECW*, vol. 12, p. 437.

183. Karl Marx, 'Panic on the London Stock Exchange – Strikes', 27 September 1853, *MECW*, vol. 12, p. 334.

184. Marx, 'British Constitution', pp. 55–6.

185. Karl Marx, 'Anti-Church Movement – Demonstration in Hyde Park', 25 June 1855, *MECW*, vol. 14, p. 303.

186. Marx, 'Future Results of British Rule in India', p. 222.

187. Marx, 'Speech at the Anniversary of *The People's Paper*', pp. 655–6.

188. 'Karl Marx to Ferdinand Lassalle', 15 September 1860, *MECW*, vol. 41, p. 194.

189. 'Karl Marx to Friedrich Engels', 7 January 1858, *MECW*, vol. 40, p. 242.
190. 'Jenny Marx to Louise Weydemeyer', 16 March 1861, *MECW*, vol. 41, p. 576.
191. Ibid., p. 575.
192. 'Friedrich Engels to Karl Marx', 25 January 1858, *MECW*, vol. 40, p. 253. For an account of the subsequent lives of Karl's circle, see Ashton, *Little Germany*, pp. 112–28.
193. In October 1858, Wilhelm, the Crown Prince of Prussia, became regent for his ailing brother, Friedrich Wilhelm IV. In 1848, he had been notorious for advocating royal withdrawal from Berlin, followed by bombardment and military reconquest of the city. By the end of the 1850s, the influence of his consort, Augusta, and a spell of exile in England had led him to modify his position. He proclaimed a 'new era' in liberalism and appointed a ministry containing liberals as well as hard-line conservatives. For the changed political climate among the German exiles in London, see Lattek, *Revolutionary Refugees*, chs. 7 and 8.
194. 'Karl Marx to Friedrich Engels', 10 March 1859, *MECW*, vol. 40, p. 400.
195. Ibid., 18 May 1859, *MECW*, vol. 40, pp. 435–6.
196. 'Karl Marx to Ferdinand Lassalle', 22 November 1859, *MECW*, vol. 40, p. 537.
197. *Risorgimento* (the Resurgence) was the name given to the process of Italian unification, the result of a political and social movement aiming to consolidate the various different states of the Italian peninsula into a single state (or kingdom) of Italy. The process began in 1815 after the fall of Napoléon and the Congress of Vienna, and ended in 1871, when Rome became the capital of the Italian Kingdom.
198. 'Karl Marx to Ferdinand Lassalle', 22 November 1859, *MECW*, vol. 40, p. 538.
199. For an excellent account of this complicated episode, see Lattek, *Revolutionary Refugees*, ch. 8.
200. Wilhelm Liebknecht, eventually, together with August Bebel, leader of the German Social Democratic Party, had been brought up in Giessen, and studied philosophy, theology and philology at the universities of Giessen, Berlin and Marburg. After getting into trouble as a student radical, Liebknecht decided to emigrate to the United States, but was diverted by the invitation to teach in a progressive school in Switzerland, where he became a journalist and reported on the Swiss civil war of 1847 for the *Mannheimer Abendzeitung*. In 1848, he went to Paris and joined Herwegh's German Legion and was arrested in Baden. Released in a crowd action, he participated in the Campaign for the Federal Constitution in Baden as an adjutant of Gustav Struve. He escaped to Switzerland, where he met Engels, and then after being expelled from Switzerland fled to London, where he and his family lived from 1850 until 1862, when an amnesty for participants in the 1848 revolution enabled him to return to

Germany. He had become a member of the Communist League and he and his wife became close to the Marx family, taking in their children when Jenny Marx went down with smallpox in 1860. Despite this, Karl did not wholly trust him, because of his independent-mindedness. In the face of Karl's disapproval he had rejoined the CABV after the split of 1850, maintaining his 'right to serve the party in a way that seemed most appropriate to me'. Liebknecht had considered it 'crazy tactics for a working men's party to seclude itself away up above the workers in a theoretic air castle; without working men, no working men's party, and the labourers we must take as we find them'. See Liebknecht, *Karl Marx: Biographical Memoirs*, p. 72.

201. 'Karl Marx to Ferdinand Lassalle', 6 November 1859, *MECW*, vol. 40, p. 518.
202. 'Karl Marx to Friedrich Engels', 12 February 1859, *MECW*, vol. 40, p. 393.
203. Karl Marx, 'The French Disarmament', *Das Volk*, 30 July 1859, *MECW*, vol. 16, p. 443.
204. Karl Marx, 'Invasion!', *Das Volk*, 30 July 1859, *MECW*, vol. 16, p. 441.
205. Charles Darwin, *The Descent of Man*, 2 vols., London, J. Murray, 1871, vol. 1, pp. 1, 4, 230.
206. Marx, *Herr Vogt*, p. 134.
207. 'Karl Marx to Ferdinand Lassalle', 14 November 1859, *MECW*, vol. 40, p. 525.
208. Cited in Lattek, *Revolutionary Refugees*, p. 211.
209. Marx, *Herr Vogt*, p. 26.
210. Marx, *Herr Vogt*, pp. 117, 152, 178.
211. 'Friedrich Engels to Karl Marx', 19 December 1860, *MECW*, vol. 41, p. 231.
212. Liebknecht, *Karl Marx: Biographical Memoirs*, p. 75.
213. See Lattek, *Revolutionary Refugees*, p. 212; Marx, *Herr Vogt*, p. 117. After the fall of the Second Empire, the French republican government in 1871 published documents showing that, in August 1859, Vogt had received 40,000 francs from the emperor's private fund. See Boris Nicolaievsky and Otto Maenchen-Helfen, *Karl Marx: Man and Fighter*, trans. G. David and E. Mosbacher, London, Allen Lane, 1973 [1933], p. 266.
214. 'Karl Marx to Ferdinand Freiligrath', 23 February 1860, *MECW*, vol. 41, p. 54.
215. One of the Saint-Simonians' main slogans, adopted from Saint-Simon's *New Christianity* (1825), was 'the speediest amelioration of the moral, physical and intellectual lot of the poorest and most numerous class'.
216. 'Ferdinand Freiligrath to Karl Marx', 28 February 1860, *MEGA*, III, x, p. 320. Eduard von Müller-Tellering, a lawyer and a democrat, worked as Vienna correspondent for the *Neue Rheinische Zeitung*. The general tenor of his articles was anti-Slav and anti-Semitic. After the revolution, he emigrated, first to England and then to the USA. He criticized Marx and his Party in the press. Charles Fleury (real name Carl Krause) was a London merchant, Prussian spy and police agent.

217. 'Karl Marx to Friedrich Engels', 11 December 1858, *MECW*, vol. 40, p. 359.

218. On the politics of the Schiller Festival, see Lattek, *Revolutionary Refugees*, pp. 215-17.

219. 'Karl Marx to Ferdinand Freiligrath', 29 February 1860, *MECW*, vol. 41, p. 87.

220. Kapp, *Eleanor Marx*, vol. 1, p. 291.

221. Ibid., pp. 289-97.

222. Ibid.

223. Terrell Carver, *Friedrich Engels: His Life and Thought*, Basingstoke, Macmillan, 1991, pp. 164-5.

224. Paul Thomas, *Karl Marx*, London, Reaktion Books, 2012, pp. 120-22.

225. Heinrich Gemkow and Rolf Hecker, 'Unbekannte Documente über Marx' Sohn Friedrich Demuth', *Beiträge zur Geschichte der Arbeiterbewegung*, 4/1994, pp. 43-59. For current assessments of the evidence, see Francis Wheen, *Karl Marx*, London, Fourth Estate, 1999, pp. 170-77; Jonathan Sperber, *Karl Marx: A Nineteenth-Century Life*, New York, Liveright Publishing Corporation, 2013, pp. 262-3.

10 THE *CRITIQUE OF POLITICAL ECONOMY*

1. The term '*Grundrisse*' means 'outline' or 'sketch'.

2. 'Karl Marx to Friedrich Engels', 8 December 1857, *MECW*, vol. 40, p. 217.

3. 'Karl Marx to Ferdinand Lassalle', 22 February 1858, *MECW*, vol. 40, pp. 270-71; ibid., p. 27.

4. Karl Marx, *Foundations of the Critique of Political Economy, Grundrisse*, *MECW*, Passim.

5. Ibid., 12 November 1858, p. 354.

6. 'Jenny Marx to Friedrich Engels', 9 April 1858, *MECW*, vol. 40, p. 569.

7. 'Karl Marx to Friedrich Engels', 31 May 1858, *MECW*, vol. 40, p. 318.

8. See Locke's comparison between the position of the day labourer in England and that of American tribes, cited in Gareth Stedman Jones, *An End to Poverty?: A Historical Debate*, London, Profile Books, 2004, pp. 11-12; and see Istvan Hont, 'An Introduction', in *Jealousy of Trade: International Competition and the Nation-State in Historical Perspective*, Cambridge, Mass., Harvard University Press, 2005. On 'oriental despotism', see François Bernier, *Voyages contenant la description des états du Grand Mogol*, Paris, 1830. What was later perceived as the economic stagnation of 'oriental' regimes was particularly attributed to the lack of intermediate institutions between ruler and subject and a corresponding lack of adequate legal recognition of private property.

9. I have preferred to follow Karl's own terminology – 'bourgeois economy' or 'bourgeois society' – since these terms retain the ambiguity of the German –

bürgerliche Gesellschaft, which can either mean 'bourgeois' or 'civil' society, and was the term employed by Hegel in *The Philosophy of Right* to describe what is rendered in English as 'civil society'. Hegel's separation between civil society and the state had been the initial focus of Karl's critique in 1843. 'Capitalism' – in German, *Kapitalismus* – was a neologism which came into existence around 1900 and was associated with Georg Simmel.

10. David Ricardo, *The Principles of Political Economy and Taxation*, London, John Murray, 1817. Ricardo had argued that relative prices were determined by the amount of labour time embodied in them.

11. Karl Marx, *The Poverty of Philosophy*, *MECW*, vol. 6, pp. 138 and 139–44.

12. Karl's notes on Ricardo in 1850–51 are to be found in *MEGA*, IV, vii, pp. 316–28 (mainly concerned with money); *MEGA*, IV, viii, pp. 17, 40, 190–99, 326–32, 350–73, 381–96, 402–5, 409–26 (this involved a substantial re-reading of the *Principles* with excerpts mainly on value, rent and wages, machinery); *MEGA*, IV, ix, pp. 159–63 (on low price of corn and agricultural protection). Keith Tribe observes that the way in which Marx moves back and forth in his note-taking strongly suggests that 'he is seeking material for a line of thought he has already formed': Keith Tribe, 'Karl Marx's "Critique of Political Economy": A Critique', in *The Economy of the Word: Language, History and Economics*, Oxford, Oxford University Press, 2015, p. 208.

13. Marx, *Poverty of Philosophy*, p. 132.

14. 'Karl Marx to Friedrich Engels', 2 April 1858, *MECW*, vol. 40, p. 298.

15. Karl Marx, *Economic Manuscripts of 1857–58 (Grundrisse)*, *MECW*, vol. 28, p. 523.

16. Andrew Ure, *The Philosophy of Manufactures: or, An Exposition of the Scientific, Moral and Commercial Economy of the Factory System of Great Britain*, London, Charles Knight, 1835; Charles Babbage, *On the Economy of Machinery and Manufactures*, London, Charles Knight, 1832.

17. Marx, *Economic Manuscripts of 1857–58*, p. 131.

18. Ibid., p. 133.

19. Ibid., p. 134 (capitals in original text).

20. Ibid., vol. 28, p. 230.

21. Ibid., p. 334.

22. Adam Smith, *An Inquiry into the Nature and Causes of the Wealth of Nations*, ed. Edwin Cannan, Chicago, University of Chicago Press, 1976 [1776], book 1, ch. 11, p. 17.

23. Marx, 'Introduction' to *Economic Manuscripts of 1857–58*, pp. 17–18.

24. Ibid., p. 18.

25. Ibid.

26. Marx, *Economic Manuscripts of 1857–58*, pp. 413, 420.

27. Ibid., pp. 409–10.
28. Ibid., vol. 29, p. 126.
29. Ibid., p. 233.
30. Ibid., vol. 28, pp. 410, 417.
31. Ibid., p. 465.
32. 'Among the Germanic peoples where the individual family chiefs settled in forests, separated by long distances, the commune exists even *outwardly* merely by virtue of the periodic gatherings of its members, although their unity *in-itself* is posited in descent, language, common past and history, etc.': ibid., p. 407. At this point, Karl reiterated the interpretation of early German history found in Justus Möser. But in the late 1860s, after reading the work of Maurer, he changed his position quite dramatically. See Chapter 12.
33. In Karl's words, although the determination of (commodity) form was simple, they were '*not posited*' in this determination. Ibid., p. 160.
34. The choice of 'the commodity' as the starting point of his analysis both in 1859 and in 1867 was a practical way of resolving his indecision about how to begin his account in 1857–8. If ideas were originally the articulations of forms of activity found in the world of everyday practice, should the exposition be ordered according to a sequence of concepts, arranged according to their importance in bourgeois society or in terms of their historical order of appearance? In the 'Introduction', although thinking derived from concrete empirical problems, such as those concerning states and populations in the seventeenth century, starting from abstract general relations, like division of labour, money, value, etc., as was the custom in the following century, was 'obviously the correct scientific method'. Marx, 'Introduction' to ibid., pp. 37–8.
35. Marx, *Economic Manuscripts of 1857–58*, p. 158.
36. Ibid., pp. 99–100.
37. Ibid., pp. 156–8.
38. Ibid., pp. 430–34.
39. Ibid., pp. 185, 206–7, 431, 433.
40. Ibid., pp. 433–4.
41. Ibid., pp. 186–7.
42. Marx, 'Introduction' to ibid., p. 42. This incidentally emphasizes Karl's proximity to Hegel rather than Darwin. Darwinists would surely have turned the statement around: the anatomy of the ape is the key to the anatomy of man.
43. See, for example, his conceptual organization of capital according to 'generality', 'particularity' and 'singularity': Marx, *Economic Manuscripts of 1857–58*, pp. 205–6.
44. Ibid., p. 89.

45. Karl Marx, 'Critique of the Hegelian Dialectic and Philosophy as a Whole', *MECW*, vol. 3, pp. 332–3.

46. 'Karl Marx to Friedrich Engels', 16 January 1858, *MECW*, vol. 40, p. 249.

47. Marx, *Economic Manuscripts of 1857–58*, p. 197.

48. Ibid., pp. 31, 36.

49. Ibid., p. 464.

50. Ibid., p. 17.

51. Alfred Darimon, *De la réforme des banques*, Paris, Guillaumin, 1856; Marx, *Economic Manuscripts of 1857–58*, pp. 51–78.

52. Ibid., p. 349.

53. Karl Marx, *Capital*, vol. I: *A Critique of Political Economy*, 1867, *MECW*, vol. 35, p. 186.

54. Marx, *Economic Manuscripts of 1857–58*, p. 185.

55. Ibid., p. 186.

56. Ibid., p. 438; ibid., vol. 29, p. 233.

57. Ibid., vol. 28, p. 245.

58. Ibid., p. 433.

59. Ibid., p. 94.

60. Ibid., pp. 381–2.

61. Ibid., pp. 131–3; ibid., vol. 29, p. 8.

62. Ibid., vol. 28, p. 459.

63. Ibid., p. 337.

64. Ibid., p. 342.

65. Ibid., vol. 29, pp. 82–3, 94.

66. Ibid., p. 133.

67. Ibid., vol. 28, pp. 390–91.

68. Ibid., vol. 29, pp. 91, 97.

69. Ibid., p. 91.

70. Ibid., vol. 28, p. 466.

71. Although he conceded that 'really free work, e.g. the composition of music, is also the most damnable difficult, demanding the most intensive effort': ibid., p. 530.

72. Marx, 'Introduction' to ibid., pp. 46–8. But he was unable to come up with an analogous explanation of the relationship between Roman civil law and modern production: ibid., p. 46.

73. Marx, *Economic Manuscripts of 1857–58*, vol. 28, p. 411.

74. Ibid., p. 337.

75. The importance of Carey was somewhat greater than was implied in the discussion in the *Grundrisse*. See Chapter 9.

76. John Stuart Mill's *Principles of Political Economy*, first edition 1848, was the most influential economic treatise of the age. It was notable in particular for its argument that political argument must concern distribution

rather than production, and for its critical but sympathetic treatment of socialism. Thomas Tooke (1774–1858) was famous for his six-volume *History of Prices*, which appeared between 1838 and 1857. It traced the financial and commercial history of Britain between 1793 and 1856. Originally a supporter of bullionism and the currency theory – the thinking that underlay Peel's Bank Charter Act of 1844 – he came to support the ready convertibility of paper money on demand.

77. The aim of the Land Tenure Reform Association was to abolish primogeniture and entailment. The Land and Labour League, whose aim to achieve the nationalization of the land, was closely connected with the International.

78. See Terry Peach, *Interpreting Ricardo*, Cambridge, Cambridge University Press, 1993, pp. 173–4.

79. David Ricardo, *Des principes de l'économie politique et de l'impôt*, Paris, J. P. Aillaud, 1835, pp. 17–19, cited in Tribe, *Economy of the Word*, ch. 6, pp. 25, 28. This edition included a translation of McCulloch's *Memoir of the Life and Writings of David Ricardo, Esq. M.P.*, which originally appeared in London in 1825.

80. Marx, *Economic Manuscripts of 1857–58*, *MECW*, vol. 28, p. 483.

81. Ibid., p. 484.

82. For a clarifying discussion of the issue, see G. A. Cohen, 'The Labour Theory of Value and the Concept of Exploitation', in G. A. Cohen, *History, Labour and Freedom: Themes from Marx*, Oxford, Oxford University Press, 1988, pp. 209–39. For a contemporary nineteenth-century discussion of the issue see Anton Menger, *The Right to the Whole Produce of Labour: The Origin and Development of the Theory of Labour's Claim to the Whole Product of Industry*, trans. M. E. Tanner, London, Macmillan, 1899 [1886].

Menger believed that unlike his German rival Rodbertus, who had repeated the thoughts of French socialists, of the Saint-Simonians and Proudhon, 'Marx is completely under the influence of the earlier English socialists, and more particularly of William Thompson. Leaving out of account the mathematical formulae by which Marx rather obscures than elucidates his argument, the whole theory of surplus value, its conception, its name and the estimates of its amount are borrowed in all essentials from Thompson's writings': Menger, *Right to the Whole Produce of Labour*, p. 101.

83. Marx, *Capital*, vol. I, p. 46.

84. Ibid., p. 48.

85. As Gerry Cohen observed, 'If anything is the *paradigm* of exploitation for Marx, it is the exploitation of the feudal serf, who does not, according to Marx, produce value, since his product is not marketed and is therefore not a commodity': Cohen, *History, Labour and Freedom*, p. 231.

86. Marx, *Economic Manuscripts of 1857–58*, *MECW*, vol. 28, pp. 249–50. Nor was the question addressed in more depth in *Capital*, see Chapter 11.

87. 'Karl Marx to Friedrich Engels', 22 July 1859, *MECW*, vol. 40, p. 473. The original comment in French, '*À quoi bon?*', was attributed by Karl to Elard Biscamp, the editor of *Das Volk*, the journal founded as the official organ of the German Workers' Educational Association. Biscamp was a radical republican journalist, originally with connections to both Kinkel and Ruge: see Christine Lattek, *Revolutionary Refugees: German Socialism in Britain, 1840–1860*, London, Routledge, 2006, pp. 203–6. The journal ran from 7 May to 20 August 1859, and in its last six weeks came under Karl's control.

88. 'Jenny Marx to Friedrich Engels', 9 April 1858, *MECW*, vol. 40, p. 569.

89. 'Karl Marx to Friedrich Engels', 21 January 1859, *MECW*, vol. 40, p. 369.

90. Ibid., 15 July 1858, p. 328.

91. Ibid., 11, 16 and 17 December 1858, 21 January 1859, pp. 359, 361, 363, 369.

92. 'Karl Marx to Ferdinand Lassalle', 22 February 1858, *MECW*, vol. 40, p. 270.

93. Ibid., 11 March 1858, p. 287.

94. 'Karl Marx to Friedrich Engels', 29 March 1858, *MECW*, vol. 40, p. 295.

95. Ibid., 2 April 1858, pp. 303–4.

96. 'Friedrich Engels to Karl Marx', 9 April 1858, *MECW*, vol. 40, p. 304.

97. 'Karl Marx to Ferdinand Lassalle', 31 May 1858, *MECW*, vol. 40, p. 315.

98. 'Karl Marx to Friedrich Engels', 29 November 1858, *MECW*, vol. 40, p. 358.

99. 'Karl Marx to Ferdinand Lassalle', 12 November 1858, *MECW*, vol. 40, pp. 354–5.

100. 'Karl Marx to Friedrich Engels', 13–15 January 1859, *MECW*, vol. 40, p. 368 (bold in the original).

101. Ibid.

102. 'Karl Marx to Joseph Weydemeyer', 1 February 1859, *MECW*, vol. 40, p. 376.

103. Ibid., p. 377.

104. 'Karl Marx to Friedrich Engels', 22 July 1859, *MECW*, vol. 40, p. 473.

105. Ibid., p. 473.

106. Ibid., 25 May 1859, p. 450.

107. 'Friedrich Engels to Karl Marx', 15 July 1859, *MECW*, vol. 4., p. 465; 'Karl Marx to Friedrich Engels', 19 July 1859, *MECW*, vol. 40, p. 471.

108. 'Friedrich Engels to Karl Marx', 3 August 1859, *MECW*, vol. 40, p. 478.

109. Ibid., 14 February 1859, *MECW*, vol. 40, p. 386; 'Karl Marx to Friedrich Engels', 22 February 1859, *MECW*, vol. 40, p. 389.

110. 'Karl Marx to Ferdinand Lassalle', 6 November 1859, *MECW*, vol. 40, p. 518.

111. It was not mentioned in Albert Schäffle's *Quintessence of Socialism* of 1874; nor was it referred to in Edward Aveling's *The Student's Marx* of 1892.

112. Karl Marx, 'Preface' to *A Contribution to the Critique of Political Economy*, 1859, *MECW*, vol. 29, p. 263.

113. For the importance of the Historical School of Law and its relevance to Karl's work, see Gareth Stedman Jones (ed.), *Karl Marx and Friedrich Engels: The Communist Manifesto*, Penguin Books, London, 2002, pp. 148–61.

114. Friedrich Engels, 'Karl Marx, *A Contribution to the Critique of Political Economy*', *MECW*, vol. 16, pp. 469, 473, 474–5.

115. Marx, 'Preface' to *Contribution to the Critique*, p. 263.

116. Karl Marx, *Economic Manuscripts of 1861–63 (A Contribution to the Critique of Political Economy: Third Chapter)*, *MECW*, vol. 30, p. 93.

117. Ibid., p. 313.

118. Ibid., pp. 92–3.

119. Ibid., pp. 95–6.

120. Kautsky rearranged the order in which theories were discussed. The original and unedited manuscript was published in 1977 as part of the *Marx-Engels-Gesamtausgabe*. The translations which appeared in volumes 30, 31 and 33 of the *Marx–Engels Collected Works* were taken from the *MEGA* edition.

121. For Lassalle, see Chapter 11, pp. 437–48.

122. 'Karl Marx to Ludwig Kugelmann', 28 December 1862, *MECW*, vol. 41, p. 435. Kugelmann had been put in touch with Marx by Freiligrath.

123. The plan is to be found in the concluding section of *Theories of Surplus Value*, *MEGA*, XI, iii.v, pp. 1861–2.

124. Karl Marx, 'Chapter Six. Results of the Direct Production Process', *MECW*, vol. 34, pp. 359, 362.

125. Ibid., pp. 427, 431.

126. Ibid., p. 398.

127. Ibid., p. 399.

128. Ibid., pp. 429, 439, 440.

129. Ibid., pp. 463, 460.

130. 'Karl Marx to Ludwig Kugelmann', 13 October 1866, *MECW*, vol. 42, p. 328.

131. Marx, 'Chapter Six. Results of the Direct Production Process', pp. 362, 375.

132. Ibid., pp. 362–3.

133. Ibid., p. 384.

134. Eugen von Böhm-Bawerk, *Karl Marx and the Close of His System: A Criticism*, trans. Alice M. Macdonald, London, T. Fisher Unwin, 1898.

135. See David McLellan, *Karl Marx: His Life and Thought*, London, Macmillan, 1973, pp. 337–8.

136. 'Karl Marx to Friedrich Engels', 31 July 1865, *MECW*, vol. 42, p. 173.

137. Ibid., 5 August 1865, p. 175.

138. 'Friedrich Engels to Karl Marx', 10 February 1866, *MECW*, vol. 42, p. 226; 'Karl Marx to Friedrich Engels', 13 February 1866, *MECW*, vol. 42, p. 228.

139. 'Jenny Marx to Ludwig Kugelmann', 26 February 1866, *MECW*, vol. 42, pp. 573–4.

140. 'Friedrich Engels to Karl Marx', 22 June 1867, *MECW*, vol. 42, p. 382.

141. 'Karl Marx to Friedrich Engels', 27 June 1867, *MECW*, vol. 42, pp. 390–91; 'Karl Marx to Ludwig Kugelmann', 13 July 1867, *MECW*, vol. 42, p. 396; and Marx, 'Preface to the First German Edition', in *Capital*, vol. I, p. 7. The appendix was published in the first edition. See Karl Marx, 'Anhang zu Kapital I, 1. Die Werthform', in *Das Kapital*, vol. I: *Kritik der politischen Oekonomie*, Hildesheim, Gerstenberg, 1980 (this is a facsimile of the first German edition, Hamburg, Verlag von Otto Meissner, 1867), pp. 764–84.

142. Marx, *Capital*, vol. I, p. 49.

143. Ibid., pp. 58, 74.

144. Ibid., pp. 86–7.

145. Ibid., pp. 176–7 ('Rhodes is here, leap here and NOW!'). The quotation is from one of Aesop's fables – an answer to someone who claimed they had once made an immense leap in Rhodes.

146. Ibid., Part VII: p. 564.

147. Marx, *Economic Manuscripts of 1857–58*, *MECW*, vol. 28, pp. 381–2.

148. Marx, *Capital*, vol. I, p. 705.

149. Marx, 'Preface to the First German Edition', in *Capital*, vol. I, p. 9.

150. Marx, *Capital*, vol. I, p. 750.

151. Marx, 'Afterword to the Second German Edition', 1873, in *Capital*, vol. I, pp. 12–20.

152. Ibid., pp. 18–19.

153. G. W. F. Hegel, *The Encyclopaedia: Logic*, trans. T. F. Geraets, W. A. Suchting and H. S. Harris, Indianapolis, Hackett, 1991, paras 217–18, p. 292.

154. G. W. F. Hegel, *Lectures on Natural Right and Political Science: The First Philosophy of Right*, trans. J. Michael Stewart and Peter C. Hodgson, Berkeley, University of California Press, 1995, para 123, p. 222.

155. Hegel uses the notion of 'subsumption' in relation to his argument for the identity of subject and predicate. 'Subsumption . . . is only the *application* of the universal to a particular or singular posited *under* it in accordance with an indeterminate representation, one of lesser quantity'. G. W. F. Hegel, *The Science of Logic*, trans. and ed. George di Giovanni, Cambridge, Cambridge University Press, 2010, p. 555.

156. Marx, 'Afterword to the Second German Edition', in *Capital*, vol. I, p. 19.

157. Ibid.

158. Marx, *Capital*, vol. I, p. 707.

159. Ibid., pp. 623–34; the term 'reserve army of labour' was first used by the Chartists.

160. Ibid., p. 507.

161. Ibid., p. 723.

162. Nassau Senior in his *Letters on the Factory Act* in 1837 claimed that the whole net profit was derived from the last hour of the working day, based on the mistaken assumption that the turnover period was invariable. The wage fund doctrine assumed that the amount of capital available in a given year to pay wages was unchanging. Therefore, if population changed, so would the wages of the workers. If population is increased, but the amount of money available to pay as wages stayed the same, workers might earn less.

163. One of the more immediate effects of the impact made by his work was its central role in initiating a debate upon the origins and nature of the industrial revolution in Britain. It was as a result of reading *Capital* in French translation that Arnold Toynbee was inspired to begin work on what was posthumously published as *Lectures on the Industrial Revolution in England*, London, Rivingtons, 1884. On Toynbee's intellectual formation, see Alon Kadish, *Apostle Arnold: The Life and Death of Arnold Toynbee, 1852–1883*, Durham, NC, Duke University Press, 1986.

11 *CAPITAL*, SOCIAL DEMOCRACY AND THE INTERNATIONAL

1. I have used the term 'transnational', following the usage by Marcel van der Linden in his *Transnational Labour History: Explorations*, Studies in Labour History, Aldershot, Ashgate, 2003, ch. 2, as a term preceding the consolidation of the new nation-states in Europe from the 1870s.

2. 'Jenny Marx to Friedrich Engels', beginning of November 1863, *MECW*, vol. 41, p. 585.

3. 'Karl Marx to Friedrich Engels', 4 July 1864, *MECW*, vol. 41, p. 546.

4. Ibid., 4 November 1864, vol. 42, p. 12; ibid., 14 November 1864, p. 22; 'Friedrich Engels to Karl Marx', 16 November 1864, *MECW*, vol. 42, p. 23; 'Karl Marx to Friedrich Engels', 2 December 1864, *MECW*, vol. 42, p. 51.

5. The supposed similarity between the Blanquist position and that espoused by Karl was more imaginary than real. Blanquists were more concerned about the divisions of 1792–3 between the Hébertistes and the Robespierrists than about Karl's conception of the modern class struggle. The only known contact between Karl and Blanqui occurred in 1864, when, at Blanqui's request, his follower Dr Watteau sent Karl a copy of Gustave Tridon, *Les Hébertistes*, Paris, 1864. See Alan B. Spitzer, *The Revolutionary Theories*

of Louis Auguste Blanqui, New York, Columbia University Press, 1957, pp. 114–15.

6. On the decline of Chartism, see Margot C. Finn, *After Chartism: Class and Nation in English Radical Politics, 1848–1874*, Cambridge, Cambridge University Press, 1993; Miles Taylor, *The Decline of British Radicalism 1847–1860*, Oxford, Clarendon Press, 1995; Jonathan Parry, *The Rise and Fall of Liberal Government in Victorian Britain*, New Haven/London, Yale University Press, 1993, Part III.

7. On the changing politics of Ernest Jones, see Miles Taylor, *Ernest Jones, Chartism and the Romance of Politics 1819–1869*, Oxford, Oxford University Press, 2003, pp. 137–210.

8. 'Karl Marx to Friedrich Engels', 24 November 1857, *MECW*, vol. 40, p. 210.

9. Ibid., 9 April 1863, vol. 41, p. 468.

10. 'Friedrich Engels to Karl Marx', 8 April 1863, *MECW*, vol. 41, p. 465.

11. Its reappearance was made possible because of its use by the prosecution in the trial of the Social Democratic leaders Wilhelm Liebknecht and August Bebel, for their 'treasonous' opposition to Prussia's war with France. The prosecution claimed that their treachery had been fuelled by the *Manifesto*'s assertion that 'the working men have no country'. However, by that stage, the *Manifesto* was no longer seen, even by its authors, as contemporary political polemic, but rather as a 'historical document'. It was only in the twentieth century, as a result of the Russian Revolution of 1917 and the foundation of the Comintern, that the pronouncements of the *Manifesto* acquired an actuality which they had never possessed in the previous century.

12. 'Karl Marx to Ferdinand Lassalle', 22 November 1859, *MECW*, vol. 40, p. 538.

13. Ibid., 23 February 1860, vol. 41, pp. 58–9. The rumour suggested that Lassalle had betrayed the workers of Düsseldorf and had embezzled funds. This distrust had been endorsed by Engels, who appears to have feared Lassalle, both because he was independent-minded and because he feared that Lassalle's charm might win Karl over.

14. 'Ferdinand Lassalle to Friedrich Engels and Karl Marx', 26–29 February 1860, *MEGA*, III, ix, p. 162.

15. Karl was obsessed by the fear that Lassalle would plagiarize his work. But Lassalle's approach was quite distinct. His economic thinking drew upon Karl's work, but combined it with a Hegelian conception of the state, a French-based advocacy of state-supported cooperatives and scepticism about trade union action, derived from what he construed to be Ricardo's 'iron law of wages'. He drew also upon the Prussian *Staatswissenschaft* tradition, particularly the writings of Johann Karl Rodbertus, for his portrayal of capitalism as a harsh exploitative system. See David Lindenfeld, *The*

Practical Imagination: The German Sciences of State in the Nineteenth Century, Chicago, Chicago University Press, 1997, pp. 186–7.

16. 'Ferdinand Lassalle to Karl Marx', 6 March 1859, *MEGA*, III, ix, pp. 336–8.

17. Ferdinand Lassalle, *Die Philosophie Herakleitos des Dunkeln von Ephesos*, Berlin, F. Duncker, 1858.

18. 'Ferdinand Lassalle to Karl Marx', 6 March 1859, *MEGA*, III, ix, pp. 336–8.

19. Ibid.

20. Ibid., 11 September 1860, *MEGA*, III, xi, p. 147; 'Karl Marx to Ferdinand Lassalle', 15 September 1860, *MECW*, vol. 41, p. 193.

21. 'Ferdinand Lassalle to Karl Marx', 11 March 1860, *MEGA*, III, x, p. 372.

22. 'Karl Marx to Friedrich Engels', 29 January 1861, *MECW*, vol. 41, p. 252.

23. 'Karl Marx to Ferdinand Lassalle', 15 February 1861, *MECW*, vol. 41, p. 263; ibid., 7 March 1861, pp. 267–8.

24. Ibid., 15 February 1861, p. 263.

25. 'Karl Marx to Antoinette Philips', 24 March 1861, *MECW*, vol. 41, pp. 269–72.

26. Pfuel had been Prime Minister of Prussia in 1848 and responsible for the harsh suppression of the revolt in Posen. Since then, however, he had become radicalized. According to Karl, Pfuel was now eighty-two, 'but still mentally alert and become very radical. He has, by the by, fallen out of favour and is ranked by the Court with the Jacobins, atheists etc.': 'Karl Marx to Friedrich Engels', 7 May 1861, *MECW*, vol. 41, p. 280.

27. Ibid., 10 May 1861, pp. 286–7.

28. 'Karl Marx to Antoinette Phillips', 24 March 1861, *MECW*, vol. 41, pp. 271–2.

29. 'Karl Marx to Ferdinand Lassalle', 8 May 1861, *MECW*, vol. 41, p. 283. For once, he referred to her in generous terms – 'the old woman . . . intrigued me by her exceedingly subtle esprit and unshakeable equanimity'.

30. Ibid., pp. 283–4.

31. Ibid., 29 May 1861, p. 291.

32. 'Jenny Marx to Friedrich Engels', beginning of April 1861, *MECW*, vol. 41, p. 579.

33. Ferdinand Lassalle, *Die Theorie der erworbenen Rechte und der Collision der Gesetze: unter besonderer Berücksichtigung des Römischen, Französischen und Preussischen Rechts*, Leipzig, Brochaus, 1861; 'Karl Marx to Ferdinand Lassalle', 11 June 1861, *MECW*, vol. 41, pp. 293–4.

34. 'Karl Marx to Friedrich Engels', 10 May 1861, *MECW*, vol. 41, p. 289; ibid., 7 May 1861, p. 280.

35. 'Karl Marx to Antoinette Philips', 24 March 1861, *MECW*, vol. 41, pp. 271–2.

36. Ibid., 17 July 1861, p. 313.

37. 'Karl Marx to Ferdinand Lassalle', 28 April 1862, *MECW*, vol. 41, p. 356.

38. The Exhibition, an international trade fair in which thirty-six countries were represented, was held on the ground which now houses the Science Museum and the Natural History Museum in South Kensington. It ran from 1 May to 1 November 1862. After the Exhibition was over, the iron and glass structure was dismantled and much of the material reused in the construction of Alexandra Palace.

39. 'Karl Marx to Ferdinand Lassalle', 16 June 1862, *MECW*, vol. 41, p. 379.

40. 'Jenny Marx to Ferdinand Lassalle', 5 May 1861, in Ferdinand Lassalle, *Nachgelassene Briefe und Schriften*, 3 vols., ed. Gustav Mayer, Stuttgart, Deutsche Verlags-Anstalt, 1921–5, vol. 3, pp. 358–9.

41. 'Karl Marx to Friedrich Engels', 30 July 1862, *MECW*, vol. 41, p. 389.

42. Ibid., p. 390.

43. Jenny Marx, 'A Short Sketch of an Eventful Life', in Institut Marksizma–Leninzma, *Reminiscences of Marx and Engels*, Moscow, Foreign Languages Publishing House, 1957, p. 000.

44. 'Karl Marx to Friedrich Engels', 30 July 1862, *MECW*, vol. 41, p. 390.

45. Ibid., p. 389.

46. 'Ferdinand Lassalle to Karl Marx', 6 November 1862, *MEGA*, III, xii, p. 264.

47. 'Karl Marx to Ferdinand Lassalle', 7 November 1862, *MECW*, vol. 41, pp. 424–5.

48. Ferdinand Lassalle, 'Über Verfassungswesen', April 1862, in *Reden und Schriften: Aus der Arbeiteragitation 1862–1864*, ed. F. Jenaczek, Munich, Deutscher Taschenbuch Verlag, 1970, p. 80.

49. Édouard Bernstein, *Ferdinand Lassalle: Le Réformateur social*, Paris, Rivière, 1913, p. 121.

50. 'Karl Marx to Dr Kugelmann', 23 February 1865, *MECW*, vol. 42, p. 101.

51. 'Karl Marx to Johann von Schweitzer', 13 October 1868, *MECW*, vol. 43, p. 133.

52. 'Karl Marx to Dr Kugelmann', 23 February 1865, *MECW*, vol. 42, p. 102.

53. Friedrich Engels, 'The Prussian Military Question and the German Workers' Party', February 1865, *MECW*, vol. 20, pp. 77–9; and see Roger Morgan, *The German Social Democrats and the First International, 1864–1872*, Cambridge, Cambridge University Press, 1965, pp. 1–12.

54. 'Karl Liebknecht to Karl Marx', 3 June 1864, in Georg Eckert (ed.), *Wilhelm Liebknecht: Briefwechsel mit Karl Marx und Friedrich Engels*, The Hague, Mouton, 1963, pp. 33–4.

55. 'Karl Marx to Friedrich Engels', 7 June 1864, *MECW*, vol. 41, p. 537.

56. 'Karl Marx to Sophie von Hatzfeldt', 12 September 1864, *MECW*, vol. 41, p. 563.

57. Ibid., p. 560.

58. 'Karl Marx to Friedrich Engels', 30 January 1865, *MECW*, vol. 42, p. 71; ibid., 18 February 1865, p. 97.

59. 'Johann von Schweitzer to Karl Marx', 11 February 1865, *MEGA*, III, xiii, p. 229. But by 1867 their differences had narrowed, in the light of Bismarck's alliance with the liberals.

60. 'Karl Marx to Friedrich Engels', 7 September 1864, *MECW*, vol. 41, p. 561.

61. See Alan B. Spitzer, *Old Hatreds and Young Hopes: The French Carbonari against the Bourbon Restoration*, Cambridge, Mass., Harvard University Press, 1971, chs. 2 and 3.

62. Ludwig Börne, *Lettres écrites de Paris pendant les années 1830 et 1831*, trans. F. Guiran, Paris, Paulin, 1832, p. 19.

63. On the religious basis of Mazzini's anti-clericalism and its proximity to English traditions of 'rational dissent', see Eugenio Biagini, 'Mazzini and Anticlericalism: The English Exile', in C. A. Bayly and E. F. Biagini (eds.), *Giuseppe Mazzini and the Globalisation of Democratic Nationalism 1830–1920*, Proceedings of the British Academy, no. 152, Oxford, Oxford University Press, 2008, pp. 145–66.

64. See Karma Nabulsi, 'Patriotism and Internationalism in the "Oath of Allegiance" to Young Europe', *European Journal of Political Theory*, 5/1 (January 2006), pp. 61– 70; Karma Nabulsi, *Traditions of War: Occupation, Resistance, and the Law*, Oxford, Oxford University Press, 1999, pp. 177–241; Stefano Recchia and Nadia Urbinati (eds.), *A Cosmopolitanism of Nations: Giuseppe Mazzini's Writings on Democracy, Nation Building, and International Relations*, Princeton, Princeton University Press, 2009.

65. The aftermath of this debacle is memorably described in E. H. Carr, *The Romantic Exiles: A Nineteenth-Century Portrait Gallery*, London, Victor Gollancz, 1933.

66. Dieter Langewiesche, 'Revolution in Germany: Constitutional State – Nation State – Social Reform', in D. Dowe, H.-G. Haupt, D. Langewiesche and J. Sperber (eds.), *Europe in 1848: Revolution and Reform*, New York/Oxford, Berghahn, 2001, pp. 120–43.

67. Giuseppe Garibaldi, *An Autobiography*, trans. William, London, Routledge, Warne and Routledge, 1861, p. 37; Garibaldi derived his cosmopolitan republican nationalism from a blending of the ideals of Mazzini's Young Italy with the global gospel propagated in *The Doctrine of Saint-Simon*. His position on the republic was not stable. After 1860, he turned away from a monarchical and Piedmontese solution for Italy, becoming increasingly anti-clerical and socialist. See Lucy Riall, *Garibaldi: Invention of a Hero*, New Haven/London, Yale University Press, 2007, p. 2.

68. Negative views of the role played by nationalism in the twentieth century led to a neglect of its nineteenth-century transnational dimensions and to a downplaying of its importance as part of republican and socialist sentiment. During the 1860s, apart from Karl and his friends, the only radical grouping that adopted a hostile attitude towards the politics of subject

nations was that of Cobden, Bright and the 'Manchester School'. See Finn, *After Chartism*, ch. 1; Derek Beales, 'Garibaldi in England: The Politics of Italian Enthusiasm', in John A. Davis and Paul Ginsborg (eds.), *Society and Politics in the Age of the Risorgimento: Essays in Honour of Denis Mack Smith*, Cambridge, Cambridge University Press, 1991, pp. 184–216.

69. Finn, *After Chartism*, pp. 217–24.

70. See Duncan A. Campbell, *English Public Opinion and the American Civil War*, London, Royal Historical Society/Boydell Press, 2003.

71. 'Karl Marx to Joseph Weydemeyer', 29 November 1864, *MECW*, vol. 42, p. 44; Yvonne Kapp, *Eleanor Marx*, 2 vols., London, Lawrence & Wishart, 1972, vol. 1, p. 34.

72. Henry Collins and Chimen Abramsky, *Karl Marx and the British Labour Movement: Years of the First International*, London, Macmillan, 1965, p. 24. On the O'Brienites, see Stan Shipley, *Club Life and Socialism in mid-Victorian London*, History Workshop Pamphlets, no. 5, Oxford, 1973.

73. Cited in Finn, *After Chartism*, p. 214.

74. 'Karl Marx to Friedrich Engels', 4 November 1864, *MECW*, vol. 42, pp. 16, 17.

75. See van der Linden, *Transnational Labour History*, ch. 1.

76. See Peter Hall, *The Industries of London since 1861*, London, Hutchinson University Library, 1962; Gareth Stedman Jones, *Outcast London: A Study in the Relationship between Classes in Victorian Society*, Oxford, Clarendon Press, 1971 (4th edn, London, Verso, 2013), part 1.

77. On the importance of the new 'amalgamated' trade unions, see Thomas Jones, 'George Odger, Robert Applegarth, and the First International Working Men's Association', unpublished MA dissertation, King's College London, 2007; Alastair Reid, *United We Stand: A History of Britain's Trade Unions*, London, Penguin Books, 2005, pp. 95–101.

78. Sidney and Beatrice Webb, *The History of Trade Unionism*, London, Longmans, 1902, chs. 4 and 5.

79. 'Rules of the London Trades Council', cited in F. M. Leventhal, *Respectable Radical: George Howell and Victorian Working Class Politics*, London, Weidenfeld and Nicolson, 1971, p. 37.

80. Cited in George Howell, 'The History of the International Association', *Nineteenth Century*, vol. IV, July 1878, p. 24.

81. Collins and Abramsky, *Karl Marx and the British Labour Movement*, pp. 18, 35. Much to Mazzini's annoyance, however, admiration for his notions of duty and the 'union of labour and capital' did not get in the way of an enthusiastic reception by the International's General Council of the 'Inaugural Address' and its admixture of Mazzinian sentiment with a class-specific appeal to 'proletarians'. See below, pp. 463–5.

82. Howell, 'History of the International Association', p. 25.

83. Compare the ease and speed of a journey by rail and steamer with the eighteenth-century difficulties of journeys between London and Paris described in *A Tale of Two Cities*.

84. The scale and extent of the cosmopolitan ambition of the English Trade Society leaders, both social and political, has been highlighted in Jones, 'George Odger, Robert Applegarth'. His dissertation provides a corrective to previous interpretations, which tended to categorize the views of English trade unionists as limited, ignorant or in need of Karl's theoretical guidance.

85. David McLellan, *Karl Marx: His Life and Thought*, London, Macmillan, 1973, p. 363. The minority consisted of three Frenchmen, two Italians and two Germans.

86. Edward Spencer Beesly, 'The International Working Men's Association', *Fortnightly Review*, 1 November 1870, reprinted in *MEGA*, I, xxi, p. 1069.

87. Howell, 'History of the International Association', p. 31. According to Howell, 'Its enormous strength was a fiction existing only in the brain of some of those who had been terrified into the belief of its vast power and resources, with ramifications in every part of the world, and paid agents ready for every emergency.'

88. 'Meeting of the General Council of the International Working Men's Association', 20 August 1867, *MEGA*, I, xx, p. 587. His particular worry was that disarmament in the rest of Europe would 'leave Russia alone in the possession of the means to make war on the rest of Europe', ibid., p. 586.

89. 'The Fourth Annual Report of the General Council', 1868, *MEGA*, I, xxi, p. 86.

90. On Bakunin, see below, pp. **510–29**.

91. Beesly, 'International Working Men's Association', p. 1078; ibid.

92. See Julian P. W. Archer, *The First International in France 1864–1872: Its Origins, Theories and Impact*, Lanham, Md Oxford, University Press of America, 1997, pp. 96–7.

93. Beesly, 'International Working Men's Association', p. 1072; and van der Linden, *Transnational Labour History*, ch. 1.

94. 'Karl Marx to Friedrich Engels', 4 November 1864, *MECW*, vol. 42, pp. 16–19.

95. This part of the 'Address' drew extensively upon the sources he was at the same time researching for Section 5 of Chapter XXV of Volume I of *Capital*, 'Illustrations of the General Law of Capitalist Accumulation', *MECW*, vol. 35, pp. 642–703.

96. Gladstone's announcement was less callous than the 'Inaugural Address' made it sound. For Gladstone also claimed that 'the augmentation' was 'of indirect benefit to the labourer' and that 'the average condition of the British labourer . . . has improved during the last twenty years to a degree that we know to be extraordinary'. A controversy later developed about whether

Karl was guilty of misquotation. The attack was first made in 1872 by Lujo Brentano, a supporter of the German Historical School of Economics, and the issue was raised again in 1883, in a dispute between a Cambridge scientist and enthusiast for profit-sharing, William Sedley Taylor, and Karl's daughter, Eleanor.

97. Karl Marx, 'Address of the International Working Men's Association' ('Inaugural Address'), October 1864, *MEGA*, I, xx, pp. 8–9.

98. Ibid., pp. 4–12.

99. Ibid.; 'Karl Marx to Friedrich Engels', 4 November 1864, *MECW*, vol. 42, p. 18.

100. Beesly, 'International Working Men's Association', p. 1068.

101. Cited in Leventhal, *Respectable Radical*, p. 53.

102. Karl Marx, *Capital* , vol. I, p. 750. This famous flight of rhetoric, enunciated in cryptic Hegelian phrases, bore little relation to the rest of the volume. It stood in place of what might have been a more substantive conclusion, had Karl been able to publish the complete work in 1867.

103. 'Karl Marx to Friedrich Engels', 7 May 1867, *MECW*, vol. 42, p. 371.

104. 'Friedrich Engels to Karl Marx', 29 January 1867, 15 August 1867, *MECW*, vol. 42, pp. 344, 402.

105. The importance of these passages has been highlighted in Shlomo Avineri, *The Social and Political Thought of Karl Marx*, Cambridge, Cambridge University Press, 1968, pp. 176–82.

106. In the first edition of 1867, it is stated, 'In England ist der Umwälzungsprozess mit Händen greifbar': Karl Marx, 'Vorwort', in *Das Kapital*, vol. I: *Kritik der politischen Oekonomie*, Hildesheim, Gerstenberg, 1980 (this is a facsimile of the first German edition, Hamburg, Verlag von Otto Meissner, 1867), p. xi. The translation twenty years later by Samuel Moore and Edward Aveling read, 'In England the progress of social disintegration is palpable': *Capital*, vol. I: *A Critique of Political Economy*, *MECW*, vol. 35, p. 9. This loses the immediacy of the sense of upheaval in the original text.

107. Karl Marx, 'Speech at the Hague Congress of the International', 18 September 1872, in H. Gerth (ed.), *The First International: Minutes of the Hague Congress of 1872*, Madison, University of Wisconsin Press, 1958, p. 236.

108. Karl Marx, 'Speech at the Polish Meeting', 22 January 1867, *MECW*, vol. 20, pp. 200–201.

109. He attributed 'the limitation of the working day' to 'legislative interference', but this would never have happened 'without the working men's continuous pressure from without'. Karl Marx, 'Draft for Value, Price and Profit', *MEGA*, I, xx, p. 184.

110. Marx, *Capital*, vol. I, pp. 306–7. The Latin quotation comes from Virgil's *Aeneid*, 'What a great change from that time!'

111. Ibid., p. 706.

112. Ibid., p. 739.

113. 'Karl Marx to Ferdinand Lassalle', 11 June 1861, *MECW*, vol. 41, p. 294.

114. Karl Marx, *Capital*, vol. III: *The Process of Capitalist Production as a Whole*, *MECW*, vol. 37, pp. 434–5.

115. Ibid., p. 436.

116. Ibid., p. 438.

117. Marx, 'Address of the International Working Men's Association', p. 10.

118. Cited in Collins and Abramsky, *Karl Marx and the British Labour Movement*, p. 123.

119. Beesly, 'International Working Men's Association', p. 1078.

120. Karl summarized his argument in 'Notes for the Report on Value, Price and Profit', *MECW*, vol. 20, p. 338. It was published posthumously in 1898 by Edward Aveling and Eleanor Marx as *Value, Price and Profit*: see *MECW*, vol. 20, pp. 101–49.

121. 'Central Council Meeting', 20 June 1865, *MEGA*, I, xx, p. 334.

122. 'Karl Marx to Dr Kugelmann', 29 November 1864, *MECW*, vol. 42, p. 45.

123. Ibid., 15 January 1866, p. 221.

124. Karl Marx, 'Marx über Gewerksgenossenschaften', *MEGA*, I, xxi, p. 906; and see pp. 2141–3. The description of the encounter by four metalworkers was originally written up by one of them, Johann Hamann, in a trade union journal, *Allgemeine Deutsche Metallarbeiterschaft*, and then reprinted in *Volksstaat*. The importance of this discussion, which had always been omitted from previous editions of *Marx–Engels Works*, has been highlighted by Jürgen Herres, editor of the 2009 *MEGA*, I, xxi, which covers the period September 1867–March 1871; see the forthcoming publication of the Paris Conference on the 150th Anniversary of the International (*150 Years Ago: The First International*, Paris, 19–20 June 2014, forthcoming Brill).

125. 'Karl Marx to Dr Kugelmann', 23 February 1865, *MECW*, vol. 42, p. 105.

126. Ibid., 9 October 1866, p. 326.

127. Karl Marx, 'Instructions for the Delegates of the Provisional General Council: The Different Questions', August 1866, *MECW*, vol. 20, pp. 185–94.

128. 'Karl Marx to Friedrich Engels', 2 April 1866, *MECW*, vol. 42, p. 253. These backers included the Christian Socialist, author of *Tom Brown's Schooldays* and cooperator, Thomas Hughes, and the editor of the *Nonconformist*, Alfred Miall.

129. 'Karl Marx to Dr Kugelmann', 23 February 1865, *MECW*, vol. 42, p. 105.

130. 'Karl Marx to Friedrich Engels', 25 February 1865, *MECW*, vol. 42, p. 108.

131. Ibid., 1 May 1865, p. 150.

132. 'Karl Marx to Dr Kugelmann', 15 January 1866, *MECW*, vol. 42, p. 221.

133. 'Karl Marx to Friedrich Engels', 7 July 1866, *MECW*, vol. 42, pp. 289–90.

134. 'Karl Marx to Dr Kugelmann', 9 October 1866, *MECW*, vol. 42, p. 327.

135. Ibid., 13 October 1866, pp. 328–9.

136. 'Karl Marx to Friedrich Engels', 11 September 1867, *MECW*, vol. 42, p. 424.

137. 'Karl Marx to Dr Kugelmann', 13 October 1866, *MECW*, vol. 42, p. 328.

138. It should be remembered that Max Weber constructed his concept of charisma with Gladstone in mind.

139. Frederic Harrison, 'The Transit of Power', *Fortnightly Review*, April 1868, pp. 384–5.

140. Cited in Royden Harrison, *Before the Socialists: Studies in Labour and Politics 1861–1881*, London, Routledge and Kegan Paul, 1965, pp. 86–7.

141. 'Karl Marx to Friedrich Engels', 2 April 1866, *MECW*, vol. 42, p. 253; ibid., 27 July 1866, p. 300.

142. 'Karl Marx to Friedrich Engels', 2 April 1866, *MECW*, vol. 42, p. 253.

143. 'Karl Marx to Johann Philipp Becker', 31 August 1866, *MECW*, vol. 42, p. 314.

144. On 6 May 1867, there was another flashpoint, in which a demonstration of over 100,000 assembled in the park, despite a government prohibition, and Walpole was forced to resign. But this seems quickly to have been forgotten. Karl was out the country at the time, and there was no mention of the event in his correspondence. See Harrison, *Before the Socialists*, pp. 97–9.

145. See ibid., pp. 78–137.

146. W. F. Moneypenny and G. E. Buckle, *The Life of Benjamin Disraeli, Earl of Beaconsfield*, 2 vols., London, John Murray, 1929, vol. 2, p. 274.

147. Parry, *Rise and Fall of Liberal Government*, p. 216.

148. For the background to the emergence of Fenianism, see R. F. Foster, *Modern Ireland: 1600–1972*, London, Allen Lane, 1988, ch. 16.

149. 'Karl Marx to Friedrich Engels', 14 December 1867, *MECW*, vol. 42, p. 501.

150. 'Karl Marx to Dr Kugelmann', 6 April 1868, *MECW*, vol. 43, p. 3.

151. See his preparatory notes, *MECW*, vol. 21, pp. 212–317.

152. 'Friedrich Engels to Laura Marx', 23 September 1867, *MECW*, vol. 42, p. 431; 'Friedrich Engels to Dr Kugelmann', 12 October 1867, *MECW*, vol. 42, p. 444.

153. 'Karl Marx to Friedrich Engels', 2 November 1867, *MECW*, vol. 42, p. 460; ibid., 28 November 1867, p. 478.

154. Ibid., p. 479; 'Friedrich Engels to Karl Marx', 29 November 1867, *MECW*, vol. 42, p. 483.

155. 'Meeting of the General Council and of Members and Friends of the Association', 19 November 1867, *MEGA*, I, xxi, p. 526.

156. Cited in Harrison, *Before the Socialists*, p. 141.

157. Compare Marx's 'Draft of a Speech on the "Fenian Question"' for the Meeting of the General Council of the International Working Men's Association', 26 November 1867, and 'Entwurf des Vortrags über den Fenianismus im Deutschen Arbeiterbildungsverein London am 16. Dezember 1867', *MEGA*, I, xxi, pp. 15–32.

158. 'Karl Marx to Friedrich Engels', 2 November 1867, *MECW*, vol. 42, pp. 460–61.

159. Ibid., 30 November 1867, pp. 486–7.

160. 'Karl Marx to Dr Kugelmann', 6 April 1868, *MECW*, vol. 43, p. 3.

161. E. S. Beesly, 1867, cited in Harrison, *Before the Socialists*, p. 143.

162. 'Karl Marx to Dr Kugelmann', 6 April 1868, *MECW*, vol. 43, p. 4.

163. 'Jenny Marx to Dr Kugelmann', 30 October 1869, *MECW*, vol. 43, p. 546.

164. 'Meeting of the General Council', 16 November 1869, *MEGA*, I, xxi, pp. 727–30.

165. Ibid., 23 November 1869, pp. 728–9, 731–4.

166. 'Karl Marx to Dr Kugelmann', 29 November 1869, *MECW*, vol. 43, p. 390.

167. 'Karl Marx to Friedrich Engels', 10 December 1869, *MECW*, vol. 43, p. 397.

168. Collins and Abramsky, *Karl Marx and the British Labour Movement*, p. 169.

169. 'The General Council to the Federal Council of Romance Switzerland', 1 January 1870, *MECW*, vol. 21, pp. 84–91.

170. Karl Marx, 'Circulaire du Conseil Général de l'Association Internationale des Travailleurs au Conseil Fédéral de la Suisse Romande du 1er janvier 1870', *Entstehung und Überlieferung*, *MEGA*, I, xxi (Apparat), pp. 1465–70.

171. 'Karl Marx to Dr Kugelmann', 10 April 1868, *MECW*, vol. 43, p. 4; pointing to the election of O'Donovan Rossa in the following year, Jenny made a similar assumption. 'Religious fanaticism is dying a natural death, the hostility of Catholics and Protestants is at an end, there is a split in the Orange camp, and Orangemen, Ribbonmen and Fenians are uniting against their common enemy, the British government. Consequently, the influence of the Priests is vanishing; the Irish movement is no longer in their hands': 'Jenny Marx to Dr Kugelmann', 27 December 1869, *MECW*, vol. 43, p. 549.

172. 'Karl Marx to Laura and Paul Lafargue', 5 March 1870, *MECW*, vol. 43, p. 449.

173. The strikers and their spokesmen increasingly often justified their demands in the language, supplied by popular political economy, of supply and demand. Significantly, also, the state had kept discreetly in the background. So far as possible, it had avoided the use of troops and the making of arrests. There were no show trials or deportations of trade unionists, as there had been in the case of the 'Tolpuddle Martyrs' twenty years before, and no significant threats to stiffen anti-strike legislation. Furthermore, the toehold gained by striking Lancashire textile operatives in 1853–4 had grown by the end of the decade into elaborate bargaining procedures between employers and operatives across the cotton region and the beginnings of forms of arbitration in the Nottingham hosiery industry.

174. For references, see Gareth Stedman Jones, 'Some Notes on Karl Marx and the English Labour Movement', *History Workshop*, 18 (Autumn 1984), pp. 124–37.

175. 'Report of the Fourth Annual Congress of the International Working Men's Association', p. 18, cited in Collins and Abramsky, *Karl Marx and the British Labour Movement*, p. 98.

176. 'Jenny Marx to Ludwig Kugelmann', 17 July 1870, *MECW*, vol. 43, p. 563.

177. 'Karl Marx to Friedrich Engels', 20 July 1870, *MECW*, vol. 44, pp. 3–4, 13; Karl Marx to Paul and Laura Lafargue, 28 July 1870, *MECW*, vol. 44, p. 14.

178. 'First Address of the General Council of the International Working Men's Association on the Franco-Prussian War', 23 July 1870, *MECW*, vol. 22, pp. 3–8.

179. 'Meeting of the General Council', 2 August 1870, *MEGA*, I, xxi, p. 814; the emphasis upon peace was especially appreciated. The Peace Society supported the printing of 30,000 copies of the 'Address'.

180. 'Friedrich Engels to Karl Marx', 22 July 1870, *MECW*, vol. 44, p. 6.

181. 'Karl Marx to Friedrich Engels', 17 August 1870, *MECW*, vol. 44, p. 51.

182. 'Second Address on the Franco-Prussian War', 9 September 1870, *MECW*, vol. 22, pp. 264, 267.

183. 'Karl Marx to Friedrich Sorge', 1 September 1870, *MECW*, vol. 44, p. 57.

184. See Christopher Clark, 'From 1848 to Christian Democracy', in Ira Katznelson and Gareth Stedman Jones (eds.), *Religion and the Political Imagination*, Cambridge, Cambridge University Press, 2010, pp. 190–213.

185. Robert Tombs, *The Paris Commune 1871*, London, Longman, 1999, p. 57.

186. Cited in John Merriman, *Massacre: The Life and Death of the Paris Commune of 1871*, New Haven, Yale University Press, 2014, p. 45.

187. Tombs, *Paris Commune*, Appendix 1, pp. 219 and 78–9.

188. See Merriman, *Massacre*, p. 63.

189. Cited in Tombs, *Paris Commune*, p. 117.

190. Ibid., pp. 114–15.

191. See K. Steven Vincent, *Between Marxism and Anarchism: Benoît Malon and French Reformist Socialism*, Berkeley/Oxford, University of California Press, 1992, pp. 14–16.

192. Nineteenth-century claims about the numbers killed, ranging from 10,000 to 40,000, are excessive. Current estimates are based upon the records of morgues and other official sources. See Robert Tombs, 'How Bloody was *La Semaine sanglante* of *1871*?', *Historical Journal*, 55/3 (2012), pp. 679–704.

193. 'Meeting of the General Council', 21 March 1871, *MEGA*, I, xxii, pp. 522–3.

194. 'Meeting of the General Council', 18 April 1871, *MEGA*, I, xxii, p. 537.

195. 'Karl Marx to Dr Kugelmann', 12 April 1871, *MECW*, vol. 44, p. 132. This judgement was similar to that put forward by Engels at the General

Council on 11 April, but it did not take account of the fact that in the first week leading up to the elections of 26 March, the National Guard continued to hope that it would be possible to negotiate with Versailles. Secondly, given the failure of all their previous sorties from the city, it is not at all clear that the Parisians would have succeeded in overcoming Versailles.

196. Karl Marx, *The Civil War in France: Address of the General Council of the International Working Men's Association*, *MECW*, vol. 22, p. 320.

197. Ibid., p. 328. It would be more accurate to say that these institutions had removed themselves with the retreat of the government to Versailles. It was also argued that 'after every revolution marking a progressive phase in the class struggle, the purely repressive character of the State power' stood out 'in bolder and bolder relief'. Presented as an empirical claim, this was arguable. But presented as part of a tendential path accompanying the development of modern industry, it was wrong. State power during the Third Republic was less repressive than it had been under the Second Empire. For this reason, the argument that Bonaparte's Empire was 'the only form of government possible at a time when the bourgeoisie had already lost, and the working class had not yet acquired, the faculty of ruling the nation' (ibid., p. 330) was also shown to be unfounded.

198. This point is well made in Avineri, *Social and Political Thought*, pp. 241–2.

199. Marx, *Civil War in France*, pp. 334–5.

200. Ibid.

201. Karl Marx, 'First Draft of *The Civil War in France*', *MECW*, vol. 22, p. 499.

202. Marx, *Civil War in France*, pp. 348, 353.

203. Ibid., pp. 342–3.

204. Ibid., p. 341.

205. 'Karl Marx to Friedrich Engels', 6 September 1870, *MECW*, vol. 44, pp. 64–5.

206. 'Karl Marx to Edward Beesly', 19 October 1870, *MECW*, vol. 44, pp. 88–9.

207. This was reported by the Austrian socialist, turned police agent, Heinrich Oberwinder in his *Mémoires* of 1887, cited in Boris Nicolaievsky and Otto Maenchen-Helfen, *Karl Marx: Man and Fighter*, trans. G. David and E. Mosbacher, London, Allen Lane, 1973 [1933], p. 347.

208. 'Karl Marx to Dr Kugelmann', 17 April 1871, *MECW*, vol. 44, pp. 136–7.

209. During the siege, Thiers had authorized a moratorium on the payment of bills and rents until 13 March, but he refused to renew it. Between 13 and 18 March, 150,000 claims for the payment of rent and bills were lodged. The *Commune* renewed the moratorium. See Avineri, *Social and Political Thought*, p. 247.

210. Marx, *Civil War in France*, p. 337. In the 'First Draft', he wrote, 'for the first time petty and *moyenne* middle class has openly rallied round the

workmen's Revolution and proclaimed it the only means to its own eman-
cipation and that of France. It forms with them the bulk of the National
Guard, and sits with them in the Commune, it mediates for them in the
Union Républicaine': Marx, 'First Draft', p. 496.

211. Marx, 'First Draft', p. 496.
212. Marx, *Civil War in France*, p. 339.
213. Marx, 'First Draft', p. 498.
214. Ibid., p. 487.
215. He considered that 'the empire, and Imperialism, with its mere mockery of
Parliament, is the *régime* now flourishing in most of the great military
states of the continent'. Karl Marx, 'Second Draft of *The Civil War in
France*', *MECW*, vol. 22, p. 533.
216. Marx, *Civil War in France*, p. 332.
217. Ibid.
218. Ibid., p. 335. See also the 'First Draft', where the transition to associated
labour is likened to 'the long process of development of new conditions'
which had resulted in the transition from slavery to serfdom and from
serfdom to free labour. 'The working class know that they have to pass
through different phases of class struggle. They know that the superseding
of the economical conditions of the slavery of labour by the conditions of
free and associated labour can only be the progressive work of time': Marx,
'First Draft', p. 491.
219. McLellan, *Karl Marx: His Life and Thought*, p. 400.
220. 'Karl Marx to Dr Kugelmann', 18 June 1871, *MECW*, vol. 44, p. 158.
221. Collins and Abramsky, *Karl Marx and the British Labour Movement*, pp.
211, 215.
222. Marx, *Civil War in France*, p. 355.
223. 'Citizen Marx' told the General Council, 'the English press acted as police
and bloodhounds for Thiers ... The press knew full well the objects and
principles of the International ... and yet it circulated reports to the effect
that the Association included the Fenian brotherhood, the Carbonari, ceased
to exist 1830, the Marianne, Ditto 1854 and other secret Societies.' 'Meeting
of the General Council', 6 June 1871, *MEGA*, I, xxii, p. 560.
224. 'Karl Marx to Dr Kugelmann', 27 July 1871, *MECW*, vol. 44, p. 177.
225. Marx, *Civil War in France*, p. 324.
226. Ibid., p. 352.
227. Thomas Wright, *Our New Masters*, London, Strahan, 1873, pp. 194–9
228. 'Meeting of the General Council', 20 June 1871, *MEGA*, I, xxii, pp. 565–6.
229. 'Eleanor Marx to the Aberdeen Socialist Society', 17 March 1893, cited in
Kapp, *Eleanor Marx*, pp. 134–6.
230. 'Jenny Marx to Ludwig and Gertrud Kugelmann', 21–22 December 1871,
MECW, vol. 44, p. 566. In a more light-hearted vein, she also commented

on her father's efforts to help. Not only had he had to 'fight with all the Governments of the ruling classes', but 'into the bargain, he has hand to hand combats with the "fat, fair and forty" landladies, who attack him, because this or that *Communeux* hasn't paid his rent. Just as he has lost himself in the *abstrakten Gedanken*, in rushes Mrs Smith or Mrs Brown. If only the *Figaro* knew this – what a feuilleton would be offered to his readers!': ibid.

231. 'Declaration to the French People', Tombs, *Paris Commune*, pp. 217–18.

232. James Guillaume, *L'Internationale: Documents et souvenirs (1864–1878)*, Paris, Société nouvelle de librairie et d'édition, 1905, vol. 1, part II, p. 192.

233. The only reference was critical and historical. The 'communal constitution', he argued, 'had been mistaken for an attempt to break up into a federation of small States, as dreamt of by Montesquieu and the Girondins'. Marx, *Civil War in France*, p. 333.

234. Hence Karl's hostility to the word; less than a year before, he had confided to Engels that he hoped for a Prussian victory in the war, because 'centralisation of STATE POWER' would be 'beneficial for the centralisation of the German working class' and 'would also mean the predominance of *our* theory over Proudhon's'. 'Karl Marx to Friedrich Engels', 20 July 1870, *MECW*, vol. 44, pp. 3–4.

235. Archer, *First International in France*, p. 43.

236. César De Paepe (1841–90) was a doctor who had graduated at the Université Libre de Bruxelles. After initially siding with the Jura Federalists in the 1872 split in the International, he came to support the necessity of a social-democratic state for the provision of social services, especially a public health service. In 1877, he helped to establish *Le Socialisme progressif*, a journal which emphasized the role of trade unions and an evolutionary form of socialism. For the significance of his activities in the First International, see William Whitham, 'César De Paepe and the Politics of Collective Property', M.Phil. dissertation, Cambridge University, 2015.

237. Paul Thomas, *Karl Marx and the Anarchists*, London, Routledge and Kegan Paul, 1980, p. 278.

238. William Whitham, 'Anarchism and Federalism in the International Working Men's Association 1864–1877', BA Thesis, Harvard University, 2014, pp. 48–9; Archer, *First International in France*, p. 196.

239. Whitham, 'Anarchism and Federalism', p. 29; G. M. Stekloff, *History of the First International*, London, M. Lawrence, 1928, pp. 141–2.

240. Alexander Herzen, *My Past and Thoughts: The Memoirs of Alexander Herzen*, trans. C. Garnett, New York, A. A. Knopf, 1968, vol. 3, pp. 1351–2. Aleksey Khomyakov was famous among the Moscow intelligentsia of the 1840s for his scepticism about Western Europe and his rehabilitation of Byzantine history and culture: see Pavel V. Annenkov, *The Extraordinary Decade: Literary Memoirs*, ed. Arthur P. Mendel, Ann Arbor, University of Michigan Press, 1968 [1881], pp. 92–101.

241. Annenkov, *Extraordinary Decade*, p. 21.

242. In my approach to Bakunin, I have been greatly indebted to the research and findings of Diana Siclovan. She emphasizes the lasting importance of Bakunin's pre-1848 beliefs, restated, but not fundamentally altered, in the 1860s. See Diana Siclovan, 'Mikhail Bakunin and the Modern Republic 1840–1867', History Dissertation, Cambridge University, 2009.

243. Herzen, *My Past and Thoughts*, vol. 3, p. 1351.

244. M. Bakunin, *Le Catéchisme révolutionnaire*, March 1866, cited in Siclovan, 'Mikhail Bakunin and the Modern Republic', p. 44.

245. Mikhail Bakunin, 'La Question slave', August 1867, p. 3, cited in Siclovan, 'Mikhail Bakunin and the Modern Republic', p. 44. As this passage shows, the term 'anarchist' was not one to which much weight should be attached during this period. For 'anarchist', in Bakunin's writings, simply meant 'federalist', or elsewhere 'socialist'.

246. See Whitham, 'Anarchism and Federalism'.

247. Vyrubov, quoted by E. H. Carr in *Michael Bakunin*, London, Macmillan Press, 1975 [1937], p. 343; or James Joll, *The Anarchists*, London, Eyre and Spottiswoode, 1964, p. 98.

248. Cited in Thomas, *Marx and the Anarchists*, pp. 303–4.

249. Ibid., p. 306.

250. The text of a letter written by Bakunin in 1872, cited in ibid. p. 305.

251. Ibid., pp. 318–19.

252. 'Karl Marx to Friedrich Engels', 4 November 1864, *MECW*, vol. 42, pp. 18–19; ibid., 11 April 1865, p. 140.

253. See the *Neue Rheinische Zeitung*, 5 July 1848. These allegations were withdrawn when George Sand intervened and declared them to have no basis.

254. 'Karl Marx to Friedrich Engels', 4 October 1867, *MECW*, vol. 42, p. 434.

255. 'Mikhail Bakunin to Karl Marx', 22 December 1868, in Guillaume, *L'Internationale*, vol. 1, pp. 103. 170–79.

256. 'Karl Marx to Friedrich Engels', 15 December 1868, *MECW*, vol. 43, p. 190.

257. 'Karl Marx to Friedrich Engels', 14 March 1869, *MECW*, vol. 43, p. 240.

258. 'Meeting of the General Council', 8 August 1871, *MEGA*, I, xxii, p. 591

259. 'Meeting of the General Council', 25 July and 15 August 1871, *MEGA*, I, xxii, pp. 582, 594.

260. Ibid.

261. 'Karl Marx to Jenny Marx', 23 September 1871, *MECW*, vol. 44, p. 220.

262. For a first-hand account of the proceedings at Sonvilliers, see Guillaume, *L'Internationale*, vol. 2, 1907, part IV, pp. 232–44.

263. Karl Marx and Friedrich Engels, 'Fictitious Splits in the International', 5 March 1872, *MECW*, vol. 23, p. 89.

264. For a compelling account of Bakunin's relationship with Nechaev, and more generally the relationships between exiles after 1848, see Carr, *Romantic Exiles*, ch. 14.

265. See, for instance, Marx and Engels, 'Fictitious splits in the International', p. 89.

266. Ibid., pp. 79–123. The pamphlet failed to silence opponents and in Italy Carlo Cafiero accused its authors of 'washing dirty linen in public', while Bakunin considered that 'Mr Marx' had employed his 'habitual weapon, a heap of filth'. See Thomas, *Marx and the Anarchists*, pp. 324–5.

267. 'Karl Marx to César De Paepe', 24 November 1871, *MECW*, vol. 44, pp. 263–4.

268. 'Karl Marx to Dr Kugelmann', 29 July 1872, *MECW*, vol. 44, p. 413.

269. Michael Bakunin, *Statism and Anarchy*, ed. and trans. Marshall Shatz, Cambridge, Cambridge University Press, 1990 [1873], p. 3.

270. L. B. Namier, *1848: The Revolution of the Intellectuals*, London, Oxford Unversity Press, 1971 [1944].

271. Bakunin, *Statism and Anarchy*, p. 194.

272. Ibid.

273. Ibid., pp. 130–31, 140.

274. Ibid., pp. 181, 180, 142, 176.

275. Ibid., pp. 177–8, 23–4.

276. Ibid., pp. 23–4, 177–8.

277. Ibid., p. 141.

278. Ibid., pp. 177, 182, 189.

279. Karl Marx, 'Notes on Bakunin's *Statehood and Anarchy*', April 1874–January 1875, *MECW*, vol. 24, p. 518.

280. Ibid., p. 519.

281. Ibid., pp. 520–521.

282. John Stuart Mill, *Autobiography*, London, Longmans, Green, Reader and Dyer, 1873, p. 694.

283. 'General Council to the Federal Council', pp. 86–8.

284. '(On Trade Unions) Minutes of London Conference of the International', 20 September 1871, *MECW*, vol. 22, p. 614.

285. Gerth (ed.), *First International*, p. 262; but he took a much harder line on the exclusion of 'Section Twelve', the one moment of possible encounter between the International and the representatives of American feminism. Karl considered it an organisation 'got up primarily to forward the chances of Mrs Victoria Woodhull' and to propagate 'those pet doctrines of her party, such as free love, spiritualism, etc.'. He claimed that it was 'composed exclusively of bogus reformers, middle class quacks and trading politicians'. Ibid., p. 264.

286. 'Karl Marx to Wilhelm Liebknecht', 11 February 1878, *MECW*, vol. 45, p. 299.

287. Gerth (ed.), *First International*, p. 285.

288. 'Karl Marx to César De Paepe', 28 May 1872, *MECW*, vol. 44, p. 387.

289. 'Karl Marx to Friedrich Engels', 17 August 1870, *MECW*, vol. 44, p. 51.

290. 'Karl Marx to Sigfrid Meyer', 21 January 1871, *MECW*, vol. 44, p. 102.

291. 'Karl Marx to his Daughters Jenny, Laura and Eleanor', 13 June 1871, *MECW*, vol. 44, p. 153.

292. Ibid.

293. For a full account of the sisters' experiences in the Pyrenees, see Kapp, *Eleanor Marx*, vol. 1, pp. 126–32.

294. 'Karl Marx to Ludwig Kugelmann', 27 July 1871, *MECW*, vol. 44, p. 176.

295. 'Friedrich Engels to Elizabeth Engels', 21 October 1871, *MECW*, vol. 44, p. 229.

296. 'Karl Marx to Friedrich Engels', 15 August 1870, *MECW*, vol. 44, p. 45.

297. 'Karl Marx to Frederick Bolte', 23 November 1871, *MECW*, vol. 44, p. 256.

298. 'Karl Marx to Karl Liebknecht', 17 November 1871, *MECW*, vol. 44, pp. 247–8.

299. 'Karl Marx to César De Paepe', 24 November 1871, *MECW*, vol. 44, p. 263.

300. 'Karl Marx to Paul Lafargue', 21 March 1872, *MECW*, vol. 44, p. 347

12 BACK TO THE FUTURE

1. Karl's idea of the second volume encompassed both Book II on 'The Process of Circulation of Capital' and Book III on 'The Process of Capitalist Production as a Whole'. A third volume was to deal with the history of economic theory. Engels posthumously published Book II and Book III as separate volumes, while Kautsky published the putative third volume as *Theories of Surplus Value*.

2. See Engels, 'Preface to the First German Edition of *Capital*, Book II: *The Process of Circulation of Capital*', *MECW*, vol. 36, pp. 6–9; according to Eleanor Marx, Engels was 'supposed to make something' out of the material for Book II, ibid., pp. 9–10.

3. 'Karl Marx to Maurice Lachâtre', 18 March 1872, *MECW*, vol. 44, p. 344.

4. 'Karl Marx to Laura Lafargue', 28 February 1872, *MECW*, vol. 44, p. 327; 'Karl Marx to Nikolai Danielson', 28 May 1872, *MECW*, vol. 44, p. 385. Karl not only made stylistic changes to make the book more readable in French, but also attempted to make his book politically more appealing by making small but significant changes in his picture of capitalism,

the factory and the nature of work. See Julia Catherine Nicholls, 'French Revolutionary Thought after the Paris Commune, 1871–1885', Ph.D. thesis, Queen Mary University of London, 2015, ch. 3.

5. 'Friedrich Engels to Ludwig Kugelmann', 1 July 1873, *MECW*, vol. 44, pp. 515–16.

6. Ibid., 28 April 1871, pp. 142–3. Kugelmann lived in Hanover.

7. The tensions were also generated by the failure of both Karl and Jenny to recognize the engagement of Eleanor ('Tussy') to the French *Communard* Lissagaray.

8. 'Karl Marx to Friedrich Sorge', 4 August 1874, MECW, vol. 45, p. 28. Friedrich Sorge (1828–1906) took part in the German Revolution of 1848 and afterwards emigrated, first to Switzerland, then to Belgium and finally, in 1852, to the USA. He was the organizer of the American section of the International.

9. 'Karl Marx to Nikolai Danielson', 12 August 1874, *MECW*, vol. 44, p. 522.

10. Karl Marx, *Capital*, vol. III: *The Process of Capitalist Production as a Whole*, *MECW*, vol. 37, p. 240.

11. This question is discussed in sections 5 and 6 of this chapter. The theory of universal development is plainly implied in the original 'Preface to the First German Edition of *Capital*', p. 9.

12. 'Karl Marx to Ludwig Kugelmann', 18 May 1874, *MECW*, vol. 45, p. 17.

13. 'Karl Marx to Friedrich Engels', 18 September 1874, *MECW*, vol. 45, p. 46; 'Eleanor Marx to Jenny Longuet', 5 September 1874, cited in Olga Meier (ed.), *The Daughters of Karl Marx: Family Correspondence 1866–1898*, Harmondsworth, Penguin Books, 1982, p. 117.

14. This passage from Franziska Kugelmann, *Reminiscences*, 1926, is reproduced in David McLellan (ed.), *Karl Marx: Interviews and Recollections*, London, Macmillan, 1981, pp. 286–7. Marx apparently could not tolerate this 'over-zealous' stance 'in a man so much younger than he and took [it] for an encroachment upon his freedom'.

15. 'Friedrich Engels to Wilhelm Bracke', 11 October 1875, *MECW*, vol. 45, p. 96.

16. 'Friedrich Engels to Ludwig Kugelmann', 20 October 1876, *MECW*, vol. 45, p. 162.

17. 'Karl Marx to Nikolai Danielson', 15 November 1878, *MECW*, vol. 45, p. 343.

18. 'Karl Marx to Nikolai Danielson', 10 April 1879, *MECW*, vol. 45, p. 354.

19. 'Friedrich Engels to August Bebel', 30 August 1883, *MECW*, vol. 47, p. 53.

20. 'Friedrich Engels to Friedrich Sorge', 12 September 1874, *MECW*, vol. 45, p. 44; it is estimated that at its height there were around 1,000–1,200 French refugees.

21. 'Jenny Marx to Karl Liebknecht', 26 May 1872, *MECW*, vol. 44, p. 580.

22. Yvonne Kapp, *Eleanor Marx*, 2 vols., London, Lawrence & Wishart, 1972, vol. 1, p. 184; this book remains the definitive study of the life of the Marx family. But see also the challenging recent biography by Rachel Holmes, *Eleanor Marx: A Life*, London, Bloomsburry, 2014.

23. Ibid., p. 217.

24. 'Jenny Marx to Wilhelm Liebknecht', 26 May 1872, *MECW*, vol. 44, p. 581.

25. Ibid.

26. 'Friedrich Engels to Laura Lafargue', 11 March 1872, *MECW*, vol. 44, p. 339.

27. 'Jenny Marx to Friedrich Sorge', 20–21 January 1877, *MECW*, vol. 45, pp. 447–8.

28. 'Friedrich Engels to Friedrich Sorge, 12–17 September 1874, *MECW*, vol. 45, p. 44.

29. See Leslie Derfler, *Paul Lafargue and the Founding of French Marxism 1842–1882*, Cambridge, Mass., Harvard University Press, 1991, pp. 154–5; see also *Correspondence of Friedrich Engels and Paul and Laura Lafargue*, 3 vols., Moscow, Foreign Languages Publishing House, 1959–60.

30. 'Friedrich Engels to Paul Lafargue', 12 September 1880, *MECW*, vol. 46, p. 32.

31. Lafargue later wrote, 'the manifesto of the civil war drawn up by Marx for the General Council invested the Commune with a socialist character that it had certainly not possessed during its ephemeral existence. The Communist refugees thereafter took themselves quite seriously as representing a socialism of which they did not know a single letter.' Paul Lafargue, 'Socialism in France from 1876 to 1896', *Fortnightly Review*, September 1897, cited in Chushichi Tsuzuki, *The Life of Eleanor Marx, 1855–1898: A Socialist Tragedy*, Oxford, Clarendon Press, 1967, pp. 33–4.

32. 'Eleanor Marx to Jenny Longuet', 7 November 1872, in Meier (ed.), *Daughters of Karl Marx*, p. 113; it seems also that thereafter Eleanor and Laura were not on speaking terms.

33. 'Karl Marx to Friedrich Engels', 23 May 1873, *MECW*, vol. 44, p. 496.

34. Ibid., 30 November 1873, pp. 342–3.

35. 'Karl Marx to Ludwig Kugelmann', 19 January 1874, *MECW*, vol. 45, p. 3.

36. Ibid., 18 May 1874, p. 17.

37. Bottigelli Archives, cited in Kapp, *Eleanor Marx*, vol. 1, pp. 153–4.

38. 'Karl Marx to Friedrich Engels', 14 August 1874, *MECW*, vol. 45, p. 34. See also Rachel Holmes, *Eleanor Marx: A Life*, London, Bloomsbury, 2014, pp. 119–24. Eleanor's symptoms appeared similar to those of anorexia nervosa, first fully analysed as a medical condition in Sir William Gull's study *Anorexia Nervosa* in 1873. But it was not until the 1930s that doctors began to understand that eating disorders were in part psychological and emotional rather than wholly physical.

39. Ibid., 19 August 1876, p. 136.

40. Ibid., 23 July 1877, p. 245.

41. Ibid., 17 August 1877, p. 268.

42. 'Karl Marx to Jenny Longuet', 18 August 1881, *MECW*, vol. 46, p. 134.

43. 'Eleanor Marx to Olive Schreiner', 16 June 1884, cited in Kapp, *Eleanor Marx*, vol. 1, p. 221.

44. 'Karl Marx to Laura Lafargue', 4 January 1882, *MECW*, vol. 46, p. 169.

45. 'Karl Marx to Friedrich Engels', 11 November 1882, *MECW*, vol. 46, p. 375.

46. Derfler, *Paul Lafargue*, pp. 158–9.

47. 'Friedrich Engels to Eduard Bernstein', 2–3 November 1882, *MECW*, vol. 46, p. 356.

48. Eleanor Marx, 'Introduction' to *History of the Commune of 1871 from the French of Lissagaray*, New York, International Publishing Company, 1898.

49. Cited in Werner Blumenberg, *Portrait of Marx: An Illustrated Biography*, trans. Douglas Scott, New York, Herder & Herder, 1972, p. 123.

50. 'Karl Marx to Maurice Lachâtre', 12 October 1872, *MECW*, vol. 44, p. 438.

51. 'Karl Marx to Friedrich Sorge', 4 August 1874, *MECW*, vol. 45, p. 30.

52. See Patrick Hutton, *The Cult of the Revolutionary Tradition: The Blanquists in French Politics, 1864–1893*, Berkeley, University of California Press, 1981, chs. v–vii.

53. Henry Mayers Hyndman, *The Record of an Adventurous Life*, London, Macmillan, 1911, p. 272.

54. Ibid., p. 285; Hyndman's book was written for the radical Democratic Federation, which he founded in 1881. In 1884, the Federation renamed itself the Social Democratic Federation, the first explicitly socialist political organization in Britain.

55. Guesde had to rebut claims that he and his colleagues were 'submitting to the will of a man who lived in London outside any party control': see Boris Nicolaievsky and Otto Maenchen-Helfen, *Karl Marx: Man and Fighter*, trans. G. David and E. Mosbacher, London, Allen Lane, 1973 [1933], p. 402. There were also frequent allusions to Karl's Prussian origins: see 'Karl Marx to Friedrich Engels', 30 October 1882, *MECW*, vol. 46, p. 339.

56. *Woodhull and Claflin's Weekly*, 12 August 1871, and see Shlomo Avineri, *The Social and Political Thought of Karl Marx*, Cambridge, Cambridge University Press, 1968, pp. 202–20.

57. Karl Marx, 'On the Hague Congress: A Correspondent's Report of a Speech Made at a Meeting in Amsterdam on September 8 1872', *MECW*, vol. 23, p. 255.

58. Ferdinand Lassalle, 'Arbeiterprogramm', in *Reden und Schriften: Aus der Arbeiteragitation 1862–1864*, ed. Friedrich Jenaczek, Munich, Deutscher Taschenbuch Verlag, 1970, p. 48.

59. Lassalle, 'Was Nun?', in *Reden und Schriften*, pp. 104, 110.

60. 'Karl Marx to Johann Baptist von Schweitzer', 13 October 1868, *MECW*, vol. 43, pp. 132–3.

61. 'Friedrich Engels to Karl Marx', 7 August 1865, *MECW*, vol. 42, p. 178.

62. Karl Marx, *The Civil War in France*, *MECW*, vol. 22, p. 334.

63. Cited in Susanne Miller and Heinrich Potthoff, *A History of German Social Democracy from 1848 to the Present*, Leamington Spa, Berg, 1986, p. 31.

64. August Bebel, *My Life*, London, T. Fisher Unwin, 1912, p. 278.

65. 'Karl Marx to Wilhelm Bracke', 5 May 1875, *MECW*, vol. 24, p. 77.

66. Karl Marx, 'Marginal Notes on the Programme of the German Workers' Party', 1875, *MECW*, vol. 24, p. 95. 'Dictatorship of the proletariat' was a phrase much employed by twentieth-century Communists. Lenin declared it 'the very essence of Marx's teaching' and it became the principal justification of the one-party state. But Karl's use of the phrase was very infrequent – in fact he only made two public references to the term, both in 1850 – and was principally related to the question of sovereignty. This is best illustrated by the use he made of the notion of dictatorship in the *Neue Rheinische Zeitung* in 1848: 'From the beginning we reproached Camphausen [the liberal Prime Minister] for not acting dictatorially, for not shattering and eliminating the remnants of old institutions' (*Neue Rheinische Zeitung*, 14 September 1848 (no. 102), *MECW*, vol. 7, p. 431). The situation to which he was referring was that created by the 18 March uprising in Berlin, which resulted in the monarch being forced to convene a new Prussian Assembly elected on the basis of universal male suffrage. The question then was whether sovereignty now belonged to the Assembly or remained with the monarchy, still relying upon divine right and the undiminished material support of the army and the bureaucracy. In September 1848, this produced a ministerial crisis: the cabinet resigned after being instructed by the Assembly to curb the assaults of the army upon the popularly constituted militia. Ministers protested that this was a legislative incursion into the realm of executive prerogative and a violation of the constitutional principle of separation of powers. But Karl in his journalism protested that they were 'still on revolutionary ground and the pretence we have already reached a stage of a constituted, an established constitutional monarchy only leads to collisions. Every provisional condition of state following a revolution', he went on, 'requires a dictatorship and an energetic dictatorship at that.'

Karl's awareness of the choices posed by this extra-legal situation was especially well-informed as a result of his study of the history of the Convention of 1792. The conflict faced by the Camphausen ministry was not dissimilar to that of the early years of the French Revolution, notably the discussion of the 'suspensive veto', the power left to the king despite the election of the National Assembly. But, in the French case, the problem had been resolved by the king himself. In June 1791, two years into the Revolution, Louis XVI had attempted to escape, having reneged on all measures enacted by the National Assembly since the fall of the Bastille. Once the monarchy lost power and legitimacy, the sovereignty of the people was no longer contested. Crowd action resulted in the massacre of prisoners, the declaration of a republic, the trial and execution of the monarch, and the summoning of a Convention to establish a new constitution. In a private letter (only published by Engels in 1891 after Karl's death) objecting to the Gotha Programme's idea of a people's state (*Volksstaat*), Karl's picture continued the usage of 1848: 'Between capitalist and communist society lies the period of the revolutionary transformation of the one into the other. There corresponds to this also a political transition period, in which the state can be nothing but the revolutionary dictatorship of the proletariat.'

67. Friedrich Engels, 'A Critique of the Draft Social-Democratic Programme of 1891', *MECW*, vol. 27, p. 227; and see Vernon Lidtke, 'German Socialism and Social Democracy 1860–1900', in Gareth Stedman Jones and Gregory Claeys (eds.), *The Cambridge History of Nineteenth-Century Political Thought*, Cambridge, Cambridge University Press, 2011, pp. 804–5.

68. As Bebel remarked, the programme indeed 'left much to be desired . . . yet it was all that could be achieved at the time'. And, he continued, 'it will be seen that it was not an easy matter to satisfy the two old gentlemen in London. What was really a clever tactical move on our part and the result of prudent calculation they regarded as mere weakness'. Bebel, *My Life*, pp. 286–7.

69. Friedrich Engels, 'Preface' to *Ludwig Feuerbach and the End of Classical German Philosophy*, 21 February 1888, *MECW*, vol. 26, pp. 519–20.

70. Paradoxically, anti-socialist laws increased the prominence of the Party as an electoral organization. While leading officials had to move newspapers or journals abroad, Social Democrats were still able to stand in *Reichstag*, state and local elections.

71. 'Karl Marx to Friedrich Engels', 8 January 1868, *MECW*, vol. 42, p. 513; 'Karl Marx to Ludwig Kugelmann', 6 March 1846, *MECW*, vol. 42, p. 544.

72. David Riazanov, *Karl Marx and Friedrich Engels: An Introduction to Their Lives and Work*, London, Monthly Review Press, 1973 [1927], p. 210.

73. Benedikt Kautsky (ed.), *Friedrich Engels' Briefwechsel mit Karl Kautsky*, Vienna, Danubia-Verlag, 1955, p. 477.

74. Friedrich Engels, *Herr Eugen Dühring's Revolution in Science*, *MECW*, vol. 25, p. 27.

75. Friedrich Engels, *Socialism: Utopian and Scientific*, *MECW*, vol. 24, p. 304.

76. Engels, *Herr Eugen Dühring*, pp. 145–6.

77. Ibid., p. 268.

78. Ibid., p. 265.

79. Ibid., p. 267.

80. Ibid., p. 268. As Shlomo Avineri has pointed out, there was a considerable difference between Engels' idea of '*Absterben des Staates*', a biological idea, and Karl's use of the term '*Aufhebung des Staates*', a Hegelian term which implied the abolition and transcendence of the distinction between state and civil society. This meant not that the state would shed one function after another, but that 'the public power would lose its political character'. The choice of persons to perform particular functions would be no different from the choice of a craftsman to execute a particular task, like making a pair of shoes. See Avineri, *Social and Political Thought*, pp. 202–20. The idea that 'the government of persons' would be replaced by the 'administration of things' was Saint-Simonian in origin.

81. Cited in Lidtke, 'German Socialism and Social Democracy', p. 799.

82. 'August Bebel to Friedrich Engels', 28 March 1881, in Werner Blumenberg (ed.), *August Bebels Briefwechsel mit Friedrich Engels*, The Hague, Mouton, 1965, p. 106.

83. 'Programme of the Social Democratic Party of Germany, Erfurt 1891', in Miller and Potthoff, *History of German Social Democracy*, p. 240.

84. Friedrich Engels, 'Second Preface to *Herr Dühring*', 23 September 1885, *MECW*, vol. 25, p. 11.

85. Ibid., p. 23.

86. Friedrich Engels, 'Draft of a Speech at the Graveside of Karl Marx', 14–17 March 1883, *MECW*, vol. 24, p. 463.

87. Engels, *Herr Eugen Dühring*, p. 270.

88. Karl Kautsky, *Ethics and the Materialist Conception of History*, Chicago, C. H. Kerr and Company 1914 [1906], pp. 96–7, 102. The 'materialist conception of history' provided insight into 'the laws of development and of the movements of the social organism, its forces and organs': ibid., p. 201.

89. Karl Marx, 'Afterword to the Second German Edition', in *Capital*, vol. I: *A Critique of Political Economy*, *MECW*, vol. 35, pp. 18–19. Among other claims cited with approval in that passage, it was stated: 'Marx treats the social movement as a process of natural history, governed by laws not only independent of human will, consciousness and intelligence, but rather, on the contrary, determining that will, consciousness and intelligence . . .

That is to say, that not the idea, but the material phenomenon alone can serve as its starting-point.'

90. Engels, *Herr Eugen Dühring*, Part II, ch. X, *MECW*, vol. 25, pp. 211–44. Apart from criticizing his treatment of the Greeks, Karl was mainly concerned to defend his view of the importance of William Petty, and to mock the arguments of David Hume.

91. Hyndman, *Record of an Adventurous Life*, p. 279.

92. 'Programme of the Social Democratic Party of Germany, Erfurt 1891', p. 240.

93. 'Friedrich Engels to August Bebel', 4 April 1885, *MECW*, vol. 47, p. 271.

94. Marx, *Capital*, vol. III, p. 245.

95. Friedrich Engels, 'Karl Marx's Funeral', *MECW*, vol. 24, p. 467.

96. The claim originated in a misfiling in the archives at his family home at Down of one of the letters written by Darwin. The letter politely refusing a dedication was written not to Karl, but to Edward Aveling (Eleanor Marx's partner). Karl did send a copy of the second, 1873 edition of *Capital* to Darwin, probably at the urging of Engels.

97. 'Karl Marx to Friedrich Engels', 7 August 1866, *MECW*, vol. 42, p. 304.

98. Charles Darwin, *The Descent of Man*, 2 vols., London, J. Murray, 1871, vol. 1, pp. 96–7.

99. Karl Marx, *Economic and Philosophical Manuscripts of 1844*, *MECW*, vol. 3, p. 337.

100. Ibid., pp. 275, 276.

101. 'Karl Marx to Friedrich Engels', 18 January 1861, *MECW*, vol. 41, pp. 246–7.

102. Ibid., 18 June 1862, p. 381.

103. Ibid., 7 August 1866, *MECW*, vol. 42, pp. 304–5.

104. 'Friedrich Engels to Karl Marx', 2 October 1866, *MECW*, vol. 42, p. 320; and see also ibid., 5 October 1866, pp. 323–4.

105. 'Karl Marx to Dr Kugelmann', 9 October 1866, *MECW*, vol. 42, p. 327.

106. Gareth Stedman Jones (ed.), *Karl Marx and Friedrich Engels: The Communist Manifesto*, London, Penguin Books, 2002, p. 224.

107. Karl Marx, 'The British Rule in India', 10 June 1853, *MECW*, vol. 12, p. 128.

108. Karl Marx, *A Contribution to the Critique of Political Economy*, 1859, *MECW*, vol. 29, p. 275; Karl Marx, *Capital*, vol. I: *A Critique of Political Economy*, *MECW*, vol. 35, p. 88.

109. 'Karl Marx to Friedrich Engels', 7 November 1868, *MECW*, vol. 35, p. 9.

110. Karl Marx, *Das Kapital*, vol. I: *Kritik der politischen Oekonomie*, Hildesheim, Gerstenberg, 1980 (this is a fascimile of the first German edition, Hamburg, Verlag von Otto Meissner, 1867), p. 763. Even in 1870, when he had first begun to read Russian, his attitudes towards the Populist

view of the Russian village commune remained the same. In a critical note appended to his annotation of Flerovskii's 'Peasant Reform and the Communal Ownership of Land', Karl wrote, 'From this rubbish, it emerges that Russian communal property is compatible with Russian barbarism, but not with bourgeois civilisation'. Cited in H. Wada, 'Marx and Revolutionary Russia', in Teodor Shanin (ed.), *Late Marx and the Russian Road*, London, Routledge & Kegan Paul, 1983, p. 45.

111. For a detailed analysis of the changes of plan occurring in the successive drafts and plans of his critique of political economy, see James D. White, *Karl Marx and the Intellectual Origins of Dialectical Materialism*, Basingstoke, Macmillan, 1996, ch. 4.

112. Karl Marx, 'The So-Called Primitive Accumulation', in *Capital*, vol. I, Part VIII, *MECW*, vol. 35, pp. 704–61.

113. Justus Möser, *Osnabrückische Geschichte*, 2nd edn, Berlin/Stettin, 1780 Nicolai, vol. 1, p. 10; and for a survey of eighteenth- and nineteenth-century German and French theories of early landownership, see Alfons Dopsch, *The Economic and Social Foundations of European Civilization*, London, Kegan Paul, Trench, Trubner, 1937 [Vienna, 1923–4], ch. 1.

114. Justus Möser, 'Preface' to *Osnabrückische Geschichte*, Osnabrück, Schmid, 1768, pp. [ix–x].

115. Möser, *Osnabrückische Geschichte*, 2nd edn, vol. 1, p. 13.

116. K. F. Eichhorn, 'Über den Ursprung der städtischen Verfassung in Deutschland', *Zeitschrift für geschichtliche Rechtswissenschaft*, 1 (1815), p. 172, cited in Dopsch, *Economic and Social Foundations*, p. 7.

117. See Adam Kuper, *The Invention of Primitive Society: Transformations of an Illusion*, London, Routledge, 1988, p. 22.

118. John Mitchell Kemble, *The Saxons in England: A History of the English Commonwealth till the Period of the Norman Conquest*, London, Longman, Brown, Green and Longmans, 1849, vol. 1, pp. 53–4.

119. William Stubbs, *The Constitutional History of England, in Its Origins and Development*, 3 vols., Oxford, Clarendon Press, 1874, vol. 1, p. 11; J. W. Burrow, *A Liberal Descent: Victorian Historians and the English Past*, Cambridge, Cambridge University Press, 1981, p. 110.

120. Edward A. Freeman, *The Chief Periods of European History: Six Lectures Read in the University of Oxford in Trinity Term, 1885*, London, Macmillan, 1886, p. 64.

121. Cited in Burrow, *Liberal Descent*, p. 176, n. 106.

122. John Richard Green, *A Short History of the English People, with Maps and Tables*, London, Macmillan, 1874, p. 4.

123. This shift of position was registered in the successive editions of Eichhorn's *Deutsche Staats- und Rechtsgeschichte*. Dopsch claimed that Eichhorn's study, which went through many editions, gradually became the standard

history of German law, and that 'his Mark theory was destined to become the cornerstone of the whole constitutional and legal history of that country'. Dopsch, *Economic and Social Foundations*, p. 8.

124. On the findings of Olufsen and Hanssen, see Hans-Peter Harstick, *Karl Marx und die zeitgenössische Verfassungsgeschichtsschreibung*, Münster, 1974, pp. xxxviii–xlii.

125. August von Haxthausen, *Über die Agrarverfassung in den Fürstenthümern Paderborn und Corvey und deren Conflicte in der gegenwärtigen Zeit: nebst Vorschlägen, die den Grund und Boden belastenden Rechte und Verbindlichkeiten daselbst aufzulösen*, Berlin, Reimer, 1829. Haxthausen was from the Catholic nobility of Westphalia, and was an enthusiast for aristocratic paternalism and an 'organic' theory of society, of the kind advocated by Adam Müller. He was a critic of the spread of market relations into the countryside. In the 1830s, his work was greatly admired by the Crown Prince, Friedrich Wilhelm, who urged the Ministry of Justice to provide financial support for him to report on agrarian relations in the Prussian provinces. His work was strongly criticized in the western provinces, especially the Rhineland, where he was accused of ignorance of the law. The Interior Minister, von Schuckmann, considered his work mainly to be propaganda, supported by little more than anecdote. The ministry withdrew support for his work in 1842.

Since his work met with an increasingly frosty reception in Prussia, he shifted his attention to an allegedly primitive Slavic agrarian constitution which supposedly replicated patterns still existing in the more remote areas of Germany, including the uplands of Trier (though, as he admitted, his claims were only based on hearsay). See August von Haxthausen, *Über den Ursprung und die Grundlagen der Verfassung in den ehemals slavischen Ländern Deutschlands, im Allgemeinen und des Herzogthums Pommern im Besondern: eine Einladungsschrift zur Erörterung und litterarischen Besprechung*, Berlin, Krause, 1842.

On the strength of these findings, he was invited by the Russian imperial government to travel through the country and report on the state of the peasantry. He made the trip in the winter of 1843–4. Knowing no Russian, he worked through an interpreter; he stayed mainly in the towns, especially Moscow, where Russian Slavophil intellectuals predictably accepted his claims. He published the first two volumes of *Studien über die inneren Zustände, das Volksleben und insbesondere die ländlichen Einrichtungen Russlands* in 1846, with a final volume in 1852. It was translated into French, English and Russian. Despite its fanciful assumptions and its feeble basis in fact, the study was immediately accepted not only by Slavophils, but also by the radical intelligentsia, notably by Alexander Herzen and Nicolai Chernyshevsky. See Tracy Dennison and A. W. Carus, 'The Invention of the Russian Rural Commune: Haxthausen and the Evidence', *Historical Journal*, 46/03 (September 2003), pp. 561–82.

126. Harstick, *Karl Marx und die zeitgenössische Verfassungsgeschichtschreibung*, pp. xxxviii–xlii.

127. Georg Ludwig von Maurer, *Einleitung zur Geschichte der Mark-, Hof-, Dorf- und Stadtverfassung und der öffentlichen Gewalt*, Vienna, Brand, 1896 [1854].

128. Dithmarsch, north-east of Hamburg, possessed a high degree of autonomy. It was famous for its dykes and reclamation of land from the sea, and also for its resistance to feudalism and its establishment of an independent peasant republic in the fifteenth century.

129. Maurer, *Mark-, Hof-, Dorf- und Stadtverfassung*, pp. 1–6.

130. Henry Sumner Maine, *Village-Communities in the East and West: Six Lectures Delivered at Oxford*, London, J. Murray, 1871, p. 11.

131. Maine, *Village-Communities*, pp. 6–7.

132. Burrow, *Liberal Descent*, p. 169.

133. Kemble, *Saxons in England*, vol. 1, p. 74; Maine, *Village-Communities*, p. 9.

134. Ibid., p. 12.

135. Henry Sumner Maine, *Ancient Law: Its Connection with the Early History of Society and Its Relation to Modern Ideas*, 1861, London, J. Murray, p. 170.

136. Henry Sumner Maine, 'The Decay of Feudal Property in France and England', *Fortnightly Review*, vol. 21 (new series), April 1877, pp. 465, 467.

137. See Kuper, *Invention of Primitive Society*, pp. 29–32; Karuna Mantena, *Alibis of Empire: Henry Maine and the Ends of Liberal Imperialism*, Princeton, Princeton University Press, 2010, pp. 98–107.

138. Maine, *Ancient Law*, pp. 89, 120.

139. Maine, *Village-Communities*, pp. 76, 77.

140. See Erwin Nasse, *On the Agricultural Community of the Middle Ages, and Inclosures of the Sixteenth Century in England*, trans. Colonel H. A. Ouvry, London, Macmillan, 1871.

141. Henry Sumner Maine, *Lectures on the Early History of Institutions*, London, J. Murray, 1875, pp. 1–2.

142. The works in which Herzen developed his position were *From the Other Shore*, written in 1848 and 1849, the first German edition appearing in 1855, and *The Russian People and Socialism: An Open Letter to Jules Michelet*, written in French and published in 1851.

143. 'Karl Marx to Friedrich Engels', 14 March 1868, *MECW*, vol. 42, p. 547.

144. Ibid., 25 March 1868, pp. 557–8.

145. Karl Marx, drafts of the letter to Vera Zasulich, 'First Draft', February/March 1881, *MECW*, vol. 24, p. 350. Vera Zasulich, on behalf of the members of Black Repartition, had written to Karl on 16 February 1881,

asking about the future of the village commune. Karl wrote four drafts of a reply, finally sending a reply on 8 March 1881.

146. Maurer, *Mark-, Hof-, Dorf- und Stadtverfassung*, pp. xxxvii–xxxviii.

147. 'Karl Marx to Friedrich Engels', 25 March 1868, *MECW*, vol. 42, p. 557.

148. August von Haxthausen, *Studies on the Interior of Russia*, ed. S. Frederick Starr, Chicago, University of Chicago Press, 1972, p. 281.

149. White, *Karl Marx*, p. 224.

150. Marx, *Capital*, vol. I, p. 90. What is translated as 'direct relations of subjection' in the German original reads 'unmittelbaren Herrschafts- und Knechtschafts-verhältnissen', terms which standardly referred to lordship and bondage: see Marx, *Kapital*, vol. I, p. 40. This would suggest that Karl included Russian serfdom in this list of 'ancient Asian and other ancient modes of production'.

151. Even in 1870, when he had first begun to read Russian, his attitude towards the Populist view of the Russian village commune remained the same. In a critical note appended to his annotation of Flerovskii's 'Peasant Reform and the Communal Ownership of Land', Karl wrote, 'From this rubbish, it emerges that Russian communal property is compatible with Russian barbarism, but not with bourgeois civilisation'. Cited in Wada, 'Marx and Revolutionary Russia', p. 45.

152. Georgi Plekhanov (1856–1918), a founder of the social-democratic movement in Russia. Originally an active Populist, he turned against the terrorist tactics of Populism, and formed a breakaway group, *Chernyi Peredel* (Black Repartition). In 1880, he was forced to leave Russia and spent the next thirty-seven years in exile in Geneva. It was there after a period of study in 1882–3 that he declared himself a 'Marxist'. In September 1883, Plekhanov joined with Axelrod, Lev Dutsch, Vasily Ignatov and Vera Zasulich to found the first Russian Marxist political grouping, the Emancipation of Labour Group. Among those attracted to the group were Peter Struve, Iulii Martov and Vladimir Ulianov (Lenin).

Vera Zasulich (1849–1919), originally a supporter of Bakunin and acquaintance of Nechaev, in 1878 shot and seriously wounded Colonel Fyodor Trepov, the governor of St Petersburg. Acquitted at her trial she escaped to Geneva, where she co-founded the Emancipation of Labour Group.

153. Marx, drafts of the letter to Vera Zasulich, February–March 1881, pp. 353, 354, 363, 368.

154. Cited in Wada, 'Marx and Revolutionary Russia', p. 48. This essay is invaluable in its meticulous tracking of Karl's changing position on Russia in the 1870s.

155. Marx, 'Afterword to the Second German Edition', in *Capital*, vol. I, p. 15. By contrast, Engels was not prepared to abandon the coupling of the village commune with despotism. In *Anti-Dühring*, he stated, 'Where the ancient communities have continued to exist, they have for thousands of years

formed the basis of the cruellest form of state, Oriental despotism, from India to Russia. It was only where these communities dissolved that the peoples made progress of themselves': Engels, *Herr Eugen Dühring*, p. 168.

156. Karl drafted but did not send a letter to Nicolai Mikhailovsky, the editor of *Otechestvenniye Zapiski*. Mikhailovsky described *Capital* as a 'historico-philosophical theory of universal progress' which argued that every country would undergo the same process of peasant expropriation as that experienced by England and assumed that Karl's attitude to Populism was summed up by his denunciation of Herzen. Karl referred him to the 1875 French edition and his praise of Chernyshevsky, implying that he shared the analysis of the Populists. See Wada, 'Marx and Revolutionary Russia', pp. 57–60. For the letter, see *MECW*, vol. 24, pp. 196–201.

157. Marx, drafts of the letter to Vera Zasulich, 'First Draft', pp. 357, 360.

158. Ibid., 'Second Draft', p. 361. But it should not be forgotten that this draft letter was never sent.

159. In the twentieth century, the story of Karl's changing views about revolution in Russia, and 'skipping a stage', was generally treated as a particular response to the Russian situation and Russian interest in *Capital*. It was of particular interest since 'Marxism' in late-nineteenth-century Russia was associated with the rejection of the Populist position. This was true both of Plekhanov, the so-called 'father of Russian Marxism', and his Geneva-based Group for the Emancipation of Labour, and of Lenin, whose *Development of Capitalism in Russia* had appeared in 1899.

160. 'Karl Marx to Friedrich Adolf Sorge', 17 September 1877, *MECW*, vol. 45, p. 278.

161. 'Karl Marx to Friedrich Engels', 14 June 1853, *MECW*, vol. 24, p. 352.

162. Marx, drafts of the letter to Vera Zasulich, 'First Draft', p. 352.

163. Karl Marx, 'Excerpts from M. M. Kovalevsky, *Obščinnoe Zemlevladenie. Pričiny, khod i posledstvija ego razloženija*, Part One, Moscow 1879', in Lawrence Krader, *The Asiatic Mode of Production: Sources, Development and Critique in the Writings of Karl Marx*, Assen, Van Gorcum, 1975, p. 406.

164. Marx, drafts of the letter to Vera Zasulich, 'First Draft' and 'Third Draft', pp. 359, 365.

165. As Karl had written to Kugelmann about his theoretical approach in 1862, 'On the basis thus provided', his argument 'could easily be pursued by others . . . with the exception, perhaps, of the relationship between the various forms of state and the various economic structures of society'. 'Karl Marx to Ludwig Kugelmann', 28 December 1862, *MECW*, vol. 41, p. 435.

166. See Donald Kelley, 'The Science of Anthropology: An Essay on the Very Old Marx', *Journal of the History of Ideas*, 45 (1984), pp. 245–63.

167. Marx, drafts of the letter to Vera Zasulich, 'First Draft', p. 349.

168. Ibid., 'Second Draft', pp. 361, 362.

169. Ibid., 'First Draft', p. 360.

170. Ibid., pp. 358–9.

171. Karl's comment in the original reads, 'Dch. d. Grecian gens gukt d. Wilde (Iroquois z.B.) aber auch unverkennbar durch.' Karl Marx, 'Excerpts from Lewis Henry Morgan, *Ancient Society*', in Lawrence Krader (ed.), *The Ethnological Notebooks of Karl Marx*, Assen, Van Gorcum, 1974, p. 198.

172. Lewis Henry Morgan, *Ancient Society, or, Researches in the Lines of Human Progress from Savagery through Barbarism to Civilisation*, London, Macmillan, 1877.

173. Marx, 'Excerpts from Lewis Henry Morgan', in Krader (ed.), *Ethnological Notebooks*, p. 120. For Fourier's theory, see Gareth Stedman Jones and Ian Patterson (eds.), *Charles Fourier: The Theory of the Four Movements*, Cambridge, Cambridge University Press, 1996, pp. 56–74.

174. Marx, 'Excerpts from Lewis Henry Morgan', in Krader (ed.), *Ethnological Notebooks*, p. 102. Here there was a clear contrast to be found with the approach of Darwin. Darwin's only direct intervention in the debate about primitive society was to disagree with McLennan about 'the promiscuity' of 'the horde', and to argue that sexual jealousy among savages had from the beginning led to the inculcation of female chastity as a virtue and therefore to the establishment of orderly sexual relations: Darwin, *Descent of Man*, vol. 1, pp. 96–7.

175. For the position he had adopted in 1844, see especially *Economic and Philosophical Manuscripts of 1844*, *MECW*, vol. 3, pp. 229–349.

176. Karl Marx, 'Excerpts from Henry Sumner Maine, *Lectures on the Early History of Institutions*', in Krader (ed.), *Ethnological Notebooks*, p. 324.

177. Johann Jakob Bachofen, *Das Mutterrecht*, Stuttgart, Krais & Hoffmann, 1861; John Ferguson McLennan, *Primitive Marriage: An Inquiry into the Origin of the Form of Capture in Marriage Ceremonies*, Edinburgh, Adam and Charles Black, 1865; Morgan, *Ancient Society*.

178. Marx, 'Excerpts from Henry Sumner Maine', in Krader (ed.), *Ethnological Notebooks*, p. 326.

179. Ibid., p. 292.

180. Ibid., p. 329.

181. Marx, drafts of the letter to Vera Zasulich, 'First Draft', p. 350. Karl cited the argument of Morgan, 'an American writer quite free from any suspicion of revolutionary tendencies', that '"the new system" towards which modern society tends "will be a REVIVAL IN SUPERIOR FORM of an archaic social type". So we must not let ourselves be alarmed at the word "archaic".'

182. Not least because the period of the 'Great Depression' was also a period in which wage-earners experienced a substantial increase in their standard of

living. According to Karl Borchardt, between 1880 and 1895 German workers experienced their greatest rise in real wages in the nineteenth century.

183. 'Karl Marx to Vera Zasulich', 8 March 1881, *MECW*, vol. 46, p. 71. This was essentially the same as the fourth draft of this letter: see *MECW*, vol. 24, pp. 370–71. For further exploration of this theme, see Gareth Stedman Jones, 'Radicalism and the Extra-European World: The Case of Karl Marx', in Duncan Bell (ed.), *Victorian Visions of Global Order: Empire and International Relations in Nineteenth-Century Political Thought*, Cambridge, Cambridge University Press, 1997, pp. 186–214.

184. Karl Marx and Friedrich Engels, 'Preface to the Russian Edition of 1882', in Stedman Jones (ed.), *Communist Manifesto*, p. 196.

185. 'Karl Marx to Friedrich Engels', 1 March 1882, *MECW*, vol. 46, p. 213.

186. David McLellan, *Karl Marx: His Life and Thought*, London, Macmillan, 1973, p. 450.

187. Eleanor Marx, 'Illness and Death of Marx', in McLellan (ed.), *Karl Marx: Interviews and Recollections*, p. 128.

EPILOGUE

1. François Guizot, *Essais sur l'histoire de France . . . pour servir de complément aux observations sur l'histoire de France de l'Abbé Mably*, Paris, J. L. J. Brière, 1823, p. 111.

2. Fustel de Coulanges, *Le Problème des origines de la propriété foncière*, Brussels, Alfred Vromant et Cie, 1889; an English translation appeared soon afterwards. See Fustel de Coulanges, *The Origin of Property in Land*, trans. Margaret Ashley, with an introductory chapter on the English manor by W. J. Ashley, London, Swan Sonnenschein, 1891.

3. Frederic Seebohm, *The English Village Community – Examined in Its Relations to the Manorial and Tribal Systems and the Common or Open Field System of Husbandry: An Essay in Economic History*, London, Longmans, Green & Co., 1883; Ashley, 'Introductory Essay', in de Coulanges, *Origin of Property in Land*; Paul Vinogradoff, *Villainage in England: Essays in English Medieval History*, Oxford, Clarendon Press, 1968 [1892].

4. Simon J. Cook, 'The Making of the English: English History, British Identity, Aryan Villages, 1870–1914', *Journal of the History of Ideas*, 75/4 (October 2014), pp. 629–49; and for a more general study of Marshall's early formation, see Simon J. Cook, *The Intellectual Foundations of Alfred Marshall's Economic Science: A Rounded Globe of Knowledge*, Cambridge, Cambridge University Press, 2009.

5. de Coulanges, *Origin of Property in Land*, pp. 122, 127.

6. See Karl Lamprecht, *Deutsches Wirtschaftsleben im Mittelalter*, 4 vols., Leipzig, A. Dürr, 1885–6, vol. 1, pp. 451ff.; A. Dopsch, *The Economic and Social Foundations of European Civilization*, London, Kegan Paul, Trench, Trubner, 1937 [Vienna, 1923–4], p. 27.

7. de Coulanges, *Origin of Property in Land*, pp. 110–11.

8. 'Friedrich Engels to Karl Marx', 15 December 1882, *MECW*, vol. 46, p. 400. This letter contains a fairly comprehensive demolition of Maurer's approach.

9. Friedrich Engels, 'Afterword' (1894) to 'On Social Relations in Russia', 1875, *MECW*, vol. 27, pp. 424, 431. This was a postscript to the reissue of an attack by Engels on Petr Tkatchev, a follower of Herzen, Haxthausen and Bakunin.

10. Ibid., pp. 425–6.

11. Lewis Henry Morgan, *Ancient Society, or, Researches in the Lines of Human Progress from Savagery through Barbarism to Civilisation*, ed. Eleanor Burke Leacock, Cleveland, World Pub. Co., 1963 [1877], p. 462.

12. On McIlvaine and his liberal Calvinist congregation, see Adam Kuper, *The Invention of Primitive Society: Transformations of an Illusion*, London, Routledge, 1988, pp. 43–6.

13. Lewis Henry Morgan, *The American Beaver and His Works*, Philadelphia, J. B. Lippincott & Co., 1868.

14. Kuper, *Invention of Primitive Society*, pp. 51–8.

15. George Grote, *History of Greece*, 3rd edition, London, John Murray, 1851.

16. Morgan, *Ancient Society*, p. 554.

17. 'Karl Marx to Friedrich Engels', 7 August 1866, *MECW*, vol. 42, p. 304; ibid., 3 October 1866, p. 322.

18. G. Plekhanov [N. Beltov], *The Development of the Monist View of History*, Moscow, Foreign Languages Publishing House, 1956 [1895], pp. 129–30.

19. Ibid., p. 218.

20. David Riazanov (ed.), *Marx–Engels Archiv: Zeitschrift des Marx–Engels-Instituts in Moskau*, Frankfurt am Main, Marx-Engels Archiv Verlagsgesellschaft, 1928, vol. 1, pp. 309–45. All serious studies of Marx are hugely indebted to the pioneer work of collecting and editing the writings and correspondence of Marx accomplished by David Riazanov. The first volume of the *Marx–Engels Gesamtausgabe* began in 1927, and since 1991 has been continued by the Berlin-Brandenburgische Akademie der Wissenschaften.

An outspoken critic of Stalin, Riazanov refused to compromise scholarly principles. He was dismissed from the Marx–Engels Institute, which he founded in Moscow in 1921, and was shot in Moscow in 1938. For an account of Riazanov's scholarly achievements and career, see Jonathan Beecher and Valerii N. Formichev, 'French Socialism in Lenin's and Stalin's Moscow: David Riazanov and the French Archive of the Marx–Engels Institute', *Journal of Modern History*, 78/1 (March 2006), pp. 119–43.

21. As discussed earlier, where Karl had considered that the Russian village commune could provide a direct starting point or element of regeneration in Russian society. See also Vera Zasulich to Karl Marx, 16 February 1881. 'This question is a question of life and death, in my opinion, especially for our socialist party. Even the personal destiny of our socialist revolutionaries will depend upon the way you decide to answer it': 'Vera Zasulich to Karl Marx', 16 February 1881, *Marx–Engels Archiv*, vol. 1, p. 316.

22. Ibid., p. 309. According to the rumours circulating in Geneva at the time and for several years afterwards, it was claimed in 1879 that Karl had even offered to write a pamphlet on the question.

23. The letter was so completely forgotten that, for example, Axelrod, who was in Romania in the winter of 1880–81 (the time needing to be considered for the receipt of the letter), remembered nothing about the letter Vera Zasulich received, or conversation about this letter, which it undoubtedly occasioned – nor any other thing relating to it. Ibid., p. 310.

Bibliography

References to the works of Marx and Engels are to be found in the following editions:

Scholarly editions

Karl Marx-Friedrich Engels Historisch-Kritische Gesamtausgabe (*MEGA*), Berlin, 1927–35
Karl Marx, Friedrich Engels Gesamtausgabe, Berlin 1977–

Popular editions

Karl Marx and Friedrich Engels, *Werke* (*MEW*), 43 vols., Berlin, 1956–1990
Karl Marx and Friedrich Engels Collected Works (*MECW*), 50 vols., Moscow, London and New York, 1975–2005

The history of the Marx–Engels archives and their publication in the twentieth century was far from straightforward. At Marx's death in 1883, his papers were bequeathed to Engels, who in turn left them to Marx' daughters, first to Eleanor until her death in 1898, and then to Laura Lafargue until her own in 1910. Engels in 1895 bequeathed his own papers to the German Social Democratic Party (SPD), with August Bebel and Eduard Bernstein acting as trustees. After 1910, the bulk of the Marx papers were added to the Engels papers and deposited in the archives of the Social Democratic Party in Berlin.

The idea of publishing the works of Marx (and possibly of Engels) was discussed at a meeting of Austro-Marxists in 1910. Nothing came of it. But after the Russian Revolution it was taken up by David Ryazanov in Moscow in the 1920s, and he was allowed to copy the papers in Berlin. He planned the original publication of the *Historisch-Kritische Gesamtausgabe* (*MEGA*), an edition of forty-two volumes to be published in Frankfurt and Berlin. Twelve volumes were published between 1927 and 1941, but collaboration between the SPD and Moscow had already ended in 1928, after Soviet Communism entered an ultra-left phase. Hitler's seizure of power and the escalation of Stalinist terror in the 1930s resulted in the execution of Ryazanov and the termination of the project. The Marx–Engels papers were taken to Holland, and during the Second World War to England. They had been sold to a Dutch insurance company, which donated them to the International Institute of Social History (IISH) in Amsterdam.

After Stalin's death in 1956, renewed interest in the continuation of *MEGA* was expressed by the Moscow and Berlin Institutes of Marxism–Leninism. Collaboration with the Amsterdam Institute was necessary as two thirds of the archival material was kept in Amsterdam, and the rest in Moscow. But this was impossible, since the Communist Party insisted upon political control of the project. Nevertheless, a more modest and unofficial form of cooperation did emerge and, between 1972 and 1991, thirty-six volumes resulted from it.

Despite these unpromising beginnings, much of the scholarship accompanying the publication of these volumes was of high quality and acquired authoritative status. But the publication of each volume continued to be conceived in a Marxist–Leninist framework. This means that the entire *MEGA* series before the 1990s has to be treated with caution. Not only were there politically inspired omissions, but in some important instances – the *1844 Manuscripts* or the *German Ideology* for instance – published volumes suffered from distortion of the organization, intention and status of the texts.

The *Marx-Engels-Werke* (*MEW*) was published in forty-three volumes in Berlin between 1956 and 1990 and was intended for a wider readership. Likewise, the *Karl Marx and Friedrich Engels Collected Works* (*MECW*), published in Moscow, London and New York between 1975 and 2005 in fifty volumes, was aimed at a lay public. But since these editions were also published under Communist Party editorial control, their reliability is as limited as that of *MEGA*.

Following the fall of the Berlin Wall and the closure of the Institutes of Marxism–Leninism in Berlin and Moscow 1990, the continued publication of the works was entrusted to the newly established *Internationale Marx-Engels-Stiftung* in Amsterdam. For some time, the future of the project remained in doubt owing to a lack of sufficient funding. But from 1993 groups supported by the Amsterdam Institute, the *Karl-Marx-Haus* in Trier and the European Research Council were entrusted with the production of specific volumes. In Germany itself as a result of a decision by the German Chancellor, Helmut Kohl, financial support for the production of the *MEGA* was provided under the auspices of the *Berlin-Brandenburgische Akademie der Wissenschaften*.

The completion of the project is planned for 2025, a century after it was first conceived. Of the planned 114 volumes, sixty-two have so far been produced.

OTHER PRIMARY DOCUMENTS

Karl Marx, *Das Kapital: Kritik der politischen Ökonomie*, Hildesheim, Gerstenberg, 1980 [Meissner, Hamburg, 1867 (Urausgabe – first edition)]

Karl Marx, *Grundrisse: Foundations of the Critique of Political Economy (Rough Draft)*, trans. Martin Nicolaus, London, Allen Lane and New Left Review, 1973

H. Gerth (ed.), *The First International: Minutes of the Hague Congress of 1872*, Madison, Wisc., University of Wisconsin Press, 1958

Deutsch-Französische Jahrbücher, eds. Arnold Ruge and Karl Marx, Leipzig, Verlag Philipp Reclam jun, 1973 [1844]

Vorwärts! Parise Signale aus Kunst, Wissenschaft, Theater, Musik und geselligen Leben, publ. by Heinrich Börnstein with the collaboration of L. F. C. Bernays, A. Ruge, H. Heine, K. Marx and F. Engels, 1844–5 (repr. Zentralantiquariat der Deutschen Demokratischen Republik, Leipzig, 1975)

Neue Rheinische Zeitung, Organ der Demokratie, 2 vols., 1848–9 (editor-in-chief Karl Marx; eds. Heinrich Bürgers, Ernst Dronke, Friedrich Engels, Ferdinand Freiligrath, Georg Weerth, Ferdinand Wolff, Wilhelm Wolff), Glashütten im Taunus, Verlag Detlev Auvermann KG, 1973)

PRIMARY SOURCES

Annenkov, Pavel V., *The Extraordinary Decade: Literary Memoirs*, ed. Arthur P. Mendel, Ann Arbor, University of Michigan Press, 1968 [1881]

Babbage, Charles, *On the Economy of Machinery and Manufactures*, London, Charles Knight, 1832

Bachofen, Johann Jakob, *Das Mutterrecht*, Stuttgart, Krais and Hoffman, 1861

Bakunin, Michael, *Statism and Anarchy*, trans. and ed. Marshall S. Shatz, Cambridge, Cambridge University Press, 1990 [1873]

Bauer, Bruno, *Briefwechsel zwischen Bruno Bauer und Edgar Bauer während der Jahre 1839–1842 aus Bonn und Berlin*, Charlottenburg, Egbert Bauer, 1844

———, *The Trumpet of the Last Judgement against Hegel the Atheist and Anti-Christ: An Ultimatum*, trans. Lawrence Stepelevich, Lewiston, NY, Edwin Mellen Press, 1989 [1841]

Bauer, Edgar, *Bruno Bauer und seine Gegner*, Berlin, Jonas, 1842

Bebel, August, *My Life*, London, T. F. Unwin, 1912

Bebel, August, and Eduard Bernstein (eds.), *Der Briefwechsel zwischen F. Engels und K. Marx*, 4 vols., Stuttgart, Dietz, 1913

Bernier, François, *Voyages contenant la description des États du Grand Mogol*, Paris, Imprimé aux frais du gouvernement, 1830

Blanc, Louis, *The History of Ten Years 1830–1840*, 2 vols., London, Chapman and Hall, 1844–5

——, *Révolution Française: Histoire de dix ans, 1830–1840*, 5 vols., Paris, Pagnerre, 1841–4

Blumenberg, Werner (ed.), *August Bebels Briefwechsel mit Friedrich Engels*, The Hague, Mouton, 1965

Bluntschli, Johann Caspar (ed.), *Die Kommunisten in der Schweiz nach den bei Weitling vorgefundenen Papieren* ('Communists in Switzerland According to Papers Found in Weitling's Possession'), Zurich, Druck von Orell, 1843 (repr. 1972, Glashütten im Taunus, Auvermann)

Böhm-Bawerk, Eugen von, *Karl Marx and the Close of His System: A Criticism*, trans. Alice M. Macdonald, with a preface by James Bonar, London, T. Fisher Unwin, 1898

——, *Zum Abschluss des Marxschen Systems*, Berlin, Haering, 1896

Born, Stefan, *Erinnerungen eines Achtundvierzigers*, Leipzig, G. H. Meyer, 1898

Börne, Ludwig, *Lettres écrites de Paris pendant les années 1830 et 1831*, trans. F. Guiran, Paris, Paulin, 1832

Börnstein, Heinrich, *Fünfundsiebzig Jahre in der alten und neuen Welt: Memoiren eines Unbedeutenden*, 2 vols., Leipzig, Otto Wigand, 1884

Buchez, Philippe Joseph B., and Pierre Célestin M. Roux-Lavergne, *Histoire parlementaire de la Révolution française*, 40 vols., Paris, Paulin, 1833–8

Buret, Eugène, *De la misère des classes laborieuses en Angleterre et en France*, Paris, Paulin, 1840

Carey, Henry Charles,*The Slave Trade, Domestic and Foreign: Why It Exists, and How It May be Extinguished*, London, Sampson Low, Son and Co., 1853

Carlyle, Thomas, *Chartism*, London, James Fraser, 1839

——, *The French Revolution: A History*, London, James Fraser, 1837

Coulanges, Fustel de, *The Origin of Property in Land*, translated by Margaret Ashley with an introductory chapter on the English manor by W.J. Ashley, London, Swan Sonnenschein, 1891

——, *Le Problème des origines de la propriété foncière*, Bruxelles, Alfred Vromant, 1889

Darimon, Alfred, *De la réforme des banques*, Paris, Guillaumin, 1856

Darwin, Charles, *The Descent of Man*, London, 2 vols., J. Murray, 1871

De Staël, Madame, *De l'Allemagne*, Paris, Firmin Didot Frères, 1860

Dronke, Ernst, *Berlin*, Darmstadt, Neuwied Luchterhand, 1974 [Frankfurt am Main, J. Rütten, 1846]

Correspondence of Frederick Engels and Paul and Laura Lafargue, 3 vols., Moscow, Foreign Languages Publishing House, 1959–60

Friedrich Engels' Briefwechsel mit Karl Kautsky, Vienna, Danubia-Verlag, 1955

Feuerbach, Ludwig, *The Essence of Christianity* [*Das Wesen des Christentums*], trans. Marian Evans, London, J. Chapman, 1854

——, *Sämmtliche Werke*, Leipzig, Otto Wigand, 1846

Flaubert, Gustave, *A Sentimental Education*, ed. and trans. Douglas Parmée, Oxford, Oxford University Press, 1989

Freeman, Edward A., *Chief Periods of European History: Six Lectures Read in the University of Oxford in Trinity Term, 1885*, London, Macmillan, 1886

Garibaldi, Giuseppe, *Autobiography of Giuseppe Garibaldi*, trans. Alice Werner, London, W. Smith and Innes, 1889

Green, John Richard, *A Short History of the English People with Maps and Tables*, London, Macmillan, 1874

Greville, Charles, *The Greville Memoirs. Second Part: A Journal of the Reign of Queen Victoria from 1837 to 1852*, vol. 3, London, Longmans, 1885

Grote, George, *History of Greece*, 3rd edn, London, John Murray, 1851

Grün, Karl, *Ausgewählte Schriften in Zwei Bänden*, ed. Manuela Köppe, Berlin, Akademie Verlag, 2005

Guillaume, James, *L'Internationale: Documents et souvenirs (1864–1878)*, vols. 1 and 2, Paris, Société nouvelle de librairie et d'édition, 1905

Guizot, François, *Essais sur l'histoire de France, pour servir de complément aux Observations sur l'histoire de France de l'Abbé Mably*, Paris, J. L. J. Brière, 1823

Haxthausen, August von, *Studies on the Interior of Russia*, ed. S. Frederick Starr, Chicago, University of Chicago Press, 1972

———, *Über die Agrarverfassung in den Fürstenthümern Paderborn und Corvey und deren Conflicte in der gegenwärtigen Zeit nebst Vorschlägen, die den Grund und Boden belastenden Rechte und Verbindlichkeiten daselbst aufzulösen*, Berlin, Reimer, 1829

Haxthausen, August von, *Über den Ursprung und die Grundlagen der Verfassung in den ehemals slavischen Ländern Deutschlands im Allgemeinen und des Herzogthums Pommern im Besondern*, Berlin, Krause, 1842

Hegel, G. W. F., *Elements of the Philosophy of Right*, ed. A.W. Wood, Cambridge, Cambridge University Press, 1991 [1821]

———, *The Encyclopaedia: Logic*, trans. T. F. Garaets, W. F. Suchting and H. S. Harris, Indianapolis, Hackett, 1991

———, *Lectures on the History of Philosophy*, 3 vols., trans. E. S. Haldane and Frances H. Simson, Lincoln, Nebr., University of Nebraska Press, , 1995

———, *Lectures on Natural Right and Political Science: The First Philosophy of Right*, eds. J. Michael Stewart and Peter C. Hodgson, Berkeley, Calif., University of California Press, 1996

———, *Phenomenology of Spirit*, trans. A. V. Miller, Oxford, Clarendon Press, 1979

———, *The Science of Logic*, trans. and ed. George di Giovanni, Cambridge, Cambridge University Press, 2010

Heine, Heinrich, *Ludwig Börne: Recollections of a Revolutionist*, trans. Thomas S. Egan, London, Newman, 1881

———, *On the History of Religion and Philosophy in Germany and Other Writings*, ed. T. Pinkard, Cambridge, Cambridge University Press, 2007

Herwegh, Marcel (ed.), *Briefe von und an Georg Herwegh*, 2nd edn, Munich, A. Langen, 1898

Herzen, Alexander, *My Past and Thoughts: Memoirs of Alexander Herzen*, vol. II, New York, A. A. Knopf, 1968

———, *My Past and Thoughts: Memoirs of Alexander Herzen*, vol. III, London, Chatto and Windus, 1968

Hess, Moses, *Briefwechsel*, ed. Edmund Silberner, The Hague, Mouton, 1959

———, *The Holy History of Mankind and Other Writings*, ed. Shlomo Avineri, Cambridge, Cambridge University Press, 2004

Hundt, Martin (ed.), *Der Bund der Kommunisten 1836–1852*, Berlin, Akademie-Verlag Dietz, 1988

Hyndman, Henry Myers, *The Record of an Adventurous Life*, London, Macmillan, 1911

Institut Marksizma-Leninzma, *Reminiscences of Marx and Engels*, Moscow, Foreign Languages Publishing House, 1957

Kant, Immanuel, *Kant's Political Writings*, ed. Hans Reiss, Cambridge, Cambridge University Press, 1970

———, *On History*, ed. Lewis White Beck, Indianapolis, Bobbs-Merrill, 1980

———, *Religion within the Boundaries of Mere Reason and Other Writings*, eds. Allen G. Wood and George di Giovanni, Cambridge, Cambridge University Press, 1998 [1793]

Kautsky, Karl, *Ethics and the Materialist Conception of History*, Chicago, C. H. Kerr and Company, 1914 [1906]

Kautsky, K., Jr (ed.), *August Bebels' Briefwechsel mit Karl Kautsky*, Assen, Van Gorcum & Co., 1971

Kemble, John Mitchell, *Saxons in England: A History of the English Commonwealth till the Period of the Norman Conquest*, London, Longman, Brown, Green and Longmans, 1849

Köppen, Karl Friedrich, *Ausgewählte Schriften in zwei Bänden*, ed. Heinz H. Pepperle, vol. 1, Berlin, Akademie Verlag, 2003

Lamprecht, Karl, *Deutsches Wirtschaftsleben im Mittelalter*, 4 vols., Leipzig, A. Dürr, 1885–6

Lassalle, Ferdinand, *Nachgelassene Briefe und Schriften*, 3 vols., ed. Gustav Meyer, Stuttgart, Deutsche Verlags-Anstalt, 1921–5

———, *Die Philosophie Herakleitos des Dunkeln von Ephesos*, Berlin, F. Duncker, 1858

———, *Reden und Schriften: Aus der Arbeiteragitation 1862–1864*, ed. Friedrich Jenaczek, Munich, Deutscher Taschenbuch Verlag, 1970

———, *Die Theorie der erworbenen Rechte und der Collision der Gesetz: unter besonderer Berücksichtigung des* römischen, *französischen und preussischen Rechts*, Leipzig, Brochaus, 1861

Liebknecht, Wilhelm, *Karl Marx: Biographical Memoirs*, London, Journeyman Press, 1975 [1901]

————, *Wilhelm Liebknecht: Briefwechsel mit Karl Marx und Friedrich Engels*, ed. Georg Eckert, The Hague, Mouton, 1963

Maine, Henry Sumner, *Ancient Law: Its Connection with the Early History of Society and Its Relation to Modern Ideas*, London, J. Murray, 1895 [1861]

————, *Lectures on the Early History of Institutions*, London, J. Murray, 1875

————, *Village-Communities in the East and West: Six Lectures Delivered at Oxford*, London, J. Murray, 1871

Marx, Eleanor, *History of the Commune of 1871 from the French of Lissagaray*, New York, International Publishing Company, 1898

Marx, Karl, *Love Poems of Karl Marx*, eds. Reinhard Lettau and Lawrence Ferlinghetti, City Light Books, San Francisco, 1977

————, *Value, Price and Profit*, ed. E. Aveling, London, Sonnenschein, 1898

Marx–Engels–Lenin Institute, *Karl Marx: Chronik seines Lebens in Einzeldaten. Zusammengestellt vom Marx-Engels-Lenin-Institut Moskau*, Moscow/Glashütten, Auvermann, 1971 [1931]

Maurer, Georg Ludwig von, *Einleitung zur Geschichte der Mark-, Hof-, Dorf- und Stadtverfassung und der öffentlichen Gewalt*, Vienna, Brand, 1896

Mayer, Gustav, *Friedrich Engels: Eine Biographie*, 2 vols., repr. Berlin, Dietz, 1970 [1919, 1932]

———— *Radikalismus, Sozialismus und bürgerliche Demokratie*, Frankfurt am Main, Suhrkamp, 1969

Mazzini, Giuseppe, *A Cosmopolitanism of Nations: Giuseppe Mazzini's Writings on Democracy, Nation Building, and International Relations*, eds. Stefano Recchia and Nadia Urbinati, Princeton, NJ, Princeton University Press, 2009

McLennan, John Ferguson, *Primitive Marriage: An Enquiry into the Origin of the Form of Capture in Marriage Ceremonies*, Edinburgh, Black, 1865

Meier, Olga (ed.), *The Daughters of Karl Marx: Family Correspondence 1866–1898*, London, Deutsch, 1982

Menger, Anton, *The Right to the Whole Produce of Labour: The Origin and Development of the Theory of Labour's Claim to the Whole Product of Industry*, trans. M. E. Tanner, London, Macmillan, 1889 [1886]

Mercier, Louis Sébastien, *Néologie ou Vocabulaire de mots nouveaux*, Paris, Moussard, 1803

Meyen, Eduard, *Hallische Jahrbücher für deutsche Wissenschaft und Kunst*, Leipzig, Verlag von Otto Wigand, no. 193, 12 August 1840

Moneypenny, William Flavelle, and George Earle Buckle, *The Life of Benjamin Disraeli, Earl of Beaconsfield*, 2 vols., London, John Murray, 1929

Mönke, Wolfgang (ed.), *Moses Hess: Philosophische und Sozialistische Schriften 1837–1850*, Vaduz, Topos Verlag, 1980

Monz, Heinz, *Karl Marx: Grundlagen der Entwicklung zu Leben und Werk*, Trier, Verlag Neu, 1973

————, *Karl Marx und Trier: Verhältnisse, Beziehungen, Einflüsse*, Trier, Verlag Neu, 1964

————, *Zur Persönlichkeit von Marx' Schwiegervater Johann Ludwig von Westphalen, Schriften aus dem Karl-Marx-Haus*, Trier, no. 9, 1973

Morgan, Lewis. H., *The American Beaver and His Works*, Philadelphia, J. B. Lippincott and Co., 1868

————, *Ancient Society, or Researches in the Lines of Human Progress from Savagery through Barbarism to Civilization*, ed. Eleanor Burke Leacock, Cleveland, World Pub. Co., 1963 [1877]

Möser, Justus, *Osnabrückische Geschichte*, 2nd edn, Berlin, 1780

Nasse, Erwin, *On the Agricultural Community of the Middle Ages, and Inclosures of the Sixteenth Century in England*, trans. Colonel H. A. Ouvry, London, Macmillan, 1871

Plekhanov, G. (N. Beltov), *The Development of the Monist View of History*, Moscow, Foreign Languages Publishing House, 1956 [1895]

Riazanov, David, *Karl Marx and Friedrich Engels: An Introduction to Their Lives and Work*, London, Monthly Review Press, 1973 [1927]

———— (ed.), *Marx-Engels-Archiv: Zeitschrift des Marx-Engels-Instituts in Moskau*, Frankfurt am Main, Marx-Engels-Archiv Verlags-Gesellschaft, 1928

Ricardo, David, *Des Principes de l'Économie Politique et de l'Impôt*, Paris, J. P. Aillaud, 1835

————, *The Principles of Political Economy and Taxation*, London, John Murray, 1817

Rousseau, J.-J., *The Social Contract and Other Later Political Writings*, ed. Victor Gourevitch, Cambridge, Cambridge University Press, 1997

Ruge, Arnold, *Arnold Ruges Briefwechsel und Tagebuchblätter aus den Jahren 1825–1880*, ed. Paul Nerrlich, Berlin, Weidmann, 1886

————, *Zwei Jahre in Paris: Studien und Erinnerungen*, 2 vols., Leipzig, W. Jurany, 1846

Rumohr, Carl Friedrich von, *Italienische Forschungen*, Berlin and Stettin, Nicolai'sche Buchhandlung, 1827

Sass, Friedrich, *Berlin in seiner neuesten Zeit und Entwicklung*, Leipzig, Koffka, 1846

Savigny, Friedrich Karl von, *The History of the Roman Law in the Middle Ages*, trans. E. Cathcart, Edinburgh, A. Black, 1829

————, *Of the Vocation of Our Age for Legislation and Jurisprudence*, trans. Abraham Hayward, London, Littlewood and Co., 1828

————, *Von Savigny's Treatise on Possession or the Jus Possessionis of the Civil Law*, trans. Erskine Perry, London, Sweet, 1848

Schlegel, Friedrich von, *Kritische-Friedrich-Schlegel-Ausgabe*, vol. VI, Munich, F. Schöningh, 1961

Seebohm, Frederic, *The English Village Community – Examined in Its Relation to the Manorial and Tribal Systems and the Common or Open Field System of Husbandry – an Essay in Economic History*, London, Longman, Green and co., 1883

Seiler, Sebastian, *Das Komplott vom 13. Juni 1849, oder der letzte Sieg der Bourgeoisie in Frankreich*, Hamburg, Joffman und Campe, 1850

Sismondi, J.-C.-L. Simonde de, *Nouveaux principes d'économie politique, ou, De la richesse dans ses rapports avec la population*, 2 vols., Paris, Chez Delaunay, 1819

Smith, Adam, *An Inquiry into the Nature and Causes of the Wealth of Nations*, ed. Edwin Cannan, Chicago, University of Chicago Press, 1976 [1776]

Stein, Lorenz von, *Der Socialismus und Communismus des heutigen Frankreichs: ein Beitrag zur Zeitgeschichte*, 2nd edn, Leipzig, Otto Wigand, 1848

Stekloff, G. M., *History of the First International*, London, M. Lawrence, 1928

Stern, Daniel, *Histoire de la Révolution de 1848*, Paris, André Balland, 1985 [1850–52]

Stirner, Max, *The Ego and Its Own*, ed. David Leopold, Cambridge, Cambridge University Press, 1995 [1845]

Stubbs, William, *Constitutional History of England, in Its Origins and Development*, 3 vols., Oxford, Clarendon Press, 1875

Tocqueville, Alexis de, *Recollections*, eds. J. P. Mayer and A. P. Kerr, trans. G. Lawrence, London, Macdonald, 1970

Toussenel, Alphonse, *Les Juifs, rois de l'époque: Histoire de la féodalité financière*, Paris, G. de Gonet, 1845

Toynbee, Arnold, *Lectures on the Industrial Revolution in England*, London, Rivingtons, 1884

Ure, Andrew, *The Philosophy of Manufactures; or, an Exposition of the Scientific, Moral and Commercial Economy of the Factory System of Great Britain*, London, Charles Knight, 1835

Vinogradoff, Paul, *Villainage in England: Essays in English Medieval History*, Oxford, Clarendon Press, 1968 [1892]

Vizetelly, Henry, *Berlin under the New Empire: Its Institutions, Inhabitants, Industry, Monuments, Museums, Social Life, Manners, and Amusements*, London, Tinsley, 1879

Webb, Sidney and Beatrice, *A History of Trade Unionism*, London, Longmans, 1902

Wright, Thomas, *Our New Masters*, London, Strahan and Co., 1873

SECONDARY SOURCES

Agulhon, Maurice, *1848, ou L'Apprentissage de la République 1848–1852*, Paris, Éditions du Seuil, 1973

Alexandrian, Sarane, *Le Socialisme Romantique*, Paris, Éditions du Seuil, 1979

Anchel, Robert, *Napoléon et les Juifs*, Paris, Presses Universitaires de France, 1928

Anderson, Kevin. B., *Marx at the Margins: On Nationalism, Ethnicity, and Non-Western Societies*, Chicago, University of Chicago Press, 2010

Archer, Julian P. W., *The First International in France 1864–1872: Its Origins, Theories and Impact*, Lanham, Md/Oxford, University Press of America, 1997

Ashton, Rosemary, *Little Germany: Exile and Asylum in Victorian England*, Oxford, Oxford University Press, 1986

Avineri, Shlomo, *The Social and Political Thought of Karl Marx*, Cambridge, Cambridge University Press, 1968

Baker, Keith, 'Fixing the French Constitution', in *Inventing the French Revolution: Essays on French Political Culture in the Eighteenth Century*, Cambridge, Cambridge University Press, 1990

Barclay, David E., *Frederick William IV and the Prussian Monarchy 1840–1861*, Oxford, Clarendon Press, 1995

Barclay, David E., and Eric D. Weitz (eds.), *Between Reform and Revolution: German Socialism and Communism from 1840 to 1990*, New York, Berghahn, 1998

Bayly, C. A., and E. S. Biagini (eds.), *Giuseppe Mazzini and the Globalisation of Democratic Nationalism 1830–1920*, London, Proceedings of the British Academy (no. 152), 2008

Beiser, Frederick C., *The Fate of Reason: German Philosophy from Kant to Fichte*, Cambridge Mass., Harvard University Press, 1987

Beiser, Frederick C., *The Romantic Imperative: The Concept of Early German Romanticism*, Cambridge, Mass., Harvard University Press, 2003

Beecher, Jonathan, *Victor Considérant and the Rise and Fall of French Romantic Socialism*, Berkeley, Calif., University of California Press, 2001

Bell, Duncan (ed.), *Victorian Visions of Global Order: Empire and International Relations in Nineteenth-Century Political Thought*, Cambridge, Cambridge University Press, 1997

Berenson, Edward, *Populist Religion and Left-Wing Politics in France, 1830–1852*, Princeton, NJ, Princeton University Press, 1984

Berlin, Isaiah, *Karl Marx: His Life and Environment*, 4th edn, Oxford, Oxford University Press, 1978 [1939]

Bernstein, Édouard, *Ferdinand Lassalle: Le Réformateur social*, Paris, Rivière, 1913

Blumenberg, Werner, *Portrait of Marx: An Illustrated Biography*, trans. Douglas Scott, New York, Herder and Herder, 1972

Blumenkranz, B. (ed.), *Histoire des Juifs en France*, Toulouse, E. Privat, 1972

Breckman, Warren, *Marx, the Young Hegelians, and the Origins of Radical Social Theory: Dethroning the Self*, Cambridge, Cambridge University Press, 1999

Brunner, Otto, Werner Conze and Reinhart Koselleck (eds.), *Geschichtliche Grundbegriffe: Historisches Lexikon sur Politisch-Sozialen Sprache in Deutschland* (vol. 1), 8 vols., Stuttgart, Klett-Cotta, 1972–97

Burrow, J. W., *A Liberal Descent: Victorian Historians and the English Past*, Cambridge, Cambridge University Press, 1981

Bush, M. L. (ed.), *Social Orders and Social Classes in Europe since 1500: Studies in Social Stratification*, London, Longman, 1992

Campbell, Duncan A., *English Public Opinion and the American Civil War*, London, Royal Historical Society/Boydell Press, 2003

Carr, Edward Hallet, *Michael Bakunin*, London, Macmillan Press, 1975 [1937]

——, *The Romantic Exiles: A Nineteenth-Century Portrait Gallery*, London, V. Gollancz, 1933

Carver, Terrell, and Daniel Blank, *Marx and Engels's 'German Ideology' Manuscripts: Presentation and Analysis of the 'Feuerbach Chapter'*, New York, Palgrave Macmillan, 2014

Catholic World, The, 6/34 (1868)

Claeys, Gregory, *Imperial Sceptics: British Critics of Empire, 1850–1920*, Cambridge, Cambridge University Press, 2010

Clark, Christopher, *Iron Kingdom: The Rise and Downfall of Prussia, 1600–1947*, London, Allen Lane, 2006

Cohen, G. A., *History, Labour and Freedom: Themes from Marx*, Oxford, Oxford University Press, 1988

Collins, Henry, and Chimen Abramsky, *Karl Marx and the British Labour Movement: Years of the First International*, London, Macmillan, 1965

Conze, Werner (ed.), *Staat und Gesellschaft im deutschen Vormärz 1815–1848*, Stuttgart, E. Klett, 1962 (*Industrielle Welt*, vol. 1)

Cook, Simon J., *The Intellectual Foundations of Alfred Marshall's Economic Science: A Rounded Globe of Knowledge*, Cambridge, Cambridge University Press, 2009

Cornu, Auguste, *Karl Marx et Friedrich Engels: Leur vie et leur oeuvre*, vol. 1, Paris, Presses Universitaires de France, 1955

Cottier, Georges, *L'Athéisme du jeune Marx: ses origines hégéliennes*, Paris, Vrin, 1969

Daumard, Adeline, *Les Bourgeois et la bourgeoisie en France depuis 1815*, Paris, Flammarion, 1987

Davis, John A., and Paul Ginsborg (eds.), *Society and Politics in the Age of the Risorgimento: Essays in Honour of Denis Mack Smith*, Cambridge, Cambridge University Press, 1991

Demetz, Peter, *Marx, Engels and the Poets: Origins of Marxist Literary Criticism*, Chicago, University of Chicago Press, 1967

Derfler, Leslie, *Paul Lafargue and the Founding of French Marxism 1842–1882*, Cambridge, Mass., Harvard University Press, 1991

Dopsch, Alfons, *The Economic and Social Foundations of European Civilisation*, London, Kegan Paul, 1937 [1923–4]

Dowe, Dieter, *Aktion und Organisation: Arbeiterbewegung, Sozialistische und Kommunistische Bewegung in der Preussischen Rheinprovinz 1820–1852*, Hanover, Verlag für Literatur und Zeitgeschehen, 1970

Dowe, Dieter, Heinz-Gerhard Haupt, Dieter Langewiesche and Jonathan Sperber (eds.), *Europe in 1848: Revolution and Reform*, New York/Oxford, Berghahn, 2001

Draper, Hal, *"The Dictatorship of the Proletariat" from Marx to Lenin*, New York, Monthly Review Press, 1987

Droz, Jacques, *L'Allemagne et la Révolution française*, Paris, Presses Universitaires de Paris, 1949

Duveau, Georges, *1848: The Making of a Revolution*, London, Routledge and Kegan Paul, 1967

Elster, John, *Making Sense of Marx*, Cambridge, Cambridge University Press, 1985

Evans, David Owen, *Le Socialisme Romantique: Pierre Leroux et ses contemporains*, Paris, M. Rivière, 1948

Finn, Margot C., *After Chartism: Class and Nation in English Radical Politics, 1848–1874*, Cambridge, Cambridge University Press, 1993

Floud, Roderick, and Paul Johnson (eds.), *The Cambridge Economic History of Modern Britain*, vol.1: *Industrialisation, 1700–1860*, Cambridge, Cambridge University Press, 2004

Foster, Robert Fitzroy, *Modern Ireland 1600–1972*, London, Allen Lane, 1988

Fried, Albert, and Ronald Sanders (eds.), *Socialist Thought: A Documentary History*, Edinburgh, Edinburgh University Press, 1964

Furet, François, *Marx et La Révolution française*, Paris, Flammarion, 1986

Gabriel, Mary, *Love and Capital: Karl and Jenny Marx and the Birth of a Revolution*, Boston, Mass., Little Brown, 2011

Gielkens, Jan, *Karl Marx und seine niederländischen Verwandten: Eine kommentierte Quellenedition, Schriften aus dem Karl-Marx Haus, Trier*, no. 50, 1999

Gillis, John R., *The Prussian Bureaucracy in Crisis, 1840–1860: Origins of an Administrative Ethos*, Stanford, Calif., Stanford University Press, 1971

Gourevitch, Alex, *From Slavery to the Cooperative Commonwealth: Labour and Republican Liberty in the Nineteenth Century*, Cambridge, Cambridge University Press, 2015

Grandjonc, Jacques, *Marx et les Communistes allemands à Paris, Vorwärts 1844: Contribution à l'étude de la naissance du Marxisme*, Paris, F. Maspero, 1974

Gruner, Shirley M., *Economic Materialism and Social Moralism: A Study in the History of Ideas in France from the Latter Part of the 18th Century to the Middle of the 19th Century*, The Hague, Mouton, 1973

Guillemin, Henri, *La Première Résurrection de la République: 24 février 1848*, Paris, Gallimard, 1967

Hall, Peter, *The Industries of London since 1861*, London, Hutchinson University Library, 1961

Hammen, Oscar J., *The Red '48ers: Karl Marx and Friedrich Engels*, New York, Scribner, 1969

Hanfi, Zawar (ed.), *The Fiery Brook: Selected Writings of Ludwig Feuerbach*, New York, Doubleday, 1972

Harris, Henry Silton, *Hegel's Development: Toward the Sunlight, 1770–1801*, Oxford, Clarendon Press, 1972

Harrison, Royden, *Before the Socialists: Studies in Labour and Politics 1861–1881*, London, Routledge and K. Paul, 1965

Harstick, Hans-Peter, *Karl Marx und die Zeitgenossische Verfassungsgeschichtsschreibung*, Munster, 1974

Haubtmann, Pierre, *Proudhon, Marx et la pensée allemande*, Grenoble, Presses Universitaires de Grenoble, 1981

Healey, Edna, *Wives of Fame : Mary Livingstone, Jenny Marx, Emma Darwin*, London, Sidgwick and Jackson, 1986

Hellman, Robert J., *Berlin, the Red Room and White Beer: The "Free" Hegelian Radicals in the 1840s*, Washington, Three Continents Press, 2006

Hodenberg, Christina von, *Aufstand der Weber: die Revolte von 1844 und ihr Aufstieg zum Mythos*, Bonn, Dietz, 1997

Hoffheimer, Michael H., *Eduard Gans and the Hegelian Philosophy of Law*, Dordrecht, Kluwer Academic Publishers, 1995

Holmes, Rachel, *Eleanor Marx: A Life*, London, Bloomsbury, 2014

Hont, Istvan, *Jealousy of Trade: International Competition and the Nation-State in Historical Perspective*, Cambridge, Mass., Harvard University Press, 2005

Hont, Jacques d', *De Hegel à Marx*, Paris, Presses Universitaires de Paris, 1972

Hunt, Richard N., *The Political Ideas of Marx and Engels,* 2 vols., London, Macmillan, 1974 and 1984

Hunt, Tristram, *The Frock-Coated Communist: The Revolutionary Life of Friedrich Engels*, London, Allen Lane, 2009

Hutton, Patrick, *The Cult of the Revolutionary Tradition: The Blanquists in French Politics, 1864–1893*, Berkeley, Calif., University of California Press, 1981

Inwood, Michael, *A Hegel Dictionary*, Oxford, Blackwell, 1992

Jaeschke, W., *Reason in Religion: The Foundations of Hegel's Philosophy of Religion*, trans. J. Michael Stewart and Peter C. Hodgson, Berkeley, Calif., University of California Press, 1990

Johnson, Christopher H., *Utopian Communism in France, 1839–1851*, Ithaca, NY, Cornell University Press, 1974

Joll, James, *The Anarchists*, London, Eyre and Spottiswoode, 1964

Jones, Thomas, 'George Odger, Robert Applegarth, and the First International Working Men's Association', MA dissertation, King's College London, 2007

Kadish, Alon, *Apostle Arnold: The Life and Death of Arnold Toynbee, 1852–1883*, Durham, NC, Duke University Press, 1986

Kant, Immanuel, *Religion within the Boundaries of Mere Reason and Other Writings*, eds. Allen Wood and George di Giovanni, Cambridge, Cambridge University Press, 1998

Kapp, Yvonne, *Eleanor Marx*, 2 vols., London, Lawrence and Wishart, 1972

Katznelson, Ira, and Gareth Stedman Jones (eds.), *Religion and the Political Imagination*, Cambridge, Cambridge University Press, 2010

Kocka, Jürgen (ed.), *Bürgertum im 19. Jahrhundert: Deutschland im europäischen Vergleich*, 3 vols., Göttingen, Vandenhoeck & Ruprecht, 1995

Koselleck, Reinhart, and Klaus Schreiner, *Bürgerschaft: Rezeption und Innovation der Begrifflichkeit vom Hohen Mittelalter bis ins 19. Jahrhundert*, Stuttgart, Kletta-Cotta, 1994

Krader, Lawrence, *The Asiatic Mode of Production: Sources, Development and Critique in the Writings of Karl Marx*, Assen, Van Gorcum, 1975

Kriedte, Peter, Hans Medick and Jürgen Schlumbohn, *Industrialisierung vor der Industrialisierung: Gewerbliche Warenproduktion auf dem Land in der Formationsperiode des Kapitalismus*, Göttingen, Vandenhoeck & Ruprecht, 1977

Kuper, Adam, *The Invention of Primitive Society: Transformations of an Illusion*, London, Routledge, 1988

Lange, Erhard, *Die Promotion von Karl Marx: Jena 1841. Eine Quellenedition*, Berlin, Dietz Verlag, 1983

Lattek, Christine, *Revolutionary Refugees: German Socialism in Britain, 1840–1860*, London, Routledge, 2006

Laufner, Richard, 'Die Familie Marx und die Trierer Judenschaft', *Schriften aus dem Karl-Marx-Haus, Trier*, no. 14, 1975

Leopold, David, *The Young Karl Marx: German Philosophy, Modern Politics and Human Flourishing*, Cambridge, Cambridge University Press, 2007

Leventhal, F. M., *Respectable Radical: George Howell and Victorian Working-Class Politics*, London, Weidenfeld and Nicolson, 1971

Lewis, Hanna Ballin (ed.), *A Year of Revolutions: Fanny Lewald's Recollections of 1848*, Providence, RI/Oxford, Berghahn, 1997

Lifshitz, Mikhail, *The Philosophy of Art of Karl Marx*, trans. Ralph B. Winn, London, Pluto Press, 1973 [Moscow, 1933]

Lindenfeld, David, *The Practical Imagination: The German Sciences of State in the Nineteenth Century*, Chicago, Chicago University Press, 1997

Lidtke, Vernon, *The Outlawed Party: Social Democracy in Germany, 1878–1890*, Princeton, NJ, Princeton University Press, 1966

Löwy, Michael, *The Theory of Revolution in the Young Marx*, Leiden, Brill, 2003

Maguire, John M., *Marx's Theory of Politics*, Cambridge, Cambridge University Press, 1978

Mantena, Karuna, *Alibis of Empire: Henry Maine and the Ends of Liberal Imperialism*, Princeton, NJ, Princeton University Press, 2010

Mastellone, Salvo, *Mazzini and Marx: Thoughts upon Democracy in Europe*, London, Praeger, 2003

Matthews, R. C. O., *A Study in Trade-Cycle History: Economic Fluctuations in Great Britain 1833–1842*, Cambridge, Cambridge University Press, 1954

Maza, Sarah, *The Myth of the French Bourgeoisie: An Essay on the Social Imaginary, 1750–1850*, Cambridge, Mass., Harvard University Press, 2003

McLellan, David, *Karl Marx: His Life and Thought*, London, Macmillan, 1973

——— (ed.), *Karl Marx: Interviews and Recollections*, London, Barnes and Noble, 1981

McManners, John, *The French Revolution and the Church*, London, SPCK, 1969

Meier, Olga (ed.), *The Daughters of Karl Marx: Family Correspondence 1866–1898*, Harmondsworth, Penguin, 1982

Mehring, Franz, *Karl Marx: The Story of His Life*, trans. Edward Fitzgerald, London, John Lane, 1936 [1918]

Merriman, John M., *The Life and Death of the Paris Commune of 1871*, New Haven, Conn., Yale University Press, 2014

Miller, Susanne, and Heinrich Pothoff, *A History of German Social Democracy from 1848 to the Present*, Leamington Spa, Berg, 1986

Moggach, Douglas, *The Philosophy and Politics of Bruno Bauer*, Cambridge, Cambridge University Press, 2003

——— (ed.), *The New Hegelians: Politics and Philosophy in the Hegelian School*, New York, Cambridge University Press, 2006

——— (ed.), *Politics, Religion and Art: Hegelian Debates*, Evanston, Ill., Northwestern University Press, 2011

Morgan, Roger, *The German Social Democrats and the First International, 1864–1872*, Cambridge, Cambridge University Press, 1965

Nabulsi, Karma, *Traditions of War, Occupation, Resistance, and the Law*, Oxford, Oxford University Press, 1998

Namier, Lewis Bernstein, *1848: The Revolution of the Intellectuals*, London, Oxford University Press, 1971 [1944]

Nicholls, Julia Catherine, 'French Revolutionary Thought after the Paris Commune, 1871–1885', Ph.D. thesis, Queen Mary University of London, 2015

Nicolaevsky, Boris, and Otto Mönke, *Karl Marx, Man and Fighter*, trans. G. David and E. Mosbacher, London, Allen Lane, 1973 [1933]

Nicolin, Günther, *Hegel in Berichten seiner Zeitgenossen*, Hamburg, F. Meiner, 1970

Nisbet, H. B. (ed.), *Lessing: Philosophical and Theological Writings*, Cambridge, Cambridge University Press, 2005

Parry, Jonathan, *The Rise and Fall of Liberal Government in Victorian Britain*, New Haven, Conn./London, Yale University Press, 1993

Peach, Terry, *Interpreting Ricardo*, Cambridge, Cambridge University Press, 1993

Pilbeam, Pamela M., *The Middle Classes in Europe 1789–1914: France, Germany, Italy and Russia*, Basingstoke, Macmillan Education, 1990

Pinkard, Terry, *Hegel: A Biography*, Cambridge, Cambridge University Press, 2000

Prawer, Siegbert Salomon, *Karl Marx and World Literature*, Oxford, Clarendon Press, 1976

Puhle, H. J. (ed.), *Bürger in der Gesellschaft der Neuzeit*, Göttingen, Vanhoeck & Ruprecht, 1991

Reid, Alastair, *United We Stand: A History of Britain's Trade Unions*, London, Penguin Books, 2005

Riall, Lucy, *Garibaldi, Invention of a Hero*, New Haven, Conn./London, Yale University Press, 2007

Riedel, Manfred, *Between Tradition and Revolution: The Hegelian Transformation of Political Philosophy*, Cambridge, Cambridge University Press, 1984

Rosanvallon, Pierre, *Le Moment Guizot*, Paris, Gallimard, 1985

——, *Le Sacré du Citoyen: Histoire du Suffrage Universel in France*, Paris, Gallimard, 1992

Rosdolsky, Roman, *The Making of Marx's 'Capital'*, London, Pluto Press, 1977

Rose, Margaret, *Marx's Lost Aesthetic: Karl Marx and the Visual Arts*, Cambridge, Cambridge University Press, 1984

Rowe, Michael, *From Reich to State: The Rhineland in the Revolutionary Age, 1780–1830*, Cambridge, Cambridge University Press, 2003

Rubel, Maximilien, *Karl Marx devant le Bonapartisme*, Paris, Mouton, 1960

——, *Marx: Life and Works*, London, Macmillan, 1980

Sassoon, Donald, *One Hundred Years of Socialism: The Western European Left in the Twentieth Century*, London, I. B. Tauris, 1996

Schulze, Hagen, *The Course of German Nationalism: From Frederick the Great to Bismarck, 1763–1837*, Cambridge, Cambridge University Press, 1991

Sepinwall, Alyssa Goldstein, *The Abbé Grégoire and the French Revolution: The Making of Modern Universalism*, Berkeley, Calif., University of California Press, 2005

Shanin, Teodor (ed.), *The Late Marx and the Russian Road*, London, Routledge and Kegan Paul, 1983

Siclovan, Diana, 'Lorenz Stein and German Socialism, 1835–1872', Ph.D. thesis, Cambridge, 2014

——, 'Mikhail Bakunin and the Modern Republic 1840–1867, Cambridge University history dissertation, 2009

——, 'The Project of *Vergesellschaftung*, 1843–1851', M.Phil. dissertation, Cambridge, 2010

Somerhausen, Luc, *L'Humanisme agissant de Karl Marx*, Paris, Richard-Masse, 1946

Sorkin, David, *The Transformation of German Jewry 1780–1840*, Oxford, Oxford University Press, 1987

Sperber, Jonathan, *Rhineland Radicals: The Democratic Movement and the Revolution of 1848–1849*, Princeton, NJ, Princeton University Press, 1991

Sperber, Jonathan, *Karl Marx: A Nineteenth Century Life*, New York, Liveright Publishing Corporation, 2013

Spitzer, Alan Barrie, *Old Hatreds and Young Hopes: The French Carbonari against the Bourbon Restoration*, Cambridge, Mass., Harvard University Press, 1971

——, *The Revolutionary Theories of Louis Auguste Blanqui*, New York, Columbia University Press, 1957

Stearns, Peter N., *The Revolutions of 1848*, London, Weidenfeld and Nicolson, 1974

Stedman Jones, Gareth, *An End to Poverty: A Historical Debate,* London, Profile Books, 2004

——, *Languages of Class*, Cambridge, Cambridge University Press, 1983

——, *Outcast London: A Study in the Relationship between Classes in Victorian Society*, Oxford, Clarendon Press, 1971 [4th edn, Verso, 2013]

—— (ed.), *Karl Marx and Friedrich Engels: The Communist Manifesto*, London, Penguin Books, 2002

Stedman Jones, Gareth, and Gregory Claeys (eds.), *The Cambridge History of Nineteenth-Century Political Thought,* Cambridge, Cambridge University Press, 2011

Stedman Jones, Gareth, and Ian Patterson (eds.), *Charles Fourier: The Theory of the Four Movements*, Cambridge, Cambridge University Press, 1996

Stepelevich, Lawrence S. (ed.), *The Young Hegelians: An Anthology*, Cambridge, Cambridge University Press, 1983

Sweezy, Paul M., *The Theory of Capitalist Development: Principles of Marxian Political Economy*, New York, Monthly Review Press, 1968

Tackett, Timothy, *Becoming a Revolutionary: The Deputies of the French National Assembly and the Emergence of a Revolutionary Culture (1789–1790)*, Princeton, NJ, Princeton University Press, 1996

Taylor, Miles, *The Decline of British Radicalism 1847–1860*, Oxford, Clarendon Press, 1995

——, *Ernest Jones, Chartism and the Romance of Politics 1819–1869*, Oxford, Oxford University Press, 2003

Thomas, Paul, *Karl Marx and the Anarchists*, London, Routledge and Kegan Paul, 1980

Toews, John E., *Hegelianism: The Path toward Dialectical Humanism, 1805–1841*, Cambridge, Cambridge University Press, 1980

Tombs, Robert, *The Paris Commune 1871*, London, Longman, 1999

Traugott, Mark, *Armies of the Poor: Determinants of Working-Class Participation in the Parisian Insurrection of June 1848*, Princeton, NJ, Princeton University Press, 1985

Tsuzuki, Chushichi, *The Life of Eleanor Marx, 1855–1898: A Socialist Tragedy*, Oxford, Clarendon Press, 1967

Tribe, Keith, *The Economy of the Word: Language, History and Economics,* Oxford, Oxford University Press, 2015

——, *Governing Economy: The Reformation of German Economic Discourse 1750–1840*, Cambridge, Cambridge University Press, 1988

Tuchinsky, Adam, *Horace Greeley's New York Tribune: Civil War Era Socialism and the Crisis of Free Labour*, Ithaca, Cornell University Press, 2009

Tudor, Henry and J. M. (eds.), *Marxism and Social Democracy: The Revisionist Debate 1896–1898*, Cambridge, Cambridge University Press, 1998 van der Linden, Maurice, *Transnational Labour History: Explorations*, Studies in Labour History, Aldershot, Ashgate, 2003

Vincent, K. Steven, *Between Marxism and Anarchism: Benoît Malon and French Reformist Socialism*, Berkeley, Calif./Oxford, University of California Press, 1992

Walker, John (ed.) *The Impact of Idealism: The Legacy of Post-Kantian German Thought*, vol. II: *Historical, Social and Political Thought*, Cambridge, Cambridge University Press, 2013

Watanabe-O'Kelly, Helen, *The Cambridge History of German Literature*, Cambridge, Cambridge University Press, 1997

Wehler, Hans-Ulrich (ed.), *Moderne deutsche Sozialgeschichte*, Köln, Kiepenheuer & Witsch, 1973

Wheen, Francis, *Karl Marx*, London, Fourth Estate, 1999

White, James D., *Karl Marx and the Intellectual Origins of Dialectical Materialism*, London, Macmillan, 1996

Whitham, William P., 'Anarchism and Federalism in the International Working Men's Association 1864–1877', Harvard BA thesis, 2014

Whitham, William P., 'César De Paepe and the Politics of Collective property', Cambridge M.Phil. dissertation, 2015

Whitman, James Q., *The Legacy of Roman Law in the German Romantic Era: Historical Vision and Legal Change*, Princeton, NJ, Princeton University Press, 1990

Wilkinson, Elizabeth M., and L. A. Willoughby (eds.), *F. Schiller: On the Aesthetic Education of Man, in a Series of Letters*, Oxford, Clarendon Press, 1982

Winch, Donald, and Patrick K. O'Brien (eds.), *The Political Economy of British Historical Experience, 1688–1914*, Oxford, Oxford University Press, 2002

Wolff, Horst-Peter, *Eduard Gumpert (1834–1893): Ein deutscher Arzt in Manchester*, Liebenwalde, Selbstverlag, 2015

Wrigley, E. A., *Continuity, Chance and Change: The Character of the Industrial Revolution in England*, Cambridge, Cambridge University Press, 1988

JOURNALS

Beecher Jonathan, and Valerii N. Formichev 'French Socialism in Lenin's and Stalin's Moscow: David Riazanov and the French Archive of the Marx–Engels Institute', *Journal of Modern History*, 78/1 (March 2006), pp. 119–43

Breckman, Warren, 'Ludwig Feuerbach and the Political Theology of Restoration', *History of Political Thought*, 13/3 (1992), pp. 437–62

Carver, Terrell, 'The German Ideology Never Took Place', *History of Political Thought*, vol. 31, Spring 2010, pp.107–27

Cook, Simon J., 'The Making of the English: English History, British Identity, Aryan Villages, 1870–1914', *Journal of the History of Ideas*, 75/4 (October 2014), pp. 629–49

Dennison, Tracy, and A. W. Carus, 'The Invention of the Russian Rural Commune: Haxthausen and the Evidence', *Historical Journal*, 46/3 (September 2003)

Eichhorn, Karl Friedrich,'Über den Ursprung der städtischen Verfassung in Deutschland', *Zeitschrift für geschichtliche Rechtswissenschaft* (1), 1815

Fay, Margaret, 'The Influence of Adam Smith on Marx's Theory of Alienation', *Science and Society*, 47/2 (Summer 1983), pp. 129–51

Gruner, Shirley, 'The Revolution of July 1830 and the Expression "Bourgeoisie"', *Historical Journal*, 11/3 (1968), pp. 462–71

Harrison, Frederic, 'The Transit of Power', *Fortnightly Review*, London, Chapman and Hall, April 1868

Hirsch, Helmut, 'Karl Friedrich Köppen: Der intimste Berliner Freund Marxens', *International Review of Social History*, vol. 1 (1936)

Howell, George, 'The History of the International Association', *Nineteenth Century*, vol. IV (July 1878), pp. 19–39

Kelley, Donald, 'The Metaphysics of Law: An Essay on the Very Young Marx', *American Historical Review*, 83/2 (1978), pp. 350–67

——, 'The Science of Anthropology: An Essay on the Very Old Marx', *Journal of the History of Ideas*, 4/2 (1984), pp. 245– 63

Levine, Norman, 'The German Historical School of Law and the Origins of Historical Materialism', *Journal of the History of Ideas*, 48 (1987), pp. 431–51

Liberles, Robert, 'From *Toleration* to *Verbesserung*: German and English Debates on the Jews in the Eighteenth Century', *Central European History*, 22/1 (1989)

Lidtke, Vernon, 'German Socialism and Social Democracy 1860–1900', in Gareth Stedman Jones and Gregory Claeys (eds.), *Cambridge History of Nineteenth Century Political Thought*, Cambridge, Cambridge University Press, 2011

Mah, Harold, 'The French Revolution and the Problem of German Modernity: Hegel, Heine, and Marx', *New German Critique*, no. 50 (Spring–Summer 1990)

Maine, Henry Sumner, 'The Decay of Feudal Property in France and England', *Fortnightly Review*, vol. 21, April 1877

Nabulsi, Karma, 'Patriotism and Internationalism in the "Oath of Allegiance" to "Young Europe"', *European Journal of Political Theory*, 5/61 (January 2006)

O'Boyle, Leonore, 'The Problem of an Excess of Educated Men in Western Europe, 1800–1850', *Journal of Modern History*, 42 (1970), pp. 471–95

Rojahn, Jürgen, 'Marxismus – Marx – Geschichtswissenschaft. Der Fall der sog. "Ökonomisch-philosophischen Manuskripte aus dem Jahre 1844"', *International Review of Social History*, 28/1 (April 1983), pp. 2–49

Shipley, Stan, *Club Life and Socialism in mid-Victorian London*, History Workshop Pamphlets, no. 5, Oxford, 1973

Stommel, Karl, 'Der Armenarzt, Dr. Andreas Gottschalk, der erste Kölner Arbeiterführer, 1848', *Annalen des Historischen Vereins für den Niederrhein* 166, Cologne, 1964

Stedman Jones, Gareth, 'The Mid-Century Crisis and the 1848 Revolutions', *Theory and Society*, 12/4 (July 1983)

———, 'Some Notes on Karl Marx and the English Labour Movement', *History Workshop*, no. 18 (Autumn 1984)

———, 'Voir sans entendre: Engels, Manchester et l'observation sociale en 1844', *Genèses*, 22/1 (1996), pp. 4–17

Tombs, Robert, 'How bloody was *La Semaine sanglante* of 1871?', *Historical Journal*, 55/3 (2012), pp. 679–704

Index